Criminology

Second Edition

Other Titles of Related Interest

SAGE Text/Reader Series in Criminology and Criminal Justice

Craig Hemmens, Series Editor

Criminology
The Essentials
Second Edition

Anthony Walsh
Boise State University

Los Angeles | London | New Delhi
Singapore | Washington DC

Los Angeles | London | New Delhi
Singapore | Washington DC

FOR INFORMATION:

SAGE Publications, Inc.
2455 Teller Road
Thousand Oaks, California 91320
E-mail: order@sagepub.com

SAGE Publications Ltd.
1 Oliver's Yard
55 City Road
London, EC1Y 1SP
United Kingdom

SAGE Publications India Pvt. Ltd.
B 1/I 1 Mohan Cooperative Industrial Area
Mathura Road, New Delhi 110 044
India

SAGE Publications Asia-Pacific Pte. Ltd.
3 Church Street
#10-04 Samsung Hub
Singapore 048763

Acquisitions Editor: Jerry Westby
Editorial Assistant: Laura Kirkhoff
Digital Content Editor: Rachael Leblond
Production Editor: Jane Haenel
Copy Editor: Mark Bast
Typesetter: C&M Digitals (P) Ltd.
Proofreader: Pam Suwinsky
Indexer: Joan Shapiro
Cover Designer: Candice Harman
Marketing Manager: Terra Schultz

Copyright © 2015 by SAGE Publications, Inc.

Printed in the United States of America

Library of Congress Cataloging-in-Publication Data

Walsh, Anthony, 1941–
Criminology : the essentials / Anthony Walsh, Boise State University—2nd edition.

pages cm
Includes bibliographical references and index.

ISBN 978-1-4833-5069-1 (pbk. : alk. paper)

1. Criminology. 2. Criminal behavior. I. Title.

HV6025.W3654 2016
364—dc23   2014008564

This book is printed on acid-free paper.

15 16 17 18 10 9 8 7 6 5 4 3 2

Brief Contents

Detailed Contents

Preface

There are a number of excellent criminological textbooks available to students and professors, so why this one? The reason is that the typical textbook has become inordinately expensive (often as high as $150), which is a true hardship for many students today. Many of the books are filled with enormous amounts of information that cannot possibly be digested in one semester. Additionally, there is so much to try to cover that professors may be reluctant to bring in additional materials such as journal articles that he or she may consider very important.

By way of contrast, this book provides the essentials of criminology in a compact and affordable volume. It covers all the material that is necessary to know and eliminates what is merely nice to know. It does not inundate students with scores of minor facts that may turn them glassy-eyed, but does engage them in straightforward language with the latest advances in criminology from a variety of disciplines (and it costs them one-half to one-third of the price charged for the more glitzy hardback texts). This book can serve as the primary text for an undergraduate course in criminology or as the primary text for a graduate course when supplemented by additional readings available on the SAGE website.

❖ Structure of the Book

This book uses the typical outline for criminology textbook topics and sections, beginning with the definitions of crime and criminology and measuring crime, proceeding into theories of crime and criminality, and then delving into typologies. I depart from the typical textbook sequencing in one way only, that of the ordering of the theory chapters. The typical criminology textbook begins with a discussion of biological and psychological theories and proceeds to demolish concepts that others demolished decades ago, such as atavism and the XYY syndrome. Having shown how wrong these concepts were, and leaving the impression that those concepts exhaust the content of modern biological and psychological theories, they proceed to sociological theories.

Unfortunately, this is the exact opposite of the way that normal science operates. Normal science begins with observations and descriptions of phenomena on a large (macro) scale and then asks a series of "why" questions that systematically takes it down to lower levels of analysis. Wholes are wonderful meaningful things, and holistic explanations are fine as far as they go. But they only go so far before they exhaust their explanatory power and before the data require a more elementary look. This is how medical epidemiologists go about tracking down the causes of exotic diseases and why philosophers of science agree that holistic accounts describe phenomena, whereas reductionist (examining a phenomenon at a more fundamental level) accounts explain them. Scientists typically observe and describe what is on the surface of a phenomenon and then seek to dig deeper to find the fundamental mechanisms that drive the phenomenon.

In the natural sciences, useful observations go in both holistic and reductionist directions, such as from quarks to the cosmos in physics and from nucleotides to ecological systems in biology. There is no zero-sum competition between levels of analysis in these sciences, nor should there be in ours. Thus, following our discussion of the early schools, we begin with the most holistic (social structural) theories. These theories describe elements of whole societies that are supposedly conducive to high rates of criminal behavior such as capitalism or racial heterogeneity. Because only a small proportion of people exposed to these alleged criminogenic forces commit crimes, we must move down to social process theories that talk about how individuals interpret and respond to structural forces. We then have to move to more individualistic (psychosocial) theories that focus on the traits and abilities of individuals that would lead them to arrive at different interpretations than other individuals and finally to theories (biosocial) that try to pin down the exact mechanisms underlying these predilections.

❖ What's New in the Second Edition?

A number of changes have been made to the second edition based on suggestions from users of the first edition. All the statistical information gathered from official sources (e.g., UR, NCVS, NIBRS) has been updated from the latest sources available.

There seems to be something of a consensus among the reviewers that victimology is becoming increasingly more important to include in any discussion of criminology. Consequently, I have moved victimology to Chapter 3 and added significantly to its scope.

A discussion of deterrence theory and the death penalty has been added to the chapter on the early classical and positivist schools of criminology (Chapter 4). This chapter is the first to include another addition to this second edition called Theory in Action. Each subsequent chapter includes such a section focusing on a particularly interesting case from real life that helps to illustrate the theories presented in them.

There was also a call for more choice-type theories, such as rational choice and routine activities theories, from reviewers. Thus, a chapter has been added (Chapter 5) that covers these theories as well as a theory that calls itself the enemy of rational choice—cultural or anarchic criminology. This theory focuses on emotions as the driving force behind criminality, and its inclusion provides us an opportunity to discuss the sorely neglected area of emotion in both instigating and preventing criminal behavior.

It was also considered desirable to separate corporate crime and organized crime into two chapters rather than combining them into one chapter as was done in the first edition. This provided me with more leeway to discuss important issues in these areas, particularly the subprime mortgage scandal that adversely affected so many people while enriching the few.

These many additions have naturally increased the number of pages in this book. I hope you will agree that this edition has increased qualitatively in direct proportion to its quantitative expansion.

❖ Acknowledgments

I would first of all like to thank the ever jovial executive editor Jerry Westby for his faith in this project from the beginning. Thanks also for the commitment of his very able colleague and assistant MaryAnn Vail. This tireless twosome kept up a most useful dialogue between authors, publisher, and a number of excellent reviewers. The copy editor, Mark Bast, spotted every errant comma, dangling participle, missing reference, and misspelled word in the manuscript, for which

I am truly thankful. The production editor, Jane Haenel, made sure everything went quickly and smoothly thereafter. Thank you one and all.

I am also most grateful for the reviewers who spent considerable time providing me with the benefit of their expertise during the writing and rewriting phase of the book's production. Their input and encouragement has undoubtedly made the book better than it would otherwise have been. These expert criminologists for the first edition are Gennifer Furst, William Paterson University; Scott Maggard, Old Dominion University; Heather Melton, The University of Utah; Allison Payne, Villanova University; Kelly Asmussen, Peru State College; Tracey Steele, Wright State University; Linda Tobin, Austin Community College; and Steven Egger, University of Houston. For this edition the reviewers are Lisa Bates-Lester, University of North Florida; Kate Melody Burmon, Northeastern University; James M. Cook, University of Maine at Augusta; Jennifer L. Lanterman, University of Nevada, Reno; Patrick F. McCarty, Rutgers University; Trinidad Morales III, The University of Texas at El Paso; Angela Overton, Georgia State University; and Evelyn J. Patterson, Vanderbilt University.

Most of all, I would like to acknowledge the love and support of my most wonderful and drop-dead gorgeous wife, Grace Jean (aka "Grace the face"). Grace's love and support have sustained me for so long that I cannot imagine life without her; she is a real treasure and the center of my universe: Szeretlek nagyonsok, Gracie.

❖ Instructor Teaching Site

A password-protected site, available at **www.sagepub.com/walshess2e,** features resources that have been designed to help instructors plan and teach their courses. These resources include an extensive test bank, chapter-specific PowerPoint presentations, lecture notes, video and web resources, and links to SAGE journal articles.

❖ Student Study Site

An open-access study site is available at **www.sagepub.com/walshess2e.** This site includes mobile-friendly eFlashcards and web quizzes, as well as links to web resources, video resources, and full-text SAGE journal articles.

This book is dedicated to my wife, Grace; my parents, Lawrence and Winifred; my sons, Robert and Michael; my stepdaughters, Heidi and Kasey; my grandchildren, Robbie, Ryan, Mikey, Randy, Christopher, Stevie, Ashlyn, Morgan, and Vivien; and to my great-grandchildren, Kaelyn, Logan, and Keagan.

CHAPTER 1

An Overview of Crime and Criminology

In 1996, Iraqi refugees Majed Al-Timimy, 28, and Latif Al-Husani, 34, married the daughters, aged 13 and 14, of a fellow Iraqi refugee in Lincoln, Nebraska. The marriages took place according to Muslim custom, and everything seemed to be going well for a while until one of the girls ran away and the concerned father and her husband reported it to the police. It was at this point that American and Iraqi norms of legality and morality clashed head-on. Under Nebraska law, people under 17 years old cannot marry, so both grooms and the girls' father and mother were arrested and charged with a variety of crimes from child endangerment to statutory rape.

According to an Iraqi woman interviewed by the police (herself married at 12 in Iraq), both girls were excited and happy about the wedding. The Iraqi community was shocked that these men faced up to 50 years in prison for their actions, as would have been earlier generations of Americans who were legally permitted to marry girls of this age. The men were sentenced to 4 to 6 years in prison and paroled in 2000 with conditions that they have no contact with their "wives." Thus something that is legally and morally permissible in one culture can be severely punished in another. Were the actions of these men child sex abuse or simply unremarkable marital sex? Which culture is right? Can we really ask such a question? Is Iraqi culture "more right" than American culture given that marrying girls of that age was permissible here too at one time? Most importantly for our purposes, how can criminologists hope to study crime scientifically if what constitutes a crime is relative to time and place?

LEARNING OBJECTIVES

- Understand the difficulty of defining crime and the difference between crime and criminality
- Know the difference between *mala in se* and *mala prohibita* crimes
- Understand the legal process required to "officially" become criminal
- Realize how thinking about crime and criminality is time and culture bound
- Understand what theory is, how it is formulated, and how theory functions in science
- Be aware of the role of ideology in criminology
- Understand the relationship between theory and policy in criminology

❖ What Is Criminology?

The 19th-century American novelist Nathaniel Hawthorne opens his famous book *The Scarlet Letter* with these words of wisdom: "The founders of a new colony, whatever Utopia of human virtue and happiness they might originally project, have invariably recognized it among their earliest practical necessities to allot a portion of the virgin soil as a cemetery, and another portion as the site of a prison" (2003, p. 1). Hawthorne is reminding us of two things we cannot avoid—death and human vice—and that we must make provisions for both. Perhaps because criminals reveal humanity's dark side, people are drawn to endless movies and television shows that explore the darker side of human nature (wasn't *Breaking Bad*'s Walter White much more interesting as a methamphetamine peddler than as a high school chemistry teacher?). It is this dark but fascinating side of the human character that criminology explores.

Criminology is an interdisciplinary science that gathers and analyzes data on various aspects of criminal, delinquent, and general antisocial behavior. It is different from the discipline of criminal justice, which is concerned with how the criminal justice system investigates, prosecutes, and controls or supervises individuals who have committed crimes. Criminology examines why those individuals committed crimes that got them ensnarled in the criminal justice system in the first place. As with all scientific disciplines, the goal of criminology is to understand its subject matter and to determine how that understanding can benefit society. In pursuit of this understanding, criminologists ask questions such as the following:

- Why do crime rates vary from time to time and from culture to culture?

- Why are some individuals more prone to committing crime than others?

- Why do crime rates vary across ages, genders, and racial/ethnic groups?

- Why are some harmful acts criminalized and not others?

- What can we do to prevent crime?

By a *scientific* study of crime and criminal behavior we mean that criminologists use the scientific method to try to answer their questions rather than just philosophizing about them from their armchairs. The scientific method is a tool for separating truth from error by demanding evidence for any conclusions criminologists arrive at. Evidence is obtained by formulating hypotheses derived from theory that are rigorously tested with data in such a way that others following the same method can replicate the study. By following the scientific method, criminologists hope to build a body of verified knowledge that may help policymakers and police and correctional officials in their battle against crime.

❖ What Is Crime?

The term *criminal* can and has been applied to many types of behavior, some of which nearly all of us have been guilty of at some time in our lives. We can all think of acts that we feel *ought* to be criminal but are not or acts that should not be criminal but are. The list of things that someone or another at different times and at different places may consider to be crimes is very large, with only a few being defined as criminal by the law in the United States at this time. Despite these difficulties, we need a definition of crime in order to proceed. The most often quoted definition is that of Paul Tappan (1947), who defined **crime** as "an intentional act in violation of the criminal law committed without defense or excuse, and penalized by the state" (p. 100). A crime is thus an act in violation of a criminal law for which a punishment is prescribed; the person committing it must have intended to do so and must have done so without legally acceptable defense or justification.

Tappan's definition is strictly a legal one that reminds us that the state, and only the state, has the power to define an act as criminal. Hypothetically a society could eradicate crime tomorrow simply by canceling all of its criminal statutes. Of course, this would not eliminate the behavior specified by the law as crimes; in fact, the behavior would doubtless increase since the behavior could no longer be officially punished. While it is absurd to think that any society would try to solve its crime problem by eliminating its criminal statutes, legislative bodies are continually revising, adding to, and deleting from their criminal statutes.

Crime as a Moving Target

Almost every vice is somewhere and sometimes a virtue. There are numerous examples of acts defined as crimes in one country being tolerated and even expected behavior in another, as demonstrated in the vignette at the beginning of this chapter. We might congratulate ourselves for protecting young girls from the kind of fate that befell the 13- and 14-year-old girls in the vignette, but in 1885 no state in the United States had an age of consent above 12 (Friedman, 2005). Laws also vary within the same culture from time to time as well as across different cultures. Until the Harrison Narcotics Act of 1914 there were few legal restrictions in the United States on the sale, possession, or use of most drugs such as heroin and cocaine. Following the Harrison Act, many drugs became controlled substances and their sale and possession a crime, and a brand-new class of criminals was created overnight.

Crimes pass out of existence also, even acts that had been considered crimes for centuries. Until the United States Supreme Court invalidated sodomy (anal or oral sex) statutes in *Lawrence v. Texas* in 2003, sodomy was legally punishable in many states, even between consenting spouses. Likewise, burning the American flag had serious legal consequences until 1989 when the Supreme Court ruled anti-flag-burning statutes unconstitutional in *Texas v. Johnson*. What constitutes a crime, then, can be defined in or out of existence by the courts or by legislators. As long as human societies remain diverse and dynamic, there will always be a moving target of activities with the potential for nomination as crimes, as well as illegal activities nominated for decriminalization.

If what constitutes crime differs across time and place, how can criminologists hope to agree on a scientific explanation for crime and criminal behavior? Science is about making universal statements about stably defined phenomena. Atoms, the gas laws, DNA, the laws of thermodynamics, photosynthesis, and so on are not defined or evaluated differently by scientists around the globe according to local customs or ideological preferences. But what we call "crime" keeps moving around, and because it does some criminologists have declared it impossible to generalize about what is and is not "real" crime.

What these criminologists are saying is that crime is a socially constructed phenomenon that lacks any "real" objective essence and is defined into existence rather than discovered. Of course, in a trivial sense everything is socially constructed. Nature does not reveal herself to us sorted into ready-labeled packages, so humans must do it for her. *Social construction* means nothing more than humans have perceived a phenomenon, named it, and categorized it according to some classificatory rule that makes note of the similarities and differences among the things being classified. Most classification schemes are not arbitrary; if they were we would not be able to make sense of anything. Categories have empirically meaningful referents and are used to impose order on the diversity of human experience, although arguments exist about just how coherent that order is.

Crime as a Subcategory of Social Harms

So, what *can* we say about crime; how *can* we conceive of it in ways that at least most people would agree are logical, consistent, and correspond with their view of reality? When all is said and done, crime is a subcategory of all harmful acts that range from simple things like smoking to very serious things like murder. Some harmful acts such as smoking tobacco and drinking to excess are not considered anyone's business other than the actor's if they take place in private or even in public if the person indulging in those things creates no annoyance to others.

Socially (as opposed to private) harmful acts are those deemed to be in need of regulation (e.g., health standards, air pollution), but not by the criminal law except under exceptional circumstance. Private wrongs (such as someone reneging on a contract) are socially harmful, but not sufficiently so to require the heavy hand of the criminal law. Such wrongs are regulated by the civil law in which the wronged party (the plaintiff) rather than the state initiates legal action and the defendant does not risk deprivation of his or her liberty if the plaintiff prevails.

Further along the continuum we find a category of harmful acts considered so socially harmful that they come under the scope of the criminal justice system. Even here we are still confronted with the problem of human judgment in determining what goes into this subcategory. But this is true all along the line; smoking was once actually considered rather healthy, and air pollution and other unhealthy environmental conditions were simply facts of life about which nothing could be done. Categorization always requires a series of human judgments, but that does not necessarily render the categorizations arbitrary.

The harm caused by criminal activity is financially and emotionally very costly. The emotional pain and suffering borne by crime victims is obviously impossible to quantify, but many estimates of the financial harm are available. Most estimates focus on the costs of running the criminal justice system, which includes the salaries and benefits of personnel and the maintenance costs of buildings (offices, jails, prisons, stations) and equipment (vehicles, weapons, uniforms). Added to these costs are the costs associated with each crime (the average cost per incident multiplied by the number of incidents as reported to the police). All these costs combined are estimates of the *direct* costs of crime.

The *indirect* costs of crime must also be considered as part of the burden. These costs include all manner of surveillance and security devices, protective devices (guns, alarms, security guards) and insurance costs, medical services, and the productivity and taxes lost of incarcerated individuals. From a variety of government sources, McCollister, French, and Fang (2010) estimate that each year crime results in approximately $15 billion in economic losses to victims and $179 billion in government expenditures on police protection, judicial and legal activities, and corrections. The tangible and intangible financial cost per murder is estimated at $8,982,907, and per rape it is $240,776. These figures do not reflect the severe psychological and emotional costs to victims and their families.

Beyond Social Construction: The Stationary Core Crimes

Few people would argue that an act is not arbitrarily categorized or is not seriously harmful if it is universally condemned. That is, there is a core of offenses defined as wrong at almost all times and in almost all cultures. Some of the strongest evidence in support of the stationary core perspective comes from the International Criminal Police Organization (Interpol), headquartered in Lyon, France. Interpol serves as a repository for crime statistics from each of its 188 member nations. Interpol's data show that such acts as murder, assault, rape, and theft are considered serious crimes in every single country (Walsh & Ellis, 2007). Individuals or groups may differ on the ordering of the seriousness of these crimes, but they are still universally condemned. There are societies in which so-called honor killings are culturally accepted, but this does not contradict the contention that murder is inherently wrong. Even in countries in which the practice exists, honor killing is contrary to the law, although it is rarely prosecuted or is treated leniently if it is. Honor killings typically involve families murdering their daughters, mostly because they have "dishonored" the family by engaging in an unsanctioned sexual relationship or because they are romantically involved with someone the family's culture deems undesirable.

Criminologists call these universally condemned crimes *mala in se* ("inherently evil"). Crimes that are time and culture bound are described as *mala prohibita* ("evil because they are prohibited"). But how can we know that an act is inherently bad? The litmus test for determining a mala in se crime is that no one except under the most bizarre of circumstances would want to be victimized by one (see Box 1.1). While millions of people seek to be "victimized" by prostitutes, drug dealers, and bookies, no one wants to be murdered, raped, robbed, or have their property stolen. Being victimized by such actions evokes physiological reactions (anger, helplessness, sadness, depression, a desire for revenge) in all cultures and would do so even if the acts were not punishable by law or custom. Mala in se crimes engage these emotions not because some legislative body has defined them as wrong, but because they hammer at our deepest concerns. Evolutionary scientists propose that these built-in emotional mechanisms exist because mala in se crimes threatened the survival and reproductive success of our distant ancestors (the ultimate concerns of all sexually reproducing animals) and that they function to strongly motivate people to try to prevent such acts from occurring and punishing them if they do (O'Manique, 2003; Walsh, 2000).

Box 1.1

Mala in Se or *Mala Prohibita*? The Cannibal and His Willing Victim

We have said that the litmus test for a mala in se crime is that no one would want to be a victim of such a crime. You would think that killing, butchering, and eating another human being would certainly pass such a test. But what if the cannibal's dinner was a willing victim and the country in which the cannibal and his victim lived had no law forbidding cannibalism? This strange state of affairs existed in Rotenburg in central Germany in 2001. Germany's own Hannibal Lecter, one Armin Meiwes, had advertised online seeking volunteers for "slaughter and consumption." Among the over 200 replies Meiwes received was an e-mail from Bernd-Jurgen Brandes (a successful software engineer) stating, "I am your meat." Meiwes and Brandes videotaped their agreement, and Meiwes taped the subsequent killing and butchering of Brandes. Brandes stated on the tape that being eaten would be the "fulfillment of my dream."

The prosecution in this case argued for a conviction of murder and "disturbing the peace of the dead," which would have gotten Meiwes a life sentence. The defense argued that what Meiwes had done was simply to assist Brandes in his suicide, which carried a 5-year sentence. The panel of judges hearing the case agreed that Meiwes could not be convicted of murder, split the difference, and handed Meiwes an 8 1/2-year prison sentence in January of 2004. However, the prosecution appealed the case, and on retrial Meiwes was convicted of murder and sentenced to life imprisonment.

In common law countries such as the United States, Meiwes would have been convicted of murder because one person cannot give another the consent to kill him or her—you can give your consent to many things, but not this. What Meiwes committed was clearly a mala in se crime, and Brandes's consent doesn't change that at all. The behavior of both men was obviously bizarre, and just because we find instances in which people do want to be victimized by acts that 99.9% of their fellow humans would find repugnant does not change the inherent badness of those acts.

Figure 1.1 illustrates the relationship of core crimes (mala in se) to acts that have been arbitrarily defined (mala prohibita) as crimes and all harmful acts that may potentially be criminalized. The figure is inspired by John Hagan's (1985) effort to distinguish between "real" crimes and "socially constructed" arbitrary crimes by examining the three highly interrelated concepts of *consensus* (the degree of public agreement on the seriousness of an act), the *severity* of penalties attached to an act, and the level of *harm* attached to an act.

❖ Criminality

Perhaps we can avoid altogether the problem of defining crimes by studying individuals who commit predatory *harmful* acts, regardless of the legal status of the acts. Criminologists do this when they study criminality. **Criminality** is a clinical or scientific term rather than a legal one and one that can be defined independently of legal definitions of crimes. Crime is an intentional act of commission or omission contrary to the law and is a property of society; criminality is a property of individuals that signals the willingness to commit crimes and other harmful acts. Criminality is a trait that lies on a continuum ranging from saint to sociopath and is composed of a mixture of other traits such as callousness, low empathy, impulsiveness, and negative emotionality that also vary greatly among people. People can use and abuse others for personal gain regardless of whether the means used have been defined as criminal; it is the propensity to do this that defines criminality independent of the labeling of an act as a crime or of the person being legally defined as a criminal.

Defining criminality as a continuous trait acknowledges that there is no sharp line separating individuals with respect to this trait—it is not a trait that one has or does not have. Just about everyone at some point in life has committed an act or two in violation of the law, perhaps even a mala in se act. But that doesn't make us all criminals; if it did the term would become virtually synonymous with being human. The point is, we are all situated somewhere on the criminality continuum, just as our heights range from the truly short to the truly tall. Some are so extreme in height that any reasonable person would call them "tall." Likewise, a small number of individuals have violated so many criminal statutes over such a long period of time that few would question the appropriateness of calling them "criminals." Thus, both height and criminality can be thought of as existing along a continuum, even though the words we use often imply that people's heights

Figure 1.1

Mala in Se and *Mala Prohibita* Crimes as Subsets of all Harms

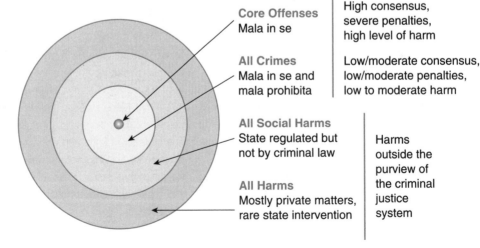

Core Offenses
Mala in se

High consensus, severe penalties, high level of harm

All Crimes
Mala in se and mala prohibita

Low/moderate consensus, low/moderate penalties, low to moderate harm

All Social Harms
State regulated but not by criminal law

Harms outside the purview of the criminal justice system

All Harms
Mostly private matters, rare state intervention

and criminal tendencies come in discrete categories (tall/short, criminal/noncriminal). In other words, just as height varies in fine gradations, so too does involvement in crime.

The Legal Making of a Criminal

Regardless of any criminal traits, no one is "officially" a criminal until he or she has been defined as such by the law, which makes it necessary to briefly discuss the process of arriving at that definition. The legal answer to the question "Who is a criminal?" is that he or she is someone who has committed a crime and has been judged guilty of having done so. Before the law can properly call a person a criminal, it must go through a series of actions governed by well-defined legal rules guiding the serious business of officially labeling a person a criminal. The upcoming section, An Excursion Through the American Criminal Justice System, shows the processing of a suspect in the American criminal justice system from arrest to trial and beyond, illustrated in Figure 1.2.

What Constitutes a Crime?

Corpus delicti is a Latin term meaning "body of the crime" and refers to the elements of an act that must be present in order to legally define it as a crime. All crimes have their own specific elements, which are the essential constituent parts that define the act as criminal. In addition to their specific elements, all crimes share a set of general elements or principles underlying and supporting the specific elements. There are five principles to be satisfied before a person is "officially" labeled a criminal, but in actuality it is only necessary for the state to prove *actus reus* and mens rea to satisfy corpus delicti. The other principles are typically automatically proven in the course of proving actus reus and mens rea.

Actus reus means "guilty act" and refers to the principle that a person must commit some forbidden act or neglect some mandatory act before he or she can be subjected to criminal sanctions. In effect, this principle of law means that people cannot be criminally prosecuted for thinking something or being something, only for *doing* something. This prevents governments from passing laws criminalizing statuses and systems of thought they don't like. For instance, although drunken behavior may be a punishable crime, *being* an alcoholic cannot be punished because "being" something is a status, not an act.

Mens rea means "guilty mind" and refers to whether or not the suspect had a wrongful purpose in mind when carrying out the actus reus. For instance, although receiving stolen property is a criminal offense, if you were to buy a stolen television set from an acquaintance without knowing it had been stolen, you would have lacked mens rea and would not be subject to prosecution. If you were to be prosecuted the state would have to prove that you knew the television was stolen. Negligence, recklessness, or carelessness that results in some harmful consequences, even though not intended, *does not* excuse such behavior from criminal prosecution under mens rea. Conditions that may preclude prosecution under this principle are self-defense, defense of others, youthfulness (a person under 7 years of age cannot be held responsible), insanity (although being found insane does not preclude confinement), and extreme duress or coercion.

Concurrence means that the act (actus reus) and the mental state (mens rea) concur in the sense that the criminal intention actuates the criminal act. For instance, if John sets out with his tools to burglarize Mary's apartment and takes her TV, he has fused the guilty mind with the wrongful act and has therefore committed burglary. However, assume John and Mary are friends who habitually visit each other's apartment unannounced. One day John decides to visit Mary, finds her not at home, and walks in and suddenly decides that he could sell Mary's TV for drug money. Although the loss to Mary is the same in both scenarios, in the latter instance John cannot be charged with burglary because he did not enter her apartment "by force or fraud," the crucial element needed to satisfy such a charge. In this case, the concurrence of guilty mind and wrongful act occurred after lawful entry, so he is only charged with theft, a less serious crime.

Causation refers to the necessity to establish a causal link between the criminal act and the harm suffered. This causal link must be proximate, not ultimate. Suppose Tony wounds Frank in a knife fight. Being macho, Frank attends to the wound himself. Three weeks later, the wound becomes severely infected and results in his death. Can Tony be charged with murder? Although the wounding led to Frank's death (the ultimate cause), Frank's disregard for the seriousness of his injury was the most proximate cause of his death. The question the law asks in cases like this is, "What would any reasonable person do?" Most people would agree that the reasonable person would have sought medical treatment. This being the case, Tony cannot be charged with homicide; the most he could be charged with is aggravated assault.

Harm refers to the negative impact a crime has either to the victim or to the general values of the community. Although the harm caused by the criminal act is often obvious, the harm caused by many so-called "victimless" crimes is often less obvious, although some such crimes can cause more social harm in the long run than many crimes with obvious victims.

❖ An Excursion Through the American Criminal Justice System

The best way to explain the process of becoming a legal criminal is to follow the processing of felony cases from arrest to trial and beyond. There are many points at which the arrested person may be shunted off the criminal justice conveyor belt via the discretionary decisions of a variety of criminal justice officials. This process varies in some specifics from state to state, but the principles underlying the specifics are uniform. Presented here are the stages and procedures that are most common among our 50 states' court systems.

Arrest A felony suspect first enters the criminal justice system by arrest. When a person has been legally detained to answer criminal charges, he or she has been arrested. Some arrests are made on the basis of an arrest warrant, which is an official document signed by a judge on the basis of evidence presented by law enforcement indicating that the person named in the warrant has probably committed a crime. The warrant authorizes the police to make an arrest, although the great majority of arrests are initiated by the police without a warrant. A police officer making a warrantless arrest is held to the same legal constraints involved in making application for a warrant. To make a legal felony arrest the officer must have probable cause. Probable cause means that the officer must possess a set of facts that would lead a reasonable person to conclude that the arrested person had committed a crime. Although a person can be stopped on the basis of an officer's suspicion and frisked for a weapon, he or she cannot be arrested on the basis of suspicion alone. It is only after an arrest that the Fifth Amendment right against self-incrimination comes into play.

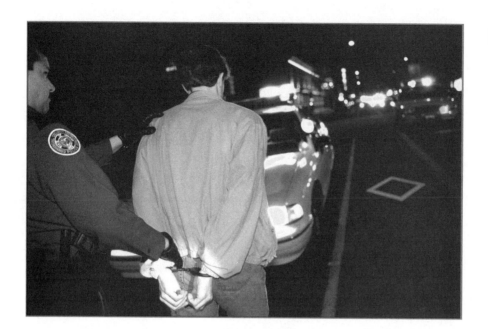

Photo 1.1

Police officer takes suspect into custody. A felony suspect enters the criminal justice system by arrest.

Preliminary hearing After arrest and booking into the county jail, the suspect must be presented in court for the preliminary hearing before a magistrate or judge at the earliest opportunity. The preliminary hearing has two purposes: to advise suspects of their constitutional rights and of the charges against them and to set bail. The suspect may be released on monetary bail on his or her "own recognizance." If bail is denied it is usually because of the gravity of the crime, the risk the suspect poses to the community, or the risk that the suspect might flee the court's jurisdiction. There is no constitutional right to bail. The Eighth Amendment only states that "excessive bail shall not be required." The traditional assumption has been that bail is only designed to assure the suspect's appearance at the next court hearing and that *excessive* means that the amount set should be within the suspect's means.

Preliminary arraignment The preliminary arraignment is a proceeding before a magistrate or judge in which three major matters must be decided: whether or not a crime has actually been committed, whether or not there are reasonable grounds to believe that the person before the bench committed it, and whether or not the crime was committed in the jurisdiction of the court. These matters determine if the suspect's arrest and detention are legal. The onus of proving the legality of the suspect's arrest and detention is on the prosecutor, who must establish probable cause and present the court with evidence pertinent to the suspect's probable guilt. This is usually a relatively easy matter for the prosecutor since defense attorneys rarely cross-examine witnesses or introduce their own evidence at this point, their primary use of the preliminary hearing being only to discover the strength of the prosecutor's case.

The grand jury If the prosecutor is successful, the suspect is bound over to a higher court for further processing. Prior to the suspect's next court appearance, prosecutors in some states must seek an indictment (a document formally charging the suspect with a specific crime or crimes) from a grand jury. The grand jury, so called to distinguish it from the "petit"

Figure 1.2

The Sequence of Events Leading to a Person Being Labeled a Criminal

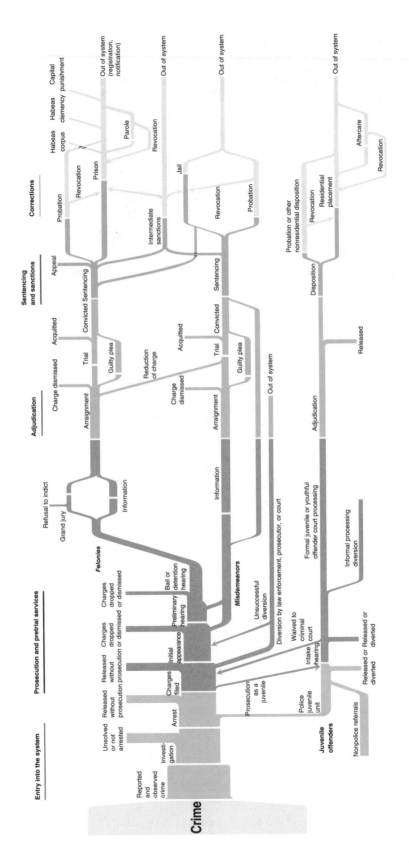

Source: U.S. Bureau of Justice Statistics, 1998

Note: This chart gives a simplified view of caseflow through the criminal justice system. Procedures vary among jurisdictions. The weights of the lines are not intended to show actual size of caseloads.

or trial jury, is nominally an investigatory body and a buffer between the awesome power of the state and its citizens, but some see it as a historical anachronism that serves only prosecutorial purposes. The grand jury is composed of citizens chosen from voter or automobile registration lists and numbers anywhere from 7 to 23 members.

Arraignment Armed with an indictment (or an *information* in states not requiring grand jury proceedings), the prosecutor files the case against the accused in felony court (variably called a district, superior, or common pleas court), which sets a date for arraignment. The arraignment proceeding is the first time a defendant has the opportunity to respond to the charges against him or her. After the charges are read to the defendant, he or she must then enter a formal response to them, known as a plea. The plea alternatives are guilty, not guilty, or no contest. A guilty plea is usually the result of a plea bargain agreement concluded before the arraignment. About 90% of all felony cases in the United States are settled by plea bargains in which the state extends some benefit to defendants, such as reduced charges, in exchange for their cooperation. By pleading guilty, defendants give up their right to be proven guilty "beyond a reasonable doubt," their right against self-incrimination, and the right to appeal.

A "not guilty" plea results in a date being set for trial; a "guilty" or "no contest" plea results in a date being set for sentencing.

The trial A trial by a jury of one's peers is a Sixth Amendment right and is an examination of the facts of a case by a judge or a jury for the purpose of reaching a judgment. The trial is an adversarial process pitting the prosecutor against the defense attorney, with each side trying to "vanquish" the other. There is no sense that each side is interested in seeking truth or justice in this totally partisan process. It is the task of the judge to ensure that both sides play by the rules. The prosecution's job is a little more difficult than the defense's since it must "prove beyond a reasonable doubt" that the accused is indeed guilty. Except in states that allow for non-unanimous jury decisions, the defense need only plant the seed of reasonable doubt in the mind of one stubborn juror to upset the prosecution's case.

Having heard the facts of the case, and having been instructed by the judge on the principles of law pertaining to it, the jury is charged with reaching a verdict. The jury's verdict may be guilty or not guilty, or if it cannot reach a verdict (a "hung" jury), the judge may declare a mistrial. A hung jury results in either dismissal of the charges by the prosecutor or in a retrial. If the verdict is guilty, in most cases the judge will delay sentencing to allow time for a presentence investigation report to be prepared. It is at the point of conviction (or entering a plea of guilty) that the person officially becomes a criminal.

Probation Presentence investigation reports (PSI) are prepared by probation officers and contain a variety of information about the crime and the offender's background (criminal record, education and work history, marital status, substance abuse, and attitude). On the basis of this information, the probation officer offers a sentencing recommendation. The most important factors influencing these recommendations are crime seriousness and the defendant's criminal history. A judge may place the offender on probation, the most common sentence in the United States today. A probation sentence is a suspended commitment to prison, and if at any time during their probationary period offenders do not abide by the imposed probation conditions (consisting of a variety of general and offender-specific conditions), they may face revocation of probation and the imposition of the original prison sentence. Probation officers supervise and monitor offenders' behavior and assure that all conditions of probation are adhered to. Probation officers thus function as both social workers and law enforcement officers, sometimes conflicting roles that officers may find difficult to reconcile.

Photo 1.2

The Sixth Amendment guarantees the right to trial by an impartial jury.

Incarceration If the sentence imposed for a felony conviction is some form of incarceration, the judge has the option of sentencing the offender to a state penitentiary, a county jail, or a county work release program. The latter two options are almost invariably imposed as supplements to probation orders.

Parole Parole is a conditional release from prison granted to inmates prior to the completion of their sentences. An inmate is granted parole by an administrative body called a parole board, which decides for or against parole based on such factors as inmate behavior while incarcerated and the urgency of the need for cell space. Once released on parole, parole officers, whose job is almost identical to that of probation officers, supervise parolees. In many states, probation and parole officers are one and the same. The primary difference between probation and parole is that probationers are under the supervision of the courts and parolees are under the supervision of the state department of corrections. Revocation of probation is a judicial function; revocation of parole is an executive administrative function.

❖ A Short History of Criminology

The Supernatural Era

Criminology is a young discipline, although humans have probably been theorizing about crime and its causes ever since they first made rules and observed others breaking them. What and how people thought about crime and criminals (as well as all other things) in the past was strongly influenced by the social and intellectual currents of their time. This is no less true of what and how modern criminologists think about crime and criminals. In prescientific days, explanations for bad behavior were often of a religious or spiritual nature. Disastrous natural events such as famines and floods were seen as divine punishment for some transgression, and criminals were considered to be possessed by evil spirits. The standard of innocence for an accused person was the survival of some sort of ordeal, such as being bound hand and feet and thrown into a river. If the accused survived the ordeal (which few, if any, ever did), he or she was considered under God's protection and therefore innocent. At other times, survival was a viewed as a sign of evil (the devil's protection), and the person was executed (Drapkin, 1989).

The Renaissance

The Renaissance was a period lasting approximately from 1450 to 1600 that saw a change in thinking away from the pure God-centered supernaturalism of the Middle Ages to more human-centered naturalism. *Renaissance* literally means "rebirth" and refers to the rediscovery of the thinking traditions of the ancient Greeks. The sciences and arts were becoming important, the printing press was invented, and Christopher Columbus "discovered" America during this period. In short, the Renaissance began to mold human thinking away from the absolute authority of received opinion and toward a way that would eventually lead to the modern scientific method. Many during this period believed that the human character and personality are transparent in physical appearance. Such folk wisdom was systematized by an Italian physician named Giambattista della Porta, who developed a theory of human personality called physiognomy in 1558. Porta claimed that the study of physical appearance, particularly of the face, could reveal much about a person's personality and character. Thieves, for instance, were said to have large lips and sharp vision.

The Enlightenment

Another major thrust toward the emergence of the modern world was the Enlightenment, a period approximately from 1650 to 1800. It might be said that the Renaissance provided a key to the human mind and the Enlightenment opened the door. Whereas the Renaissance is associated with advances in art, literature, music, and philosophy, the Enlightenment is associated with advances in mathematics, science, and the dignity and worth of the individual as exemplified by a concern for human rights. This concern led to reforms in criminal justice systems throughout Europe, a process given a major push by Cesare Becarria's work *On Crime and Punishment* that ushered in the so-called classical school. The classical school emphasized human rationality and free will in its explanations for criminal behavior.

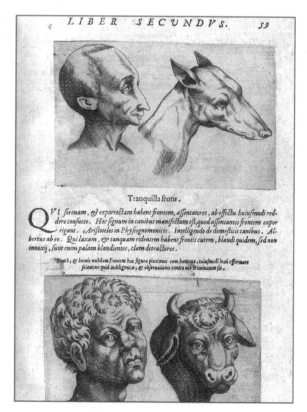

Photo 1.3

One of Giambattista Della Porta's illustrations. Physiogonomists were fascinated by the apparent similarities of some people's faces with animals.

The Industrial Revolution and the Age of Science

Modern criminology began to take shape in the 19th century with the increasing faith that science could provide answers for everything. This period saw the harnessing of the forces of nature to build and operate the great machines that drove the Industrial Revolution and the strides made in biology by Charles Darwin's works on evolution. Criminology saw the beginning of the so-called positivist school during this period. Theories of character, such as phrenology, abounded. The basic idea behind phrenology was that cognitive and personality functions are localized in the brain and that the parts regulating the most dominant functions were bigger than parts regulating the less dominant ones. Criminals were said to have large bumps on parts of the skull thought to regulate craftiness, brutishness, and moral insensibility and small bumps in such "localities" as intelligence, honor, and piety. The biggest impact during this period, however, was made by Cesare Lombroso's theory of atavism, or the born criminal. Criminologists from this point on were obsessed with measuring, sorting, and sifting all kinds of data about criminal behavior. The main stumbling block to criminological advancement during this period was the inadequacy of its research. The intricacies of scientifically valid research design and measurement were not appreciated, and statistical techniques were truly primitive by today's standards. The early classical and positivist thinkers are discussed at length in Chapter 4.

The Progressive Era

The so-called Progressive Era (about 1890 to 1920) ushered in new social ideologies and new ways of thinking about crime. It was an era of liberal efforts to bring about social reform as unions, women, and other disadvantaged groups of people struggled for recognition. Criminology largely turned away from what was disparaged as "biological determinism," which implied that nothing could be done to reform criminals, to cultural or social determinism. If behavior is caused by what people experience in their environments, it was thought that all we had to do to change their behavior was to change their environment. It was during this period that sociology became the disciplinary home of criminology. Criminology became less interested in why individuals commit crime from biological or psychological points of view to a concern with aggregate-level data (e.g., social structures, neighborhoods, subcultures); that is, where is crime most prevalent and among what groups? It was during this period that the so-called structural theories of crime (discussed in Chapter 6), such as the Chicago school of social ecology, were formulated. Anomie strain theory was another structural/cultural theory that emerged somewhat later (1938). This theory was doubtless influenced strongly by the American experience of the Great Depression and by the exclusion of African Americans from many areas of American society.

The period from the 1950s through the early 1970s saw considerable dissatisfaction with the strong structural approach, which many viewed as proceeding as if individuals were almost irrelevant to explaining criminal behavior. Criminological theory moved toward integrating psychology and sociology during this period and strongly emphasized the importance of socialization. Control theories were highly popular at this time, as was labeling theory; these are addressed in Chapter 7.

The Critical Period

Because the latter part of this period was a time of great civil unrest in the United States (the anti–Vietnam War, civil rights, women's, and gay rights movements) it also saw the emergence of several theories, such as conflict theory, that were highly critical of American society. These theories extended to earlier works of Marxist criminologists, who tended to believe that the only real cause of crime was capitalism. These theories provided little new in terms of our understanding of "street" criminal behavior, but they did spark an interest in white-collar crime and how laws were made by the powerful and applied against the powerless. These theories are addressed in Chapter 8. Perhaps in response to these theories, and perhaps because of a new conservative mood in the United States, theories with the classical taste for free will and rationality embedded in them reemerged in the 1980s. These were rational choice and routine activities theories, discussed in Chapter 5.

The Modern Period

The late 1990s and early 2000s saw a resurgence of biosocial theories. These theories view behavior as the result of biological factors interacting with past and present environments. Biosocial theories have been on the periphery of criminology since its beginning but have been hampered by perceptions of them as driven by an illiberal agenda and by the inability to "get inside" the mysteries of hereditary and the workings of the brain. The truly spectacular advances in the observational techniques (e.g., brain scan methods, $10 cheek swabs to test DNA) in the genetic and neurosciences over the last three decades have made these things less mysterious, and social scientists are increasingly realizing that there is nothing illiberal about recognizing the biology basis of human nature.

Lilly, Cullen, and Ball (2007) note that the most dramatic developments in science come most often from new observational techniques rather than new developments in theory. No science advances without the technology at its disposal to plumb its depths. Many chemists in the late 19th century refused to accept the existence of atoms, but chemistry advanced by leaps and bounds when the discipline as a whole finally accepted the atomic theory of matter (we are even able to see atoms with a scanning tunneling microscope, invented in 1981). Criminology is in a position today similar to that of chemists 150 years ago. The concepts, methods, and measuring devices available to us today may do for the progress of criminology what physics did for chemistry, what chemistry did for biology, and what biology is doing for psychology. Exceptionally ambitious longitudinal studies carried out over decades in concert with medical and biological scientists, such as the Dunedin Multidisciplinary Health and Development Study (Moffitt, 1993), the National Longitudinal Study of Adolescent Health (Udry, 2003), and the National Youth Survey (Menard, Mihalic, & Huizinga, 2001) are able to gather a wealth of genetic, neurological, physiological, psychological, and sociological data. Paus (2010) discusses four evolving long-term studies that are brain imaging 400 to 2,000 subjects at a time and collecting large volumes of behavioral and cognitive data (e.g., socioeconomic status, maternal smoking and drinking,

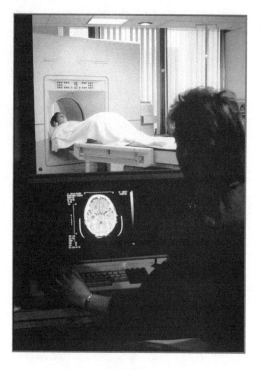

Photo 1.4

Functional Magnetic Resonance Imaging (fMRI) machines can tell us a lot about the functioning of the brain and how that functioning is related to behavior.

stressful life events, antisocial behavior, IQ, personality profiles). Three of these four studies are also collecting DNA data. Integrating these hard data into criminology will no more rob it of its autonomy than physics robbed chemistry or chemistry robbed biology. For those who agree with this assessment, this is an exciting time to study criminology!

❖ The Role of Theory in Criminology

When an FBI agent asked the Depression-era bank robber Willie Sutton why he robbed banks, Sutton replied, "Because that's where the money is" (Sutton & Linn, 1976, p. 120). In his witty way, Sutton was offering a theory explaining bank robbery: If we put a certain kind of personality and learning together with opportunity and coveted resources, we get bank robbery. This is what theory making is all about: trying to grasp how all the known factors related to (or correlated with) a phenomenon such as crime are linked together in noncoincidental ways to produce an effect.

Just as medical scientists want to find out what causes disease, criminologists are interested in finding out factors that cause criminal behavior. Just as there are risk factors related to becoming ill, there are a variety of risk factors that may lead to criminal behavior. The first step in a long chain leading to the detection of causes is to discover correlates related to the phenomenon of interest. To discover if two things (we call them factors or variables) are co-related, we have to determine if they vary together; i.e., if one of the variables changes (goes up or down) when the other variable changes.

Take gender, the most thoroughly documented correlate of criminal behavior ever identified. Literally thousands of studies throughout the world, some European studies going back five or six centuries, consistently report strong gender differences in criminal behavior, and the more serious the crime the greater the difference (Ellis & Walsh, 2000). In other words, as we move from one category of the gender variable (female to male), the prevalence and incidence of crime rises dramatically. However, establishing *why* gender is such a strong correlate of crime is the real challenge. Of course, variables can vary together coincidentally rather than causally. When we consistently find correlations between criminal behavior and some other factor it is tempting to assume that something causal is going on, but a correlation *suggests* causation; it does not establish it. Resisting the tendency to jump to causal conclusions from correlations is the first lesson of statistics. Establishing *causal* connections between and among correlates is the business of theory.

Photo 1.5

Bank robber Willie Sutton at the courthouse for his trial.

What Is Theory?

A **theory** is a set of logically interconnected propositions explaining how observed facts within a domain of interest are related and from which a number of hypotheses can be derived and tested. Theories should provide logical explanations of an area of interest by fitting the discovered facts into a coherent pattern. Not only should they be capable of making sense of relevant empirical facts so far discovered, they should provide practical guidance for researchers looking for yet undiscovered facts. This guidance takes the form of a series of statements that can be logically deduced from the assertions of the theory called **hypotheses**, which are statements about relationships between and among factors we expect to find based on the logic of our theories. Theories provide the raw material (the ideas) for generating hypotheses, and hypotheses support or fail to support theories by exposing them to empirical (based on experiment and observation) testing.

Theories are devised to explain how a number of correlates may actually be causally related to criminal behavior rather than simply associated with it. When we talk of causes we do not mean that when X is present Y *will* occur in a completely prescribed way. We mean that when X is present Y has a certain *probability* of occurring and perhaps only then if X is present along with factors A, B, and C. Criminologists have never uncovered a necessary cause (a factor that *must* be present for criminal behavior to occur and in the absence of which criminal behavior has never occurred) or a sufficient cause (a factor that is able to produce criminal behavior without being augmented by some other factor).

Theories thus both help us to make sense of a diversity of facts and even tell us where to look for more facts. We all use theory every day to fit diverse facts together. A detective confronted with a number of facts about a mysterious murder must fit them together, even though their meaning and relatedness to one another is ambiguous and perhaps even contradictory. Using years of experience, training, and good common sense the detective constructs a theory linking those facts together so that they begin to make some sense, to begin to tell their story. An initial theory derived from the available facts then guides the detective in the search for additional facts in a series of "*if* this is true, *then* this should be true" statements (this is what scientists call hypotheses). There may be many false starts as our detective misinterprets some facts, fails to uncover others, and considers some to be relevant when they are not. Good detectives, like good scientists, will adjust their theory as new facts warrant; poor detectives and poor scientists will stand by their favored theory by not looking for more facts or by ignoring, downplaying, or hiding contrary facts that come to their attention.

What Is a Good Theory?

The physical and natural sciences enjoy a great deal of agreement about what constitutes the core body of knowledge within their disciplines and thus have few competing theories, especially at the most general levels. Within criminology, and the social/behavioral sciences in general, there is little agreement about the nature of the phenomena we study, and so we suffer an embarrassment of theoretical riches (see Table 1.1). Given the number of criminological theories, students may be forgiven for asking which one is true. Scientists never use the term *truth* in scientific discourse; rather, they tend to ask which theory is most useful. Criteria for judging the merits of a theory are summarized here from Ellis, Hartley, and Walsh (2010).

1. *Predictive accuracy.* A theory must not only be backward looking in the sense that it harmoniously fits known facts together, it must also be forward looking, telling researchers where they should find new facts. That is, a theory has merit and is useful to the extent that it accurately predicted what is later observed; it has generated a large number of research hypotheses that have supported it. This is the most important criterion.

2. *Predictive scope.* This refers to the scope or range of the theory and thus the scope or range of the hypotheses that can be derived from it. That is, how much of the empirical world falls under the explanatory umbrella of Theory A compared to how

much falls under Theory B. As the predictive scope of a theory widens, it tends to get more complicated.

3. *Simplicity.* If two competing theories are essentially equal in terms of the first two criteria, then the less complicated one is considered more "elegant."

4. *Falsifiability.* A theory is never proven true, but it must have the quality of being falsifiable or disprovable. If a theory is formulated in such a way that no amount of evidence could possibly falsify it, then the theory is of little use.

How to Think About Theories

You will be a lot less concerned about the numerous theories in criminology if you realize that different theories deal with different levels of analysis. A **level of analysis** is that segment of the phenomenon of interest that is measured and analyzed. We can ask about causes of crime at the levels of whole societies, subcultures, neighborhoods, families, or individuals. If the question asks about crime rates in societies (such as Japan versus the United States), the answers must address sociocultural differences among different societies or in the same society at different times. Conversely, if crime rates are found to be related to the degree of industrialization or racial and ethnic diversity in societies, this tells us nothing about why some people or groups in an industrialized and racially heterogeneous society commit crimes and other people and groups in the same society do not. To answer questions about individuals and groups we need theories about individuals and groups. Generally speaking, questions of cause and effect must be answered at the same level of analysis at which they were posed; thus different theories are required at different levels. This is not to say, however, that we do not have theories that attempt to span multiple levels of analysis.

To span different levels of analysis we have to understand how factors included in different levels interact (how each is both affected by and affects the other). Crime rates can change drastically from time to time without any corresponding change in the gene pool or personalities of the people in the population. Because causes can only be sought among factors that vary, changing sociocultural environments must be the only causes of changing crime rates. What environmental changes do, however, is raise or lower individual thresholds for engaging in crime, and some people have lower thresholds than others. People with weak criminal propensities (or high prosocial propensities) require high levels of environmental instigation to commit crimes, but some individuals engage in criminal behavior in the most benign of environments. Whether an individual crosses the threshold to commit criminal acts depends on where his or her personal threshold is set interacting with where the environmental threshold is set. At this level, then, we need to have a firm grasp both on individual characteristics and how they interact with a variety of environmental conditions.

❖ Ideology in Criminological Theory

In addition to criminological theorizing being linked to the social and intellectual climate of the times, it is also strongly linked to ideology. **Ideology** is a way of looking at the world, a general emotional picture of "how things should be." It is often so strongly held that it narrows the mind and inflames the passions, leading to a selective interpretation and understanding of evidence rather than an objective and rational evaluation of it. Ideology forms, shapes, and colors our concepts of crime and its causes in ways that lead to a tendency to accept or reject new evidence according to how well or poorly it fits our ideology.

A criminological theory is at least partly shaped by ideology, and those who feel drawn to a particular theory owe a great deal of their attraction to it to the fact that they share the theory's vision (Cullen, 2005). This observation reminds us of the Indian parable of the six blind men feeling different parts of an elephant. Each man described the elephant according to the part of its anatomy he had felt, but each failed to appreciate the descriptions of the others who felt different parts. The men fell into dispute and departed in anger, each convinced of the utter stupidity of the others. The point is that ideology often leads criminologists to "feel" only parts of the criminological elephant, to confuse the parts with the whole, and even to question the intelligence and motives (e.g., having some kind of political agenda) of others who have examined different parts of the criminological elephant. Criminology is, however, slowly moving toward the realization that criminal behavior must be examined at all levels from neurons to neighborhoods if it is ever to come to terms with the whole.

According to economist and philosopher Thomas Sowell (1987), two contrasting visions have shaped thoughts about human nature throughout history, and these visions are in constant conflict with each other. The first of these visions is the **constrained vision**, so called because believers in this vision view human activities as constrained by an innate human nature that is self-centered and largely unalterable. The **unconstrained vision** denies an innate human nature, viewing it as formed anew in each different culture. The unconstrained vision also believes that human nature is perfectible, a view scoffed at by those who profess the constrained vision. A major difference between the two visions is that the constrained vision says "this is how the world *is*," and the unconstrained vision says "this is how the world *should be*." For instance, unconstrained visionaries might ask what causes crime or poverty, but constrained visionaries would ask the opposite questions—what causes a well-ordered society and wealth? Note that this implies that unconstrained visionaries believe that crime and poverty are deviations from the norm and need to be explained. Constrained visionaries see crime and poverty as historically normal and inevitable (albeit regrettable) and believe that what has to be understood are the conditions that prevent them. The major fault line in criminology lies in these visions. Theories broadly classified as social learning theories see crime as caused, and theories broadly classified as social control theories see crime as inevitable unless steps are taken to prevent it.

The evidence that ideology is linked to which theories criminologists favor is strong. Cooper, Walsh, and Ellis (2010) surveyed 379 criminologists and asked them which theory best explained serious criminal behavior. As you see from Table 1.1, 24 theories were represented. Obviously they cannot all "best explain serious criminal behavior," so something other than evidence led them to their choices, and the best predictor was criminologists' self-reported ideology, divided into conservative, moderate, liberal, and radical. The "$X^2 = 134.6$, $p < 0.001$" notation means that such a result could be found by chance in less than one time in 1,000 similar samplings. We can thus be quite confident that the finding can be generalized beyond the sample to other criminologists, especially since this study repeated a previous study of a different group of criminologists with the same results (Walsh & Ellis, 2004). When reading this text try to understand where the originators, supporters, and detractors of any particular theory being discussed are "coming from" ideologically as well as theoretically.

❖ Connecting Criminological Theory and Social Policy

Theories of crime imply that changing the conditions the theory holds responsible for causing crime can reduce it and even prevent it. I say "imply" because few theorists are explicit about

Table 1.1

Theories Favored by Criminologists Cross-Tabulated by Self-Reported Political Ideology

Theory Favored*	Political Ideology				
	Conservative	Moderate	Liberal	Radical	Total
Social learning (2, 6)	1	22	22	5	50
Life course/developmental (n/a, 11)	3	8	28	3	42
Social control (1, 1)	0	14	27	1	42
Social disorganization (7, 14)	0	11	26	3	40
Self control (n/a, 2)	3	6	15	0	24
Biosocial (n/a, 12)	5	5	11	0	21
Rational choice	2	7	11	1	21
Conflict (n/a, 4)	0	2	8	6	16
Critical (10, 18)	0	0	8	8	16
Differential association (4, 3)	1	4	10	1	16
Age-graded developmental	1	5	7	0	13
Strain (n/a, 8)	0	3	9	0	12
Dual-pathway developmental (n/a, 5)	1	0	10	0	11
Routine activities (n/a, 9)	1	2	8	0	11
General strain	0	2	4	1	7
Institutional anomie	0	1	5	0	6
Interactional	0	1	5	0	6
Opportunity (5, 15)	1	2	2	0	5
Ecological (n/a, 23)	1	1	2	0	4
Labeling (6, 17)	0	1	2	1	4
Psychological	0	1	3	0	4
Classical (n/a, 20)	0	3	0	0	3
Feminist (n/a, 10)	0	0	2	1	3
Anomie (9, 6)	0	1	1	0	2
TOTAL	20	102	226	31	379

Source: Cooper, Walsh, & Ellis, 2010

$X^2 = 134.6$, $p < 0.001$

*Numbers in parentheses represent ranking of theories in the Ellis and Hoffman (1990) and Walsh and Ellis (2004) surveys. Theories without ranking or designated n/a (not applicable) were not represented in those surveys.

the public policy implications of their work. Scientists are primarily concerned with gaining knowledge for its own sake; they are only secondarily concerned with how useful that knowledge may be to practitioners and policymakers. Conversely, policymakers are less concerned with hypothesized "causes" of a problem and more concerned with what can be done about the problem that is politically, practically, and financially feasible.

Policy is simply a decided course of action designed to solve some problem selected from among alternative courses of action. Solving a social problem means attempting to reduce the level of the problem currently being experienced or to enact strategies that try to prevent it from occurring in the first place. Social science findings can and have been used to help policymakers determine which course of action to follow to "do something" about the crime problem, but many other concerns policymakers must consider go beyond maintaining consistency with social science theory and data. The question of "what to do about crime" involves political and financial considerations, the urgency of other problems competing for scarce financial resources (schools, highways, environmental protection, public housing, national defense), and a host of other major and minor considerations deemed important by various segments of the population.

Policy choices are, at bottom, value choices, and as such only those policy recommendations that are ideologically palatable are likely to be implemented. Given all of these extratheoretical considerations, it would be unfair to base our judgment of a theory's power solely by its impact on public policy. Even if some aspects of policy are theory based, unless all recommendations of the theory are fully implemented, the success or failure of the policy cannot be considered evidence of theoretical failure anymore than a baker can blame a recipe for a lousy cake if he or she neglects to include all the ingredients it calls for.

Connecting problems with solutions is a tricky business in all areas of government policymaking, but nowhere is it more difficult than in criminal justice. No single strategy can be expected to produce significant results, and a strategy may sometimes make matters worse. For example, President Johnson's "War on Poverty" was supposed to have a significant impact on the crime problem by attacking what informed opinion of the time considered its "root cause." Programs and policies developed to reduce poverty currently involve 126 federal (as well as state) programs that have spent almost $15 *trillion* over the past 40 years (Tanner, 2012). However, reducing poverty had no effect on reducing crime; in fact, crime rose to record levels as poverty was falling during the latter period of the 20th century (Walsh & Ellis, 2007). Another high-profile example of failed policy is the Volstead Act of 1919 that prohibited the manufacture and sale of alcohol in the United States. Although based on a true premise (alcohol is a major factor in facilitating violent crime), it failed because it ushered in a wild period of crime as gangs fought over control of the illegal alcohol market. The current war on drugs has had similar negative consequences. Policies attempting to control human behavior often have effects unanticipated by policymakers or by the theories that may have driven their policies.

Nevertheless, every theory has policy implications deducible from its primary assumptions and propositions. The deep and lasting effects of the classical theories on legal systems around the world have long been noted, but the broad generalities about human nature contained in those theories offer little specific advice on ways to change criminals or to reduce their numbers. Although we caution against using the performance of a theory's public policy recommendations as a major criterion to evaluate its power, the fact remains that a good theory *should* offer useful practical recommendations, and we discuss the policy implications of each theory.

Summary

- Criminology is the scientific study of crime and criminals. It is an interdisciplinary/multidisciplinary study, although criminology has yet to integrate these disciplines in any comprehensive way.

- The definition of crime is problematic because acts defined as criminal vary across time and culture. Many criminologists believe that because crimes are defined into existence we cannot determine what constitutes real crimes and criminals. However, there is a stationary core of crimes that are universally condemned and always have been. These are predatory crimes that cause serious harm and are defined as mala in se, or "inherently bad" crimes, as opposed to mala prohibita, or "bad because they are forbidden" crimes.

- A person is not "officially" a criminal until such time as he or she has been found guilty beyond a reasonable doubt of having committed a crime. In order to prove that he or she did, the state has to prove corpus delicti ("the body of the crime"), which essentially means that he or she committed a criminal act (actus reus) with full awareness that the act was wrong (mens rea—guilty mind). Other basic principles—concurrence, harm, and causation—are proven in the process of proving corpus delicti.

- The history of criminology shows that the cultural and intellectual climate of the time strongly influences how scholars think about and study crime and criminality. The Renaissance brought more secular thinking, the Enlightenment more humane and rational thinking, the Industrial Revolution more scientific thinking, and the Progressive Era a reform-oriented criminology reminiscent of the classical school.

- Advances in any science are also constrained by the tools available to test theories. The ever-improving concepts, methods, and techniques available from modern genetics, neuroscience, and other biological sciences should add immeasurably to criminology's knowledge base in the near future.

- Theory is the "bread and butter" of any science, including criminology. There are many contending theories seeking to explain crime and criminality. Although we do not observe such theoretical disagreement in the more established sciences, the social/behavioral sciences are young, and human behavior is extremely difficult to study.

- When judging among the various theories we have to keep certain things in mind, including the predictive accuracy, scope, simplicity, and falsifiability. We must also remember that crime and criminality can be discussed at many levels (society-wide, subcultural, family, or individual) and that a theory that may do a good job of predicting crime at one level may do a poor job at another level.

- Theories can also be offered at different levels of analysis—whole societies, subcultures, neighborhoods, families, and individuals. They may focus on the evolutionary history of the species, the individual's subjective appraisal of a situation, or any other temporal level in between. A full account of an individual's behavior may have to take all these levels into consideration because any behavior arises from an individual's propensities interacting with the environmental situation as that individual perceives it. This is why we approach criminology from social, psychosocial, and biosocial perspectives.

- Criminologists have traditionally examined only aspects of criminal behavior that they find congenial to their ideology and, unfortunately, often malign those who focus on other aspects. The main ideological dividing line in criminology is between constrained visionaries (primarily conservatives who tend to favor explanations of behavior that focus on the individual) and unconstrained visionaries (mostly liberals who tend to favor structural or cultural explanations).

- All theories have explicit or implicit recommendation for policy since they posit causes of crime or criminality. Removing those alleged causes should reduce crime if the theory is correct, but the complex nature of crime and criminality make policy decisions based on them very risky indeed. Policymakers must consider many other issues demanding scarce resources, so the policy content of a theory should never be used to pass judgment on the usefulness of theory for criminologists.

Exercises and Discussion Questions

1. Which of the following acts do you consider mala in se crimes, mala prohibita crimes, or no crime at all? Defend your choices.

   A. drug possession. B. vandalism. C. drunk driving. D. collaborating with the enemy. E. sale of alcohol to minors. F. fraud. G. spouse abuse. H. adult male having consensual sex with underage person. I. prostitution. J. homosexual behavior. K. pornography.

2. Why are new observational techniques such as DNA testing and brain scans useful to criminologists?

3. Discuss the relationship among theories, facts, and hypotheses.

4. Why is it important to consider ideology when evaluating criminologists' work? Is it possible for criminologists to divorce their ideology from their work?

5. Large-scale policies aimed at reducing crime (think of Prohibition and the War on Poverty) rarely have the desired effect. Can you think of any good reasons why this is so?

6. Go to www.lsus.edu/offices-and-services/community-outreach/the-journal-of-ideology/archives for the online journal *Quarterly Journal of Ideology*. Click on *archive* and find and read "Ideology: Criminology's Achilles' Heel." What does this article say about the "conflict of visions" in criminology?

Useful Websites

Anderson, K. Social constructionism and belief causation. http://philosophy.stanford.edu/apps/stanfordphilosophy/files/wysiwyg_images/anderson.pdf.

Critical Criminology. www.critcrim.org.

Conflict Criminology. www.criminology.com/resources/understanding-criminology-theories.

Learning Theories of Crime. http://criminology.wikia.com/wiki/Social_Learning_Theory.

Links to Criminological Theory. www.criminology.com/resources/understanding-criminology-theories.

Chapter Terms

Actus reus	Crime	Level of analysis
Arraignment	Criminality	*Mala in se*
Arrest	Criminology	*Mala prohibita*
Causation	Grand jury	*Mens rea*
Concurrence	Harm	Policy
Constrained vision	Hypotheses	Theory
Corpus delicti	Ideology	Unconstrained vision

CHAPTER 2

Measuring Crime and Criminal Behavior

A weary English bobby (a popular nickname for British police officers) patrolling his foot beat on a chilly November night hears the unmistakable sounds of sexual activity from the dark entranceway of a closed greengrocer's shop. He smiles to himself and tiptoes toward the sound. When he reaches the entranceway he switches on his flashlight and booms out the favorite line of the stereotypical bobby: "What's goin' on 'ere then?" The squeaking couple immediately come to attention and adjust their dress before the young man—obviously still in a state of arousal—stammers, "Why, nothing, constable." The officer recognizes the woman as a local "slapper" (prostitute) and he vaguely recognizes the man (more of a boy of around 17 really) as a local supermarket worker. The constable reasons that he should arrest both parties for public indecency, but that would entail about an hour of paperwork (an hour in the warm police station with a nice cup of tea sounded good though) and lead to the profound embarrassment of the poor boy. He finally decides to give the boy some sound advice about sexually transmitted diseases and a stern warning to the woman and sends them both on their way.

This short story illustrates that official statistics measure police behavior as much as they measure crime. Sir Josiah Stamp, director of the Bank of England in the 1920s, cynically stated this criticism: "The government are very keen on amassing statistics. They collect them, raise them to the nth power, take the cube root and prepare wonderful diagrams. But you must never forget that every one of these figures comes in the first instance from the village watchmen, who just puts down what he damn pleases" (in Nettler, 1984, p. 39). We don't recommend this kind of cynicism, but we do counsel that you keep a healthy skepticism about statistics as you read this chapter.

LEARNING OBJECTIVES

- Know the primary sources of criminologists' crime data
- Understand the strengths and weaknesses of each source
- Be able to give examples of how these sources can resolve criminological arguments
- Understand the pitfalls of comparing international crime data
- Understand the difficulties in explaining crime trends over long periods

❖ Categorizing and Measuring Crime and Criminal Behavior

When attempting to understand, predict, and control any social problem, including the crime problem, the first step is to determine its extent. Gauging the extent of the problem means discovering how much of it there is, where and when it occurs most often, and among what social categories it occurs most frequently. It also helps our endeavors if we have knowledge of the patterns and trends of the problem over time. Note that we did not address "why" questions (why does crime occur; why is it increasing or decreasing, who commits it and why, and so on); such questions can only be adequately addressed after we have reliable data about the extent of the problem. However, all social statistics are suspect to some extent, and crime statistics are perhaps the most suspect of all. They are collected from many different sources in many different ways and have passed through many sieves of judgment before being recorded.

There is a wide variety of data provided by government and private sources to help us come to grips with America's crime problem, all with their particular strengths and weaknesses. The major data sources can be grouped into three broad categories: official statistics, victimization survey data, and self-reported data. Official statistics are those derived from the routine functioning of the criminal justice system. The most basic category of official statistics comes from the calls made to police by victims or witnesses and by crimes the police discover on patrol. Other major categories of official crime data consist of information about arrests, about convictions, and about correctional (prison, probation/parole) populations.

❖ Uniform Crime Reports: Counting Crime Officially

The primary source of official crime statistics in the United States is the annual **Uniform Crime Reports** (UCR) compiled by the Federal Bureau of Investigation (FBI). The UCR reports crimes known to the nation's police and sheriff's departments and the number of arrests made by these agencies; federal crimes are not included. Offenses known to the police are recorded whether or not an arrest is made or an arrested person is subsequently prosecuted and convicted. Participation in the UCR reporting program is voluntary, and thus all agencies do not participate. This is unfortunate for anyone hoping for comprehensive crime data. In 2012 law enforcement agencies active in the UCR program represented more than 308 million inhabitants of the United States—98.1% of the total population (FBI, 2013a). This means that crimes committed in the jurisdictions of agencies representing about 1.9% of the population (about 9.5 million people) were not included in the UCR data.

The UCR reports the number of each crime reported to the police as well as its rate of occurrence. The rate of a given crime is the actual number of reported crimes standardized by some unit of the population. We expect the raw number of crimes to increase as the population increases, so comparing the number of crimes reported today with the number reported 30 years ago, or the number of crimes reported in New York with the number reported in Wyoming, tells us little without considering population differences. For instance, California reported 1,884 murders to the FBI in 2012, and Louisiana reported 495. In which state are you most likely to be murdered? We can't say unless we take their respective populations into consideration. To obtain a **crime rate** we divide the number of reported crimes in a state by its population and multiply the quotient by 100,000, as in the following comparison of California and Louisiana rates.

Photo 2.1

The J. Edgar Hoover building, headquarters of the FBI, in Washington, D.C. Annual Uniform Crime Reports are compiled by the FBI after local, county, and state criminal justice agencies send in their annual crime data.

$$\text{Rate} = \frac{\text{CA murders} = 1,884}{\text{CA population} = 38,041,430} = .000049 \times 100,000 = 4.9$$

$$\text{Rate} = \frac{\text{LA murders} = 495}{\text{LA population} = 4,601,893} = .000107 \times 100,000 = 10.7$$

Thus a person in Louisiana is at over twice the risk (10.7 versus 4.9 murders per 100,000 population) of being murdered than he or she is in California. This statement is based on the statewide rate; the actual risk will vary widely from person to person based on such factors as age, race, sex, socioeconomic status (SES), neighborhood, and urban versus rural residence.

The UCR separates crimes into two categories: **Part I offenses** (or **index crimes**) and **Part II offenses**. Part I offenses include four violent (homicide, assault, forcible rape, and robbery) and four property offenses (larceny/theft, burglary, motor vehicle theft, and arson). Notice that these are all universally condemned *mala in se* offenses. Part I offenses correspond with what most people think of as "serious" crime. Part II offenses are treated as less serious and are recorded based on arrests made rather than cases reported to the police. Part II offense figures understate the extent of criminal offending far more than is the case with Part I figures because only a very small proportion of these crimes result in arrest.

The FBI's famous crime clock is presented in Figure 2.1. The clock shows how often in an average day one of the index crimes was reported in 2012; these are only rough estimates and should not be taken literally because many crimes are not reported.

Cleared Offenses

For law enforcement purposes, a **cleared offense** is when at least one person is arrested, charged, and turned over for prosecution. If a person is arrested and charged for a Part I offense the UCR records the crime as cleared *by arrest*. A crime may also be cleared by *exceptional*

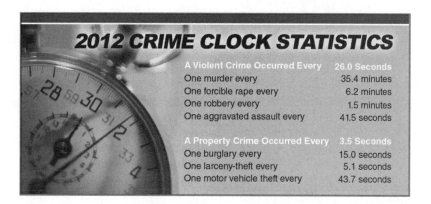

Figure 2.1

The FBI Crime Clock

Source: FBI, 2013a

means when the police have identified a suspect and have enough evidence to support arrest, but he or she could not be taken into custody immediately or at all. Such circumstances exist when the suspect dies or is in a location where the police cannot presently gain custody. For instance, he or she is in custody on other charges in another jurisdiction or is residing in a country with no extradition treaty with the United States. As can be seen in Figure 2.2, which gives 2012 clearance rates, violent crimes are more likely to be cleared than property crimes because violent crime investigations are pursued more vigorously and because victims of such crimes may be able to identify the perpetrator(s).

Table 2.1 is a page from the 2013 UCR listing all Part I and II crimes broken down by sex and percentage change in crime rates from 2003 to 2012. This provides us the male/female differences in arrests (as well as the increases or decreases in their respective rates of offending) and provides for interesting discussions of why these gender differences exist. Part II crimes are those listed as "other assaults" and all offenses listed below that category.

Crime Trends

The UCR is very useful for tracking crime trends. Table 2.2 shows trends from 1990 to 2009 (FBI, 2010). Note that total crime has dropped just over 40% (5,802.7 − 3,465.5 = 2,337.2/5,802.7 = .40278 or ≈ 40.3%) in that time frame. It is much easier to note that crime increased or decreased by some percentage over a specified time period than it is to explain why it did so, however. Despite the accumulation of tons of factual data, it is difficult to arrive at a sturdy conclusion that fit them together to everyone's satisfaction. Facts only describe events; they do not explain them. Any explanation for major fluctuations in crime rates requires an understanding of the historical, social, political, economic, and demographic processes unfolding around the same time that increases or decreases in crime are recorded and how those processes interact. The effects of any particular process on crime may be immediate, such as a series of riots and general mayhem following some perceived injustice, or they may only be felt a decade or so down the road, such as an economic policy decision that later affects job creation. Whatever process or alleged cause we examine, you should keep in mind that just as there is no single cause of crime or criminality, there is no single cause that explains crime trends.

Year	Violent	Property
1963	168.2	2,021.1
1993	747.1	4,740.0
2003	475.8	3,591.2

Table 2.1

Ten-Year Arrest Trends for Part I and Part II Crimes by Sex

Offense Charged	Male Total			Male Under 18			Female Total			Female Under 18		
	2003	2012	Percent Change	2003	2012	Percent Change	2003	2012	Percent Change	2003	2012	Percent Change
TOTAL	6,904,010	6,028,378	−12.7	1,017,933	622,485	−38.8	2,080,990	2,140,934	+2.9	385,564	259,043	−32.8
Murder and nonnegligent manslaughter	7,353	6,303	−14.3	637	403	−36.7	905	830	−8.3	66	40	−39.4
Forcible rape	16,578	11,782	−28.9	2,585	1,657	−35.9	210	109	−48.1	44	25	−43.2
Robbery	63,555	59,033	−7.1	14,904	11,831	−20.6	7,512	9,032	+20.2	1,497	1,369	−8.6
Aggravated assault	239,489	201,049	−16.1	30,876	17,279	−44.0	62,450	59,103	−5.4	9,456	5,840	−38.2
Burglary	170,581	161,450	−5.4	50,456	31,926	−36.7	28,275	32,432	+14.7	6,866	4,498	−34.5
Larceny-theft	486,870	488,888	+0.4	135,857	88,715	−34.7	288,894	374,332	+29.6	88,043	64,268	−27.0
Motor vehicle theft	78,642	37,237	−52.6	22,493	7,083	−68.5	15,531	8,833	−43.1	4,656	1,320	−71.6
Arson	9,153	6,476	−29.2	4,902	2,567	−47.6	1,718	1,436	−16.4	695	447	−35.7
Violent crime	326,975	278,167	−14.9	49,002	31,170	−36.4	71,077	69,074	−2.8	11,063	7,274	−34.2
Property crime	745,246	694,051	−6.9	213,708	130,291	−39.0	334,418	417,033	+24.7	100,260	70,533	−29.6
Other assaults	622,089	577,611	−7.1	107,045	71,954	−32.8	199,426	222,923	+11.8	51,241	41,665	−18.7
Forgery and counterfeiting	45,818	28,225	−38.4	2,076	685	−67.0	31,184	16,823	−46.1	1,170	270	−76.9
Fraud	120,139	62,673	−47.8	3,648	2,156	−40.9	101,513	42,809	−57.8	1,896	1,059	−44.1
Embezzlement	6,301	5,605	−11.0	522	185	−64.6	6,426	5,376	−16.3	351	124	−64.7
Stolen property; buying, receiving, possessing	71,587	53,781	−24.9	14,304	7,442	−48.0	16,038	13,736	−14.4	2,539	1,461	−42.5

Offense Charged	Male						Female					
	Total			Under 18			Total			Under 18		
	2003	2012	Percent Change	2003	2012	Percent Change	2003	2012	Percent Change	2003	2012	Percent Change
Vandalism	153,555	122,544	−20.2	63,188	34,251	−45.8	29,910	30,460	+1.8	10,142	6,438	−36.5
Weapons; carrying, possessing, etc.	102,092	90,790	−11.1	23,275	14,607	−37.2	9,001	8,065	−10.4	2,741	1,530	−44.2
Prostitution and commercialized vice	16,382	11,977	−26.9	248	139	−44.0	32,131	24,954	−22.3	707	425	−39.9
Sex offenses (except forcible rape) and prostitution	54,794	43,629	−20.4	11,207	7,711	−31.2	5,361	3,740	−30.2	1,182	865	−26.8
Drug abuse violations	887,736	817,198	−7.9	104,941	75,510	−28.0	203,212	211,020	+3.8	21,841	16,042	−26.6
Gambling	3,694	2,284	−38.2	402	160	−60.2	697	525	+24.7	25	15	−40.0
Offenses against the family and children	68,432	52,719	−23.0	2,689	1,310	−51.3	20,346	18,710	−8.0	1,681	834	−50.4
Driving under the influence	780,679	649,664	−16.8	11,044	4,676	−57.7	174,545	211,019	+20.9	2,827	1,619	−42.7
Liquor laws	311,799	217,530	−30.2	61,238	34,194	−44.2	109,377	90,661	−17.1	33,199	22,779	−31.4
Drunkenness	324,213	286,633	−11.6	8,988	5,006	−44.3	54,153	64,202	+18.6	2,669	1,867	−30.0
Disorderly conduct	312,480	249,828	−20.0	88,951	49,943	−43.9	108,318	99,540	−8.1	40,157	27,742	−30.9
Vagrancy	15,521	13,647	−12.1	1,041	463	−55.5	4,266	3,057	−28.3	342	117	−65.8
All other offenses (except traffic)	1,868,452	1,734,857	−7.2	184,390	115,667	−37.3	540,912	573,146	+6.0	70,852	42,323	−40.3
Suspicion	1,447	828	−42.8	282	174	−38.3	269	281	+4.5	91	68	−25.3
Curfew and loitering law violations	66,026	34,965	−47.0	66,026	34,965	−47.0	28,679	14,061	−51.0	28,679	14,061	−51.0

Figure 2.2

Percentage of Crimes Cleared by Arrest or Exceptional Means in 2012

Source: FBI, 2013a

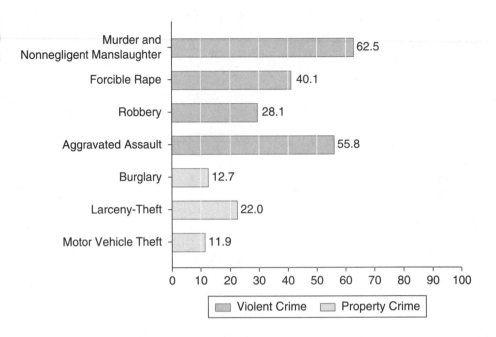

| Table 2.2 |

Crime Rates From 1990 to 2009

Year	Crime	Violent Crime	Property Crime	Murder	Rape	Robbery	Assault	Burglary	Larceny-Theft	Motor Vehicle Theft
1990	5,802.7	729.6	5,073.1	9.4	41.1	256.3	422.9	1,232.2	3,185.1	655.8
1991	5,898.4	758.2	5,140.2	9.8	42.3	272.7	433.4	1,252.1	3,229.1	659.0
1992	5,661.4	757.7	4,903.7	9.3	42.8	263.7	441.9	1,168.4	3,103.6	631.6
1993	5,487.1	747.1	4,740.0	9.5	41.1	256.0	440.5	1,099.7	3,033.9	606.3
1994	5,373.8	713.6	4,660.2	9.0	39.3	237.8	427.6	1,042.1	3,026.9	591.3
1995	5,275.0	684.5	4,590.5	8.2	37.1	220.9	418.3	987.0	3,043.2	560.3
1996	5,087.6	636.6	4,451.0	7.4	36.3	201.9	391.0	945.0	2,980.3	525.7
1997	4,927.3	611.0	4,316.3	6.8	35.9	186.2	382.1	918.8	2,891.8	505.7
1998	4,620.1	567.6	4,052.5	6.3	34.5	165.5	361.4	863.2	2,729.5	459.9
1999	4,266.6	523.0	3,743.6	5.7	32.8	150.1	334.3	770.4	2,550.7	422.5
2000	4,124.8	506.5	3,618.3	5.5	32.0	145.0	324.0	728.8	2,477.3	412.2
2001	4,162.6	504.5	3,658.1	5.6	31.8	148.5	318.6	741.8	2,485.7	430.5
2002	4,125.0	494.4	3,630.6	5.6	33.1	146.1	309.5	747.0	2,450.7	432.9
2003	4,067.0	475.8	3,591.2	5.7	32.3	142.5	295.4	741.0	2,416.5	433.7
2004	3,977.3	463.2	3,514.1	5.5	32.4	136.7	288.6	730.3	2,362.3	421.5

Year	Crime	Violent Crime	Property Crime	Murder	Rape	Robbery	Assault	Burglary	Larceny-Theft	Motor Vehicle Theft
2005	3,900.5	469.0	3,431.5	5.6	31.8	140.8	290.8	726.9	2,287.8	416.8
2006	3,838.3	480.6	3,357.7	5.8	31.7	150.6	292.6	735.2	2,221.4	401.1
2007	3,748.8	472.0	3,276.8	5.7	30.5	148.4	287.4	726.0	2,186.3	364.6
2008	3,669.0	457.5	3,211.5	5.4	29.7	145.7	276.7	732.1	2,164.5	315.0
2009	3,465.5	429.4	3,036.1	5.0	28.7	133.0	262.8	716.3	2,060.9	258.8

Source: FBI, 2010

Examine the UCR violent and property crime rates per 100,000 for 1963, 1993, and 2003 just listed and ask yourself whether crime has gone up or down. If we compare 1993 with 2003 we conclude that crime dropped significantly, but if we take 1963 as our beginning year and compare it with 2003, we conclude that crime has gone up significantly. Whether crime has "gone up" or "gone down" thus depends on what years we choose to look at. Interpretations of crime trends should be read with caution because the author may have chosen a beginning and ending year to support his or her favored explanation. So before we begin to congratulate or berate ourselves because the crime rate has gone up or down, it is wise to ask "Compared to what year?"

Take also the murder rate trends from 1900 to 2006 presented in Figure 2.3. The graph looks like a rugged mountain range with peaks and troughs, indicating that at some points in American history murder rates were more than twice as high as they were at other points. The 1900 rate of 1.0 per 100,000 is highly suspect given the descriptions of life in such cities as New York and Boston at the turn of the century, as well as the still semicivilized condition of much of the western United States. We should never take national statistics at face value unless we are very sure of their quality, and national reporting of crime statistics was in a terrible state in the early part of the 20th century.

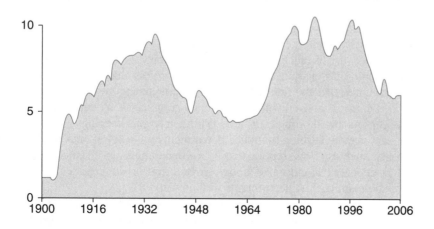

Figure 2.3

Murder Rates in the United States, 1900 to 2006

Source: U.S. Bureau of Justice Statistics, 2010

With the advent of the UCR in 1930 national data became somewhat more reliable. The homicide rate started a steep climb after the Volstead Act prohibiting the production and sale of alcohol took effect in 1920 as gangs fought over the lucrative and now illegal alcohol market. The rate started to fall with the repeal of the Volstead Act in 1933, which effectively removed criminals from the alcohol business. It dropped even further during World War II when most young men (the age category that commits the lion's share of crime) were in uniform and overseas, showed a sharp rise when they returned, and then settled into a relatively peaceful period from the 1950s to early 1960s. Murder rates then started a precipitous rise beginning in the late 1960s.

The late 1960s through the mid-1970s was a period of tumultuous changes in American society. Opposition to the Vietnam War combined with the civil rights and feminist movements led to the widespread questioning by many of the fundamental values of American society. When values and norms are questioned, they become weaker in their ability to regulate behavior. The weakened power of traditional social norms to control behavior led to all kinds of experimentation with alternative lifestyles, including the use of drugs. The emergence of crack cocaine in the early 1980s led to a period of gang wars over sales territory; just like the gang wars over alcohol did in the 1920s. Crack cocaine is easier to make, conceal, and sell than barrels of beer or bottles of whiskey, so crack dealing is more of an "equal opportunity" enterprise than supplying illegal alcohol was. Numerous young "gang bangers" took advantage of the opportunity for easy money, sparking a decade-long street war with other like-minded individuals.

The decrease in the homicide rate in the early 1990s can be attributed to several factors, including a large decrease in the crack market and in gang warfare as territories became consolidated by the strong pushing out the weak. Severe penalties for the sale and possession of crack and the danger from others trafficking in the same market may have also driven out many dealers.

Problems With the UCR

UCR data have limitations that restrict their usefulness for criminological research, particularly research seeking to uncover causes of crime. Some of the more serious of these limitations are outlined here.

- The UCR data significantly underrepresent the actual number of criminal events in the United States each year. According to a nationwide victim survey, only 44% of victims of violent crime and 34% of victims of property crime indicated reporting their victimization to the police (Truman, Langton, & Planty, 2013). Victims are more likely to report violent crimes if injuries are serious and are more likely to report property crimes when losses are high. Females are more likely than males to report violent victimization; males and females are about equally as likely to report property victimization.
- Federal crimes such as highly costly white-collar crimes such as stock market fraud, hazardous waste dumping, tax evasion, and false claims for professional services are not included.
- Crimes committed in the jurisdictions of nonparticipating law enforcement agencies are not included in the data. Even with full voluntary compliance, all departments would not be equally as efficient and thorough (or honest) in their record keeping.
- Crime data may be falsified by police departments for political reasons. The National Center for Policy Analysis (1998) reports that police departments in Philadelphia, New York, Atlanta, and Boca Raton, Florida, had underreported and/or downgraded crimes in their localities (and these are just the departments we know about).
- The UCR even underreports crimes known to the police because of the FBI's hierarchy rule. The **hierarchy rule** requires police to report only the highest (most serious) offense

committed in a multiple-offense single incident to the FBI and to ignore the others. For instance, if a man robs five patrons in a bar, pistol-whips one patron who tried to resist, locks the victims in the beer cooler, and then rapes the female bartender, only the rape is reported to the FBI. Arson is the sole exception to this rule. If some other violent or property crime is committed in conjunction with arson, both offenses are reported.

Problems With Comparing International Crime Rates

Problems such as the hierarchy rule and the ways in which different nations record crime make it extremely difficult to compare crime rates across nations. For instance, which two nations have the highest rate of recorded kidnappings in the world: (A) Australia and Canada or (B) Columbia and Mexico? The answer is *A*. According to United Nations figures for 2012, Australia has 17 kidnappings per 100,000 and Canada 12.7, compared with 0.6 in Columbia and 1.1 in Mexico (Alexander, 2013). If you are skeptical, you have learned the lesson from the opening vignette. According to Alexander (2013), these differences are simply a matter of how the different countries define kidnapping. In Australia or Canada, "if a divorced parent takes a child for the weekend, and the other parent objects and reports it to the police, the police will record the incident as a kidnapping." In most countries, "real" kidnapping is unlawfully seizing and carrying away a person by force or fraud and detaining that person against his or her will with the purpose of committing some other crime (rape, slavery, a ransom demand).

Photo 2.2

Is this considered kidnapping? It depends on what country you live in. This illustrates the difficulties in collecting and comparing crime statistics internationally.

Another example is Sweden's rape rate, which is officially the highest in the world, but is it "really"? The Swedes record every incident of sexual violence separately, so if a woman goes to the police and tells them that her partner raped her at least once a month over the last year, the police will record 12 separate events (Alexander, 2013). In the United States it would be recorded as a single incident—one case of rape. So, it is not just the village watchman who "puts down what he damn pleases" that confounds our efforts to make comparisons, but also the legal peculiarities of each country or changing emphases on different crimes and changing police practices.

Then there is the problem of the efficiency, accuracy, capacity, and honesty of the police in various countries in recording and reporting their crimes, especially homicides. Figure 2.4 compares rates of homicides reported by countries in various subregions of the world by the criminal justice system and by various health agencies such as the World Health Organization (Harrendorf, Heiskanen, & Malby, 2010). Note in general that in the less developed countries the homicides recorded by public health agencies greatly outnumber those recorded by the developed countries. Also note that in the more developed regions there is hardly any discrepancy between criminal justice and public health sources of data.

Figure 2.4

Average Subregion
Homicide Rates
According to
Criminal Justice and
Public Health Data

Source: Harrendorf,
Heiskanen, & Malby, 2010

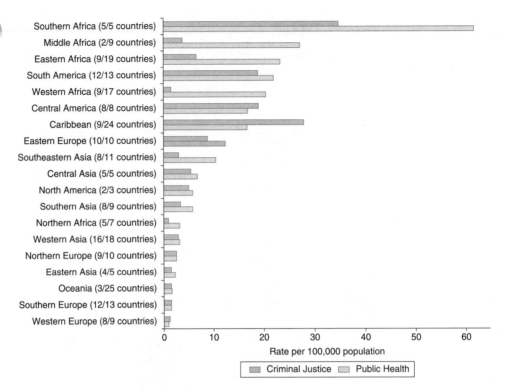

❖ NIBRS: The "New and Improved" UCR

Efforts to improve the reliability and validity of official statistics are occurring all the time, with the most ambitious being the **National Incident-Based Reporting System** (NIBRS). NIBRS began in 1982 and is designed for the collection of more detailed and more comprehensive crime statistics than those of the UCR (which it is supposed to replace). As opposed to the current UCR, which monitors only a relatively few crimes and gathers few details associated with them, NIBRS collects data on 46 "Group A" offenses and 11 "Group B" offenses. There is no hierarchy rule under the NIBRS system; it reports multiple victims, multiple offenders, and multiple crimes that may be part of the same incident. It also provides information about the circumstances of the offense and about victim and offender characteristics, such as offender/victim relationship and age, sex, and race of victims and perpetrators (if known). According to the Incident-Based Reporting Resource Center (2013), "As of June 2012, 32 states have been certified to report NIBRS to the FBI, and three additional states and the District of Columbia have individual agencies submitting NIBRS data. Approximately 29% of the population is covered by NIBRS reporting, representing 27% of the nation's reported crime and 43% of law enforcement agencies." Unfortunately, many police departments lack the manpower and technical expertise to collect and process the wide and detailed range of information that is part of each crime incident their officers deal with, and administrators see little benefit to their department to justify the effort (Dunworth, 2001).

NIBRS, the UCR, and Police Bias in Arrests

NIBRS may miss an awful lot of crime, but it makes up for it in other areas. Because NIBRS data provide information about the offender and the victim (victims can identify physical characteristics of perpetrators), they can be used to try to resolve some important criminological issues. One issue is the disproportionately high rate of arrest for African Americans in the United States. The question for criminologists is this: Is the disproportion in arrests the result of disproportionately high black involvement in crime or the result of discriminatory arrest patterns of police? For instance, although they constitute only about 13% of the population, African Americans

Photo 2.3

The use of technology by police has been credited in part for crime reduction in the 1990s.

accounted for 38.5% of arrests for all violent crimes and 29.3% for all property crimes according to the 2013 UCR. As long as we only had raw arrest data from the UCR, we could argue without end about whether the data reflect police bias or disproportionate black involvement in crime.

This issue was explored by D'Alessio and Stolzenberg (2003) using NIBRS data from 17 states and 335,619 arrests for rape, robbery, and aggravated and simple assault. Their results indicate the odds of arrest for robbery, aggravated assault, and simple assault were significantly greater for white offenders than for black offenders, but there was no significant racial difference in the probability of arrest for rape. In other words, white offenders were more likely to be arrested for violent crimes other than rape (blacks and whites were arrested with almost equal probability for rape). For instance, African Americans committed 5,278 robberies in those states for which only 21.4% were arrested; whites committed 2,620 robberies for which 30.8% were arrested. The researchers concluded that the disproportionately high black arrest rate is attributable to disproportionately higher black involvement in crime. Similar results based on NIBRS data were found in Pope and Snyder's (2003) analysis of 102,905 violent incidents committed by juveniles; that is, white juveniles were significantly more likely to be arrested than black juveniles even though African American juveniles were more involved in violent incidents.

❖ Crime Victimization Survey Data and Their Problems

Crime victimization surveys involve asking large numbers of people if they have been criminally victimized within some specified time frame regardless of whether they reported the incident to police. Census Bureau personnel interview a nationally representative sample of people age 12 or over on behalf of the Bureau of Justice Statistics (BJS) twice each year. This survey is known as the **National Crime Victimization Survey** (NCVS), and in 2012, 162,940 people from 93,390 households were interviewed (Truman, Langton, & Planty, 2013). The NCVS requests information on crimes committed against individuals and households, the circumstances of the offense, and personal information about victims (age, sex, race, income, and education level) and offenders (approximate age, sex, race, and victim/offender relationship). Figure 2.5 presents highlights from the 2013 NCVS report.

Victimization surveys have their own problems that make them almost as suspect as the UCR. Some of these problems include the following:

- Crimes such as drug dealing and all "victimless" crimes such as prostitution and gambling are not revealed in such surveys for obvious reasons. And because murder victims cannot be interviewed, this most serious of crimes is not included.

Figure 2.5

Highlights From
the 2012 Criminal
Victimization Survey

Source: Truman, Langton,
& Planty, 2013

- The rate of violent victimization increased from 226 victimizations per 1,000 persons age 12 or older in 2011 to 26.1 in 2012. Crime not reported to police and simple assault accounted for the majority of this increase.
- Violent victimizations not reported to police increased from 10.8 per 1,000 persons in 2011 to 14.0 in 2012
- The apparent increase in the number and rate of serious violent crime from 2011 to 2012 was not statistically significant.
- The rate of property crime increased from 138.7 per 1,000 households in 2011 to 155.8 in 2012.

- From 2011 to 2012, there were no statistically significant changes in the rates of domestic violence, violence involving an injury, or firearm violence.
- In 2012, 44% of violent victimizations and 54% of serious violent victimizations were reported to police.
- There was no significant change in the percentage of crime victims receiving assistance from victim service agencies from 2011 to 2012 (about 8%).
- Violent crime rates increased slightly in 2012 for blacks but remained stable for whites and Hispanics.
- In 2012, residents in urban areas continued to experience the highest rate of violent crime.

- Because NCVS only surveys households, crimes committed against commercial establishments such as stores, bars, and factories are not included. This exclusion results in a huge underestimate of crimes such as burglaries, robberies, theft, and vandalism.
- Victimization data do not have to meet any stringent legal or evidentiary standards in order to be reported as an offense; if the respondent says he or she was robbed (it may have actually been a theft or a burglary), a robbery is recorded. UCR data, on the other hand, pass through the legal sieve to determine whether the reported incident was indeed a robbery.
- Other problems involve memory lapses, providing answers the respondent thinks the interviewer wants to hear, forgetting an incident, embellishing an incident, and any number of other misunderstandings, ambiguities, and even downright lies that occur when one person is asking another about his or her life experiences.
- Consistent with the previous point, there are suggestions that just as underreporting plagues UCR data, overreporting may plague NCVS data (O'Brien, 2001). Whatever the case may be, we find many anomalies when comparing the two sources of data. For instance, substantially more crimes appear in police records than NCVS victims claim to have reported to the police. The discrepancy is easily explained for burglary and motor vehicle theft because the NCVS does not include commercial establishments in their reports. It is more difficult to explain discrepancies in violent crime, however. One explanation for this is that the NCVS does not include victims less than 12 years of age whereas the UCR does, although it is difficult to believe that children under 12 account for 15 to 20% of the violent victimization known to the police.

NCVS researchers are aware of the problems that arise when asking people to recall victimization and have initiated many interview improvements in their methodology, one of which is the bounding interview. This technique involves comparing reported incidents from the same household in the current interview with those reported 6 months earlier. When a report appears to be a duplicate, the respondent is reminded of the earlier report and asked if the new report represents the incident previously mentioned or if it is different. Other techniques used to minimize some of the reported problems mentioned are available on the NCVS website at www.icpsr.umich.edu/NACJD/NCVS. Figure 2.6 provides an example of the kinds of questions asked by NCVS survey workers.

29. How were you attacked? Any other way?

Mark (X) all that apply.

FIELD REPRESENTATIVE – *If raped, ASK –*

Do you mean forced or coerced sexual intercourse?

If No, ASK – **What do you mean?**

If tried to rape, ASK –

Do you mean attempted forced or coerced sexual intercourse?

If No, ASK – **What do you mean?**

646	1 ☐ Raped
	2 ☐ Tried to rape
	3 ☐ Sexual assault other than rape or attempted rape
	4 ☐ Shot
	5 ☐ Shot at (but missed)
	6 ☐ Hit with gun held in hand
647	7 ☐ Stabbed/cut with knife/sharp weapon
	8 ☐ Attempted attack with knife/sharp weapon
	9 ☐ Hit by object (other than gun) held in hand
	10 ☐ Hit by thrown object
648	11 ☐ Attempted attack with weapon other than gun/knife/sharp weapon
	12 ☐ Hit, slapped, knocked down
	13 ☐ Grabbed, held, tripped, jumped, pushed, etc.
	14 ☐ Other – *Specify* ↗

30. Did the offender THREATEN to hurt you before you were actually attacked?

649	1 ☐ Yes
	2 ☐ No
	3 ☐ Other – *Specify* ↗

31. What were the injuries you suffered, if any? Anything else?

Mark (X) all that apply.

FIELD REPRESENTATIVE – *If raped and box 1 in item 29 is NOT marked, ASK –*

Do you mean forced or coerced sexual intercourse?

If No, ASK – **What do you mean?**

If attempted rape and box 2 in item 29 is NOT marked, ASK –

Do you mean attempted forced or coerced sexual intercourse?

If No, ASK – **What do you mean?**

655	1 ☐ None – **SKIP** to 40
	2 ☐ Raped
	3 ☐ Attempted rape
	4 ☐ Sexual assault other than rape or attempted rape
	5 ☐ Knife or stab wounds
	6 ☐ Gun shot, bullet wounds
656	7 ☐ Broken bones or teeth knocked out
	8 ☐ Internal injuries
	9 ☐ Knocked unconscious
	10 ☐ Bruises, black eye, cuts, scratches, swelling, chipped teeth
	11 ☐ Other – *Specify* ↗

32. ASK OR VERIFY –
Were any of the injuries caused by a weapon other than a gun or knife?

| 657 | 1 ☐ Yes – *Ask 33* |
| | 2 ☐ No – **SKIP** to 34 |

33. Which injuries were caused by a weapon OTHER than a gun or knife?

Enter code(s) from 31.

| 658 | ☐ | ☐ | ☐ |
| | Code | Code | Code |

34. Were you injured to the extent that you received any medical care, including self treatment?

| 659 | 1 ☐ Yes – *Ask 35* |
| | 2 ☐ No – **SKIP** to 40 |

35. Where did you receive this care? Anywhere else?

Mark (X) all that apply.

660	1 ☐ At the scene
	2 ☐ At home/neighbor's/friend's
	3 ☐ Health unit at work/school, first aid station at a stadium/park, etc.
	4 ☐ Doctor's office/health clinic
	5 ☐ Emergency room at hospital/emergency clinic
	6 ☐ Hospital (other than emergency room)
	7 ☐ Other – *Specify* ↗

Figure 2.6

Examples of NCVS Victimization Questions

Source: Catalano, 2006

❖ Areas of Agreement Between the UCR and NCVS

To the extent that two or more data sources tell us the same thing, our confidence in both is increased. The UCR and NCVS agree on the demographics of crime in that they both tell us that males, the young, the poor, and African Americans are more likely to be perpetrators and victims of crime than are females, older persons, wealthier persons, and persons of other races. Both sources also agree as to the geographic areas and times of the year when crimes are more likely to occur. Over a 3-year period, O'Brien (2001) found that NCVS victims reported that 91.5% of those who robbed them and 87.7% of their aggravated assault assailants were male, as were 91.2% and 84.3%, respectively, of those arrested for those offenses. Likewise, NCVS victims reported that 64.1% of those who robbed them and 40% of their aggravated assault assailants were African American. These percentages fit the UCR arrest statistics for race almost exactly; 62.2% arrested for robbery were African American, as were 40% of those arrested for aggravated assault. Thus, the two data sets agree almost perfectly with respect to these two violent crimes.

Comparisons of UCR and NCVS data have often proven very useful to resolve issues such as these. Another such issue is the so-called masculinization hypothesis put forward by some feminist criminologists. The essence of this hypothesis is that women are becoming more "masculinized" as a result of assuming "male" roles in the workforce and that this is reflected in the increased rates of female arrests for violent crimes. Darrell Steffensmeier and his colleagues (2006) used a comparison of data trends reported in the UCR and NCVS from 1980 to 2003 to explore the issue of whether the violent crime gap between males and females is closing. They found that both sources reported little or no changes in the gender ratio for violent crimes such as murder, rape, and robbery but that the UCR reports indicated a sharp rise in assaults by females. Does this mean that women became more violent over the period examined, or does the increase reflect the behavior of the police more than the behavior of women? The authors conclude that net-widening policy shifts have escalated the arrest proneness of females for "criminal assault" (e.g., policing physical attacks or threats of marginal seriousness) rather than women having become any more violent. In other words, UCR increases in female arrests for simple assault are explained by changes in police policy in the form of mandatory arrests for domestic violence. This is something that could not have been determined without examining both data sources. The addition of the NCVS and NIBRS to the nation's crime databases thus has great utility for settling some major quarrels among criminologists of different ideological persuasions, although not to the satisfaction of everyone.

Note from Table 2.1 that this trend was still in evidence comparing UCR arrests for aggravated assault and simple (labeled "other assaults" in the table) assault from 2003 to 2012. In contradiction to the masculinization hypothesis, female aggravated assault decreased by 5.4%. During the same period, female arrests for simple assault increased by 11.8%, a figure that in conjunction with the female decrease in other violent offenses favors the police behavior hypothesis.

❖ Self-Report Crime Surveys and Their Problems

Self-report surveys of offending provide a way for criminologists to collect data without having to rely on government sources. Questionnaires used in these surveys typically provide a list of offenses and request subjects to check each offense they recall having committed and how often. Sometimes asked is if they have ever been arrested and if so, how many times. Self-reported surveys have relied primarily on college and high school students for subjects, although prison inmates and probationers/parolees have also been surveyed.

The greatest strength of self-report research is that researchers can correlate a variety of characteristics of respondents with their admitted offenses that go beyond the demographics of age, race, and gender. For instance, they can attempt to measure various constructs thought to be associated with offending, such as impulsiveness, empathy, and sensation seeking, as well as

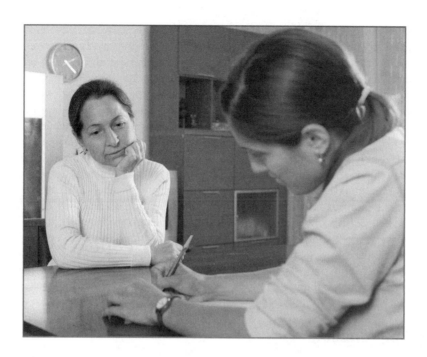

Photo 2.4

A woman completing a self-report survey. When using self-report data we must ask ourselves, "How accurate are people's memories? Do people lie on surveys?"

their peer associations and their attitudes. The evidence indicates that self-report crime measures provide largely accurate information about some illegal act sometime in their lives. However, there are a number of reasons why self-report crime surveys also provide a distorted picture of criminal involvement.

- The majority of self-reported studies surveyed "convenience" samples of high school and college students, populations in which we don't expect to find many seriously criminally involved individuals. Most self-report studies thus eliminate the very people we are most interested in gathering information about. One strength of the self-report method, however, is that it appears to capture the extent of illegal drug usage among high school and college students, something that neither the UCR nor the NCVS attempt to do.

- Self-report studies typically uncover only fairly trivial antisocial acts such as fighting, stealing items worth less than $5, smoking, and truancy. Almost everyone has committed one or more of these acts. These are hardly acts that help us to understand the nature of serious crime. A connected problem is that some researchers lump respondents who report one delinquent act together with adjudicated delinquents who break the law in many different ways many different times.

- Even though most people are forthright in revealing minor antisocial behaviors, most people do not have a serious criminal history, and those who do have a distinct tendency to underreport their crimes (Hindelang, Hirschi, & Weis, 1981). As the number of crimes people commit increases, so does the proportion of offenses they withhold reporting, with those arrested for the most serious offenses having the greatest probability of denial (Farrington, 1982).

- Males tend to report their antisocial activities less honestly than females, and African Americans less honestly than other racial groups (Cernkovich, Giordano, & Rudolph, 2000; Kim, Fendrich, & Wislar, 2000). This evidence renders any statements about gender or racial differences regarding antisocial behavior based on self-report data suspect. When it comes to relying on self-report data to assess the nature and extent of serious crime it is well to remember the gambler's dictum: "Never trust an animal that talks."

We should not end on a pessimistic note about self-reports, however. Several studies have addressed the accuracy and honesty of self-reported offenses in various ways, and the results have generally been encouraging, at least for uncovering the extent of minor offenses. On average, known delinquents and criminals disclose almost three times as many offenses as nondelinquents. Many of the major multimillion-dollar longitudinal studies taking place today have built-in safeguards against researchers naively taking subjects at their word. A number of studies verify self-report accounts with police records and other social agencies, a practice that further helps us to gain a grasp on the reliability of self-report studies. For instance, a large longitudinal (a study following the same people across the life span) cohort study (studying a set of individuals who share a common characteristic, such as being born in the same month in the same geographic area) showed that individuals from the lowest social class category reported 3.21 times more offenses than individuals from the highest social class category (Fergusson, Swain-Campbell, & Horwood, 2004). However, when researchers compared individuals from these two classes for official juvenile and adult arrests, the members of the lowest class had 25.82 times more officially recorded arrests than members of the highest class. Thus, the more actively involved delinquents or criminals do report more antisocial behavior than others, but they also tend to greatly underreport them.

❖ Crime Mapping

Crime statistics are also gathered by individual police departments for their own use in the battle against crime in their jurisdictions. These statistics enable police departments to view areas and trends across time periods (the where, when, and how of crime) so they can allocate their resources where and when they are most needed. The most sophisticated of these methods is known as crime mapping. **Crime mapping** is the use of modern technology such as Geographic Information Systems (GIS) by police departments to "map" (visualize) and analyze patterns of crime.

The geography of a city can strongly influence crime because the features and characteristics of an area of a city or town can make it easier or more difficult for crime to occur (Kumar & Chandrasekar, 2011). For instance, the location of alleys, buildings, and open spaces, as well as the houses and businesses that occupy the areas, such as bars, pawn shops, derelict buildings, schools, parks, and factories, all affect the likelihood that a crime will or will not occur. By combining such geographic information with police report data and then displaying the information on a computerized map, police analysts find it to be an effective way to analyze where, when, and how crime occurs. To accomplish such mapping, information about all serious criminal incidents is fed into a computer equipped with special software, allowing analysts to pinpoint crime hot spots and other trends and patterns over time. This is the basis for intelligence- or information-based policing, which has been enormously useful to police departments in their relentless battles with crime. Figure 2.7 is an example of the pattern of homicides by location and methods of killing in Washington, DC, from 2004 to 2006.

❖ White-Collar Crime: The FBI's Financial Crimes Report

The only "white-collar" crimes, that is, crimes committed by guile as opposed to force, listed in the UCR are embezzlement, forgery/counterfeiting, and fraud, which are mostly committed by individuals. There is, however, a separate accounting of major white-collar crimes committed by organized groups (banks, law firms, medical practices, and corporations) called the **Financial Crimes Report** (FBI, 2012). This report is issued each year by the FBI and contains results of investigations carried out by the Financial Crimes Section (FCS) of the FBI. The role of the FCS is to oversee the investigation of financial fraud and to supervise the forfeiture of assets from individuals engaged in such crimes. The FCS is composed of the Asset Forfeiture/Money Laundering Unit (AF/MLU), the Economic Crimes Unit (ECU), the Health Care Fraud Unit (HCFU), the Forensic Accountant Unit (FAU), and the National Mortgage Fraud Team (NMFT).

The crimes investigated by the Financial Crimes Section are more fully discussed in the white-collar crime chapter, but here we highlight the FBI's major successes in 2011 as reported in the 2012 *Financial Crimes Report to the Public*. FBI investigations led to 242 indictments and 241 convictions for corporate fraud, mostly cases involving fraudulent accounting and insider trading. The FBI obtained $2.4 billion in restitution and $16.1 million in fines from convicted corporate criminals. As Figure 2.7 indicates, an ever-growing number of corporate fraud cases have been investigated since the beginning of the current recession in 2007. This may reflect greater levels of corporate fraud, greater emphasis on such cases, or both.

The FBI also obtained 520 indictments and 394 convictions for securities/commodities fraud—market manipulation, Ponzi schemes, cyberscams, foreign currency exchange fraud, and so on. As a result of these investigations, the FBI recovered $36 million and obtained $8.8 billion in restitution, $752 million in forfeitures, and $113 million in fines.

In the health care field, the FBI investigated 2,690 cases resulting in 1,676 indictments and 736 convictions. This type of fraud involves billing for services not provided, duplicate claims, medically unnecessary services, and kickbacks for referring patients for services paid for by Medicare/Medicaid. The FBI obtained $1.2 billion in restitution, $1 billion in fines, $96 million in seizures, $320 million in restitution, and $1 billion in settlements in 2011.

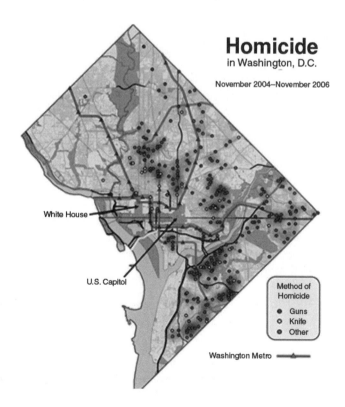

Homicide
in Washington, D.C.

November 2004–November 2006

White House

U.S. Capitol

Method of Homicide
● Guns
○ Knife
◉ Other

Washington Metro ━━━

Figure 2.7

Mapping Homicide Locations and Methods in Washington, D.C.

Source: District of Columbia, 2014

Because of tighter underwriting standards, mortgage frauds were at their lowest levels since 2001. Mortgage frauds include foreclosure rescue schemes and a wide variety of other types of misrepresentations or omissions aimed at distressed homeowners who bought homes under greatly relaxed loan standards prior to the 2007 housing crash. In 2011, the FBI had 2,691 pending mortgage fraud cases and obtained convictions on 1,082 criminals. It obtained $1.38 billion in restitution, $116.3 million in fines, and $23 million in seizures/forfeitures.

Finally, the FBI obtained 521 indictments and 429 convictions for financial institution fraud, a type of crime that includes embezzlement, check fraud, counterfeit negotiable instruments, check kiting, and fraud contributing to the failure of financial institutions. These convictions resulted in $1.38 billion in restitution, $116.3 million in fines (being exactly the same values as listed for mortgage fraud, these first two figures may have been erroneously listed twice), and $15.7 million in seizures.

❖ The Dark Figure of Crime

The **dark** (or hidden) **figure of crime** is that portion of the total crimes committed each year that never comes to light. Figure 2.9 presents three diagrams that show the dark figures for the three major measures of criminal behavior. (The dark figures are represented by the dark shading in each diagram.)

Each diagram shows the degree of seriousness to which crimes are most likely to be detected by each measure ("victimless" crimes excluded). In the top diagram displaying UCR data, you can see that very few trivial offenses are reported in official statistics, and most of those that are will be dismissed as unfounded by the police. For official statistics, then, the dark figures are highly concentrated at the nonserious end of the crime spectrum.

The middle diagram reveals that the dark figures for victimization data are primarily concentrated in the nonserious end of the spectrum also, although to a lesser degree than in the case of official data. The failure of victimization data to pick up these minor offenses is largely due to survey subjects not remembering all incidences of victimization.

In the bottom diagram we see that most of the dark figures in the case of self-reports are concentrated in the upper end of the seriousness continuum rather than the lower end. This is partly due to the fact that nearly all self-report surveys exclude most persistent serious offenders from their subject pools and that many of the most serious offenders who remain in self-report subject pools do not reveal the full extent of their criminal histories.

Figure 2.8

Corporate Fraud
Pending Cases,
2007–2011

Source: FBI, 2012

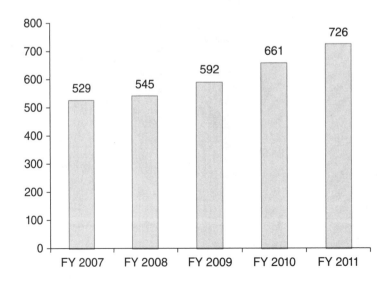

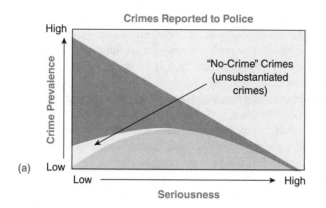

(a)

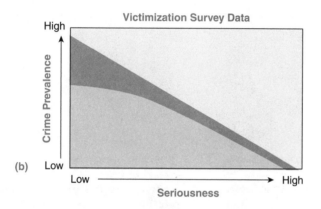

(b)

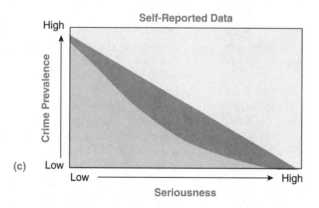

(c)

Figure 2.9

Differing
Proportions
of Reported/
Unreported Crimes
for the Three Major
Measures of Crime

Light shading =
proportion of crimes
reported. Dark shading =
proportion not reported.

❖ What Can We Conclude About the Three Main Measures of Crime in America?

All three of the main measures of crime in America are imperfect, and which one of them is "best" depends on what we want to know. UCR data are still probably the best single source for studying serious crimes and, indeed, the only one for studying murder rates and circumstances.

NIBRS is best for a more comprehensive picture of criminal events such as the demographics (sex, race, age) of offenders and victims, although it is not as nationally representative as either the UCR or the NCVS. For studying less serious but much more common crimes, either victimization or self-report survey data are best. If the interest is in drug offenses, self-reports are the preferable data source.

Because all three data sources converge on some very important points about crime, they enable us to proceed with at least some confidence in our endeavors to understand the "whys" of crime. The basic demographics of crime constitute the raw social facts that are the building blocks of our criminological theories. If street crime is concentrated among the lower socioeconomic classes and in the poorest neighborhoods, we can begin to ask such things as whether poverty "causes" crime or if some other variable or set of variables causes both. Is social disorganization in a neighborhood independent of the people living in it or completely dependent on the people living in it? Why do females always and everywhere commit far less crime (particularly the most serious crimes) than males? These and many dozens of other why questions can be asked once we have a firm grip on the raw facts supplied by the methods described in this chapter.

Summary

- Crime and criminal behavior are measured in several ways in the United States. The oldest measure is the FBI's Uniform Crime Reports (UCR), which is a tabulation of all crimes reported to the police in most of the jurisdictions in the United States in the previous year. The UCR is divided into two parts: Part I records the eight index crimes (murder, rape, robbery, aggravated assault, burglary, larceny, theft, and arson), and Part II records arrests made for all other crimes.

- UCR data seriously underestimate the extent of crime because they only record reported crimes, ignores drug offenses, and only reports the most serious crime in a multiple-crime event. The problems with the UCR led to the implementation of the National Incident-Based Reporting System (NIBRS).

- The second major source of crime statistics is the National Crime Victimization Survey (NCVS). This survey consists of many thousands of interviews of householders throughout the United States asking them about their crime victimization (if any) during the previous 6 months. The NCVS also has problems because it leaves out crimes against commercial establishments and relies exclusively on the memory and the word of interviewees.

- The third source of crime data is self-report data collected by criminologists themselves. The advantage of self-report data is that they are derived "from the horse's mouth," and typically the questionnaires used ask about "victimless" offenses not covered in either the UCR or NCVS. The major problems with self-report data are that they do not capture serious criminal behavior and is subject to dishonesty in the form of underreporting, especially underreporting by those most seriously involved in criminal activity.

- The UCR, NCVS, and self-report data come to different conclusions on a variety of points, but they agree about where, when, and among whom crime is most prevalent and the fact that crime has fallen dramatically in the United States over the past decade. Taken together, then, we have a fairly reliable picture of the correlates of crime from which to develop our theories about explanatory mechanisms.

- The FBI's Financial Crimes Report is the "white-collar" version of the UCR. This report focuses on ongoing and completed investigations of many kinds of white-collar crimes such as insider trading, fraudulent schemes, and medical fraud.

- The "dark figure" of crime refers to the amount of crime that goes unreported and unknown every year. All measures of criminal activity discussed in this chapter have weaknesses that obscure an unknown amount of crime, but taken together they provide a roughly accurate picture of annual crime rates in the United States.

Exercises and Discussion Questions

1. Go to the website www.fbi.gov/wanted/topten for the FBI's 10 most wanted and research the background and crimes of one of the men listed there. Then write a one- to two-page summary and report to the class.

2. Do you think it wise to make "authoritative" statements or formulate theories of criminal behavior, especially serious criminal behavior, based on self-report data?

3. Can you think of other problems possibly associated with asking people about their delinquent or criminal behavior or their victimization other than those discussed in the chapter?

4. If you were the American "crime czar," what would you do to get the various law enforcement agencies to fully implement NIBRS? (No, you can't just order them to do so.)

Useful Websites

Bureau of Justice Statistics. www.bjs.gov.
National Archive of Criminal Justice Data. www .icpsr.umich.edu/NACJD.
National Crime Victimization Survey Resource Guide. www.icpsr.umich.edu/NACJD/NCVS.

National Incident-Based Reporting System Resource Guide. www.icpsr.umich.edu/NACJD/NIBRS.
Uniform Crime Reports. www.fbi.gov/ucr/ucr.htm.

Chapter Terms

Cleared offenses

Crime mapping

Crime rate

Dark figure of crime

Financial Crimes Report

Hierarchy rule

National Crime Victimization Survey (NCVS)

National Incident-Based Reporting System (NIBRS)

Part I offenses (or index crimes)

Part II offenses

Self-report surveys

Uniform Crime Reports (UCR)

CHAPTER 3

Victimology

Exploring the Experience of Victimization

John Sutcliff's entire adult life has been devoted to the sexual seduction of teenage boys. At the age of 33 he was arrested and sentenced to prison for sexually assaulting a 13-year-old boy who was a member of his "Big Brother's Club." By his own admission he had sexually molested over 200 "members" of his club. John's favorite activity with these boys was giving and receiving enemas. John became involved with the fetish while enrolled in a residential boy's school where many of the boys were subjected to enemas administered in front of the entire dormitory.

 After his release from prison, John became much more "scientific" in his efforts to procure victims. A "theoretical" paper he wrote indicated that father-absent boys were "ripe" for seduction, and he would entice them with his friendly ways and with a houseful of electronic equipment he would teach the boys to repair and operate. He weeded out boys with a father in the home and would spend at least 6 weeks grooming each victim. He used systematic desensitization techniques, starting with simply getting the boys to agree to type in answers to innocuous questions and escalating to having them view pornographic homosexual pictures and giving them "pretend" enemas, actual enemas, and enemas accompanied by sexual activity. With each successive approximation toward John's goal the boys were reinforced by material and nonmaterial rewards (friendship, attention, praise) that made the final events seem almost natural.

 John's activities came to light when U.S. postal inspectors found a package containing pictures, letters, and tapes John exchanged with like-minded individuals. On the basis of this evidence the police raided John's home and found neatly cataloged files detailing 475 boys that he had seduced. His methods were so successful that his actions were never reported to the authorities (indeed, some of the boys were recruited for him by earlier victims). Some of his earlier victims still kept in touch with him and were victimizing boys themselves. Only one victim agreed to testify, but John was allowed to plea to one count of lewd and lascivious conduct. He received a sentence of 1 year and was paroled after serving 10 months, thus serving 15.7 hours for each of his 475 known victims. This case illustrates how victims (totally innocent as children) can be turned into victimizers (totally responsible as adults) and how the distinction between victim and perpetrator can sometimes be blurred.

LEARNING OBJECTIVES

- Understand the need for victimology both theoretically and practically
- Know why victims and perpetrators are often interchangeable
- Understand the extent of workplace and school violence
- Know the reasons behind and the extent of human trafficking and its devastating effects on its victims
- Be able to articulate the risk factors for child molestation
- Know the facts about domestic violence and the primary risk factors
- Be able to articulate the theories of victimization
- Know what the criminal justice system is doing (or not doing) for crime victims

❖ The Emergence of Victimology

Victims of crimes are very often the overlooked parties in criminology, but except for minor public order crimes, for every criminal act there is necessarily a victim. Criminologists have spent decades trying to determine the factors that contribute to making a person a criminal, but it wasn't until German criminologist Hans von Hentig's (1941) work that they began seriously thinking about the role of the victim. It turned out that although victimization can be an unfortunate random event in which the victim is simply in the wrong place at the wrong time, in many cases of victimization, there is a systematic pattern if one looks closely enough. Just as criminologists want to find out why some people commit crimes and others do not, and why some who commit crimes commit more crimes than others, victimologists want to discover why some people become victims and why some victims become repeat victims.

Victimology is a subfield of criminology that specializes in studying the victims of crime. Victimologists study the series of events that typically lead to victimization acts of various kinds in attempts to arrive at general theories of victimization and insights relevant to how victimization can be avoided. They also examine the way victims are treated in the criminal justice system in its attempts to compensate crime victims and attend to their practical and emotional needs (Karmen, 2005). Criminologists interested in perpetrators of crime ask what the risk factors for becoming involved in crime are. Criminologists interested in victims of crime ask pretty much the same question; i.e., why are some individuals, households, groups, and other entities targeted and others are not (Doerner & Lab, 2002)?

The labels "offender" and "victim" are sometimes blurred distinctions that hide the details of the interactions of the offender/victim dyad. Burglars often prey on their own kind, robbers prey on drug dealers, and homicides are frequently the outcome of minor arguments in which the victim was the instigator. As victimologist Andrew Karmen (2005) put it, "Predators prey on each other as well as upon innocent members of the public. . . . When youth gangs feud with each other by carrying out 'drive-by' shootings, the young members who get gunned down are casualties of their own brand of retaliatory street justice" (p. 14). Of course, we should not think of all victims, or even most victims, this way. There are millions of innocent victims who in no way contribute to their victimization, and even lawbreakers can be genuine victims deserving of protection and redress in the criminal courts.

❖ Who Gets Victimized?

Becoming a victim is a process encompassing a host of systematic environmental, demographic, and personal characteristics, and rarely is it totally random. According to the 2013 NCVS study, the individual most likely to be victimized is a young black unmarried male living in poverty in an urban environment. Victimization, like criminal behavior, drops precipitously from 25 years of age onward and with increasing household income, and being married is a protective factor against victimization and crime (Truman, Langton, & Planty, 2013).

Victim characteristics also differ according to the type of crime. Females were 4.3 times more likely than males to be victimized by rape/sexual assault, but males were 1.6 times more likely to be victimized by aggravated assault. Females are more likely to be victimized by someone they know, and males tend to be victimized by strangers. Blacks were 1.7 times more likely than "other races" (Asian, American Indian/Alaskan Native) to be victims of aggravated assault but slightly

Table 3.1

Victimization Rates for Violent and Property Crimes Reported and Not Reported to Police in 2003, 2011, and 2012

Type of Crime	Reported to Police			Not Reported to Police		
	2003	2011	2012	2003	2011	2012
Violent crime	15.2	11.1	11.5	16.2	10.8	14.0
Rape/sexual assault	0.8	0.3	0.4	0.6	0.7	0.9
Robbery	1.9	1.4	1.6	1.1	0.7	1.2
Assault	12.6	9.4	9.6	14.6	9.4	11.9
Aggravated assault	3.2	2.7	2.4	2.3	1.2	1.3
Simple assault	9.4	6.6	7.2	12.2	8.2	10.6
Domestic violence	3.5	3.1	2.6	2.6	2.1	2.0
Intimate partner violence	2.6	2.0	1.6	1.6	1.3	1.3
Violent crime involving injury	4.7	3.4	3.5	3.5	1.9	2.4
Serious violent crime	5.8	4.4	4.3	4.0	2.6	3.5
Serious domestic violence	1.7	0.8	1.0	0.9	0.6	0.6
Serious intimate partner violence	1.3	0.6	0.6	0.7	0.4	0.4
Serious violent crime involving weapons	4.2	3.1	3.0	2.7	1.4	2.3
Serious violent crime involving injury	2.5	1.8	1.6	1.3	0.8	1.2
Property crime	65.1	51.1	52.2	106.4	86.1	101.9
Burglary	17.2	15.1	16.4	14.5	13.6	13.2
Motor vehicle theft	6.9	4.2	4.0	2.0	0.9	1.1
Theft	41.0	31.8	31.9	89.9	71.6	87.7

Source: Truman, Langton, & Planty, 2013

less likely than whites to be victims of simple assault. Individuals 65 or older were 20 times less likely than individuals 20 to 24 to be victimized by any type of violent crime but slightly more likely to be victimized by a personal theft (Truman, Langton, & Planty, 2013). Table 3.1 shows the rate of reported victimizations in 2012 compared with 2011 and 2003 in the 2013 NCVS survey and the percentage reported and not reported to the police.

❖ Victimization in the Workplace

Two important demographic variables not included in the 2012 NCVS report are victimization at work and at school. It is important to consider these variables since most of us spend the majority of our waking hours either at work or at school.

Highlights of the United States Department of Justice (Harrell, 2011) report on workplace violence are shown in Figure 3.1 This report dealt with workplace violence from 1993 to 2009 and found that the rate declined by 62% during that time. Males were 62.9% of victims, 77.9% of all victims were white, and the age most likely to be victimized falls within the 35–49 category. The three occupations most at risk were security guards (a rate of 30.2 per 1,000), police officers (30.2), and corrections officers (33.0). Homicides were 21% of all occupational fatalities for women, with relatives or domestic partners committing 39% of female occupational homicide. Homicide accounted for only 9% of male workplace fatalities, which were most likely to be perpetrated by robbers. The most dangerous jobs are those in which workers must deal with the public in a protective (police officers) or supervisory (probation/parole and correctional officers) capacity. Those who work alone and are relatively isolated from others, who work at night, and who work with money (cab drivers, convenience store clerks) are also more at risk. The safest job category was university professor.

Workplace Victimization Protection

Many businesses and law enforcement agencies have instituted programs to prevent workplace violence that have gone a long way to reducing its occurrence and minimizing injuries when

- From 2002 to 2009, the rate of nonfatal workplace violence has declined by 35%, following a 62% decline in the rate from 1993 to 2002.
- The average annual rate of workplace violence between 2005 and 2009 (5 violent crimes per 1,000 employed persons age 16 or older) was about one-third the rate of nonworkplace violence (16 violent crimes per 1,000 employed persons age 16 or older) and violence against persons not employed (17 violent crimes per 1,000 persons age 16 or older).
- Between 2005 and 2009, law enforcement officers, security guards, and bartenders had the highest rates of nonfatal workplace violence.

- Strangers committed the greatest proportion of nonfatal workplace violence against males (53%) and females (41%) between 2005 and 2009.
- Among workplace homicides that occurred between 2005 and 2009, about 28% involved victims in sales and related occupations and about 17% involved victims in protective service occupations.
- About 70% of workplace homicides were committed by robbers and other assailants while about 21% were committed by work associates between 2005 and 2009.
- Between 2005 and 2009, while firearms were used in 5% of nonfatal workplace violence, shootings accounted for 80% of workplace homicides.

Figure 3.1

Highlights of 2011 Report on Workplace Violence

Source: Harrell, 2011

Figure 3.2

Types of Workplace Violent Crimes and Methods Used Between 1993 and 2009

Source: National Center for Victims of Violence, 2012

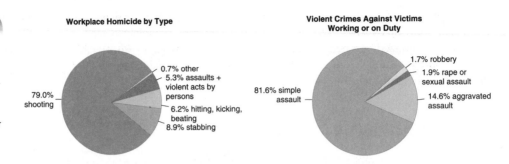

Workplace Homicide by Type

- 79.0% shooting
- 0.7% other
- 5.3% assaults + violent acts by persons
- 6.2% hitting, kicking, beating
- 8.9% stabbing

Violent Crimes Against Victims Working or on Duty

- 81.6% simple assault
- 1.7% robbery
- 1.9% rape or sexual assault
- 14.6% aggravated assault

it does happen. These programs stress that workplace violence does not occur at random and that employers and employees should develop an awareness of indicators of possible threats and the implementation of action plans to deescalate potentially violent situations. Another component of a mind-set promoting survival entails employees becoming stakeholders in their own safety and security. The FBI recommends the development of "shooter" scenarios akin to that of fire drills to "inoculate" employees against the stress of such threats and to produce a more fluid and rapid response in the event of a real incident (Romano, Levi-Minzi, Rugala, & Van Hasselt, 2011). Figure 3.3 represents the FBI's model of trained and untrained responses to the possibility of workplace victimization that emphasizes the necessity of potential victims to take responsibility for their own safety. In many ways this is a model we can all adapt to our own particular situations, whether at home, work, school, or play.

Figure 3.3

The Contrast Between Trained and Untrained Responses to Possible Workplace Violence

Source: Romano et al., 2011

Incident of Workplace Violence

Startle and Fear

Trained Response	Untrained Response
Anxious	Panic
Recall	Disbelief
Prepare	Denial
Commit to Act	Helplessness

❖ Victimization in the Schools

Public perceptions of victimization at the nation's schools are fueled by isolated but horrendous events such as Adam Lanza's fatal shooting of 20 children and six adults at Sandy Hook Elementary School in Connecticut in 2012. The truth is that our schools are some of the safest places to be. DeVoe, Bauer, and Hill's (2012) nationwide study of school crime and safety found that less than 1% of all juvenile homicides and suicides occurred at school during the period studied. Only 2.8% of students reported being victims of theft and 1.1% being victims of violence (mostly simple assault), with only 0.3% reporting a serious violent victimization. A larger percentage of males were victims of any crime at school (4.6%) than females (3.2%).

Bullying, which also gets a lot of press, is not as prevalent as we are sometimes led to believe (26.5% reported being bullied in some manner in 2008–2009). Figure 3.4 shows the percentage of students from 6th to 12th grade who reported being bullied during the 2008–2009 school year broken down by self-reported types of crime victimization. For instance, 92% of students who said they had been victims of a violent crime reported that they had also been bullied versus 27% of those who reported no victimization at all. Note that "traditional" bullying means everything from insults and name calling to assault and destroying the victim's property. "Electronic bullying" means anything designed to hurt sent by electronic means (e-mail, Facebook, text messages, and so forth).

Cyberbullying can have more devastating effects than physical bullying, especially if it is of a sexual nature, because it can be witnessed by anyone who logs on. For instance, high school freshman Kenneth Weishuhn committed suicide after being repeatedly electronically harassed and threatened after he "came out" as being gay. Similarly, college student Tyler Clementi committed suicide after a gay encounter with another man in his dorm was secretly videoed and streamed over the Internet by fellow students. Then there was high school senior Jessica Logan who killed herself after her ex-boyfriend sent a nude photograph of her around the school, precipitating a long stream of bullying in which she was called a "slut" and a "whore." Figure 3.5 provides a breakdown of the various means by which people are electronically bullied.

❖ Human Trafficking

The most horrible form of victimization is arguably slavery, although we have another name for it today—human trafficking. **Human trafficking** is defined by the United Nations Convention Against Transnational Organized Crime in *The Trafficking Protocol of the Universal Declaration of Human Rights* as

The recruitment, transportation, transfer, harbouring or receipt of persons, by means of threat or use of force or other forms of coercion, of abduction, of fraud, of deception, of the abuse of power or of a position of vulnerability or of the giving or receiving of payments or benefits to achieve the consent of a person having control over another person, for the purpose

Photo 3.1

Cyberbullying can have potentially devastating effects, even leading to violence and suicide. What do you think this young cyberbullying victim is feeling right now?

Figure 3.4

Percentage of
Students Age
12 Through 18
Reporting Being
Bullied by Traditional
Means at School or
Electronic Means
Anywhere: School
Year 2008–2009

Source: DeVoe et al., 2012

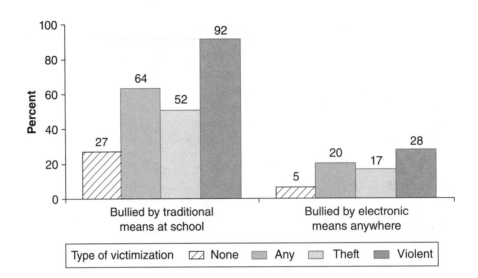

Figure 3.5

Where Cyberbullying
Occurs

Source: David-Ferdon &
Hertz, 2009

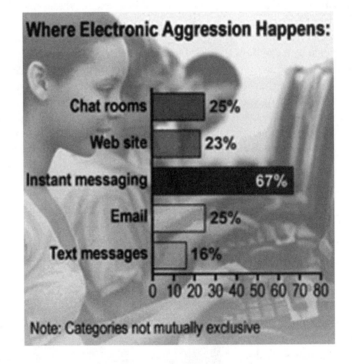

of exploitation. Exploitation shall include, at a minimum, the exploitation of the prostitution of others or other forms of sexual exploitation, forced labour or services, slavery or practices similar to slavery, servitude or the removal of organs. (2004, p. 42)

It is quite bizarre to think that 200 years after the British fought costly wars to end the transatlantic slave trade that we are still talking about it happening in the 21st century. According to a U.S. Department of State (2013) report on human trafficking, "It is estimated that as many as 27 million men, women, and children around the world are victims of what is often described with the umbrella term 'human trafficking.'"

Julia Davidson (2010) argues that this modern form of slavery is often worse than the old open legal slavery where slaves were given some degree of autonomy. Modern slavery is illegal and thus must be hidden. Because of the illegality and often severe criminal penalties attached to trafficking in first-world countries, the people that control modern-day slaves use a variety of methods to do so. According to the U.S. Department of State (2013), these include confiscating all identifying documents; isolating victims; constantly accompanying victims; restricting access to food, clothing, medical care, and sleep; requiring long work days; and otherwise abusing and intimidating their victims into becoming physically and psychologically dependent on their captors.

The source countries for human trafficking are almost invariably poor third-world countries with corrupt law enforcement and few employment opportunities, and the destination countries are usually, but not always, rich countries. Trafficked humans may be used in their own countries in brothels and sweatshops. Women and children are typically used as prostitutes; most males are used as forced labor. It is obviously a highly profitable enterprise for the traffickers, and it is no surprise that organized crime groups participate in smuggling humans, just as they are involved in smuggling drugs. It is estimated that human trafficking is second only to the illegal drug market in terms of profitability, netting the traffickers from $5 to $9 billion a year according to a United Nations (2004) report. Since that time, however, the number of victims has risen while costs have declined for the trafficker. As Heather Smith (2011) explains, "Coupled with the fact that trafficked sex slaves are the single most profitable type of slave, costing on average $1,895 each but generating $29,210 annually, [there are] stark predictions about the likely growth in commercial sex slavery in the future" (p. 271). Figure 3.6 offers a thumbnail sketch of human trafficking from the Immigration and Customs Enforcement (ICE) Department. ICE is mandated to control all kinds of smuggling into the United States, and Figure 3.7 gives trafficking figures specific to the United States.

❖ Sexual Assault of Children: Who Gets Victimized?

The sexual assault of children is perhaps the most prevalent crime against humanity in the United States, with approximately two-thirds of incarcerated sex offenders having offended against children (Talbot, Gilligan, Carter, & Matson, 2002). It is problematic to accurately gauge the prevalence of child molesting, with rates depending on how broad or how narrowly molesting is defined. According to the National Center for Victims of Crime (NCVC; 2010) the percentage of children in the United States experiencing sexual abuse sometime during their childhood is 20% for girls and 5% for boys. Girls are more likely to be abused within the family, and boys are more likely to be victimized by acquaintances outside of the family and by strangers (NCVC, 2010; Turner, Finkelhor, & Ormrod, 2006). The strongest single predictor of victimization for girls is having a stepfather or mother's live-in boyfriend in the house. Stepfathers are about five times more likely to sexually abuse their daughters than are biological fathers, and the strongest predictor for boys is growing up in a father-absent home (Turner et al., 2006). There are many other factors predictive of child sexual abuse, and the more factors present the more likely abuse is to occur.

Finkelhor (1984) developed a risk factor checklist for the likelihood of girls' victimization containing the following predictors:

1. Living with a stepfather or mother's live-in boyfriend

2. Living without biological mother

3. Not close to mother

Figure 3.6

Thumbnail Sketch of
Human Trafficking
From ICE

Source: U.S. Immigration
and Customs Enforcement,
2013

Human Trafficking
A Global Problem

Prostitution. Servitude. Forced Labor.

Each year, hundreds of thousands of innocent men, women and children
are exploited in human trafficking schemes.

ICE is a leader in the global fight against trafficking.

By targeting trafficking organizations while providing support to victims, ICE
is working to dismantle the criminal infrastructure behind human trafficking.

Common Trafficking Indicators

- Victim does not have ID or travel documents.
- Victim has been coached in talking to law enforcement and immigration officials.
- Victim is in forced labor situation or sex trade.
- Victim's salary is garnished to pay off smuggling fees.
- Victim is denied freedom of movement.
- Victim or family is threatened with harm if escape is attempted.
- Victim is threatened with deportation or arrest.
- Victim has been harmed or denied food, water, sleep or medical care.
- Victim is denied contact with friends or family.
- Victim is not allowed to socialize or attend religious services.

Trafficking vs. Smuggling

Human Trafficking is defined as:

- Sex trafficking in which a commercial sex act is induced by force, fraud or coercion, or in which the person induced to perform such act is younger than 18; or
- The recruitment, harboring, transportation, provision or obtaining of a person for labor or services, through the use of force, fraud or coercion for the purpose of subjection to involuntary servitude, peonage, debt bondage or slavery.

Human Smuggling is defined as:

- The importation of people into the United States involving deliberate evasion of immigration laws. This offense includes bringing illegal aliens into the country, as well as the unlawful transportation and harboring of aliens already in the United States.

Figure 3.7

Human Trafficking
Figures Specific to
the United States

Source: U.S. Department
of State, 2012

- 14,500–17,500: estimated number of people trafficked into the United States each year
- 50% of people trafficked into the U.S. each year are children
- 800,000 people are trafficked worldwide each year
- East Asia/Pacific is the region that is the largest source of people who are trafficked into the U.S each year

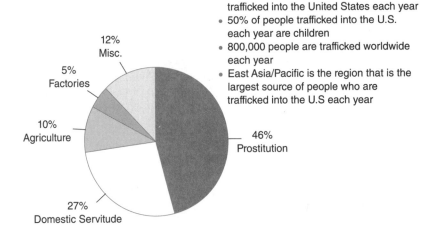

12% Misc.

5% Factories

10% Agriculture

46% Prostitution

27% Domestic Servitude

4. Mother never finished high school

5. Sex-punitive mother

6. No physical affection from (biological) father

7. Family income under $10,000 (in 1980 dollars; $28,416 in 2013 dollars)

8. Two friends or fewer in childhood

Finkelhor found that the probability of victimization was virtually zero among girls with none of the predictors in their background and rose steadily to 66% among girls with five predictors. Given the large number of divorces, out-of-wedlock births, and reconstituted families we are seeing in the United States, these risk factors for sexual abuse will be experienced by an increasing number of children. The victimization of children in domestic situations is particularly heinous, and we need to know under what circumstances it is most prevalent. It seems that every research program examining this problem finds that it is most likely to occur in homes in which children do not reside with both biological parents. A national representative sample of over 2,000 children ages 2 through 9 found that children of single parents were 6.7 times more likely to witness family violence, 3.9 times more likely to be maltreated, and 2.7 times more likely to be sexually assaulted than children with both biological parents present. The figures for stepparent families were even worse at 9.2, 4.6, and 4.3, respectively (Turner et al., 2006). This same study found that stepchildren were 9.2 times more likely to witness family violence, 4.6 times more likely to be maltreated, and 4.3 times more likely to be sexually assaulted than children living with two biological parents. A girl living with a stepfather or mother's live-in boyfriend is approximately 65 times more likely to be fatally abused than a child living with both biological parents (Daly & Wilson, 1996)

❖ Domestic Violence Victimization

Domestic violence victimization encompasses a variety of acts and refers to any abusive act (physical, sexual, or psychological) that occurs within a domestic setting. Family violence is the most prevalent form of violence in the United States today, and most of that is intimate-partner (spouse or lover) violence (Tolan, Gorman-Smith, & Henry, 2006). Except for minor forms of abuse, intimate-partner violence is overwhelmingly committed by males against females, although when females commit such violence they are more likely to use a weapon to equalize the size and strength difference between the sexes (Smith & Farole, 2009). However, while just over one-third of all murders of females in the United States are committed by intimate partners, less than 4% of males are killed by intimate partners (Rennison, 2003).

Violent victimization of spouses or lovers perpetrated by males is primarily driven by male sexual ownership, jealousy, and suspicion of infidelity. Evidence from around the world indicates that the single most important cause of domestic violence (including homicide) is

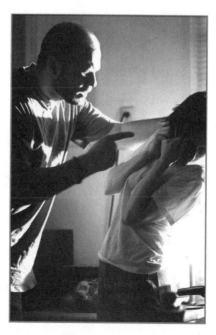

Photo 3.2

Intimate-partner violence is predominately committed by males against females.

male jealousy and suspicion of infidelity (Lepowsky, 1994). DNA data indicate that from 1% to 30% (depending on the culture or subculture) of children are fathered by someone other than the presumed father (Birkenhead & Moller, 1992). The threat of cuckoldry (being fooled into raising someone else's child) is thus real, which suggests that male violence against spouses and lovers should be most common in environments where the threat of infidelity is most real. Such environments would be those in which marriages are most precarious, where moral restrictions on premarital and extramarital sexual relationships are weakest, and where out-of-wedlock birth rates are highest (Graham-Kevan & Archer, 2009).

Although by no means limited to the lower classes, domestic violence is most often committed by competitively disadvantaged (CD) males (Graham-Kevan & Archer, 2009). CD males have low mate value because they have less to offer in terms of resources or prospects of acquiring them, which tends to make their mates less desirous of maintaining the relationship with them and seek other partners. Lacking alternative means of controlling their partner's behavior, CD males may turn to violently coercive tactics to intimidate them. This may be one of the reasons why intimate personal violence is two to three times more prevalent and more deadly among African American males than among males of other races (Hampton, Oliver, & Magarian, 2003). Hampton and his colleagues (2003) also list the anger and frustration born of poverty and unemployment, the reluctance of black females to report incidents, and the general fractious and antagonistic relationship that allegedly exists between black men and women as reasons. Figure 3.8 shows the victimization rates by annual household income of victims. Figure 3.9 offers highlights from the Bureau of Justice Statistics' 2012 special report on intimate-partner violence.

❖ Identity Theft and Other Forms of Cybervictimization

Identity theft is the use of someone else's personal information without his or her permission to fraudulently obtain goods or services. According to a Federal Trade Commission (2010) report, 279,389 complaints of identity theft were filed in 2009, although it estimates that about 9 million people actually are victims of identity theft in some form. The cost to the economy is approximately $50 billion a year. Identity theft can range from a criminal's short-term use of a stolen or lost credit card to the long-term use of a person's complete biographical information

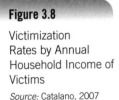

Figure 3.8

Victimization Rates by Annual Household Income of Victims

Source: Catalano, 2007

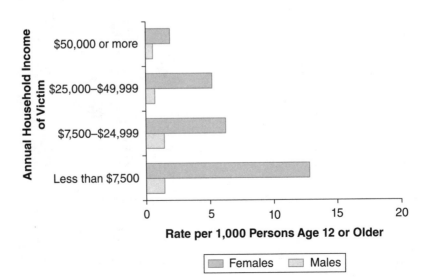

• From 1994 to 2010, the overall rate of intimate partner violence in the United States declined by 64%, from 9.8 victimizations per 1,000 persons age 12 or older to 3.6 per 1,000. • Intimate partner violence declined by more than 60% for both males and females from 1994 to 2010. • From 1994 to 2010, about 4 in 5 victims of intimate partner violence were female. • Females ages 18 to 24 and 25 to 34 generally experienced the highest rates of intimate partner violence.	• Compared to every other age group, a smaller percentage of female victims ages 12 to 17 were previously victimized by the same offender. • The rate of intimate partner violence for Hispanic females declined 78%, from 18.8 victimizations per 1,000 in 1994 to 4.1 per 1,000 in 2010. • Females living in households comprised of one female adult with children experienced intimate partner violence at a rate more than 10 times higher than households with married adults with children and 6 times higher than households with one female only.

Figure 3.9

Highlights From Special Report on Intimate Violence 1993–2010

Source: Catalano, 2012

(name, social security number, and other identifiers) to "clone" the victim's identity and to commit multiple crimes that may be attributed to the victim.

Criminals gain access to the personal information of others in a variety of ways. They can steal it, buy it, or simply be given it by their unwary victims. People are continually providing confidential information to all sorts of businesses and agencies that goes into huge data banks that may be legitimately accessed by employees and stolen, or they can be "hacked" and have their information stolen. Credit card numbers can be copied during a financial transaction such as when a restaurant server takes your card for processing, or numbers can be surreptitiously recorded on a skimming device, which is typically a cigarette-pack-size device run across a credit card to record the electronic information in the magnetic strip. This information is then used to make duplicate cards. Thieves can also steal original checks left in mailboxes for pickup, copy the information on them, and buy duplicate checks from mail-order firms.

Most stolen identity information is not for the personal use of the thief but for sale to others. An organization of about 4,000 individuals called the Shadowcrew stole large volumes of personal information for many years and arrogantly advertised and sold it on websites worldwide. If you wanted to buy card numbers with security codes you could get 50 of them for $200; if you wanted the same thing complete with the original owner's social security number and date of birth you would only have to pay $40 each (Levy & Stone, 2005). Leading members of the Shadowcrew were arrested by the U.S. Secret Service in 2004, effectively closing the business that authorities estimated had trafficked at least 1.5 million credit and bank cards, account numbers, and other counterfeit documents such as passports and driver's licenses (U.S. Department of Justice, 2004). The consequences of identity theft victimization are illustrated in the story of Michelle Brown.

THEORY IN ACTION: A Case of Cybervictimization and Its Consequences

With the advent of the computer age we are all victims in waiting. The ability to victimize someone without coming remotely within contact of that person means that the strongest among us can be viciously "attacked" by the weakest. One of the most terrifying fictional depictions of cybervictimization is provided in the movie *The Net*. In this movie, Angela Bennett, played by Sandra Bullock, is a computer expert who has her life turned into a nightmare

(Continued)

THEORY IN ACTION (Continued)

when her records are wiped clean and she is given a new identity by people who want to destroy her. Her new identity came complete with a police record, and the rest of the movie is about her struggles to find out who has done this to her and why. Another movie with the same theme, *Identity Theft: The Michelle Brown Story*, is based on a true story of identity theft victimization.

Michelle Brown, a 29-year-old white female, is one of a number of real-life Angela Bennetts whose nightmare began in January 1998. While Michelle did not have her records erased, she had them "cloned" by a woman who gained access to her personal information. Her identity clone was Heddi Larae Ille, a 33-year-old white female with no physical resemblance to Michelle at all. With a line of credit established with Michelle's social security number and driver's license number, Heddi racked up $1,443 in phone bills, bought a $32,000 automobile, had $4,800 worth of liposuction, and bought numerous other items. Worse yet, Heddi was arrested as Michelle Brown for smuggling 3,000 pounds of marijuana into Texas from Mexico. Michelle was thus named in the indictment and listed as a DEA informant. Returning from a trip overseas, Michelle (the real one) was detained

for over an hour at LAX because the DEA had posed a lookout for her. Only a phone call from a police detective aware of Michelle's predicament got her released. Heddi was arrested and booked again under Michelle's identity for grand theft and possession of stolen property in 1999. Her true identity finally came to light, and she was sentenced to 73 months in federal prison and 24 months in state prison.

Michelle presented her story before a U.S. Senate committee on identity theft. She also informed them of the traumatic effects her victimization had on her life. She said that she spent over 500 hours (the equivalent of 12 1/2 workweeks) trying to unravel the mess, lost countless hours of sleep, lost her appetite, and lost a valued 3-year relationship with her boyfriend. She added that she also "lost identification with the person I really was inside and shut myself out of social functions because of the negativity this caused in my life." She indicated that she was afraid to leave the country again in case her name is still on some country's computer listing her as "wanted." Michelle's case, admittedly a particularly horrible one, is just one of the many thousands of such cases that occur annually in the United States.

Another type of cybervictimization is *phishing*, which as the name implies, involves thieves casting thousands of fraudulent e-mails into the cyberpond asking for personal information and waiting for someone to bite. Phishers may send out official looking e-mails with a bank logo asking recipients to "update" their information or telling them that their account may have been fraudulently used and that the bank needs to "verify" their personal information. One study indicated that 40% of recipients of one fraudulent bank e-mail believed it to be real (Kshetri, 2006).

A victim may also be literally scared into providing their information. Imagine receiving an e-mail from "Lolita Productions" telling you that your credit card has been billed $99.95 for the first two child pornography DVDs and that it will be automatically billed $49.95 each month for further DVDs. The message also says that if you want to cancel membership you should e-mail back with full credit card details "for verification." Knowing the penalties for possessing child porn, you may be anxious to do anything to free yourself from the electronic embrace of Lolita Productions.

The most notorious phishers are the so-called Nigerian frauds run by Nigerian organized crime groups. E-mails have been received by millions of people the world over. A small number of people fall for it. These people are first asked to send a small amount of money (perhaps $200 or less) to "cover expenses" but are suckered into sending ever-larger amounts as "complications" arise. Some of the more gullible have even been lured to Nigeria with their cash and have been killed (Baines, 1996).

❖ Victimization Theories

Victimization can occur at any time or place without warning. Who could have predicted someone gassing her car at the filling station would be gunned down by Washington, DC, Beltway snipers John Muhammad and Lee Malvo in 2002? Or that the typist at his desk in the World Trade Center would be obliterated seconds later by a passenger jet on September 11? There is no systemic way to evaluate events such as these from a victimology perspective. But as previously noted, many victimizing events are not random or unpredictable. Criminologists no longer view victims as simply passive players in crime who were unfortunate enough to be in the wrong place at the wrong time (as of course were the victims of 9/11 and the DC snipers). In the majority of cases, victims are now seen as individuals who in some way, knowingly or unknowingly, passively or actively, influenced their victimization. Obviously, the role of the victim, however provocative it may be, is never a necessary and sufficient cause of his or her victimization and therefore cannot fully explain the actions of the person committing the criminal act.

Victim Precipitation Theory

Victim precipitation theory was first presented by von Hentig (1941) and applies only to violent victimization. Its basic premise is that by acting in certain provocative ways some individuals initiate a chain of events that lead to their victimization. Most murders of spouses and boyfriends by women, for example, are victim precipitated in that the "perpetrator" is defending herself from the victim (Mann, 1990). Likewise, serious delinquent and criminal behavior and serious victimization are inextricably linked. Schaffer and Ruback (2002), for instance, found that violent offenders, all other things being statistically controlled, are about twice as likely as nonviolent offenders to be victimized themselves. Furthermore, past victimization is the best predictor of future victimization (odds ratio = 5.7, which means that if you were victimized in Year 1, the odds of you being victimized in Year 2 are 5.7 times greater than if you were not victimized in Year 1). Another study using data from the longitudinal Pittsburgh and Denver studies of delinquency risk factors (e.g., low SES, single-parent household, hyperactivity, impulsiveness, drug usage) showed that the same factors predicted victimization as well (Loeber, Kalb, & Huizinga, 2001). As seen in Figure 3.10, overall, 50% of seriously violent delinquents were themselves violently victimized, compared with 10% of nondelinquents from the same neighborhoods.

Victim precipitation theory has been most contentious when applied to rape victims ever since Menachem Amir's (1971) study of police records found that 19% of forcible rapes were supposedly victim precipitated. Amir defined victim-precipitated rape as a case in which the victim initially agreed to sexual relations and then reneged. A number of surveys of high school and college students have shown that a majority of males and a significant minority of females believe that it is justifiable for a man to use violence to obtain sex if the victim had "led him on" (Herman, 1991). For this reason many criminologists have disparaged victim precipitation theory as victim blaming, although it was never meant to be that. Hopefully, the attitudes revealed in these 1980s surveys have diminished with the greater awareness of the horrible nature of this crime and a greater awareness that women have every right to change their minds even if they have "excited" their partners by mild petting.

Figure 3.10

Male Victimization
Rates by Number
of Risk Factors for
Delinquency

Source: Loeber et al., 2001

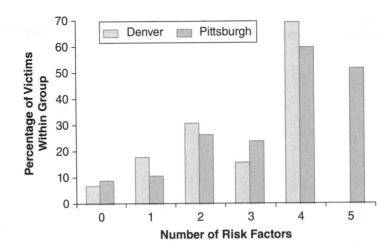

Figure 3.11 provides four scenarios illustrating various levels of victim/offender responsibility from the victim precipitation perspective. In the first scenario, the woman who stabbed her husband after suffering years of abuse is judged blameless, although some lacking a little in empathy and understanding of the psychology of domestic abuse may argue that she must take some responsibility for remaining in the relationship. In the second scenario, both the offender and the victim were engaging in a minor vice crime and both are judged equally responsible for the crime (morally he should not have been there and was careless with his wallet). In the third scenario, the victim facilitated the crime by carelessly leaving his keys in the car. In the last scenario, the child is totally innocent of any responsibility for what happened to her. We want to strongly emphasize that whatever the degree of responsibility, "responsibility" does not mean "guilt."

Routine Activities Theory/Lifestyle Theory

Routine activities theory and **lifestyle theory** are separate entities, but in victimology they are similar enough to warrant being merged into one (Doerner & Lab, 2002). Routine

Figure 3.11

Four Scenarios
Illustrating
the Degree of
Victim/Offender
Responsibility
According to Victim
Precipitation Theory

Degree of Criminal Intent of the Perpetrator			
None ⟶	**Some** ⟶	**More** ⟶	**Much**
Victim Provocation A woman who has suffered years of abuse stabs and kills her husband in self-defense as he is beating her again.	*Equal Responsibility* Victim using the services of a prostitute leaves his wallet on the bed stand and leaves. She decides to keep the money in his wallet.	*Victim Facilitation* Victim leaves keys in his car while he runs into a store. A teenager impulsively steals the car and wrecks it.	*Victim Innocent* A sex offender kidnaps a screaming young girl from a playground and molests her.
Much ⟵	**More** ⟵	**Some** ⟵	**None** ⟵
Degree of Victim Facilitation or Provocation/Precipitation			

activities theory stresses that criminal behavior takes place via the interaction of three variables that reflect individuals' everyday routine activities: (1) the presence of motivated offenders, (2) the availability of suitable targets, and (3) the absence of capable guardians. The basic idea of lifestyle theory is that there are certain lifestyles (routine activities) that disproportionately expose some people to high risk for victimization. Lifestyles are the routine patterned activities that people engage in on a daily basis, both obligatory (e.g., work related) and optional (e.g., recreational). A high-risk lifestyle may be getting involved with deviant peer groups or drugs, in just "hanging out" or frequenting bars until late into the night and drinking heavily. Routine activities/lifestyle theory explains some of the data relating to demographic profiles and risk presented by Loeber et al. (2001) discussed earlier. Males, the young, the unmarried, and the poor are more at risk for victimization than females, older people, married people, and more affluent people because they have riskier lifestyles. On average, the lifestyles of the former are more active and action oriented than the latter.

These lifestyles sometimes lead to repeat victimization. Prior victimization has been called "arguably the best readily available predictor of future victimization," and it "appears a robust finding across crime types and data sources" (Tseloni & Pease, 2003, p. 196). Lisa Bostaph (2004) reviews the literature on what she calls "career victims," and among the various interesting research findings on this phenomenon she lists the following attributable to lifestyle patterns:

- A British crime survey that found that 20.2% of the respondents were victims of 81.2% of all offenses

- A study that found 24% of rape victims had been raped before

- A study of assault victims in the Netherlands that found 11.3% of victims accounted for 25.3% of hospital admissions for assault over 25 years

- A study reporting that 67% of sexual assault victims had experienced prior sexual assaults

Photo 3.3

It's never a smart idea to run around with peers "with an attitude"—victimization is often just around the corner.

Why we see so much repeat victimization is an important question on victimology's research agenda. The explanations offered by various theorists almost inevitably revolve around routine activities theory—a motivated offender taking advantage of a suitable victim lacking capable guardians. The repeat victimization of domestic partners or children occurs because the perpetrator is typically supposed to be the capable guardian, and the "suitable targets" are often trapped in the same household as the motivated offenders. Over time, such victims may come to accept victimization as normal and inevitable.

Repeat victims of violent assault are often found to frequent places known to have violent reputations, such as going to certain bars with the stated intention of getting drunk and involved in fights (Farrell, Phillips, & Pease, 1995). These individuals can be either or both repeat offenders and repeat victims.

Most of the research in routine activities/lifestyle theory has been done on rape victimization. Bonnie Fisher and her colleagues' (2001) national sample of college women found that 2.8% had been raped, although 46.5 % of this 2.8% whom Fisher and her colleagues defined as rape victims said that they did not experience the event as rape. Fisher and colleagues (2001) report that four lifestyle factors are consistently found to increase the risk of sexual assault: (1) frequently drinking enough to get drunk, (2) being unmarried, (3) having previously been a victim of sexual assault, and (4) living on campus (for on-campus victimization only). A later study by Daigle, Fisher, and Cullen (2008) among 4,432 college females found that a mere 3.3% of them experienced 45.2% of all the forcible sexual incidents reported in the study. The major factor that appears to distinguish one-time from repeat victims is that one-time victims take steps to avoid circumstances that led to their victimization whereas repeat victims tend not to. It is also possible that repeat victims suffer from what has been called *traumatic sexualization*, which is the result of prior victimization by someone the victim trusted. This can lead to risk taking and provocative behavior. Such victimization can also undermine trust in others and lead to feelings of powerlessness. All of these symptoms increase the risk of revictimization (Reid & Sullivan, 2009).

❖ Is Victimology "Blaming the Victim"?

Some victim advocates reject victimology theories as "victim blaming." Victimologists counter by emphasizing that victimologist do not "blame" victims and that they simply explore the process of victimization with the goal of understanding and *preventing* it. Although victimology research is used to develop crime prevention strategies, not to berate victims, some victim advocates even reject "as ideologically tainted" crime-prevention tips endorsed by victimologists (Karmen, 2005, p. 129). Victimologists maintain, however, that crime prevention tips and strategies are ignored at our peril. We all agree that we *should* be able to leave our cars unlocked, sleep with the windows open in summer, leave our doors unlocked, frequent any bar we choose, and walk down any alley in any neighborhood at any time we please, but we cannot. The essence of the workplace violence prevention strategies recommended by the FBI and implemented by companies around the United States is that we must take some responsibility for our own safety. If we do not, we will be helpless and passive pawns in the hands of those who would victimize us (Romano et al., 2011).

It is agreed that it is indicative of a double standard when we warn our young women not to get drunk lest they become victims of rape, and I can appreciate the point of those who say we should be loudly warning our young men not to take advantage of impaired women instead. Of course, it is never wise to get drunk whatever one's gender, because it opens everyone to possible victimization (not to mention accidents). Common sense demands that we take what steps we can to safeguard ourselves and our property in this imperfect world.

Crime prevention tips are really no different from tips we get all the time about staying healthy: eat right, exercise, and quit smoking if you want to avoid health problems. Similarly, avoid certain places, dress sensibly, don't provoke, take reasonable precautionary measures, and don't drink too much if you want to avoid victimization. Victims deserve our sympathy even if they somehow provoked or facilitated their own victimization. Victimologists do not "blame"; they simply remind us that complete innocence and full responsibility lie on a continuum.

❖ The Consequences of Victimization

Some crime victims suffer lifelong pain from wounds and some suffer permanent disability, but for the majority of victims the worst consequences are psychological. We all like to think that we live in a safe, predictable, and lawful world in which people treat one another decently. When we are victimized this comfortable "just world" view is shattered. With victimization come stressful feelings of shock, personal vulnerability, anger, fear of further victimization, and suspicion of others.

Victimization also produces feelings of depression, guilt, self-blame, and lowered self-esteem and self-efficacy. Rape in particular has these consequences for its victims ("Did I contribute to it?" "Could I have done more to prevent it?"). The shock, anger, and depression that typically afflict a rape victim are known as **rape trauma syndrome**, which is similar to post-traumatic stress disorder (reexperiencing the event via "flashbacks," avoiding anything at all associated with the event, and a general numbness of affect) often suffered by those who have experienced the horrors of war (van Berlo & Ensink, 2000). Victimization "also changes one's perceptions of and beliefs about others in society. It does so by indicating others as sources of threat and harm rather than sources of support" (Macmillan, 2001, p. 12).

Victims of property crimes, particularly burglary, also have the foundations of their world shaken. The home is supposed to be a personal sanctuary of safety and security, and when it is "touched" by an intruder some victims describe it as the "rape" of their home (Bartol, 2002, p. 336). A British study of burglary victims found that 65% reacted with anger and 30% with fear of revictimization, and 29% suffered insomnia as a consequence. The type and severity of these reactions were structured by victims' place in the social structure, with those most likely to be affected being women, older and poorer individuals, and residents of single-parent households (Mawby, 2001). Finally, note the trauma, stress, wasted time, and lost relationships suffered by Michelle Brown (see Theory in Action box) after being victimized by a person she neither knew nor had ever seen. This underlies the contention that each one of us is a victim in waiting.

In summing up the consequences of victimization, we note that just as offending behavior shapes the life course trajectories of offenders, violent victimization helps to shape the life course trajectories of victims. Scott Menard's (2002) study of the National Survey of Youth samples, a longitudinal study involving individuals from age 11 to 33, found that violent victimization during adolescence has pervasive effects on problem outcomes as adults. Figure 3.12 shows that the expected probability of a variety of negative outcomes in adulthood is much greater for victims of violence during adolescence than nonvictims during the same period.

❖ Victimization and the Criminal Justice System

Until fairly recently the victim had been the forgotten party in the criminal justice system. In the United States crime is considered an act against the state rather than against the individual

Figure 3.12

Percentage of Adolescent Victims and Nonvictims of Violence Expected to Experience Adult Problem Outcomes

Source: Menard, 2002

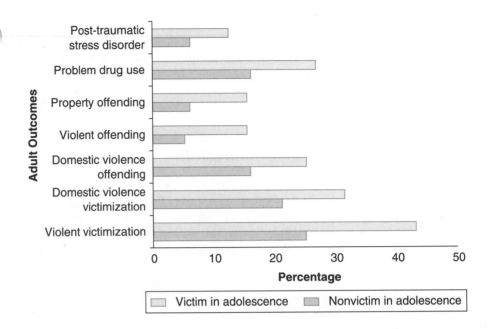

who was actually victimized. In 2004 the Senate passed a crime victim's bill of rights that has gone some considerable way to recognizing the previously discounted victim. Although these rights apply only to victims of federal crimes, all 50 states have implemented constitutional amendments or promulgated bills guaranteeing similar rights. We owe much of this increased attention to victim issues to the women's movement and to feminist criminologists.

Crime Victim's Bill of Rights

1. The right to be reasonably protected from the accused

2. The right to reasonable, accurate, and timely notice of any public proceeding involving the crime or of any release or escape of the accused

3. The right not to be excluded from any such public proceeding

4. The right to be reasonably heard at any public proceeding involving release, plea, or sentencing

5. The right to confer with the attorney for the government in the case

6. The right to full and timely restitution as provided in law

7. The right to proceedings free from unreasonable delay

8. The right to be treated with fairness and with respect for the victim's dignity and privacy

Source: Senate Bill S2329, April 21, 2004

Crime victims are eligible for partial compensation from the state to cover medical and living expenses incurred as a result of their victimization. All 50 states and all United States protectorates have established programs that typically cover what private insurance does not, assuming the state has sufficient funds. According to the National Association of Crime Victim Compensation Board (NACVCB; 2005), in 2004 victims of violent crime nationwide received a total of $426 million in compensation, with the majority (51%) going for medical expenses.

❖ Victim-Offender Reconciliation Programs (VORPs)

VORPs are an integral component of restorative justice philosophy. Many crime victims are seeking fairness, justice, and restitution *as defined by them* (restorative justice) as opposed to revenge and punishment. Central to the VORP process is the bringing together of victim and offender in face-to-face meetings mediated by a person trained in mediation theory and practice (Walsh & Stohr, 2010). Meetings are voluntary for both offender and victim and are designed to iron out ways in which the offender can make amends for the hurt and damage caused to the victim.

Photo 3.4

A trained mediator assisting a victim in sharing with the offender. Could you forgive your victimizer?

Victims participating in VORPs gain the opportunity to make offenders aware of their feelings of personal violation and loss and to lay out their proposals for how offenders can restore the situation. Offenders are afforded the opportunity to see firsthand the pain they have caused their victims and perhaps even to express remorse. The mediator assists the parties in developing a contract agreeable to both. The mediator monitors the terms of the contract and may schedule further face-to-face meetings.

VORPs are used most often in the juvenile system but rarely used for personal violent crimes in either juvenile or adult systems. Where they are used, about 60% of victims invited to participate actually become involved, and a high percentage (mid- to high 90s) result in signed contracts (Coates, 1990). Mark Umbreit and his colleagues (1994) sum up the various satisfactions expressed by victims who participate in VORPs:

1. Meeting offenders helped reduce their fear of being revictimized.

2. They appreciated the opportunity to tell offenders how they felt.

3. Being personally involved in the justice process was satisfying to them.

4. They gained insight into the crime and into the offender's situation.

5. They received restitution.

However, VORPs do not suit all victims, especially those who feel that the wrong done to them cannot so easily be "put right," and want the offender punished (Olson & Dzur, 2004).

Summary

- Victimology is the study of the risk factors for and consequences of victimization and criminal justice approaches dealing with victims and victimization. The risk factors for victimization are basically the same as the risk factors for victimizing in terms of gender, race, age, SES, personal characteristics, and neighborhood.

- Although the NCVS tells us much about victimization in the United States, there is little information relating to victimization occurring in the two places we spend most of our time—at work or school. Workplace violence usually occurs against people who deal with the public in a protective or supervisory capacity or against those who work alone with money.

- Serious physical victimization in our schools is relatively rare, but electronic bullying is ever growing and can have even more hurtful consequences (including suicide) than physical bullying.

- The most insidious form of victimization today is arguably human trafficking, which in effect is a modern form of slavery. People of all ages and sexes are trafficked, but the vast majority are girls and women who are used primarily as captive prostitutes.

- The sexual assault of children is possibly the most prevalent crime against humanity in the United States, with estimates of 20% of girls and 5% of boys being victimized. The greatest risk for child victimization is living with a male who is not the biological father of the child.

- Domestic violence (mostly intimate-partner violence) is the most prevalent form of violence in the United States today. Much of it is driven by jealousy and real or imaged infidelity and is most likely to be committed by competitively disadvantaged males.

- Theories of victimization such as victim precipitation theory and routine activities/lifestyle theory examine the victim's role in facilitating or precipitating his or her victimization. This is not "victim blaming," but rather an effort to understand and prevent victimization. Victimologists apportion responsibility within the victim/offender dyad on a continuum from complete victim innocence to victim precipitation.

- The consequences of victimization can be devastating both physically and psychologically. Although the severity of the psychological consequences of the same sort of victimization can vary widely according to the characteristics of the victim, consequences can range from short-lived anger to post-traumatic stress disorder, especially for victims of rape.

- Until fairly recently victims were the forgotten party in a criminal justice system that tended to think of them only as "evidence" or witnesses. Things have changed over the last 25 years with the passage of a victim's rights bill by the federal government and all 50 states. There are also various victim-centered programs designed to ease the pains of victimization, such as victim compensation.

Exercises and Discussion Questions

1. Interview a willing classmate or friend who has been victimized by a serious crime and ask about his or her feelings shortly after victimization and now. Did it change his or her attitudes about crime and punishment?

2. Is it a surprise to you that perpetrators of crimes are more likely to also be victims of crime than people in general? Why or why not?

3. Discuss the various ways that human trafficking is like slavery.

4. Go to your state's official website and look up funding levels and what services are available to crime victims.

5. Discuss how learning about victimology helps you to further understand offending behavior.

6. Domestic violence has been falling dramatically over the last 10 to 20 years. Is this attributable to mandatory arrest policies or to some other factor?

7. In your opinion, does the criminal justice system do enough to guarantee victims' rights? What other steps can be taken to lessen the harm suffered by victims in the aftermath of being victimized?

Useful Websites

American Society of Victimology. www.american-society-victimology.us.

International Victimology Website. www.victimology.nl.

National Crime Victimization Survey Resource Guide. www.icpsr.umich.edu/NACJD/NCVS.

National Incident-Based Reporting System Resource Guide. www.icpsr.umich.edu/NACJD/NIBRS.

The World Society of Victimology. www.worldsocietyofvictimology.org.

Chapter Terms

Domestic violence

Human trafficking

Identity theft

Rape trauma syndrome

Routine activities/lifestyle theory

Victim precipitation theory

Victimology

CHAPTER 4

The Early Schools of Criminology

"Lisa" is a 30-year-old mother of three children aged 8, 6, and 4. Her husband left her a year ago for another woman, and his present whereabouts are unknown. Because Lisa only has a 10th-grade education and because she cannot afford child care costs, she was forced onto the welfare rolls. When Christmas rolled around she had no money to buy her children any presents, so she took a temporary Christmas job at the local Wal-Mart store where she earned $1,200 over a two-month period. Lisa did not report this income to the welfare authorities as required by law; a welfare audit uncovered her crime. The terrified and deeply ashamed Lisa pled guilty to grand theft, which carries a possible sentence of 2 years in prison and was referred to the probation department for a presentence investigation report (PSI) and sentencing recommendation.

"Chris" is a 30-something male with a record of thefts and other crimes committed since he was 10 years old. Chris also pled guilty before the same judge on the same day and was likewise referred for a PSI. Chris had stolen money and parts totaling $1,200 from an auto parts store during one of his very brief periods of employment.

These two cases point to a perennial debate among criminal justice scholars, with one side favoring the so-called classical school position and the other favoring the positivist position. Both positions are ultimately about the role of punishment in deterring crime, but the classical position maintains that punishment should fit the crime and nothing else; i.e., all people convicted of similar crimes should receive the same punishment regardless of any differences they may have. Both Lisa and Chris freely chose to commit the crime, and the fact that Chris has a record and Lisa does not is irrelevant. The positivist position is that punishment should fit the offender and be appropriate to rehabilitation. Lisa's and Chris's crimes were motivated by very different considerations, and Lisa and Chris are very different people morally. Blindly applying similar punishments to similar crimes without considering the possible consequences is pure folly. Think about these two cases as you read about classical and positivist thought about human nature, punishment, and deterrence.

LEARNING OBJECTIVES

- Understand the assumptions about human nature held by the classical school
- Know the elements of punishment outlined by Beccaria
- Understand Bentham's "sovereign masters" concept and what it means in terms of understanding criminal behavior
- Understand the differences between the classical and positivist schools
- Know the ideas put forth by Lombroso and how they have influenced modern criminology
- Understand specific and general deterrence in the context of perceptual deterrence theory
- Be able to expound on the legacies of the classical and positivist schools

❖ Preclassical Notions of Crime and Criminals

As discussed in Chapter 1, prior to the 18th century, explanations for a wide variety of phenomena, including criminal behavior, tended to be of a religious or spiritual nature. Good fortune and disaster alike were frequently attributed to good or evil supernatural forces. A simple extension of this worldview was to define crime as the result of demonic possession or the evil abuse of free will. Because of the legacy of original sin, all human beings were considered born sinners, and so it made no sense to ask questions like "What causes crime?" The gift of the grace of God kept men and women on the straight and narrow, and if they deviated from this line it was because God was no longer their guiding compass. That being so, it made sense to "beat the devil out of them" by the most hideous and sadistic means to save their immortal souls.

Demonological explanations for criminal behavior began to wane in the 18th century with the beginning of a period historians call the **Enlightenment**, which was essentially a major shift in the way people began to view the world and their place in it. This new worldview questioned traditional religious and political values, such as absolute monarchy and demonic possession. In their place it substituted humanism, rationalism, and a belief in the primacy of the natural over the supernatural world. Enlightenment thinkers believed in the dignity and worth of the individual, a view that would eventually find expression in the law and in the treatment of criminal offenders.

❖ The Classical School: The Calculating Criminal

Modern criminology is the product of two main schools of thought: the classical school originating in the 18th century and the positivist school originating in the 19th century. You may ask yourselves why a discussion of the "old masters" is necessary; after all, you don't see such discussions in physics, chemistry, or biology texts. The reason for this is that unlike those disciplines that have long solved the issues that perplexed their founders, modern criminology is still battling the same problem that confronted its pioneers. That issue, of course, is the problem of explaining crime and criminality in a way that satisfies everyone regardless of his or her sociopolitical ideology. Thus the works of the criminological pioneers are of more than passing interest to us.

The father of classical criminology is the Italian nobleman and professor of law, Cesare Bonesana, Marchese di Beccaria. In 1764, Beccaria published a call for the reform of judicial and penal systems throughout Europe called *On Crimes and Punishment* (1764/1963). The book is a passionate plea to reform the criminal justice system, humanize and rationalize the law, and make punishment more just and humane. Beccaria emphasized the idea that citizens give up certain rights in order to gain protection from the state (the so-called social contract). Although laws are supposed to be compacts between citizens and the state, they were often arbitrary and cruel. Beccaria believed that equals should be treated equally and unequals unequally according to relevant differences. By *equal* and *unequal* he was referring to the crimes offenders had committed, which was the only "relevant difference" to be considered, not their social standing or any other aspect of their lives. Under this principle, Lisa would be punished exactly the same way as Chris. Beccaria also believed that judges should not have the authority to interpret laws; they should simply apply the punishment for a given offense statutorily defined by the legislature.

Beccaria felt that the responsibility of determining the facts of a case should be placed in the hands of ordinary citizens, not simply a judge who had little idea what life was like for the ordinary person: "I consider an excellent law that which assigns popular jurors, taken by lot, to assist the chief judge . . . that each man ought to be judged by his peers" (1963, p. 21). He was also very much against the practice of using torture to obtain confessions and other information from

Photo 4.1

Cesare Beccaria, father of classical criminology/criminal justice.

suspects and was against the use of capital punishment (but believed corporal punishment was appropriate for violent offenders). Capital punishment could not be an effective deterrent according to Beccaria because it was too quick. Life imprisonment would be more effective.

Beccaria made no effort to plumb the depths of criminal character or motivation, arguing that crime is simply the result of "the despotic spirit which is in every man" (1963, p. 12). He also argued that the tendency of man to give in to the "despotic spirit" had to be countered by the threat of punishment, which had to be certain, swift, and severe enough to outweigh any benefits offenders get from crime if they are to be deterred from future crime. He elaborated on these three elements of punishment as follows:

Certainty: "The certainty of punishment, even if it be moderate, will always make a stronger impression than the fear of another which is more terrible but combined with the hope of impunity" (p. 58).

Swiftness: "The more promptly and the more closely punishment follows upon the commission of a crime, the more just and useful will it be" (p. 55).

Severity: "For a punishment to attain its end, the evil which it inflicts has only to exceed the advantage derivable from the crime; in this excess of evil one should include the . . . loss of the good which the crime might have produced. All beyond this is superfluous and for that reason tyrannical" (p. 43).

Jeremy Bentham and Human Nature

Another prominent figure of the classical school was British lawyer and philosopher Jeremy Bentham. His major work, *Principles of Morals and Legislation* (1789/1948), is essentially a philosophy of social control based on the **principle of utility**, which prescribed "the greatest happiness for the greatest number." The principle posits that any human action should be judged moral or immoral by its effect on the happiness of the community. Thus the proper function of the legislature is to pass laws aimed at maximizing the pleasure and minimizing the pain of the largest number in society—"the greatest good for the greatest number" (1948, p. 151). If legislators are to legislate according to the principle of utility, they must understand human motivation and behavior. For Bentham this was easily summed up: "Nature has placed mankind under the governance of two sovereign masters, pain and pleasure. It is for them alone to point out what we ought to do, as well as to determine what we shall do" (p. 125). In other words, if we are to understand any form of behavior and what motivates it, we have to do so with reference to the "sovereign masters"; that is, our efforts to maximize our pleasure and minimize our pain, whether in conforming or deviant ways. This is what we refer to as the "classical" or "constrained" view of human nature.

The classical explanation of criminal behavior and how to prevent it can be derived from the Enlightenment assumption that human nature is hedonistic, rational, and endowed with free will. **Hedonism** is a doctrine whose central idea is that happiness (pleasure) is the main goal of life. All other life goals are seen only as instrumentally desirable; that is, they are only desirable as means to the end of achieving pleasure or avoiding pain. Thus hedonism is the greatest single motivator of human action. Of course, happiness and how to achieve it means different things for different people.

Rational behavior is that consistent with logic. People are said to behave rationally when we observe a logical "fit" between the goals they strive for and means they use to achieve them. The goal of human rationality is self-interest, and self-interest governs our behavior whether in conforming or deviant directions. The issue of rationality is an important one in criminology and is addressed further in Chapter 5.

Hedonism and rationality are combined in the concept of the **hedonistic calculus**, a method by which individuals are assumed to logically weigh the anticipated benefits of a given course of action against its possible costs. If the balance of consequences of a contemplated action is thought to enhance pleasure and/or minimize pain, then individuals will pursue it; if not, they will not.

Free will enables human beings to purposely and deliberately choose to follow a calculated course of action. Therefore, if people seek to increase their pleasures illegally, they do so freely and with full knowledge of the wrongness of their acts, and thus society has a perfectly legitimate right to punish those who harm it.

It follows from these assumptions about human nature that if crime is to be deterred punishment (pain) must exceed the gain (pleasure) gained from it. Criminals will weigh the costs against the benefits of crime and desist if, on balance, the costs exceed the benefits. Bentham went somewhat further than Beccaria by devoting a great deal of energy (and his own money) to arguing for the development of prisons as punitive substitutes for torture, execution, or transportation to overseas penal colonies. He designed a prison called the *panopticon* ("all seeing"), which was to be a circular "inspection house" enabling guards to constantly see their charges, thus requiring fewer staff (see drawing of the panopticon that follows). Because prisoners could always be seen without seeing who was watching them or when they were being watched, the belief was that the perception of constant scrutiny would develop into self-monitoring. Bentham felt that prisoners could be put to useful work and thus pay for their own keep with the hoped-for added benefit that they would acquire the habit of honest labor.

❖ The Rise of Positivism

Classicists defined criminal acts as natural consequences of the unrestrained human tendency to seek pleasure; simple hedonistic abuses of free will. The problem with such an explanation, if accepted without qualification, is that it provides little possibility of further investigation. In the 19th century, criminologists began to move away from the classical assumptions, especially the assumption of free will as it is commonly understood, and toward a more scientific view of human behavior. This is not to say that hedonism, rationality, and free will are mythical human attributes. Rationality and free will may define the "essence" of human nature because they are the attributes that most distinguish humans from other animals, but to accept these constructs in pure form poses difficulties for science, a method of inquiry that seeks measurable "causes" of phenomena that can be verified (replicated) by different scientists.

Photo 4.3

Jeremy Bentham's panopticon prison design.

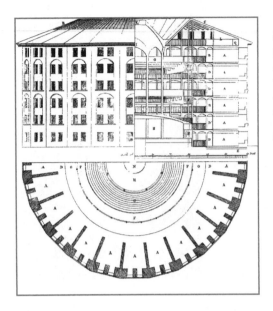

The increasingly popular view among criminologists of this period was that crime resulted from internal and/or external forces impinging on individuals, biasing or even completely determining their behavioral choices. This position became known as determinism. **Determinism** simply means that events have causes that precede them. As noted in Chapter 1, determinism does not mean that if X is present Y *will* occur; that is strong determinism, which has all but disappeared from science. Determinists only say that if X is present then Y has a *certain probability* of occurring. The adherents of such probabilistic determinism were known as positivists.

Just as the spirit of reason in the 18th century ushered in the classical school, the spirit of science in the second half of the 19th century ushered in the positivist school. The term **positivism** in the social sciences is used to designate the extension of the scientific method—from which more *positive* knowledge can be obtained—to social life. Positivists in the human sciences insisted on divorcing science from metaphysics and morals and looking only at what is and not what ought to be. The writings of natural scientists, particularly those of Charles Darwin on evolution, generated a major new way of thinking about human nature just as revolutionary as the writings of the Enlightenment philosophers a century earlier. The flattering image of human beings that emerged from the Enlightenment gave way to the evolutionary view that we are different only in degree from other animal forms and that science could explain human behavior just as it could explain events in the nonhuman world. Positivist criminologists were more concerned with discovering biological, psychological, or social determinants of criminal behavior than with the classical concerns of legal and penal reforms.

Enrico Ferri, one of the early positivists, gives us perhaps the best short description of the differences between classical and positivist criminology. Note that even back then criminologists from different schools of thought were taking jabs at one another: "We are empirical *scientists*; you lot are just armchair *speculators*":

> For them [the classicists] the facts should give place to syllogisms [reasoning from a taken-for-granted premise to a logical conclusion]; for us [positivists] the facts govern and no reasoning can occur without starting from the facts. For them science only needs paper, pen, and ink and the rest comes from a brain stuffed with . . . abundant reading of books. . . . For us science requires spending a long time in examining the facts one by one, evaluating them, reducing them to a common denominator, [and] extracting the central idea from them. For them a syllogism or an anecdote suffices to demolish a myriad of facts gathered by years of observation and analysis; for us, the reverse is true. (in Curran & Renzetti, 2001, p. 16)

Bentham: A Bridge Between the Classical and Positivist Schools

There is not always the sharp discontinuity between the classical and positivist schools that we are sometimes led to believe. For instance, although traditionally placed firmly in the classical camp, the work of Jeremy Bentham may be considered a bridge between the two schools. Despite Bentham's classical view of human nature, he never lost sight of its intricacies. While always maintaining the freedom of the will, he argued that it was moved by "motives" arising from the "bodily senses," which were differentially felt by people according to certain internal and external factors. Estimates of the value of pleasures and pains are to be considered with reference to four circumstances: intensity (severity), duration, certainty, and propinquity (how soon after the crime pleasure or pain is forthcoming) (Bentham, 1948, p. 151). In expressing these views, Bentham added to Beccaria's insight by showing how they cohered with human nature as classical scholars viewed it. He devoted an entire chapter of *A Fragment on Government* to 32 biological, psychological, and social factors (e.g., intelligence, temperament, personality, gender, age, education, occupation) that he thought of as "circumstances influencing sensibility" (1789/1948, Chapter VI). Although he only devoted a single paragraph to each one, the fact that he recognized internal and external constraints on free will and rationality leads us to believe that Bentham may have been both the last of the classical criminologists and the first of the positivist criminologists.

Photo 4.4

Charles Darwin, the man who forever changed our view of human nature.

Cartographic Criminology

Some of the earliest positivist attempts to leave the armchair and collect facts about crime in order to understand it came from cartographers. Cartographers are scholars who employ maps and other geographic information in their research, and those who employ these methods to study crime are called **cartographic criminologists**. Rather than exploring why individuals commit crimes, cartographic criminologists are more interested in where and when criminal behavior is most prevalent. Cartographic criminology is an early version of modern crime mapping discussed in Chapter 2.

The first publication of detailed statistics relating to criminal activity for an entire country occurred in France in 1827, more than 100 years before the publication of the first edition of the Uniform Crime Reports (UCR) in the United States. This work was used by two scholars to make statements about crime and its causes that anticipated by about a century those of theories we explore in Chapter 6. The first was a Frenchman named Andre-Michel Guerry, and the other was a Belgian named Lambert-Adolphe-Jacques Quetelet. Quetelet compared crime rates in France across ages, sexes, and seasons. He saw the same reflections in his data that we see today in the American UCR—that is, young males living in poor neighborhoods commit a disproportionate amount of crime. He thought sociologically about crime before the discipline officially existed, writing that "society prepares the crime and the guilty is only the instrument by which it is accomplished" (in Vold & Bernard, 1986, p. 132).

Both Quetelet and Guerry discounted the idea that crime is caused by poverty per se, noting that the wealthiest regions of France had the greatest level of property crime. However, Guerry noted that the overall level of wealth in a region does not necessarily correspond to the level of wealth among all its citizens and that being poor amid riches (as in urban France), not being poor per se (as in rural France), is the condition that produces the most "misery" (today we call this relative deprivation). He also noted that among the factors affecting crime are areas "where a frequent mixture of people takes place, and where the inequality of fortune is most felt" (in Rennie, 1978, p. 36).

Guerry produced many fine-shaded ecological maps to represent crime rates in different areas. This method of presenting data crossed the English Channel to influence British researchers Henry Mayhew and Joseph Fletcher. Using British crime data from the 1830s to 1840s, both men independently mapped out the concentration of various kinds of criminal activity across England and Wales, as well as other factors such as population density and rates of out-of-wedlock births. They came to many of the same conclusions that U.S. researchers would later come to (i.e., crime and delinquency are concentrated in poor neighborhoods undergoing population changes). Many British cities were experiencing the same demographic changes in the early 1800s that American cities were to experience in the early 1900s. Rural people flocked to the big cities to obtain work in the new factory system, and in the obscurity of these cities of strangers, social bonds weakened, morals declined, and crime flourished (Levin & Lindesmith, 1971).

Given the many conclusions of the cartographic school that are consistent with modern ecological criminology, it is surprising that more attention is not paid to it. The influence of the school declined in the latter part of the 19th century as interest started to focus more on the individual criminal and less on his or her environment. It would reemerge in Chicago in the early 20th century as human social ecology.

Biological Positivism: Cesare Lombroso and the Born Criminal

Five years after Charles Darwin shocked the world with the publication of his theory of evolution, an Italian army physician named Cesare Lombroso published *Criminal Man* (1876), which is considered the first book devoted solely to the causes of criminality ever written. Lombroso is widely acclaimed as the father of modern criminology, although he is often criticized for the views put forth in his book. His basic idea was that many (not all, as is commonly assumed) criminals are born criminal and that they are evolutionary "throwbacks" to an earlier form of life. The term used to describe the appearance of organisms resembling ancestral (prehuman) forms of life is **atavism**. Lombroso was influenced by Ernst Haeckel's famous biogenetic law, which stated that ontogeny (individual development) recapitulates phylogeny (evolutionary development of the species). Criminals were thus considered "throwbacks" to a more primitive stage of evolution and could be identified by a number of measurable physical stigmata. These stigmata included protruding jaws, drooping eyes, large ears, twisted and flatish noses, long arms relative to the lower limbs, sloping shoulders, and a coccyx that resembled "the stump of a tail" (Lombroso-Ferrero, 1911/1972, pp. 10–21).

Photo 4.5

One of Lombroso's skull collection; note the markings indicating where specific traits or talents were thought to be located.

The concept of atavism highlights an important point of difference between the classical and positivist schools: While the classicists viewed criminals and noncriminals as essentially similar beings who simply chose different pathways in life, positivists viewed them as being quite different beings. Lombroso was just one of many who sought to understand behavioral phenomena with reference to the principles of evolution as they were understood at the time. If humankind was just at one end of the continuum of animal life, it made sense to many people that criminals—who acted "beastly" and lacked reasoned conscience—were biologically inferior beings belonging to an earlier "uncivilized" evolutionary period.

In addition to the atavistic "born criminal," Lombroso identified two other types: the **insane criminal** and the **criminaloid**. Although insane criminals bore some stigmata, they were not born criminals; rather, they become criminals as a result "of an alteration of the brain, which completely upsets their moral nature" (1911/1972, p. 74). Among the ranks of Lombroso's insane criminals were alcoholics, kleptomaniacs, nymphomaniacs, and child molesters. Criminaloids had none of the physical peculiarities of the born or insane criminal and were considered less dangerous. Criminaloids were further categorized as habitual criminals, who become so by contact with other criminals, the abuse of alcohol, or other "distressing circumstances"; juridical criminals, who fall afoul of the law by accident; and the criminal by passion, hotheaded and impulsive persons who commit violent acts when provoked.

Although Lombroso is best remembered for his concept of the atavistic born criminal, in his later work, *Crime: Its Causes and Remedies* (Lombroso, 1911/1968), he listed a bewildering variety of possible "causes," including unlikely candidates such as tobacco, hair color, and "goitrous districts." Notwithstanding Lombroso's recognition that crime has multiple causes, he still argued that "organic causes" accounted for 35% to 40% of the "fatal influence" on crime.

Raffael Garofalo: Natural Crime and Offender Peculiarities

Lombroso and two of his Italian contemporaries, Raffael Garofalo and Enrico Ferri, founded what became known as the **Italian school of criminology**. Both Garofalo and Ferri were lawyers who accepted the positivist notion that behavior has discoverable causes. Garofalo, who coined the term *criminology* in 1885 (1885/1968), is perhaps best known for his efforts to formulate a "natural" definition of crime. Classical thinkers accepted the legal definition of crime uncritically— crime is what the law says it is. This appeared to be rather arbitrary and "unscientific" to Garofalo (like the Anglo American system of linear measurement) who wanted to anchor his definition of crime in something natural (like tying linear measurement to the circumference of the earth, as in the metric system). Garofalo felt that definitions of crime should be anchored in human nature, by which he meant that a given act would be considered a crime only if it was universally condemned, and it would be universally condemned if it offended the natural altruistic sentiments of probity (integrity, honesty) and pity (compassion, sympathy). The hallmarks of criminality were the relative lack of the altruistic sentiments for Garofalo.

As we saw in Chapter 1, Garofalo's "natural crimes" are evil in themselves (*mala in se*), whereas other kinds of crimes (*mala prohibita*) are wrong only because they have been made wrong by the law. Garofalo rejected the classical principle that punishment should fit the crime, arguing instead that it should fit the criminal. Under this principle, Lisa and Chris in our vignette would be treated quite differently. Garofalo believed that criminals have little control over their actions. This repudiation of moral responsibility and fitting the punishment to the offender would eventually lead to sentencing aimed at the humane goals of treatment and rehabilitation. But treatment and rehabilitation were of no concern to Garofalo, for whom the only question to be considered at sentencing was the danger the offender posed to society judged by what he referred to as offenders' peculiarities, which was essentially the degree to which they lacked probity and pity.

Garofalo developed four categories of criminals, each meriting different forms of punishment: extreme, impulsive, professional, and endemic. Society could only be defended from extreme criminals (who completely lacked the altruistic sentiments) by swiftly executing them, regardless of the crime for which they were being punished. Impulsive criminals, a category that included alcoholics and the insane, were to be imprisoned. Professional criminals were psychologically normal individuals who use the hedonistic calculus before committing their crimes and thus require "elimination," either by life imprisonment or transportation to a penal colony overseas. Endemic crimes, by which Garofalo meant crimes peculiar to a given region (mala prohibita crimes), could best be controlled by changes in the law.

THEORY IN ACTION: Giuseppe Villella: Atavism, Ideology, and Racism

Very little is known about Giuseppe Villella, who is often referred to as a "notorious brigand," other than that he was born in 1803 in Saint Lucia Motta, in southern Italy, and died in prison in 1872. We know that he was sentenced three times for theft and arson, but Italian records only indicate that he was "suspected" of brigandage (robbery). However, Villella became immortalized because the central idea of Lombroso's work resulted from an autopsy Lombroso performed on his body, particularly his skull. As Lombroso explains,

At the sight of that skull, I seemed to see all of a sudden, lighted up as a vast plain under a flaming sky, the problem of the nature of the criminal—an atavistic being who reproduces in his person the ferocious instincts of primitive humanity and the inferior animals. Thus were explained anatomically the enormous jaws, high cheek bones, prominent superciliary arches, solitary lines in the palms, extreme size of the orbits, handle-shaped or sensile ears found in criminals, savages and apes, insensibility to pain, extremely acute sight, tattooing, excessive idleness, love of orgies, and the irresistible craving for evil for its own sake, the desire not only to extinguish life in the victim, but to mutilate the corpse, tear its flesh and drink its blood.

As Lombroso contemplated Villella's skull, the feature that got him most excited was a depression or indent on the occiput (the back of the skull), which he called the median occipital fossa, which essentially means an "indentation in the middle of the brain's occipital lobe." This indentation was in a space normally occupied by something called the occipital crest. This anatomical feature reminded him of the skulls of "inferior races and the lower types of apes, rodents, and birds." This is the origin of Lombroso's use of the term *atavism* to describe criminals with supposed physical characteristics resembling prehuman forms of animal life.

We can see from Villella's picture that he wasn't exactly an Italian maiden's dream, but the picture was taken in prison when he was 69 years old and suffering from tuberculosis and scurvy. Furthermore, there was never any indication that Giuseppe ever killed anyone, never mind "mutilate[ing] the corpse, tear[ing] its flesh and drink[ing] its blood." Modern Italian historians see Lombroso's characterization of Villella as politically motivated at a time just after the unification of Italy, when prosperous northern Italians looked down on the peasantry of southern Italy. There had been a lot of intermittent fighting among and between various regions of what is now Italy for 60 years prior to Italian unification in 1870, and many atrocities were committed by northern Italian troops, particularly in the area from which Villella came. Consequently, many people labeled as "brigands" were actually people who actively resisted northern troops. Because of this, the people of Saint Lucia Motta have demanded the return of Villella's remains (now on display in the Lombroso Museum) to be given a Christian burial.

Lombroso's theory strongly illustrates what was said about the role of ideology in formulating theories about

THEORY IN ACTION (Continued)

human behavior. Northern and southern Italians had been at each other's throats for decades, and attrocities had been committed by both sides. Lombroso (subconsciously or not) may have wanted to both blame the attrocities committed by the south on their "animal" natures and excuse those committed by the north. He even considered northern and southern Italians to be of different races, so his ideas may also be considered racist. Thus, while Lombroso did criminology a service in one sense, he is still considered the archytypical example of how ideology and personal prejudices can infect supposedly scientific theories.

Discussion Questions

1. Look up "minor physical anomalies" on any search engine and determine if these anomalies could be the "stigmata" that Lombroso wrote about.
2. Do you think there is such a thing as a "born criminal"? Look up "psychopathy" and see what leading scholars in this area think.
3. Although Lombroso was very wrong about many things, in what way can he be said to have done criminology a service?

Sources: Gibson, 2002; Jones, 2009

Enrico Ferri and Social Defense

Ferri, like Garofalo, dismissed the notion of free will as myth, and he derived the same policy implications from its dismissal. Prepositivistic notions of culpability, moral responsibility, and intent were to be subordinate to an assessment of the offender's strength of resistance to the criminal impulse, with the express purpose of averting future danger to society. He believed that moral insensibility and lack of foresight, underscored by low intelligence, were the criminal's most marked characteristics: The criminal has "defective resistance to criminal tendencies and temptations, due to that ill-balanced impulsiveness which characterizes children and savages" (Ferri, 1897/1917, p. 11).

Ferri's primary concern was social preservation, not the nature of criminal behavior. With Lombroso and Garofalo, Ferri was instrumental in formulating the concept of **social defense** as the rationale for punishment. This theory of punishment asserts that its purpose is not to deter or to rehabilitate but to defend society from criminal predation. Ferri reasoned that the characteristics of criminals prevented them from basing their behavior on rational calculus principles, so how could such behavior be deterred, and how could born criminals be rehabilitated? Given the assumptions of biological positivism, the only reasonable rationale for punishing offenders is to incapacitate them for as long as possible so that they no longer pose a threat to the peace and security of society. This theory of punishment provides us with an excellent example of how our assumptions about human nature drive our policies for dealing with crime and criminals.

❖ Deterrence and Choice: Pain Versus Gain

Deterring criminal behavior is a major concern of both the classical and positivist schools of criminology. That people respond to incentives and are deterred by the threat of punishment is taken for granted by almost everyone and is the philosophical foundation behind all systems of criminal law. Deterrence theory can be encapsulated by the principle central to a school of psychology called behaviorism (or operant psychology) stating that behavior is governed by its consequences. That is, if a behavior is followed by something rewarding, the behavior tends to be repeated; if followed by something unpleasant, it tends not to be repeated. A positive consequence of crime for criminals is that it affords them something they want for little effort; a negative consequence is the possible punishment attached to their crimes.

Deterrence is the prevention of criminal acts by the use or threat of punishment and may be either specific or general. **Specific deterrence** refers to the effect of punishment on the future behavior of the person who experiences the punishment. For specific deterrence to work, a previously punished person must make a mental connection between an intended criminal act and the punitive consequences suffered as a result of similar acts committed in the past. Unfortunately, such connections, if made, rarely have the socially desired effect, either because memories of the previous consequences were insufficiently emotionally strong or the offender discounted them.

Committing another crime after previously being punished for one is called **recidivism** ("falling back" into criminal behavior). Recidivism is a lot more common among ex-convicts than repentance and rehabilitation. According to the U. S. Bureau of Justice Statistics (BJS; 2007), about 33% of released prisoners in the United States recidivate within 6 months of release, and over 66% recidivate by the third year after release. These are just the ones who are caught, so we can safely say that there is very little specific deterrent effect attached to punishing people with imprisonment. Released offenders accumulated 4.1 million arrests before their imprisonment and another 744,000 within 3 years of release. The highest recidivism rates were for robbers (70.2%), burglars (74%), larcenists (74.6%), auto thieves (78.8%), and for possessing, using, or selling illegal weapons (70.2%). The offenders least likely to recidivate were rapists (2.5%) and murders (1.2%). According to the BJS (2007), these recidivism rates are quite stable from year to year.

The effect of punishment on future behavior also depends on the **contrast effect**, which is the distinction between the circumstances of punishment and the usual life experience of the person being punished. The prospect of incarceration is a nightmarish contrast for those who enjoy a loving family and a valued career. The mere prospect of experiencing the embarrassment of public disgrace threatening families and careers is a strong deterrent for people embedded in a prosocial lifestyle. For people lacking these things, punishment has minimal effect because the negative contrast between the punishment and their everyday lives is minimal. Like many other things in life, the irony is that specific deterrence works best for those who need deterring the least and works least for those who need deterring the most.

General deterrence is the preventive effect of the threat of punishment on the general population; that is, on *potential* offenders. Punishing offenders serves as an example to the rest of us of what may happen if we violate the law. As Radzinowicz and King (1979) put it, "People are not sent to prison primarily for their own good, or even in the hope that they will be cured of crime. . . . It is used as a warning and deterrent to others" (p. 296). The threat of punishment for law violators doubtless deters a large but unknown number of individuals who might commit crimes if no such system existed. Of course, most people probably never seriously think of committing crimes and thus never consciously think of punishment. They simply habitually ignore criminal opportunities because the contrast effect is subconsciously part and parcel of their very being.

Perceptual Deterrence Theory

Perceptual deterrence theory is concerned with how individuals respond to the perceived as opposed to objective cost properties of their criminal decisions. A statutory punishment, however certain, swift, and severe it may be, will not deter a potential criminal if he or she does not perceive its existence or the possibility of being caught and convicted. Put otherwise, the objective properties of punishment can only be effective if potential offenders consciously realize and understand their presence and the risk attached to their activities.

Criminals are certainly aware that they will be punished for their crimes if caught, but the issue explored by perceptual deterrence theory is their awareness of changes in criminal justice policy that lead to increased or decreased probabilities of being apprehended or of changes in the severity of the punishment for a given crime. The more offenders commit a crime and get away with it, the more they downgrade punishment probabilities; the more they are caught and punished, the more they upgrade them.

Take drunk driving as an example of perceptual deterrence. In 1982 there were 9.1 alcohol-related fatalities per 100,000 people, and in 2008 there were 3.9 per 100,000, an impressive 57% decrease (National Highway Traffic Safety Commission [NHTSC], 2009). The NHTSC attribute this welcome reduction in fatalities to drastically increased penalties for drunk driving, increased police emphasis on enforcing DUI laws, and campaigns to inform the public that society is no longer treating drunk driving lightly but rather as a serious crime that could lead to someone's death.

The Minneapolis Domestic Violence Experiment (Buzawa & Buzawa, 2003) is another application of perceptual deterrence theory. In this study, police officers were randomly assigned to respond to domestic violence calls in one of three ways: (1) separate parties and order one of them to leave, (2) inform both parties of alternatives to violence, such as attending dispute resolution centers or counseling, and (3) arrest the abuser. It was shown that 24% of those ordered to leave, 19% advised of alternatives, and 10% of those arrested engaged in further domestic violence. Arrests apparently perceived as "cracking down" thus had more of a deterrent effect than the other two less intrusive alternatives.

These examples provide strong support for perceptual deterrence theory (that is, people are less likely to break the law if they become aware of punitive changes in the law's stance), but the spoiler is that just about all adult Americans drive, and many also partake of alcohol. Then there is the domestic violence data. According to the National Coalition Against Domestic Violence (2009), there are over 1.3 million cases of reported domestic violence in the United States each year, but many of the most serious cases are never reported for fear of reprisal. Many domestic violence calls may thus be the result of relatively minor events committed by otherwise law-abiding citizens. What we see with these studies are examples of general deterrence affecting people aware that they have a lot to lose (shame, embarrassment, hefty fines, lawyer's fees, loss of license, insurance rate increases, and perhaps even a stint in jail).

What about the effect of perceptual deterrence on people who lack all these things and who see jail as little more than an occupational hazard; in other words, the effect on individuals who are seriously criminally involved? Paternoster (2010) cites a number of studies demonstrating that 20% to 30% of the crime drop from its peak in the early 1990s is attributable to the approximately 52% increase in the imprisonment rate in the United States. As he put it, "There is a general consensus that the decline in crime is, at least in part, due to more and longer prison sentences, with much of the controversy being over how much of an effect" (p. 801).

Paternoster (2010) also cites a large number of studies, however, that find the correlation between objective punishments and subjective perceptions of them to be negligible. If this is so, by what mechanism has the objectively increased likelihood of imprisonment in the United States resulted in the crime drop? The problem is that we cannot determine from the correlation between raw incarceration rates and dropping crime rates if we are witnessing a *deterrent* effect (has crime declined because more people have perceived a greater punitive effect?) or an *incapacitation* effect (has crime declined because more people are behind bars and thus not at liberty to commit crimes on the outside?). Incarcerating chronic offenders indisputably has an incapacitation effect, but the impact of it in terms of deterring others aware of their incarceration is far from certain. Paternoster (2010) concludes his massive review of the deterrence literature:

Finally, while there may be disagreement about the magnitude, there does seem to be a modest inverse relationship between the perceived certainty of punishment and crime [as certainty goes up, crime goes down], but no real evidence of a deterrent effect for severity, and no real knowledge base about the celerity [swiftness] of punishment. (p. 818)

An example of deterrence from a certainty rather than severity-of-punishment point of view is the jaw-dropping decrease in crime in New York City from the early 1990s to the present. From 1990 to 2009, the homicide, robbery, and burglary rates dropped 82%, 84%, and 85%, respectively, while the city's incarceration rate decreased by 28% (Zimring, 2013). These decreases are more than twice the national average, so how were they achieved? Beginning in 1990, New York City decided to invest in smart preventative policing rather than reactive incarceration, adding more than 7,000 new police officers and training them to be more aggressive and to focus on high-crime settings. This is known as "zero-tolerance" policing and involves stops and pat-downs looking for weapons and not tolerating minor infractions. Some have criticized this as targeting minorities, but it has been the minority communities that have benefitted most from smart and aggressive policing—it is very hard to argue with success rates such as those Zimring (2013) provides.

Deterrence and the Death Penalty

Nowhere is the effectiveness (or lack of) of deterrence more passionately argued than in the case of the death penalty. The death penalty is unique in that it is the only punishment required to demonstrate its deterrent effect to validate its constitutionality. We take it for granted that penalties applied to other crimes have a general deterrent effect, if not necessarily the desired specific effect. It is obvious that the threat of the death penalty fails every time a murder is committed, and we can easily document the number of these failures. On the other hand, it is just as obvious that we cannot count the times the death penalty threat may have succeeded since we cannot count nonevents. That is, we cannot know how many (if any) people who might otherwise have committed murder did not do so for fear of losing their own lives.

The deterrence argument is divided between those who state "conclusively" that it deters and those who also state "conclusively" that it does not. Deterrence studies going back to 1925 have looked at homicide rates in neighboring states with and without the death penalty or homicide rates before and after abolition in states that abolished capital punishment. These studies almost always show that the death penalty had no discernible effect on reducing homicides and that most abolitionist states had lower homicide rates than most death penalty states (Nagin & Pepper, 2012). This is illustrated in Figure 4.1. However, we cannot say that most non–death penalty states had lower homicide rates in 2009 (or any other year) than death penalty states because they did not *have* the death penalty. Maryland, which had the second highest homicide rate in 2009, is now a non–death penalty state, which may make the graph a little less visually dramatic. Some non–death penalty states had higher homicide rates than some death penalty states, and perhaps some death penalty states retain the death penalty *because* they have a high homicide rate.

The opposing sides in the deterrence argument tend to be sociologists and criminologists on one side and economists on the other. "In contrast to economics studies, most of the sociological studies find no deterrence," asserts Joanna Shepherd (2005, pp. 214–218). Similarly, Bushway and Reuter (2008) tell us that "economists and criminologists have actively butted heads over the topic of deterrence almost since economists began studying the topic [and] have clashed heatedly over empirical research on the death penalty since the 1970s" (pp. 390–391). The deterrent

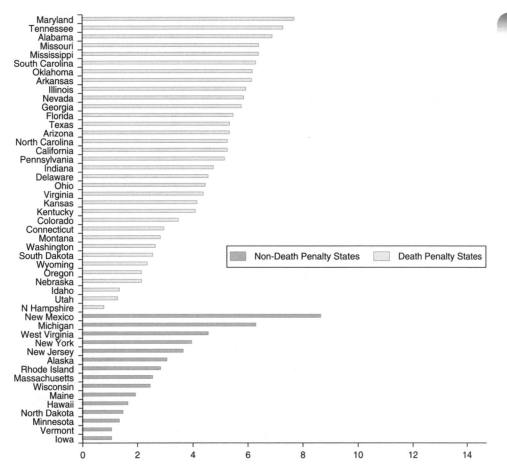

Figure 4.1

Murder Rates in States With and Without the Death Penalty in 2009

Source: Death Penalty Information Center, 2011

effect of punishment is thus taken for granted by economists, who share the classical view of human nature (Kirchgassner, 2011), but most criminologists are sociologically trained (Cooper, Walsh, & Ellis, 2010) and tend to be either agnostic about human nature or deny that such a thing exists.

Although no studies could be found assessing the opinions of a wide range of economists on the death penalty, in Radelet and Lacock's (2009) poll of 77 prominent criminologists asking them if they believed the death penalty to be a deterrent to further murder, 88.2% agreed or strongly agreed that it was not. Likewise, a poll of 500 police chiefs found that 63% disagreed with the statement that "the death penalty significantly reduces the number of homicides" (Dieter, 2009).

It is difficult to tease any deterrent effect out of the death penalty because of its rarity; only about 2% to 6% (depending on jurisdiction) of murders are tried as capital cases (Berk, Li, & Hickman, 2005), and only 15% of people sentenced to death since the death penalty was reinstated in 1976 have actually been executed (Nagin & Pepper, 2012). If a person is sentenced to death, the time lapse between conviction and execution has increased from an average of 14.4 months in the 1950s to an average of 174 months (14.5 years) in 2010 (Snell, 2011). Thus, while the death penalty is certainly severe, it is far from being certain or swift.

The confusion over the issue led to the National Academy of Science convening a subcommittee (the Committee on Deterrence and the Death Penalty [CDDP]) of criminologists, sociologists, economists, and statisticians to try to reach a conclusion. The CDDP examined the results of all credible death penalty studies up to 2011 and concluded that the evidence is "inconclusive." The committee also recommended that deterrence studies not be used to influence judicial deliberations. The committee's conclusion reads:

> The committee concludes that research to date on the effect of capital punishment on homicide is not informative about whether capital punishment decreases, increases, or has no effect on homicide rates. Therefore, the committee recommends that these studies not be used to inform deliberations requiring judgments about the effect of the death penalty on homicide. Consequently, claims that research demonstrates that capital punishment decreases or increases the homicide rate by a specified amount or has no effect on the homicide rate should not influence policy judgments about capital punishment. (Nagin & Pepper, 2012, p. 102)

So, What About Deterrence? Is the United States Hard or Soft on Crime?

The United States is perceived to be soft on crime by many laypersons, and therefore its punishments are not likely to have much of a deterrent effect. But if we define hardness or softness in terms of incarceration rates, the numbers do not support that perception because the United States has the highest incarceration rate in the world. Figure 4.2 shows incarceration rates per 100,000 for selected countries in 2012. Using incarceration rates per 100,000 *citizens* is not the same as the rate per 100,000 *criminals*, however. The greater incarceration rate in the United States may be justified if the United States has more criminals than these other countries. Of course, no one knows how many criminals any country has, but we can get a rough estimate from a country's crime rates. For instance, the U.S. homicide rate is about five times that of England and Wales, which roughly matches the U.S.'s five times greater incarceration rate. However, when it comes to property crimes, Americans are about in the middle of the pack of nations in terms of the probability of being victimized by property crime (less than in England and Wales, incidentally). This fact notwithstanding, burglars serve an average of 16.2 months in prison in the United States, compared with 6.8 months in Britain and 5.3 months in Canada (Mauer, 2005), which makes the United States harder on crime than its closest cultural relatives and suggests that

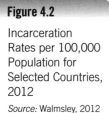

Figure 4.2

Incarceration Rates per 100,000 Population for Selected Countries, 2012

Source: Walmsley, 2012

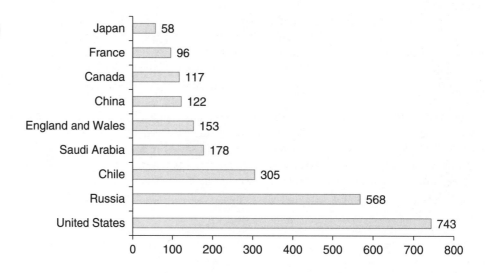

we may be overusing incarceration to address our crime problem. Alternatively, from a crime control perspective, these other nations can be seen as excessively soft on crime at the expense of rising crime rates, although crime has fallen in those countries since the 1990s also.

If we define hardness/softness in terms of alternative punishments and/or the conditions of confinement, then the United States is "soft" on crime, although a better term would be *humane*. For instance, although we see that China has an incarceration rate more than five times lower than the United States, it is by far the world's leader in the proportion of its criminals it executes each year (Stohr & Walsh, 2012). Also, punishment in some Arab Islamic countries such as Saudi Arabia often includes barbaric corporal punishments for offenses considered relatively minor in the West. For instance, the British embassy in Saudi Arabia issues a publication called *Information Pack for British Prisoners in Saudi Arabia* to British nationals arrested there informing them of what the British government can and cannot do for them. This publication lists the punishments individuals may expect if convicted—not exactly reassuring material to read in one's cell:

> The Saudi courts impose a number of severe physical punishments. The death penalty can be imposed for a wide range of offences including murder, rape, armed robbery, repeated drug use, apostasy, adultery, witchcraft and sorcery and can be carried out by beheading with a sword, stoning or firing squad, followed by crucifixion. (British Foreign Office, 2013, p. 9)

So, is the United States softer or harder on crime than other countries? The answer obviously depends on how we conceptualize and measure the concepts of hardness and softness and with which countries we compare ourselves. Compared with countries that share our democratic ideals, we are tough (because of our retention of the death penalty, some would even say barbaric) on crime; compared with countries most distant from Anglo American ideals, we are extremely soft, and for that we should be grateful. But regardless of hardness or softness, we have to remember that the effects of deterrence depend far more on the certainty and swiftness of punishment, not its severity, and most assuredly on the contrast effect.

❖ Evaluation of the Classical and Early Positivist Schools

The **classical school** is a school of philosophical jurisprudence bent on establishing a set of reformist moral values in criminal justice, not a school of empirical data collection and analysis attempting to build a theory of criminality. Regardless of their influence on criminological theory, the influence of the classical theorists on the legal and penal systems of Europe and North America was huge. Many European monarchs of the 18th century were moved to adopt their principles, and the U.S. Constitution and the 1789 French *Declaration of the Rights of Man* were very much influenced by them.

All criminal justice systems in the world assume the classical position that persons are free agents who deserve to be punished when they transgress the law. We may also recognize many of the ideas championed by Beccaria in such rights as freedom from cruel and unusual punishment, the right to a speedy trial, and the right to confront one's accusers, contained in the Bill of Rights and other documents at the heart of Western legal systems today. The emphasis on rationality, free will, and personal responsibility within the modern legal system reflects the once radical image of human beings posited by the great Enlightenment thinkers. We shall see in the next chapter that disenchantment with positivism during the latter quarter of the 20th century led some criminologists to reembrace classical principles in their theorizing.

Because it embraces scientific principles, the positivist school is highly influential in criminology today. Although Lombroso tends to be reviled and ridiculed as a biological determinist today, some criminologists, while acknowledging Lombroso's many errors in logic, research design, measurement, and elitist and sexist ideas, insist that his contributions are both misunderstood and undervalued. His methodology, although very badly flawed by modern standards, was an improvement over previous attempts to understand criminal behavior (Gibson, 2002). Lilly, Cullen, and Ball (2011) sum up Lombroso's legacy: "He took the logic of the causes of crime away from sin and placed it in the realm of science, where it remains today" (p. 25). From Lombroso on, there has been an enduring commitment to sort, sift, and measure all sorts of biological, psychological, and social variables in an attempt to get to the bottom of criminal behavior.

Table 4.1 summarizes major differences between the classical and positivist schools.

Table 4.1

Summary and Comparisons of the Classical and Positivist Schools

	Classical	Positivist
Historical Period	18th-century Enlightenment, early period of Industrial Revolution	19th-century Age of Reason, mid–Industrial Revolution
Leading Figures	Cesare Becarria, Jeremy Bentham	Cesare Lombroso, Raffael Garofalo, Enrico Ferri
Purpose of School	To reform and humanize the legal and penal systems	To apply the scientific method to the study of crime and criminality
Image of Human Nature	Humans are hedonistic, rational, and have free will. Our behavior is motivated by maximizing pleasure and minimizing pain.	Human behavior is determined by psychological, biological, or social forces that constrain our rationality and free will.
Image of Criminals	Criminals are essentially the same as noncriminals. They commit crimes after calculating costs and benefits.	Criminals are different from noncriminals. They commit crimes because they are inferior in some way.
Definition of Crime	Strictly legal; crime is whatever the law says it is.	Based on universal human abhorrence; crime should be limited to inherently evil (mala in se) acts.
Purpose of Punishment	To deter. Punishment is to be applied equally to all offenders committing the same crime. Judicial discretion to be limited.	Social defense. Punishment to be applied differently to different offenders based on relevant differences and should be rehabilitative.

❖ Policy and Prevention: Implications of Deterrence Theories

The answer to crime for classical deterrence theorists is to increase the certainty of apprehension and the swiftness of punishment and to assess whether the severity of punishment for a given crime really outweighs the benefits criminals obtain from it. More police on the streets and increased efficiency in processing criminals through the system from arrest to the imposition of punishment might be a recommendation to improve certainty. However, the swiftness aspect would certainly run up against constitutional issues in a system purposely designed to make it as difficult as possible to convict suspects (Walsh & Hemmens, 2011).

"Get tough on crime" messages are the kinds of simple, easily implemented solutions that policymakers love—build prisons and fill 'em up. This takes care of the severity aspect. But getting tough is expensive, as many legislative bodies have found out. Many states started putting more and more offenders behind bars for longer periods and implemented mandatory sentencing laws in the 1980s but soon found their prisons so overcrowded that the courts intervened. This resulted in the repeal of some states' mandatory sentencing laws and the institution of early release programs. Thus, releasing offenders to the streets became the solution to a current problem, but that solution *was* the problem a few years earlier (Gilsinian, 1991). This goes to show how remarkably complicated and even perverse policy decisions can be and why we should not judge a criminological theory based on its impact (or lack of) on public policy.

The methods resulting in the remarkable success in crime reduction in New York City are obvious policy recommendations derived from deterrence theory. At the heart of these methods is **CompStat** (COMParative STATistics), a police management and accountability process that has been implemented across the nation. CompStat employs computer-based systems that map crime to geographic areas and identify problems, thus enabling police administrators to devise strategies and tactics to reduce crime and solve a variety of other problems. Its major function has been to provide senior police administrators with ammunition enabling them to hold precinct commanders and other senior officers accountable for problem areas under their jurisdiction identified by CompStat. To take full advantage of this system requires well-trained and educated administrative police officers and sufficient manpower to implement the strategies and tactics they devise.

Summary

- The classical school of criminology began during the Enlightenment with the work of Cesare Beccaria, whose aim was to reform an arbitrary and cruel system of criminal justice.

- Jeremy Bentham, best known for his concept of the hedonistic calculus, was another leading figure. The hedonistic calculus summarized the classical notion of human nature as hedonistic, rational, and possessed of free will.

- The positivist school aimed at substituting the methods of science for the armchair philosophizing of the classicists; i.e., they sought measurable causes of behavior.

- The cartographic criminologists such as Guerry, Quetelet, Mayhew, and Fletcher were among the first positivists. These scholars studied maps and statistics to pinpoint where and when crime was most likely to occur.

- Cesare Lombroso is widely considered the father of criminology. His work was much influenced by evolutionary thought as he understood it. Lombroso saw criminals as atavistic "throwbacks" to an earlier evolutionary period who could be identified by a number of bodily stigmata.

- Other early positivists included Raffael Garofalo and Enrico Ferri. Garofalo was interested in developing a "natural" definition of crime and in generating categories of criminals for the purpose of determining what should be done with them. Ferri was instrumental in formulating the concept of social defense as the only justification for punishment.

- Deterrence theories are concerned with the prevention of crime. They differentiate between specific deterrence—the effect of punishment on those directly experiencing it—and general deterrence—the effect of the threat of punishment on the general population.

- Perceptual deterrence theory posits that before an objective punishment can affect an offender's behavior he or she must be consciously aware that it exists. Awareness of increased penalties strongly influences the behavior of the general public (general deterrence) but does not seem to affect the behavior of the criminally involved.

■ Our discussion of the death penalty noted the difficulty inherent in showing whether or not it constitutes a deterrent. It is rarely imposed and even more rarely carried out. Studies by economists tend to show that it is a deterrent, while studies by sociologists and criminologists tend to show that

it is not. The Committee on Deterrence and the Death Penalty concluded that the issue has not been settled either way.

■ The question of whether the United States is "hard" or "soft" on crime depends on what countries we compare it with. We may be tougher than other Western nations if our measure is incarceration rates, but we are softer than non-Western countries that practice barbaric punishments.

Exercises and Discussion Questions

1. If humans are primarily motivated by the hedonistic calculus, is simple deterrence the answer to the crime problem?

2. What advantages (or disadvantages) does positivism offer us over classicism?

3. Is Ferri's social defense rationale for punishment preferable to one emphasizing rehabilitation of offenders?

4. Use any search engine and type in "Beccaria preventing crime." How do Beccaria's ideas compare

with those of the positivists on preventing crime? What is Beccaria's idea of "real crime," and how does it compare with Garofalo's?

5. What is it that prevents most people from committing serious crimes that does not prevent criminals from doing so?

6. Would you like to see the criminal penalties applied by the Chinese and the Saudi Arabians applied in the United States in order to reduce crime to a minimum?

Useful Websites

Biological and psychological positivism. http://criminology.fsu.edu/crimtheory/week4.htm

The classical school. http://criminology.fsu.edu/crimtheory/week3.htm

Chapter Terms

Atavism

Cartographic criminologists

Classical school

CompStat

Contrast effect

Criminaloid

Determinism

Deterrence

Enlightenment

Free will

General deterrence

Hedonism

Hedonistic calculus

Insane criminal

Italian school of criminology

Perceptual deterrence theory

Positivism

Principle of utility

Rational

Recidivism

Social defense

Specific deterrence

CHAPTER 5

Crime as Choice

Rationality, Emotion, and Criminal Behavior

It is a given that we all strive to maximize our pleasure and to minimize our pain and that we all devise strategies we believe to be reasonable to attain this goal. Most people go about this by reasoning that if they want the finer material things in life (such as a Lexus parked in front of the mansion on the hill) shared with a kind, considerate, and beautiful wife or handsome husband and a couple of healthy and intelligent children, they must prepare themselves by working and studying hard and settling into a lucrative career. This is exactly what Bill Gates did, and now he's the world's richest man. Of course, Gates is a product of a solidly upper-middle-class intact home, and he is remarkably intelligent (his biography lists his IQ in the 150–160 range), ambitious, and conscientious, so it is no wonder that he never reasoned that knocking off the local convenience store or selling crack was in his best interest. Gates had much too much to lose, and such thoughts probably never crossed his mind anyway.

Then we have Charles Manson, the illegitimate son of a 16-year-old runaway girl who raised him in a series of grungy motels and who once sold him for a pitcher of beer. Charlie also wanted to maximize his pleasure and minimize his pain, but he reasoned that this was best achieved by stealing, robbing, burglarizing, and founding a hippie cult featuring an abundance of sex, drugs, and rock 'n' roll. As of 2014, Manson was 80 years old; 58 of those years have been spent locked up in juvenile and adult facilities. Was Manson stupid and irrational? No; prison testing showed him to have an IQ of 109. While this is not in Gates's league, it is in the bright-average range. Neither was he unaware that his lifestyle would lead to the pains of imprisonment given his numerous incarcerations before his death sentence for murder (commuted to life in prison in 1972). Charlie simply relished the thrills and fruits of crime because they were immediate, while punishment was only a distant "maybe," and he had very little to lose anyway. Thus, while everyone has the same basic general motive behind their behavior, how different people view "the good life" and what they consider to be the optimal way to achieve it depends on a host of developmental, personality, emotional, and environmental factors that impinge on their rational decisions. Keep this in mind as you read about "crime as choice" in this chapter.

- Be able to articulate the nature of rationality and its constraints
- Understand the assumptions and key strengths and weaknesses of rational choice, routine activities, and cultural/anarchic theories
- Be aware of the criticisms aimed at all three theories
- Understand cultural criminology's point about the primacy of emotions in motivating criminal behavior
- Understand what primary and secondary emotions are and how they function to both facilitate and prevent criminal activity
- Know the crime prevention policy recommendations offered by the three theories

❖ Returning to Classic Assumptions of Human Nature

The positivist school of thought emphasizing the scientific method and eliminating what was considered metaphysical assumptions about human nature, such as rationality and free will, held a tight rein in criminology for almost a century after its emergence. However, a combination of high crime rates, the failure of existing positivist theories to adequately account for high crime rates, and the emergence of a more conservative attitude in the late 1970s and early 1980s saw a swing away from the ideals of positivism back to the classical notion that offenders are rational actors responsible for their own actions. One of the principal complaints made by more conservative criminologists such as Hirschi and Hindelang (1977), Wilson (1976), and Wilson and Herrnstein (1985) was that many criminological theories wanted to trace "root causes" of crime to society and to exonerate delinquents and criminals from any blame for their actions. According to these critics, viewing offenders as blameless strips them of their humanity and paints them as pawns of capricious environmental winds and leads offenders to view themselves as victims, a deadly trap from which they may never escape. To illustrate such attitudes, Boyd Sharp (2006, p. 3) cited a *Calvin and Hobbes* cartoon in which Calvin says,

> I have concluded that nothing bad I do is my fault. . . . I'm a helpless victim of countless bad influences. An unwholesome culture panders to my undeveloped values and it pushes me into misbehavior. I take no responsibility for my behavior. I'm an innocent pawn of society.

Sharp's point is that criminals come to think like Calvin in the context of a society where many people prefer to claim victimhood rather than personal responsibility (McDonald's made me fat, the Marlboro man made me smoke, and so forth). Criminals are eager to accept authoritative pronouncements that excuse their behavior, and defense lawyers are equally quick to argue them in court. All of this reinforces the patterns of criminal denial that treatment providers in corrections (prison counselors, probation and parole officers, social workers) find so frustrating (Sharp, 2006; Walsh & Stohr, 2010). Thus there were a variety of reasons that many of the classical ideas about criminal offending reemerged when they did.

Two popular theories based on neoclassical (a term meaning revival and/or new interpretation of the classical school) ideas of human nature are rational choice theory and routine activities theory. These theories share what Thomas Sowell (1987; see Chapter 1) calls a constrained vision. The most common thread of the two theories is that they emphasize the roles of criminal situations and opportunities and the ratio of benefits to risks in making decisions about whether to engage in criminal behavior. This is contrary to most other theories in this book that focus to various extents on offenders' personal and social characteristics such as impulsiveness, callousness, social class, gender, and age. In other words, rational choice and routine activities theories are concerned with crime rather than criminality.

A theory called cultural criminology directly opposes both these theories, and it emphasizes the role of emotions in instigating criminal behavior rather than rationality. Cultural criminology maintains that criminology (and social science in general) has had a much too rational view of human beings and their behavior and that it has seriously neglected the role of emotions (Ferrell, 2004). Cultural criminologists agree with evolutionary scholars that emotions are more important than rationality in human social decision making because they functioned long before our vaunted rational faculties evolved as the basis for social interaction (Suwa et al., 2009). Despite this big difference in emphasis, cultural criminology shares with rational choice and routine activities theories the rejection of positivist and deterministic "background" theories in favor of examining the "foreground" of crime. The **foreground of crime** is defined as the immediate situation and the thought processes of the individual criminal at the time of the crime, while the **background of crime** refers to everything that person is (age, race, gender, impulsive, drug abuser) or has experienced (abuse, poverty, broken home, drugs) that may have led him or her to think that way. The inclusion of cultural criminology offers us an opportunity to explore the much neglected role of emotions in criminology in terms of the roles they play both in instigating and preventing criminal behavior.

❖ Rational Choice Theory

Rational choice theory is based on the basic tenets of classical theory and would thus dismiss Calvin as a whiner who needs to pull up his socks and take charge of his life. Recall that the central beliefs of the classical school are that people freely choose their behavior and that they do so motivated by the hedonistic calculus. In other words, all behavior, good or bad, is designed to produce some net advantage for the actor. Furthermore, because people are rational they will respond to incentives and disincentives in such a way as to maximize pleasure and minimize pain. Criminal behavior, like all other behavior, is motivated by many things. It could be anger, greed, lust, thrills, jealousy, revenge, status, peer approval, or any number of other reasons. Whatever the reason, at bottom it is all about attempts to gain some sort of personal satisfaction (pleasure) or to remove some source of irritation (pain). This does not mean that neoclassical criminologists have extreme visions of a will free of any causal chains. Rational choice theorists are "soft determinists" because while they believe that criminal behavior is ultimately a choice, the choice is made in the context of personal and situational constraints and opportunities. In other words, rational choice theorists substitute extreme versions of the classical free will concept for that of human agency.

Human agency is a concept that maintains humans have the capacity to make choices and the responsibility to make moral ones regardless of internal or external constraints on one's ability to do so. This is a form of free will compatible with determinism, because it recognizes both the internal and external constraints that limit our ability to do as we please. Because rational choice theory grants offenders the dignity of possessing agency, just as nonoffenders purposely weigh options before deciding on a course of action, so do offenders before deciding to commit a crime. Therefore, "he or she can be held responsible for that choice and can be legitimately punished" (Clarke & Cornish, 2001, p. 25).

What Is Rationality?

It is important to understand rationality and its limits if we are to understand criminal offending and devise effective ways to deter it. Rationality is a desirable quality said to be inherent in human beings. Although rationality is defined somewhat differently in different disciplines, the basic notion is that rationality is the state of having good sense and sound judgment. Good sense and sound judgment are said to be present when we base our choices on the evidence before us at any given time and when we revise our reasoning (and hence our behavior) as new evidence arises. Rationality should not be confused with morality because rationality's goal is self-interest, and self-interest governs behavior whether in conforming or deviant directions. Crime is rational (at least in the short run) if criminals employ reason and act purposely to gain desired ends. Rationality is thus the quality of thinking and behaving in accordance with logic and reason such that one's reality is an ordered and intelligible system for achieving goals and solving problems.

The notion of rationality in the social sciences is indebted to German economist and sociologist Max Weber. Weber conceived of two broad types of rationality. The first is ***zweckrationalitat*** ("purpose" or "instrumental" rationality). Weber assumed this self-serving means-ends rationality to be innate: "Personal self-interest is already fixed by genetic inheritance in all human individuals and needs no further fixing there by external imposition" (in Wallace, 1990, p. 209). In other words, Weber was in agreement with the classical scholars that rationality is a part of human nature pressed into service to assure we meet goals that serve our interests.

Weber also posited a learned rationality called ***wertrationalitat*** ("value" rationality). This type of rationality is related to a value such as honor, or to duty to some revered entity (one's nation, group, God) or idea (patriotism, ideology, religion), which may appear to observers to be antithetical to instrumental rationality. Examples include Catholic priests taking vows of poverty, obedience, and chastity or terrorists blowing themselves up along with busloads of kids in the belief that it is pleasing to God. *Zweckrationalitat* thus points us to reasoned means of attaining a goal, and *wertrationalitat* helps to define those means and goals in terms of norms and values.

What Are the Constraints on Rationality?

A rational decision is one that is reasoned to be optimal for achieving a goal, but rationality is subjective (personal and biased) and bounded (it has limits). Given that it is subjective and bounded, unwanted outcomes can be produced by rational strategies. This is because we do not all make the same calculations or arrive at the same plan when pursuing the same goals. Just like Bill Gates and Charles Manson, we all contemplate our anticipated actions with less than perfect knowledge, with different mind-sets, and with different reasoning abilities. In other words, we may think we are behaving in ways that best serve our self-interest, but our behavior may bring unwanted results because we are ignorant of some things and misinterpret others. We do the best we can to order our decisions relating to our self-interest with the knowledge and understanding we have about the possible outcomes of a particular course of action. All people have mental models of the world and behave rationally with respect to them, even if others might consider our behavior to be irrational. Criminals behave rationally from their private models of reality and "are generally doing the best they can within the limits of time, resources, and information available to them. This is why we characterize their decision making as rational, albeit in a limited way" (Clarke & Cornish, 2001, p. 25).

Photo 5.1

Burglar taking advantage of an isolated back entrance; rational if he accomplishes goal, but immoral.

Rather than focusing on the nature and backgrounds of criminals, rational choice theorists simply assume criminally motivated offenders will always be with us and focus on the process of their choices to offend (the foreground rather than the background of crime). This process is known as **choice structuring** and is defined as "the constellation of opportunities, costs, and benefits attaching to particular kinds of crime" (Cornish & Clarke, 1987, p. 993). We all make choices all the time, but making good ones that maximize the probability that they will result in the desired outcome requires a strategy that structures them. For instance, experienced burglars have to take a variety of factors into consideration before burglarizing a home. They will already have in their heads a general strategy that structures their thinking about where to go, when to go, and what to do to successfully burgle a house. Thus, criminal events require motivated offenders meeting situations they perceive as an opportunity to acquire something they want, such as the bank robber Willie Sutton we met in Chapter 1 viewing a bank. Each criminal event is the result of a series of choice-structuring decisions to initiate the event, continue with it, or desist. Each particular kind of crime is the result of a series of different decisions that can only be explained on their own terms: the decision to rape is arrived at quite differently than the decision to burglarize. The simple basics of rational choice theory are illustrated in Figure 5.1.

Routine Activities Theory

We have already briefly discussed **routine activities theory** in Chapter 3 in the context of victimization. The theory was devised by Lawrence Cohen and Marcus Felson (1979) in the tradition of rational choice theory and attempts to explain crime rates in different societies and neighborhoods without invoking individual differences in criminal propensity. They do this by pointing to the routine activities in that society or neighborhood. Routine activities are defined as "recurrent and prevalent activities which provide for basic population and individual needs" (Cohen & Felson, 1979, p. 593). In other words, routine activities are the normal day-to-day activity patterns that characterize a particular place that either invite or dissuade crime. Take for example the significant increase in the burglary rate in the United States in the 1960s. According to Cohen and Felson (1979), this was almost entirely attributable to the increasing numbers of women entering the workforce, which meant there were fewer people at home to guard it and thus more opportunities for criminals as homes "routinely" were left unoccupied during the day.

Routine activity theory discounts what others see as causes of crime such as poverty, unemployment, and inequality, pointing out that crime increased dramatically with the expansion of the welfare state from the 1960s onward that was supposed to address these things (Walsh & Ellis, 2007). Society's affluence is as much a "cause" of crime as its poverty because affluence brings

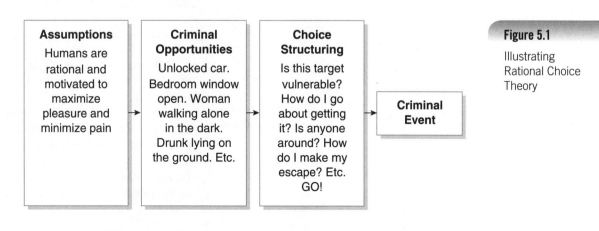

Figure 5.1

Illustrating Rational Choice Theory

with it many opportunities for crime. Of course, it's not that the average affluent person commits more crimes than the average poor person; rather, a general level of affluence makes more things available to steal, rob, loot, and kill for. Additionally, convenience stores and ATM machines competing for their share of the general affluence stay open all hours of the day and night, thus making them convenient for robbers and thieves as well as for shoppers. Affluence may also "cause" crime by flaunting itself in the faces of the poor. An affluent society offers many targets for the not-so-affluent who want "their share" of the pie. Increased crime may be the price we have to pay for increased affluence, especially if affluence is not more evenly distributed.

According to Cohen and Felson (1979), crime is the result of *motivated offenders* meeting *suitable targets* that lack *capable guardians*. This is illustrated in Figure 5.2. If these three elements do not converge in time and space, crime is not likely to occur. Motivated offenders are individuals willing and able to commit crimes. Suitable targets are persons that offenders view as vulnerable or attractive who possess something they want or are objects they want to possess. Capable guardians are persons (mates, patrolling police, concerned neighbors, and so on) or things (alarms, locked doors, well-lit streets, and so forth) that deter criminal activity. For instance, in their early work Cohen and Felson (1979) established that people, especially females, living alone are more likely to be victimized both for personal and property crimes because they are likely to be out alone at night (in bars, home alone, or walking alone) and lack anyone to help in guarding themselves or their property.

Cohen and Felson take motivated offenders for granted and do not attempt to explain their existence. The theory is thus very much like rational choice theory in that it describes situations in which criminal victimization is likely to occur. In poor disorganized communities there is never a shortage of motivated offenders, and although the pickings are generally slim in such areas, victimization is more prevalent in them than in more affluent areas (Truman, Langton, & Planty, 2013). One of the obvious reasons for high victimization rates in poor disorganized areas (besides the abundance of motivated offenders) is that residents of such areas tend to lack capable guardians for either their persons or their property.

Routine activities theory looks at crime from the points of view of both the offender and of crime prevention efforts. A crime will only be committed when a motivated offender believes he or she has found something worth stealing or someone to victimize lacking a capable guardian. Because of disrupted families, transient neighbors, poverty, and all the other negative aspects of disorganized neighborhoods, except for police patrols, capable guardians are in short supply. Crime is a "situation," and crime rates can go up or down depending on how these situations (routine activities) change without any changes in offender motivation or in the prevalence of motivated offenders.

Take murder for example. The FBI (2013a) indicates that in 2012 only 62.5% of homicides were cleared by the police as opposed to 90% in 1960 (Keel, Jarvis, & Muirhead, 2009). This means that about one out of three murderers got away with it in the United States in 2012 versus one out of 10 in 1960. The clearance rate was

Figure 5.2

Routine Activities Theory's Model of When a Criminal Event Is Likely to Occur

A likely offender

CRIME

A suitable target

The absence of a capable guardian

even lower in cities with the highest homicide rates, such as Chicago, where in 2008 it was 35%; it was 22% in New Orleans and just 21% in Detroit (Hargrove, 2010). The lessening ability of the police to act as capable guardians in those cities yields to the perception that "I can get away with it," as apparently four out of five murderers did in Detroit in 2008. The ever-increasing prevalence of single-parent households means more vulnerable women and children lacking capable guardians. As we saw in Chapter 3, single-parent households also mean a highly elevated risk of abuse and neglect, which is likely to result in more motivated offenders as well (Kruk, 2012). Note that out-of-wedlock births, falling marriage rates, and rising divorces rates are becoming "routine" activities in the United States in certain areas, and according to this theory, there is no need to turn to individual traits to explain high crime rates existing there. Recurring situations conducive to acquiring resources with minimal effort also tempt more individuals to take advantage of them.

Evaluation of Rational Choice and Routine Activities Theories

Rational choice and routine activities theories have been criticized on many fronts. Both theories resonate most with conservatives because they aver that offenders are thinking agents who must be held responsible for their actions. Although this position grants criminals the dignity of having reasoned control over their lives, liberals tend not to like it because the "free agent" position naturally leads to a retributivist stance on punishment (punishment based on just desserts) (Lilly, Cullen, & Ball, 2011).

The most glaring criticism, however, is the assumption of rationality. It is assumed that everyone agrees that all humans of sound mind are rational in the classical sense of wanting to maximize their pleasure and minimize their pain. But if everyone is rational, rationality is a constant and thus cannot by itself explain something as variable as human behavior. What we need to adequately explain behavior are the factors that affect offenders' rationality but do not affect nonoffenders' rationality and vice versa. That is, what leads a person like Charlie Manson to decide, quite rationally, that increasing his pleasure means immediate gratification (a drug fix now, a woman for tonight), and minimizing his pain (boredom, drug craving) is best met by robbery and other crimes, while a person like Bill Gates decides, just as rationally, that his needs are best met by delaying gratification, attending college, getting a good job, getting married, and settling down? In other words, what should interest criminologists the most are the factors that lead people to exercise the rationality they have in common in radically different ways.

It would seem that the typical criminal's rationality is severely "bounded." We continually see more than two-thirds of released criminals going back to prison, and that is hardly maximizing pleasure and minimizing pain (Stohr & Walsh, 2012). As we have seen, criminals are rational from their own limited point of view, and they do weigh costs and benefits. But like the rest of us, criminals are not walking calculating machines who routinely take time to weigh the pros and cons of their every move. As van den Haag (2003) puts it, "Law abiding people habitually ignore criminal opportunities. Law breakers habitually discount the risk of punishment. Neither calculates" (p. 47). As Jack Katz (1988) explains, "The hardman triumphs, after all, by *inducing others* to calculate the costs and benefits" (p. 235, emphasis added). The bottom line is that incentives and disincentives to law-abiding or criminal behavior are perceived differently because of ingrained habits. It is the development of these habitual ways of responding to opportunities that interests most criminologists.

Routine activities theory is a different proposition because it makes no explicit assumptions about offenders other than that their motives are to "gain quick pleasure and avoid imminent pain" (Felson, 1998, p. 23). In other words, routine activities theorists implicitly agree with Beccaria that criminals are not fundamentally different from noncriminals and that everyone may be motivated to commit a crime at some point in his or her life if the benefits are large enough and the possible costs are negligible. Because the theory concentrates on crime as a process of unfolding events rather than the motivated offender, it appeals to those who see individual difference explanations as stigmatizing and wish to avoid them. On the other hand, there are those who criticize the theory for ignoring the social conditions they see as giving rise to motivated offenders. Liberal critics view the theory's focus on narrow crime prevention as granting society permission to avoid discussing such issues as poverty and inequality.

Criminologists whose interests lie in scientific discovery rather than practical crime prevention also criticize the theory for its narrow focus (not that they deny the value of crime prevention, of course). These individuals point out that while it is true that anyone may be tempted to commit a crime if the ratio of benefit to cost is high, few people ever commit a serious crime. Criminologists of this persuasion point out that chronic criminals do not just bump into criminal opportunities; they actively create them, even if the benefits of doing so are paltry compared to the possible costs (DeLisi & Conis, 2012). We should thus like to know what differentiates criminals who make a conscious decision to lead a life of crime and have no intention of pursuing a straight life from noncriminals, one-time, or short-term criminals. These criminologists are interested in the differences in the developmental histories (which include all social, cultural, and environmental variables) and differences in genetics and brain functioning between chronic criminals and noncriminals (Walsh & Bolen, 2012; Wright & Beaver, 2012).

In defense of routine activities theory, we might point out that once criminal dispositions have been acquired, it seems very difficult to change the motivated offender. Likewise, the so-called root causes of poverty, as we saw previously, have been impervious to solutions despite state and federal programs spending billions of dollars every year battling them (Tanner, 2012). Thus, it makes sense to focus on strategies that make it more difficult to commit crimes. Routine activities theorists also point out that they are not in competition with criminologists who focus on individual differences or on social conditions that give rise to motivated offenders. They insist that they are simply taking them for granted and have staked out "criminal opportunities" and practical crime prevention strategies as their domain of research.

❖ Cultural Criminology

Cultural criminology (sometimes called anarchic criminology) is a relatively new theory that seemingly attracts disenchanted members of the radical left (thus the anarchic label). This theory is included here for two major reasons: (1) it positions itself in direct opposition to rational choice theory, and (2) it provides an opportunity to discuss a prime motivator of behavior that is emphasized by cultural criminology but is seriously neglected in mainstream criminology—emotion.

According to Lilly, Cullen, and Ball (2011), "The enemy of cultural criminology is the state and an administrative criminology that advocates rational choice theory" (p. 226). Cultural criminologists thus tend to be politically engaged radicals who attack theories favored by conservatives and liberals alike and who have a special distaste for viewing criminals as rational calculators. This theory looks at much of modern crime as the result of the breakdown of culture in the context of a destabilizing economic globalization (Hayward & Young, 2004). They see the old Western culture of stable families and secure full employment with good pay morphing into the "McDonaldsization" of work and a culture that has become obsessed with consumerism, hedonism, sex, and violence (Young, 2003).

Differences in pop music starkly illustrate what cultural criminologists mean about the difference between the morality of the old and new cultures. In the 1950s we had Pat Boone—hand on heart—crooning softly to his special lady in "April Love" that "every star's a wishing star that shines for you" and Elvis Presley serenading his love by telling her that "you have made my life complete, and I love you so" in "Love Me Tender." Fast-forward half a century and we have Lil Wayne—hand on crotch—wailing in "Every Girl" to no one in particular: "I wish I could fuck every girl in the world" and Pitbull barking that his "ho" of the moment has "got an ass like a donkey, with a monkey, look like King Kong," in "I Know You Want Me."

To explain the kind of psychology underlying the cultural degradation that cultural criminologists perceive, they introduce the concept of *anelpis*, a Greek term meaning "without hope." Hall and Winlow (2004) apply this term to describe "a historically unique section of humanity, which cannot be described as an 'underclass' in the structural sense because their wage needs have been priced out of the global market" (p. 277). The state of mind of the

Photo 5.2

Cultural criminologists explain modern crime as the result of the breakdown of culture. Through that lens, Lil Wayne becomes a living symbol of the anelpis culture of consumerism, sex, drugs, and violence.

anelpis is described as "the presence of virtually total cynicism and nihilism: virtually no opinion, no realistic expectations, no hope and no fear of authority" (p. 277). This image is of a subsection of Western populations trapped in permanent economic recession that has abandoned all patterns of rational thought and reverted to a more primitive state of being animated primarily by negative emotions such as humiliation, anger, resentment, and rage (Hall, 2000). Cultural criminologists see much of criminal and other transgressive behaviors as attempts to escape these negative emotions and to assert their humanity. For such people "rules are transgressed because they are there, risk is a challenge, not a deterrent" (Young, 2003, p. 319).

Ironically, this view of cultural breakdown is shared by conservative criminologists who see the dominance of a liberal worldview starting in the late 1960s as one that "undermined traditional values and authority. A culture that had emphasized self-control and discipline was replaced by a culture trumpeting moral relativism and an insidious permissiveness" (Cullen & Agnew, 2006, p. 459). Note that while cultural criminologists trace cultural breakdown to economic globalization and relentless poverty, which in turn *produces* the anelpis mind-set, conservative criminologists trace it to the culture itself; that is, changes in cultural values and norms of behavior are the *products* of cultural degradation. Cultural criminologists thus emphasize financial poverty and conservative criminologists emphasize moral poverty.

The Relationship of Rationality and Emotion

Because both rationality and emotion initiate behavior, the relationship between them has long interested philosophers. Enlightenment philosopher Immanuel Kant called the emotions "pathological," and his contemporary Gottfried Leibniz called them "confused passions" (in Walsh, 2014, p. 85). Cultural criminologists maintain that social science has been so gripped by the Enlightenment's view of emotions and its emphasis on reason that it has seriously neglected the role of emotions in directing human behavior (Kirman, Livet, & Teschl, 2010). But even during the Enlightenment there were those such as philosopher David Hume who believed that emotion drove our behavior more than rationality. Hume considered our species to be *Homo emovere* ("emoting man") rather than *Homo sapiens* ("wise man"), with our reason providing only rationales for doing what we feel like doing. For Hume, we perceive a situation, experience emotions, pass judgment on the event based on the emotion it evokes, and then provide reasons for that judgment.

If criminologists think about the role of emotions at all, they tend to see them as Kant and Leibniz did—as toxic enemies of reason that instigate only negative behavior and have no adaptive positive function of their own. For instance, the frustration, envy, and resentment evoked when some people observe someone else's good fortune (what criminologists call relative deprivation) is said to lead to anger and then to stimulate criminal behavior to placate those emotions and to obtain what is envied (Smith, Pettigrew, Pippin, & Bialosiewitz, 2012). To put it another way, emotion is seen as *intervening* between a perception and an action as follows:

$$\text{relative deprivation} \rightarrow \text{resentment/envy} \rightarrow \text{anger/crime.}$$

On the other hand, cultural criminologists view emotions as primary causes of a great deal of criminal behavior. For them, the emotion motivating crime is not a fleeting perception but rather a permanent fixture of many criminals' mental lives. While crime is assumed to alleviate the negative emotions constantly felt by the anelpis, positive emotional satisfaction in the form of "thrills" gained by transgressing the legal and moral norms of society is more important. Cultural criminologists see the rational calculator view of the criminal as offering us a flawed image of bloodless individuals devoid of passion (Ferrell, 2004). The primary appeal of crime for them is its intrinsic rewards; the thrills and the rush of taking risks and getting away with it, not the frequently negligible material rewards of crime. Studies of street criminals by researchers such as Katz (1988) and De Haan and Vos (2003) paint a picture of "unreasonable" individuals seduced by a life of action who value their "badass" reputations more than monetary success. According to Jack Katz (1988), the materialistic (monetary) motive for criminal activity emphasized by many criminologists is characterized by an "overwhelmingly inadequacy for grasping the experiential facts of crime" (p. 314). For Katz and other cultural criminologists, most criminals are impulsively motivated by short-run hedonism, which is expressive, malicious, and destructive, rather than the instrument for attaining material wants.

The scanty monetary gains and dismal long-term consequences of a criminal lifestyle make it difficult to think of most crime as simply an alternative way to achieve monetary success, as some theories maintain. Cultural criminologists reveal criminals' own accounts of crime that tell us there is something that makes crime appealing for its own sake regardless of material rewards. Chronic criminals are certainly motivated by the need for fast cash to feed their "every night is Saturday night" lifestyles, but interviews with criminals find that the internal rewards of committing expressive crimes are powerful motivators (Wood, Gove, Wilson, & Cochran, 1997). As Jock Young (2003) put it, "The sensual nature of crime, the adrenaline rushes of edgework—voluntary illicit risk-taking and the dialectic of fear and pleasure . . . all point to a wide swath of crime that is expressive rather than narrowly instrumental" (p. 391). The neurobiological details of this "dialectic of fear and pleasure" have been revealed in terms of a complex interplay of brain chemicals before, during, and after the commission of a crime (Gove & Wilmoth, 2003).

But this "emotional edgework" is not without considerations of material costs and benefits and thus not devoid of instrumental rationality. Willie Sutton (the bank robber we met in Chapter 1 and featured in the Theory in Action segment of this chapter) plainly enjoyed the visceral rush of crime. When asked why he robbed banks he replied: "Because I enjoyed it. I was more alive when I was inside a bank, robbing it, than at any other time in my life." But as we have seen, he would also answer "Because that's where the money is" (Sutton & Linn, 1976, p. 120). The *meaning* of bank robbery is different for Willie, the bank manager, and society at large. It is the analysis of these differences—especially the meaning crime has for the criminal—that cultural criminology emphasizes.

Evaluating Cultural Criminology

Cultural criminology has done the discipline a service by emphasizing the role of emotions in the commission of crimes, because emotions have long been treated only peripherally in criminology. We need to understand the foreground of crime (the criminal's experience of a crime; what it means to him or her at the moment) emphasized by this theory as well as the background (the criminal's objective placement in the social order) of crime emphasized by other theories. Although rational choice and routine activities theories also emphasize the foreground, cultural criminology differs in emphasizing the emotional rather than the rational aspects of the foreground. Looking at crime from offenders' subjective points of view allows us insight into their thought processes, motives, values, and emotions. This is valuable as long as we don't find ourselves excusing their behavior, as cultural criminologists are inclined to do. The anarchic quality of the theory pushes itself to the front time and again in its constant reference to state repression and oppression and its calls for resistance. "Anarchic criminology" is thus a more apt description for this brand of criminology than "cultural criminology." Their negative view of social control agents (police, judges, probation/parole officers, and so on), their often romanticized view of criminals, and their general disdain for empirical science (a position shared by most critical theories) makes it clear that this is a highly politicized theory of criminology.

Nevertheless, the theory's focus on the impact of economic globalism on workplace practices such as the loss of manufacturing jobs in the Western world, as well as their replacement by "flexible" and insecure part-time jobs from which workers can be fired "at will," tells us much about the sense of insecurity and hopelessness of many low-level workers and provides reasons why they may well retreat into the underground economy. The concept of the anelpis that describes the very lowest members of society whose lives are saturated with all things that traditional morality finds repugnant is a useful one. The question here is whether this group's existence is a function of the effects of globalization on the culture, as cultural criminologists maintain, or is cultural degradation spawned by the permissive attitudes exemplified by the rap music and behavior of performers such as Lil Wayne and Pitbull, as conservative criminologists maintain. Of course, these things can, and do, have reciprocal effects on each other.

THEORY IN ACTION: "Slick Willie" Sutton—"Where the Money Is"

Willie Sutton, aka "Willie the Actor" and "Slick Willie," was America's most prolific bank robber from the 1920s through the 1950s. Sutton gained his nicknames because of his ability to disguise himself and his daring ability in executing bank robberies. During his 40-year criminal career, he stole an estimated $2 million but paid for it by spending more than half of his adult life in prison. Although less well-known to the general public than other Depression-era gangsters such as Al Capone, he was in many ways both more interesting and more successful than most of them (he lived to a ripe old age of 79). As one of his biographers, J. R. Moehringer, described him, "Smarter than Machine Gun Kelly, saner than Pretty Boy Floyd, more likable than Legs Diamond, more peaceable than Dutch Schultz, more romantic than Bonnie and Clyde, Sutton saw bank robbery as high art and went about it with an artist's single-minded zeal." He was educated only to the eighth-grade level, but he was very wise in the ways of the law, dispensing legal advice freely to fellow prison inmates. His intelligence was also demonstrated in his three successful prison escapes.

Willie was born in the squalid slums of Irishtown, Brooklyn, into an Irish American family in 1901. He was the fourth of five children born to his impoverished parents in a hardworking family that was strict but not abusive

(Continued)

THEORY IN ACTION (Continued)

or neglectful. Although he endured the hardship of a level of poverty no modern American is allowed to suffer, neither he nor his equally impoverished peers who took to crime fell to the squalid moral level exemplified by those described by cultural criminologists as anelpis. Indeed, it has been claimed that this dapper, well-dressed man would never finish robbing a bank when a woman screamed or a baby cried and always showed deep respect for the "fair sex."

Photo 5.3

Bank robber Willie "The Actor" Sutton.

In many ways Willie is a poster child for both those criminologists who emphasize rationality and those who emphasize emotion. He did legitimate work for short periods—his longest period lasted 8 months, ironically, in a bank. His choice structuring was very involved before making his clandestine bank "withdrawals" dressed as a cop, maintenance worker, security guard, or window washer. He rarely went for the teller, preferring to go for the motherlode in the vault. Willie clearly planned all his bank heists very carefully, and he was much admired by his underworld cohorts for his coolly planned and executed prison escapes. This side of Willie clearly illustrates the rational component of his criminal activities. Recall that I earlier quoted Willie's reply to the question of why he robbed banks: "Because that's where the money is. Go where the money is . . . and go there often." After all, Willie loved the ladies and he loved to gamble, and these pursuits cost money.

However, there are many indications that the thrill of crime, of transgressing the law and getting away with it, the euphoria of feeling alive and authentic, was perhaps his primary motivation. He was committing burglaries and thefts by age 9 and was attracted to the bawdy beer joints frequented by sailors. In his autobiography, partly ghostwritten by Edward Linn, *Where the Money Was: The Memoirs of a Bank Robber*, Sutton gives what he himself considered the real reason he robbed banks. "Why did I rob banks? Because I enjoyed it. I loved it. I was more alive when I was inside a bank, robbing it, than at any other time in my life. I enjoyed everything about it so much that one or two weeks later I'd be out looking for the next job. But to me the money was the chips, that's all." The money being just "chips," of course, refers to gambling chips that are simply the tools of gambling, not the rewards per se. This all sounds very much like a man essentially addicted to the adrenaline rush of crime and relatively impervious to the negative consequences of it.

Discussion Questions

1. Determine if a classmate is willing to reveal if he or she has ever committed a crime such as shoplifting and got away with it. Ask him or her how they felt before, during, and after the event.

2. Willie and his compatriots grew up in a time in which there were no government programs designed to help the poor and in which poverty conditions were far greater than they are today. Why do you think those conditions never led to the values, attitudes, and behaviors that cultural criminologists attribute to the anelpis?

3. Willie, and many other infamous crooks of the Depression era, have biographies, movies, and novels featuring their criminal careers devoured by the public. Yet we rarely, if ever, see the lives of people who did constructive, valuable, and philanthropic things during that era featured. What does that tell you about human nature and its attractions?

Sources: Moehringer, 2012; Sutton & Linn, 1976

❖ Emotions and Their Functions

If emotions are so important, we must understand what they are and how they engage behavior. **Emotions** are subjective feelings of varying strength prompted by nervous system arousal in response to some perceived event. They are situated in the limbic system, a set of brain structures that predate by at least a million years the evolution of the brain structures where our reasoning power is housed (Suwa et al., 2009). Former president of the American Sociological Association, Douglas Massey (2002) put it this way: "Emotionality clearly preceded rationality in evolutionary sequence, and as rationality developed it did not replace emotionality as the basis for human interaction. Rather, rational abilities were gradually added to preexisting and simultaneously developing emotional capacities" (p. 15). Jonathan Haidt (2001) put it even more strongly: "It [emotion] comes first in phylogeny [the developmental history of the species], it emerges first in ontogeny [the developmental history of the individual], it is triggered more quickly in real-time judgments, and it is more powerful and irrevocable [than rationality] when the two systems yield conflicting judgments" (p. 819).

Modern neuroscience has demonstrated time and again that emotion and rationality, far from being antagonists as often assumed, are two inseparably linked components of all that we think and do. Brain imaging research has shown that emotion and cognition are fully *physically* integrated in an area of the brain called the lateral prefrontal cortex that weighs rational and emotional information coming in from their respective brain areas to guide human actions (Pessoa, 2008). It is worth noting that a defining characteristic of some of our worst criminals is their inability to "tie" the brain's rational and emotional networks together (Pitchford, 2001; Wiebe, 2011). Chronic criminals are perfectly capable of reasoning; it is mainly their poorly developed emotional systems that cause them to discount their knowledge of moral norms and to behave according to immediate self-gratification (Walsh & Bolen, 2012).

Primary and Secondary Emotions

Psychologists distinguish between primary emotions (e.g., anger, fear, disgust, joy) and secondary emotions. The secondary (often called the "social" emotions) are mixtures of the primary emotions just as the secondary colors are mixtures of the primary colors. Far from being pathological (which of course they can be), the primary emotions have been enormously useful in the evolution of our species. Fear, anger, and disgust focus our attention on an immediate problem and narrow responses toward some corrective strategy. Anger directed at injustice may prevent it, and fear and disgust motivate escape and avoidance.

The social emotions, such as empathy, shame, embarrassment, and guilt, are retrofitted to the primary emotions as a mixture that broadens rather than narrows our focus and are integral to developing and strengthening social bonds (Fredrickson, 2003). They evolved as essential parts of our social intelligence and serve as clues as to the kinds of relationships (cooperative vs. uncooperative) we are likely to have with others. Emotions such as empathy and guilt serve to adjust our social behavior by arousing, focusing, and modifying brain activity in ways that lead most people to habitually choose prosocial rather than antisocial responses when presented with "a suitable target lacking a capable guardian." Taking advantage of a criminal opportunity may be more rational in the short term because it gets one resources with little effort, but it is self-defeating in the long run. Short-term rewards are easier to appreciate than long-term consequences, and thus criminals have the tendency to abandon consideration of the latter when confronted with temptation. It is the immediate warnings sounded by the social emotions that lead others to attend to the long-term consequences of their behavior despite temptation.

Important Crime-Preventing Social Emotions

Positive emotions that function to prevent criminal behavior have been practically ignored in criminology. It hardly needs pointing out that empathy—the cognitive and emotional ability to understand the feelings and distress of others—is important to social life. Empathy is an ancient capacity predating the emergence of the human species and evolved rapidly in the context of parental care (de Waal, 2008). Because we feel distress personally when witnessing the distress of others, we alleviate our own distress if we can help to alleviate the distress of others. Empathy channels helping behavior in social species because it moves us to rapidly access a situation and respond to it without having to rely on time-consuming conscious reflection to determine our response (Roach & Pease, 2013).

Because individuals in social groups react toward others who violate social expectations, it is adaptive for humans to have evolved social emotions such as guilt and shame to monitor and constrain negative impulses. When we do things that have a negative effect on ourselves or on others, it is useful to be aware of them and to be appropriately motivated to take some remedial action. Guilt involves anxiety, remorse, and concern about how one's actions have negatively impacted others, and it motivates both avoidance and approach behavior. Because guilt is psychologically punitive, it motivates one not to repeat the transgression (avoidance), and because it also moves one toward reparative behavior (apologies, restitution) it motivates approach behavior. As we might expect, guilt is positively related to empathy since persons are not likely to feel bad about offending others if they are indifferent to them (Silfver & Klaus, 2007).

Guilt is other-centered because it focuses our thoughts on recognizing the rights and respect of others and how we have violated them. Shame, on the other hand, is more self-centered because it involves an appraisal of self-worth in light of what one has done to be ashamed of. Unlike guilt, shame is a private thing, with only the person experiencing it being aware of the origin of the emotion. The object of shame is thus the self ("I *am* a bad person") rather than an event as is guilt ("I *did* a bad thing").

Emotions are thus integral to understanding criminal behavior. You may have noticed that the social emotions are part and parcel of what we call the conscience. The bite of conscience is what keeps many of us on the straight and narrow, and it is the lack of this bite that grants criminals permission to prey on others. There are thus criminologists who consider the lack of functioning social emotions to be of more concern than the lack of rationality (Tibbetts, 2003; Wiebe, 2011). After all, even the worst criminals are well aware intellectually of right and wrong; the trouble is that their weak social emotions allow them to discount that knowledge.

❖ Policy and Prevention: Implications of Rational Choice and Routine Activities Theories

As we saw in the previous chapter, the assumption of rational offenders is shared by legal systems around the world. The law in Western countries also recognizes that rationality is bounded in its acknowledgment of the existence of mitigating circumstances when punishing convicted criminals. Although the assumption of rationality may be questionable for some, it is considered prudent to abide by it for the practical purposes of crime prevention.

The key to preventing crime from these theories is reducing criminal opportunities by minimizing the occasions where potential offenders and suitable targets intersect. This is to be done by arranging the environment to make it more difficult and more risky to offend. What do we mean by "arranging the environment"? Well, if you were the kind of motivated rational criminal assumed by neoclassical theorists, what sort of questions would you ask yourself at the potential crime site before you made your decision on whether to commit the crime? I bet that among them would be the following: "Is there a quick way out of the area after the job is done?" "How vulnerable are the targets (is the car unlocked, is the door open, is the girl alone)?" "What are my chances of being seen by people in the area?" "If people in this area do see me, do they look likely to do something about it?" These are rational questions potential lawbreakers ask themselves all the time. The policy implications of the assumptions of rational criminals boil down to trying to arrange things in time and space in such a way that criminals will dissuade themselves from committing crimes by maximizing the probability that the answers to these and other such questions criminals ask themselves will lead them to conclude that committing a criminal act is too risky.

Rational choice and routine activities theories thus shift the policy focus from large and costly social programs such as antipoverty programs to target hardening. They shift attention away from policies designed to change offenders' attitudes and behavior toward making it more difficult and more costly for them to offend. Examples of target hardening include antitheft devices on automobiles, home alarms, the use of vandal-resistant materials on public property, improved city lighting, surveillance cameras in stores and at public gathering places, check guarantee cards, banning the sale of alcohol at sporting events, neighborhood watches, and curfews for teenagers. Neoclassical theorists would be especially likely to recommend that the police concentrate their efforts on so-called hot spots rather than spreading themselves around. As we have seen, this is precisely the intelligence-based policing made possible by CompStat programs across the nation (Zimring, 2013). Hot spots are places identified by crime mapping where not only serious crimes occur, but also numerous minor antisocial acts such as public drunkenness and urination, fights, and vandalism. Neoclassical theorists argue that such acts should not be ignored because they contribute to further deterioration of a neighborhood and invite worse crimes.

Many of the crime prevention recommendations of neoclassical theorists revolve around the concept of environmental design. Environmental design is primarily concerned with **defensible space**, defined as "a model for residential environments which inhibit crime by creating the physical expression of a social fabric that defends itself" (Newman, 1972, p. 3). It endeavors to bring people together into a tribelike sense of community by designing the physical environment

Photo 5.4

Target hardening such as installing surveillance cameras or home alarm systems makes it more difficult for criminals to commit crimes.

so as to awaken the human sense of territoriality. The best possible physical environment for the growth of crime is the large barracks-like blocks of apartments with few entrances, private spaces, and demarcation barriers that say "this space is mine." Families must be given back a sense of ownership, for if everything is "owned" in common (elevators, walkways and staircases, balconies, grass and shrubberies) then no one takes care of it, and it deteriorates rapidly. Streets must be strategically arranged, both to generate a sense of belonging to "my special little neighborhood" and so criminals cannot easily access or escape the neighborhood.

❖ Policy and Prevention: Implications of Cultural Criminology

As a highly politicized theory disdainful of all neoclassical assumptions, cultural criminology tends to also discount the crime prevention efforts derived from these assumptions (Farrell, 2010). When writing about crime prevention, cultural criminologists are more likely to point out the pitfalls of situational crime prevention (such as criminals moving to less guarded areas—crime displacement—when they perceive crime in one area is too difficult and risky) than to offer their own preventative suggestions (Hayward, 2007). In fact, Farrell (2010) asserts that cultural criminology offers "little, if anything, useful to inform crime reduction efforts" (p. 60). Since much of the blame for predatory criminality is placed at the door of capitalism (Hayward, 2012), the only solution to the crime problem for cultural criminologists seems to be to replace the free market economy with a more government-controlled command economy.

As mentioned in Chapter 1, however, it is unfair to judge a theory solely on its policy recommendations (or lack of them). Cultural criminology is not interested in primary crime prevention, but rather in understanding the expressive motives of a certain class of offender—those who supposedly have given up hope of ever effectively participating successfully in mainstream society. While cultural criminologists seem unable to draw any practical applications from their theory, understanding the minds and motives of motivated offenders, even offenders primarily moved by emotions and "damn the consequences" rather than rationality may lead others to devise ways of effectively dealing with these offenders in the future.

Table 5.1 summarizes the key concepts of each of the theories presented in this chapter, as well as their strengths and weaknesses.

Table 5.1

Summarizing Rational Choice, Routine Activities, and Cultural Theories

Theory	Key Concepts	Strengths	Weaknesses
Rational Choice	Individualistic theory. All people, including criminals, are self-interested persons seeking to maximize pleasure and minimize pain. Before engaging in any behavior, people weigh the costs and benefits. Because criminals have agency, they are responsible for their behavior and should be punished accordingly.	Brings back the idea of individual responsibility. Grants criminals the dignity of agency and does not allow for excuse making. Even though the assumption of rationality may be scientifically questionable, it may be prudent to accept it.	Recognizes that rationality is bounded but ignores the fact. We would like to know why something is rational for one person and not another. Assumes that all crime is instrumental; ignores the emotional appeal of crime.

Theory	Key Concepts	Strengths	Weaknesses
Routine Activities	Ignores criminality and concentrates on crime as an event. Crime occurs in the context of everyday routine activities in some geographic area. Crime is an event at the confluence of a motivated offender meeting a suitable target that lacks a capable guardian.	Can explain changing crime rates without having to account for increases or decreases in motivated offenders or why they are motivated. Accounts for crime rates in an area in terms of its normal activities. Offers practical crime prevention strategies.	Simply assumes motivated offenders and does not try to account for them. Ignores what some consider "root causes" of crime such as poverty and inequality, as well as the personality traits of motivated offenders.
Cultural or Anarchic Criminology	Opposes both the capitalist state and ideas of rational offenders. Globalization has led to cultural breakdown, which has led to a subset of individuals called anelpis who are without hope. These people are motivated to commit crime by emotions, both to get rid of negative emotions and to achieve thrills. Material gain is only a small part of criminal motivation.	Explains high crime rates among the most severely disadvantaged members of society. Brings a much neglected concept into the explanation of criminal behavior—emotion. Explains crime in which the financial gains are negligible or absent. Tries to explain cultural breakdown.	Appears to be more politically than scientifically motivated. Primarily accounts for crime among anelpis. Ignores the fact that there are many crimes motivated by materialism that are rationally planned and carried out.

Summary

- Neoclassical theories reemerged in the form of rational choice and routine activities theories in the 1970s. These theories assume that humans are rational and self-seeking, although rationality is bounded by knowledge levels and thinking abilities. They downplay personal and background factors influencing choices in favor of analyzing the processes leading to offenders' choices to offend.

- Rational choice theory concentrates on how offenders structure their choices when making decisions about whether or not to offend, and routine activities theory looks at a criminal event as a motivated offender meeting a suitable target lacking a capable guardian. These ideas show how crime rates can go up or down without a change in the prevalence of motivated offenders by increasing or decreasing suitable targets and capable guardians.

- Cultural criminology shares with rational choice and routine activities theories its emphasis on the foreground of crime rather than the background.

However, cultural criminologists disdain the perspective and ideology of rational choice and routine activities theories. Cultural criminology emphasizes the power of emotions (the thrill and the rush of edgework) to stimulate crime as opposed to bloodless rational cost/benefit calculations.

- The concept of anelpis is an important one in cultural criminology. *Anelpis* is a term meaning "without hope" and applied by cultural criminologists to describe the lowest segment of society marked by cynicism and nihilism, no realistic expectations, no hope, and no fear of authority who are ruled primarily by their emotions.

- Evolutionary biologists inform us that emotions have been tremendously useful as the basis for social interaction for hundreds of thousands of years, and neuroscientists tell us that rationality and emotion are two inseparable components of all we say and do. When our emotions and our rationality are in opposition, emotions tend to win out.

- Social emotions such as empathy, guilt, and shame are powerful evolved devices that function to minimize occasions of hurtful antisocial behavior. They are part of what we call our conscience, which is what psychopaths and chronic criminals lack; they do not lack rationality.
- The policy and prevention strategies derived from rational choice and routine activities theories boil down to making it more difficult, and thus less rewarding, for criminals to commit a crime by hardening targets. That is, arranging the physical environment in such a way that the intersection of a motivated offender and suitable targets intersecting is less likely. The nature of cultural criminology is such that it offers no immediate practical recommendations for reducing crime.

Exercises and Discussion Questions

1. Discuss the notion that criminal behavior is just as rational as noncriminal behavior.

2. Why are rational choice and routine activities theories broadly considered conservative?

3. Give examples of some routine activities that practically invite crime.

4. Take a position on whether rationality or emotions are more important in understanding criminal behavior.

5. Who are the anelpis, and how do you think they became the way they are? In other words, is it economic poverty as cultural criminologists contend, or is it moral poverty as conservative criminologists contend?

6. Why (or why not) is target hardening preferable to other anticrime strategies such as reducing poverty?

Useful Websites

Cultural criminology. www.albany.edu/scj/jcjpc/vol3is2/culture.html.

Rational choice theory. www.umsl.edu/~keelr/200/ratchoc.html.

Routine activities theory. www.children.gov.on.ca/htdocs/English/topics/youthandthelaw/roots/volume5/chapter03_rational_choice.aspx.

Chapter Terms

Anelpis	Defensible space	Rational choice theory
Background of crime	Emotions	Routine activities theory
Choice structuring	Foreground of crime	*Wertrationalitat*
Cultural criminology	Human agency	*Zweckrationalitat*

CHAPTER 6

Social Structural Theories

On June 15, 1975, 12-year-old Kody Scott graduated from elementary school in Los Angeles. During the ceremony, his thoughts were on "the hood" and his one ambition in life, which was to join the Eight Tray Crips, become a "ghetto star," and major in murder, robbery, and general mayhem. He went straight from the graduation to his initiation into the gang, which involved taking part in the gunning down of 15 members of a rival faction of L.A.'s other notorious gang, the Bloods. Two years later, during a robbery in which the victim tried to run, Kody beat and stomped the man into a coma. A police officer at the scene said that "whoever did this is a monster," a name Kody proudly took as his street moniker. Monster did time in juvenile detention and then served several prison terms. During one of these terms, he converted to Afrocentric Islam and changed his name to Sanyika Shakur. He also wrote Monster: The Autobiography of an L.A. Gang Member, which provides a frightening portrayal of the violence of ghetto life. Shakur was paroled in 1995; returned to prison on parole violations in 1996, 1997, and 1998; and again was incarcerated for a shooting in 2000. Paroled again sometime later, he was rearrested in 2004 for "battery with great bodily harm" and again sent to prison. After being paroled for this offense, he was arrested in 2008 for carjacking and robbery and sentenced to 6 years and was paroled (yet again!) in 2012.

Shakur was allegedly the illegitimate son of an ex-football player named Dick Bass. His mother subsequently married another man and had four more children. She divorced their father when Shakur was 6 years old and had to raise the children alone. Shakur was mistreated by his stepfather and never included in family outings. He spent almost all his childhood in the wild and chaotic streets, which he says was the only thing that really interested him. As you read this chapter about disorganized neighborhoods, blocked opportunities to legitimate success, and lower-class values, try to imagine Shakur at the center of it all and how these things may have shaped his life.

LEARNING OBJECTIVES

- Understand the basic premise of the social structural tradition
- Be able to explain the assumptions of human ecology theory, its major finding, and criticisms aimed at it
- Be able to describe the evolution of the anomie tradition and how the various versions differ
- Understand how many of these theories, while remaining structural, implicitly appeal to psychological constructs
- Know the basic ideas of subcultural theories—how they form and how the status concerns of young males are met in those subcultures
- Know why gangs are formed, what their function is, and how they relate to social structure

❖ The Social Structural Tradition

Almost all sociological theories of crime touch on social structure to some degree. **Social structure** is the framework of social institutions—the family and educational, religious, economic, and political institutions that operate to structure the patterns of relationships members of a society have with one another. Structural theorists maintain that wholes (societies, institutions, groups) are greater than the sums of their parts, that these wholes are real and enjoy an existence of their own separate from their individual members. Although groups cannot exist apart from the individuals who comprise them, once formed they take on an existence independent of any one individual. Structural theorists work from assumptions made from general models of society and to deduce everyday experiences of individuals from those models. Their philosophy is summed up in Quetelet's proposition as stated in Chapter 4: "Society prepares the crime and individuals are only the instruments that give it life." They are thus interested in seeking the social structural causes of crime rather than why particular individuals commit crimes.

Structural criminologists tend to assume that human nature is socially constructed, an unconstrained vision position that avers that all human traits and characteristics are specific to local cultures. This is in opposition to the constrained vision that maintains that there is a human nature common to all cultures, although cultures determine the form of its expression (Mallon, 2007). Given the socially constructed assumption, the task of structural criminologists is to discover why good social animals commit antisocial acts. If human nature is socially constructed, the presence of criminals reflects defective social practices such as poverty, competitiveness, inequality, and discrimination rather than defective human materials such as impulsiveness or lacking in empathy.

Broadly speaking, structural theorists follow one of two general models of society—the consensus perspective or the conflict perspective. This chapter examines the **consensus perspective** (sometimes known as the functionalist perspective), which views society as a system of mutually sustaining parts and characterized by broad normative consensus. Functionalists often draw analogies with the physical body comprising specialized parts (heart, lungs, brains, kidneys, and so on) that function in unison to keep the whole body healthy. When any one of these parts malfunctions, all the other parts, and thus the whole body, are negatively affected. Likewise, because social institutions are also integrated parts of a larger whole (the social body), a change in any part affects the proper functioning of the entire social system. Anything that threatens that normative consensus is dysfunctional and therefore undesirable. Consensus theorists are aware that conflicts between individuals and groups with different interests occur. However, they believe these conflicts can be patched up by a mostly neutral legal system that all parties are said to respect. The legal system functions as society's "immune system" protecting the other social institutions from harm. Law is said to reflect society's deeply held values and is deemed legitimate by almost all segments of society.

❖ The Chicago School of Ecology

The first criminological theory to be developed in the United States was human ecology, developed at the University of Chicago in the 1920s and 1930s primarily through the works of Clifford Shaw and Henry McKay (1972). The Chicago school borrowed heavily from biological ecology with the intent of "achieving a thorough-going natural science treatment of human behavior" (Hawley, 1944, p. 400). *Ecology* is a biological term describing the interrelationships of plants and animals and their environment, how each affects and is affected by the other. Long-term occupation of a particular ecological niche implies a high level of adaptation to the point that the niche becomes a "natural area" for the organisms occupying it. Sometimes nonnative species may invade these niches and come to dominate them, even driving the former species to extinction. Anyone living in the southeastern United States is familiar with the huge problems caused by an alien plant introduced from Japan called kudzu. Kudzu is a fast-growing weed that outcompetes all native flora by growing around them, blocking their sunlight, siphoning off their moisture, and eventually suffocating them. This biological process of invasion, dominance, and succession, describing the course of occupation of ecological niches by species of plant or animal life previously occupied by other species, was borrowed whole and imported into human ecology.

Human ecology describes the interrelations of human beings and the environments in which they live and views the city as a kind of superorganism with areas differentially adaptive for different ethnic groups (e.g., Little Italy, Chinatown). When natural areas are invaded by alien ethnic groups, large increases in deviant behavior ensue. In their analysis of Cook County Juvenile Court records spanning the years from 1900 to 1933, Shaw and McKay (1972) noted that the majority of delinquents always came from the same neighborhoods. This suggested the existence of natural areas that facilitated crime and delinquency independent of other factors. Their findings also increased confidence among sociologists in their assertion that the environment was more important than ethnic group or individual differences in explaining criminal behavior. It was not claimed that residential areas "caused" crime, but rather that crime was heavily concentrated in certain neighborhoods regardless of the ethnic identities of their residents.

Previous research in **social ecology** characterized the spatial patterns of American U.S. cities as radiating outward from central business and industrial areas in a series of concentric circles, or ecological zones. As shown in Figure 6.1, Zone I was the Loop area of Chicago, and Zone II was the factory zone around which earlier Chicago residents had built their homes but was then inhabited by the poorest residents. This was the so-called **transition zone** where social changes leading to delinquency mostly occurred. This zone was inhabited by native and foreign immigrants because the cheapest rents were there. In response to increasing factory expansion, some Zone II residents invaded Zone III, the zone of working-class homes, making this zone less desirable, and those who could afford to do so moved out. Successive waves of immigrants invaded and occupied these old inner-city neighborhoods, just as they had in the British cities studied by Mayhew and Fletcher in the 1800s, discussed in Chapter 4. This process had a rippling effect, like a stone dropped in a river. Successive waves of newcomers to the poorest neighborhoods precipitate constant movement from zone to zone as more established groups seek to escape the intrusion of the newcomers. Urban decay and crime are consequences of this population movement. Note that delinquency rates decreased linearly from 9.8 incidents per 100 juveniles in the poorest zone (the inner semicircle in Figure 6.1) to 1.8 per 100 in the most affluent zone (the outer semicircle).

❖ Social Disorganization

The decline in crime and delinquency that occurred from the inner city outward was not in itself theoretically significant or useful. What Shaw and McKay needed was a mechanism that explained it. That mechanism was **social disorganization**, by which they meant the breakdown of the power of informal community norms regulating conduct. Social disorganization is created by the continuous redistribution of neighborhood populations, bringing with them a wide variety of cultural traditions sometimes at odds with traditional American middle-class norms of behavior. Neighborhoods invaded by members of alien racial or ethnic groups became rife with conflicting values and conduct norms and lost their sense of community. The movie *Gran Torino*, starring Clint Eastwood, highlights the alienation felt by Eastwood's character as his neighborhood, formerly populated by white working-class families, became populated by Asian immigrants.

Figure 6.1

Zone Map of Male Delinquents in Chicago 1925–1933

Source: Shaw & McKay, 1972, p. 69. Copyright © by the University of Chicago Press. Reproduced with permission. All rights reserved.

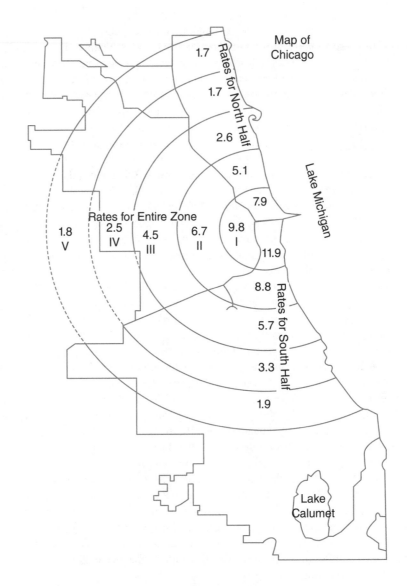

Social disorganization impacts crime and delinquency in two ways. First, the lack of informal social controls within neighborhoods facilitates crime by failing to inhibit it. Second, in the absence of prosocial values, a set of values supporting antisocial behavior is likely to develop to fill the vacuum. Slum youths thus have both negative and positive inducements to crime and delinquency, represented by the absence of social controls and the presence of delinquent values, respectively. These conditions are transmitted across generations until they become intrinsic properties of the neighborhood. Figure 6.2 is a diagrammatic presentation of the theory.

Shaw and McKay worked under the assumption that effective neighborhoods were characterized by warm emotional bonds based on shared ethnicity and values and that social control was born from this shared intimacy. Although rooted in the social disorganization approach, Robert Sampson (2004) updated the notion of neighborhood control of crime without reference to the narrow focus of traditional ethnicity-based emotional ties with his concept of collective efficacy.

Influx of immigrants into cities looking for work and congregating in poorest areas → Value conflicts and decrease in formal and informal social controls lead to **Social Disorganization** → Deterioration of neighborhood and development of delinquent values → **Delinquency and Crime**

Figure 6.2

Diagrammatic Presentation of Social Disorganization Theory

Collective efficacy is the shared power of a group of connected and engaged individuals to influence the maintenance of public order. Modern neighborhoods exercise social control based on shared rational goals using shared expectations that others can be counted on to take action to prevent crime (neighborhood watches, voluntary associations, demand for police services, and so on). As we would expect from individuals bonded by shared interests rather than shared ethnic ties, neighborhood collective efficacy is dynamic and task specific rather than static and generalized. A study by Sampson, Raudenbush, and Earls (1997) surveyed individuals, rather than looking only at census data as Shaw and McKay had, and found that collective efficacy had a positive impact on crime rates in Chicago. We should note the same things that predict the loss of collective efficacy—concentrated poverty, lack of home ownership, rundown buildings, family disruptions, and so on—are the same things that predict social disorganization. These factors accounted for 70% of the variance in collective efficacy among the 343 neighborhood clusters examined. Thus it would seem that like deterrence, collective efficacy works least where it is needed the most.

❖ Evaluation of Social Ecology/Social Disorganization Theory

Shaw and McKay's theory points out that crime is concentrated in socially disorganized areas inhabited by economically deprived people. But causal direction has always been a problem. Are neighborhoods run down and criminogenic because people with personal characteristics conducive to both crime and poverty populate them, or do neighborhoods somehow "cause" crime independent of the characteristics of people living there? After all, when formerly blighted areas become "gentrified" and middle-class people move in, the neighborhood is no longer "criminogenic." Some theorists argue that ecological factors have no independent effect on crime once the human composition of areas is taken into consideration. Others argue the opposite, while still others argue that people and places are equally important in explaining crime.

The "people versus places" argument was best stated by Ruth Kornhauser's (1978) question: "How do we know that area differences in delinquency rates result from the aggregated characteristics of communities rather than the characteristics of individuals selectively aggregated into communities?" (p. 104). In other words, do neighborhoods make people or do people make neighborhoods? Obviously, choices people make are often constrained by factors beyond their power to control, but people must bear some responsibility for the state of their environments. The people versus places issue has been well researched, with the overall conclusion being that neighborhoods do have effects independent of individual differences, although individual differences matter more (Webster, MacDonald, & Simpson, 2006; Wright, 2009).

Related to this issue, Osgood and Chambers's (2003) large study of social disorganization theory in rural settings also traced social disorganization to high population turnover and ethnic diversity but identified high rates of female-headed households as the most important factor in explaining crime rates. The most notable finding of the study was that "a 10 percent increase in female-headed households was associated with a 73- to 100-percent higher rate of arrest for all offenses except homicide [a 10% increase in female-headed households was associated with a 33% increase in homicide]" (Osgood & Chambers, 2003, p. 6). Another study looking at both neighborhood and individual influence on crime (Wikstrom & Loeber, 2000) concluded that neighborhood effects were only related to delinquency for boys who began committing delinquent acts at adolescence and that boys who began prior to adolescence were equally delinquent across all 90 Pittsburgh neighborhoods they studied.

Ecological theory cannot account for why the majority of people in disorganized neighborhoods do not commit serious crimes or why among those who do, a very small minority commits the majority of them. The concept of **ecological fallacy** states that we cannot make inferences about individuals and groups on the basis of information derived from the larger population of which they are a part. Even Shaw and McKay (1972) showed that Asians and Jews living in high-crime areas had very low crime rates. To find high crime rates in a neighborhood with a large Asian population and then to assume that Asians commit crimes at a rate matching the neighborhood rate is an example of the ecological fallacy. Low Asian crime rates in high-crime neighborhoods also suggested that the rejection of group and individual differences as explanations for crime and delinquency was premature.

❖ The Anomie/Strain Tradition

Durkheim's Concept of Anomie

French sociologist Émile Durkheim provided criminology with one of its most revered and enduring concepts: anomie. *Anomie* is a term meaning "lacking in norms." Of course, no society can lack norms and be a society; what is really meant by *anomie* is a breakdown or weakening of existing norms. Norms can be weakened if there are an abundance of contradictory norms, a situation that exists when people with different backgrounds live side by side, as we saw in the discussion of human ecology. Durkheim was greatly concerned with social solidarity and the threat posed to it by social change.

Durkheim distinguished between mechanical and organic solidarity. **Mechanical solidarity** exists in small prestate societies in which individuals share common experiences and circumstances and thus common values and strong emotional ties to the collectivity. This is basically the same idea at the societal level that Shaw and McKay emphasized at the neighborhood level. Under these circumstances informal social controls are strong and antisocial behavior is minimal. **Organic solidarity** is characteristic of modern societies with high degrees of occupational specialization and diversity of experiences and circumstances. This diversity weakens common values and social bonds, and antisocial behavior grows.

Durkheim argued that because crime is found at all times and in all societies, it is a normal and inevitable social phenomenon and even socially useful (functional) in that it serves to identify the limits of acceptable behavior. Too much repression of deviant behavior would lead to a pathological conformity that would stifle creativity, progress, and personal freedom. Crime is one of the prices we pay for personal freedom and for social progress. Durkheim (1982) even asserted that when crime drops significantly below average levels (such as in wartime) it is sign that something is wrong.

Although Durkheim (1982) believed that crime was "a normal phenomenon of normal sociology," he did not imply that the criminal "is an individual normally constituted from the biological and psychological points of view" (pp. 106–107). He also asserted that in any society there are always individuals who "diverge to some extent from the collective type," and among them is the "criminal character" (p. 101). Durkheim thus left room for psychologists and biologists to get into the criminology game.

Durkheim (1951) also set the stage for later extensions of anomie theory by addressing "strains" when he wrote that although human beings are similar in their "essential qualities, one sort of hereditary will always exist, that of natural talent" (p. 251). The crux of the crime problem at the individual level is that "human activity naturally aspires beyond assignable limits and sets itself unattainable goals" (1951, p. 247). When people get less than they expect they are ripe for criminal behavior.

Robert Merton's Extension of Anomie Theory

Robert Merton (1938) expanded anomie theory based on agreement with Durkheim that the inability to attain resources legitimately generates unhappiness (strain) and sometimes leads to efforts to obtain them illegitimately, to develop his **strain theory**. Whereas social disorganization theory assumes that the *rejection* of conventional middle-class values via the intergenerational transmission of deviant values was productive of crime, Merton argued that it was the *acceptance* of middle-class values that generated crime by placing too much emphasis on financial success. The central feature of Merton's theory is that American culture defines monetary success (the "American Dream") as the predominant cultural goal for which all its citizens should aspire while at the same time American social structure restricts access to legitimate means of attaining it to certain segments of the population. The disjunction between cultural goals and the structural impediments to achieving them is the anomic gap in which crime is bred.

There are a number of differences between Durkheim and Merton on the notion of anomie. Durkheim had a constrained naturalistic view of human nature while Merton had a social structuralist view. This difference led Durkheim to see society as the "good guy" preventing the natural greedy impulses of individuals from using criminal means to obtain resources. Merton's unconstrained vision, however, led him to view society (at least, capitalist society) as a negative force that *motivated* such behavior. Rather than anomie being an occasional condition arising

Photo 6.1

Strain theories presume that lower-class citizens envy the rich but, lacking the means to become productive, often turn to crime as an alternative pathway. These brand-new condos were built by tearing down some of the neighboring high-rise slum buildings in Cabrini Green. Police patrol the streets that separate the new housing, unaffordable to the ghetto residents, making sure that the new condos are safe from burglaries or robberies.

in periods of rapid social change as Durkheim saw it, Merton viewed it as a permanent condition of society caused by the disjunction between goals and opportunities. For Merton, crime is woven into the fabric of American society because it arises from **conformity** to American values—a way disadvantaged people get what they have been taught to want—not from deviation from its values due to weakening of social bonds. For Durkheim, the freeing of natural greed, acquisitiveness, egoism, deviance, and crime are *consequences* of anomie; for Merton they are socially constructed traits that are the *causes* of anomie (Passas, 1995).

Merton identified five **modes of adaptation** people adopt in response to this societal pressure, all of which, with the exception of conformity, are deviant.

1. *Conformity* is the most common mode of adaptation because most people have the means of legally attaining cultural goals at their disposal. Conformists accept the success goals of American society and the prescribed means of attaining them (hard work, education, persistence, dedication).

2. *Ritualism* is the adaptation of the nine-to-five slugger who has given up on ever achieving material success but who nevertheless continues to work within legitimate boundaries because he or she accepts the legitimacy of the opportunity structure.

3. *Innovation* is the mode of adaptation most associated with crime. For Merton, crime is an innovative avenue to success—a method by which deprived people (the not-so-deprived also) get what they have been taught by their culture to want.

4. *Retreatism* is adopted by those who reject both the cultural goals and the institutionalized means of attaining them. Retreatists drop out of society and often take refuge in drugs, alcohol, and transience and are frequently in trouble with the law.

5. *Rebellion* is the adaptation of those who reject both the goals and the means of American society but wish to substitute alternative legitimate goals and alternative legitimate means. Rebels may be committed to some alternative political system, such as socialism, which was Merton's preference. The cultural and structural context and the modes of adaptation to it are illustrated diagrammatically in Figure 6.3.

Merton never systematically explored why certain individuals took on one adaptation rather than another. In a sense, his theory of crime is about the envy and resentment his innovators feel about being left out of the American Dream. The power of relative deprivation is often accompanied by negative self-feelings, which in turn may motivate adoption of deviant coping patterns (Stiles, Liu, & Kaplan, 2000). Whatever the route to one adaptation or the other may be, Merton's anomie strain theory has generated a great deal of interest and theoretical extension over the decades.

Institutional Anomie Theory

Institutional anomie theory (IAT) extends anomie theory and claims that "high crime rates are intrinsic to American society: in short, at all social levels *America is organized for crime*" (Messner & Rosenfeld, 2001, p. 5, emphasis added). Messner and Rosenfeld show that inequality in the United States is not an aberration of the American Dream but an expression of it: "A competitive allocation of monetary rewards [that] requires both winners and losers, and winning

Cultural and Structural Context

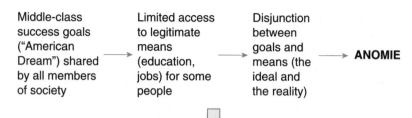

| Middle-class success goals ("American Dream") shared by all members of society | → | Limited access to legitimate means (education, jobs) for some people | → | Disjunction between goals and means (the ideal and the reality) | → | **ANOMIE** |

Figure 6.3

Diagrammatic Presentation of Anomie/Strain Theory

Social-Psychological Response

Individuals adapt to anomie by accepting or rejecting goals and means

GOALS	MEANS	MODE OF ADAPTATION TO ANOMIE
Accepts	Accepts	→ CONFORMITY (nondeviant)
Rejects	Accepts	→ RITUALISM (deviant, noncriminal)
Rejects	Rejects	→ RETREATISM (deviant, probably criminal)
Accepts	Rejects	→ INNOVATION (deviant, criminal)
Rejects	Rejects	→ REBELLION (deviant, substitute new goals and means)

and losing have meaning only when rewards are distributed unequally" (2001, p. 9). From this position a meritocracy (a society in which the greatest rewards go to those who merit them most by virtue of their talents and efforts) is both criminogenic and unfair. Sawhill and Morton (2007) also question the fairness of the American meritocracy when they write, "People are born with different genetic endowments and are raised in different families over which they have no control, raising fundamental questions about the fairness of even a perfectly functioning meritocracy" (p. 4).

IAT posits that the root of the problem is the subjugation of all other social institutions to the economy in the United States. American culture devalues the noneconomic function and roles of other social institutions and obliges them to accommodate themselves to economic requirements. Messner and Rosenfeld claim that a great deal of the focus of the family, religion, education, law, and government is brought to bear on instilling in Americans the beliefs and values of the marketplace to the detriment of the institution-specific beliefs and values they are supposed to inculcate. The dominance of the economy thus disrupts and devalues the prosocial functioning of the other institutions and substitutes an overweening concern for the pursuit of monetary rewards that, in common with Merton, IAT sees as profoundly criminogenic.

Messner and Rosenfeld's plan to reduce crime is called **decommodification**. *Commodification* means the transformation of social relationships formerly untainted by economic considerations into commodities. Thus decommodification refers to policies intended to free social relationships from economic considerations by freeing the other social institutions from the domination of the economy. For instance, few people complain about finding time for their jobs as opposed to finding time for their family, and how many students go to college "to get a job" rather than for the love of learning? Freeing people from economic domination would allow individuals to construct their lives unconstrained by market considerations. According to IAT, this would reduce what they see as cutthroat competition, which in return would reduce crime.

Robert Agnew's General Strain Theory

Robert Agnew has made several attempts to fine-tune and reformulate strain theory, culminating in his **general strain theory**. Agnew identifies several other sources of strain besides the disjunction between expectations and actual achievements. Strain can also result from the removal of positive stimuli (Agnew uses the word *stimuli* to cover both physical and abstract things), such as the loss of a boyfriend or girlfriend or a job. These problems may induce delinquency or crime via efforts to prevent or regain the loss via illegal means or to gain revenge on those deemed responsible for the loss. Strain also arises from the presentation of negative stimuli such as child abuse or neglect and negative school experiences. These can lead to delinquency and crime via efforts to escape negative stimuli by running away from home and truancy.

We all experience multiple strains throughout our lives, but the impact of strain differs according to its magnitude, recency, duration, and clustering (miseries that cluster together produce a whole greater than the sum of its parts and may overwhelm coping resources). Agnew (2002) tells us that strain can result in crime and delinquency through the development of a generally negative attitude about other people: "Repeated or chronic strain may lead to a hostile attitude—a general dislike and suspicion of others and an associated tendency to respond in an aggressive manner" (p. 119). Thus Agnew views crime and delinquency as primarily the result of negative emotions that arise from strains, particularly from negative relationships with others, and not only from Merton's blocked opportunities to financial success. The negative emotion most involved in crime is anger. Agnew asserts that people are most likely to react with anger when they blame their negative situations or relationships on others, and this anger leads to a desire for revenge.

One of the most positive aspects of general strain theory is Broidy and Agnew's (1997) discussion of gender differences in the experiencing of negative emotions. Broidy and Agnew argue that females experience more strain in their lives than males but also commit much less crime, and they want to explore why. They find that males and females are burdened with different concerns and respond differently emotionally to failures to deal with these concerns satisfactorily. Whereas males are more concerned with material success, females are more concerned with maintaining close relationships with others. Unfulfilled male concerns can thus lead to property crimes to fulfill them, but female concerns cannot be fulfilled by crime. Broidy and Agnew also find that while males are more likely to respond to strain with anger, females are more likely to respond with both depression and anger. Unlike male anger, female anger is likely to be accompanied by fear, guilt, and shame, and females are more likely to blame themselves for their anger. Male anger is accompanied by moral outrage and placing the blame on others, and males are less concerned about hurting others. Broidy and Agnew (1997) claim that general strain theory is able to explain a lot about gender differences in criminal behavior.

Although Agnew added much to the understanding of crime from a strain perspective, his greatest contribution is to remind us that the most important factor is not strain per se but *how one copes with it*. Although no one is happy when strained and may curse and throw things, few of us cope with it by committing crimes. How we cope with strain depends on things such as the level of social support we enjoy; the number, frequency, duration, and intensity of the strain-inducing circumstances we face; and what kind of persons we are. According to Agnew (2002), the individual traits that differentiate people who cope poorly with strain and others who cope well include "temperament, intelligence, creativity, problem-solving skills, interpersonal skills, self-efficacy, and self-esteem." He goes on to say that "these traits affect the selection of coping strategies by influencing the individual's sensitivity to objective strains and the ability to engage in cognitive, emotional, and behavioral coping" (p. 123).

Thus crime is more likely when individuals have the personality traits leading them to low tolerance for strain. Among a large sample of youths, Agnew, Brezina, Wright, and Cullen (2002) found that youths with high levels of negative emotionality (the tendency to react to situations with anger and irritation) and low constraint (low self-control) were more likely than other youths to respond to strain with criminal behavior. Of course, these and the other traits Agnew mentions may also be the traits that move people in one or the other of Merton's adaptations—negative and impulsive people are not very likely to achieve legitimate financial success. In adding these traits, Agnew has moved the anomie/strain tradition away from its "pure" sociological origins toward a more interdisciplinary future.

❖ Extending Anomie: Subcultural Theories

A number of Merton's former students took Merton's basic ideas to develop what are known as subcultural theories. Subcultures emerge when a significant number of people feel alienated or are segregated from the larger culture and forge a lifestyle different from the mainstream culture and often at odds with it. Albert Cohen (1955) proposed a subcultural theory explaining how lower-class youths adapt to the limited avenues of success open to them. Cohen maintained that most criminal behavior in lower-class neighborhoods is not a rational method of acquiring financial assets as Merton claimed, but is rather an expression of short-run hedonism. **Short-run hedonism** means the actor is seeking immediate gratification of his or her desires without regard for any long-term consequences, just like the anelpis of cultural criminology discussed in the previous chapter. Much delinquent behavior is nonutilitarian, malicious, and negative and turns middle-class norms of behavior upside down (e.g., destroying rather than creating).

Because lower-class boys cannot adjust to what Cohen calls **middle-class measuring rods**, they experience a status frustration and spawn an oppositional culture with behavioral norms consciously contrary to those of the middle class. Cohen saw criminal subcultures as a kind of mass reaction formation to the problem of blocked opportunities, although he saw **status frustration**, not blocked opportunities, as the real problem. Lower-class youth desire approval and status ("juice," "street cred") like everyone else but seek it via alternate means. To gain status and respect, members of criminal subcultures establish "new norms, new criteria of status which defines as meritorious the characteristics they *do* possess, the kinds of conduct of which they *are* capable" (Cohen, 1955, p. 66, emphasis in original). These status criteria are most often physical, such as being ready and able to respond violently to challenges to one's manhood or gaining a reputation as a "stud."

Another influential extension of strain theory is Cloward and Ohlin's (1960) **opportunity structure theory**. Cloward and Ohlin accepted that delinquents and criminals want middle-class financial success but have little interest in its usual indicators, preferring "big cars," "flashy clothes," and "swell dames" (1960, p. 96). Their biggest contribution, however, was to point out that just as there are barriers to achieving legitimate success, there are barriers to achieving illegitimate (criminal) success—it takes more than talent and motivation to make it within either the legitimate or illegitimate opportunity structures. To obtain illegitimate opportunities, would-be crooks need a friend, relative, or acquaintance who can show them "the ropes." Youths born into an established and organized delinquent subculture—the illegitimate "opportunity structure"—have a career advantage over "wannabe" outsiders. Individuals within an illegitimate opportunity structure join criminal gangs. The best example of this type of gang is organized crime gangs such as the Mafia, which has a pool of aspiring "sponsored" recruits.

Cloward and Ohlin identified two other gang types that develop from the frustration in lower-class culture: conflict gangs and retreatist gangs. Conflict gangs are generated in slum areas with a high degree of transience and instability as opposed to stable areas with an established illegitimate opportunity structure. Members of these loose-knit gangs commit senseless acts of

Photo 6.2

Members of criminal subcultures seek status and respect through alternate means, placing value on the ability to respond violently to challenges and maintain "street cred."

violence and vandalism, and their efforts to make a living from criminal activity tend to be "individualistic, unorganized, petty, poorly paid and unprotected" (Cloward & Ohlin, 1960, p. 73). Retreatist gang members are more "escapist" in their attitudes than conflict gang members in that almost all of them abuse drugs and/or alcohol. In both conflict and retreatist gangs, the concern is not with remote goals but rather with the immediate gratification of present wants.

Walter Miller's Focal Concerns

Walter Miller's theory was based on a very large study sponsored by the National Institute of Health and conducted by Miller and seven trained social workers who maintained daily contact with subjects "for a total time period of about thirteen worker years" (Miller, 1958, p. 6). Miller took issue with the idea that gangs are formed as a *reaction* to status deprivation. Criminals may resent the middle class, but it is not a matter of "If you can't join 'em, lick 'em," because their resentment is born out of envy for what middle-class people have, not for what they are. Middle-class traits such as hard work, stable habits, and responsibility are not appealing to them. Miller asserted that lower-class values must be viewed on their own terms and not as simple negations of those of the middle class. He also identified six interrelated **focal concerns** as part of a value system and lifestyle from the realities of life on the bottom rung of society:

1. *Trouble* is something to stay out of most of the time, but life is trouble and trouble is something that confers status if it is the right kind (being able to handle oneself).

2. *Toughness* is very important to the status of lower-class males: being strong, brave, macho, sexually aggressive, unsentimental, and "not taking any shit."

3. *Smartness* refers to street smarts, the ability to survive on the streets using one's wits.

4. *Excitement* is the search for fun, often defined in terms of fighting, sexual adventurism, gambling, and getting drunk or stoned.

5. *Fate* is a belief that the locus of control is external to oneself.

6. *Autonomy* means personal freedom, being outside the control of authority figures such as teachers, employers, and the police and thus being able to "do my own thing."

The hard-core lower-class lifestyle typified by these focal concerns catches those engaged in it in a web of situations that virtually guarantee delinquent and criminal activities. The search for *excitement* leads to sexual adventures in which little preventative care is taken (*fate*), and the desire for personal freedom (*autonomy*) is likely to preclude marriage if pregnancy results. Miller was concerned that many lower-class males thus grow up in homes lacking a father or any other significant male role model. This leaves them with little supervision and leads them to seek their male identities in what Miller (1958) called "one-sex peer units" (male gangs) (p. 14).

Miller's ideas are given strong support by Elijah Anderson's ethnographic work in African American neighborhoods in Philadelphia (1999). The concentration of disadvantages in such neighborhoods has spawned a hostile oppositional culture spurning most things valued by middle-class America, as in "rap music that encourages its young listeners to kill cops, to rape, and the like" (1999, p. 107). Anderson points out that although there are many "decent" families in these neighborhoods, the cultural ambiance is set by "street" families, which often makes it necessary for decent people to "code switch" (adopt street values) to survive. Striving for education and upward mobility is viewed as "dissing" the neighborhood, and street people do what they can to prevent their "decent counterparts from . . . acting white" (Anderson, 1999, p. 65). The street code is primarily a campaign for respect ("juice") achieved by exaggerated displays of manhood, defined in terms of toughness and sexuality, in a gang context.

THEORY IN ACTION: Anthony and Nathaniel Cook and Oppositional Culture

From early 1979 to September 1981, Anthony and Nathaniel Cook committed a series of racially motivated vicious murders that would make them Toledo, Ohio's, most notorious killers ever. Although it was later learned that Anthony committed his first murder in 1973, the first known murder as a sibling team began after Anthony was released from prison after serving 6 years for armed robbery. In May of 1979, a series of badly beaten bodies were found in culverts, ditches, and car trunks all around Toledo, beginning with the abduction of a courting couple. The male of this couple was shot and killed and his girlfriend was raped and stabbed but survived. The rampage ended when Anthony was arrested for the shooting death of Peter Sawicki. This murder occurred as Anthony was raping Sawicki's daughter after he had shot her boyfriend. Sawicki had heard the shot and his daughter's screams, tried to intervene, and was killed (his daughter escaped and called the police). Cook was sentenced to life for Sawicki's murder and the nonfatal shooting of Sawicki's daughter's boyfriend, but 17 years were to go by before DNA evidence revealed the full extent of the Cook brothers' murderous rampage.

Anthony and Nathaniel Cook were born in Mobile, Alabama, in 1949 and 1958, respectively, when the state was highly racially segregated. The family, which included seven other children, migrated to Toledo, Ohio, but the parents divorced, leaving their unemployed mother to care for their nine children. Anthony became a problem child after the divorce, as did the oldest brother, Hayes Cook II, who was imprisoned for rape. Anthony dropped out of school, soon became streetwise, and was arrested for armed robbery and sent to prison in 1973. Anthony complained that he was ill treated by white guards in prison and often declared that whites were his enemies.

Photo 6.3

Anthony (*right*) and Nathaniel (*left*) Cook at sentencing hearing in 2000.

It was shortly after his release from prison that Anthony and Nathaniel went on their deadly killing spree, which they supposedly dubbed "honky hunting." The most heinous murder committed by them was the kidnapping, torture, rape, and murder of 12-year-old Dawn Backes. Cook was suspected of this murder from the beginning, but the crime was not solved until the district attorney was persuaded to revisit the evidence with new DNA technology in 1998, which identified both Cook brothers as serial killers. The brothers pled guilty to nine murders. Anthony was given additional life sentences and Nathaniel was sentenced to 20 years.

To what theory can we appeal to explain such evil behavior? The Cooks were certainly raised in adverse family circumstances in socially disorganized neighborhoods, but so were millions of other people who never killed anyone, never mind became serial killers. Neither

(Continued)

THEORY IN ACTION (Continued)

can we appeal to anomie in Nathaniel's case since he had a well-paying job as a long-haul truck driver. The murders were clearly racially motivated, so perhaps subcultural opposition to mainstream (white) society animated Anthony, if not Nathaniel, because he never committed another major crime after Anthony was sent away for the Sawicki murder. Despite being in prison for armed robbery, and despite having killed 22-year-old Vickie Lynn Small prior to his imprisonment, Anthony Cook considered himself to be the victim of mistreatment by white guards. He seemed determined to seek revenge for his perceived victimization by engaging in a frenzy of rape and murder of whites.

Discussion Questions

1. Criminological theories seek to offer "rational" explanations for criminal behavior. Is there any rational explanation for the behavior of Anthony Cook found in any of the theories in this chapter or previous chapters?

2. If you had to explain Nathaniel's behavior (who only committed murders at the instigation of his older brother), what, if any, theory in this chapter would suffice?

3. How would you personally account for the Cook brothers' behavior?

Sources: Stiles, 2007, and the *Toledo Blade* (numerous stories on the case, particularly in 2000)

❖ Street Gangs Today

Street gangs have changed and expanded dramatically since the days of the classical studies of Cohen, Cloward and Ohlin, and Miller, but explanations for their formation remain much the same. That is, gangs are spawned in subcultures where mainstream values are spurned (Anderson, 1999). An accepted definition of a gang is "any transpersonal group of youths that shows a willingness to use deadly force to claim and defend territory, attack rival gangs, extort or rob money, or engage in other criminal behavior as an activity associated with its group, and is recognized by itself and its immediate community as a distinct dangerous entity" (Sanders, 1994, p. 20). Figures from the 2012 National Youth Gang Survey (NYGS) estimated that there were 29,900 gangs and 782,500 gang members in 2011 and that approximately half of all homicides in Chicago and Los Angeles in that year were gang related (NYGS, 2012).

Gang membership has increased dramatically since theorists such as Cohen were writing in the 1950s and 1960s. The increase has been largely attributed to the loss of millions of manufacturing jobs in the United States (Moore & Hagedorn, 2001, p. 2), a loss that has hit our most vulnerable citizens, the young and the uneducated, hardest. As cultural criminologist emphasize, the deindustrialization of America set in motion a chain of events creating a large segment of the population that has become economically marginalized and socially isolated from mainstream culture.

Marginalized and isolated people (mainly African Americans and Hispanics) have become known as the "underclass" or the "truly disadvantaged" (Wilson, 1987, p. 8), and the neighborhoods where they live are fertile soil for the growth of gangs. As shown in Figure 6.4, the NYGS (2012) survey of the racial/ethnic composition of gangs found that 46% were Hispanic, 35% black, 11% white, and 7% "other." It is estimated that over 25% of black males aged 15 to 24 in Los Angeles County are members of the nation's two most notorious youth gangs, the Crips and the Bloods (Shelden, Tracy, & Brown, 2001, p. 28).

Why Do Young People Join Gangs?

Irving Spergel (1995) writes that "youths join gangs for many reasons: status, security, money, power, excitement, and/or new experiences" (pp. 108–109). Joining a gang has become a

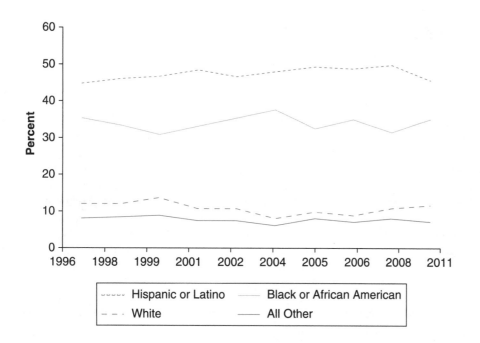

Figure 6.4

Race/Ethnicity of
Gang Members
1996–2011

Source: National Youth
Gang Survey Analysis,
2012

survival imperative in some areas
where unaffiliated youths are likely
to be victimized. Having "homies"
watching your back makes you feel
safe and secure. Gang membership
also provides means of satisfying
belongingness needs—having a
place in the world among people
who care. Gang members often display their belonging through initiation rites, secret gang signals, special
clothing, "colors," and tattoos, all of
which shout out loud: "I belong!" "I'm

Photo 6.4

Crips gang
members in Los
Angeles flash
gang signs.
Gangs claim to
replace the family
cohesiveness the
youth may not
have at home,
while symbols
such as colors
and signs clearly
demarcate
members from
outsiders or rival
gangs.

valued!" A youth camp counselor describes this function of gangs well: "The gang serves emotional needs. You feel wanted. You feel welcome. You feel important. And there is discipline
and there are rules" (Bing, 1991, p. 12).

Social institutions (especially the family and the economy) satisfy most needs for most of us,
but in the virtual absence of the influence of these institutions in the lives of those most affected
by the economic and demographic transitions of the past few decades, the gang offers an attractive substitute means of achieving these needs. Thus the gang functions for many of its members
as family, friendship group, play group, protective agency, educational institution, and employer.

As a structuralist sociologist, Martin Sanchez-Jankowski (2003) would like to focus less on the
psychological rewards of gang membership and more on the relationship between the structure
of society and the structure of gangs. He argues in the tradition of IAT, stating that the competitive
nature of American society requires winners and losers, and gangs are composed of society's losers.
Sanchez-Jankowski also sees gang members in Mertonian fashion as accepting the economic principles of America and seeking economic success within the confines of the limited opportunities
they perceive as being available to them.

❖ Evaluation of the Anomie/Strain and Subcultural Tradition

The anomie-strain tradition has had a large impact on theory generation in criminology. Because of the emphasis on monetary success in the United States, Merton's theory should best explain rational crimes netting perpetrators monetary gain. For instance, Bartol and Bartol (1989) claim that anomie theory's strength lies in its "ability to explain why utilitarian crimes rates are so high in one society (e.g., the United States) and so low in another (e.g., England)" (p. 110). Ever since the mid-1980s, however, England has had higher rates of utilitarian crimes (e.g., burglary, auto theft) than the United States (Kesteren, Mayhew, & Nieuwbeerta, 2000). It is nonutilitarian crimes such as murder, rape, and assault that are more common in the United States than in England, which supports Cohen's contention that much of American lower-class crime is emotionally driven, nonutilitarian, and malicious rather than rationally instrumental.

Agnew (1997) points out a potentially fatal flaw in Merton's anomie/strain theory. A strict interpretation of it should lead us to predict a sharp increase in criminal behavior in late adolescence/early adulthood when many such individuals begin to seriously enter the job market. If there is a disjunction between cultural goals and structural impediments to achieving them, a number of young adults entering the job market will feel its bite for the first time and respond with one of Merton's deviant adaptations. However, just when the alleged cause of criminal behavior becomes most salient for young people, we observe a significant decrease in antisocial behavior among them rather than an increase (see the discussion of the age-crime curve in Chapter 11).

Another flaw is that Merton never attempts to explain what it is that sorts individuals into his modes of adaptation beyond citing class-based socialization practices. In other words, he is basically saying that social class causes social class, and social class determines the mode of adaptation. Agnew's general strain theory has attempted to account for the mode adopted by pointing to personality traits that help individuals to deal with strain—which is something we all experience in our lives—constructively rather than destructively, which may also sort people into different social classes (Wright, 2009).

IAT's claim that the United States' strong emphasis on competitive meritocracy makes it more anomic than other developed societies is not supported by the available evidence. Using data from the 1981 and 1991 World Values Survey, a massive annual undertaking covering 70% of the world's population, Cao (2000) found that the United States was well below the total average anomie score of all countries. It was also found that the anomie scores of all eastern European countries (with economies directly opposite of capitalism until the 1990s), and several other capitalist countries (e.g., Canada, Britain, France, Germany, Spain), also had higher scores. While one might quibble about the measure of anomie used, the available evidence does not support the contention that the American economic system generates high levels of anomie, which in turn drives the American crime rate.

The subcultural theories look at patterned ways of life in areas whose members set themselves apart and pride themselves in their distinctiveness. It is this patterned way of life that sustains delinquent values and goals. However, a number of theorists have cast doubt as to whether there are distinct lower-class subcultures in this sense. It is difficult to imagine that lower-class subcultures arose by consciously taking steps to turn middle-class norms on their head, as Cohen's reaction formation hypothesis supposes. Yet there are areas in our cities in which middle-class values are disdained, not because they are defined as middle class, but rather because they demand self-control, delayed gratification, and the disciplined application of effort (Anderson, 1999).

Miller's work was criticized by Tittle (1983), who asked if the middle and upper classes embrace values opposite those of the lower class: Do they "value weakness, stupidity, boredom, and dependency?" (p. 341). This is a strange criticism because Miller (1958) explicitly states that these concerns are not confined to the lower classes; it is their meaning and the ways they are expressed "that differs both in rank order and weighting" (p. 6). Presumably we all understand that toughness, excitement, smartness, and autonomy mean vastly different things to middle- and lower-class individuals.

As we have seen, Elijah Anderson supports Cohen and Miller in his contention that the street code is primarily a campaign for respect ("juice") achieved by exaggerated displays of manhood, defined in terms of toughness and sexuality. These displays contribute greatly to the high rates of violence and out-of-wedlock births in the kinds of neighborhoods Anderson (and Cohen and Miller before him) describes. If these theorists are correct about the role of fate in lower-class life, then the whole anomie/strain argument about blocked opportunities may be off-base. If lower-class individuals perceive their opportunities in a fatalistic "live-for-the-moment" way, or spurn them as antithetical to the street code, their visions of reality and the values imparted by their subculture are blocking their legitimate success. Of course, one might argue that fatalism is generated by perceived blocked opportunities as well.

The anomie/strain tradition does not link crime straightforwardly to poverty but sees it having criminogenic effects only when coupled with a competitive culture that ties self-worth to monetary success. This leads us to a major issue in criminology: Does poverty cause crime or does crime cause poverty? Prominent criminologist Robert Sampson (2000) notes that "everyone believes that 'poverty causes crime' it seems; in fact, I have heard many a senior sociologist express frustration as to why criminologists would waste time with theories outside the poverty paradigm. The reason we do . . . is that the facts demand it" (p. 711). Frank Schmalleger (2004) also notes that the underlying assumption of all structural theories is that the "root causes" of crime are poverty and various social injustices. But as he also notes, "Some now argue the inverse of the 'root causes' argument, saying that poverty and what appear to be social injustices are produced by crime, rather than the other way around" (p. 223). This is an extremely important question, the answer to which points to opposite policy implications. Of course, neither may cause the other because some third set of variables may cause both crime and poverty.

❖ Policy and Prevention: Implications of Social Structural Theories

If social disorganized slum neighborhoods are the "root cause" of crime, what feasible policy strategies might be recommended to public policymakers? One of the first things you might want to suggest would be the strengthening of community life, but how do we go about it? Clifford Shaw began by securing funds for the **Chicago Area Project** (CAP), which consisted of a number of programs aimed at generating or strengthening a sense of community in neighborhoods with the help and cooperation of schools, churches, recreational clubs, trade unions, and businesses. Athletic leagues, various kinds of clubs, summer camps, and many other activities were formed to busy the idle hands of the young. "Street corner" counselors were hired to offer advice to youths and to mediate with the police on their behalf when they got into trouble. Neighborhood residents were encouraged to form committees to resolve neighborhood problems.

Despite the money and energy invested in CAP from 1932 to 1957, its effects were never evaluated in any systematic way. Similar programs in other cities had a number of positive outcomes, but their impact on crime and delinquency rates was negligible. Writing about the overall impact of CAP-type programs, Rosenbaum, Lurigio, and Davis (1998) concluded that there were "few positive program effects. The local programs did not affect official crime rates and in some cases were associated with adverse change in survey-based victimization rates" (p. 214).

Table 6.1

Summarizing Social Structural Theories

Theory	Key Concepts	Strengths	Weaknesses
Social Ecology/Social Disorganization	Poverty concentrates people of different cultural backgrounds and generates cultural conflict. The breakdown of informal social controls leads to social disorganization, and peer group gangs replace social institutions as socializers.	Explains high crime rates in certain areas. Accounts for intergenerational transmission of deviant values and predicts crime rates from neighborhood characteristics.	Cannot account for individuals and groups in the same neighborhood who are crime free or why a few individuals commit a highly disproportionate share of crime.
Anomie (Durkheim)	Rapid social change leads to social deregulation and the weakening of restraining social norms. This unleashes "insatiable appetites," which some seek to satisfy through criminal activity.	Emphasizes the power of norms and social solidarity to restrain crime and points to situations that weaken them.	Concentrates on whole societies and ignores differences in areas that are differentially affected by social deregulation.
Anomie/Strain (Merton)	All members of American society are socialized to want to attain monetary success, but some are denied access to legitimate means of attaining it. These people may then resort to crime to achieve what they have been taught to want.	Explains high crime rates among the disadvantaged and how cultural norms create conflict and crime. Explains various means of adapting to strain.	Does not explain why individuals similarly affected by strain do not react (adapt) similarly.
Institutional Anomie	America is literally organized for crime due to its overweening emphasis on the economy and material success. All other institutions are devalued and must accommodate themselves to the requirements of the economy.	Explains why crime rates are higher in America than in other capitalist societies. Points to decommodification as crime reduction strategy.	Concentrates on a single cause of crime. Should predict high rates of property crime in America rather than violent crime, but the opposite is true.
General Strain	There are multiple sources of strain, and strain differs along numerous dimensions. Strain is the result of negative emotions that arise from negative relationships with others and sociocultural forces. Individual characteristics help us to cope poorly or well with strain.	Reminds us that strain is multifaceted and that how we cope with it is more important than its existence. Adds individual traits and characteristics to the theory.	Criticized by structural theorists as reductionist for its emphasis on individual traits and because it fails to explore the structural origins of strain.
Subcultural Theories	Much delinquency is short-run hedonism rather than utilitarian. Lower-class youths cannot live up to middle-class measuring rods and thus develop status frustration. They seek status in ways peculiar to the subculture. Subcultural youths do not have equal illegitimate opportunities for attaining success. Those who have such opportunities join criminal gangs; those who don't join retreatist and conflict gangs and engage in mindless violence and vandalism.	Extends the scope of anomie theory and integrates social disorganization theory. Focuses on processes by which lower-class youths adapt to their disadvantages and shows that illegitimate opportunities are also denied to some. Explains the patterned way of life that sustains delinquent values and goals.	Explains subcultural crime and delinquency only. There is some question as to whether a distinct lower-class culture exists in the sense that it is supported by proscriptive values that require antisocial behavior.

The ideas of anomie/strain theory had tremendous impact on public policy via President Lyndon Johnson's War on Poverty. The reasoning was that since crime is perceived as an activity engaged in mostly by the poor, fewer poor people would mean fewer crimes. The poverty rate fell, but the expected bonus of crime reduction did not materialize. As many billions of tax dollars were spent on antipoverty programs during the three decades separating 1963 and 1993, crime rates soared. Specifically, as the poverty rate in the United States *decreased* by about 23%, we saw an overall *increase* in the crime rate of approximately 350% (Walsh & Ellis, 2007).

If crime is caused by a disjunction between cultural values emphasizing success for all and a social structure denying access to legitimate means of achieving it to some, rather than poverty per se, then the cure for crime is to increase opportunities or dampen aspirations. The latter option is not unacceptable to policymakers of either the right or the left, so we are left with the task of trying to increase opportunities. Following in the footsteps of CAP, Richard Cloward and Lloyd Ohlin developed a delinquency prevention project known as Mobilization for Youth (MFY), which concentrated on expanding legitimate opportunities for disadvantaged youths via a number of educational, training, and job placement programs. MFY programs received generous private, state, and federal funds and served as models for such federal programs as Head Start, the job corps, the Comprehensive Employment and Training Act (CETA), affirmative action, and many others (LaFree, Drass, & O'Day, 1992).

Some unknown number of people were diverted from a life of crime because of the opportunities presented to them by such programs, but unfortunately their heyday occurred at the same time the United States was undergoing a huge jump in crime from 1965 to 1980. This unfortunate convergence provided conservatives and neoclassical criminologists with arguments against the use of social welfare policies to combat crime and toward the kinds of crime control mechanisms addressed in Chapter 5.

The policy recommendation of institutional anomie theory would be to tame the power of the market via decommodification. For instance, the decision to have children could be freed from economic considerations by granting government-guaranteed maternity leave benefits and family allowances/income support, and higher education could be accessible to all people with talent without regard for the financial ability to pay. In other words, policies that ensure an adequate level of material well-being that is not so completely dependent on an individual's performance in the marketplace.

If this sounds too socialistic, you may be surprised to learn that many items on the 1928 economic platform of the American Socialist Party have been adopted in the United States. These items include a 40-hour workweek, unemployment benefits, social security, public works, legal trade unions, child labor laws, and government unemployment offices. Other reforms predating 1928, such as a graduated income tax, free education for all children, and the abolition of child labor, have been so integrated into American life that few today would call them "socialist" or "un-American," although they all have their origins in left-wing thought (Walsh, 2009).

Any policy recommendations derived from subcultural theories would not differ from those derived from ecological or anomie/strain theories. Changing a subculture is extremely difficult. Insofar as a subculture is a patterned way of life, we cannot attack the problem in parts and expect to change the whole. One possible strategy would be to disperse "problem families" throughout a city rather than concentrating them in block-type projects as is typically done. But even if this was politically feasible, rather than breaking up the subculture and its values, it may result in its displaced carriers "infecting" areas previously insulated from deviant values.

The gang problem offers obvious policy recommendations in theory, such as increasing low-skill work opportunities by somehow convincing American companies from moving them overseas and by strengthening the other social institutions for which gangs are a substitute. Gangs will always be a problem while legitimate social institutions in our poorest areas are too weak to provide young people with their basic needs.

Summary

- Social structural theories focus on social forces that influence people to commit criminal acts. Ecological theory emphasizes that "deviant places" can cause delinquent and criminal behavior regardless of the personal characteristics of individuals residing there. Such areas are characterized by social disorganization, which results from diverse cultural traditions within slum areas.

- One of the most interesting early findings of this perspective is that the same slum areas continued to have the highest crime rates in a city regardless of the ethnic or racial composition of its inhabitants. More recent ecological studies find that neighborhoods do have effects independent of the people who live in them, but most effects are mediated by individual differences.

- Collective efficacy is the opposite of social disorganization but does not focus on emotional bonds tied to ethnicity. The concept is about a neighborhood's ability to mobilize its residents as an effective force to fight problems, including crime.

- Anomie/strain theories focus on the strain generated by society's emphasis on success goals coupled with its denial of access to some to legitimate opportunities to achieve success. Merton's strain theory focuses on the ways people adapt to this situation via conformity, ritualism, retreatism, rebellion, and innovation (the modes of adaptation). Although the latter four modes are "deviant," they are not all criminal. The innovator and the retreatist modes are considered the most criminal.

- Institutional anomie theory argues that the United States is literally organized for crime because the institutional balance of power strongly favors the economy. All other American institutions are subordinate to our highly competitive economy, and the competition would be meaningless if there were not both winners and losers.

- General strain theory argues that there are many other sources of strain besides Merton's disjunction between goals and means. These strains result in negative emotions that adversely affect relationships with others and may lead to crime. The important thing is not strain, however, but how people cope with it. Among the many attributes Agnew lists as coping resources are temperament, intelligence, and self-esteem.

- Subcultural strain theories have slightly different emphases. Albert Cohen noted that lower-class boys, knowing they cannot live up to the middle-class measuring rods, form oppositional gangs that perpetuate an oppositional subculture. These gangs usually reject both the goals and the means of middle-class society, as gauged by the malicious and nonutilitarian nature of many of their crimes.

- Walter Miller augments Cohen's assertion that lower-class culture is oppositional to middle-class culture with his theory of focal concerns. Focal concerns—trouble, toughness, smartness, excitement, fate, and autonomy—are behavioral norms of lower-class culture that command strong emotional attention. Miller's thesis is supported by later work done by Elijah Anderson.

- Cloward and Ohlin emphasize that people have differential access to illegitimate, as well as legitimate, means to success and that sociological and psychological factors limit a person's access to both.

- Youth gangs have been noted throughout recorded history. The prevalence of gangs in the United States is greater than ever before and has been attributable to the deindustrialization of America. Deindustrialization has affected minorities the most and has tended to leave a sizable number of them marginalized from mainstream society and living in disorganized neighborhoods. The gang becomes an attractive option to many of these youths because it offers them many of the things the ineffective social institutions in those neighborhoods do not.

Exercises and Discussion Questions

1. What is your position on "kinds of people versus kinds of places" argument in ecological theory? Do places matter independent of the people living in them? If they both matter, which do you think matters more?

2. Is the American stress on material success good or bad overall? Is greed "good"? Does it drive the economy? Would we be better off psychologically with less?

3. Are lower-class delinquents reacting against middle-class values as Cohen contends, or is there a lower-class culture with its own set of values and attitudes to which delinquents are conforming, as Miller contends?

4. Go to the latest version of the UCR and determine the 10 cities with the highest crime rates. Then use any Internet search engine and determine the average income and unemployment rates of those cities. Is there a pattern?

5. Debate whether poverty causes crime, crime causes poverty, or something else causes both poverty and crime.

Useful Websites

Chicago Area Project. www.chicagoareaproject.org.
The Chicago school of ecology. www.csiss.org/classics/content/26.
Émile Durkheim. www.emile-durkheim.com.

General strain theory. www.criminology.fsu.edu/crimtheory/agnew.htm.
Youth gangs. www.ncjrs.gov/pdffiles/167249.pdf.

Chapter Terms

Anomie

Chicago Area Project

Collective efficacy

Conformity

Consensus or functionalist perspective

Decommodification

Ecological fallacy

Focal concerns

General strain theory

Human ecology

Institutional anomie theory

Mechanical solidarity

Middle-class measuring rods

Modes of adaptation

Opportunity structure theory

Organic solidarity

Short-run hedonism

Social disorganization

Social ecology

Social structure

Status frustration

Strain theory

Transition zone

CHAPTER 7

Social Process Theories

The social structural theories discussed in the previous chapter only explain part of the possible reason that Kody Scott chose the path in life he did. Not all who experience the same conditions turn out the same way; indeed, only one of Kody's brothers ran afoul of the law. The social process theories discussed in this chapter take us a step further in understanding Kody's choices. Two of the theories in this chapter tell us that criminal behavior is learned in association with peers and that we choose to repeat behaviors that are rewarding to us. After he shot and killed the Blood gang members in his initiation, Kody tells us that he lay in bed that night feeling guilty and ashamed of his actions and that he knew they were wrong. Nevertheless, when the time came to do the same thing again, he chose to do what his peers told him to do because he valued their praise and approval more than anything else in life. His fellow Crips also provided him with rationales and justifications for his actions that neutralized his guilt.

On a personal level, he plainly lacked self-control; he was impulsive, hedonistic, and angry. Theorists in this chapter tell us that self-control is developed by consistent parental monitoring, supervision, and discipline, but his weary single mother lacked the time, resources, or incentive to provide Kody with proper parenting. From the youngest age, he came and went as he pleased. His autobiography makes it plain that he was something of a "feral child," big enough, mean enough, and guiltless enough to be free to satisfy any and all urges as they arose. This chapter details many of the social processes by which Kody came to be the monster he claims himself to be.

LEARNING OBJECTIVES

- Understand the basic premise of social process theories and how they differ from that of social structural theories
- Understand differential association theory and the criticisms surrounding it
- Know how social learning theory improved differential association theory
- Understand the fundamental differences in terms of Sowell's visions between social learning and social- and self-control theories.
- Understand how labeling and neutralizing theory lead to different policy recommendations

❖ The Social Process Tradition

Social process criminologists operate from a sociological perspective known as **symbolic interactionism**. Symbolic interactionists focus on how people interpret and define their social reality and the meanings they attach to it in the process of interacting with one another via language (symbols). Social process theorists believe that if we wish to understand social behavior we have to understand how individuals subjectively perceive their social reality and how they interact with others to create, sustain, and change it. The perspective is summed up in the Thomas theorem: "If men [and women] define situations as real, they are real in their consequences" (in Nettler, 1978, p. 272). The processes most stressed are socialization and cultural conflict; that is, social process theorists seek to describe criminal and delinquent socialization (how antisocial attitudes and behavior are learned) and how social conflict "pressures" individuals into committing antisocial acts. Some process theories focus on the reverse process of learning prosocial attitudes and behavior in the face of temptations to do otherwise. All social process theories represent the joining of sociology and psychology to varying extents.

❖ Differential Association Theory

Differential association theory (DAT) is the brainchild of Edwin Sutherland, whose ambition was to devise a theory that could explain both individual criminality and aggregate crime rates by identifying conditions that must be present for crime to occur and that are absent when crime is absent. In common with social ecologists, Sutherland stressed that where people grow up—the social context in which they are embedded—matters greatly to the patterns of behavior they exhibit. His theory attempted to provide mechanisms by which factors such as social disorganization led to crime. Like Walter Miller in his focal concerns theory, Sutherland saw lower-class culture as having its own integrity, and he disdained the phrase *social disorganization* as insulting, substituting *differential social organization*. Although Sutherland explicitly denied the role of psychology in crime and delinquency, his theory is implicitly (some would say explicitly) psychological in that it focuses on the process of becoming delinquent via subjective social definitions of reality and attitude formation. He laid out his theory in the form of the following nine propositions:

1. Criminal behavior is learned.

2. Criminal behavior is learned in interaction with other persons in a process of communication.

3. The principal part of the learning of criminal behavior occurs within intimate personal groups.

4. When criminal behavior is learned, the learning includes techniques of committing the crime, which are sometimes very complicated and sometimes simple and the specific direction of motives, drives, rationalizations, and attitudes.

5. The specific direction of motives and drives is learned from definitions of the legal codes as favorable or unfavorable.

6. A person becomes delinquent because of an excess of definitions favorable to violation of law over definitions unfavorable to violation of the law.

7. Differential associations may vary in frequency, duration, priority, and intensity.

8. The process of learning criminal behavior by association with criminal and non-criminal patterns involves all of the mechanisms in any other learning.

9. While criminal behavior is an expression of general needs and values, it is not explained by those needs and values, since noncriminal behavior is an expression of the same needs and values. (Sutherland & Cressey, 1974, p. 75)

Photo 7.1

A young boy imitates the gang signs of an older gang member, emphasizing the differential association theory that criminal behavior is learned by intimate social groups.

These nine propositions outline the process by which individuals come to acquire attitudes favorable to criminal behavior, which may be summarized by saying that criminal behavior is learned in intimate social groups. By emphasizing social learning, DAT wants to guide criminologists away from the notion that criminal behavior is the result of biological or psychological abnormalities or invented anew by each criminal. According to DAT, criminality is not the result of individual traits, nor learned from impersonal communication from movies or magazines and the like. The learning of criminal behavior involves the same culturally transmitted mechanisms involved in any other learning and includes specific skills and techniques for committing crimes, as well as the motives, rationalizations, justifications, and attitudes of criminals.

The theory asserts that humans, like chameleons, take on the hues and colors of their environments, blending in and conforming with natural ease. Most Americans probably like baseball, hot dogs, apple pie, and Chevrolets, as a Chevrolet commercial used to remind us. But do we prefer these things over, say, soccer, bratwurst, strudel, and Volkswagens because the former are demonstrably superior to the latter or simply because we are Americans and not Germans? We view the world differentially according to the attitudes, beliefs, and expectations of the groups around which our lives revolve; it could hardly be otherwise, particularly in our formative years. Sutherland's basic premise is that delinquent behavior is learned just as readily as we learn to play the games, enjoy the food, and drive the cars that are integral parts of our cultural lives.

The key proposition in DAT is Number 6: "A person becomes delinquent because of an excess of definitions favorable to violations of law over definitions unfavorable to violations of law" (Sutherland & Cressey, 1974, p. 75). Learning criminal conduct is a process of modeling the self after and identifying with individuals we respect and value. **Definitions** refer to the meanings our experiences have for us, how we see things, our attitudes, values, and habitual ways of viewing the world.

Definitions become favorable to law violation according to the frequency, duration, priority, and intensity of exposure to them. That is, the earlier we are exposed to criminal definitions, the more often we are exposed to them, the longer they last, and the more strongly we are attached to those who supply us with them, the more likely we are to commit criminal acts when opportunities to do so arise. As we have already seen, antisocial definitions are more likely to be learned in lower-class neighborhoods. In such neighborhoods children are surrounded by antisocial definitions (the code of the streets, focal concerns) and cannot help being influenced by them regardless of their individual characteristics. Figure 7.1 illustrates the process of differential association theory from its origins in lower-class areas, to the process of learning definitions favorable to law violation, and finally to crime and delinquency.

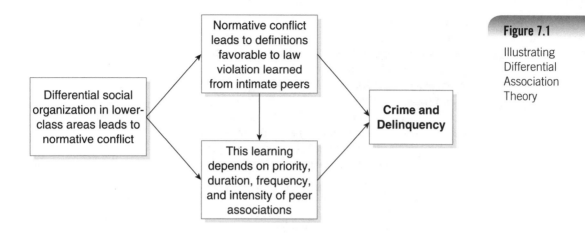

Figure 7.1

Illustrating
Differential
Association
Theory

Evaluation of Differential Association Theory

DAT is in the unconstrained vision camp in that it assumes that antisocial behavior is learned, not something that comes naturally in the absence of prosocial training. As one early critic of DAT (no doubt a constrained visionary) asked, "What is there to be learned about simple lying, taking things that belong to another, fighting and sex play?" (Glueck, 1956, p. 94). Individuals certainly learn to get better at doing these things in their associations with other like-minded individuals, but do they have to be taught them, or do they have to be taught how to curb them? What constitutes moral behavior, and how to consider the rights and feelings of others?

DAT is also criticized for ignoring individual differences in the propensity to associate with antisocial peers. Individual traits do sort people in different relationship patterns—as numerous studies of relationship patterns attest (Rodkin, Farmer, Pearl, & Van Acker, 2000). Differential association may thus be a case of birds of a feather flocking together rather than of innocents joining a flock and then changing their feathers. In this scenario, their flocking facilitates and accentuates their activities but does not "cause" them. Reviews typically find that delinquent behavior *precedes* gang membership and that association with other delinquents simply speeds up and enhances delinquency among the predisposed rather than acting as a stimulator of uncharacteristic behavior among the innocent. As Gottfredson (2006) summarized a number of studies addressing this issue, "The evidence is consistent with the proposition that much of the variance in peer effects on delinquency is attributable to the selection effect of like individuals associating together" (p. 92).

Despite his later rejection of individual differences, Sutherland recognized that they affect relationship patterns in his 1939 statement: "Individual differences among people in respect to personal characteristics or social situations cause crime only as they affect differential association or frequency and consistency of contacts with criminal patterns" (1939, p. 8). Sutherland was specifying a path in which differential association clearly *intervenes* between individual differences and crime as follows:

Individual differences → Contact with criminal patterns → Crime.

In defense of DAT, the concept of differential social organization accounts for the associations people have. Children associate, play, and become friendly with individuals in the neighborhoods their parents provide. In certain neighborhoods, delinquent peers may indeed "cause" delinquency among youths who are otherwise insulated from it, as well as facilitate and accelerate it among others attracted to it. The causal order criticism may be valid for children growing up in better neighborhoods with equal access to both pro- and antisocial peers, but not for kids growing up in the urban slums where prosocial peers are rare. Ronald Akers (1999) responded to the "birds of a feather" adage with the equally pithy reply: "If you lie down with dogs you get up with fleas" (p. 480).

Mark Warr (2002) criticizes DAT for having a singular vision of peer influence. Warr makes a distinction between two approaches to the influence of delinquent peers—private acceptance and compliance. Compliance is "going through the motions" of delinquent activity without privately accepting the appropriateness of what one is doing. Private acceptance refers to both the public and private acceptance of the attitudes, values, and behavior of the delinquent group, and so once a delinquent career is initiated the person will continue offending across the life span. Warr (2002) says DAT was formulated only with private acceptance in mind while ignoring the idea of compliance. We know that the great majority of delinquents limit their offending to adolescence (are temporary compliers) and do not become adult criminals (Caspi & Moffit, 1995).

❖ Social Learning Theory

As we saw in Table 1.1 in Chapter 1, social learning theory, associated primarily with Ronald Akers, was the theory most frequently chosen by criminologists surveyed in 2007 as that which best explains variance in criminal behavior (50 out of 379, or 13.2% chose it). Akers's **social learning theory** (SLT) goes beyond looking solely at learned "definitions favorable" to getting involved in delinquency to look at mechanisms that lead individuals to either continue or desist from it. Akers and his colleague Robert Burgess (1966) applied the powerful concepts of operant psychology to this issue and claimed it was the differential reinforcement of behavior that either amplified of extinguished criminal behavior. **Differential reinforcement** is defined as "the balance of anticipated or actual rewards and punishments that follow or are consequences of behavior" (Akers, 2009, p. 67).

While psychological principles are central to SLT, Akers (2002) insists that it is in the same sociological tradition of DAT and that it retains all the processes found in Sutherland's theory, albeit modified and clarified. The difference is that for some the processes move in prosocial directions and for others in antisocial directions. Rarely is this an all-or-nothing process; rather, the direction the process takes reflects a balance of influences, which can fluctuate over time. Rather than focusing solely on differential association as a mechanism to explain a person's social behavior, SLT theory focuses on four: (1) differential association, (2) differential reinforcement, (3) imitation, and (4) definitions. The debt to DAT can be seen in these four principles said to affect the individual's probability of committing law violations. Law violation will happen when

1. He or she differentially associates with others who commit, model, and support violations of social and legal norms (differential association).

2. The violative behavior is differentially reinforced over behavior in conformity to the norm (differential reinforcement).

3. He or she is more exposed to and observes more deviant than conforming models (imitation).

4. His or her own learned definitions are favorable toward committing the deviant acts (excess of definitions). (Akers, 1998, p. 51)

The most important of these four principles is differential reinforcement, which is based on the principles of operant psychology. **Operant psychology** is a theory of learning asserting that behavior is governed by its consequences. When we behave we "operate" on the environment and generate consequences in the form of feedback from others that we interpret in terms of the positive or negative consequences it has for us. Behavior has two general consequences: it is reinforced or it is punished. The most effective reinforcements and punishments are social and derived primarily from one's intimate social groups. Behavior that has positive consequences for the actor is said to reinforce that behavior, making it more likely the behavior will be repeated in similar situations. Behavior that is punished is less likely to be repeated and may even be extinguished (see Figure 7.2).

Reinforcement is either positive or negative. The loot from a robbery or status achieved by facing down rivals is an example of positive reinforcement. Negative reinforcement occurs when some aversive condition is avoided or removed, such as the removal of a street reputation as a "punk" following some act of bravado. Both examples strengthen criminal behavior and thus result in its amplification.

Reinforcement Increases a Behavior	Punishment Decreases a Behavior
Positive Reinforcement (something rewarding received)	**Positive Punishment** (something punishing applied)
Negative Reinforcement (something punishing avoided)	**Negative Punishment** (something rewarding lost)

Figure 7.2

Illustrating Types of Reinforcement and Punishment

Punishment, which leads to the weakening or eliminating of the behavior preceding it, can also be positive or negative. Positive punishment is the application of something undesirable, such as a prison term. Negative punishment is the removal of a pleasant stimulus, such as the loss of status in a street gang. The acquisition of Sutherland's "definitions favorable" to antisocial behavior (or prosocial behavior, for that matter) thus depends on each individual's history of reinforcement and punishment.

In any peer group each member has reciprocal effects on every other member via his or her participation in the reinforcement/punishment process. Of course, what is reinforcing for some may be punishing for others. For teens who value the approval of their parents and teachers, an arrest is punishment. For teens who value the approval of antisocial peers, such an outcome is a reinforcer since it marks them officially as a "bad ass." The social context is thus an extremely important component of SLT because most learning takes place in the presence of others who provide both the social context and the available reinforcers or punishments.

Photo 7.2

Discriminative stimuli, such as this purse in an unlocked car, are present before a crime takes place and signal reward to the potential perpetrator.

Discrimination is another important component of SLT. Whereas reinforcements or punishments *follow* behavior, discriminative stimuli are present *before* the behavior occurs and helps to determine it. Discriminative stimuli are signals or clues transmitted by others indicating the kinds of behaviors that will be rewarded or punished in a particular social context. Consider the different social signals presented to a person stopped in the street by a little girl, a clergyman, a Hell's Angel, a police officer, an aggressive wino, or the person's mother, and then consider his or her possible responses. The person's response will represent what he or she has previously learned (personally or vicariously) about those people or others like them. In other words, discrimination involves learning to distinguish between stimuli that have been reinforced or punished in the past with similar stimuli you expect will result in the same response in the future. For instance, an unlocked car with the keys in it (a suitable target lacking a capable guardian) is a discriminative stimulus that signals "immediate reward" for the criminal, but for the average person it probably signals nothing other than how foolish the owner is.

Evaluation of Social Learning Theory

Many of the same criticisms applicable to DAT are also applicable to SLT and won't be repeated. SLT adds some meat to DAT by specifying how definitions favorable to law violation are learned by operant conditioning, although it neglects the role of individual differences in the ease or difficulty with which persons learn. Some people find general hell-raising more exciting (and thus more reinforcing) than others. Some people are more susceptible to short-term rewards because they are especially impulsive, and some are better able to appreciate the long-term rewards of behaving well.

In other words, all complex behavior is social learning, so it does not help much to say that crime is socially learned. What we really need to know is why some people are inclined to learn one thing and other people other things and what makes them successful or failures in their learning endeavors. Thus, Cao (2004) says that in common with DAT, SLT assumes "a passive and unintentional actor who lacks individuality . . . and [is] better at explaining the transmission of criminal behavior than its origins." Because of their "limited conception of human nature, learning theories generally also ignore the differential receptivity of individuals to criminal messages" (p. 97). In other words, some individuals are more ready to engage in aggressive behavior than others because of the nature of their personalities and will find such behavior is reinforced in delinquent areas. As criminologist Gwynn Nettler (1984) so well put it, "Constitutions affect the impact of environment. What we learn and how well we learn it depends on constitution. . . . The fire that melts the butter hardens the egg" (p. 295).

In response to criticism that SLT neglects individual differences, Akers (1999) disagrees: "An individual in a low crime group or category who is nevertheless more exposed to criminal associations, models, definitions, and reinforcement than someone in a high crime group or category will have a higher probability of committing criminal or deviant acts" (p. 482). But this is an explanation in terms of different *environments*, not in terms of different *individuals*. As if to vindicate Cao's (2004) observation, it assumes automaton-like individuals entering different environments at one end and emerging out the other as criminal or not criminal based solely on their exposure to different environments, and what they bring with them to the environment is ignored.

❖ The Social Control Tradition

Social control theories do a 180-degree turn from social learning theories. According to Franklin, Gau, and Pratt (2010), scholars from the "control" and "learning" camps vehemently disagree with one another on a number of issues relating to crime and criminals. Looking back to Chapter 1 and our discussion of ideology, criminologists who favor a control orientation tend to identify themselves as conservatives and moderates, and criminologists who favor a learning orientation tend to identify themselves as liberals and radicals (Cooper, Walsh, & Ellis, 2010). Learning theories assume that criminal behavior requires some learned motivation for it to emerge, whereas control theories assume that criminal behavior requires no such special motivation; rather, such behavior arises from natural motivations that we must learn to curb. Both sets of theories talk of learning but emphasize different things to be learned—antisocial or prosocial behavior.

To ensure a peaceful and predictable social existence, all societies have created mechanisms designed to minimize nonconformity and deviance that we may collectively call **social control**. Both Durkheim's anomie theory and Shaw and McKay's ecological theory may be viewed as control theories because they point to circumstances (anomie or social disorganization) that lessen the social control of individuals' behavior. Social control may be direct, formal, and coercive, as exemplified by uniformed symbols of the state. But indirect and informal social control is preferable because it produces prosocial behavior regardless of the presence or absence of external coercion. Obeying society's rules of proper conduct because we believe the rules are right and just, not simply because we fear formal sanctions, means we have our own internalized police officer and judge in the form of something called a conscience.

Travis Hirschi's Social Bond Theory

There are a variety of control theories, but the most popular is Travis Hirschi's (1969) **social bond theory**. Other than rational choice and routine activities theories, previous theories we have examined assume crime is learned by basically good people living in bad environments and ask, "What causes crime?" Control theorists believe this question reveals a faulty understanding of human nature and that the real question is not why some people behave badly but why most of us behave well most of the time. They tell us that we behave well if our ties to prosocial others are strong, but we may revert to predatory self-interest if they are not. After all, children who are not properly socialized hit, kick, bite, steal, and scream whenever the mood strikes them. They have to be taught not to do these things, which in the absence of training "come naturally." In this tradition it is society that is "good," and human beings, in the absence of the proper training, who become "bad." Gwynn Nettler (1984) said it most colorfully: "If we grow up 'naturally,' without cultivation, like weeds, we grow up like weeds—rank" (p. 313).

Virtually all developmental experts agree that "weediness" will be the natural outcome for children not subjected to controls in the form of prosocial socialization. A longitudinal observational study of children from 2 to 12 years of age found that the frequency of hitting, biting, and kicking peaked at 27 months and declined by about 66% by age 12 (Tibbetts & Hemmens, 2010). Tremblay (2008) sums up the literature on this issue by stating, "By monitoring the development of physical aggression from infancy onwards, recent longitudinal studies show that human infants spontaneously use physical aggression and that humans learn not to physically aggress rather than learn to aggress" (p. 2619). From this perspective criminals are simply toddlers grown big and strong.

Social control theory is thus about the role of social relationships that bind people to the social order and prevent antisocial behavior. This is the classical view of human nature and very much in the constrained vision camp. Antisocial behavior will emerge automatically if controls are lacking; it needs no special learning or motivating factors since human beings are assumed to be naturally self-centered. The classical assumption of self-interested persons anxious to experience pleasure and avoid pain is there, but the theory tries to account for why some people pursue their self-interest in legitimate ways and others do not, with primary emphasis on socialization practices that do or do not produce individuals capable of reigning in their natural instincts.

Four Elements of the Social Bond

Hirschi formulated his theory with some foundational facts about the "typical" criminal and found him to be a young male who grew up in a fatherless home in an urban slum, is unemployed, and has a history of difficulty in school. From this he deduced that those most likely to commit crimes lack the four elements of the social bond that form the foundation of prosocial behavior: attachment, commitment, involvement, and belief.

Photo 7.3

Attachment to parents provides the foundation for attachment to social institutions and to commitment to a prosocial career, involvement in prosocial activities, a belief in prosocial values, and the foundation for a happy and law-abiding life.

Attachment is the emotional component of conformity and refers to the emotional bonds existing between the individual and key social institutions such as the family and the school. Attachment to prosocial others is the foundation for all other social bonds because it leads us to feel valued, respected, and admired and to value the favorable judgments of those to whom we are attached. A good deal of our behavior can be seen as attempts to gain favorable judgments from people and groups we care about. Lack of attachment to parents and lack of respect for their wishes easily spills over into a lack of attachment and respect for the broader social groupings of which the child is a part. Much of the controlling power of others outside the family lies in the threat of reporting misbehavior to parents. If the child has little respect for parental sanctions, the control exercised by others has little effect because parental control has little effect: "If a person feels no emotional attachment to a person or institution, the rules [of that person or institution] tend to be denied legitimacy" (Hirschi, 1969, p. 127).

Commitment is the rational component of conformity and refers to a lifestyle in which one has invested considerable time and energy in the pursuit of a lawful career. People who invest heavily in a lawful career have a valuable stake in conformity and are not likely to risk it by engaging in crime. School dropouts and the unemployed do not have a strong investment in conventional behavior and therefore risk less by committing crime. Acquiring a stake in conformity requires disciplined application to tasks that children do not relish but complete in order to gain approval from parents. Attachment is thus the essential foundation for commitment to a prosocial lifestyle.

Involvement is a direct consequence of commitment; it is a part of an overall conventional pattern of existence. Involvement is a matter of time and energy constrictions placed on us by the demands of our lawful activities that reduce exposure to illegal opportunities. Conversely, noninvolvement in conventional activities increases the possibility of exposure to illegal activities. As Hirschi (1969) put it, "Idle hands are the devil's workshop" (p. 187).

Belief refers to the acceptance of the social norms regulating conduct. Persons lacking attachment, commitment, and involvement tend not to believe in conventional morality. A belief system empty of conventional morality is concerned only with narrow self-interest. Unlike differential association theory, control theory does not view a criminal belief system as motivating criminal behavior. Rather, criminals act according to their urges and then justify or rationalize their behavior with a set of statements such as "Suckers deserve what they get," and "Do onto others as they would do onto you—only do it first." For control theorists, behavior gives birth to the belief rather than vice versa. It is important to realize that crime is not motivated by the absence of any of the social bonds; their absence merely represents social deficiencies that result in a reduction of the perceived potential costs of committing it.

Gottfredson and Hirschi's Low Self-Control Theory

With colleague Michael Gottfredson, in 1990 Hirschi moved from explaining crime and delinquency in terms of social control toward explaining it in terms of self-control. **Self-control** is defined as the "extent to which [different people] are vulnerable to the temptations of the moment" (Gottfredson & Hirschi, 1990, p. 87). **Self-control theory** accepts the classical idea that crimes are the result of unrestrained natural human impulses to enhance pleasure and avoid pain. These impulses often lead to crimes, which Gottfredson and Hirschi (1990) define as "acts of force or fraud undertaken in pursuit of self-interest" (p. 15). Most crimes, they assert, are spontaneous acts requiring little skill and earn the criminal minimal short-term satisfaction. People with low self-control possess the following personal traits that put them at risk for criminal offending:

- They are oriented to the present rather than to the future, and crime affords them immediate rather than delayed gratification.

- They are risk taking and physical as opposed to cautious and cognitive, and crime provides them with exciting and risky adventures.

- They lack patience, persistence, and diligence, and crime provides them with quick and easy ways to obtain money, sex, revenge, and so forth.

- They are self-centered and insensitive, so they can commit crimes without experiencing pangs of guilt for causing the suffering of others. (1990, pp. 89–90)

According to Gottfredson and Hirschi, low self-control is established early in childhood, tends to persist throughout life, and is the result of incompetent parenting. It is important to realize that children *do not* learn low self-control; low self-control is the default outcome that occurs in the absence of adequate socialization. As Brannigan (1997) puts it, "In the absence of interaction designed to promote empathy, identification, delayed gratification, a long time horizon, and prosocial values, the infant appears to exhibit older evolutionary scripts of adaptation which favour immediate gratification and egoism" (p. 425). Parental warmth, nurturance, vigilance, and the willingness to practice "tough love" are necessary to forge self-control in offspring. Other factors that may result in low self-control include parental criminality (criminals are not very successful in socializing their children), family size (the larger the family, the more difficult it is to monitor behavior), single-parent families (two parents are generally better than one), and working mothers, which negatively impact the development of children's self-control if no substitute monitor is provided (Gottfredson & Hirschi, 1990, pp. 100–105).

Gottfredson and Hirschi argue that children acquire or fail to acquire self-control in the first decade of life, after which the attained level of control remains stable across the life course. Subsequent experiences, situations, and circumstances have little independent effect on the probability of offending. Because low self-control is a stable component of a criminal personality, most criminals typically fail in anything that requires long-term commitment, such as school, employment, and marriage, because such commitments get in the way of immediate satisfaction of their desires. Note that self-control is not a motivator of any act; it is a brake, not an accelerator.

The Role of Opportunity

Low self-control is not sufficient in itself to account for offending. Because Gottfredson and Hirschi consider it to be stable across the life course, variation in criminal behavior cannot be explained by variation in self-control (they seem to be saying that all who lack self-control have equal levels of low self-control). What explains variation in criminal behavior among low self-control individuals is variation in the *opportunities* to commit it. A criminal **opportunity** is "a situation that presents itself to someone with low self-control by which he or she can immediately satisfy needs with minimal mental or physical effort" (1990, pp. 12–13).

Self-control theory is thus similar to routine activities theory in this respect: crime is the result of people with low self-control (a motivated offender) meeting a criminal opportunity (a suitable target lacking a capable guardian). The difference is that low self-control theory emphasizes the motivated offender and ignores the target and the guardian while routine activities theory does the opposite. Gottfredson and Hirschi illustrate what they mean by the intersection of low self-control and opportunity by describing typical criminal incidents as not the culmination of foresight and planning but as opportunities (an open door, an unlocked car with keys in the ignition, a vulnerable person walking down a dark alley) witnessed by someone ready to take advantage of them.

Integrating Social- and Self-Control Theories

Given the emphasis on parental guidance in the development of self-control, many criminologists wondered for a long time why the elements of the social bond are absent in self-control theory. After all, both theories assume a natural inclination to pursue selfish interests with little effort and without regard for others, and both maintain that what distinguishes law-abiding people from criminals are the controls that prevent the former from acting on their natural impulses. Hirschi (2004) has addressed this concern by assuming that, like self-control, "differences in social control are stable, that social control and self-control are the same thing" (p. 543). He welds the two theories together with two simple sentences: "Self-control is the set of inhibitions one carries with one wherever one goes. Their character may be initially described by going to the elements of the bond identified by social control theory: Attachment, commitment, involvement, and belief" (2004, pp. 543–544). Hirschi is now saying that self-control and the social control exercised by others in the family, school, and workplace mutually affect one another constantly across the life course and that self- and social-control theories may now be considered integrated. This integration is illustrated in Figure 7.3.

Evaluation of Social- and Self-Control Theories

Criminologists ranked social- and self-control theories as the most empirically supported theories for decades, but they were only ranked 3 and 5, respectively, in the 2007 survey discussed in Chapter 1. However, if we combine both theories and treat them as one, as Hirschi now does, more contemporary criminologists (66, or 17.4%) checked it as the theory that best explains criminal behavior. Both versions of control theory agree that the family is central to the developmental of mechanisms that affect criminal behavior, and because of this they have been criticized for neglecting social structure (Grasmick, Tittle, Bursik, & Arneklev, 1993). Critics feel that if the family is so important, the social, economic, and political factors that impede stable and nurturing families should be addressed. Control theorists might respond that whatever those things may be, they are not within the purview of control theory, which attempts to explain the *consequences* of weak and disrupted families, not why they are disrupted.

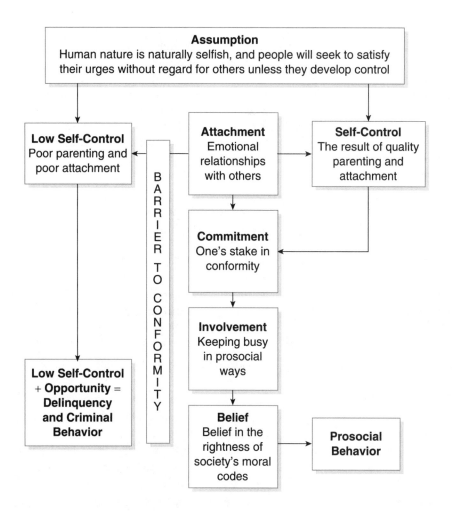

Figure 7.3

Hirschi's
Integration of
Social- and Self-
Control Theories

It is also often pointed out that a person can be emotionally attached to deviant parents and deviant peers, and thus his or her own deviant behavior can be viewed as conforming to deviant expectations. This might be the sort of criticism followers of differential association theory might express. The problem here is that Hirschi is expressly referring to attachment to prosocial others as a way to explain prosocial behavior and not to all attachments (Franklin, Gau, & Pratt, 2010).

A major criticism of self-control theory arises from the claim that it is a *general* theory meant to explain *all* crime. Although most common street crimes are impulsive spontaneous acts, many others are not. White-collar criminals, organized-crime criminals, serial killers, and terrorists, among others, typically plan their crimes extensively. It is too simplistic to claim that crime can be explained by the single tendency of low self-control. In other words, low self-control cannot be a necessary and sufficient explanation of criminality (nor can any other single risk factor).

Self-control theory has also been criticized for attributing variation in people's level of self-control solely to variation in parental behavior and ignoring child effects. The child development literature makes it clear that socialization is a two-way street in which parental behavior is shaped by the evocative behavior of the child just as much as the child's behavior is shaped by his or her parents (Harris, 1998). All parents with two or more children know this. Low self-control may be something children bring with them to the socialization process rather than a product of the failure of that process. This is supported by a number of studies that have found a strong genetic component to low self-control (Wright & Beaver, 2005; Wright, Beaver, Delisi, & Vaughn, 2008). As Lilly, Cullen, and Ball (2007) point out, "Research suggests that parents may affect levels of self control less by their parenting styles and more by genetic transmission" (p. 110). This certainly does not mean that parenting doesn't matter; loving and conscientious parents mean more than anything else to the healthy development of children. It only means that if we are to understand self-control at a more sophisticated level we must use genetically informed samples and assess the influences of children's behavior on parenting styles.

THEORY IN ACTION: Lionel Tate and Social- and Self-Control

Lionel Tate, weighing in at 170 pounds, became the youngest person in American history to be sentenced to life in prison in 2001. He had been convicted of the vicious beating death of 6-year-old, 48-pound Tiffany Eunick in his mother's apartment in 1999 when he was 12 years old. Tiffany's autopsy revealed that she suffered a ruptured spleen, numerous lacerations, a fractured skull, brain contusions, a bleeding brain, broken ribs, a lacerated and partially detached liver, and kidney hemorrhaging. Upon discovering the body, Tate's mother, a Florida Highway Patrol officer who had brought Tiffany home for the evening to babysit her, called the police and Lionel was taken into custody.

Photo 7.4

Lionel Tate cries after a judge sentences him to life in prison, making him the youngest person in American history to receive that sentence.

After serving 3 years, Tate's conviction was thrown out on a legal technicality (his mental competency had not been evaluated). Mental testing concluded that Tate did not suffer from any form of mental illness (he had tried to fake mental illness) but that he certainly had a high potential for violence, uncontrolled feelings of anger, resentment, and poor impulse control. He subsequently pled guilty to second-degree murder and was sentenced to a year of house arrest and 10 years' probation coupled with counseling and community service hours. In 2005, Tate violated his probation after robbing a pizza deliveryman at gunpoint and assaulting the occupant of the apartment to which the pizza was being delivered. He was sentenced to 30 years in prison for these offenses and for violating his probation.

Lionel Tate was born on January 30, 1987, to John and Kathleen Tate. The couple divorced shortly afterward, with John having very little presence in Lionel's life thereafter. Lionel spent his formative years living either with his mother or with various relatives. Because of the lack of proper parental supervision, he grew up street-smart and displayed major levels of antisocial behavior for years prior to his murder of Tiffany. He was in constant trouble from the age of 5 for fighting, assault, lying, stealing, and bullying and was suspended from school 15 times. At such times, Kathleen would go to Lionel's school in her police uniform and make excuses for him. She even described Tiffany's killing as a "tragic accident" and claiming that Lionel was completely innocent.

Tate's case involves a troubled boy who grew up in a fatherless home in a relatively crime-ridden area and who did poorly in school. In short, Lionel possessed all of Hirschi's "foundational facts" predictive of the lack of the four elements of the social bond. In trouble from an early age for many things, including violent bullying, he also clearly lacked self-control. Rather than disciplining Lionel, his mother constantly excused his behavior. She may even have been able to prevent Tiffany's murder had she done more to monitor the behavior of her clearly antisocial son. She evidently shouted at Lionel not to be

THEORY IN ACTION (Continued)

so noisy as he and Tiffany were "playing" upstairs and did not go upstairs to investigate what was going on for over 40 minutes after Tiffany's death.

This case clearly illustrates the importance of a two-parent family for the supervision of children. Kathleen had perhaps tried her best, but the shift work and overtime requirements involved in police work left her little time or energy for her parental duties after she and Lionel were deserted by John. Thus, to quote Nettler again, Lionel was allowed to "grow up naturally"; that is, without care and cultivation mixed with the right amount of tough love.

Discussion Questions

1. Discuss whether someone who committed a crime (even a heinous one such as Tate's) at the age of 12 should be given life in prison.

2. Does Lionel's story fit any other theory we have discussed better than control theory?

3. What do you think should have been done with Lionel? Would he continue to commit crimes if released tomorrow (he was 26 years old as of 2013)?

Sources: Blanco, n.d.; Woodhouse, 2010

❖ Labeling Theory: The Irony of Social Reaction

Do you believe there is any truth to the old saying, "Give a dog a bad name and he'll live up to it"? There are those who do, and one school of criminological thought takes seriously the power of bad labels to stigmatize and, by doing so, evoke the very behavior the labels signify. The school of thought is known as labeling theory (LT). Other theories may recognize that the stigma of a criminal label can have unintended negative consequences, but only this theory grants the labeling process a central role in explaining crime and deviance. The labeling perspective is interesting and provocative; unlike most other theories it does not ask why crime rates vary or why individuals differ in their propensity to commit crime. Rather, it asks why some behaviors are labeled criminal and not others and thus shifts the focus from the actor (the criminal) to the reactor (the criminal justice system). In doing this, LT looks for the causes of crime *after* the crime has been committed, discovered, and punished.

LT is often traced to Frank Tannenbaum's *Crime and the Community*, which emphasized that a major part in the making of a criminal is the process of identifying and labeling a person as such—the "dramatizing of evil" by which "the person becomes the thing he is described as being" (1938, p. 20). Tannenbaum viewed the labeling of a person as a "criminal" as a self-fulfilling prophesy (a definition of something that becomes true if it is believed and acted upon), which means that processing law violators through the criminal justice system, rather than deterring them from future criminal behavior, embeds them further in a criminal lifestyle.

For labeling theorists, crime has no objective reality and is defined into existence rather than discovered. There is no crime independent of cultural values and norms, which are embodied in the judgments and reactions of others. To put it simply, no act is by its "nature" criminal, because acts do not have natures until they are witnessed and judged good or bad by others. This ignores the fact that *mala in se* crimes (murder, rape, robbery, aggravated assault, and theft offenses) are recognized as crimes in all 180 countries supplying data to INTERPOL (Walsh & Ellis, 2007).

LT distinguishes between primary and secondary deviance (Lemert, 1974). **Primary deviance** is the initial nonconforming act that comes to the attention of the authorities. Primary deviance can arise for a wide variety of reasons, but these reasons are of little interest because they have only marginal effects on the offender's self-concept as a criminal or noncriminal, and it is the individual's self-concept that is crucial in LT. The idea that primary deviance is of little consequence was derived by examining self-report studies of crime and delinquency. Official statistics consistently show higher arrest rates for the poor and underprivileged than for the middle class, but self-report data (mostly asking about extremely minor deviant acts) tended to show no significant differences among groups in offending. In other words, these data tell us that no specific group of individuals (including even males vis-à-vis females for some labeling theorists) is prone to commit crimes than any other group, thus the overrepresentation of some groups in official statistics reflects police bias (Paternoster & Iovanni, 1989). Primary deviance is of interest to labeling theorists only insofar as it is detected and reacted to by individuals with power to pin a stigmatizing label on the rule breaker. According to LT, being caught in an act of primary deviance is either the result of police bias or sheer bad luck; the real criminogenic experience comes *after* a person is caught and labeled. The central concern of LT is thus to explain the consequences of being labeled.

Secondary deviance results from society's reaction to primary deviance. The stigma of a criminal label may result in people becoming more criminal than they would have been had they not been caught. This may occur in two ways. First, labeled persons may alter their self-concepts in conformity with the label ("Yes, I am a criminal and will act more like one in future"). Second, the label may exclude them from conventional employment and lead to the loss of conventional friends. This may lead them to seek illegitimate opportunities to fulfill their financial needs and to seek other criminals to fulfill their friendship needs, which further strengthens their growing conception of themselves as "really" criminal. The criminal label becomes a self-fulfilling prophesy because it is a more powerful label than other social labels that offenders may claim.

The most important consideration is thus the change of an offender's identity that supposedly results from the formal application of a deviant label. If the criminal label is successfully applied, it leads to the offender's reevaluation of his or her self-concept as a criminal, which then increases the probability of further criminal activity (secondary deviance). Labeling theorists do not assert that this process is inevitable; there are many exceptions to the "rule." Being labeled delinquent or criminal engages the emotion of shame in some people and the emotion of pride in others—it all depends on the person and his or her circumstances and circle of friends (Topalli, 2005). Some offenders resist labeling by denying or downplaying the seriousness of their actions and may be successful at disavowing their deviance, even if formally labeled. Being arrested can have the effect of deterring future criminal activity—think back to Chapter 4 and the concept of the contrast effect, as well as how formal arrest and increased penalties have had dramatic effects on reducing drunk driving and domestic violence. At the opposite pole, there are those who actively seek the criminal or delinquent label as a badge of pride—think about how Kody Scott proudly embraced the "monster" label the police officer pinned on him and how also in Chapter 4 that formal punishment has little effect on people who are arrested after they have become deeply embedded in crime.

Although only four criminologists (just over 1%) of those surveyed in Figure 1.1 considered LT to be the theory that best explained criminal behavior, there has been a resurgence in the theory in recent years (Petrosino, Turpin-Petrosino, & Guckenburg, 2010). These new labeling theorists no longer make the claim that state intervention is a major cause of crime. Rather, they propose that it is a risk factor contributing to continued criminal involvement. It is not news to anyone, of course, that the more often a person is arrested and the longer a person is incarcerated the more likely it is that the person will offend again. The issue is to what extent the labeling process is the "cause" of this habitual return to crime.

Sykes and Matza's Neutralization Theory

Sykes and Matza's neutralization theory (NT) attacks differential association's failure to explain why some people drift in and out of crime rather than being consistently criminal. It also runs counter to the assumption of DAT and subcultural theories that give the impression that criminal behavior is endowed with positive value and condoned as morally right. It is difficult to believe that most criminals do not know "deep down" that their behavior is wrong: "If there existed in fact a delinquent subculture such that the delinquent viewed his behavior as morally correct," he or she would show no shame when caught but would instead show "indignation or a sense of martyrdom" (Sykes & Matza, 2002, p. 145). NT suggests that delinquents and criminals know their behavior is wrong, but they justify it on a number of grounds. In other words, they neutralize any sense of shame or guilt for having committed some wrongful act, which means that they are at least minimally attached to conventional norms. NT also runs counter to labeling theory because it shows how delinquents resist labeling rather than passively accepting it. Sykes and Matza's five **techniques of neutralization** follow.

- *Denial of responsibility* shifts the blame for a deviant act away from the actor: "I know she's only 6, but she seduced me."

- *Denial of injury* is an offender's claim that no "real" offense occurred because no one was harmed: "He got his car back, and his insurance covers the damage, doesn't it?"

- *Denial of victim* implies that the victim got what he or she deserves: "I guess I did beat her up, but she kept nagging; hell, she asked for it!"

- *Condemnation of the condemners* involves attempts by the offender to share guilt with the condemners (parents, police, probation officers) by asserting that their behavior is just bad as his or hers: "You drink booze, I smoke grass; what's the difference?"

- *Appeal to higher loyalties* elevates the offender's moral integrity by claiming altruistic motives: "I have to cover my homies' backs don't I?"

The motive behind employing these techniques is assumed to be the maintenance of a noncriminal self-image by individuals who have committed a criminal act and who have been asked to explain why. Such individuals "define the situation" in a way that mitigates the seriousness of their acts and simultaneously protects the image they have of themselves as non-criminals. If we engage in behavior we consider morally wrong but find that behavior rewarding, we tend to develop a form of psychological discomfort called **cognitive dissonance**. It is this contradiction—belief in the validity of the moral order coupled with noncompliance with it—that generates cognitive dissonance or, in this context, guilt and shame. The elimination of uncomfortable inconsistencies between attitudes and behavior then becomes a powerful motive to change one or the other. Psychologists tell us that we find it a lot easier to make our attitudes consistent with our behavior than to change the behavior to conform with our attitudes if the behavior is rewarding (Wood & Wood, 1997).

A less benign interpretation of the use of these techniques is that rather than trying to protect their self-images, they are seeking to mitigate their punishment or at least to "share" it with some convenient other. Conversely, intensive interviews with hard-core criminals indicate they strive to maintain an image consistent with inner-city street codes, not with conventional ones; i.e., "they neutralize being good rather than being bad" (Topalli, 2005, p. 798).

Evaluation of Labeling and Neutralization Theories

Ronald Akers criticizes LT for coming close to asserting that the original causes of delinquent and criminal behavior (primary deviance) do not matter with its overemphasis on the importance of official labeling. He continues: "One sometimes gets the impression from reading this literature that people go about minding their own business, and then—wham—bad society come along and slaps them with a stigmatized label. Forced into the role of deviant the individual has little choice but to be deviant" (in Bernard, Snipes, & Gerould, 2010, p. 230). Of course, labels can stigmatize and lead to social exclusion for prosocial relationships and gainful employment and push offenders into the company of other criminally stigmatized individuals, thus increasing the likelihood of further antisocial behavior. It goes without saying that punishing convicted felons with imprisonment certainly creates stigma, puts convicts in the company of other criminals, and diminishes the person's opportunities for a subsequent prosocial lifestyle, but the alternative (not arresting and punishing) "is neither politically expedient nor likely to be popular with the general public" (Restivo & Lanier, 2013, p. 20).

One of the positive elements of neutralization theory is that it eliminates much of the overdetermined image of subcultural values implied in subcultural theories. Many delinquents are no more completely committed to antisocial values than they are to prosocial values. Neutralization techniques are not viewed as "causes" of antisocial behavior; rather, they are a set of justifications that loosen moral constraints and allow offenders to drift in and out of antisocial behavior because they are able to "neutralize" these constraints.

One of the major problems with the theory is that it says nothing about the origins of the antisocial behavior the actors seek to neutralize. To be a causal theory of criminal behavior rather than an explanation of the post hoc process of rationalization, it would have to show that individuals *first* neutralize their moral beliefs and *then* engage in antisocial acts. Some studies have found that neutralization techniques were able to explain future deviance, but this should not surprise anyone since persons in a position where they have to explain their offending behavior are more likely than those not in such a position to offend in the future—past is prologue regardless of our explanations of it.

❖ Policy and Prevention: Implications of Social Process Theories

Where we see the cause(s) of crime is where we assume we will find the solution. However, although they deal with different units of analysis, very few policy recommendations not discussed in ecological and strain theories can be gleaned from DAT or SLT. The bottom line for all subcultural theories is that lower-class neighborhoods harbor values and attitudes conducive to criminal behavior. Thus, if learning crime and delinquency within a particular culture is the problem, then changing relative aspects of that culture is the answer. However, we have already seen that attempts to do that have met with only meager success at best.

Because DAT concerns itself with the influence of role models in intimate peer groups, the provision of prosocial role models to replace antisocial ones is an obvious thought. Probation and parole authorities have long recognized the importance of keeping convicted felons away from each other, making it a revocable offense to "associate with known felons." As every probation and parole officer knows, however, this is easier said than done. Programs that bring youths together for prosocial purposes, such as sports leagues and community projects, might be high on the agenda of any policymaker using differential association as a guide. But the lure of "the streets" and of the friends they have grown up with remains a powerful force retarding rehabilitation. The good news is that most delinquents will desist as they mature, and the breakup of the friendship group by the incarceration, migration, death, or marriage of some of its members will break the grip of antisocial behavior for many of the remaining members (Sampson & Laub, 1999).

The policy implications derivable from social control and self-control theories have to do with the family. Given the importance of nurturance and attachment, both versions of control theory support the idea of early family intervention designed to cultivate these things. Families with children in almost all advanced nations receive support via family allowances and receive paid maternal leave, but such programs do not exist in the United States, which shows that politics and ideology dictate the direction of criminal justice policy more than criminological theory.

Other attempts to increase bonding to social institutions would concentrate on increasing children's involvement in a variety of prosocial activities and programs centered in and around the school. These programs provide prosocial models, teach moral beliefs such as personal responsibility, and keep youths busy in meaningful and challenging ways. Social control theory might recommend more vocationally oriented classes to keep less academically inclined students bonded to school.

Neither version of control theory would advise increased employment opportunities as a way to control crime. The assumption of control theory is that people who are attached and who possess self-control will do fine in the job market as it is, and increasing job opportunities for those lacking attachment and self-control will have minimal effect. Because low self-control is the result of the absence of inhibiting forces typically experienced in early childhood, Gottfredson and Hirschi (1997) are pessimistic about the ability of less powerful inhibiting forces (such as the threat of punishment) present in later life to deter crime. They also see little use in satisfying the wants and needs other theories view as important in reducing crime (e.g., reducing poverty, improving neighborhoods) because crime's appeal is its provision of immediate gains and minimal cost. In short, "society" is neither the cause of nor the solution to crime.

Gottfredson and Hirschi advocate some of the same policies (e.g., target hardening) advocated by rational choice and routine activities to reduce criminal opportunities. However, the most important policy recommendation is to strengthen families and improve parenting skills, especially skills relevant to teaching self-control. It is only by working with and through families that society can do anything about crime in the long run. Gottfredson and Hirschi's (1997) most important recommendation is this: "Delaying pregnancy among unmarried girls would probably do more to affect the long-term crime rates than all the criminal justice programs combined" (p. 33).

If the causes of primary deviance are secondary to the labeling process, then preventative efforts should focus on "noninterventionism" ("Leave the kids alone, they'll grow out of it"). This advice may be prudent for teenage pot smokers or runaways but hardly wise for teenage robbers and rapists. LT advises that such delinquents should be "treated" rather than "punished," although it is deemed necessary to punish on many occasions. Restivo and Lanier (2013) suggest that minor offenders (particularly juveniles) should be confronted and shamed for what they have done, but not in a degrading way, and then reintegrated into the community in ways that avoid stigmatization.

Labeling theory had an effect on criminal justice policy far in excess of what its empirical support warrants. If it is correct that official societal reaction to primary deviance amplifies and promotes more of the same, the logical policy recommendation is that we should ignore primary deviance for the sake of alleviating secondary deviance. Labeling theory recommends that we allow offenders to protect their self-images as noncriminals by not challenging their "techniques of neutralization." Juveniles must be particularly protected from labeling. To a large extent, juvenile authorities have implemented diversion programs for all but the most serious offenders. Diversion programs allow juvenile offenders to avoid formal sanctioning by the court in favor

Table 7.1

Summarizing Social Process Theories

Theory	Key Concepts	Strengths	Weaknesses
Differential Association	Crime is learned in association with peers holding definitions favorable to law violation. Most likely to occur in differentially organized (lower-class) neighborhoods.	Explains the onset of offending and the power of peer pressure and the need to be accepted by the peer group.	Neglects possibility of like seeking like (birds of a feather). Does not make distinction between private accepters and temporary compliers.
Social Learning	Definitions favorable to law violation depend on history of reinforcement and punishment. Excess rewards for criminal behavior perpetuate it.	Adds powerful concepts of operant psychology to explain how people learn criminal behavior. Links sociology to psychology.	Neglects individual differences affecting what is reinforcing to whom and the ease or difficulty with which one learns.
Social Bonding	Bonds to social institutions prevent crime, which otherwise comes naturally. The bonds are attachment, commitment, involvement, and belief.	The most popular and empirically supported theory. Emphasizes importance of the family and provides workable policy recommendations.	Neglects structural variables contributing to family instability and to loss of occupational opportunities. Neglects differences in the ease with which attachment is achieved.
Self-Control	Low self-control explains all crime and analogous acts. Low self-control occurs in the absence of proper parenting. Exposure to criminal opportunities explains differences in criminal behavior among low-self-control individuals.	Identifies a single measurable trait as responsible for many antisocial behaviors. Accords well with the impulsive nature of most criminal behavior. Links sociology to psychology.	Claims too much for a single trait. Neglects child influences on parenting behavior and the effects of genes on low self-control.
Labeling	Crime has no independent reality. Original primary deviance is unimportant; what is important is the labeling process, which leads to secondary (continuing) deviance. Labeling people criminal leads them to organize their self-concepts around that label.	Explains consequences of labeling with a "master status." Identifies the social construction of crime and points to the power of some (the powerful) to criminalize the acts of others (the powerless).	The neglect of causes of primary deviance. Advice that criminals should be treated not punished contradicts the theory that there is nothing intrinsically bad about crime and therefore there is nothing to "treat."
Neutralization	Delinquents and criminals learn to neutralize moral constraints and thus their guilt for committing crimes. They drift in and out of crime.	Emphasizes that criminals are no more fully committed to antisocial attitudes than they are to prosocial attitudes. Shows how criminals handle feelings of guilt.	Says nothing about the origins of behavior being neutralized. More a theory of antisocial rationalization than of crime.

of completing various informal requirements of the program such as completing a counseling program, paying restitution, and perhaps completing some community service hours determined by a juvenile probation officer rather than a judge. These programs tend to have positive results in preventing recidivism (Wilson & Hoge, 2013).

The only policy implication of neutralization theory is the opposite of that of labeling theory; i.e., criminal justice agents charged with managing offenders (probation/parole officers) should strongly challenge their excuse making. If offenders come to believe their own rationalizations, rehabilitative efforts will become more difficult. Thus, offenders must be shown that their thinking patterns have negative long-term consequences for them.

Summary

- Social process theories emphasize how people perceive their reality and how these perceptions structure their behavior. DAT is a learning theory that emphasizes the power of peer associations and the definitions favorable to law violation found within them to be the cause of crime and delinquency.
- SLT adds to DAT by stressing the mechanisms by which "definitions favorable" are learned. Behavior is either reinforced (rewarded) or punished. Behavior that is rewarded tends to be repeated; behavior that is punished tends not to be. Discriminative stimuli provide signals for the kinds of behaviors likely to be rewarding or punishing and are based on what we have learned about those stimuli in the past.
- Control theories are in many ways the opposite of DAT and SLT because they don't ask why people commit crimes but why most of us do not. Crime comes naturally to those who are not either socially or self-controlled. Hirschi speaks of the social bonds (attachment, commitment, involvement, and belief) that keep us on the straight and narrow. These are not causes of crime; rather they are bonds, the absence of which allows our natural impulses to emerge.
- Gottfredson and Hirschi's self-control theory move the focus from social- to self-control, although our experiences within the family are still vital to learn self-control. Low self-control must be paired with a criminal opportunity for crime to occur. Hirschi has now integrated social- and self-control theories, stating that they are "the same thing."
- Labeling theory is not interested in why some people commit crimes (primary deviance), believing that the only thing that differentiates criminals from the rest of us is that they have been caught and labeled. The real problem for LT is the affixing of a deviant label because it changes the person's self-concept, and he or she then engages in secondary deviance in conformity with the label.
- Sykes and Matza's neutralization theory is contrary to labeling theory because it focuses on individuals' attempts to resist being labeled criminal by offering justifications or excuses for their behavior.

Exercises and Discussion Question

1. Without indicating a particular theory, does the social structural or social process approach to explaining crime and criminality make most sense to you?

2. Compare differential association theory with control theory in terms of their respective assumptions about human nature. Which assumption makes more sense to you?

3. Is a delinquent or criminal label applied to someone sufficient in most cases to change a person's self-concept enough to lead him or her to continue offending?

4. Gottfredson and Hirschi claim that parents are to blame for an individual's lack of self-control. Are there some children who are simply more difficult to socialize than others? Are they rather than their parents at fault for their lack of self-control?

5. Why is attachment the most important of the four social bonds?

Useful Websites

Control theories of crime. http://sitemason.vanderbilt
.edu/files/l/l3Bguk/soccon.

Differential association theory. www.criminology.fsu
.edu/crimtheory/sutherland.html.

Labeling theories of crime. www.historylearningsite
.co.uk/labelling_theory.htm.

Learning theories of crime. http://criminology.fsu.edu/
crimtheory/learning.htm.

Social control theories. www.criminology.fsu.edu/
crimtheory/hirschi.htm.

Chapter Terms

Attachment

Belief

Cognitive dissonance

Commitment

Definitions

Differential association theory

Differential reinforcement

Discrimination

Involvement

Operant psychology

Opportunity

Primary deviance

Punishment

Reinforcement

Secondary deviance

Self-control

Self-control theory

Social bond theory

Social control

Social learning theory

Symbolic interactionism

Techniques of neutralization

CHAPTER 8

Critical and Feminist Theories

At the heart of the theories in this chapter is social stratification by class and power, the most "politicized" of all criminological theories. Sanyika Shakur, aka Kody Scott, came to embrace this critical and politicized view of society as he grew older and converted to Afrocentric Islam. Shakur was very much a member of the class Karl Marx called the lumpenproletariat, which is the very bottom of the class hierarchy. Many critical theorists would view Shakur's criminality as justifiable rebellion against class and racial exploitation. Shakur wanted all the material rewards of American capitalism, but he perceived that the only way he could get them was through crime. Shakur was a total egoist, but many Marxists would excuse this as a trait nourished by capitalism, which they consider the "root cause" of crime. From his earliest days he was on the fringes of a society he plainly disdained. He referred to whites as "Americans" to emphasize his distance from them and to black cops as "Negroes" to distinguish them from the "New African Man." He called himself a "student of revolutionary science" and advocated a separate black nation in America.

Conflict concepts dominated Shakur's life as he battled the Bloods and other Crip "sets" with interests at odds with his set. It is easy to imagine his violent acts as the outlet of a desperate man struggling against feelings of class and race inferiority. Perhaps he was only able to achieve a sense of power when he held the fate of another human being in his hands. His fragile narcissism often exploded into violent fury whenever he felt himself being "dissed." How much of Shakur's behavior and the behavior of youth gangs in general is explained by the concepts of critical theories? Is violent conflict a justifiable response to class and race inequality in a democratic society, or are there more productive ways to resolve social issues?

LEARNING OBJECTIVES

- Understand the underlying assumptions of critical theories
- Note the difference between the way modern Marxists perceive crime and criminals versus the way Karl Marx himself did
- Be aware of the many ways that Marxist and conflict theorists view concepts such as crime, class, and conflict
- Understand why women's liberation has been linked to female crime
- Know reasons why females differ from males so much in criminal behavior
- Know the policy recommendations of critical and feminists theories

❖ The Conflict Perspective of Society

Although all sociological theories of crime contain elements of social conflict, consensus theories tend to judge alternative normative systems from the point of view of mainstream values, and they do not call for major restructuring of society. Theories presented in this chapter do just that and concentrate on power relationships as explanatory variables to the exclusion of almost everything else. They view criminal behavior, the law, and the penalties imposed for breaking the law as originating in the deep inequalities of power and resources in society. For conflict theorists, the law is not a neutral system of dispute settlement designed to protect everyone, but rather the tool of the privileged who criminalize acts contrary to their interests.

Critical criminology is an umbrella term for a variety of theories united only by the assumption that conflict and power relations between various classes of people best characterize the nature of society. Adherents of these diverse theories are not of one mind; they quarrel among themselves, and they coin new names for their theories such as *conflict, radical, critical, new criminology, radical human rights criminology, Marxist, neo-Marxist,* and *left realists.* It is fair to say that there is far more agreement among them about what they are against (the status quo) than what they are for (Hill & Robertson, 2003). These theories differ in subtle philosophical and theoretical ways within the general framework of the conflict model of society.

You don't have to be a radical or even a liberal to acknowledge that great inequalities of wealth and power exist in every society and that the wealthy classes have the upper hand in all things. History is full of examples: Plutarch wrote of the conflicts generated by disparity in wealth in Athens in 594 BC (Durrant & Durrant, 1968), and U.S. president John Adams wrote that American society in the late 18th century was divided into "a small group of rich men and a great mass of poor engaged in a constant class struggle" (Adams, 1778/1971, p. 221).

❖ Karl Marx and Revolution

Karl Marx is the father of critical criminology. The core of Marxism is the concept of **class struggle**: "Freeman and slave, patrician and plebian, lord and serf, guildmaster and journeyman, in a word, oppressor and oppressed, stood in constant opposition to one another" (Marx & Engels, 1948, p. 9). The oppressors in Marx's time were the owners of the means of production (the **bourgeoisie**), and the oppressed were the workers (the **proletariat**). The bourgeoisie strive to keep the cost of labor at a minimum, and the proletariat strive to sell its labor at the highest possible price. These opposing goals are the major source of conflict in a capitalist society. The bourgeoisie enjoy the upper hand because capitalist societies have large armies of unemployed workers anxious to secure work at any price, thus driving down the cost of labor. According to Marx, these economic and social arrangements—the material conditions of people's lives—determine what they will know, believe, and value and how they will behave.

Marx and his collaborator Freidrich Engels were disdainful of criminals, describing them in terms that would make a New York cop proud: "The dangerous class, the social scum, that rotting mass thrown off by the lowest layers of the old society" (1948, p. 22). These folks (described by Marx and Engels in a way that reminds us of the *anelpis* of cultural criminology) are from a third class in society—the *lumpenproletariat* (the "rag" proletariat). These folks would play no decisive role in the expected revolution. For Marx and Engels (1965) crime was simply the product of unjust and alienating social conditions—"the struggle of the isolated individual against the prevailing conditions" (p. 367). This became known as the **primitive rebellion hypothesis**, one of the best modern statements of which is Bohm's (2001): "Crime in capitalist societies is often a rational response to the circumstances in which people find themselves" (p. 115).

Another concept central to critical criminology is alienation (Smith & Bohm, 2008). **Alienation** describes the distancing of individuals from something. For Marx, most individuals in capitalist societies were alienated from work (which they believed should be creative and enjoyable), which led to alienation from themselves and from others. Work is central to Marx's thought because he believed that while nonhuman animals instinctively act on the environment *as given* to satisfy their immediate needs, humans distinguish themselves from animals by consciously *creating* their environment instead of just submitting to it. Alienation is the result of this discord between one's species being and one's behavior (e.g., mindlessly noncreative work as opposed to creative work). Marx thought wage labor dehumanized human beings by taking from them their creative advantage over other animals—robbing them of the species being (in effect, their human nature) and reducing them to the level of animals.

When individuals become alienated from themselves they become alienated from others and from their society in general. Alienated individuals may then treat others as mere objects to be exploited and victimized as they themselves are supposedly exploited and victimized by the capitalist system. Since the great majority of wage workers do not experience their work as creative activity, they are all dehumanized ritualists (to borrow from Merton's modes of adaptation). If we accept this notion, then perhaps one can view criminals as heroic rebels struggling to rehumanize themselves, as some modern Marxist criminologists have done.

Willem Bonger: The First Marxist Criminologist

Dutch criminologist Willem Bonger's *Criminality and Economic Conditions* (1905/1969) is the first work devoted to a Marxist analysis of crime. For Bonger the roots of crime lay in the exploitive and alienating conditions of capitalism, although some individuals are at greater risk for crime than others because people vary in their "innate **social sentiments**"—altruism (an active concern for the well-being of others) and its opposite, egoism (a concern only for one's own selfish interests). Bonger believed that capitalism generates egoism and blunts altruism because it relies on competition for valuable resources, setting person against person and group against group, leaving the losers to their miserable fates. Thus all individuals in capitalist societies are infected by egoism, and all are thus prone to crime—the poor out of economic necessity, the rich and the middle class from pure greed. Poverty was a major cause of crime for Bonger, particularly its effects on family structure (broken homes) and poor parental supervision of their children. Because of his emphasis on family structure and what he saw as the moral deficits of the poor, Bonger has been criticized by other Marxists, but he firmly believed that only by transforming society from capitalism to socialism would it be possible to regain the altruistic sentiment and reduce crime.

Modern Marxist Criminology

Contrary to Marx, modern Marxist criminologists tend to excuse criminals. William Chambliss (1976) views some criminal behavior to be "no more than the 'rightful' behavior of persons exploited by the extant economic relationships" (p. 6), and Ian Taylor (1999) sees the convict as "an additional victim of the routine operations of a capitalist system—a victim, that is of 'processes of reproduction' of social and racial inequality" (p. 151). David Greenberg (1981) even elevated Marx's despised criminals to the status of revolutionary leaders: "Criminals, rather than the working class, might be the vanguard of the revolution" (p. 28). Marxist criminologists view the class struggle as the *only* source of *all* crime, accuse other criminologists of being parties to class oppression, and view "real" crime as violations of human rights, such as racism, sexism, imperialism, and capitalism.

Tony Platt even wrote that "it is not too far-fetched to characterize many criminologists as domestic war criminals" (in Siegel, 1986, p. 276).

In the 1980s Marxists calling themselves **left realists** began to acknowledge predatory street crime as a *real* source of concern among the working class, who are the primary victims of it. Left realists understood that they have to translate their concern for the poor into practical, *realistic* social policies. This theoretical shift signals a move away from the former singular emphasis on the political economy to embrace the interrelatedness of the offender, the victim, the community, and the state in the causes of crime. It also signals a return to a more orthodox Marxist view of criminals as people whose activities are against the interests of the working and ruling classes. Although unashamedly socialist in orientation, left realists have been criticized by more traditional Marxists who see their advocacy of solutions to the crime problem within the context of capitalism as a sellout (Bohm, 2001).

❖ Conflict Theory: Max Weber and Power and Conflict

In common with Marx, Max Weber (1864–1920) saw societal relationships as best characterized by conflict. They differed on three key points, however: First, while Marx saw cultural ideas as molded by its economic system, Weber saw a culture's economic system molded by its ideas. Second, whereas Marx emphasized economic conflict between only two social classes, Weber saw conflict arising from multiple sources, with economic conflict often subordinate to other conflicts. Third, Marx envisioned the end of conflict with the destruction of capitalism, while Weber contended that capitalism will always exist, regardless of the social, economic, or political nature of society, and that it was functional because of its role in bringing disputes into the open for public debate.

Even though individuals and groups enjoying great wealth, prestige, and power have the resources necessary to impose their values on others with fewer resources, Weber viewed the various class divisions in society as normal, inevitable, and acceptable, as do many contemporary conflict theorists (Curran & Renzetti, 2001). As opposed to Marx's concentration on two great classes (the bourgeoisie and the proletariat) based only on economic interests, Weber focused of three types of social groups that form and dissolve as their interests change—class, party, and status. A class group shares only common economic interests, and *party* refers to political groups. Status groups are the only truly social groups because members hold common values, live common lifestyles, and share a sense of belonging. For Weber the law is a resource by which the powerful are able to impose their will on others by criminalizing acts contrary to their class interests. Because of this, wrote Weber, "Criminality exists in all societies and is the result of the political struggle among different groups attempting to promote or enhance their life chances" (in Bartollas, 2005, p. 179).

George Vold produced a version of conflict theory that moved conflict away from an emphasis on value and normative conflicts (as in the Chicago ecological tradition) to include conflicts of interest. Vold saw social life as a continual struggle to maintain or improve one's own group's interests—workers against management, race against race, ecologists against land developers, and the young against adult authority—with new interest groups continually forming and disbanding as conflicts arise and are resolved. Conflicts between youth gangs and adult authorities were of particular concern to Vold, who saw gangs in conflict with the values and interests of just about every other interest group, including those of other gangs (as in the Crips versus Bloods, for example). Gangs are examples of **minority power groups**, or groups whose interests are sufficiently on the margins of mainstream society such that just about all their activities are criminalized. Minority power groups are excellent examples of Weber's status groups in which status depends almost solely on adherence to a particular lifestyle: "Status honour is normally expressed by the fact that above all else a specific *style of life* is expected from all those who wish to belong to the circle" (Weber, 1978, p. 1028, emphasis in original). Vold's theory concentrates entirely on the clash of individuals loyally upholding their differing group interests and is not concerned with crimes unrelated to group conflict.

Like Weber, Vold viewed conflict as normal and socially desirable. Conflict is a way of assuring social change and, in the long run, a way of assuring social stability. A society that stifles conflict in the name of order stagnates and has no mechanisms for change short of revolution. Since social change is inevitable, it is preferable that it occur peacefully and incrementally (evolutionary) rather than violently (revolutionary). Even 19th-century archconservative British philosopher Edmund Burke saw that conflict is functional in this regard, writing that "a state without the means of some change is without means of its conservation" (in Walsh & Hemmens, 2000, p. 214).

Conflict criminology differs from Marxist criminology in that it concentrates on the *processes* of value conflict and lawmaking rather than on the social structural elements underlying those things. It is also relatively silent about how the powerful got to be powerful and makes no value judgments about crime (is it the activities of "social scum" or of "revolutionaries"?). Conflict theorists simply analyze the power relationships underlying the act of criminalization.

Because Marist and conflict theories are frequently confused with one another, Table 8.1 summarizes the differences between them on key concepts.

❖ Peacemaking Criminology

Perhaps because of the implosion of socialist societies around the world, Lilly, Cullen, and Ball (2011) see many strands of conflict theory "metamorph[izing] in the form of peacemaking criminology" (p. 193). **Peacemaking criminology** is a fairly recent addition to the growing number of theories in criminology and has drawn a number of former Marxists into its fold. It is situated squarely in the postmodernist tradition (a tradition that rejects the notion that the scientific view is better than any other view and disparages the claim that any method of understanding can be objective). Peacemaking criminologists reject the "modernist" view aimed at understanding, explaining, predicting, and controlling crime and appeal for a diversity of views in which none are disparaged and all are legitimized. They reject the notion that the scientific view is any better than any other view and that we can ever "know" something objectively. For them, "criminology's search for causes of crime is bankrupt because even the question is framed by androcentric, sexist, classist, and racist definitions of crime, criminality, and cause" (Pollock, 1999, p. 146). In its peacemaking endeavors it relies heavily on "appreciative relativism," a position that holds all points of view, including those of criminals, as relative and worthy of appreciation. It is a compassionate and spiritual criminology that has much of its philosophical roots in humanistic religion.

Peacemaking criminology's basic philosophy is similar to the 1960s hippie adage "Make love, not war," without the sexual overtones. It shudders at the current "war on crime" metaphor and wants to substitute "peace on crime." The idea of making peace on crime is perhaps best captured by Kay Harris (1991) in writing that we "need to reject the idea that those who cause injury or harm to others should suffer severance of the common bonds of respect and concern that binds members of a community. We should relinquish the notion that it is acceptable to try to 'get rid of' another person whether through execution, banishment, or caging away people about whom we do not care" (p. 93). While recognizing that many criminals should be incarcerated, peacemaking criminologists aver that an overemphasis on punishing criminals escalates violence. Richard Quinney has called the American criminal justice system the moral equivalent

Table 8.1

Comparing Marxist and Conflict Theory on Major Concepts

Concept	Marxist	Conflict
Origin of conflict	The powerful oppress the powerless (e.g., the bourgeoisie oppressing the proletariat under capitalism).	It is generated by many factors regardless of the political and economic system.
Nature of conflict	It is socially bad and must and will be eliminated in a socialist system.	It is socially useful and necessary and cannot be eliminated.
Major participants in conflict	The owners of the means of production and the workers are engaged in the only conflict that matters.	Conflict takes place everywhere among all sorts of interest groups.
Social class	Only two classes defined by their relationship to the means of production: the bourgeoisie and proletariat. The aristocracy and the lumpenproletariat are parasite classes that will be eliminated.	There are number of different classes in society defined by their relative wealth, status, and power.
Concept of the law	It is the tool of the ruling class that criminalizes the activities of the workers harmful to its interests and ignores its own socially harmful behavior.	The law favors the powerful, but not any one particular group. The greater the wealth, power, and prestige a group has, the more likely the law will favor it.
Concept of crime	Some view crime as the revolutionary actions of the downtrodden, others view it as the socially harmful acts of "class traitors," and others see it as violations of human rights.	Conflict theorists refuse to pass moral judgment because they view criminal conduct as morally neutral with no intrinsic properties that distinguish it from conforming behavior. Crime doesn't exist until a powerful interest group is able to criminalize the activities of another less powerful group.
Cause of crime	The dehumanizing conditions of capitalism. Capitalism generates egoism and alienates people from themselves and from others.	The distribution of political power that leads to some interest groups being able to criminalize the acts of other interest groups.
Cure for crime	With the overthrow of the capitalist mode of production, the natural goodness of humanity will emerge, and there will be no more criminal behavior.	As long as people have different interests and as long as some groups have more power than others, crime will exist. Since interest and power differentials are part of the human condition, crime will always be with us.

of war and notes that war naturally invites resistance by those it is waged against. He further adds that when society resists criminal victimization, it "must be in compassion and love, not in terms of the violence that is being resisted" (in Vold, Bernard, & Snipes, 1998, p. 274).

In place of imprisoning offenders, peacemaking criminologists advocate **restorative justice**, which is basically a system of mediation and conflict resolution. Restorative justice is primarily oriented toward repairing the harm caused by crime and typically involves face-to-face confrontations between victim and perpetrator to arrive at mutually agreeable solution to "restore" the situation to what it was before the crime (Champion, 2005). Restorative justice has been applauded because it humanizes justice by bringing victim and offender together to try to correct the wrong

Photo 8.1

The friendly presence of police at a large ethnic festival demonstrates the peacekeeping approach to crime prevention.

done, usually in the form of written apologizes and payment of restitution. Although developed for juveniles and primarily confined to them, restorative justice has also been applied to non-violent adult offenders in a number of countries as well as the United States. The belief behind restorative justice is that, to the extent that both victim and victimizer come to see that justice is attained when a violation of one person by another is made right by the violator, the violator will have taken a step toward reformation and the community will be a safer place in which to live.

❖ Evaluation of Critical Theories

It is often said that Marxist theory has very little that is unique to add to criminology theory: "When Marxist theorists offer explanations of crime that go beyond simply attributing the causes of all crime to capitalism, they rely on concepts taken from the same 'traditional' criminological theories of which they have been so critical" (Akers, 1994, p. 167). Like cultural/anarchic criminologists, with whom they share their anticapitalist views, Marxists tend to ignore empirical studies, preferring historical, descriptive, and illustrative research. The tendency to romanticize criminals as revolutionaries has long been a major criticism of Marxist criminologists, although because of the influence of left realists they are less likely to do this today.

Can Marxists claim support for their argument that capitalism causes crime and socialism "cures" it? It may be true that capitalist countries in general have higher crime rates than socialist countries, but the question is whether the Marxist interpretation is correct. Lower crime rates in socialist societies may have more to do with repressive law enforcement than with any altruistic qualities supposedly intrinsic to socialism.

Marxist criminology also seems to assume that the conditions prevailing in Marx's time still exist today in advanced capitalist societies. People from all over the world have risked life and limb to get into capitalist countries because those countries are where human rights are most respected and human needs most readily accessible. Left realism realizes this and is more the reform-minded "practical" wing of Marxism than a theory of crime that has anything special to offer criminology. Indeed, "working within the system" has produced numerous changes in American society that used to be considered socialist, such as those mentioned under the policy implications of institutional anomie theory in Chapter 6.

Conflict theory is challenging and refreshing because its efforts to identify power relationships in society have applications that go beyond criminology. But there are problems with it as a theory of criminal behavior. It has even been said that "conflict theory does not attempt to explain crime; it simply identifies social conflict as a basic fact of life and a source of discriminatory treatment" (Adler, Mueller, & Laufer, 2001, p. 223). Thus, and despite their differences, both Marxist and conflict criminologists draw a fairly straight line between capitalism or conflict, respectively, and criminal behavior. With the exception of Willem Bonger and his social sentiments, theorists from these two camps rarely attempt to examine specific mechanisms that may intervene between their favored concept and crime.

According to Ronald Akers (1997), peacemaking criminologists "take the extreme position that denies crime as such really exists. Crime exists only because it is a 'discursive production,' that is, a product not only of the interaction of offenders, control agents, criminologists, or other people, or simply by talking about it. . . . This implies that there is no such thing as crime as an objective behavioral reality to be explained." He goes on to ask, "Does this mean that criminal behavior would not exist if we did not talk about it?" (pp. 176–177). This may be somewhat overstated, but one does often get the impression from reading peacemaking literature that crime is simply an invention. A similar approach is that of using arbitrary *mala prohibita* crimes to make a point about all crimes. For instance, William Chambliss correctly argued that the vagrancy laws in 12th-century England following the Black Death plague, which devastated the labor force and deprived landowners of cheap labor, were passed to curtail the mobility of laborers for the benefit of the ruling classes (the landowners). Having done this, he employed the classic "bait and switch" tactic by claiming that "what is true of the vagrancy laws is also true of the criminal law in general" (in Nettler, 1984, p. 197).

Lanier and Henry (1998) point out that "postmodernism has been sharply criticized by mainstream criminologists . . . as (1) difficult to understand, not the least because of its language; (2) nihilistic and relativistic, having no standards to judge anything as good or bad; and (3) impractical and even dangerous to disempowered groups" (p. 285). Peacemaking criminology urges us to make peace on crime, but what does this actually mean? As a number of commentators have pointed out, "being nice" is not enough to stop others from hurting us. It is undoubtedly true that the reduction of human suffering and achieving a truly just world would reduce crime, as advocates of this position contend, but advocates offer us no notion of how this can be achieved beyond counseling that we should appreciate criminals' points of view and not be so punitive.

❖ Policy and Prevention: Implications of Critical Theories

The policy implications of Marxist theory are straightforward: substitute socialism for capitalism and crime will be reduced. This position was straightforwardly expressed by Richard Quinney (1974): "Only with the collapse of capitalist society and the creation of a new society, based on socialist principles, will there be a solution to the crime problem" (p. 16). Most Marxists today realize that this is unrealistic, a fact underlined for them by the collapse of socialist states across Eastern Europe. They also realize that emphasis on a single cause of crime (the class struggle in a capitalist society) and romanticizing criminals are equally unrealistic. Rather than throw out their entire ideological agenda, left realists now temper their views while still maintaining their critical stance toward the "system." Policy recommendations made by left realists have many things in common with those made by ecological, anomie, and routine activities theorists. Community activities, neighborhood watches, community policing, dispute resolution centers, and target hardening are among the policies suggested.

Because crime is viewed as the result of conflict between interest groups with power and wealth differences, and since conflict theorists view conflict and the existence of social classes as normal, it is difficult to recommend policies *specifically* derived from conflict theory. We might logically conclude from this view of class and conflict that if these things are normal and perhaps beneficial, then so is crime in some sense. If we want to reduce crime we should equalize the distribution of power, wealth, and status, thus reducing the ability of any one group to dictate what is criminalized. Generally speaking, conflict theorists favor programs such as minimum wage laws, sharply progressive taxation, a government-controlled comprehensive health care system, paid maternal leave, and a national policy of family support as a way of reducing crime (Currie, 1989).

❖ Feminist Criminology

Concepts and Concerns of Feminist Criminology

Feminist criminology sits firmly in the critical/conflict camp of criminology. Feminists see women as oppressed both by gender inequality (their social position in a sexist culture) and by class inequality (their economic position in a capitalist society). Just as there is a wide variety of views within critical criminology as a whole, there is a wide variety of feminist positions on crime and other things. Some feminists view the answer to women's oppression as the overthrow of the two-headed monster, capitalism and patriarchy, while others simply seek reform. In the meantime, they all want to interpret female crime from a feminist perspective.

The core concept of most feminist theorizing is patriarchy. **Patriarchy** literally means "rule of the father" and is used to describe any social system that is male dominated at all levels from the family to the highest reaches of government and supported by the belief of male superiority. A patriarchal society is one in which "masculine" traits such as competitiveness, aggressiveness, autonomy, and individualism are valued, and "feminine" traits such as intimacy, connection, cooperation, nurturance, while appreciated, are downplayed (Grana, 2002). Sociologist Joan Huber (2008) views the origins of patriarchy in the different reproductive role of the sexes, with our ancestral mothers caught in a continuous cycle of gestation and lactation that has barred women from public life, first by virtue of their reproductive role and later by customs and laws that justified their exclusion. Huber (2008) maintains that to understand gender differences in almost any behavior we must understand their evolutionary logic.

Photo 8.2

Girls who run away from home often find themselves on the streets where they are preyed upon and often forced into prostitution, shoplifting, and drug trafficking.

Feminist criminologists wrestle with two major concerns, the first being "Do traditional male-centered theories of crime apply to women?" This is known as the **generalizability problem**. The generalizability problem has been defined as "the quest to find theories that account equally for male and female offending" (Irwin & Chesney-Lind, 2008, p. 839). Many feminist criminologists have concluded that male-centered theories have limited applicability to females because they focus on male frustration in their efforts to obtain success goals (status, resources) and ignore female relationship goals (marriage, family) (Leonard, 1995). Although Broidy and Agnew's (1997) discussion of gender differences in the experiencing of negative emotions in Chapter 6 is an effort to generate a general theory, some feminist scholars believe that no feminist-specific general theory is possible and that they must be content to focus on crime-specific "mini-theories" (Daly & Chesney-Lind, 2002). An example is Meda Chesney-Lind's (1995) "criminalizing girls' survival" mini-theory in which she describes a sequence of events related to efforts of parents and social control agents to closely supervise girls and notes that girls are more likely than boys to be reported for status offenses. She also notes that girls are more likely to be sexually abused than boys, that their assailants are more likely to be family members, and that a likely response is for girls to run away from home. When girls run away from such homes, they are returned by paternalistic juvenile authorities who feel it is their duty to "protect" them, which reinforces the girls' feeling of "nobody cares" and strengthens their resolve not to get caught again. When a girl is on the streets, she has to do something to survive: steal money, food, or clothing; use and sell drugs; or engage in prostitution, which may then become lifetime patterns of behavior. Chesney-Lind's point is that girls' victimization and their response to it are shaped by their status in a patriarchal society in which males dominate the family and define their daughters as property. Thus, patriarchy combines with paternalism to force girls to live "lives of escaped convicts."

Others wonder why a special feminist theory is needed since most offenders tend to be found in the same places as their male counterparts; i.e., among single-parent families located in poor socially disorganized neighborhoods. Male and female crime rates increase or decrease together across different nations and communities, indicating that females are responsive to the same environmental conditions as males (Campbell, 2009). This was recognized more than three-quarters of a century ago in Sheldon and Eleanor Glueck's *Five Hundred Delinquent Women* (1934). So demographically, at least, theories that address these factors generalize to females.

Individual-level correlates of male offending such as low self-control, low IQ, ADHD, and so forth are also correlated with female offending (Moffitt, Caspi, Rutter, & Silva, 2001), and again this is something the Gluecks pointed out in 1934. As Bennett, Farrington, and Huesmann (2005) put it, "Males and females are not raised apart and exposed to an entirely different set of developmental conditions" (p. 280). Males and females may be affected to different degrees by the same risk factors, but criminogenic risk factors are still risk factors for both genders (Steffensmeier & Haynie, 2000). Given this evidence, Daly and Chesney-Lind (2002) ask, "Why do similar processes produce a distinctive, gender-based [male] structure to crime and delinquency?"(p. 270). Daly and Chesney-Lind's question leads us to the gender ratio problem.

The **gender ratio problem** is this: "What explains the universal fact that women are far less likely than men to involve themselves in criminal activity?" (Daly & Chesney-Lind, 2002, pp. 269–270). Eileen Leonard (1995) contends that the fact of huge gender differences in criminal behavior is not in dispute by feminists or anyone else: "Women have had lower rates of crime in *all nations*, in *all communities* within nations, for *all age groups*, for *all periods in recorded history*, and for practically *all crimes*" (p. 55, emphasis in original). Why this is so has been called the "single most important fact that criminology theories must be able to explain" (Bernard, Snipes, & Gerould, 2010, p. 299). Figure 8.1 shows percentages of males and females arrested for seven of the eight FBI index crimes (FBI, 2013) in 2012. There are about nine males for every one female

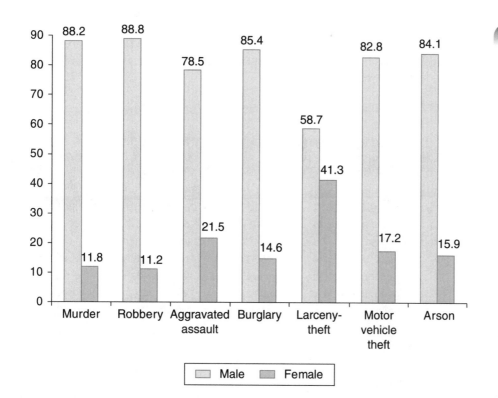

Figure 8.1

Male vs. Female Arrests for FBI Part I Crimes in 2012 by Percentage

Source: FBI, 2013

arrested for murder and robbery, but fewer than two males for every female arrested for larceny/theft. The more violent the offense, the more males dominate in its commission.

Women's Liberation and Crime

Two early attempts to answer the gender ratio problem question were Freda Adler's (1975) **masculinization hypothesis** and Rita Simon's (1975) **emancipation hypothesis**, both of which looked at the effect of the women's liberation movement on female offending. Adler's (1975) point was that the adoption of male roles would result in female attitudes and behavior becoming "masculinized" and eventually crime rates matching those of males: "In the same way that women are demanding equal opportunity in fields of legitimate endeavor, a similar number of determined women are forcing their way into the world of major crimes" (p. 13). She went on to opine that "increasing numbers of women are using guns, knives, and wits to establish themselves as full human beings, as capable of violent aggression as any man" (1975, p. 15). Adler's view was not well received by many feminists who did not share her opinion of how women might establish their humanity and who saw it as providing ammunition for those who opposed women's liberation ("We don't want our women committing crimes or becoming masculinized!").

Rita Simon's (1975) emancipation hypothesis claimed that increased participation in the workforce afforded women greater opportunities to commit job-related crime such as "fraud, embezzlement, larceny and forgery" (p. 2) and denied Adler's notion that to engage in crime women would have to become more masculine. Women are quite capable of committing crimes when the opportunity presents itself without first undergoing masculinization. Simon believed that while women's emancipation would generate an increase in nonviolent crime, it would simultaneously reduce women's violent crime by reducing the frustrations she believed they had when stuck in traditional housewife roles. Neither hypothesis proved useful in explaining the gender crime ratio because male/female arrest rates have not varied by more than 5 percentage points over the past 40 years (Campbell, 2009).

THEORY IN ACTION: Revolutionary Marxism, Gender Fluidity, and Patty Hearst

On the evening on February 4, 1974, a 19-year-old college student named Patricia (Patty) Hearst and her fiancé, Steven Weed, were enjoying a quiet evening at home in Berkeley, California, when a group of armed men and women burst into their apartment, beat up Weed, threw Patty in the trunk of a car, and drove off. Hearst's kidnapping stunned the nation and made front-page national news for months.

Photo 8.3

This poster issued by the Symbionese Liberation Army shows Patricia Hearst, as "Tania," holding a machine gun.

Her kidnappers were a radical leftist group of anti-American and anticapitalist terrorists who called themselves the Symbionese Liberation Army (SLA). The SLA was led by a prison escapee named Donald DeFreeze, who liked to be called by his "war name"—General Field Marshal Cinque. The stated goal of the SLA was to incite a guerrilla war against the U.S. government and destroy the "capitalist state." The SLA ranks included blacks and whites of both sexes from various walks of life united by their extremist views and fanned by the anti–Vietnam War sentiment rife at the time. Hearst was from an extremely wealthy and powerful family; her grandfather was newspaper magnate William Randolph Hearst, the epitome of everything the SLA hated. Shortly after her disappearance, the SLA began releasing audiotapes demanding millions of dollars in food donations and the release of their imprisoned members in exchange for her release. During this time, the

SLA apparently began abusing and brainwashing Patty, hoping to turn this "capitalist" heiress into a poster child for the revolution. It seemed to have worked, because the SLA began releasing statements by Patty indicating that she had renounced her former life and embraced the group's revolutionary agenda, taking the revolutionary name Tania. The famous picture of her posed in front of the SLA banner wielding an automatic rifle shown nearby was taken at the time of her "conversion."

Ten weeks after her abduction, Patty was captured on surveillance cameras taking part in the armed robbery of a San Francisco bank. A few weeks after the robbery, six members of the SLA, including DeFreeze, died in a fire following a massive shootout with the police in Los Angeles. Patty was not present at the house, and she and her surviving captors (or "comrades"—depending on which version of her story one believes) disappeared. The FBI captured her in San Francisco on September 18, 1975, and charged her with bank robbery and other crimes. She was defended by famous attorney F. Lee Bailey, who claimed Patty had been tortured, raped, and brainwashed into becoming a part of the SLA, but the jury found her guilty, and she was sentenced to seven years in prison. President Carter commuted her sentence after she had served two years, and she was later pardoned by President Clinton.

Was Patty a victim, a survivor, or a willing convert to a radical left-wing ideology that turned her into a criminal? She certainly did embrace the SLA ideology; upon her arrest she offered reporters a defiant clenched-fist salute and told the booking officer at the jail that her occupation was "urban guerilla." The issue is how free a "free choice" can be after brainwashing, and she was only 19 at the time of her kidnapping. She would later say that she joined the SLA because she was afraid of them and that she ran from the FBI because she was afraid of them also.

THEORY IN ACTION (Continued)

Many left-wingers believed she was a rational person who defied her bourgeois class expectations, shed her false consciousness, and logically arrived at the "right" political ideology after being exposed to it. Since capitalism is evil, it did not bother them that Patty had violated it by robbing banks and planting bombs. For their part, feminists loved how Patty demonstrated the fluidity of gender by transforming herself from a "respectable" debutant engaged to be married into a gangster's moll. She may have been Rita Adler's model (see text) for her statement that "increasing numbers of women are using guns, knives, and wits to establish themselves as full human beings, as capable of violent aggression as any man."

Whatever the case may be, the Patty Hearst story starkly illustrates the theories in this chapter. Her story unfolded at a time when many Americans were embracing the ideas put forward by any system of thought critical of American society and at a time when feminist theory was new and refreshing. Her story also illustrates the most potent and important social, economic, and political divide of the 20th century, between those who believe in a free market system (capitalism) and those who prefer a government-run command economy (socialism).

Discussion Questions

1. Check out the Patty Hearst story online through any Internet search engine or in the sources listed after the Discussion Questions. Do you think she was a spoiled rich girl out for kicks who freely joined the SLA, or did she do what she had to in order to survive?

2. Patty subsequently married and has two grown children. What, if anything, does that say to you about Patty's "transformation" into a gangster?

3. Look up the phrase *Stockholm syndrome* and explain how that may apply to Patty.

Sources: Scott, 2012; Webster, 1990

Another interpretation linking women's liberation to female crime is the **economic marginalization hypothesis**. This perspective argues that both Adler and Simon neglected to pay sufficient attention to patriarchy and the extent to which males control female labor and sexuality. Research has suggested that much of female crime is related to economic need and that women's poverty and crime rates have risen together (Hunnicutt & Broidy, 2004). According to this hypothesis, both the increasing crime and poverty rates are indirectly related to the women's liberation movement. Specifically, the women's liberation movement has generated efforts by women to free themselves from the power of men, but by doing so women have freed men from their traditional roles as providers. The decline in male respect for women has led to a large increase in out-of-wedlock births and divorce. These things have led to female-headed households and the "feminization of poverty," which motivates women to engage in economically related crimes such as prostitution, drug sales, and shoplifting (Reckdenwald & Parker, 2008).

Power-Control Theory

Despite doubts that a general feminist theory of criminal behavior is possible, there have been some attempts to formulate one, including John Hagan's power-control theory. **Power-control theory** views gender differences in antisocial behavior as a function of power differentials in the family and states that these arise from the positions these spouses occupy in the workforce. Where fathers are the sole breadwinner and mothers are housewives and/or have menial jobs, a patriarchal family structure results, especially if the father is in a position of authority at work.

The patriarchal family is one in which the workplace experiences are reproduced and is said to be "unbalanced" in favor of the father. Patriarchal families are viewed as granting greater freedom to boys to prepare them for traditional male roles while daughters are socialized to be feminine, conforming, and domesticated.

The egalitarian family develops in the absence of large differences between the work roles of parents and where the responsibility for child rearing is shared. Power relations in such families are said to be "balanced," and parents socialize male and female children similarly. Similarity of treatment will lead to sons and daughters developing similar traits, attitudes, and behaviors, which implies that girls from such families will increase their delinquent involvement. Hagan (1989) claims that while there will be large gender differences in delinquency among children from patriarchal families, egalitarian families will show smaller gender differences. According to Siegel (1992), it is not only middle-class girls who will increase their offending: "Power-control theory, then, implies that middle-class youth of *both* sexes will have higher crime rates than their lower-class peers" (p. 270).

Structured Action Theory: "Doing Gender"

Central to James Messerschmidt's **structured action theory** is the concept of hegemonic masculinity, the cultural ideal of masculinity that men are expected to live up to. **Hegemonic masculinity** is "defined through work in the paid-labor market, the subordination of women, heterosexism, and the driven uncontrollable sexuality of men" (Messerschmidt, 1993, p. 82). Although it is about living up to masculine ideals and distancing the masculine self from femininity, hegemonic masculinity is also a way to maintain patriarchy (Connell & Messerschmidt, 2005).

For Messerschmidt, gender is something males and females demonstrate and accomplish rather than something they automatically are by virtue of biological sex. Doing gender is an ongoing dynamic process by which males express their masculinity to audiences of both sexes to be socially validated. This expression can take many forms according to culture and social context, which jointly inform males of the appropriate norms of masculine behavior. To project a positive masculine image to the world, a man must learn the relevant cultural definitions of masculinity. Traditional middle-class ways of doing masculinity (proving one's manhood) include being successful in a career, having and providing for a family, being a good protector, and projecting an aura of quiet dominance as well as physical and mental strength. When males cannot or will not strive to accomplish legitimate modes of doing gender they develop alternative modes to accomplish the same result, such as engaging in crime (Merton's innovation mode of adaptation). In lower-class cultures this often involves violent confrontations over status issues because taking matters into one's own hands is seen as the only way to obtain "juice" (masculine status) on the street. Violent and criminal behavior can thus be used as a resource for accomplishing masculinity—for "doing gender."

Messerschmidt also theorizes about "doing femininity" among gang girls and women engaging in "bad girl femininity." Although violence is defined culturally as masculine behavior, Messerschmidt (2002) asserts that if females engage in it they are "not attempting increasingly to be masculine, but, rather, were engaging in physical violence authentically as girls and as a legitimate aspect of their femininity" (p. 465). Gang females do not consider themselves masculine, then, but rather as "bad." Gang girls are emphatic about their feminine identity and are "very fussy over gender display (clothes, hair, makeup) and, thus, for the most part display themselves as feminine in 'culturally approved' ways" (Messerschmidt, 2002, p. 464).

Messerschmidt wants to show that because gender is fluid and context specific, there is no incompatibility between "acting bad" and femininity. Girls and women fight to defend friends, the "hood," and "her man" from the poaching efforts of other females. He also wants to emphasize that the construction of a "bad ass" image is not a concern for gang females as it is among gang males and that it is very much subordinate to constructing a feminine image. When females fight, they are contextually "doing masculinity" just as males contextually "do femininity" when "comforting and nurturing a fellow gang member" (Messerschmidt, 2002, p. 473).

Both Hagan and Messerschmidt's theories place sole reliance on socialization and gender roles to explain differences in male-female offending. Others attempt to explain it by saying that the sexes differ in exposure to delinquent peers, that males are more influenced by peers than females, and that females have greater inhibitory morality (Mears, Ploeger, & Warr, 1998). Cullen and Agnew (2011) aver that statements such as these amount to nothing more than saying boys will be boys and girls will be girls, because they beg the questions of why males are more exposed to and more influenced by delinquent peers than females and why females have a stronger sense of morality. A standard answer to these questions is that girls are more closely supervised than boys, but controlling for supervision level results in the same gender gap in offending (Gottfredson & Hirschi, 1990), and a meta-analysis of 172 studies found a nonsignificant tendency for girls to be *less* strictly supervised than boys (Lytton & Romney, 1991).

Explanations From Evolutionary Biology and Neurobiology

Bernard, Snipes, and Gerould (2010) note that feminists such as Joan Huber have "argued that the natural reproductive differences between the sexes [ultimately] underlie male-female differences" (p. 290). These feminists note with Dianna Fishbein (1992) that "cross cultural studies do not support the prominent role of structural and cultural influences of gender-specific crime rates as the type and extent of male versus female crime remains consistent across cultures" (p. 100). The basic argument is that because the size of the gender gap varies across time and space and yet still remains constantly wide at all times and in all places, biological factors *must* play a major part (Bennett et al., 2005; Campbell, 2009). If only social factors accounted for gender differences there should be a set of cultural conditions under which crime rates would be equal for both sexes (or even higher for females), but no such conditions have ever been found (Bernard, Snipes, & Gerould, 2010). Feminists who include biological thinking in their theories assert that sex differences in dominance and aggression are seen in all human cultures from the earliest days of life and are observed in all primate and most mammalian species, and no one would evoke socialization to explain sex differences in these instances (Campbell, 2006; Hopcroft, 2009).

Neuroscientists have long known that chemistry organizes the brain in male or female directions while we are still in our mothers' wombs (Amateau & McCarthy, 2004), and it does so in such a way that males become more vulnerable to the various traits associated with antisocial behavior (Ellis, 2003). Doreen Kimura (1992) tells us that males and females come into this world with "differently wired brains," and these differences "make it almost impossible to evaluate the effects of experience independent of physiological predisposition" (p. 119). Sarah Bennett and her colleagues (2005) agree and explain the pathways from sex-differentiated brain organization to antisocial behavior:

> Males and females vary on a number of perceptual and cognitive information-processing domains that are difficult to ascribe to sex-role socialization. . . . The human brain is either masculinized or feminized structurally and chemically before birth. Genetics and the biological environment in utero [in the womb] provide the

foundation of gender differences in early brain morphology, physiology, chemistry, and nervous system development. It would be surprising if these differences did not contribute to gender differences in cognitive abilities, temperament, and ultimately, normal or antisocial behavior. (p. 273)

According to many theorists, the major explanation for gender difference in crime is differences in fear and empathy (females higher on both), traits underlain by testosterone and oxytocin (the "cuddle chemical"). Males have significantly more testosterone and females significantly more oxytocin (Herman, Putman, & van Honk, 2006). Higher testosterone equals less fear, and higher oxytocin equals greater empathy (Campbell, 2008; MacDonald & MacDonald, 2010). Shelly Taylor (2006) among others has shown how these hormones work against each other and that their levels are ultimately linked to sex-differentiated evolutionary selection for nurturing behavior. No one claims these substances are major risk (testosterone) or protective (oxytocin) factors for or against committing criminal acts, only that they are major factors underlying gender differences in the propensity to commit such acts.

Anne Campbell's Staying-Alive Hypothesis

Why do "differently wired brains" and different hormone levels between the sexes exist in the first place? No such differences arise without an evolutionary reason behind them. Biologists note that sex differences in aggression and dominance seeking are related to parental investment (time and resources devoted to parental care), not biological sex per se. It is parental investment that provokes evolutionary pressures for the selection of the mechanisms that underlie these behaviors. In some bird and fish species males contribute greater parental investment (e.g., incubating the eggs and feeding the young), and females take more risks, are more promiscuous and aggressive in courtship, have higher testosterone levels, and engage in violent competition for mates (Barash & Lipton, 2001). In these species, sex-related characteristics are the opposite of those found in species in which females assume all or most of the burden of parenting (the vast majority of species).

Anne Campbell (1999), who describes herself as a liberal evolutionary feminist, has attempted to account for the gender ratio problem using the logic of evolutionary theory in her **staying-alive hypothesis**. Her work has been characterized as "perhaps the best attempt to account for gender differences in criminality" (Roach & Pease, 2013, p. 66). Campbell's hypothesis is based on the traits of nurturing and fear coupled with male status concerns. Campbell argues that because the obligatory parental investment of females is greater than that of males, and because of the infant's greater dependence on the mother, a mother's presence is more critical to offspring survival than is a father's. She notes that offspring survival is more critical to female reproductive success (the passing of one's genes to subsequent generations—the ultimate "goal" of all life forms) than to male reproductive success. Because of the limits placed on female reproductive success by long periods of gestation and lactation, females have more investment tied up in children they already have than males, whose reproductive success is only limited by access to willing females. You are reminded that men and women are adapted to seek sexual pleasure, not reproductive success per se. Reproduction was simply a more common outcome of sexual activity in precontraceptive times.

Campbell argues that because offspring survival is so enormously important to their reproductive success, females have evolved a propensity to avoid engaging in behaviors that pose survival risks. The practice of keeping nursing children in close proximity in ancestral environments posed an elevated risk of injuring the child as well as herself if the mother placed herself in risky situations. Thus it became adaptive for females to experience many different situations as fearful. There are no sex differences in fearfulness unless a situation contains a significant risk of physical injury, and it this fear that accounts for the greater tendency of females to avoid or remove themselves from potentially violent situations and to employ low-risk strategies in competition and dispute resolution relative to males. Average differences in fear levels are strong and consistently found cross-culturally regardless of how fear is measured (Brebner, 2003; Campbell, 2009). Females do engage in competition with one another for resources and mates, of course, but it is rarely violent competition. Most of it is decidedly low key, low risk, and chronic as opposed to high-key, high-risk, and acute male competition.

Campbell's theory also focuses on gender differences in status striving. Campbell shows that when females engage in crime they almost always do so for instrumental reasons, and their crimes rarely involve risk of physical injury. There is no evidence, for instance, that female robbers crave the additional payoffs of dominance that male robbers do or seek reputations as "hard-asses." Campbell (1999) notes that while women do aggress and do steal, "they rarely do both at the same time because the equation of resources and status reflects a particularly masculine logic" (p. 210).

❖ Evaluation of Feminist Theories

In common with critical theorists, feminist theorists have generally been content to focus on descriptive studies or on crime-specific "mini-theories," such as Chesney-Lind's "Criminalizing girls' survival," that have worked well to explain female-specific offending.

Although Hagan's and Messerschmidt's theories offer some interesting insights regarding family dynamics and how gender is perceived in different social contexts, they have not moved the discipline forward. Messerschmidt's theory seems to be a rehash of the old subcultural theories in which "doing gender" is substituted for male status striving stressed by subculturists such as Albert Cohen in the 1950s.

The assertion in Hagan's power-control theory that middle-class children will have higher rates of antisocial behavior than lower-class children is contrary to all we know about the relationship between social class and crime, especially serious crime (Walsh, 2011a). However, Hagan (1989) admits that his theory best addresses minor misbehaviors such as smoking, drinking, and fighting, which leaves unaddressed the serious violent crimes that most strongly differentiate male and female offending. It is thus difficult not to agree with feminists who argue that qualitative studies of specific crimes are the best way to study female crime, although, of course, this does not address the gender ratio problem.

As previously noted, if forced to boil down the reasons for the universal sex difference in criminal behavior to their bare minimum, differences in empathy and fear would be the strongest candidates. Numerous studies show large differences in average levels of fear and empathy between males and females of all ages (reviewed in Walsh, 2011a). Empathy and fear are the natural enemies of crime for obvious reasons:

> Empathy is other oriented and prevents one from committing acts injurious to others because one has an emotional and cognitive investment in the well-being of others. Fear is self-oriented and prevents one from committing acts injurious to others out of fear of the consequences to one's self. Many other prosocial tendencies flow from these two basic foundations, such as a strong conscience, altruism, self-control, and agreeableness. (Walsh, 2011a, p. 124)

Campbell's staying-alive/high-fear hypothesis is about why females commit so little crime, not why some females commit it, but it does address the gender ratio problem. Because of its biological underpinnings, it may not be acceptable to many traditional feminists, but only four of the 27 commentators on her target article argued that strictly social theories better accounted for gender differences in crime. Campbell's hypothesis must be augmented with cultural factors because we sometimes see females committing more serious crimes than males. For instance, African American females have had higher homicide rates than white *males* ever since the UCR has existed (Barak, 1998). In 2007, the black female homicide rate was 6.2 per 100,000 and the white male rate was 5.4. This does not negate the basic gender ratio argument because *within* the African American community the gender ratio is much higher than it is in the white community. The black male homicide rate in 2007 was 39.7, which is 6.4 times the black female rate, while the white male rate (5.4) was only 2.8 times the white female rate of 1.9 (U.S. Census Bureau, 2012).

❖ Policy and Prevention: Implications of Feminist Theories

The policy recommendations of feminist theory depend on which variety of feminism we examine. Marxists seem more concerned with defeating capitalism than patriarchy; socialists are more concerned with patriarchy but have no love for capitalism; radical feminists want to abolish gender, and liberal feminists are less radical reformers who want only to abolish patriarchy (Lanier & Henry, 2010). Liberal feminist reformers have been successful in moving women into what had formerly been "male" occupations, but how the policies of other forms of feminism (abolishing capitalism and gender) could be implemented, as well as their desirability, are open to highly contentious discussion. There are all sorts of other recommendations in between, the major one being the reform of our patriarchal society. Other recommendations include the more equal (less paternalistic) treatment of girls and boys by juvenile authorities, increased educational and occupational choices for women so that those in abusive relationships can leave them, more day care centers, and so forth. Feminist theory suggests that gender sensitivity education in the schools and workplaces may lead men to abandon many of their embedded sexist ideas pertaining to the relationship between the sexes.

Feminist criminologists have impacted the criminal justice system more strongly than criminology. The efforts of feminists to fight gender stereotypes have moved women into previously all-male occupations such as police, probation/parole, and corrections officer positions and have placed more female judges on the bench and more lawyers before the bar. This has led to a greater understanding of female victims and their plight. Feminist criminologists and other feminist activists have been in the forefront in fighting such previously quasi-"acceptable" practices as sexual harassment, stalking, date rape, and child pornography. It was feminists who long pushed for mandatory arrests for domestic violence and now have it, although this has led to an increase in female as well as male arrests. Feminists also fought for other reforms such as removing the spousal exception to rape (up until the 1980s it was not legally possible for a man to rape his wife) and rape shield laws, protecting rape victims' sexual history from examination in a rape trial. Overall, feminist criminology has been quite successful in pushing for a more just, less patriarchal, and more sensitive criminal justice system.

Table 8.2

Summarizing Critical and Feminist Theories

Theory	Key Concepts	Strengths	Weaknesses
Marxist-Based Theories	Crime is the natural result of worker exploitation within a capitalist mode of production. Mindless work alienates people from their human nature. Crime will cease when there is no longer any conflict; that is, when we have a socialist classless society.	Marxist thought provides the philosophical foundation of all critical schools of criminology. Points out the constant historical battles between the haves and have-nots—the bourgeoisie and proletariat in Marx's time.	Trace every evil to a single cause—capitalism. Naïve view that conflict will cease with the coming of communism. Unrealistic policy recommendations given the collapse of socialism around the world.
Weberian Conflict-Based Theories	Crime is the result of political struggles among social groups seeking to enhance their life chances. Those with the power are able to criminalize acts of other groups that are not in the interests of the elite. Some groups are so outside the mainstream that almost all their activities are criminalized.	Emphasize that conflict is ubiquitous and can never be eliminated—nor should it be because it is necessary for social change. Conflict exists among a variety of status, class, and party groups, not just two groups as in Marxist thought.	Just as reductionist as Marxism because they reduce all crime to individual and group conflict. Also in common with Marist criminology, they neglect empirical research in favor of historical analysis and case histories.
Peacemaking	Abhors the "war on crime" metaphor and wants to substitute "peace on crime." Wants society to appreciate the views of all others, including criminals. Wants to substitute restorative justice for more punitive social responses to crime.	Provides a foil against those who advocate the "tough on crime" position. Has a quasi-religious element to it and advocates a humane and forgiving approach exemplified by restorative justice.	Criticized mostly for its naiveté and its often impenetrable prose. It wants us to make peace on crime but offers little advice on how to do this except to recommend restorative justice.
Women's Liberation Theories	Increased opportunities for women in "male" roles in the workforce will masculinize women (Adler) and eventually they will commit as much crime as males. Not necessary to become masculinized for women to commit more crime (Simon). Women's liberation has led to decline in respect for women, and men have thus abandoned their protective role, leading to feminization of poverty (Hunnicutt & Broidy).	Focus attention on female criminality and bring girls and women to the fore. Ask if "male"-centered theories apply to females and about the ubiquitous gap between male and female offending. Have had large impact on criminal justice policies.	The generalizability problem is no problem because criminals of both genders are found in the same areas. Also, the same traits that predict male offending predict female offending. Efforts to explain the gender ratio problem have relied almost exclusively on socialization.
Power-Control	Focuses on family structure—patriarchal versus egalitarian. Because of different patterns of socialization, children from patriarchal families will have greater gender difference in offending than those from egalitarian families. Claims that middle-class children will be more delinquent than lower-class children.	Explains how experiences in the larger social class context are reproduced in the family. Emphasizes family dynamics.	Relies solely on gender socialization to explain gender differences in crime and delinquency. Admits theory only explains minor misbehaviors. Claims about delinquency and class contradict what is known in that respect.

(Continued)

Table 8.2

(Continued)

Theory	Key Concepts	Strengths	Weaknesses
Structured Action	One's gender is something one demonstrates rather than something one automatically is. Males and females "do gender" differently in different social classes. In the lower classes, males doing gender means garnering "juice" through displays of toughness and sexuality. Many of these ways lead to crime.	Emphasizes the fluid nature of gender and how it is demonstrated differently in different cultures and subcultures.	Very little new in the theory regarding status striving in different areas not said in the old subcultural theories except to add females. Once again, sole reliance on socialization to explain gender differences in crime.
Staying-Alive	Gender differences in crime are ultimately traceable to sex-differentiated reproductive roles. Female survival means more to her reproductive success and thus females have evolved mechanisms—primarily fear—that deter them from engaging in risky behaviors. Status concerns are also less vital to female reproductive success, so they are less likely to engage in violent competitions with other females.	Although not billed as a theory, this hypothesis welds together plentiful data from evolutionary biology, neuroscience, psychology, and sociology into a coherent explanation for the gender ratio problem. Fear and empathy are the natural enemies of crime, and every study assessing gender differences finds females to be significantly higher in both.	Does not explain why females commit crimes, but rather why they do not. Although it integrates insights from many disciplines, it could benefit from attempting to explain anomalous facts such as the homicide gap between black females and white males.

Summary

- *Critical criminology* is a generic term encompassing many theoretical positions united by the common view that society is best characterized by conflict and power relations rather than by value consensus.
- Marxist criminologists follow the theoretical trail of Karl Marx, who posited the existence of two conflicting classes in society, the bourgeoisie and the proletariat. While some modern Marxists tend to romanticize criminals as heroic revolutionaries, Marx considered them "social scum" who preyed upon the working class. Marx is credited with introducing the terms *primitive rebellion* and *alienation* in criminology's vocabulary.

- Willem Bonger is credited with being the first Marxist criminologist. He was concerned with two opposite "social sentiments": altruism and egoism. The sentiment of altruism is killed in a capitalist social system because such a system generates competition for wealth, status, and jobs. Thus, capitalism produces egoism, which leads to criminal behavior on the part of both the poor and the rich.
- Marxists tend to view capitalism as the only cause of crime, and they insist that class and class values are generated by the material conditions of social life. Because only the material conditions of life really matter, the only way to make any serious impact on

crime is to eliminate the capitalist mode of production and institute a Marxist social order. Left realists realize that such a radical transformation is highly unlikely in modern times, and although they maintain a critical stance toward the system, they work within it in an effort to influence social policy.

■ Conflict theorists share some sentiments with Marxists but view conflict in pluralistic terms and as intrinsic to society, not something that can be eliminated. Crime is the result of the ability of powerful interest groups to criminalize the behavior of other less powerful interest groups when that behavior is contrary to their interests.

■ Conflict criminological research tends to focus on the differential treatment by the criminal justice system of individuals who are members of less powerful groups such as minorities, women, and working-class whites.

■ Peacemaking criminology is based on religious principles more than empirical science. It wants to make peace on crime, counsels us that we should appreciate the criminals' point of view, and wants us to be less punitive.

■ Feminist criminology focuses on trying to understand female offending from the feminist perspective, which contends that women are faced with special disabilities living in an oppressive sexist society.

■ The two big issues in feminist criminology are the generalizability problem (do traditional theories of crime explain female as well as male offending?) and the gender ratio problem (what accounts for the huge gap in offending between males and females?).

■ Early attempts to explain female crime from the feminist tradition emphasized the masculinization of female attitudes as they increasingly adopted "male" roles or simply that as women moved into the workforce in greater numbers they found greater opportunities to commit job-related crimes. Many feminists rejected both positions, pointing out that such theorizing provided ammunition for those who opposed the women's movement and that regardless of any increase in female offending, the male/female gap remains as wide as ever.

■ John Hagan and James Messerschmidt have formulated theories of gender difference in antisocial behavior based on socialization and gender role theories. Other feminists maintain that we cannot understand gender differences in behavior without understanding the underlying biological differences between the sexes.

■ The size and universality of the gender gap suggests to some that the most logical explanation for it must lie in some fundamental differences between the sexes rather than socialization, such as neurological and hormonal differences.

■ Anne Campbell's staying-alive hypothesis attempts to explain the gender ratio problem in terms of differential evolutionary selection pressures between the sexes. Female survival was more crucial to their reproductive success than male survival was to theirs. Natural selection exerted pressure for females to be more fearful of dangerous situations, whereas for males the seeking of dominance and status, which aided their reproductive success, often placed them in such situations.

Exercises and Discussion Questions

1. Do you think the "material conditions of life" largely determine what we will know, believe, and value and how we will behave?

2. Do you believe that social conflict is inevitable? In what ways is conflict a good thing?

3. Can inequality ever be eliminated? If we can do this, what price would we pay?

4. Do we really need a feminist criminology, or do the traditional theories suffice to explain both male and female criminality?

5. What advantages can we gain from natural science knowledge of sex differences in understanding the gender ratio problem?

6. Explain how ultimate-level explanations of gender differences in behavior, such as Campbell's staying-alive hypothesis, are or are not useful for criminologists.

Useful Websites

Conflict theory. http://criminology.fsu.edu/crimtheory/conflict.htm.

Feminist criminology. www.tulane.edu/~femtheory/journals/paper8.html.

Karl Marx. www.historyguide.org/intellect/marx.html.

Peacemaking criminology. www.greggbarak.com/whats_new_2.html.

Postmodern criminology. www.bunker8.pwp.blueyonder.co.uk/misc/pmod.htm.

Chapter Terms

Alienation

Bourgeoisie

Class struggle

Critical criminology

Economic marginalization hypothesis

Emancipation hypothesis

Gender ratio problem

Generalizability problem

Hegemonic masculinity

Left realists

Lumpenproletariat

Masculinization hypothesis

Minority power groups

Patriarchy

Peacemaking criminology

Power-control theory

Primitive rebellion hypothesis

Proletariat

Restorative justice

Social sentiments

Staying-alive hypothesis

Structured action theory

CHAPTER 9

Psychosocial Theories

Individual Traits and Criminal Behavior

Little Jimmy Caine is an emotionless, guiltless, walking id, all 5' 5" and 130 pounds of him. By the time he was 26, Jimmy had accumulated one of the worst criminal records the police in Toledo, Ohio, had ever seen: burglary, robbery, aggravated assault, rape—name it, Jimmy had done it. This little tearaway had been arrested for the brutal rape of a 45-year-old barmaid. Jimmy entered an unlocked bar after closing time to find the lone barmaid attending to some cleaning chores. Putting a knife to the terrified woman's throat, he forced her to strip and proceeded to rape her. Because she was not sexually responsive, Jimmy became angry and placed her head over the kitchen sink and tried to decapitate her. His knife was as dull as his conscience, which only increased his anger so he picked up a bottle of liquor and smashed it over her head. While the woman lay moaning at his feet, he poured more liquor over her, screaming, "I'm going to burn you up, bitch!" The noisy approach of the bar's owner sent Jimmy scurrying away like a rat who smelled the cat. He was arrested 45 minutes later casually eating a hamburger at McDonald's.

Jimmy didn't fit the demographic profile of individuals who engage in this type of crime. Although he had a slightly below-average IQ, he came from a fairly normal intact middle-class home. However, Jimmy had been in trouble since his earliest days and had been examined by a variety of psychiatrists and psychologists. Psychiatrists diagnosed him with something called conduct disorder as an 8-year-old and as having antisocial personality disorder at 18. Jimmy's case reminds us that we have to go beyond factors such as age, race, gender, and socioeconomic status to explain why individuals commit criminal acts. In this chapter we look at many of the traits psychologists and psychiatrists have examined to explain individual criminality. These explanations do not compete with sociological explanation; rather, they complement them.

❖ The Two "Great Pillars of Psychology"

This chapter is called *psychosocial* rather than *psychological* because, along with many others (e.g., Cullen & Agnew, 2011), I believe it is artificial to strictly separate social and psychological approaches. Many sociological theories—self-control, social learning, subcultural, and general strain theories, for instance, focus heavily on psychological traits. Psychosocial theories of criminal behavior are more interested in individual differences in the propensity to commit crimes than in environmental conditions that may push a person into committing a crime, although the difference is only a matter of degree. Two of the most respected modern criminologists, Francis Cullen and Robert Agnew (2011), have written that "it has become increasingly clear that biological factors, individual traits, and social factors all have an important role to play in the explanation of crime" (p. 78). We have already looked at social factors; biological factors are examined in the next chapter, and in this chapter we look at individual traits other than those examined in previous chapters.

Early theories in the psychological tradition strongly emphasized two major traits contributing to criminal behavior—intelligence and temperament—the so-called "two great pillars of differential psychology" (Chamorro-Premuzic & Furnham, 2005, p. 352). Early theorists assumed that low intelligence hampers the ability to calculate the pleasures and pains involved in undertaking criminal activity and that certain types of temperament make individuals impulsive and difficult to socialize.

One of the earliest works emphasizing low intelligence was Richard Dugdale's *"The Jukes": A Study of Crime, Pauperism, Disease, and Heredity* (1877/1895), which studied the lineage of a rural upstate New York family known for its criminal activity, to which he gave the fictitious name of "Jukes." He traced the family lineage to a colonial-era character named "Max," whose descendants remained in relative isolation and largely propagated themselves through intermarriage. Dugdale eventually traced 1,200 of Max's descendants, among whom he found numerous cases of crime, pauperism, disease, feeblemindedness, sexual promiscuity, and prostitution. Dugdale's work was widely interpreted as evidence of the hereditary nature of criminality, although Dugdale himself believed that moral education could override biological propensities.

Another early study was published by Henry Goddard in a book titled *The Kallikak Family: A Study in the Heredity of Feeble-Mindedness* (1912/1931). This study traced two family lineages of a Revolutionary War soldier named Martin Kallikak Sr., who dallied with a "feebleminded tavern girl" with whom he fathered a son. From this lineage, there issued a variety of individuals of unsavory character. Martin produced another line of descendants with a woman from a "good Quaker family," whom he married and from whose lineage emerged a number of prominent people and very few of unsavory character. From these two families with a common male ancestor and two female ancestors, one "defective" and the other "respectable," Goddard concluded that "degeneracy" was the result of "bad blood" (1931, p. 69).

❖ Intelligence

David Wechsler (who devised many of the IQ tests in use today) defined **intelligence** as "the aggregate or global capacity of the individual to act purposefully, to think rationally, and to deal effectively with his [or her] environment" (in Matarazzo, 1976, p. 79). Although some claim that IQ tests are culturally biased, according to the National Academy of Sciences (Seligman, 1992) and the American Psychological Association's Task Force on Intelligence (Neisser et al., 1995), no study designed to detect such bias has ever done so.

Although most studies of IQ today look at the brain and genes thought to be associated with it, environmental effects should not be neglected. The most important evidence of environmental effects on IQ involves the so-called **Flynn effect**. Flynn (2007) has shown that the average IQ has increased in populations in all developed countries studied by approximately 3.1 points per decade from 1932 to 2000. These gains have been seen mostly in lower socioeconomic groups as the environment has become more equal (better schooling for all, medical treatment). Things like malnutrition and mineral deficiencies that caused rickets, anemia, and many other diseases prevalent in the 1930s are virtually unknown today in developed societies (Lynn, 2009). Eppig, Fincher, and Thornhill (2010, 2011) also note the reduction of parasite infections in developed countries because such infections in early childhood consume the energy otherwise used in building the brain. IQ gains have ceased in developed countries because they have wrung all the IQ-enhancing benefits they can from the environment, although the Flynn effect is still evident in developing countries.

Flynn (2007) claims that the direct genetic effect on IQ is only about 36% (as opposed to much higher estimates claimed by others), with 64% resulting from the indirect effects of genes interacting with the environment. This gene-environment interplay results in what Dickens and Flynn (2001) call the "multiplier effect." That is, genes are usually matched with environments ("high IQ genes" with advantaged environments and "low IQ genes" with disadvantaged environments) and multiply what may have been a small genetic advantage or disadvantage at birth into a large advantage or disadvantage over time. In former times when societies were more unequal, a person born into lower-class conditions was not able to realize his or her full genetic potential, so environmental factors simply reinforced the advantage or disadvantage of genetic inheritance in a kind of "the rich get richer and the poor get poorer" fashion. Dickens and Flynn (2001) go on to say that across the time in which the Flynn effect has been working, the better environments to which successive generations have been exposed has allowed "the potency of environmental factors [to stand] out in bold relief" (p. 351).

❖ The IQ/Crime Connection

A number of reviews find the IQ/crime relationship to be robust (Ellis & Walsh, 2003; Lynam, Moffitt, & Stouthamer-Loeber, 1993). It is stronger than often indicated because most IQ studies lump together boys who commit only minor delinquent acts during their teenage years with boys who will continue to seriously and frequently offend into adulthood. Casual and less serious offenders differ from nonoffenders by only about 1 point while serious persistent offenders differ from nonoffenders by about 17 points (Gatzke-Kopp, Raine, Loeber, Stouthamer-Loeber, Steinhauer, 2002; Moffitt, 1993). Simple arithmetic tells us that pooling these two groups hides the magnitude of IQ differences between nonoffenders and serious offenders if the latter have lower IQs than the former.

David Wechsler's (1958) statement that "the most outstanding feature of the sociopath's test profile is the systematic high score on the performance as opposed to the verbal part of the scale" sparked another way of examining the relationship between IQ and antisocial behavior (p. 176). Most IQ studies look at full-scale IQ (FSIQ), which is obtained by averaging the scores on verbal (VIQ) and performance (PIQ) IQ subscales. While most people's VIQ and PIQ scores closely match, criminal offender populations are almost always found to have significantly lower than average VIQ scores, but not lower PIQ scores, than nonoffenders.

This PIQ>VIQ discrepancy is called **intellectual imbalance**. As Miller (1987) remarks, "This PIQ>VIQ relationship [is] found across studies, despite variations in age, sex, race, setting, and form of the Wechsler [IQ] scale administered, as well in differences in criteria for delinquency" (p. 120). A literature review found that overall VIQ>PIQ boys are underrepresented in delinquent populations by a factor of about 2.6, and PIQ>VIQ boys are overrepresented by a factor of about 2.2 (Walsh, 2003). A VIQ>PIQ profile appears to be a major predictor of prosocial behavior, especially among adults. Barnett, Zimmer, and McCormack (1989) found that only 0.9% of prison inmates had such a profile compared to the 18% of the general male population, a large 20-fold difference. The research on intellectual imbalance provides another example of how the role of IQ in understanding criminal behavior may be underestimated if we rely solely on full-scale IQ rather than looking deeper into the effects of verbal IQ only or of PIQ>VIQ imbalance.

The most usual explanation for the IQ/delinquency link is that it works via poor school performance, which leads to dropping out of school and then associating with delinquent peers (Ward & Tittle, 1994). The idea that IQ influences offending via its influences on school performance was supported in 89% of 158 studies based on official statistics and 77.7% based on self-reports (Ellis & Walsh, 2000). On the other hand, all 46 studies exploring the link between grade point average (GPA) and antisocial behavior established such a link. Actual performance measures of academic achievement such as GPA are probably better predictors of antisocial behavior than IQ. Academic achievement is a measure of IQ plus many other personal and situational characteristics such as conscientious study habits, ambition, and supportive parents: talent + effort.

IQ is related to a wide range of life outcomes that are themselves related to criminal and antisocial behavior such as poverty, lack of education, and unemployment. The data presented in Table 9.1 come from 12,686 white males and females in the National Longitudinal Study of Youth (NLSY). This study began in 1979 when subjects were 14 to 17 years old, and data were collected in 1989 when the subjects were 24 to 27 years old. The bottom 20% on IQ had scores of 87 and below; the top 20% had scores of 113 and above. Note the large ratios between the two groups on all outcomes. For instance, for every one person in the top 20% on IQ ever interviewed in jail or prison there were 31 in the bottom 20% interviewed in jail or prison.

❖ Temperament and Personality

It is obvious that low intelligence alone cannot explain criminal behavior. Most individuals with a below-average IQ do not commit crimes, and many people with an above-average IQ do. Many early psychological criminologists saw criminal behavior as a result of the interaction of low intelligence and a particular kind of temperament. As we have seen, IQ and temperament are given prominent roles as factors influencing how a person copes with strain and thus how insulated he or she is from criminal behavior in Robert Agnew's general strain theory discussed in Chapter 6.

Table 9.1

The Impact of High and Low IQ on Selected Life Outcomes

| | IQ Level | | |
Social Behavior	Bottom 20%	Top 20%	Ratio
Dropped out of high school	66%	2%	33.0:1
Living below poverty level	48%	5%	9.6:1
Unemployed entire previous year*	64%	4%	16.0:1
Ever interviewed in jail or prison	62%	2%	31.0:1
Chronic welfare recipient	57%	2%	28.5:1
Had child out of wedlock**	52%	3%	17.3:1

Source: Herrnstein & Murray, 1994

*Males only **Females only

Temperament is defined as "constitutionally based individual differences in reactivity and self regulation, influenced over time by genes, maturation, and experience" (Rothbart, 2012, p. 9). It is thus a person's habitual mode of emotionally responding to stimuli and is largely a function of genes governing physiological arousal patterns, although arousal systems are fine-tuned by experience. Temperamental components include mood (happy/sad), activity level (high/low), sociability (introverted/extraverted), reactivity (calm/excitable), and affect (warm/cold). These components make it easy or difficult for others to like us and to get along with us. Temperamental differences in children make some easy to socialize and others difficult. Children who throw temper tantrums and reject warm overtures from others may adversely affect the quality of parent-infant interactions regardless of their parent's temperaments and thus lead to poor parent-child attachment and all the negative consequences that result. Numerous studies have shown that parents, teachers, and peers respond to children with bad temperaments negatively and that such children find acceptance only in association with others with similar dispositions (reviewed in Caspi, 2000).

Sigmund Freud and Personality

Personality is an individual's set of relatively enduring and functionally integrated psychological characteristics that result from his or her temperament interacting with cultural and developmental experiences. There are many components of personality that psychologists call traits, some of which are associated with the probability of committing antisocial acts and some of which protect against doing so. People differ only on the strength of these traits; they are not characteristics that some people possess and others do not.

Any discussion of personality must acknowledge the role of the father of psychoanalysis, Sigmund Freud. Freud offered a broad sweeping theory of personality, and although he wrote little about crime, his ideas stimulated many criminologists.

Early psychological theorists never pondered what mental processes might intervene between their assumed causes and criminal behavior. If all people are hedonistic, why do only

Photo 9.2

Sigmund Freud, the father of Personality Psychology.

some commit crimes? If criminals are feebleminded, why don't all low-IQ people commit crimes? The psychological answer to such questions is that individuals possess different personalities, and these different personalities lead them to respond differently to identical situations.

According to Freud, the basic human personality consists of three interacting components each having separate purposes: the id, ego, and superego. The id is the biological raw material of our temperament and personality; it represents our drives and instincts for acquiring life-sustaining necessities and life's pleasures. Like a spoiled child, the id demands instant gratification of its desires and does not care if the means used to satisfy them are appropriate or injurious to self or to others. The id obeys what Freud called the pleasure principle, but because it lacks the ability to engage in the hedonistic calculus, it is often dangerous to itself as well as to others. The selfish, immoral, uncaring, antisocial id is the only aspect of the personality we are born with, so in a Freudian sense we might say that we are all Lombroso's "born criminals."

The ego and the superego are formed from the raw material of the id in the process of socialization. With the correct moral training, energy from the id is used to form the ego, or the aspect of the personality we think of as "me" or "I." The ego obeys the reality principle because it realizes that the desires and demands of the id are necessary, but they must be satisfied in socially appropriate ways if one is to avoid negative consequences. It is the ego that performs the hedonistic calculus; it does not deny the pleasure principle, it simply adjusts it to the demands of reality. Freud analogized the interaction of the ego and the id in terms of a rider and a horse. The horse (the id) supplies the raw locomotive power while the rider (the ego) supplies the goals and the direction (Freud, 1923/1976).

The superego strives for the ideal and is thus just as irrational as the id. It represents all the moral and social rules (the "do's and do not's") internalized by the person during the process of socialization and may be summed up as the conscience. Because many urges have been defined as wrong or sinful, the superego tries to suppress all the normal urges arising from the id. It is the ego's function to sort out the conflict between the antisocial demands of the id and the overly conformist demands of the censorious superego. The normal personality is one in which the ego is successful in working out compromises between its irrational partners. An abnormal personality results when either the id or the superego overwhelms the ego, resulting in psychic energy being drained from the weaker components to strengthen the stronger component. If the id is "in command" of the personality the result is a conscienceless and impulsive individual who seeks to satisfy personal needs regardless of the expense to others.

Personality Traits Positively and Negatively Associated With Criminal Behavior

Impulsiveness is perhaps the trait most often linked to criminal behavior. Impulsiveness is the tendency to act without giving much thought to the consequences. Although impulsiveness and low self-control are somewhat different constructs, they are similar enough to be treated as one. Both involve disinhibited behavior in which the actor is unable or unwilling to consider the long-term consequences of his or her behavior (Chapple & Johnson, 2007).

A review of 80 studies examining the relationship between impulsivity and criminal behavior found that 78 were positive and the remaining two were nonsignificant (Ellis & Walsh, 2000). Although impulsiveness is a potent risk factor for criminality in its own right, it becomes more potent if negative emotionality is added to the mix.

Negative emotionality refers to the tendency to experience many situations as aversive and to react to them with irritation and anger more readily than with positive affective states (McGue, Bacon, & Lykken, 1993). The trait is central to Robert Agnew's general strain theory and is strongly related to self-reported and officially recorded criminality "across countries, genders, races, and methods" (Caspi et al., 1994, p. 163). People who are low on constraint (they are impulsive) tend to be high on negative emotionality. Low levels of a brain chemical called serotonin underlie both high levels of negative emotionality and impulsivity. Caspi and his colleagues (1994) claim that low serotonin may represent a constitutional predisposition for these traits and thus a general vulnerability to criminality. Taking advantage of the relationship between these two traits, Agnew has developed a theory featuring them (discussed in Chapter 11).

Sensation seeking refers to the active desire for novel, varied, and risky sensations (Zuckerman, 1990). Sensation seekers tend to be outgoing and relatively impulsive and fearless. These other traits lead socialized sensation seekers to want to work as fire fighters, police officers, or any other job that provides physical activity, variety, and excitement. Poorly socialized sensation seekers, on the other hand, may well find their kicks in carjacking and burglary. A review of the literature found that 98.4% of the studies reported a statistically significant relationship between sensation seeking and antisocial behavior (Ellis & Walsh, 2000).

Empathy is the emotional and cognitive ability to understand the feelings and distress of others as if they were your own. The emotional component allows you to "feel" the other person's pain, and the cognitive component allows you to understand that person's pain and why he or she is feeling it. Some people carry the pains of the world on their shoulders while others couldn't care less about anyone. Most criminals fall into the "care less" category for obvious reasons—you are less likely to victimize someone if you feel and understand what the consequences may be for that person (Covell & Scalora, 2002). High empathy is thus a strong protective factor against criminal offending.

Altruism can be thought of as the action component of empathy; if you feel empathy for someone you will probably feel motivated to take some sort of action to alleviate his or her distress if you are able. As with empathy, altruism lies on a continuum, with criminals (again for obvious reasons) on the wrong end of it. Lack of empathy and altruism is considered one of the most salient characteristics of psychopaths, the worst of the worst among criminals (Fishbein, 2001). A review of 24 studies of these traits found that 23 of them were statistically significant in the predicted direction; that is, the lower the level of empathy/altruism the more the antisocial behavior (Ellis & Walsh, 2000).

Conscientiousness is a primary trait composed of several secondary traits such as well-organized, disciplined, scrupulous, responsible, and reliable at one pole and disorganized, careless, unreliable, irresponsible, and unscrupulous at the other. It is easy to see how conscientiousness could be directly related to crime through the inability of people who lack it to follow a legitimate path to the American Dream: "It is not merely a matter of talented individuals confronted with inferior schools and discriminatory hiring practices. Rather, a good deal of research indicates that many delinquents and criminals are untalented individuals who cannot compete effectively in complex industrial societies" (Vold, Bernard, &

Snipes, 1998, p. 177). In other words, persons with certain kinds of temperament do not develop the personal qualities needed to apply themselves to the long and arduous task of achieving financial success legitimately and as a consequence may attempt to obtain it through crime.

Agreeableness is the tendency to be friendly, considerate, courteous, helpful, and coopera-tive with others. Agreeable persons tend to trust others, to compromise with them, and to empathize with and aid them. This list of subtraits suggests a high degree of concern for prosocial conformity and social desirability. Disagreeable persons simply display the oppo-site characteristics—suspicion of others, unfriendly, uncooperative, unhelpful, and lacking in empathy—which all suggest a lack of concern for prosocial conformity and social desirability. While agreeable people tend to also be conscientious, this is not always the case. A person can be very conscientious at work but thoroughly disagreeable as a person (think of the greedy, egotistical, and manipulative corporate criminal), and one can be very agreeable but be thoroughly lackadaisical at work (think of the ritualist of Merton's anomie theory).

Agreeableness seems to be a better protective factor than conscientiousness. In Miller and Lynam's (2001) meta-analysis of 29 studies that compared prisoner with nonprisoner samples they found moderate to strong relationships between agreeableness and antisocial behavior and moderate relationships between conscientiousness and antisocial behavior. Miller and Lynam (2001) describe the personality of the "typical" criminal in terms of agreeableness and conscientiousness:

> Individuals who commit crimes tend to be hostile, self-centered, spiteful, jealous, and indifferent to others (i.e., low in Agreeableness). They tend to lack ambition, motivation, and perseverance, have difficulty controlling their impulses, and hold nontraditional and unconventional values and beliefs (i.e., are low in Conscientiousness). (p. 780)

Conscience and Arousal

One of the basic ideas of psychology is that different levels of physiological arousal correlate with different personality and behavioral patterns because arousal levels determine what we pay attention to, how strongly we pay attention, and the ease or difficulty of acquiring a conscience. When we ask most individuals why they don't victimize others, they tend to reply that their consciences won't let them, yet few people are aware of how their consciences were formed. A **conscience** is a complex mix of emotional and cognitive mechanisms acquired by internalizing the moral rules of our social group during socialization. People with strong con-sciences feel guilt, shame, stress, and anxiety when they violate, or even contemplate violating, these rules. A functioning conscience thus signals a successful prosocial socialization, which mostly revolves around individuals' relative sensitivity to social reward and punishment as they contemplate the approval or disapproval of their behavior by others. We must learn cogni-tively what is expected of us, but how well such lessons are learned is more a function of how they engage our emotions than how they engage rational reflection (Gao, Raine, Venerables, Dawson, & Mednick, 2010; Munoz & Anastassiou-Hadjicharalambous, 2011).

Differences in the emotional component of conscience reflect variation in **autonomic nervous system** (ANS) arousal patterns (Kochanska & Aksan, 2004). The ANS is part of the peripheral nervous system and carries out the basic housekeeping functions of the body by funneling messages from the environment to the various internal organs to keep the organism in a state of biological balance (e.g., adjusting pupil size, shivering or sweating in response to temperature). The ANS has two complementary branches: the sympathetic and parasympathetic systems. When an organism perceives a threat, the brain sends signals to the sympathetic branch to mobilize the body for vigorous action (the "fight or flight" reaction). Pupils dilate for better vision, the heart and lungs accelerate their activity, and digestion stops, among other things, all of which is aided by pumping out epinephrine (adrenaline). The parasympathetic system restores the body to homeostasis after the organism perceives the threat to be over. These processes regulating bodily functions occur automatically and never reach our conscious awareness. However, certain other messages that influence ANS functioning and do reach awareness are important for the acquisition of conscience via a process called **classical conditioning**. Figure 9.1 illustrates the various functions of the ANS.

Photo 9.3

Arousal theory states that human beings have varying internal "thermostats," which explains why people differ on the levels of arousal or stimulation they need to feel comfortable. Those already set on "high" may attempt to avoid noise, activity, or crowds. On the other hand, those who crave stimulation might climb mountains, go to loud parties, or watch slasher movies.

Classical conditioning is a form of learning different from operant conditioning discussed in Chapter 7. Operant conditioning is active (it depends on the actor's behavior) and cognitive in that it forms a conscious association between a person's behavior and its consequences. Classical conditioning, on the other hand, is mostly passive (it depends more on the level of ANS arousal than on anything the actor does) and visceral (felt in the internal organs); it simply forms a subconscious association between two paired stimuli. You may have heard about Russian psychologist Ian Pavlov's classical conditioning experiment in Psych 101 in which he conditioned dogs to salivate at the sound of a bell. Salivation is a natural ANS response to the expectation of food. A bell has no intrinsic properties that would make dogs salivate at its sound, but because Pavlov consistently paired the sound of the bell with food, the dogs learned (were conditioned) to associate the sound of the bell with food, and the sound itself became enough to make them salivate even when not paired with food.

We have all been conditioned in various ways to respond at the gut level to neutral stimuli via their association with unconditional stimuli. How did you feel when the school bell rang for recess or you heard the bells of the ice cream truck as a child? In both cases we expect that you responded with some pleasure, not because you love the sound of bells themselves, but because they signaled something you did love.

It is by way of these associations that we develop the "gut level" emotions of shame, guilt, and embarrassment that make up the emotional ("feeling") scaffolding of our consciences. Children must learn which behaviors are acceptable and which are not (the "knowledge" part of our conscience), most of which comes via parental teaching. Once children know the behavior expected of them, the degree to which emotions influence future behavior depends on the severity of the reprimand interacting with the responsiveness of their ANSs (Kochanska & Aksan, 2004; Pinel, 2000). Assuming an adequately responsive ANS, refraining from such behavior in the future is not simply a rational calculation of cost and benefits, but rather a function of the emotional component of conscience strongly discouraging it by generating unpleasant feelings.

Individuals with a readily aroused ANS are easily socialized; they learn their moral lessons well because ANS arousal ("butterflies in the stomach") is subjectively experienced as fear and anxiety, but people with an ANS resistant to arousal will not experience anxiety and fear. This sluggish ANS arousal is a good predictor of criminal behavior: "Poor fear conditioning is a predisposing factor to crime because individuals who lack fear are less likely to avoid situations, contexts and events that are associated with future punishment—resulting in a lack of conscience"

(Syngelaki, Fairchild, Moore, Savage, & van Goozen, 2012, p. 1). A hyperresponsive ANS generates high levels of fear and anxiety and is a protective factor against antisocial behavior. Studies have shown that males with hyperarousable (quick to react) ANSs living in high-crime environments are less involved with antisocial behavior than males with hypoarousable (slow to arouse) ANSs living in low-crime environments (Brennan et al., 1997; Lacourse et al., 2006). A longitudinal study of a birth cohort found that measures of poor ANS conditioning at age 3 successfully predicted

Figure 9.1

Functions of the Autonomic Nervous System

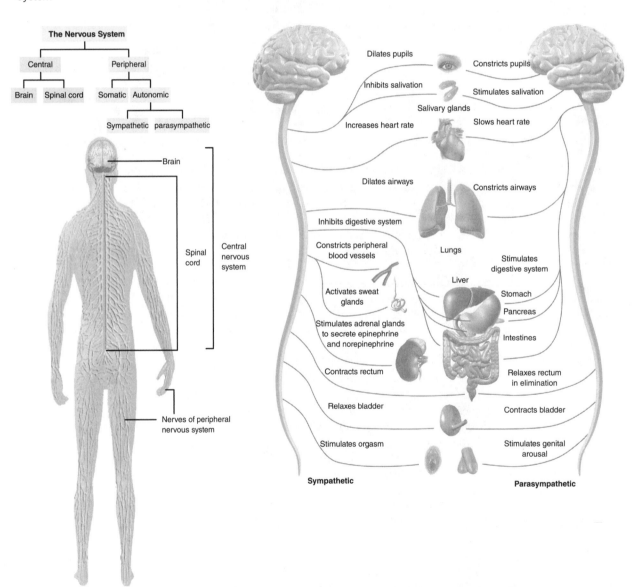

criminal offending (official records) at age 23 independent of controls for a variety of social adversities that are risk factors for criminality (Gao et al., 2010).

Individuals with relatively unresponsive ANSs are difficult to socialize because they experience little fear, shame, or guilt when they offend, even when discovered and punished. Measures of ANS arousal such as resting heart rate in childhood have enabled researchers to accurately predict which of their subjects would and would not have a criminal record at age 24 with 75% accuracy (Raine, 1997). Across a wide variety of subjects and settings it is consistently found that antisocial individuals have relatively unresponsive ANSs. This relationship exists because a hypoarousable ANS does not allow for adequate development of the social emotions. Having knowledge of what is right or wrong without that knowledge being paired with emotional arousal is rather like knowing the words to a song but not the music; not much good for the social choir.

The rational cognitive components of conscience are presumably stressed strongly in the socialization process of children from advantaged environments. If such children become delinquent and criminal, then it follows that because they lack the environmental factors that push children from less advantaged environments into crime they will be less emotionally conditionable than their peers. Variation in physiological measures will therefore be more important in accounting for antisocial behavior among higher SES individuals than in lower SES individuals, whose physiological risks are masked by psychosocial risk factors. This is consistently found and has been called the **social push hypothesis**. Scarpa and Raine (2003) define the social push hypothesis: "If an individual lacks psychosocial risk factors that predispose toward antisocial behavior yet still exhibits antisocial behavior, then the causes of this behavior are more likely to be biologically than socially based" (p. 213). However, children from lower SES environments who are difficult to condition because of a hyporeactive ANS are at greatest risk for antisocial behavior because they are also more likely, on average, to lack the cognitive skills necessary for acquiring a conscience and less likely to be consistently taught moral rules.

Cognitive Arousal

Another form of arousal of interest to psychologists is neurological arousal, the regulator of which is the brain's **reticular activating system** (RAS). The RAS is a little finger-size bundle of brain cells situated at the top of the spinal cord and can be thought of as the brain's filter system determining what incoming stimuli the higher brain centers will pay attention to (see Figure 9.2). Some individuals possess an RAS highly sensitive to incoming stimuli (augmenters), and others possess one that is unusually insensitive (reducers). Thus in identical environmental situations, some people are underaroused and other people are overaroused. Both over- and underarousal are psychologically uncomfortable. If you've ever taken your grandpa to a rap concert, or he has taken you to a chamber music recital, you'll know what I mean.

There is no conscious attempt to augment or reduce incoming stimuli; as with the ANS, augmentation or reduction in the RAS is solely a function of physiology. Augmenters tend to be people with hyperactive ANSs, and reducers tend to be people with hypoactive ANSs. Underarousal of the ANS is associated with fearlessness and underarousal of the RAS with sensation seeking. We can readily appreciate that sensation seeking and fearlessness are correlated since sensation seeking is aided by fearlessness (Raine, 1997).

Reducers are easily bored with levels of stimulation that are "just right" for most of us and continually seek to boost stimuli to more comfortable levels. They also require a high level of punishing stimuli before learning to avoid the behavior that provokes punishment and are thus unusually prone to criminal behavior. Studies have shown that relative to the general population, criminals, especially those with the most serious records, are chronically underaroused as determined by electroencephalograph (EEG) brain wave patterns, resting heart rate, and skin conductance (Ellis,

Figure 9.2

Schematic Image of the Brain Showing Various Parts of Interest

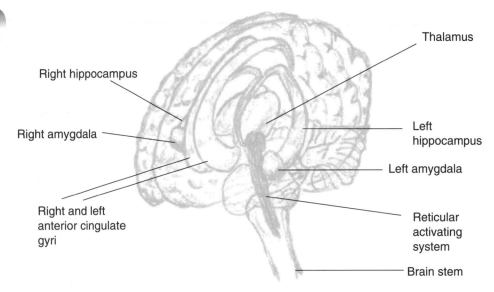

2003). EEG brainwaves reflect the electrical "chatter" of billions of brain cells. Clinicians recognize four bands of EEG brainwaves: alpha, beta, theta, and delta. Beta waves followed by alpha waves are the most rapid, and they signal when a person is alert and focused. Theta waves are emitted when a person is in a drowsy mental state, and delta waves are the slowest of them all. Most studies (about 75%) show that EEG readouts of criminals reveal that their brains are less often in the alert and focused range than are the brains of people in general (Ellis & Walsh, 2000).

Skin conductivity is measured by a meter attached to various parts of the body that records electrical responses to sweat. Sweat contains high levels of salt, and salt water is an excellent conductor of electricity. In temperature-controlled environments, increased sweating (even though the sweating may not be enough for the person to notice that he or she is sweating) occurs in response to emotional arousal. This is the basis of polygraph testing. The polygrapher asks suspects questions that evoke emotions such as guilt, shame, or embarrassment that are detected (or rather skin conductivity is detected) by the monitor. Because chronic criminals tend to have low levels of these emotions as well as lower levels of ANS arousal, they are least likely to show sweat responses to threatening questions. Thus, low skin conductivity and criminal behavior are expected to be related. In a review of this literature, all 19 studies found this relationship to be significant (Ellis & Walsh, 2000).

❖ Glen Walters's Lifestyle Theory

Perhaps the best known modern psychosocial criminological theory is Glen Walters's (1990) **lifestyle theory**. Walters believes that criminal behavior is part of a general pattern of life, or lifestyle, characterized by irresponsibility, impulsiveness, self-indulgence, negative interpersonal relationships, and the chronic willingness to violate society's rules. Lifestyle theory has three key concepts: conditions, choice, and cognition. A criminal lifestyle is the result of choices criminals make "within the limits established by our early and current biologic/environmental conditions" (Walters & White, 1989, p. 3). Thus, various biological and environmental conditions lay the foundation of future choices. Walters stresses impulsiveness and low IQ as the most important choice-biasing conditions at the individual level and attachment to significant others as the most important environmental condition. Walters's theory thus adds to rational choice theory by pointing to two important components of choice structuring.

The third concept, cognition, refers to cognitive styles people develop as a consequence of their biological/environmental conditions and the pattern of choices they have made in response to them. According to this theory, criminals display eight major cognitive features or **thinking errors** that make them what they are (Walters, 1990). Examples of criminal thinking errors are cutoff (the ability to discount the suffering of their victims), entitlement (the world owes them a living), power orientation (viewing the world in terms of weakness and strength), cognitive indolence (orientation to the present; concrete in thinking), and discontinuity (the inability to integrate thinking patterns). Little can be done to change criminal behavior until criminals change their pattern of thinking.

These thinking errors lead to four interrelated behavioral patterns or styles that almost guarantee criminality: rule breaking, interpersonal intrusiveness (intruding into the lives of others when not wanted), self-indulgence, and irresponsibility. These behavioral patterns are the result of faulty thinking patterns, which arise from the consequences (reward and punishment) of choices in early life, which are themselves influenced by biological and early environmental conditions. Figure 9.3 lays out lifestyle theory in diagrammatic form.

❖ The Antisocial Personalities

Psychopathy

Depending on whom you ask, *antisocial personality disorder*, *psychopathy*, and *sociopathy* are terms describing the same constellation of traits or separate concepts with fuzzy boundaries. We use the generic term **psychopathy**, a syndrome we can define as being characterized psychologically by egocentricity, deceitfulness, manipulativeness, selfishness, and a lack of empathy, guilt or remorse or physiologically as a syndrome characterized by the inability to tie the brain areas associated with the social emotions and rational cognition together.

Some researchers believe there is a subset of psychopaths (so-called primary psychopaths) whose behavior is biological in origin and a more numerous group (secondary psychopaths, or as others call them, sociopaths) whose behavior is mostly the result of incompetent parenting (Lykken, 1995; Walsh & Wu, 2008). Others view psychopathy not as something one is or isn't, but rather simply a name we apply to the most serious and chronic criminal offenders. Psychiatrists apply the label **antisocial personality disorder** (APD) to such criminals. APD is defined by

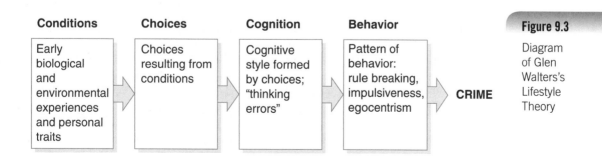

Figure 9.3

Diagram of Glen Walters's Lifestyle Theory

Photo 9.4

Serial killer Ted Bundy nonchalantly leans on the Leon County jail wall as the indictment charging him with the murder of two Florida State University coeds is read to him. Only a psychopath would show such a disinterested attitude.

the American Psychiatric Association (APA; 1994) as "a pervasive pattern of disregard for, and violation of, the rights of others that begins in childhood or early adolescence and continues into adulthood" (p. 645).

The criteria for diagnosing APD are both clinical and legal but rest primarily on behavior. Criminologists generally want to define individuals according to criteria independent of their behavior and then determine in what ways those so defined differ from individuals not so defined. The most widely used measure of psychopathy is the **Psychopathy Checklist–Revised** (PCL–R), which was devised by Robert Hare, the leading expert in psychopathy in the world today (Bartol, 2002). Using case histories and semistructured interviews that may last up to 2 hours, doctoral-level clinicians rate subjects on each of the 20 traits or behaviors listed nearby on a 3-point scale ranging from 0 to 2; a score of 30 or higher out of a possible 40 is the required cut-point in a psychopathic diagnosis. To put this number in perspective, offenders in general have an average PCL–R score of 22, and nonoffenders a score of 5 (Hare, 1996).

Statistical analyses of the PCL–R reveal that psychopathy is composed of two major factors derived from the statistical analysis of all the traits and behaviors in the PCL–R to find groups of traits and behaviors that cluster together. Two major factors arise from this process and are shown in Table 9.2. Factor 1 describes an arrangement of personality traits that indicate an overall insensitivity to the feelings of others. Factor 2 is a collection of behavioral traits reflecting an impulsive and deviant lifestyle. These two factors can exist independently but tend to be fairly strongly related (Patrick, 2006). Biological anomalies associated with psychopathy typically correlate highly with scores on Factor 1 (personality traits) but not necessarily with Factor 2 (unstable and antisocial lifestyle). Low IQ is associated with high scores on Factor 2, which describes sociopaths more than psychopaths, but not on Factor 1 (Harris, Skilling, & Rice, 2001; Patrick, 2006). Individuals who score high on Factor 1 (mostly psychopaths) are less likely than those who score high on Factor 2 (mostly sociopaths) to improve with age (Meadows & Kuehnel, 2005).

Table 9.2

Personality and Behavioral Traits Measured by Hare's PCL–R

Factor 1	Factor 2
Glibness/superficial charm	Need for stimulation/proneness to boredom
Grandiose sense of self-worth	Parasitic lifestyle
Pathological lying	Poor behavioral control
Cunning/manipulative	Promiscuous sexual behavior
Lack of remorse or guilt	Lack of realistic, long-term goals
Emotionally shallow	Impulsiveness
Callous/lack of empathy	Irresponsibility
Failure to accept responsibility for actions	Juvenile delinquency
	Early behavioral problems
	Revocation of conditional release

Robert Hare (1993) considers psychopathy to be primarily biological in origin: "I can find no convincing evidence that psychopathy is the direct result of early social or environmental factors" (p. 170). Similarly, Blair (2008) notes that "currently, there are no known environmental factors (including trauma and neglect) that can give rise to the pathophysiology seen in psychopathy" (p. 2557). Just because researchers have not found any environmental factors that *cause* psychopathy, it does not mean that such factors have no effect on how psychopathy is behaviorally *expressed*. Cesare Lombroso probably had psychopathy in mind before the term was coined with his "morally insane" born criminals, i.e., those "who appear normal in physique and intelligence but cannot distinguish good from evil" (in Gibson, 2002, p. 25). Of course, modern researchers no longer talk of criminals as evolutionary throwbacks whose behavior is "unnatural." Rather, they view psychopaths as behaving exactly as they were designed by natural selection to behave (Quinsey, 2002). This does not mean that their behavior is acceptable or that we cannot consider it *morally* pathological and punish it accordingly.

THEORY IN ACTION: Evil Minds: The Spahalski Twins

Robert and Stephen Spahalski are twin brothers born in December 1954, in Elmira, New York. Their parents were divorced when they were 12 years old. They were inseparable during their childhood, which was spent daring one another to commit more and more serious antisocial acts. On one of their stealing excursions when they were barely 17, Stephen killed a store owner. When Stephen was sentenced to prison for his crime, Robert's life fell apart as he became a crack cocaine addict and a gay prostitute. Robert was sent to prison for a 1973 burglary, and from that date onward, he was in and out of prison until 1989, when his behavior became more bizarre and deadly. Although he was more successful in avoiding major incarcerations from 1990 to 2005, it was during this time that he went on a killing spree, killing three women and one man.

(Continued)

THEORY IN ACTION (Continued)

His first known victim was Moraine Armstrong, a fellow addict and prostitute, in 1990. He then strangled Adrian Berger, his girlfriend, who was also an addict and prostitute. Neither of these murders was solved until Spahalski confessed to them in 2005. Spahalski also confessed to killing Charles Grande in 1991 after Grande had refused to pay him for his sexual services. Robert was arrested in 1991 on suspicion for committing this crime but released. Then in 2005 Spahalski was smoking crack with his girlfriend's next-door neighbor, Vivian Irizarry, when, as he explained to detectives, "all of a sudden I saw her as a demon. I freaked out." He bludgeoned and strangled the "demon" he saw and then spent the rest of the weekend on a crack binge.

After Robert came down from his extended high, he walked up to the desk at the Rochester, New York, police department and turned himself in. It was during the subsequent interrogation that he confessed to the other murders mentioned. Spahalski is suspected of other murders in upstate New York that have a number of resemblances to the murders he admits to. At trial, Robert pled not guilty by reason of insanity, claiming he suffered from post-traumatic stress disorder, and that his murders were committed in a state of drug-induced psychosis. However, he later withdrew that plea, and he was sentenced to 100 years imprisonment. When a corrections officer showed Stephen a news article about Robert's confession to four murders, he replied, "I thought I was the only murderer in the family."

As for Stephen, he was paroled in 1981 after serving 8 years for the murder of the store owner but was arrested, convicted, and sent back to prison for robbery and kidnapping in 1982. He was paroled again in 1999 and was back in prison within months on a parole violation. Released again in 2006, he was arrested for robbery in 2010 and again incarcerated.

How does one account for the evil behavior of these twins? The twins were raised in an intact home during their most formative years, both graduated high school, and there is no indication that either of them was ever physically, sexually, or psychologically abused. Their early onset of antisocial behavior indicates some sort of neurological or temperamental deficit, but none has ever been identified. The pattern of daring one another to commit ever more serious acts of antisocial behavior may have set in motion a snowball of behaviors that, once set rolling, could not be stopped. We can infer from their behavior that they have high levels of a number of traits mentioned in this chapter associated with criminal behavior and low levels of traits associated with prosocial behavior. Both were sensation seekers who relished the thrills of taking risks and getting away with it, and both obviously lacked empathy (when asked why he killed the store owner, Stephen matter-of-factly replied, "Because he deserved it").

Discussion Questions

1. Take a look at the traits and behaviors listed in Hare's PCL–R presented in this chapter and then go to http://murderpedia.org/male.S/s/spahalski-robert.htm for a more thorough treatment of Robert. Is there anything in his story that might indicate that Robert (and Stephen) are psychopaths?

2. Do you think that twins like Robert and Stephen were "destined" to behave more or less similarly by their shared genes?

3. Explain how Freud's possible account of the twins' behavior might differ from an account based on Glen Walters's lifestyle theory.

Sources: Benson, 2010; Blanco, n.d., *Robert Bruce Spahalski.*

If psychopathy is a behavioral strategy forged by evolution, there must be some biological markers that distinguish psychopaths from the rest of us. One of the most consistent physiological findings about psychopaths is their greatly reduced ability to experience the social emotions of shame, embarrassment, guilt, and empathy (Scarpa & Raine, 2003; Wiebe, 2004,

2011). Social emotions modify brain activity in ways that lead us to choose certain responses over others. Feelings of guilt, shame, and empathy prevent us from doing things (steal, lie, cheat) that might be to our immediate advantage but would cost us in reputation and future positive relationships if discovered. Hundreds of studies using many different methods have revealed over and over that the defining characteristic of psychopaths is their inability to "tie" the brain's cognitive and emotional networks together and thus to form a conscience (reviewed in Walsh & Bolen, 2012).

This inability is the strongest area of agreement among psychopathy researchers. What it essentially means is that the amygdala (part of the brain that plays a role in emotional memories, particularly fear) and the prefrontal cortex (part of the brain considered the brain's "chief executive officer") do not have strong connections in psychopaths as they do in the brains of normal people (van Honk, Harmon-Jones, Morgan, & Schutter, 2010). This certainly helps to explain the difficulties of psychopaths in processing emotions in socially approved ways.

Figure 9.2 shows the location of some brain areas mentioned in this chapter. The prefrontal cortex is a large area located just above the eyes and extends about one-third of the way from the forehead to the back of the head.

Sociopathy

As noted, some theorists believe sociopaths are different from psychopaths. Lykken (1995) colorfully describes **sociopaths** as "feral creatures, undomesticated predators, stowaways on our communal voyage who have never signed the Social Contract" and states that their behavior is "traceable to deviant learning histories interacting, perhaps, with deviant genetic predilections" (p. 22). Linda Mealey (1995) sees sociopaths as individuals who employ a "cheating strategy not as clearly tied to genotype [as the psychopath]" (p. 539). One of the biggest factors contributing to sociopathy is poor parenting, which is itself a function of the increase in the number of children being born out of wedlock (Rowe, 2002).

According to a study of 1,524 sibling pairs from different family structures taken from the National Longitudinal Survey of Youth, Cleveland and his colleagues (2000) found that, on average, unmarried mothers have a tendency to follow an impulsive and risky lifestyle and to have a number of antisocial personality traits, be more promiscuous, and to have a below-average IQ. Families headed by single mothers with children fathered by different men were found to put off-spring most at risk for antisocial behavior. Two-parent families with full siblings placed offspring at the lowest risk. Similar findings and conclusions from a large-scale British study have been reported (Moffitt & the E-Risk Study Team, 2002). Finally, Barber (2004) found that the rate of out-of-wedlock births was by far the strongest predictor of a composite measure of violent crime (murder, rape, assault) in his sample of 39 countries from Argentina to Zimbabwe.

The Office of Juvenile Justice and Delinquency Prevention (OJJDP) claims that delaying pregnancy until 20 to 21 years of age would lead to a 30% to 40% reduction in child abuse and neglect and could potentially save $4 billion ($5.8 billion in 2013 dollars) in law enforcement and corrections costs because offspring of teenage mothers are 2.7 times more likely than offspring of adult mothers to be incarcerated (Maynard & Garry, 1997).

❖ Evaluation of the Psychosocial Perspective

Psychologists like to point out that whatever social conditions may contribute to criminal behavior must influence individuals before they can affect behavior. Social factors matter and may "set the stage" for crimes, but real flesh-and-blood people commit them. Individuals are differentially

Table 9.3

Summarizing Psychosocial Theories

Theory	Key Concepts	Strengths	Weaknesses
Arousal	Because of differing ANS and RAS physiology, people differ in arousal levels they consider optimal. Underarousal under normal conditions poses an elevated risk of criminal behavior because it signals fearlessness, boredom, and poor prospects for socialization.	Allows researchers to use "harder" assessment tools such as EEGs to measure traits. Ties behavior to physiology. Explains why individuals in "good" environments commit crimes and why individuals in "bad" ones do not.	May be too individualistic for some criminologists. Puts all the "blame" on the individual's physiology. Ignores environmental effects.
Lifestyle	Crime is a patterned way of life (a lifestyle) rather than simply a behavior. Crime is caused by errors in thinking, which results from choices previously made, which are the results of early negative biological and environmental conditions.	Primarily a theory useful for correctional counselors dealing with their clients. Shows how criminals think and how these errors in thinking lead them into criminal behavior.	Concentrates only on thinking errors. Does talk about why they exist but pays scant attention to these reasons.
Antisocial Personality	There are a small stable group of individuals who may be biologically obligated to behave antisocially (psychopaths) and a larger group who behave similarly but whose numbers grow or subside with changing environmental conditions (sociopaths).	Concentrates on the scariest and most persistent criminals in our midst. Uses theories from evolutionary biology and "hard" brain imaging and physiological measures to identify psychopaths.	Some doubt the division of psychopath and sociopath as separate entities. While they are the scariest criminals, they are only a small proportion of all criminals.

vulnerable to the criminogenic forces existing in the environment because they bring different characteristics to it. This person-environment interaction is captured by the old saying "The fire that melts the butter hardens the egg." Psychologists largely take the fire (the environment) for granted and look for how the butter and eggs of our differing constitutions react to the heat of the fire. Of course, we can never take either the environment or the individual for granted because each affects and is affected by the other.

The relationship between IQ and criminal behavior has always been contentious. Adler, Mueller, and Laufer (2001) voice the familiar criticism that IQ tests are culturally biased, despite the findings of the National Academy of Sciences and the APA's Task Force on Intelligence cited earlier. They also cite the "debate" over whether genetics or the environment "determines" intelligence. This implies an either/or answer is possible, but since scientists involved in the study of intelligence unanimously agree that all traits are *necessarily* the result of both genes and environment, it is a monumental nondebate (Carey, 2003; Flynn, 2007).

One of the most pervasive criticisms of psychological theories is that they focus on "defective" or "abnormal" personalities (Akers, 1994). If by "abnormal" we mean *statistical* abnormality (below or above the average on a variety of traits), then all theories of criminality focus on abnormality. Our personalities consist of normal variation in traits we *all* possess, and these are products of the interaction of our temperaments and our developmental experiences. Lifestyle theory emphasizes that criminals are at the extremes of normal distributions of many traits but focuses mainly on how criminals think as a result of their biological constitutions and early experiences. However, there is always some risk in attaching a psychiatric label to individuals.

The use of "hard" measuring instruments to measure ANS and RAS arousal provides us with more accurate predictions about future offending than simple "paper and pencil" methods. Although we must not forget that the influences of these arousal mechanisms are strongly conditioned by the social environment. Nor should we forget that even if hard measures are better able to identify and predict, they still don't tell us how we can change criminal propensity or deal with the ethical problems involved in predicting what people "might do" in the future. Predictions about human behavior are far from foolproof, and there can be many false positives (predicting something will happen and it doesn't) as well as false negatives (predicting something won't happen and it does).

❖ Policy and Prevention: Implications of Psychosocial Theories

The best anticrime policies are environmental since they are aimed at reducing the prevalence of crime in the population. But because policies aimed at "root causes" have had little impact on the crime problem in the past (Rosenbaum, Lurigio, & Davis, 1998; Tanner, 2012) perhaps it is wise to focus efforts on those who are already committing crimes rather than on conditions external to them. A variety of such programs aimed at rehabilitating offenders operate under the assumption that criminals are rational beings plagued by ignorance of the long-term negative consequences of their offending behavior.

There is wide disagreement on how well rehabilitative programs work and even the criteria for success. Reviews of studies with strict criteria for determining success find recidivism rates lowered by from 8% to 10% (Andrews & Bonta, 1998). These small percentages do not seem like much, but they represent many thousands of crimes that were not committed. Effective rehabilitation programs use multiple treatment components; are structured and focus on developing social, academic, and employment skills; use directive cognitive-behavioral counseling methods; and provide substantial and meaningful contact between treatment personnel and offenders (Sherman et al., 1997; Walsh & Stohr, 2010).

Glen Walters's theory deals with what correctional counselors call "stinkin' thinkin'" (remember Calvin in Chapter 5?) and who see their task as guiding offenders to realize how destructive their thinking has been in their lives. Correctional counselors see offenders' problems as resulting from illogical and negative thinking about experiences that they reiterate in self-defeating monologues. The counselor's task is to strip away self-damaging ideas (such as techniques of neutralization) and beliefs by attacking them directly and challenging offenders to reinterpret their experiences in a growth-enhancing fashion. The cognitive-behavioral counselor operates from the assumption that no matter how well offenders come to understand the remote origins of their behavior, if they are unable to make the vital link between those origins and current behavioral problems, it is of no avail.

Psychopaths are poor candidates for treatment. Robert Hare states that because they are largely incapable of the empathy, warmth, and sincerity needed to develop an effective treatment relationship, treatment often makes them worse because they learn how to better push other people's buttons (Hare, 1993). Old age seems to be the only "cure" for the behaviors associated with this syndrome.

Summary

- Psychosocial criminology focuses largely on intelligence and temperament as the most important correlates of criminal behavior. Low intelligence as measured by IQ tests is thought to be linked to crime because people will low IQ are said to lack the ability to correctly calculate the costs and benefits of committing crimes, and temperament is linked to crime largely in terms of impulsiveness. Intelligence is the product of both genes and environment. We concluded that IQ is probably related to crime and delinquency through its effect on poor school performance.

- Temperament constitutes a person's habitual way of emotionally responding to stimuli. The kind of temperament we inherit makes us variably responsive to socialization, although patient and caring parents can modify a difficult temperament.

- Our personalities are formed from the joint raw material of temperament and developmental processes. A number of personality traits are associated with the probability of engaging in antisocial behavior, particularly high levels of impulsiveness, negative emotionality, and sensation seeking and low levels of conscientiousness, empathy, altruism, and moral reasoning.

- Classical conditioning via the ANS constitutes the emotional component of conscience and precedes the cognitive component. People differ in the responsiveness of their ANS, with those having a sluggish ANS being difficult to socialize. RAS arousal is also important to understanding criminal behavior because RAS reducers are chronically bored and seek to increase stimuli to alleviate that boredom. This may result in criminal behavior. Although people differ greatly in their behavior depending on their innate temperaments (a function of arousal levels), their developmental and other environmental experiences also play huge parts.

- Lifestyle theory views criminal behavior as a lifestyle rather than just another form of behavior. The lifestyle begins with biological and environmental conditions that lead criminals to make certain choices, which in turn lead to criminal cognitions. The theory focuses on these cognitions, or "thinking errors." Thinking errors lead criminals into behavioral patterns that virtually guarantee criminality. The theory was devised primarily to assist correctional counselors to change criminal thinking patterns.

- Psychopaths are at the extreme end of the antisocial personality continuum. Most researchers regard the psychopathy syndrome as biological in origin whereas some view sociopaths as formed both by genetics and the environment, with the environment playing the larger role. Many hundreds of studies have shown psychopaths to have limited ability to tie the rational and emotional components of thinking together.

- Some researchers assert that the primary cause of psychopathy is inept parenting by single mothers. Other theorists point to the fact that children born to such mothers also receive genes advantageous to antisocial behavior from both parents in addition to an environment conducive to its expression.

Exercises and Discussion Questions

1. Since psychologists have long identified temperaments as something that makes is easy or difficult to socialize children, why do you think Gottfredson and Hirschi ignored temperaments in their self-control theory?

2. Honestly rate yourself from 1 to 10 on the traits positively associated with antisocial behavior (impulsiveness, negative emotionality, and sensation seeking), then on the traits negatively related with antisocial behavior (conscientiousness, empathy, and altruism). Subtract the latter from the former. If the difference is a positive number greater than 10 or a negative number less than –10, do the results correspond to your actual behavior?

3. Explain the role low arousal of the autonomic nervous system and the reticular activating system may play in the development of psychopathy.

4. How might anomie/strain theory benefit from incorporating information on IQ and conscientiousness?

Useful Websites

IQ. www.psyonline.nl/en-iq.htm.

IQ/aggression connection. www.crimetimes.org/95c/
    w95cp10.htm.

Mental deficiency and crime. www.drtomoconnor
    .com/1060/1060lect03.htm.

Mental health. www.mentalhealth.com.

Personality disorders. www.focusas.com/
    PersonalityDisorders.html.

Chapter Terms

Agreeableness

Altruism

Antisocial personality disorder

Autonomic nervous system

Classical conditioning

Conscience

Conscientiousness

Empathy

Flynn effect

Impulsiveness

Intellectual imbalance

Intelligence

Lifestyle theory

Negative emotionality

Personality

Psychopathy

Psychopathy Checklist–Revised

Reticular activating system

Sensation seeking

Social push hypothesis

Sociopaths

Temperament

Thinking errors

CHAPTER 10

Biosocial
Approaches

In February of 1991, Stephen Mobley walked into a Domino's Pizza store in Georgia to rob it. After getting the money, Mobley forced store manager John Collins onto his knees and shot him execution style. Mobley was apprehended by Atlanta police after committing several other robberies and bragging to friends about Collins's murder. He was subsequently charged with aggravated murder and sentenced to death. In the automatic appeal to the Georgia Supreme Court to get his sentenced commuted to life in prison, his primary defense boiled down to claiming that his "genes made me do it." In support of this defense, Mobley's lawyers pointed to a Dutch study of an extended family in which for generations many of the men had histories of unprovoked violence. The Researchers took DNA samples from 24 male members of the family and found that those with violent records had a marker for a mutant or variation of a gene for the manufacture of monoamine oxidase (MAOA), an enzyme that regulates a lot of brain chemicals. Mobley's lawyers found a similar pattern of violent behavior and criminal convictions among his male relatives across the generations and requested the court for funds to conduct genetic tests on Mobley to see if he had the same genetic variant.

The court wisely denied the defense motion. Even if it were found that Mobley had the same genetic variant, it would not show that he lacked the substantial capacity to appreciate the wrongfulness of his acts or to conform to the requirements of the law. Mobley's lawyers were hoping to mitigate his sentence by appealing to a sort of genetic determinism that simply does not exist. As we shall see in this section, genes don't "make" us do anything; they simply bias us in one direction rather than another. Except in cases of extreme mental disease or defect, we are always legally and morally responsible for our behavior. Cases such as Mobley's underline the urgent need for criminologists to understand the role of genes in human behavior as that role is understood by geneticists.

LEARNING OBJECTIVES

- Understand that while all behavior is the result of genes interacting with environments, there is no gene "for" crime
- Understand the basis of heritability and what it tells us
- Be able to explain gene-environment correlation and interaction
- Understand the basic ideas behind an evolutionary view of criminality
- Differentiate between mating and parenting effort and understand how each is related to the probability of criminal behavior
- Understand how the brain "softwires" itself by experience
- Know the basics of reward dominance theory
- Understand the policy implications of biosocial criminology

❖ The Biosocial Approach

Biosocial theories have not been popular with mainstream social scientists until relatively recently because they were interpreted as a sort of "biological determinism." This kind of thinking is much rarer today as social scientists have become more sophisticated in their thinking about the interaction of biology and the environment (Robinson, 2004). There are still people who fear that "biological" theories can be used for nasty purposes, but as Bryan Vila (1994) remarks, this may be the case "only if we allow perpetuation of the ignorance that underlies these arguments" (p. 329). Bigots and hate-mongers will climb aboard any vehicle that gives their prejudices a free ride, and they have done so for centuries before genes were heard of. The bottom line, as stated by Christopher Shea (2009), is that "with study after study finding that all sorts of personal characteristics are heritable—along with behaviors shaped by those characteristics—a see-no-gene perspective is obsolete" (p. 6).

Biosocial criminologists assert that because humans have brains, genes, hormones, and an evolutionary history, they should integrate insights from the disciplines that study these things into their theories and should dismiss naïve nature *versus* nurture arguments in favor of nature *via* nurture. *Any* trait, characteristic, or behavior of *any* living thing is *always* the result of biological factors interacting with environmental factors (Beaver, 2009; Cartwright, 2000), which is why we call modern biologically informed criminology *biosocial* rather than *biological*. Biosocial criminology is not a theory; rather, it is a way of looking at criminal behavior from a wide array of biologically informed theories and methodologies. John Wright and Frank Cullen (2012) view the biosocial approach as integrative and believe "biosocial criminology can lead to a criminology that is rooted more in science and empirical observations and can link criminology to a diverse array of other disciplines and research methodologies" (p. 237). These are the developmental theories we discuss in the next chapter; this chapter sets the stage for them by outlining their foundational disciplines—genetics, neurobiology, and evolutionary psychology.

In many ways, the early positivists were biosocial in approach because they explicitly envisioned biological and environmental interaction. Their ideas and methods were primitive by today's standards, but then so were the ideas and methods of most sciences in the 19th century. Evolutionary ideas about the behavior of all animals were poorly understood; genes were unheard of, and the brain was still a mysterious locked black box. This has all changed with the sequencing of the human genome and the advent of machines that enable us to see what is going on in the brain as we think and act. For these and other reasons, biosocial research into criminality is proceeding at an explosive pace. As Lilly, Cullen, and Ball (2007) opine, "It is clear that the time has arrived for criminologists to abandon their ideological distaste for biological theories" (p. 304).

❖ Behavior Genetics

Behavior genetics studies the relative contributions of heredity and environment to behavioral and personality characteristics. The sum of the genes we get from our parents is called our **genotype**. Genes and environments work together to develop any observable and measurable trait—height, weight, IQ, impulsiveness, blood sugar levels, self-esteem, blood pressure, and so on—the sum of which constitutes the person's **phenotype**. **Genes** are segments of deoxyribonucleic acid (DNA) that code for proteins. Genes simply make proteins; the stuff that builds, maintains, and replaces the tissues in your body. Although protein products such as neurotransmitters (such as dopamine and serotonin, discussed later in this chapter) and hormones (such as testosterone) have a lot to do with how we behave or feel, they do not *cause* us to behave or feel one way or another. They *facilitate* our behavior and our feelings by producing tendencies or dispositions to respond to the environments in one way rather than in another. That is, they incline us; they do not compel us. Thus there are no genes "for" criminal behavior, but there are genes that lead to particular traits, such as low empathy or impulsiveness, that increase the probability of criminal behavior when combined with certain environments.

Biosocial criminologists use twin and adoption studies to disentangle the relative influences of genes and environments, and they tell us that genes and environments are always jointly responsible for any human characteristic (Beaver, 2009; Carey, 2003). To ask whether genes or environment is most important for a given trait is just as nonsensical as asking whether height or width is most important to the area of a rectangle because without height and width together there is no rectangle. Gene expression always depends on the environment (think of identical rose seeds planted in an English garden and in the Nevada desert, and then think about where the full genetic potential of the seeds will be realized). We can think of genes as light bulbs, and the environment as a dimmer switch. Just as the light from bulbs can be cranked up or dimmed down according to the requirements of the person operating the switch, genes are switched on, cranked up, dimmed down, and turned off depending on what the organism requires at the moment to meet specific environmental challenges.

Behavior geneticists quantify the extent to which genes influence a trait with a measure called **heritability** (symbolized as h^2), which ranges from 0.0 to 1.0. The closer h^2 is to 1.0 the more the variance (difference) in a trait in a population, not in an individual, is due to genetic factors. Since any differences among individuals can only come from two sources—genes or environment—heritability is also a measure of environmental effects ($1 - h^2$ = environmental effects). All cognitive, behavioral, and personality traits are heritable to some degree, with the traits discussed in the previous chapter such as impulsiveness and negative emotionality being in the 0.30 to 0.80 range (Carey, 2003). Thus, in addition to furthering our understanding of the role of genes, advances in genetics have yielded enormous benefits to our understanding of the environment's role in shaping behavior. As Baker, Bezdjian, and Raine (2006) put it, "The more we know about genetics of behavior, the more important the environment appears to be" (p. 44).

The environmental effects on a trait are divided into shared and nonshared. **Shared environment** refers to the environment experienced by children reared in the same family (parental SES, religion, values and attitudes, parenting style, family size, intactness of home, and neighborhood) and assumed to make them similar. **Nonshared environment** refers to unique environmental experiences that make children from the same family different. Nonshared environment can be familial or extrafamilial. Familial nonshared variables include gender, birth order, perinatal trauma, illness, and parental favoritism. Extrafamilial nonshared factors include having different peer groups and teachers; experiencing a different, time-dependent culture; and any other idiosyncratic experiences.

It is consistently found that shared environmental effects on cognitive and personality traits, although moderate during childhood, disappear almost completely in adulthood. This is *not* to say parents have no effect on children apart from the genes they provide them with. What disappear are parental effects on personality and cognitive traits that made siblings somewhat similar while they shared a home. That similarity fails to survive after the period of common rearing. The nonshared features of the environment appear to be much more salient than shared environment with respect to the formation of an individual's personality and cognitive traits. Genetic effects on personality and cognitive traits, however, continue to increase throughout the life span (Ferguson, 2010, Gottfredson, 2011; Nisbett et al., 2012).

Gene-Environment Interaction and Correlation

Gene-environment interaction and gene-environment correlation describe peoples' active transactions with their environment. All living things are designed to be responsive to their

Photo 10.1

Former major league baseball player José Canseco is sworn in at a U.S. House of Representatives baseball steroids hearing. Canseco presents a fascinating case for biosocial theories. José had a fraternal twin brother, Ozzie, who also chose a career in baseball. However, in comparison with José 462 home runs and over 1,400 RBI, Ozzie had only a "cup of coffee" in the major leagues. He came to bat only 65 times over three seasons and never hit a home run. Had he been an identical rather than a fraternal twin, might Ozzie have performed more like his brother? After finishing his baseball career, José wrote a book (*Juiced*) in which he admitted using steroids for most of his playing career and claimed that 85% of other players in his era did likewise. Because of his steroid use, many baseball experts predict José will never be elected to the Baseball Hall of Fame, though his career numbers exceed those of many current Hall of Fame players.

environments, and gene-environment interaction and gene-environment correlation help us to understand how by showing the indirect way genes help to determine what aspects of the environment will and will not be important to us. **Gene-environment interaction** (GxE) involves the commonsense notion that people are differentially sensitive to identical environmental influences and will thus respond in different ways to them. For instance, a relatively fearless and impulsive person is more likely to seize opportunities to engage in antisocial behavior than is a fearful and constrained person.

Gene-environment correlation (rGE) means that genotypes and environments are related. There are three types of G/E correlation: passive, evocative, and active.

Passive rGE is the positive association between genes and their environments due to biological parents providing children with genes linked to certain traits and an environment favorable for their expression. Children born to intellectually gifted parents, for instance, are likely to receive genes that lead to above-average intelligence and an environment in which intellectual behavior is modeled and reinforced, thus setting them on a trajectory independent (passively) of anything the child has done.

Evocative rGE refers to the way others react to the individual on the basis of his or her evocative behavior. Children bring traits with them to situations that increase or decrease the probability of evoking certain kinds of responses from others. A pleasant and well-mannered child will evoke different reactions than will a bad-tempered and ill-mannered child. Some children may be so resistant to socialization that parents may resort to coercive parenting or simply give up, either of which may worsen any antisocial tendencies and drive children to seek environments where their behavior is accepted. Evocative rGE thus serves to magnify phenotypic differences by funneling individuals into like-minded peer groups ("birds of a feather flock together").

Active rGE refers to the active seeking of environments compatible with our genetic dispositions. Active rGE becomes more pertinent as we mature and acquire the ability to take greater control of our lives. This is because within the range of possibilities available in our cultures, our genes help to determine what features of the environment will and will not be attractive to us. Active rGE assures us that our minds and personalities are not simply products of external forces and that our choices are not just passive responses to social forces and situations. We are active agents who create our own environments just as they help to create us. Genes imply human self-determination because, after all, our genes are *our* genes. As Christopher Badcock (2000) put it, "Genes don't deny human freedom; they positively guarantee it" (p. 71). Genes are constantly at our beck and call, extracting information from the environment and manufacturing the substances we need to navigate it. They are also what make us uniquely ourselves and thus resistant to environmental influences that grate against our natures. In short, genes do not constrain us, they enable us. This view of humanity is more respectful of human dignity than the blank-slate view of people as putty in the hands of environmental winds.

Figure 10.1 illustrates rGE, emphasizing that behind every gene-environment correlation GxE is operating also. Note that there is only a one-way arrow from passive to evocative rGE, but the influence runs both ways between evocative and active rGE.

Figure 10.1

Illustrating Passive, Evocative, and Active rGE and GxE Interaction

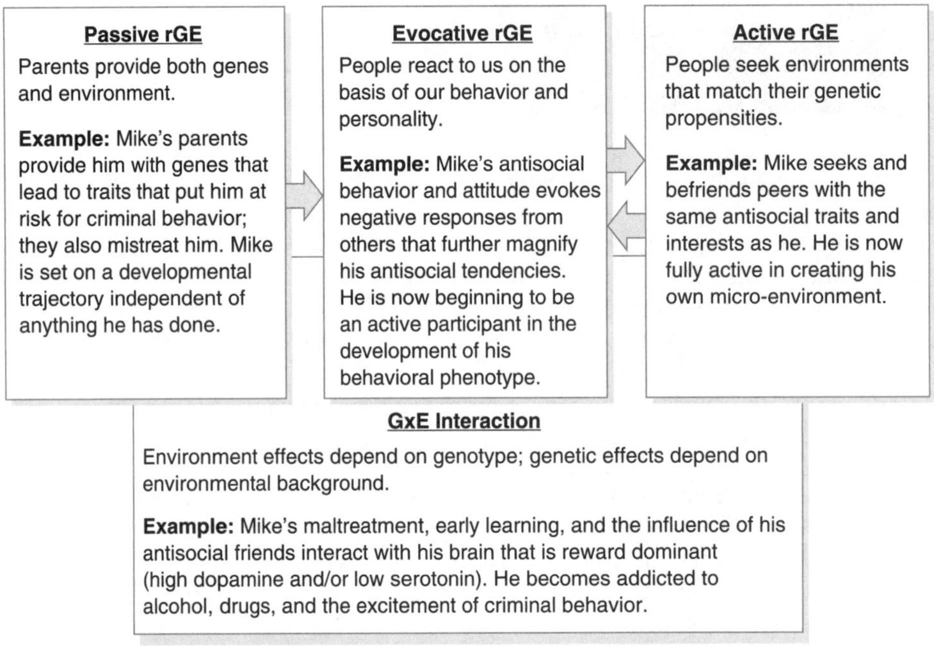

Passive rGE

Parents provide both genes and environment.

Example: Mike's parents provide him with genes that lead to traits that put him at risk for criminal behavior; they also mistreat him. Mike is set on a developmental trajectory independent of anything he has done.

Evocative rGE

People react to us on the basis of our behavior and personality.

Example: Mike's antisocial behavior and attitude evokes negative responses from others that further magnify his antisocial tendencies. He is now beginning to be an active participant in the development of his behavioral phenotype.

Active rGE

People seek environments that match their genetic propensities.

Example: Mike seeks and befriends peers with the same antisocial traits and interests as he. He is now fully active in creating his own micro-environment.

GxE Interaction

Environment effects depend on genotype; genetic effects depend on environmental background.

Example: Mike's maltreatment, early learning, and the influence of his antisocial friends interact with his brain that is reward dominant (high dopamine and/or low serotonin). He becomes addicted to alcohol, drugs, and the excitement of criminal behavior.

Behavior Genetics and Criminal Behavior

Although there are no behavior genetic theories of criminal behavior per se, behavior genetic studies are of immense importance in helping to better understand traditional criminological theories. For instance, in the previous chapter we saw how different family structures predicted antisocial behavior in large studies in both the United States (Cleveland, Wiebe, van den Oord, & Rowe, 2000) and the United Kingdom (Moffitt & the E-Risk Study Team, 2002). Both studies showed that genetic factors play a large part in sorting individuals into those structures. In both studies, families consisting of a divorced or never-married mother with children fathered by different men are the most at-risk family type for antisocial behavior, and families with full siblings with both biological parents present were least at risk. Genes, of course, contribute to the choices people make, as well as make them easy or difficult to live with.

One of those factors influencing choices is almost certainly low self-control. As we saw in Chapter 7, Gottfredson and Hirschi (1990) attributed low self-control exclusively to parental treatment. However, there are now well over 100 studies that have shown strong links between low self-control and low levels of the neurotransmitter serotonin (Crockett, Clark, Lieberman, Tabinia, & Robbins, 2010). In other words, while we all have to be taught to control our impulses, some of us are naturally easier to teach than others. Levels of serotonin are governed both by genes and the environment. That is, genes govern the base levels of serotonin a person has and how well it is regulated, but what is going on in the environment results in serotonin levels increasing and decreasing (Wright, 2011).

In terms of differential association theory and its concern with peer effects, Cleveland, Wiebe, and Rowe (2005) found that genetic factors accounted for 64% of the variance in delinquent peer affiliation. Another study of 533 monozygotic (MZ; identical) and 558 dizygotic (DZ; fraternal) twin pairs (Button et al. 2007) found that peer group affiliation was associated with genetics and that the magnitude of the genetic effects on conduct problems increased as the level of association with delinquent peers increased. A longitudinal study of peer group deviance using data from 469 MZ and 287 DZ twin pairs followed from age 8 to 25 found that as twins matured and created their own mini-worlds (active rGE) genes played an increasingly larger role in peer choice (Kendler et al., 2007). Even molecular genetics is getting into the act. Beaver, Wright, and DeLisi (2008) demonstrated a significant effect of a gene called DAT1 (discussed more fully shortly) on peer group affiliation controlling for a number of other risk variables.

Unlike the relatively strong genetic influences discovered for most human traits, genetic influence on antisocial behavior is modest, especially during the teenage years. Heritability coefficients for most traits related to antisocial behavior are typically in the 0.30 to 0.80 range, and for antisocial behavior itself, they are in the 0.40 to 0.58 range (Ferguson, 2010; Rhee & Waldman, 2002), with h^2 higher in adult than in juvenile populations. The reason for this is that a trait is something that may or may not be expressed according to what is going on in the environment. Crime and delinquency are the result of traits interacting with incentives and disincentives, as well as how well one has learned one's moral lessons. This, says David Lykken (1995), is why "the heritability of criminality is less than the more basic psychological traits [that are its constituent parts]" (p. 109). Strong genetic effects on antisocial behavior are most likely to be found only among chronic offenders who begin offending prior to puberty and who continue to do so across the life course (Moffitt & Walsh, 2003).

❖ Molecular Genetics

Heritability estimates only tell us that genes are contributing to a trait, but they do not tell us which genes; only molecular genetics can tell us this. Fortunately, we can now go straight to the DNA by genotyping individuals with a simple cheek swab. We can then look at the effects of particular types of genes among individuals who have them and who do not. As you know, we get our genes from our parents, who might both provide us with the same or different version of the same gene called an **allele**. For instance, you may have received a "brown" allele for eye color from your father and a "blue" allele from your mother. This tells us why even though every human being has the same genes that make us human, we can still be differentiated by our alleles. If we didn't have these differences, the police in crime scene investigation movies would not be able to identify suspects by the bodily fluids left behind at crime scenes.

Molecular genetic studies are being conducted with increasing frequency in criminology, with the huge National Longitudinal Study of Adolescent Health (ADD Health) yielding some very important findings. Any individual gene accounts only for a miniscule proportion of the variance in criminal behavior, and it contributes to a trait linked to criminality, *not* to criminality itself, which you remember is a composite of many different traits. Genes always have *indirect* effects on behavior via the effects of the proteins they make on human traits and abilities.

Although we only get one allele from each parent, most genes have many allelic variations geneticists call **genetic polymorphisms**. Polymorphisms are differences in DNA sequences that code for the same gene but may make more or less of the substance (say, low serotonin), or affect the gene's efficiency, which leads to slightly different functional or physical traits among individuals. Let us return to Mobley's "my MAOA gene made me do it" argument in the opening vignette to illustrate how biosocial criminologists study the effects of these gene variants.

A major longitudinal study of maltreatment looking at the role of the MAOA gene showed why only about one-half of abused or neglected children become violent adults (Caspi et al., 2002). The MAOA gene comes in variants that geneticists call "high" and "low" activity. For a variety of reasons we cannot get into here, the low-activity version is a risk factor for a number of behavioral problems, and the high-activity version is a protective factor. Neither the genetic risk nor environmental risk factors by themselves had much effect on antisocial behavior. When combined, however, the odds of having a verified arrest for a violent crime for those with both genetic (the low variant of the MAOA gene) and environmental (maltreatment) risk factors were 9.8 times greater than the odds for subjects with neither the genetic nor environmental risk. Furthermore, although the low MAOA + maltreatment subjects were only 12% of the cohort they were responsible for 44% of its criminal convictions.

The overall conclusion arrived at by a meta-analysis of the MAOA/maltreatment research was that their interaction is a significant predictor of antisocial behavior across all studies (Kim-Cohen et al., 2006). However, a study by Widom and Brzustowicz (2006) found that while the high-activity MAOA allele buffered whites from the effects of childhood abuse and neglect as it relates to antisocial behavior later in life, it did not protect nonwhites. The authors suggest that other environmental stressors, such as the high density of antisocial others in the neighborhood, may have negated the protective power of the high-activity polymorphism among nonwhites. These studies all point to the importance of studying GxE interactions—how the environment modifies the effects of genes and how genes modify the effects of the environment. There are many other genetic polymorphisms related to traits associated with antisocial behavior being examined by biosocial criminologists, but we meet just one more in the section on evolutionary psychology.

❖ The Neurosciences

Whatever the source of human behavior, it is necessarily funneled through the brain, arguably the most awe-inspiring structure in the universe. Although the brain is only about 2% of body mass, it consumes 20% of the body's energy as it perceives, evaluates, and responds to its environment (Shore, 1997). This 3-pound marvel of evolutionary design is the CEO of all that we think, feel, and do. Powerful brain imaging technologies such as PET, MRI, and fMRI have resulted in an explosion of information on the brain over the past two decades. We are a long way from fully understanding the brain, but we cannot ignore what is known about it relevant to criminology. Matt Robinson (2004) goes as far as to say that any theory of behavior "is logically incomplete if it does not discuss the role of the brain" (p. 72). As we will see, the insights criminologists can derive from neuroscience will not only buttress our theories, but may also strengthen our claims for preventative *environmental* intervention.

Softwiring the Brain by Experience

All our thoughts, feelings, emotions, and behaviors are the result of networks of billions of brain cells called **neurons** communicating with one another through substances called **neurotransmitters**. There are many transmitters and other brain chemicals, but criminologists are most interested in dopamine and serotonin. Figure 10.2 shows how neurotransmitters shunt information back and forth across the brain. Information from the environment is received from thousands of dendrites, summated in the body of the neuron and passed on electrically down the axon. When the impulse reaches the end of the axon it releases the neurotransmitters across the synaptic gap to further relay the message. The most important thing to remember here is that more "primitive" networks that control vital functions such as breathing and heart rate come "hardwired"

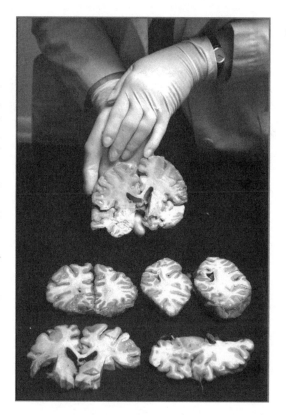

Photo 10.2

Harkening back to the 19th century, when postmortem examinations of the brains of criminals were a frequent phenomenon, the brain of serial killer John Wayne Gacy was dissected after his execution. The attempt to locate an organic explanation of his monstrous behavior was unsuccessful.

at birth, but development of the higher brain areas depends a lot on environmental "software" downloaded after birth. The message neuroscience has for us is that the experiences we encounter largely determine the patterns of our neuronal connections and thus our ability to successfully navigate our lives (Quartz & Sejnowski, 1997).

Neural networks are continually being made and selected for retention or elimination in a "use it or lose it" process governed by the strength and frequency of experience. Retention is biased in favor of networks that are most stimulated during early development (Restak, 2001). This is why bonding and attachment are so vital to human beings and why abuse and neglect are so injurious. Hormones released by chronic stress can cause neurons to die, and children with high levels of these hormones experience cognitive and social development delays (Robinson, 2004). As Perry and Pollard (1998) point out, "Experience in adults *alters* the *organized* brain, but in infants and children it *organizes* the *developing* brain" (p. 36, italics added). Brains organized by stressful and traumatic events tend to relay events along the same brain pathways laid out by early events because pathways laid down early in life are more resistant to elimination than pathways laid down later in life. A brain organized by negative events is ripe for all kinds of antisocial behavior.

Reward Dominance and Prefrontal Dysfunction Theories

If social animals are to function normally in their social groups they must possess the ability to respond to signals of reward and punishment with the socially appropriate approach and avoidance behavior. **Reward dominance theory** is a neurological theory based on the proposition that behavior is regulated by two opposing mechanisms, the **behavioral activating** (or

Figure 10.2

Neurons, Axons, Dendrites, and the Synaptic Process

Source: Alzheimer's Disease Education and Referral Center, 2011

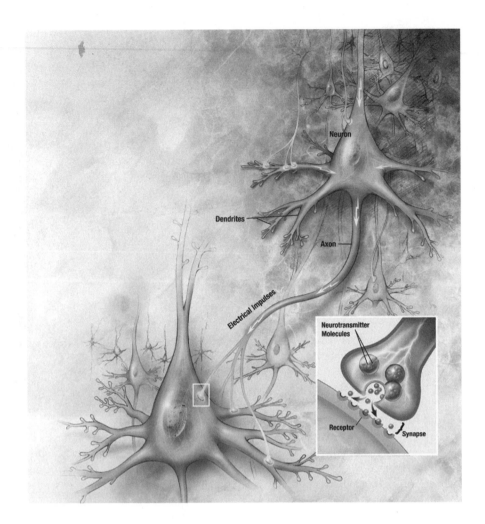

approach) **system** (BAS) and the **behavioral inhibition system** (BIS). The BAS is associated with the neurotransmitter dopamine and with pleasure areas in the brain (Gove & Wilmoth, 2003). The BIS is associated with serotonin and with brain structures that govern memory. Neurotransmitters such as dopamine and serotonin are the chemical messengers that shunt information between neural networks. Dopamine facilitates goal-directed behavior and serotonin generally modulates behavior (Depue & Collins, 1999).

The BAS is sensitive to reward and can be likened to an accelerator motivating a person to seek rewarding stimuli. The BIS is sensitive to threats of punishment and can be likened to a brake that stops a person from going too far too fast. The BAS motivates us to seek whatever affords us pleasure, and the BIS tells us when we have had enough for our own good. A normal BAS combined with a faulty BIS, or vice versa, may lead to a very impulsive person with a "craving brain" that can lead him or her into all sorts of physical, social, moral, and legal difficulties by becoming addicted to pleasures such as food, gambling, sex, alcohol, and drugs (Day & Carelli, 2007). Figure 10.3 outlines the dopamine and serotonin pathways in the brain. The VTA is the ventral tegmental area where dopamine is manufactured and sent to the nucleus accumbens, the brain's major pleasure center, as well as to the substantia nigra, another important pleasure center. The raphe nuclei are part of the reticular activating system, and their main function is to release serotonin.

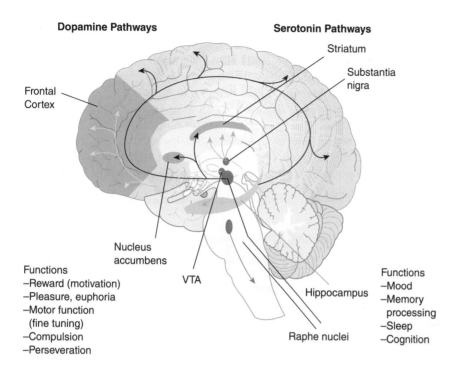

Dopamine Pathways

Serotonin Pathways

Frontal Cortex

Striatum

Substantia nigra

Nucleus accumbens

VTA

Hippocampus

Raphe nuclei

Functions
–Reward (motivation)
–Pleasure, euphoria
–Motor function
   (fine tuning)
–Compulsion
–Perseveration

Functions
–Mood
–Memory
   processing
–Sleep
–Cognition

Figure 10.3

Major Dopamine (*light brown*) and Serotonin (*black*) Pathways in the Brain

Source: National Institutes of Health, United States Department of Health and Human Services

While most of us are more or less equally sensitive to both reward and punishment (BAS/BIS balance), in some people one system might dominate the other most of the time. The theory asserts that criminals, especially chronic criminals, have a dominant BAS, which tends to make them overly sensitive to reward cues and relatively insensitive to punishment cues (Day & Carelli, 2007). Reward dominance theory provides us with hard *physical* evidence relating to the concepts of sensation seeking, impulsiveness, and low self-control we have previously discussed, since each of these traits are underlain by either a sticky accelerator (not enough dopamine) or faulty brakes (low serotonin).

A third system of behavior control is the **flight/fight system** (FFS) chemically controlled by epinephrine (adrenaline). The FFS is that part of the autonomic nervous system that mobilizes the body for vigorous action in response to threats by pumping out epinephrine. Fear and anxiety at the chemical level is epinephrine shouting its warning: "Attention, danger ahead; take action to avoid!" Having a weak FFS that whispers rather than shouts combined with a BAS that keeps shouting "Go get it," and a BIS too feeble to object, is obviously very useful when pursuing all kinds of antisocial activities. You have probably noted that reward dominance theory is very similar to Freud's notion of the battles between the id and the superego. The primary difference is that the specific brain areas and chemicals associated with approach and avoidance behavior are identified.

Another neurologically specific theory of criminal behavior is prefrontal dysfunction theory. The human **prefrontal cortex** (PFC) is a part of the brain located just above the eyes that occupies about one-third of the cerebral cortex and has been called "the most uniquely human of all brain structures" (Goldberg, 2001, p. 2). The PFC is responsible for things such as making moral judgments, planning, analyzing, synthesizing, and modulating emotions. The PFC provides us with knowledge about how other people see and think about us, thus moving us to adjust our behavior to consider their needs, concerns, and expectations of us. These PFC functions are collectively referred to as executive functions and are clearly involved in prosocial behavior. If these functions are compromised in some way via damage to the PFC, the result is often antisocial behavior.

Positron emission tomography (PET) and functional magnetic resonance imaging (fMRI) studies consistently find links between PFC activity and impulsive criminal behavior. A PET study comparing impulsive murderers with murderers whose crimes were planned found that the former showed significantly lower PFC and higher limbic system activity (indicative of emotional arousal) than the latter and other control subjects (Raine et al., 1998). Cauffman, Steinberg, and Piquero (2005) combined reward dominance and PFC dysfunctions theories in a large-scale study of incarcerated and nonincarcerated youths in California and found that seriously delinquent offenders had slower resting heart rates and performed poorly relative to nondelinquents on various cognitive functions mediated by the PFC.

THEORY IN ACTION: Genetics and Neuroscience in Court: The Brian Dugan Case

Brian James Dugan was born in 1956, the second of five children of James and Genevieve Dugan, both of whom were thought to have been alcoholics. Brian's birth was evidently traumatic and may have led to brain damage. Brian was known to torture animals and set fires (he burned down his family's garage) and was a chronic bed-wetter. These three behaviors, known as the MacDonald triad, are predictive of psychopathy. Indeed, he is one of the worst psychopaths ever diagnosed with the condition, scoring 38 out of a possible 40 on the Hare Psychopathy Checklist (see Chapter 9). While still a teenager he committed numerous assaults, burglaries, and arsons.

Photo 10.3

Brian Dugan

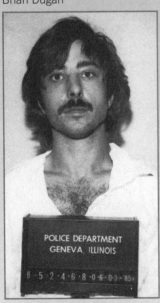

At the age of 28 in 1984, Dugan raped and murdered 27-year-old Donna Schnorr; in 1985 he raped and murdered 7-year-old Melissa Ackerman and raped a 21-year-old woman who survived the attack. Dugan previously attempted to abduct and rape other girls and women. He was arrested the day after Melissa's murder. The evidence was so overwhelming that he confessed to the murders of Ackerman and Schnorr, as well as that of 10-year-old Jeanine Nicarico who had been raped and beaten to death in 1983. His confession to Nicarico's murder was not taken seriously because two other males, Rolondo Cruz and Alejandro Hernandez, had been arrested, convicted, and sentenced to death for her murder. However, in 2002 DNA evidence conclusively linked Dugan to Nicarico's murder, and Cruz and Hernandez were released 10 years after being convicted.

In an effort to save Dugan from the death penalty, his attorneys enlisted the help of neuroscientists to scan his brain. They found that his brain showed all the classic signs of psychopathy, such as inadequate linking between the emotional and rational sides and a relatively inactive amygdala (the part of the brain that deals with emotions such as fear). Dugan's inability to engage the emotions means that he lacked empathy, shame, and guilt and was thus callously indifferent to the suffering of others. A relatively inactive amygdala signals a relative lack of fear, which leads psychopaths to take risks most other people would not. The jury was unimpressed with such evidence and voted to impose the death penalty on Dugan in 2009. However, the death penalty was abolished in Illinois in 2011, and his sentence was commuted to life in prison.

The Dugan case illustrates many concepts in this chapter, particularly rGE, as his genotype interacted with his abusive environment. He certainly illustrated a

THEORY IN ACTION (Continued)

reward-dominant brain, being addicted to drugs, alcohol, and sex (he even molested his younger brother). The case also illustrates the value and the limitations of the genetic and neurological sciences when applied to criminal justice issues. DNA evidence served to free two innocent men from death row, and that is a truly wonderful application of science, but should DNA evidence be used to mitigate punishment ("My genes made me do it")? Does the undisputed fact that Dugan is the worst kind of psychopath, and that we can actually determine this in terms of brain anatomy and functioning, mean that he has diminished responsibility for his actions ("My defective brain made me do it")? Questions such as these at the intersection of biosocial criminology and the law raise ethical and philosophical issues previous generations did not have to ponder.

Discussion Questions

1. Look up *MacDonald triad* on any search engine and discuss why childhood bedwetting, fire setting, and animal cruelty are predictors of adult psychopathy.

2. In many ways we are our brains, and our brains are us. Therefore, if our brains are not functioning normally as determined by brain scans, does that lessen our responsibility for criminal behavior? Not that a person should be totally exonerated for having such a brain, but what about using the evidence to mitigate his or her sentence?

3. Do you agree with the jury's decision to sentence Dugan to death?

Sources: Barnum & Gregory, 2009; Hughes, 2010

❖ Evolutionary Psychology

The Usefulness of an Evolutionary Framework

Evolutionary psychology explores human behavior using an evolutionary theoretical framework. Many disciplines such as economics, psychiatry, medicine, and political science are adopting the Darwinian framework as it has become increasingly obvious that it is extremely useful to understand the ultimate reasons why people do what they do and why things happen the way they do (Hacking, 2006). Criminologists operating within this framework explore how certain behaviors society now calls criminal may have been adaptive. **Adaptive behavior** is any behavior that contributes directly or indirectly to an individual's survival and reproductive success. These two evolutionary "goals" are common to all sexually reproducing organisms and are thus subject to the process of natural selection (Roach & Pease, 2013).

Evolutionary psychology complements genetics because it informs us how the genes of interest came to be present in the human gene pool in the first place. While genetics looks for what makes people different, evolutionary psychology focuses on what makes us all the same. Another basic difference is that evolutionary psychology looks at ultimate-level "why" questions (what evolutionary problem did this behavioral mechanism evolve to solve?), and geneticists look at proximate-level "how" questions (to what extent is this behavioral mechanism influenced by genes in this population at this time?). Ultimate causes are thus causes that occurred in the past that are *ultimately* responsible for something, whereas a proximate cause is one that is most immediately responsible for causing some observed behavioral outcome.

Evolutionary psychologists agree with most criminologists that although it is morally regrettable, crime is normal behavior for which everyone has the potential (Kanazawa, 2003). Evolutionary logic tells us that if criminal behavior is normal, it must have provided some evolutionary advantage for our distant ancestors. However, because modern environments are so radically different from hunter/gatherer environments, many traits selected for their adaptive value at the time may not be adaptive today. It is important to realize that it is the traits underlying criminal behavior that are the alleged adaptations, not the specific acts we call crimes (Rowe, 2002; Walsh, 2009). If behavior we now call criminal is normal, it must have conferred some evolutionary advantage on our ancestors. Judith Harris (1998) speculates about the probable traits of hunter/gatherer leaders and how they would have been useful:

> Almost all the characteristics of the "born criminal" would be, in watered-down form, useful to a male in a hunter-gatherer society and useful in his group. His lack of fear, desire for excitement, and impulsiveness made him a formidable weapon against rival groups. His aggressiveness, strength, and lack of compassion enable him to dominate his groupmates and give him first shot at hunter-gatherer perks. (pp. 299–300)

These perks were those most pertinent to survival and reproductive success—resources and women. Women would have been attracted to such men, not because they were sensitive "nice guys," but because they had status and resources within the group and were good protectors (Buss, 2005). Such traits can certainly overshoot their optimum and become liabilities, which is often the case when exercised too freely in modern evolutionarily novel societies.

Criminal behavior is a way to acquire resources illegitimately, and the traits Harris mentions are most useful in that regard. Evolutionary scientists refer to such behavior (whether it is defined as criminal or not) as cheating and think of individual traits associated with it such as impulsiveness and aggression in terms of adaptive traits all humans share at varying levels. Whether exploitation occurs depends on environmental triggers interacting with individual differences and environmental constraints. Although we all have the potential to exploit and deceive others, we are a highly social and cooperative species with minds forged by evolution to form cooperative relationships built on trust (Barkow, 2006). Cooperation is typically contingent on the reciprocity of others and is thus a tit-for-tat strategy favored by natural selection because of the benefits it confers. We cooperate with our fellows because we feel good when we do and because it identifies us as reliable and trustworthy, which confers valued social status on us.

Because cooperation occurs among groups of other cooperators, it creates niches for non-cooperators to exploit others by signaling their cooperation and then failing to follow through (Roach & Pease, 2013). Criminal behavior may thus be viewed as an extreme form of defaulting on the rules of cooperation. But cheating comes at a cost, so before deciding to do so the individual must weigh the costs and benefits of cooperating versus defaulting. Cheating is rational (not to be confused with moral) when the benefits outweigh the costs. But if cheating is so rational, how did cooperation come to be predominant in social species? The answer is that cheating is only rational in circumstances of limited interaction and communication. Frequent interaction and communication breeds trust and bonding, and cheating becomes a less rational strategy because cooperators remember and retaliate against those who have cheated them. Ultimately, cooperation is the most rational strategy in any social species because each player reaps in the future what he or she has sown in the past.

Yet we continue to see cheating behavior despite threats of exposure and retaliation. We do so because exposure and retaliation are threats only if cheats must operate within the same environment in which their reputations are known. Cheats can move from location to location meeting and cheating a series of others who are unaware of their reputation. This is the pattern of many career criminals who move from place to place, job to job, and relationship to relationship, leaving a trail of misery behind them before their reputation catches up. This is why cheats are more likely to prosper in large cities in modern societies than in small traditional communities where the threat of exposure and retaliation is great (Wiebe, 2012). Of course, the stability of the group and cultural dynamics must be considered. Even in communities containing large numbers of chronic criminals there must be some level of group loyalty and cooperation.

The Evolution of Criminal Traits: Parenting Versus Mating Effort

There are a number of evolutionary theories of crime (such as Anne Campbell's "staying-alive" hypothesis discussed in Chapter 8), all of which focus on reproductive strategies. There are two ways that members of any animal species can maximize reproductive success: parenting effort and mating effort. **Parenting effort** is the proportion of reproductive effort invested in rearing offspring, and **mating effort** is that proportion allotted to acquiring sexual partners. Mating effort is associated with traits useful for committing criminal acts. David Rowe (2002) provides us with an excellent thumbnail sketch of the traits useful to mating effort, traits that can clearly be co-opted to support criminal behavior:

> A strong sexual drive and attraction to novelty of new sexual partners is clearly one component of mating effort. An ability to appear charming and superficially interested in women while courting them would be useful. The emotional attachment, however, must be an insincere one, to prevent emotional bonding to a girlfriend or spouse. The cad may be aggressive, to coerce sex from partly willing partners and to deter rival men. He feels little remorse about lying or cheating. Impulsivity could be advantageous in a cad because mating decisions must be made quickly and without prolonged deliberation; the unconscious aim is many partners, not a high-quality partner. (pp. 62–63)

The reverse is also true—traits that facilitate parenting effort underlie other forms of prosocial activity: "Crime can be identified with the behaviors that tend to promote mating effort and

Photo 10.4

A concentration on parenting effort is strongly associated with a prosocial lifestyle; a concentration on mating effort is strongly associated with an antisocial lifestyle.

noncrime with those that tend to promote parenting effort" (Rowe, 1996, p. 270). Because female reproductive success hinges more on parenting effort than mating effort, females have evolved higher levels of the traits that facilitate it (e.g., empathy and altruism) and lower levels of traits unfavorable to it (e.g., aggressiveness) than males. Of course, both males and females engage in both mating and parenting strategies, and both genders follow a mixed mating strategy. It is only claimed that mating behavior is more typical of males and parenting effort is more typical of females.

Because humans are born more dependent than any other animal, parenting effort is particularly important to our species. Humans have thus evolved to invest more in parenting effort than any other species, but there is considerable variation within the species. Gender constitutes the largest division due to different levels of obligatory parental investment between the sexes. Female parental investment necessarily requires an enormous expenditure of time and energy, but the only *obligatory* investment of males is the time and energy spent copulating. Reproductive success for males increases in proportion to the number of females to whom they have sexual access, and thus males have an evolved propensity to seek multiple partners. Mating effort emphasizes quantity over quality (maximizing the number of offspring rather than nurturing a few), although maximizing offspring numbers is obviously not a conscious motive of any male seeking sex. The proximate motivation is sexual pleasure, with more offspring being a natural consequence (in precontraceptive days) when the strategy proved successful.

Reproductive success among our ancestral females rested primarily on their ability to secure mates to assist them in raising offspring in exchange for exclusive sexual access, and thus human females evolved a much more discriminating attitude about sexual behavior (Geary, 2000; Nedelec & Beaver, 2012). According to evolutionary biologists, the inherent conflict between the reckless and indiscriminate male mating strategy and the careful and discriminating female mating strategy drove the evolution of traits such as aggressiveness and the lowering of trait levels (relative to female levels) such as empathy and constraint that help males to overcome both male competitors and female reluctance. The important point to remember is that although these traits were designed by natural selection to facilitate mating effort, they are also useful in gaining nonsexual resources via illegitimate means (Quinsey, 2002; Walsh, 2006).

Empirical research supports the notion that an excessive concentration on mating effort is linked to criminal behavior. A review of 51 studies relating number of sex partners to criminal behavior found 50 of them to be positive, and in another review of 31 studies it was found that age of onset of sexual behavior was negatively related to criminal behavior (the earlier the age of onset, the greater the criminal activity) in all 31 (Ellis & Walsh, 2000). A British cohort study found that the most antisocial 10% of males in the cohort fathered 27% of the children (Jafee, Moffitt, Caspi, & Taylor, 2003), and anthropologists tell us there are striking differences in behavior between members of cultures that emphasize either parenting or mating strategies. Cultures emphasizing mating effort the world over exhibit behaviors (low-level parental care, hypermasculinity, transient bonding) considered antisocial in Western societies (Ember & Ember, 1998).

Molecular genetic studies also find significant relationships between sexual and criminal behavior. A study by Beaver, Wright, and Walsh (2008) tested the evolutionary claim that the most antisocial males should have the largest number of sex partners. They found the same polymorphism of the dopamine transporter gene (DAT1) that was significantly related to number of sexual partners was also significantly related to antisocial behavior. The reason for this is that one variant of the DAT1 gene is exceptionally efficient at clearing dopamine from the synaptic gap after it signals other neurons. This is problematic because it is dopamine that gives us pleasure when we engage in activities such as having sex, so if it is cleared too fast we are moved to seek more of the activity to get more pleasure (more dopamine). This constant seeking of activities to raise dopamine levels is the chemical basis of addiction to all sorts of things besides sex, such as drugs, smoking, food, gambling, and alcohol (Walsh, Johnson, & Bolen, 2012). Another study of 674 males found that those who had two copies (one allele each from their mom and dad) of the same DAT1 polymorphism had significantly more sex partners (an average of 5.66) than males who had only one or no copies (an average of 2.94), as well as significantly higher delinquency scores and scores on other kinds of risky behaviors (Guo, Tong, and Cai, 2008). In other words, this particular gene variant is typically found among "people who need high levels of excitement and stimulation to activate their reward system in the same capacity as those with normally functioning reward systems" (DeLisi, Beaver, Vaughn, & Wright, 2009, p. 1189).

❖ Other Biosocial Risk Factors for Criminality

There are numerous other biosocial risk factors for criminal behavior, but we will select only a few and relate back to issues in previous chapters to show how biological factors interact with the social context to produce behavior.

In Chapter 8 we briefly discussed testosterone (T) in the context of male-female differences, but how about its effect among males only? Rowe (2002) discusses a study of the effect of T among 4,462 males. The sample was divided into high T (upper 10%) and normal T (lower 90%) and into high and low socioeconomic status (SES). The study found that antisocial behavior more than doubled (from 14.7% to 30.1%) among low-SES/high-T males compared to low-SES/normal-T males. Among high-SES males, T levels had no effect on antisocial behavior. The interaction between T and social context is further illustrated in a longitudinal study of 1,400 boys that found T levels were unrelated to conduct problems for boys with "nondeviant" or "possibly deviant" friends, but conduct problems were greatly elevated among boys with high T who associated with "definitely deviant" peers (Maughan, 2005). Thus the effects of testosterone depend quite a lot on social context, and this illustrates once again that we cannot separate biological and environmental variables and expect to understand complex behavior.

In Chapter 9 we discussed a few environmental factors that influence IQ, but there are others. Exposure to noxious substances such as lead (Pb) is one such factor. For every microgram of Pb per deciliter of blood (µg/dl) there is an average decrease of one-half IQ point (Koller, Brown, Spurfeon, & Levy, 2004). An fMRI study found that brain grey matter was inversely related with average childhood Pb concentrations (the more the lead the less the grey matter) in young inner-city adults (Cecil et al., 2008). The average childhood blood Pb concentration of this sample was 13.3µg/dl, which is far in excess of the 2006 average of 1.5µg/dl for the U.S. general population (Bellinger, 2008). Although the grey matter lost to Pb exposure was relatively small (about 1.2%), it was concentrated in vital behavior-moderating areas responsible for executive functioning and mood regulation such as the PFC. Another study examining the relationship between blood Pb and verified criminal arrests found that after controlling for other relevant variables, for every 5µg/dl increase in blood Pb there was an increase in the probability of arrest for a violent crime of about 50% (Wright et al., 2008).

There are a number of neurological disorders that result from mothers drinking alcohol while pregnant, the most serious of which is **fetal alcohol syndrome** (FAS). FAS is the major preventable cause of low IQ known today (May & Gossage, 2008). Prenatal exposure to alcohol disrupts the migration and hookup of the embryo-fetus's developing neurons in brain areas such as the frontal lobes. It also plays havoc with a number of other brain developmental processes in the womb (Goodlett, Horn, & Zhou, 2005). Because heavy drinking is most prevalent among lower-SES individuals in deprived environments (Casswell, Pledger, & Hooper, 2003), FAS rates are higher among people living there. A review of numerous studies by the National Institute of Alcohol Abuse and Alcoholism (May & Gossage, 2008) found an average rate of FAS of about

0.26 per thousand for the middle class and about 3.4 per thousand for the lowest SES class, which is about 13 times greater. The behavioral, cognitive, and personality symptoms typically found among people suffering from FAS include low IQ, hyperactivity, impulsiveness, alcoholism, poor social skills, and poor emotional and moral development, all of which are independent risk factors for antisocial behavior (Walsh & Yun, 2011).

Many other substances have similar effects on neuron development and migration, because whatever the mother ingests so does her embryo-fetus. A common risk factor is maternal smoking, which puts her fetus at risk for hypoxia (intermittent reduction of oxygen available to the fetus that may lead to brain cell death) (Zechel et al., 2005), as well as the toxic chemical components of tobacco (Huizink & Mulder, 2006). Cohort studies (e.g., Brennan, Grekin, & Sarnoff, 1999) consistently find that maternal smoking during pregnancy predicts criminal behavior in their offspring independent of other factors. A review of a number of such studies found significantly increased risk for fetal tobacco–exposed individuals versus nonexposed individuals for various forms of antisocial behavior across diverse contexts and independent of other factors such as maternal SES and IQ (Wakschlag, Pickett, Cook, Benowitz, & Leventhal, 2002). Table 10.1 summarizes the key concepts and strengths and weaknesses of biosocial perspectives and theories

❖ Evaluation of the Biosocial Perspective

In Chapter 1 we noted Lilly, Cullen, and Ball's (2007) contention that the most dramatic developments in science come most often from new observational techniques (think of the telescope and microscope) rather than new developments in theory. The strength of biosocial approaches is that they take advantage of these new observational techniques in their ability to incorporate biological concepts and findings derived from these sophisticated physical measures into their theories. Criminologists now have access to new observational techniques in the form of DNA and neuroimaging data. Because of this, writes Matt DeLisi (2009), "Never before has the sublime interplay between nature and nurture been available for scientific discovery" (p. 266). The main stumbling block is that such studies are more difficult and far more expensive than the typical social science study. If we want genetic information we cannot simply go to the nearest high school and survey a few hundred students. Behavior genetic studies require comparing samples consisting of pairs of identical and fraternal twins and/or adoptees, and these are difficult to come by. However, new technologies have allowed us to go straight to the DNA, thus eliminating this need, but genotyping costs about $10 per individual.

It used to be difficult to make generalizations from the typical neuroimaging study because many tended to consist of a small number of known offenders matched with a control group. However, today there are a number of ambitious studies imaging anywhere from 400 to 2,000 subjects as costs continue to come down. Paus (2010) discusses four of these studies at length, including two longitudinal studies. All studies are collecting mountains of environmental, behavioral, and cognitive data (e.g., socioeconomic status, maternal smoking, drinking, stressful life events, antisocial behavior, IQ, personality profiles, and many other things). Three of the studies are also collecting DNA data. Thus biosocial studies provide criminologists with more robust evidence than they are typically able to get, and this evidence will help them to more solidly ground their theories. Biosocial analyses of many phenomena such as medical, psychiatric, and psychological problems are now all the rage in these disciplines, and many prominent sociologists and criminologists believe this approach will prove just as useful in their disciplines. One of the most exciting advances is that some universities are offering a double major in criminology and molecular genetics or neuroscience. In any event, as new discoveries are made in genetics and neuroscience, criminology can hardly ignore them.

Table 10.1

Summarizing Biosocial Perspectives and Theories

Theory or Perspective	Key Concepts	Strengths	Weaknesses
Behavior and Molecular Genetics	Genes affect behavior in interaction with environmental influences. Heritability estimates the relative contribution of genetic and environmental factor traits affecting criminality. All individual traits are at least modestly influenced by genes. Molecular genetics identifies genes underlying those traits.	Looks at both the genetic and environmental risk factors for criminal behavior. Understanding genetic contributions also identifies the contributions of the environmental. Provides "hard" evidence that illustrates mechanisms that underlie concepts in traditional theories.	Requires twin samples of twins and/or adoptees, which are difficult to come by. However, technology now enables us to go straight to the DNA in molecular genetics. Expensive and requires cooperation of lab scientists. Requires criminologists to learn some genetics.
Evolutionary Psychology	Human behavior is rooted in evolutionary history. Natural selection has favored victimizing tendencies in humans, especially males. These tendencies arose to facilitate mating effort but are useful in pursuing criminal behavior as well. Criminals emphasize mating effort over parenting effort more than males in general.	Ties criminology to evolutionary biology. Mating effort helps to explain why males are more criminal than females and why criminals tend to be more sexually promiscuous than persons in general. Emphasizes that crime is biologically "normal" (although regrettable) rather than pathological.	Gives some the impression that because crime is considered "normal" it is justified or excused. Makes assumptions about human nature that may or may not be true. While recognizing that culture is important, it tends to ignore it.
Neuroscience	Whatever its origin, all stimuli are channeled through the brain before given expression in behavior. The development of the brain is strongly influenced by early environmental experiences, especially those involving nurturance and attachment.	Shows how environmental experiences are physically "captured" by the brain. Emphasizes the importance of nurturing for optimal development of the brain. Uses sophisticated technology and provides harder observable evidence.	High cost of neuroimaging studies. Studies difficult and expensive to conduct but are getting cheaper all the time. The "hardness" of the data may lead us to accept findings too uncritically.
Reward Dominance Theory	Behavioral activating (BAS) and behavioral inhibiting system (BIS) are dopamine and serotonin driven, respectively. Among criminals the BAS tends to be dominant over the BIS. This BIS/BAS imbalance can lead to addiction to many things, including crime.	Explains why low serotonin is related to offending (low serotonin functioning = low self-control). Explains why criminality persists in some offenders because they develop a taste for the "thrill of it all," as cultural criminologists maintain.	The neurological underpinnings of the BAS and BIS are difficult to precisely identify. Nevertheless, it is a model used in many disciplines (medicine, psychology, addiction studies) interested in human behavior.
Prefrontal Dysfunction Theory	Frontal lobes control long-term planning and temper emotions and their expressions. Criminals have frontal lobes that fail to function as they do in most people, especially in terms of inhibiting actions that harm others.	Explains why moral reasoning is inversely related to involvement in persistent criminality. Explains why criminality has been linked to frontal lobe damage and to abnormal brain waves.	Dysfunction of the prefrontal lobes remains difficult to measure, even with fMRI scans. Same sampling difficulties noted for the neurosciences in general.

❖ Policy and Prevention: Implications of Biosocial Theories

It has been said that "biosocial theories may have their greatest policy applications in terms of prevention and treatment programs" (Lilly, Cullen, & Ball, 2011, p. 376). The policies suggested by the biosocial perspective are midway between the macro-level sociological suggestions aimed at whole societies and the micro-level suggestions of psychological theories aimed at already convicted criminals. Mindful of how nurturing affects both gene expression and brain development in humans, many biosocial criminologists have advocated a wide array of "nurturant" strategies such as pre- and postnatal care for all women, monitoring infants and young children through the early developmental years, paid maternal leave, nutritional programs, and a whole host of other interventions (Vila, 1997). Some of the programs, such as lead removal programs and educational programs to reduce maternal drinking and smoking, should pay generous dividends in terms of reducing IQ loss and other negative factors caused by toxic lead and maternal substance abuse. Douglas Massey (2004), former president of the American Sociological Association, called for a biosocial understanding of such things:

> By understanding and modeling the interaction between social structure and allostasis [*allostasis* refers to the dysregulation of stress response systems such as the ANS discussed in the last chapter in response to chronic levels of stress], social scientists should be able to discredit explanations of racial differences in terms of pure heredity. In an era when scientific understanding is advancing rapidly through interdisciplinary efforts, social scientists in general—and sociologists in particular—must abandon the hostility to biological science and incorporate its knowledge and understanding into their work. (p. 22)

Biosocial criminologists are typically in the forefront in advocating treatment over punishment and toward this end they have favored indeterminate over fixed sentences (Lanier & Henry, 1998). Pharmacological in conjunction with psychosocial treatments have proven to be superior to psychosocial treatment alone for syndromes (e.g., alcoholism, drug addiction) associated with criminal behavior (Robinson, 2009). Of course, there are always dangers of seeking simple medical solutions to complex social problems. Requiring sex offenders to take antiandrogen treatment to reduce the sex drive raises both medical and legal/ethical issues regardless of how effective the treatment is. Prescribing selective serotonin reuptake inhibitors such as Prozac and Zoloft helps to curb low self-control and irritability, but there is always the temptation to treat everyone the same regardless of his or her serotonin levels.

One of the greatest successes of biosocial science was its pivotal role in the United States Supreme Court's outlawing of the juvenile death penalty. In writing the 2005 majority opinion in *Roper v. Simmons*, Justice Anthony Kennedy noted the neurobiological evidence for the physical immaturity of the adolescent brain, which was brought to the Court's attention by the American Medical and Psychological Associations (Walsh & Hemmens, 2011). Thus the biosocial approach can serve to advance arguments both for prevention rather than punishment and for punishment that takes into consideration valid identifiable brain differences among people.

Matt Robinson (2009), a sociologist who has spent much of his career researching crime prevention, states that "since biosocial criminology meaningfully integrates perspective and theories from the biological and social sciences, the approach offers much hope in the area of crime prevention. At the very least, biosocial crime prevention should be far more effective than those strategies currently utilized" (p. 243). Biosocial studies provide information about *both* environmental and biological risk factors and, as such, are "more likely to refine social policies by better specification of environmental factors than to divert funds from environmental crime prevention strategies" (Morley & Hall, 2003). In other words, they will enable us to better pinpoint environmental factors that may prove fruitful in our crime prevention efforts.

Summary

- Behavior geneticists study the genetic underpinning of traits and characteristics in populations by calculating heritability coefficients. There are no genes "for" any kind of complex human behavior; genes simply bias trait values in one direction or another. This view is respectful of human dignity because it implies self-determinism because our genes are *our* genes.

- Gene/environment interaction tells us that the impact our environmental situation (e.g., living in a crime-ridden neighborhood) has on us depends on who we are, and gene/environment correlation tells us that who we are is a product of our unique genotype and the environments we find ourselves in.

- Genes have practically no influence on juvenile delinquency, probably because of the high base rate of delinquency. There are genetic effects for chronic and serious delinquents, but these few individuals tend to get "lost" in studies that combine them with those who limit their offending to adolescence. Adult criminality is much more influenced by genes. One of the reasons we find only modest genetic effects in criminality when the traits that underlie it are strongly influenced by genes is that parents have control over their children's behavior but little or none on the underlying traits.

- Evolutionary psychology focuses on why we have the traits we do and is more interested in their universality than in their variability. Crime is viewed as a normal but regrettable response to environmental conditions. By this it is meant that many human adaptations forged by natural selection in response to survival and reproductive pressures are easily co-opted to serve morally wrong purposes.

- In common with all sexually producing species, humans are preeminently concerned with our own survival and reproductive success. The traits designed to assist males in their mating efforts include many that can also assist them to secure other resources illegitimately; traits designed to assist females in their parenting efforts are conducive to prosocial behavior. Mating vs. parenting effort is not an either/or thing. Males and females engage in both at various times in their lives, it is just that mating effort is more typical of males and parenting effort is more typical of females.

- Socially cooperating species create niches that cheats can exploit to their advantage by signaling cooperation but then defaulting. Cheating is a rational strategy in the short term but invites retaliation in the long term. This is why chronic criminals rarely have successful relationships with others and why they typically die broke.

- Neuroscience tells us that genes have surrendered control of human behavior to the brain. Following genetic wiring to jump-start the process, the brain literally wires itself in response to environmental input. The softwiring of our brains is an electrochemical process that depends on the frequency and intensity of early experiences. Adverse experiences can literally physically organize the brain so that we experience the world negatively, which is why nurturing, love, and attachment are so important to the healthy development of humans.

- Reward dominance theory informs us that the brain regulates our behavior through the BIS and BAS systems. The BIS and BAS systems (underlain by serotonin and dopamine neurotransmitters, respectively) in most people are balanced, but criminals tend to have either an overactive BAS or an underactive BIS. This means their behavior is dominated by reward cues and relatively unaffected by punishment cues.

- Prefrontal dysfunction theory posits that the brain's prefrontal cortex (PFC) is vital to the so-called executive functions such as planning and modulating emotions. If the PFC is damaged in any way the individual is deficient in these executive functions and tends to be impulsive.

Exercises and Discussion Questions

1. If it could be shown with high scientific confidence that some young children inherit genes that put them at 85% risk for developing antisocial proclivities, what do you think should be done? Should their parents be warned to be especially vigilant and to seek early treatment for their children, or would such a warning tend to stigmatize children? What are the costs and benefits of each option?

2. We know that males, especially young males, are more likely to perpetrate and be victimized by violent crimes. Provide a plausible evolutionary explanation for this.

3. How might reward dominance theory add strength and coherence to low self-control theory?

4. Explain why the traits underlying mating versus parenting effort are related to crime.

5. Discuss why understanding the biological and environmental risk factors for criminal behavior is superior to understanding only one or the other in isolation.

Useful Websites

Anatomy of the brain. www.neuroguide.com/index .html.

Behavioral genetics. www.ornl.gov/sci/techresources/ Human_Genome/elsi/behavior .shtml.

Center for Evolutionary Psychology. www.cep .ucsb.edu/evolutionary psychology.

Crime Times. http://crimetimes.org.

The human brain. www.fi.edu/brain/index.htm.

Chapter Terms

Allele

Adaptive behavior

Behavior genetics

Behavioral activating system

Behavioral inhibition system

Evolutionary psychology

Fetal alcohol syndrome

Flight/fight system

Gene/environment correlation

Gene/environment interaction

Genes

Genetic polymorphisms

Genotype

Heritability

Mating effort

Neurons

Neurotransmitters

Nonshared environment

Parenting effort

Phenotype

Prefrontal cortex

Reward dominance theory

Shared environment

CHAPTER 11

Developmental Theories

From Delinquency to Crime to Desistance

Kathleen Holmes was a sweet child born to an "All-American" family in Boise, Idaho. Her parents sent her to a Catholic girls' school where she did well in her studies. All seemed to be going well for Kathy until she was 16 years old and agreed to go to a local Air Force base with two older friends from the neighborhood to meet one of the girls' boyfriends. The boyfriend brought along two of his friends, and the six of them partied with alcohol, drugs, and sex. It was Kathy's first time experiencing any of these things, and she discovered that she liked them all. Thus began a 9-year spiral into alcohol, drug, and sex addiction and into all the crimes associated with these conditions such as drug trafficking, robbery, and prostitution.

When she was 25 years old she was involved in a serious automobile accident in which she broke her pelvis, both legs, and an arm and suffered a concussion. She was charged with drunken driving and possession of methamphetamine for sale. Kathy spent 10 months recuperating from her injuries during which she was drug-, alcohol-, and sex-free. Because of her medical condition she was placed on probation. Her probation officer (P.O.) was a real "knuckle dragger" who, while brooking no nonsense, became something of a father figure to her. While she was recuperating she was often taken care of by a male nurse she described as "nerdy but nice." Her parents, who had been estranged from her for some time, became reacquainted with her, and her P.O. and nurse taught her to trust men again. She also occupied her time taking an online college course on drug addiction and counseling. She eventually married her "nerdy nurse" with her parents' blessing, and one of the honored guests was the "knuckle dragger."

Kathy's story illustrates some core ideas in this section. No matter how low a person sinks into antisocial behavior, he or she is not destined to continue the downward spiral. Certain so-called turning points in life can have a dramatic impact on a person's life. The auto accident and meeting the tough P.O. and the tender nurse would certainly qualify as significant turning points, as most certainly would marriage and the decision to continue her education. Before she became involved with "the wrong crowd," she had accumulated what is called "social capital" in the form of a good relationship with her family and good academic preparation. Although she spent most of her social capital, there was sufficient left to get her back on the right track.

❖ The Developmental Perspective: Continuity and Change

Most theories of crime implicitly assume that their favored causes are applicable across the life span and neglect changing social, economic, biological, and psychological conditions that impact the probability of criminal behavior. Most theories also imply that criminal behavior is self-perpetuating once initiated and say little about the process of desisting. In contrast to these static views, **developmental theories** are dynamic in that they emphasize individuals developing along different pathways, and as they do, factors that were previously meaningful to them (e.g., acceptance by antisocial peers) no longer are, and factors that previously meant little to them (marriage, a career) become meaningful. These theories are concerned with the onset, acceleration, and deceleration of offending and finally desisting altogether. All theories in this chapter are biosocial to varying degrees because they all integrate social, psychological, and biological factors into a developmental whole.

The Juvenile Years and the Age-Crime Curve

Offending in the early stages of life is known as **delinquency**, a legal term that distinguishes between juvenile and adult offending. Except in rare instances in which a juvenile commits murder and is waived (transferred) to adult court, juvenile offenders are not referred to as criminals. Acts forbidden by law are called delinquent acts when committed by juveniles. The term *delinquent* comes from a Latin term meaning to "leave undone," with the connotation being that juveniles have *not done* something they were supposed to (behave lawfully) rather than *done* something they were not supposed to (behave unlawfully). This subtle difference reflects the rehabilitative rather than punitive thrust of the juvenile justice system.

Figure 11.1 shows prevalence rates for criminal behavior over the life course from different times and different countries. This pattern is known as the **age-crime curve** and is formed from the statistical count of the number of known crimes committed in a population over a given period mapped according to age. The curve reflects a sharp increase in offending beginning in early adolescence, a peak in midadolescence, and then a steep decline in early adulthood followed by a steadier decline thereafter. The peak may be higher or lower at different periods, and the peak age may vary by a year or two at different times or in different places, but the peak remains. This pattern has been noted throughout history. William Shakespeare wrote in *The Winter's Tale*, "I would there be no age between ten and three-and-twenty, or that youth would sleep out the rest; for there is nothing in the between but getting

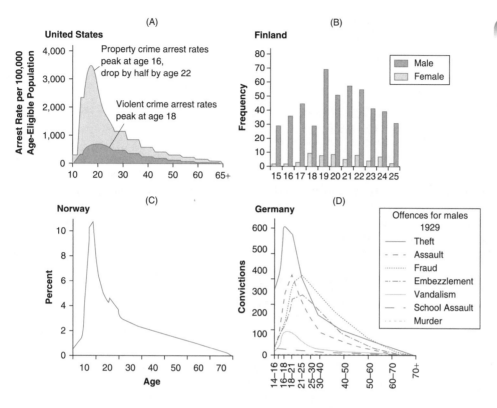

Figure 11.1

Illustrating the Age-Crime Curve in Different Countries and Times

Source: Ellis & Walsh, 2000

wenches with child, wronging the ancientry, stealing, fighting" (Act III, scene iii). Because this pattern has long been noted in all cultures around the world and at all times it has been called "the most important regularity in criminology" (Nagin & Land, 1993, p. 330) and a "law of nature" (Gottfredson & Hirschi, 1990, p. 124). By the age of 28, about 85% of all former delinquents have desisted (Caspi & Moffit, 1995).

The age-crime curve has long puzzled criminologists. Hirschi and Gottfredson (1983), for instance, admitted that "the age distribution of crime cannot be accounted for by any variable or combination of variables currently available to criminology" (p. 554). Some criminologists attempt to explain the rise in antisocial behavior in adolescence by the increase in peer involvement at this time and its decline thereafter by the decreasing influence of peers and the increasing influence of girlfriends, wives, children, and employers (Warr, 2002). However, this does not explain *why* the period between these events is so filled with antisocial behavior, *why* associations with peers so often lead to negative behavior, or why they great majority desist by age 28. Powerful brain imaging techniques are now available to help us answer these questions.

To help us to understand why adolescence is fraught with antisocial impulses and experimentation, Aaron White (2004) provides us with four key messages from the 2003 conference of the New York Academy of Sciences (NYAS), which focused on adolescent brain development, a topic that has become very popular among criminologists lately for a variety of reasons, not the least of which is the influence it had on abolishing the juvenile death penalty as discussed in the last chapter:

1. Much of the behavior characterizing adolescence is rooted in biology intermingling with environmental influences to cause teens to conflict with their parents, take more risks, and experience wide swings in emotion.

2. The lack of synchrony between a physically mature body and a still maturing nervous system may explain these behaviors.

3. Adolescents' sensitivities to rewards appear to be different than adults', prompting them to seek higher levels of novelty and stimulation to achieve the same feeling of pleasure.

4. With the right dose of guidance and understanding, adolescence can be a relatively smooth transition. (p. 4)

The NYAS statement is basically saying that the immature behavior of many adolescents is mirrored by the immaturity of their brains. The reshaping of the adolescent brain is initiated by the hormonal surges of puberty when male levels of testosterone are more than 10 times that of females (Ellis, 2003). Puberty marks the onset of the transition from childhood to adulthood and prepares us for procreation. If puberty marks the onset of adolescence, then socially defined adulthood marks its end. Socially defined adulthood means taking on socially responsible roles such as acquiring a steady job and starting one's own family that mark individuals as independent members of society. The legal definition of adulthood as 18 years of age rarely matches socially defined adulthood today, however. Young people are reaching puberty much earlier than previous generations but are confronted with an increasingly complex economy that requires much longer preparation to enter than previous generations, which constitutes "the first time in our history as a species [that] biological maturation well precedes psychosocial maturation" (Gluckman & Hanson, 2006).

Perhaps for this reason alone adolescence can be a confusing time of life. But adolescents are also experiencing profound brain changes during this period that further add to the confusion. They are experiencing changes in the ratios of excitatory to inhibitory neurotransmitters such as dopamine (the "go get it" transmitter) are peaking, while inhibitory transmitters such as serotonin ("hold your horses") are reduced (Collins, 2004). These neurohormonal changes lead many theorists (e.g., Spear, 2000; White, 2004) to conclude with Martin Daly (1996) that "there are many reasons to think that we've been designed to be maximally competitive and conflictual in young adulthood" (p. 193). We have perhaps been designed to be conflictual in adolescence to force us out of the parental nest and help us to decide which aspects of the parental generation to keep and which to discard. Adolescents are being resocialized into a somewhat different culture and need to experiment with skills that will enable them to live and mate with members of their own generation, not their parents' generation.

When the reorganization of the brain during adolescence is completed, behavior becomes more stable. McCrae (2000) and his colleagues report findings from five countries showing age-related decreases in personality traits positively related to antisocial behavior (e.g., neuroticism and risk taking) and increases in personality traits positively related to prosocial behavior (e.g., conscientiousness, agreeableness). The fine-tuning of neurological and hormonal systems occurs across the life span and in personality traits in adulthood conducive to prosocial behavior for most individuals. Likewise, Blonigen's (2010) review of studies of age-related changes in personality traits related to antisocial behavior found that a reduction in negative emotionality and an increase in conscientiousness stood out as the strongest changes. There were also moderate to large increases in agreeableness and self-control and small to moderate decreases in neuroticism (emotional instability).

Many of us have seen media accounts of how the adolescent brain changes from puberty to the mid- to late twenties. One of the most important points is that the axons (see Figure 10.2) in the adolescent prefrontal cortex are not yet fully myelinated. Myelin is a fatty substance that coats and insulates axons and allows for the rapid transmission of brain messages, just like a plastic coating around electrical wires prevents them from short-circuiting. Brains that are not fully myelinated result in a larger "time lapse" between the onset of an emotional event in the limbic system (the emotional part of the brain) and a person's rational judgment of it. In other words, there are *physical* reasons for the greater ratio of emotional to rational responses evidenced by many teens. The physical immaturity of the adolescent brain combined with a "supercharged" physiology facilitates the tendency to assign faulty attributions to situations and the intentions of others. A brain on "go slow" superimposed on a physiology on "fast-forward" explains why "many teenagers find it difficult to accurately gauge the meanings and intentions of others and to experience more stimuli as aversive during adolescence than they did as children and will do so when they are adults" (Walsh, 2002, p. 143).

❖ Risk and Protective Factors for Serious Delinquency

Some individuals possess so many risk factors that they go beyond the normal adolescent hell-raising to commit serious crimes. A **risk factor** is something that increases the probability of offending. These factors are dynamic, meaning their predictive value changes according to in which stage of the individual's development they occur, the presence of other risk and protective factors, and the immediate social circumstances. For instance, low socioeconomic status (SES) is a family risk factor, but a person with a high IQ and warm relationship with both parents is protected from the risks posed by low SES. It is typical for risk factors to cluster together. A single-parent family, for instance, is a risk factor that can lead to low SES and the financial necessity to reside in socially disorganized neighborhoods where children interact with antisocial peers. Likewise, protective factors also tend to cluster together. A report based on hundreds of studies issued by the Office of the Surgeon General of the United States (OSGUS; 2001) indicated that a 10-year-old child with six or more risk factors is approximately 10 times more likely than a child of the same age with only one risk factor to be violent by the age of 18 (see Table 11.1). We have already examined many of these risk factors (low SES, social disorganization, low IQ, lack of parental supervision, abuse), so we only examine developmental factors here.

Photo 11.1

A juvenile arrest can lead to many negative consequences, including placing a person on a path to a lifetime of crime and imprisonment.

Among the risk factors listed by OSGUS are ADHD/impulsivity, restlessness, difficulty concentrating, and aggression, which can be subsumed under the syndromes of **attention deficit with hyperactivity disorder** (ADHD) and conduct disorder (CD). ADHD is a chronic neurological condition manifested as constant restlessness, impulsiveness, difficulty with peers, disruptive behavior, short attention span, academic underachievement, risk-taking behavior, and extreme boredom. Most healthy children will show some of these symptoms at one time or another, but the symptoms cluster together to form a syndrome in ADHD children (8 out of 14 symptoms are required for diagnosis) and are chronic and more severe than simple high spirits (Durston, 2003). ADHD affects somewhere from

Table 11.1

Delinquency Risk Factors by Domain

Domain	Early Onset (Ages 6–11)	Late Onset (Ages 12–14)	Protective Factors
Individual	Being male	Restlessness	Intolerant attitude toward deviance
	ADHD/impulsivity	Difficulty concentrating[a]	High IQ
	Medical, physical problems	General offenses	Being female
	Aggression	Risk taking	Positive social orientation
	Low IQ	Aggression[a]	Perceived sanction for transgressions
	General offenses	Being male	
	Problem (antisocial) behavior	Physical violence	
	Substance abuse	Antisocial attitudes, beliefs	
	Exposure to TV violence	Crimes against persons	
	Antisocial attitudes, beliefs	Low IQ	
	Dishonesty[a]	Substance abuse	
Family	Low socioeconomic status	Poor parent-child relationship	Warm, supportive relationship with parents and other adults
	Antisocial parents	Low socioeconomic status	Parent's positive evaluation of child's peers
	Poor parent-child relationship	Harsh, lax, or inconsistent parenting	Parental monitoring
	Harsh, lax, or inconsistent parenting	Poor monitoring, supervision	
	Broken home	Antisocial parents	
	Separation from parents	Broken home	
	Abusive parents	Abusive parents	
	Neglect	Family conflict[a]	
School	Poor attitude, performance	Poor attitude, performance	Commitment to school
		Academic failure	Involvement in conventional activities
Peer group	Weak social ties	Weak social ties	Friends who engage in conventional behavior
	Antisocial peers	Antisocial, delinquent peers	
		Gang membership	
Community		Neighborhood crime, drugs	Stable, organized neighborhood
		Neighborhood disorganization	

Source: Office of the Surgeon General, 2001

a. Males only

2% to 9% of children and is four or five times more prevalent in males than in females (Levy, Hay, McStephen, Wood, & Waldman, 1997). Brain imaging studies have found differences (albeit small ones) in brain anatomy and physiology between ADHD and non-ADHD children (Raz, 2004; Sanjiv & Thaden, 2004).

Although the precise cause of ADHD is not known, genes play a large role, with heritability estimates averaging about 0.80 (Bobb, Castellanos, Addington, & Rapoport, 2005). As we might expect from our previous discussions of gene variants (polymorphisms), the genes most strongly involved in ADHD are associated with the BAS/BIS functioning of dopamine and serotonin (Bobb et al., 2005; Schilling, Walsh & Yun, 2011). Environmental factors that play a role in the etiology of ADHD are fetal exposure to drugs, alcohol, and tobacco; perinatal complications; and head trauma (Durston, 2003). Subsequent environmental factors have no causal effect, although they may worsen symptoms. ADHD symptoms generally decline in their severity with age, although about 90% of ADHD sufferers continue to display some symptoms into adulthood (Willoughby, 2003).

A review of 100 studies found that 99 reported a positive relationship between ADHD and antisocial behavior (Ellis & Walsh, 2000). ADHD individuals are consistently found to be overrepresented in juvenile detention centers, jails, and prisons worldwide (Rösler et al., 2004). Gudjonsson and colleagues' (2009) review of studies of ADHD rates among adult prison inmates using various diagnostic criteria in a number of countries found rates ranging from 24% to 67%, and a German study (Rösler et al., 2004) found that 45% of inmates had some form of ADHD (there are a number of subtypes) compared to 9.4% of a control sample. Thus ADHD is strongly related to criminal behavior, and it has been suggested that ADHD may underlie one of criminology's favored concepts—low self-control (Unnever, Cullen, & Pratt, 2003).

The probability that ADHD persons will persist in offending as adults rises dramatically if they are also diagnosed with **conduct disorder** (CD). CD is defined as "the persistent display of serious antisocial actions that are extreme given the child's developmental level and have a significant impact on the rights of others" (Lynam, 1996, p. 211). Markus Krueisi and his colleagues (1994) propose that ADHD is a product of a deficient BIS, and CD is a product of an oversensitive BAS (see Chapter 10). ADHD individuals with CD thus suffer a double disability: their dominant BAS inclining them to seek high levels of stimulation (to raise dopamine levels) and their faulty BIS leaving them with little sense of when to stop (low serotonin functioning). ADHD and CD are found to co-occur in 30% to 50% (Lynam, 1996). CD has an onset at around 5 years of age and is a neurological disorder with substantial genetic affects (Coolidge, Thede, & Young, 2000). Studies have consistently shown that ADHD, especially ADHD + CD individuals, display low ANS arousal as well (Crowell et al., 2006; Posthumus, Böcker, Raaijmakers, Van Engeland, & Matthys, 2009). Lynam (1996) describes the trajectory from ADHD + CD to criminality stating that the co-occurrence of ADHD and CD

> may tax the skills of parents and lead to the adoption of coercive child rearing techniques, which in turn may enhance the risk of antisocial behavior. Entry into school may bring academic failure and increase the child's frustration, which may increase his or her level of aggressive behavior. Finally, the peer rejection associated with hyperactivity may lead to increased social isolation and conflict with peers. (p. 22)

Patterns of Serious Delinquency

The developmental model of the progression of delinquency devised by Terrence Thornberry, David Huizinga, and Rolf Loeber (2004) focuses on the escalation of the seriousness of delinquent acts committed as boys age. The model is based on three longitudinal studies that include more than 4,000 subjects followed since 1987. What has emerged from these three studies is an image of three developmental pathways of offending, as noted in Figure 11.2. The authority conflict pathway starts before puberty with simple stubborn behavior, followed by defiance and authority avoidance. Some boys in this pathway move into the second stage (defiance/disobedience) and a few more into the authority avoidance stage. At this point, some boys progress to one of the other two pathways, but many will go no further. The covert pathway starts after puberty and involves minor offenses in Stage 1 that become progressively more serious for a few boys who enter Stage 3 on this pathway. The overt pathway progresses

Figure 11.2

Three Pathways to Boys' Disruptive Behavior and Delinquency

Source: Thornberry, Huizinga, & Loeber, 2004

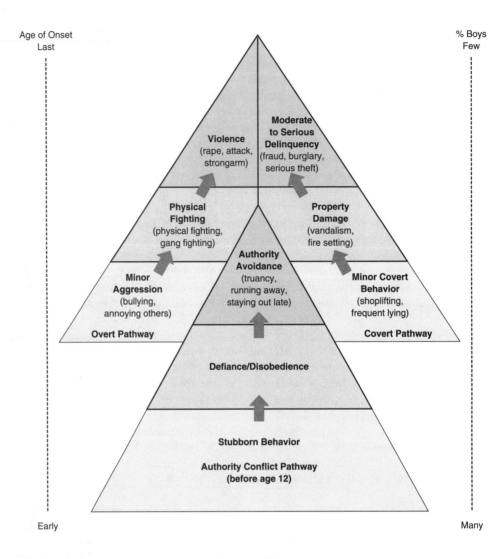

from minor aggressive acts in Stage 1 to very serious violent acts in Stage 3. The more seriously involved delinquents in the overt and covert pathways may switch back and forth between violent and property crimes. The overall take-home lesson of this model is that as boys get older, their crimes become more serious, but happily there are far fewer serious crimes.

❖ Major Developmental Theories

As already noted, developmental theories are dynamic theories concerned with the frequency, duration, and seriousness of offending behavior from onset to desistance. All theories maintain that although a criminal career may be initiated at any time, it is almost always begun in childhood or adolescence, with only about 4% initiated in adulthood (Elliot, Huizinga, & Menard, 1989). The duration of a criminal career may be limited to one offense or can last well into old age, with the frequency and seriousness of offending varying widely. Onset, frequency, duration, seriousness, and desistance depend on a variety of interacting individual and situational factors that vary across the life course.

Robert Agnew's General or "Super Traits" Theory

In his general or **"super traits" theory**, Robert Agnew identifies five life domains that contain possible crime-generating factors: personality, family, school, peers, and work. It is a developmental theory because these domains interact and feed back on one another across the life span as illustrated in Figure 11.3. Agnew suggests that personality traits set individuals on a particular developmental trajectory that influences how other people in the family, school, peer group, and work domains react to them. In other words, personality variables "condition" the effect of social variables on crime. Noting that personality traits cluster together, Agnew identifies the latent (underlying) traits of low self-control and irritability as super traits that encompass many of the traits we discussed in previous sections, such as sensation seeking, impulsivity, inattentiveness, and low empathy. People saddled with low self-control and irritable temperaments are likely to evoke negative responses from family members, school teachers, peers, and workmates that feed back and make those tendencies worse than they would have otherwise been (the feedback process of evocative gene-environment correlation discussed in Chapter 10).

Agnew (2005) states that "biological factors [ANS and brain chemistry] have a direct effect on irritability/low self-control and an indirect effect on the other life domains through [the effects of] irritability/low self-control [on them]" (p. 213). What Agnew calls irritability is analogous to the trait most psychologists call negative emotionality.

Agnew claims his theory can explain gender, race, age, and SES effects on criminality and can account for the differences between individuals who limit their offending to the adolescent years and those who offend across the life course.

In terms of gender differences, Agnew (2005) says that males are more likely to inherit irritability–low self-control than females, perhaps because in evolutionary terms these traits have aided male reproductive success by enhancing male aggressiveness and competitiveness. In terms of race differences, Agnew argues that African Americans are more likely to be poor and to receive discriminatory treatment. This and other factors may significantly increase

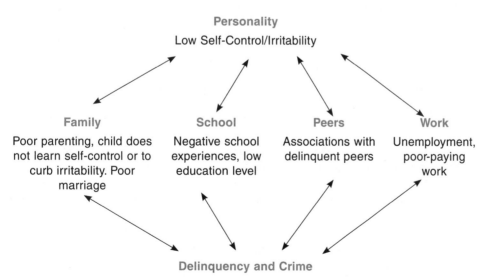

Figure 11.3

Agnew's General or "Super Traits" Theory

Personality and life domains loop back on one another in an evocative gene–environment correlation fashion. This negatively affects both the relationships the person has and his or her personality, thus further impacting criminal propensity.

irritability, and perceptions of poor job prospects may also lead to the adoption of an impulsive "live-for-the-day" lifestyle among some African Americans. Finally, in terms of SES, Agnew (2005) states that "individuals from low-SES families may be more likely to inherit these traits, as these traits may be more common among low-SES individuals" (p. 143). He also notes that low-SES individuals may not only be more likely to inherit polymorphisms related to such traits, but are also more likely than higher-SES individuals to suffer biological insults such as prenatal exposure to toxic substances and birth complications that contribute environmentally to these traits.

Agnew also notes that the immaturity of adolescent behavior is tied to the immaturity of the adolescent brain and that adolescents tend to become more irritable because their brains are undergoing a period of intense "remodeling." At the same time adolescent brains are changing, adolescents are experiencing massive hormonal surges that tend to facilitate aggression and competitiveness. Thus the neurological and endocrine changes during adolescence *temporarily* increase irritability–low self-control among adolescents who limit their offending to that period, while for those who continue to offend irritability–low self-control is a *stable* characteristic.

David Farrington's Integrated Cognitive Antisocial Potential (ICAP) Theory

David Farrington's ICAP theory integrates a number of concepts from social learning, social control, labeling, strain, and rational choice theories. However, it is mostly reminiscent of Walters's lifestyle theory stressing that early biological and environmental conditions affect choice and that these choices lead to particular cognitions, or ways of thinking. The theory is based on a longitudinal cohort study of boys born in deprived areas (thus putting all boys at environmental risk) of London. The key concepts in **integrated cognitive antisocial potential theory** are antisocial potential (AP), which is a person's risk or propensity to engage in crime, and **cognition**, which is the "thinking or decision-making process that turns potential into actual behavior" (Farrington, 2003, p. 231). AP is ordered on a continuum with relatively few people with very high levels, but levels vary over time and across life events and peak in adolescence.

Farrington distinguishes between long-term and short-term AP. Individuals with long-term AP tend to come from poor families; be poorly socialized, impulsive, and sensation seeking; and have low IQ. Short-term AP individuals suffer few or any of these deficits but may temporarily increase their AP in response to certain situations or inducements. Farrington (2003) indicates that we all have "desires for material goods, status among intimates, excitement, and sexual satisfaction, and that people choose illegitimate ways of satisfying them when they lack legitimate means of doing so, or when bored, frustrated, or drunk" (p. 231). The teenage years are particularly potent for temporarily increasing AP because not only are they years in which the desires Farrington identifies are particularly strong, but they are also the years in which many teenagers lack prosocial means of satisfying them. As we have seen, they are also the years in which teens lack full integration of the cognitive means that enable persons to make wise choices.

Short-tem AP may turn into long-term AP over time as a consequence of offending. This can happen if individuals find offending to be reinforcing either in material or psychological terms by gaining status and approval from peers. Such outcomes lead to changes in cognition such that AP is more likely to turn into actual criminal behavior in the future. Offending can also lead to criminal labeling and incarceration, which limits future legitimate opportunities to meet one's needs legitimately. Thus long-term AP can develop even in the absence of most or all of the risk factors (i.e., for social-situational reasons alone) said to predict chronic offending across the life course.

ICAP theory is also interested in the process of desisting from offending, which occurs for both social and individual reasons and at different rates according to a person's level of AP. As noted earlier, as people age they tend to become less impulsive and less easily frustrated. They also experience life changes such as marriage, steady employment, and moving to new areas, thus shifting their patterns of interaction from peers to girlfriends, wives, and children. These events decrease offending opportunities by shifting routine activities such as drinking with male peers; increase informal controls in terms of having family and work responsibilities; and change cognition in the form of reduced subjective rewards of offending because the costs are now much higher than before (the risk of losing a hard-earned stake in conformity). Potential peer approval becomes the potential disapproval of wives and other family members (Farrington, 2003).

Terrie Moffitt's Dual-Pathway Developmental Theory

Moffitt's dual-pathway developmental theory is based on findings from an ongoing longitudinal study of a New Zealand birth cohort (in its 39th year as of 2014). It has been called "the most innovative approach to age-crime relationships and life-course patterns" (Tittle, 2000, p. 68). The data available to Moffitt and her colleagues comes from collaborative efforts by scientists in sociology, criminology, psychology, medicine, genetics, and neuroscience, enabling them to test biosocial hypotheses.

It has long been known that the vast majority of youth who offend during adolescence desist and that there are a small number who continue to offend in adulthood. Moffitt calls the former **adolescent-limited (AL) offenders** and the latter **life course–persistent (LCP) offenders**. LCP offenders are individuals who begin offending prior to puberty and continue well into adulthood and who are saddled with neuropsychological and temperamental deficits manifested in low IQ, hyperactivity, inattentiveness, negatively emotionality, and low impulse control. These problems arise from a combination of genetic and environmental effects on brain development. Environmental risk factors include being the offspring of a single teenage mother, low SES, abuse/neglect, and inconsistent discipline. These related individual and environmental impairments initiate a cumulative process of negative person/environment interactions that result in a life course trajectory propelling individuals toward ever-hardening antisocial attitudes and behaviors.

Moffitt (1993) describes the antisocial trajectory of LCP offenders as one of "biting and hitting at age 4, shoplifting and truancy at age 10, selling drugs and stealing cars at age 16, robbery and rape at age 22, fraud and child abuse at age 30; the underlying disposition remains the same, but its expression changes form as new social opportunities arise at different points of development" (p. 679). This is matched by cross-situational behavioral consistency. LCP offenders "lie at home, steal from shops, cheat at school, fight in bars, and embezzle at work" (p. 679). Given this antisocial consistency across time and place, opportunities for change and legitimate success become increasingly unlikely for these individuals. While LCP offenders constituted only 7% of the cohort, they were responsible for more than 50% of all delinquent and criminal acts committed by it (Henry et al., 1996). Moreover, whereas AL offenders tend to commit relatively minor offenses such as petty theft, LCP offenders tend to be convicted of more serious crimes such as assault, robbery, and rape (Moffitt & Walsh, 2003).

As illustrated in Figure 11.3, AL offenders have a developmental history that places them on a prosocial trajectory temporarily derailed at adolescence. They are not burdened with the neuropsychological problems that weigh heavily on LCP offenders and are adequately socialized in childhood by competent parents, but they are also seeking a degree of adult autonomy. As they are doing this, "every curfew broken, car stolen, joint smoked, and baby conceived is a statement of independence. . . . Algebra does not make a statement about independence; it does not assert that a youth is entitled to be taken seriously. Crime does" (Caspi & Moffit, 1995, p. 500). AL offenders are "normal" youths adapting to the transitional events surrounding adolescence and whose offending is a social phenomenon played out in peers groups and does not reflect any stable personal deficiencies (Moffitt, 1993). At least 85% of youthful offenders are adolescent limited.

According to Moffitt, many more teens than in the past are being diverted from their prosocial life trajectories because better health and nutrition has lowered the average age of puberty while the average time needed to prepare for participation in the economy has increased. These changes have resulted in about a 5- to 10-year **maturity gap** between puberty and entry into the job market. Thus, "adolescent-limited offending is a product of an interaction between age and historical period" (Moffitt, 1993, p. 692). Filled with youthful energy, strength, and confidence and a strong desire to shed the restrictions of childhood, AL offenders are attracted to the excitement of antisocial peer groups typically led by experienced LCP delinquents. Once initiated into the group, juveniles learn the attitudes and techniques of offending through mimicking others and gain reinforcement in the form of much desired group approval and acceptance for doing so, as social learning theorists argue.

As AL offenders mature, they begin to realize that an adult criminal record will severely limit their future options. They also begin to realize that they are freer now to structure their environments consistent with their innate preferences. For some AL offenders, desistance from antisocial behavior is abrupt and for others it is a slower process. Much depends on personal characteristics and a combination of how well they were integrated into the antisocial peer group and what prosocial opportunities become available to them. AL offenders have accumulated a store of positive attachments (they elicit positive responses from prosocial others) and academic skills (they stayed in school and did reasonably well) before they started offending and even while they were offending. These attachments and skills can be called on to provide them with prosocial opportunities such as a good marriage and a good job. In Moffitt's (1993) words, AL offenders

Figure 11.4

Moffitt's Dual-Developmental Pathways

*rGE = gene-environment correlation (see Chapter 10)

Life Course–Persistent: Applicable to Congenitally Predisposed Youths

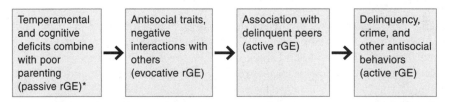

Adolescent-Limited: Applicable to Many "Normal" Youths During Adolescence

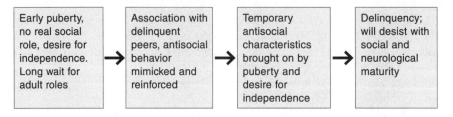

desist from offending because they are "psychologically healthy," and "healthy youths respond adaptively to changing contingencies" (p. 690).

Sampson and Laub's Age-Graded Theory

All three developmental theories we have thus far discussed posit a set of traits that set individuals on developmentally distinct pro- or antisocial pathways. However, Sampson and Laub (2005) prefer to call their age-graded theory a life-course theory rather than a developmental theory because they deny that people are necessarily locked into developmentally distinct pathways by these traits, which of course they are not. Sampson and Laub want to emphasize environmental circumstances and human agency as opposed to individual traits, although these traits are not ignored. Their theory is based on data collected in the 1930s through the 1960s by Sheldon and Eleanor Glueck (1950). Age-graded theory is essentially a social control theory extended into adulthood in that it assumes that we have to learn to be good rather than to be bad and that ties to prosocial others are particularly important to this prosocial learning process. While the bonds to parents and school are very important during childhood, and to peers during adolescence, they become less important in adulthood when new situations offer opportunities to form new social bonds that constrain offending behavior for most people.

Photo 11.2

From this series of family images taken over time, can you discern the behavioral and life course paths of the individuals depicted? One became a teen delinquent but then went on to be a law-abiding adult and, ultimately, a minister. One dropped out of a teen job to move away and marry a federal inmate who had sold a number of different drugs. Another started a career in sales but became involved in possible "Ponzi" schemes. One became a criminologist.

As with all control theories, the task of age-graded theory is not to explain why some people commit crimes but rather why most people do not. The theory assumes that factors such as low IQ, difficult temperament, SES, and broken home have only indirect effects on offending via their influence on the ease or difficulty with which bonding and socialization take place. The theory also places emphasis on the process of desisting from offending among those who start and the situational factors involved in the process rather than on individual risk factors for offending.

People who bond well with conventional others build **social capital**, which is essentially a store of positive relationships built on norms of reciprocity and trust developed over time on which the individual can draw for support when needed. People who have opened their social capital "accounts" early in life (bonding to parents and school), even though they may spend it freely as adolescents, still have quite a decent nest egg by the time they reach adulthood. They can then gather more interest in the form of a successful career and marriage (bonding to a career and a family of one's own). This accumulation of social capital provides people with a powerful stake in conformity that they are not likely to risk by engaging in criminal activity. To put it in terms of Hirschi's social bonding theory discussed in Chapter 6, social capital is the result of early attachments and commitment to parents and school and is increased in adulthood by attachments and commitments to marriages and careers.

Life is a series of transitions (or life events) that may change life trajectories in prosocial directions for persons lacking much social capital. Sampson and Laub (2005) call such events **turning points** and consider this the most important concept in their theory. Important turning points include getting married, finding a decent job, moving to a new neighborhood, or entering military service. Of course, turning points are processes rather than events, and rather than promoting change, they may accentuate antisocial tendencies or at least leave them intact. According to Gottfredson and Hirschi (1990), the problem is that "the offender tends to convert these institutions [marriage, jobs] into sources of satisfaction consistent with his previous criminal

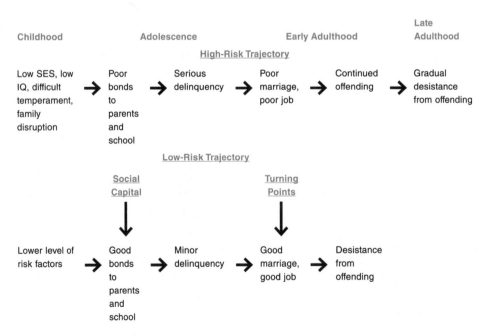

Figure 11.5

Sampson and Laub's Age-Graded Theory

Photo 11.3

Major turning points in life such as getting married and joining the military can halt a criminal career.

behavior" (p. 141). In other words, criminals expand their antisocial repertoire into domestic abuse and workplace crime.

Blonigen (2010) also takes issue with the notion that informal social controls that kick in with the acquisition of a job and a "good" marriage can account for desisting from crime. He avers that such arguments do not acknowledge the reciprocal relationship between social roles and personality traits (intelligent and conscientious people get good jobs, and agreeable people get congenial marriage partners). Put otherwise, "self selection and social influence are 'corresponsive' in their effect on personality such that social roles serve to accentuate features of an individual's personality that were already present." This process reflects "a 'niche-picking' process in which individuals chose roles consistent with their personality make-up" (Blonigen, 2010, p. 96). Nevertheless, Laub and Sampson (2003) have shown that obtaining a good job and a good marriage does reduce offending among even previously high-rate offenders. We must understand that these things represent the possibility, not the inevitability, of positive change.

As this chapter's opening vignette and the Theory in Action box illustrate, although a person may be disadvantaged by the past, he or she does not have to be a prisoner to it. Along with rational choice theory, age-graded theory strongly emphasizes human agency, defined as "the purposeful execution of choice and individual will," and some people freely chose a life of crime because they find it seductive and rewarding despite having full knowledge of the negative consequences (Sampson & Laub, 2005, p. 37). Regardless, all members of the Glueck's original delinquent sample of 500 that Sampson and Laub were able to locate ($N = 52$) had desisted from offending by age 70 regardless of whether they were defined as high-risk or low-risk as children and regardless of the level of social capital they had managed to accumulate. This supports the long-held opinion among criminologists that all criminals "age out" of crime eventually just as we all age out of participation in many of the activities we enjoyed as youths. Figure 11.5 illustrates the two life course pathways according to Sampson and Laub's theory.

THEORY IN ACTION: Jimmy Boyle, From Underworld Hero to Art Celebrity

Jimmy Boyle was born the second of four sons in 1944, in the Gorbals, the most crime-infested slum in Glasgow, Scotland. Jimmy grew up hero worshiping the "hard men" of Glasgow and dearly wanted to be one of them. His father was a well-known villain in Glasgow who died from a beating by a rival gang when Jimmy was only 6 years old. Jimmy soon fell in with a powerful criminal gang, garnering his first arrest at 13 for breaking into a chewing gum machine. In his 20s he was twice arrested and charged with murder but was not convicted, apparently because witnesses were intimidated into refusing to testify. He was later imprisoned for a serious assault acquired while practicing his profession as muscle for a loan shark and behaved so badly in prison that he soon earned the accolade he most desired—"Scotland's most violent man." After his release, he resumed his criminal ways and was convicted in 1967 of the murder of another Glasgow scoundrel named William "Babs" Rooney. Boyle always denied this murder, but he was sentenced to life imprisonment in Scotland's Barlinnie Prison anyway.

Photo 11.4

Jimmy Boyle, once touted as "Scotland's most violent man," eventually became an artist, got married, and changed his life completely.

While in prison he consistently worked to embellish his "hard Boyled" reputation by assaulting the prison governor (the warden), the "screws" (prison guards), and other inmates, as well as fermenting a number of riots. Desperate to do something—anything!—to calm Boyle down, in 1973 he was placed in the Barlinnie Prison Special Unit's rehabilitation program. This was a unit for violent offenders in which the officers outnumbered inmates. Inmates and officers would sit together and talk about various issues, and inmates were given more freedoms and responsibilities than inmates in the general population.

It was in this unit that Boyle discovered his artistic side, producing many fine sculptures (imagine putting a hammer and chisel in the hands of Scotland's most violent man!) and writing his autobiography he called *A Sense of Freedom*. Boyle also met his future wife, Sarah Trevelyan, a psychotherapist who read his book and visited him in prison; the couple now has two grown and successful children. Boyle was paroled in 1987 and took up the life of a professional sculptor. He also set up and financed a program called the Gateway Exchange to help people with addiction problems. He is now an internationally renowned sculptor, an acclaimed writer, and a drug counselor.

Jimmy Boyle's story illustrates Sampson and Laub's belief that no matter how far a person goes down the wrong road, he or she can always turn around and take another one. The "turning points" in Jimmy's life (according to Jimmy himself) were the transfer to the Barlinnie Prison Special Unit, where he learned respect and responsibility, and his marriage. But Jimmy had a special advantage that most other criminals do not have—a toolkit of prodigious talents to call on to help him mend his ways. On the other hand, he had gone down the wrong road much further that almost any other criminal—after all, he did have the label he cherished as well earned, that of "Scotland's most violent man." He may also have a touch of ADHD because he characterizes himself as "always on the go," from 4 a.m. onward. The difference is that now he has a creative outlet in his sculpting and writing for all that energy, illustrating that ADHD can be a positive thing if the incessant need for novelty is channeled into constructive endeavors.

THEORY IN ACTION (Continued)

Discussion Questions

1. Which of the theories discussed in this or other chapters do you think best fits Jimmy Boyle's onset and continuance in crime?

2. Which of the theories discussed in this chapter do you think best fits Jimmy Boyle's desistance from crime?

3. What would labeling theorists have to say about Boyle's criminal labels, which he relished?

Sources: BBC News, 1999; Smith, 1984

Table 11.2

Summary of Key Points, Strengths, and Differences of Developmental Theories

Theory	Key Points	Key Strengths	Key Differences
Agnew's General or Super Traits Theory	Low self-control and irritability set people on a trajectory leading to negative interactions with peers and the family, at school and work, and in marriage. These different domains interact and feed back on one another.	Parsimoniously integrates concepts from psychology, sociology, and biology and shows how each affects and is affected by all others. Theory states that low self-control and irritability are temporarily increased during adolescence.	Does not address the process of desisting from offending. Does not explicitly address different trajectories as in Moffitt and to a lesser extent in Farrington and Sampson and Laub.
Sampson and Laub's Age-Graded Theory	Power of informal social controls across the life course. Assumes classical notions of why people commit crimes, therefore no need to dwell too much on risk factors. Turning points in life and human agency are important. These turning points are made easier if one has accumulated significant social capital.	Emphasis on the power of life events to turn trajectories around and to facilitate desistance. Also emphasis on human agency is refreshing. All offenders will eventually desist regardless of risk factors or lack of social capital.	Unlike other theories, there is little emphasis on risk factors setting people on a particular trajectory other than bonding strength. Emphasis on inhibiting (bonding, social capital) rather than facilitating factors.
Farrington's ICAP Theory	People have varying levels of antisocial propensity (AP) due to a variety of environmental and biological factors. Few people have long-term AP, but these people tend to offend across the life course. Short-term AP tends to occur in adolescence and can change to long-term under some circumstances.	Shows how people think (cognition) translates AP into actual offending behavior. As with Moffitt's AL offenders, AP is said to increase temporarily during adolescence. It can lead to long-term AP if caught and labeled criminal because such a label limits future opportunities.	Not as much emphasis on desisting as age-graded theory but more so than Agnew and Moffitt. Less emphasis than Agnew and Moffitt on latent traits but more than Sampson and Laub. Unlike Moffitt, AP is considered a continuum rather than a distinct two-type typology.

(Continued)

Table 11.2

(Continued)

Moffitt's Dual-Pathway Theory	There are two main pathways to offending—LCP and AL. LCP offenders have neurological and temperamental difficulties exacerbated by inept parenting. LCPs offend across time and situations, begin prior to puberty, and continue well into adulthood. AL offenders are "normal" individuals temporarily derailed during adolescence.	Identifies two distinct pathways to offending rather than assuming all people are similarly affected by similar factors. Shows how the social bonds so important to age-graded theory are formed or not formed according to the characteristics of individuals.	Emphasizes a larger number of individual differences that affect offending behavior than all other theories. Also attempts to explain prevalence of offending with reference to the modern maturity gap. Differences between the two trajectory groups more defined than in other theories.

❖ Evaluation of Developmental Theories

Developmental theories offer many advantages over theories previously discussed because of their dynamic nature. They are also all biosocial to different degrees since they all integrate a number of important biological and environmental factors. It is not only consideration of the differential impact of risk factors at different junctures across the life span that distinguishes developmental theories; it is also their focus on the process of desisting from crime. Developmental theories are mostly based on longitudinal cohort data, which enables theorists to examine the links between risk factors and crime among the same individuals at every developmental stage of their lives. Longitudinal studies also enable theorists to identify causes rather than mere correlates because temporal order (which factor came first) is established among the correlates, something that cross-sectional studies (studies that sample subjects at a single moment in time) cannot do.

With the exception of Agnew's theory, all developmental theories discussed in this chapter are based on longitudinal cohort data so that theorists can examine the links between risk factors and crime among the same individuals at every developmental stage of their lives. Such data are very hard to come by and very expensive to conduct, and some theorists argue that cross-sectional studies are adequate and that longitudinal studies are an expensive luxury. Theorists making such claims are those who identify a **latent trait** (e.g., self-control) that is considered stable throughout life, thus cross-sectional studies capture characteristics of individuals at any one time, making multiyear studies redundant. Such a position ignores the interaction of the supposedly stable latent trait with vastly different life experiences as people make their journeys from cradle to grave.

In short, if there is a "gold standard" for criminological theory, developmental theories would have to be it because they are biosocial theories in that they generally integrate and consider sociological, psychological, and biological factors as a coherent whole; they follow the same individuals over long periods of time, a strategy that allows for cause/effect analysis; and they can identify characteristics that lead to onset, persistence, and desistance from crime in the same individuals.

Because low self-control and irritability (negative emotionality) are personality traits considered to be strongly influenced by low serotonin levels, Agnew's super traits theory could guide a longitudinal study in which life histories, offending records, and serotonin levels (as well as other neurohormonal substances) could be measured periodically. The relationship between low serotonin and impulsive violent behavior is consistently found and has been called "perhaps the most reliable finding in the history of psychiatry" (Fishbein, 2001, p. 15). Such longitudinal studies could tell us if at-risk individuals became even more at risk because of magnification of low self-control–high irritability due to the feedback effects of others reacting to their evocative behavior. Because neurohormonal substances are responsive to environmental contexts, significant changes in them may index important environmental changes in a person's life (Collins, 2004). We could also be informed if important turning points in subjects' lives led to decreased (or increased) offending and decreased (or increased) levels of various neurohormonal substances.

❖ Policy and Prevention: Implications of Developmental Theories

Policies designed to prevent and reduce crime derived from developmental studies do not differ from other theories but rather encompass them all and suggest a broad array of strategies. Developmental theories support the same kind of family-based nurturant strategies supported by biosocial and social and self-control theories. Regardless of any traits children may bring with them to the socialization process, however, these traits can be muted by patient and loving parenting, and as such, many developmental theories suggest family interventions as early as possible to help nurture bonds between children and their parents.

The Nurse-Family Partnership program has attempted to do this. The program began in 1978 with a sample of 400 at-risk women and girls and their infants. All mothers were unmarried, most were living in poverty, and 48% were under age 15. The women and girls were randomly assigned to four different groups, with one group (the experimental group) receiving extensive care from nurses in the form of multiple prenatal and postnatal home visitations in which the nurses gave help and advice on a variety of child care matters. The other groups received less comprehensive care for shorter periods. A 15-year follow-up study by Olds and his colleagues (1998) found that the program had many beneficial outcomes for the experimental group children and their mothers relative to the subjects in the other groups. For the mothers, there was less substance abuse, fewer subsequent illegitimate births, fewer legal difficulties, and 79% fewer verified instances of child abuse/neglect relative to the control groups. For the children, there was less substance abuse, fewer arrests, better school performance, and better all-around social adjustment.

An interesting school-based program that has been implemented in several countries and is explicitly based on the assumptions of developmental theories is the Fast Track Project (2005). Through multistage screening of over 10,000 kindergarten children they identified 891 who were at high risk for antisocial behavior. These children were impulsive, had difficult temperaments, and came from unstable families living in low-income high-crime neighborhoods. The children were divided into experimental ($n = 445$) and control ($n = 446$) groups. The experimental group was given a curriculum designed to develop social understanding and emotional communication skills and improve self-control and problem-solving skills. This group was also placed in so-called friendship groups and peer pairing designed to increase social skills and enhance friendships. Their parents received parenting effectiveness training and home visits to foster their problem-solving skills and general life management.

The program is evaluated periodically and has been found to have modest but positive outcomes. By the end of the third grade, 37% of the experimental group was judged to be free of conduct problems as opposed to 27% of the control group. By the eighth grade, 38% of the experimental group had been arrested as opposed to 42% of the control group. Although these differences are modest at best, they still reflect a good number of people saved from criminal victimization if the improvements hold in the future. If programs such as the Fast Track Project are combined with programs like the Nurse-Family Partnership we should see improved results since even kindergarten intervention may be too late in some cases. Yet developmental theories tell us that human life is characterized by dynamism and that people can change at any time. This is a note of optimism for crime control/prevention strategies.

Summary

- Developmental theories are dynamic and integrative and examine offending across the life course. Juvenile offending has been noted across time and cultures. A sharp rise in offending following puberty and a steady decline thereafter has been noted always and everywhere. Brain and hormonal scientists explain the age effect with respect to the brain and hormonal processes occurring during adolescence. At puberty a huge surge in testosterone levels is experienced and the brain undergoes a process of intensive resculpting.

- There are a wide variety of factors that put some teens more at risk for delinquent behavior than others. The factors we focused on were ADHD and CD, which are highly heritable. The co-occurrence of ADHD and CD is a particularly strong risk factor.

- Developmental theories follow individuals across the life course to determine the differential effect of risk factors for offending at different junctures.

- Agnew's super traits theory focuses on how low self-control and irritability (negative emotionality) interact with other life domains (e.g., school, work, marriage) across the life span to impact the probability of offending.

- Farrington's ICAP theory stresses antisocial potential and cognition and how these things are shaped in pro- or antisocial directions at different times and in different situations. Farrington distinguishes between long-term and short-term antisocial potential. Short-term antisocial potential occurs primarily during adolescence.

- Moffitt's theory posits a dual-pathway model consisting of adolescent-limited offenders (AL), who limit their offending to the adolescent years, and life course–persistent (LCP) offenders, who offend across the life course. LCP offenders have neurological and temperamental difficulties that set them on a developmental trajectory that leads to antisocial behavior at all ages and in all social situations. AL offenders do not suffer these disabilities and have accumulated sufficient social capital that they can resettle into a prosocial lifestyle once neurological and social maturity has been reached.

- Sampson and Laub's age-graded theory is concerned with the power of informal social control (bonds) to prevent offending. Turning points in life (e.g., marriage, new job) are important in understanding the process of offenders' desisting from crime.

Exercises and Discussion Questions

1. Why is it important that we understand what is going on biologically during adolescence?

2. If people age out of crime as well as into it, would it be a good idea to ignore all but the most serious of juvenile crimes so that we don't risk having children gain a "criminal" reputation?

3. What is social capital, and how much of it do you believe you have accumulated?

4. If only a very small number of individuals are life course–persistent offenders, shouldn't we concentrate our crime control efforts on them? If you agree with this, how do we identify them? Isn't there a danger of false-positive identification (identifying someone who will continue to offend well into adulthood when in fact he or she wouldn't have)?

5. Go to http://fasttrackproject.org/overview.php and read more about the Fast Track Project. Identify some of the specifics of the program and report to the class.

Useful Websites

ADHD. www.nimh.nih.gov/health/topics/attention-deficit-hyperactivity-disorder-adhd/index.shtml.

Developmental psychology. http://medicine.jrank.org/pages/455/Developmental-Psychology.html.

Moffitt, T. E. (1993). Adolescent-limited and life-course persistent antisocial behavior: A developmental taxonomy. *Psychological Review,* 100(4), 674–701. www.soc.umn.edu/~uggen/Moffitt_PR_93.pdf.

National Institute of Mental Health. www.nimh.nih.gov.

Office of Juvenile Justice and Delinquency Prevention .www.ojjdp.gov.

Chapter Terms

Age-crime curve

Age-graded theory

Attention deficit with hyperactivity disorder (ADHD)

Conduct disorder

Delinquency

Developmental theories

Integrated cognitive antisocial potential theory (ICAP)

Latent trait

Maturity gap

Moffitt's dual-pathway developmental theory

Risk factor

Social capital

Super traits theory

Turning points

CHAPTER 12

Crimes of Violence

On December 14, 2012, 20-year-old Adam Lanza shot his mother in her bed and drove to Sandy Hook Elementary School in Newtown, Connecticut. Arriving at the school with three of his mother's semiautomatic weapons, he shot his way through locked glass doors and fatally shot 20 children and six adult staff members. Why?

Lanza had a difficult time in school, although he was extremely intelligent. His difficulties were more in the inability to respond appropriately to social stimuli, and he was taken out of high school and home-schooled by his mother. He reportedly was only able to bond with his mother during their numerous sessions at the firing range where he became an excellent marksman. Lanza was also enamored with ultraviolent video games, especially the Call of Duty series, and reportedly would spend many hours each day playing them. After the massacre, the police found thousands of dollars worth of violent video games in the Lanza home (the Lanzas were well off; Mrs. Lanza received a handsome alimony check every month from her ex-husband, who was a company CEO).

In April of 1973, Edmund Kemper, a 6-foot-9-inch, 300-pound, 25-year-old hate machine, crept into his mother's bedroom and bludgeoned her to death. He decapitated her, had sex with her headless body, and played darts with the head. He then invited his mother's best friend over for a "surprise" dinner to honor his mother and bludgeoned and decapitated her also. He killed at least six other women and sexually assaulted their headless corpses. He even ate the flesh of some of his victims, cooking it into a macaroni casserole. But Kemper's biggest thrill was not sex, murder, or cannibalism; it was decapitation. In Kemper's own words, "You hear that little pop and pull their heads off and hold their heads up by the hair. Whipping their heads off, their body sitting there. That'd get me off."

The potential for violence is in us all, waiting to be ignited by environmental sparks, but thankfully only a miniscule few react like Lanza or Kemper. We have to ask ourselves what kind of a society glorifies sickening violence in its so-called entertainment and allows young boys to gain access to deadly weapons. At the same time, we have a society that does not provide its young with meaningful moral lessons and activities to fill their time and often laughs at the very idea of injecting morality into school curricula.

LEARNING OBJECTIVES

- Know why violent crime has dropped over the centuries
- Be able to identify types of murder and its victims and perpetrators
- Know differences between mass, spree, and serial killers
- Know the myths associated with serial killers
- Know the basics of rape, robbery, and aggravated assault
- Understand the sociological, evolutionary, and neuroscience theories of violence and their common lessons

❖ Violence in History

Just as every generation in its youth seems to think it discovered sex, every generation in its maturity seems to feel it is in the midst of an unprecedented wave of **violent crime**. If we had lived in earlier times we really would have had something to complain about. Eisener's (2001) examination of European murder rates showed a drop from a high average of 32 per 100,000 in the 13th and 14th centuries to 19, 11, 3.2, 2.6, and 1.4 per 100,000 in the subsequent five centuries. Eisener concludes that social control mechanisms such as the state's monopoly of power, the expansion of universal schooling, the rise of religious reform movements, and the organized discipline of the manufacturing workplace largely accounted for the decline in violence. The high murder rates in medieval Europe had a lot to do with the combination of the habit of bearing arms, alcohol-induced quarrels, and the absence of effective medical treatment for wounds and a trusted system of justice. His data also show clearly that violence can be controlled and that violence may be the default option when controls are lacking, as social control theories maintain. This chapter examines each of the four Part I violent crimes in the UCR, starting with murder, including mass, spree, and serial murder.

❖ Murder

Murder is "the willful (non-negligent) killing of one human being by another" (FBI, 2013a). There were 14,827 murders in the United States in 2012, a rate of 4.7 per 100,000 of the population. This is an increase of 0.4% from the 2011 estimate but less than half of the all-time high rate of 10.2 in 1980. Flint, Michigan, had the highest city homicide rate (64.9 murders per 100,000), followed by Detroit (54.6), New Orleans (53.5), St. Louis (35.5), and Baltimore (35.0). These rates are higher than European cities in the 13th century. For known offenders, 88.5% were males, 49.4% were black, 48.2% were white, and 2.4% were of other races. Note that most Hispanics—about 94%—are classified as white for FBI recording purposes. About 90% of known murders are intraracial and intrasexual. About 14% of the murders in 2012 took place within the family, as indicated by Figure 12.1. Most of the family relationships were not biological; i.e., most victims were spouses, stepchildren, and half-siblings. Only murders in which the victim-offender relationship was known are included.

In the United States, young people aged 18 through 24 are most likely to be killed. Young black males are about nine times more likely to be murdered than young white males, and young black females are about six times more likely to be murdered than young white females (Walsh & Ellis, 2007). Males are far more likely to murder than females. When females kill males, they typically kill a spouse, ex-spouse, or boyfriend in a self-defense situation (Mann, 1990). Females murdering females is very rare around the world. Daly and Wilson (2000) examined data on same-sex nonrelative murders from a number of cultures and found that female/female homicide constituted only 2.5% of the total number of murders. Even going back to England in the 13th century, female/female murder accounted for only 4.9% of the total murders (Given, 1977).

As high as the U.S. murder rate is, it is much lower than in most other countries. According to the United Nations Office on Drugs and Crime (UNODC; 2012), the United States' murder rate is many times lower than most African and Central and South American countries, which are third-world or developing countries with corrupt governments and high rates of organized crime. The U.S. murder rate in 2011 was 4.8 per 100,000, while for Honduras it was 19 times higher at 91.6. Other high-rate homicide countries include Cote d'Ivoire (56.9), Jamaica (52.2), and Venezuela (45.1). The countries suffer today from the same combination of factors, especially the absence of effective police power and of a trusted system of justice that Europe suffered from in medieval times. However, the U.S.

Figure 12.1

Murder by
Victim-Offender
Relationship, 2012

Source: FBI, 2013a

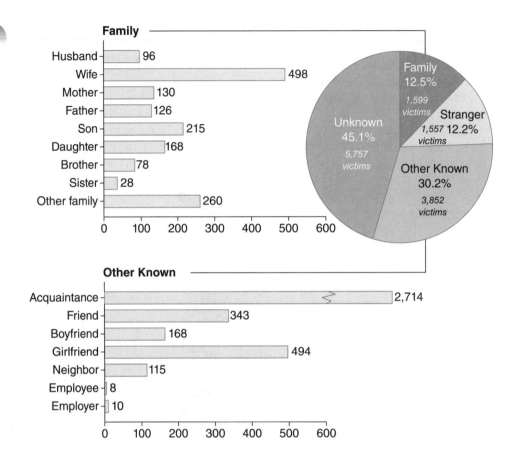

rate is considerably higher than other stable and wealthy democracies. Japan is listed as having the lowest homicide rate (0.4), which is 12 times lower than the U.S. rate. Other low-rate homicide countries include Germany (0.8), France (1.1), and the United Kingdom (1.2) (UNODC, 2012).

As we saw in Chapter 2, murder rates have dropped dramatically in the United States from the early 1990s. Much of this can be attributed to several factors, including a large decrease in the crack market and in gang warfare as territories became consolidated by the strong pushing out the weak. According to Anthony Harris and his colleagues (2002), perhaps the biggest factor in the homicide drop has been medical and technological improvements. They claim that U.S. homicide rates would be up to five times higher without those improvements, which means that we may have experienced 74,135 murders in 2012 rather than the 14,827 we did if medicine and technology were at the same level as in 1960. Cell phones for reporting incidents are everywhere, and emergency medical technicians are alerted and dispatched swiftly. Once hospitalized, victims have the benefit of all that medicine has learned from treating violent traumas since the Vietnam War, which is something to remember when comparing U.S. rates to those of other less-developed countries. Many other factors known and unknown have contributed to the fluctuations in the homicide rate observed over the course of the 20th century.

Types of Homicide

Homicide is the killing of a human being, but all homicides are not murder. A murder—or criminal homicide—is the killing of a human being without justification. A justification would be self-defense or a law enforcement agent killing someone in the performance of his or her duty to prevent harm to himself, herself, or to others. Murder is typically broken into the following four major categories (note that different states may use different terminology and slightly different definitions).

Aggravated or first-degree murder is defined as the intentional unlawful killing of one human being by another with "premeditation and deliberation." In other words, the killer had a purposeful and evil intention (malice) to kill the victim and thought about and planned it (premeditation) with full awareness of the consequences (deliberation). First-degree murder is the only kind of murder for which a convicted murderer can be executed in states that have the death penalty.

Second-degree murder (also called **voluntary manslaughter** in a number of states) is the intentional killing of another human being without premeditation and deliberation. It is murder committed in response to the mistaken belief that self-defense required the use of deadly force or in response to adequate provocation while in the heat of passion. The term *passion* can mean fear, anger, or outrage and can result from such provocations as being threatened in a bar or catching your spouse in bed with someone else. In other words, voluntary manslaughter is usually charged when the suspect had temporarily been in such a high state of emotional arousal that his or her rational faculties were impeded.

Involuntary manslaughter is a criminal homicide where an unintentional killing results from a reckless act. In such cases, the defendant is charged with consciously disregarding a substantial risk that he or she should know puts others in danger of losing their lives. The most obvious example of this is driving under the influence of alcohol or some other drug.

Negligent manslaughter is an unintentional homicide charged when a death arises from some negligent act that carries a substantial risk of death to others. Negligent homicide is charged when someone neglects to do something he or she should have rather than does something he or she should not have. Doing something someone should not have can range widely from driving an unsafe vehicle that should have been fixed to failing to comply with safety regulations in a work setting.

Photo 12.1

The driver in this photo is guilty of involuntary manslaughter because her reckless choice to drive while under the influence caused an unintentional killing.

❖ Mass, Spree, and Serial Murder

Although murder is usually considered the most serious crime a person can commit, murder for revenge or for personal gain is understandable because such motives have rational if not moral elements. The gruesome bloodlust of killers like Lanza and Kemper, however, baffles and terrifies us because it lacks any objectively rational motivation with which we can identify. We can all imagine circumstances in which we might act violently, and even kill someone, but few of us can imagine ourselves becoming mass, spree, or serial killers.

Mass and Spree Murder

Mass murder is the killing of several people at one location that begins and ends within a few minutes or hours, usually with the death of the killer by suicide. **Spree murder** is the killing of several people at different locations over a period of several days. Research suggests that the time frame involved is the only factor that differentiates mass and spree killers and that both mass and spree killers are different from the serial killer.

Mass murderers are divided into two types: those who choose specific targets the killer believes to have caused him stress (e.g., disgruntled workers) and those who attack targets having no connection with the killer but who belong to groups the killer dislikes, such as prostitutes or people of a different race. Such people rarely "just snap" and kill people at random. Most mass murderers are motivated by a hatred that simmers until some specific incident provides the flame that brings it to a boil. Marc Lepine, for instance, had been denied admission into the engineering school at the University of Montreal and sought revenge on the women who had taken his place in a "man's profession" by killing 14 women and wounding 13 (Fox & Levin, 2001, p. 119). Colin Ferguson, who killed six people and wounded 19 others on a Long Island commuter train in 1993, hated whites and claimed that "black rage" at what he saw as society's mistreatment of blacks led him to his rampage (Schmalleger, 2004). Then there was Jiverly Wong, who shot and killed 13 people and wounded four others at an immigration center in Binghamton, New York, in 2009 and then shot himself. Wong apparently disliked Americans because he felt they were prejudiced toward him (although most of his victims were fellow immigrants) and was embarrassed by his poor English (Lester, 2010). All three men methodically and selectively chose their victims on the basis of some alleged wrong done to them by a group their targeted victims represented.

The deadliest mass/spree killing in history occurred on July 22, 2011, when Anders Breivik murdered 69 teenagers on Utoya Island in Norway. Before the shooting, Breivik detonated a car bomb in Oslo killing eight, bringing his total to 77 dead and 96 injured. Breivik planned the massacre since 2009 and was deemed sane by court psychiatrists. He was sentenced to life imprisonment (there is no death penalty in Norway).

Spree killers move from victim to victim in fairly rapid succession and like mass murderers make little effort to hide their activities or avoid detection, as if driven by some frenzied compulsion. Spree killing is rare, but spree-killing teams are even rarer and are typically composed of a dominant leader and a submissive lover. The most recent spree killer team in the United States is the sniper team of John Muhammad and Lee Malvo, who killed 13 random individuals and wounded six others in the Washington, D.C., area in 2002. Although the team killed without regard to race or gender, Muhammad belonged to the Nation of Islam, which may have provided ideological impetus to his vicious spree (Hurd, 2003).

We can make relatively few generalities about mass and spree killers. Most research on these individuals comes from interviews with families and friends and sometimes notes left by the offender, because the offender typically commits suicide or is killed by police at or near the scene of the crime. Reviews of the literature (Fox & Levin, 2001; Palermo, 1997) note several commonalities shared by American mass and spree murderers:

- They are typically white males with an age range broader than that of serial killers.

- African Americans are overrepresented in terms of their proportion in the population.

- They have previously displayed impulsive, violent, frustrated, depressed, alienated, and antiauthoritarian behavior arising from a deep sense of having been wronged.

- They tend to have a morbid fascination with guns and to own many of them.

- Their behavior at the time of the crime, as well as the fact that it is typically committed in public places, makes it obvious they are unconcerned about their own death, leading some researchers to view this type of murder as an elaborate suicide attempt.

- They seem to contemplate committing murder and prepare for the act, although the time and place of the offense is not generally preestablished.

- Like crime in general, spree and mass murders increased considerably in the United States from the 1960s through the 1990s.

- The average age of all mass murderers over the past 40 years is 29.

Serial Murder

Serial murder is the killing of three or more victims over an extended period of time with a "cooling off" period in between kills (Hickey, 2006). Unlike mass and spree killers who almost invariably use guns, serial killers tend to favor "hands-on" killing, often with torture. In 2007, the FBI (2008) held a symposium on serial killers that included 135 expert law enforcement officers, mental health specialists, and criminologists who specialized in serial killing research. This group of experts put together seven commonly believed myths about serial killers.

Myth: Serial killers are all dysfunctional loners The truth is that most serial killers have families, homes, and gainful employment; some have even been churchgoers and law enforcement officers. They hide in "plain sight," which is why their neighbors are shocked to hear that such a "nice man" was a serial killer and why they are so often overlooked by law enforcement.

Myth: Serial killers are all white males The reality is that white males are underrepresented among serial killers in proportion to their numbers in the population. Hickey (2006) claims that about 44% of serial killers operating from 1995 to 2004 have been African American, which is about 3.4 times greater than expected by their proportion in the population. The Radford University's Serial Killer Information Center (Aamodt, 2013) finds that from 2000 to 2010 African Americans have been 57.9% of serial killers in the United States, whites 34%, Hispanics 7.9%, and Asian Americans 0.0%. The only *known* Asian American serial killer operating in the United States during the 20th century was Charles Ng, who, with Leonard Lake, killed at least 19 people in the early 1980s (Newton, 2000).

Myth: Serial killers are only motivated by sex While sexual lust is the major motivation of many serial killers, there are many other motivations such as thrill seeking, attention getting, anger, financial gain, religious or ideological reasons, and perhaps the greatest—a sense of power.

Myth: Serial killers travel and operate interstate While a number of serial killers travel around the country trolling for victims, most conduct their operations within a well-defined geographic comfort zone where they feel confident. This comfort zone typically centers around their home or place of employment.

Myth: Serial killers cannot stop killing While most serial killers do continue to kill until they are caught or die, there are some well-known killers who may have stopped for years before starting again. For instance, Dennis Rader, the infamous BTK ("Bind, Torture, Kill") serial killer, murdered 10 victims from 1974 to 1991 and did not kill again. He was caught in 2005 because he wanted to tell his side of the story when someone was writing a book about the unsolved BTK killings.

Myth: All serial killers are insane or evil geniuses Most serial killers probably fit the criteria for psychopathy or antisocial personality disorder, but only a very few qualify as mentally ill (e.g., schizophrenic) or legally insane. Neither are they geniuses who are able to outsmart the law at every turn. The IQs of serial killers vary considerably; the genius myth probably derives from the published IQs of particularly infamous serial killers such as Ed Kemper (IQ = 136) and Ted Bundy (IQ = 124) (Walsh & Ellis, 2007). The Radford Serial Killer data (Aamodt, 2013) found that the median IQ was 87.5 (half of the serial killers scoring above that number and half below) and the mean (average) was 95 (5 points below the American population mean). The U.S. serial killer with the lowest IQ is Simon Pirela, (four victims) with an IQ of 57, and the serial killer with the highest IQ (160) is Theodore Kaczynski, a PhD mathematics professor known as the "unabomber" who killed three and injured 23 in a spate of bombings from 1978 to 1995.

Myth: Serial killers want to get caught This is far from true and probably derives from amateur psychoanalysis. Serial killers plan their crimes (the target selection, acquisition, control, and disposal) with great care, getting better at it with each victim. They often have such feelings of power that, contrary to wanting to get caught, they feel they *cannot* be caught.

Myth: Serial killers are never women This myth is not listed by the FBI but one we address anyway because there are female serial killers. As the Photo 12.2 shows, serial killers are found among both sexes and all races and ethnic groups. Ottis Toole murdered at least six victims but claimed more, Aileen Wournos killed seven, and John Thomas killed at least 17. When Aileen Wuornos was arrested in 1991 and charged with the shooting deaths of seven males whom she had picked up while working as a prostitute she was dubbed "America's first woman serial killer" because she fit the definition of a "true" serial killer as

Photo 12.2

Serial killers come from both sexes and all races.

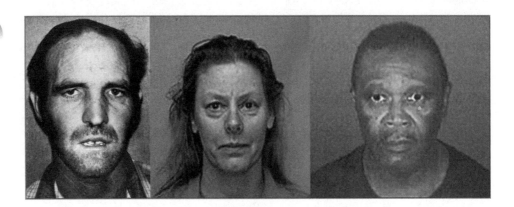

a person who kills for no rational motive (Keeney & Heide, 1995). Yet there had been a number of others before her. Nursing home proprietor Amy Archer-Gilligan, who may have murdered up to 100 patients in her charge from 1907 to 1914, like most female serial killers, killed for financial reasons. Thus the key distinction between male and female serial killers may be that "there are no female counterparts to a Bundy or a Gacy, to whom sex or sexual violence is a part of the murder pattern" (Segrave, 1992, p. 5).

Prevalence of Serial Killing

No one knows exactly how many serial killers there are at any given time or how many murders per year are attributable to them. Figure 12.2 presents the number and rates of serial killers per million in the United States from 1900 to 2010 broken into decades. For instance, the last bar represents the 245 known serial killers operating from 2000 to 2010. The increase in the rate of killers from the 1950s to the 1990s is probably only partly a real increase. An unknown portion of the increase may be attributed to improved law enforcement methods initiated during the latter period. The increase in other forms of homicide, including spree and mass murder, during the same period, however, leads us to conclude that a good part of the reported increase in serial killers represents a real increase.

Typology of Serial Killers

Although all serial killers have a common killing goal, they have different psychological motives. Holmes and DeBurger (1998) have provided a typology that divides serial killers into four broad

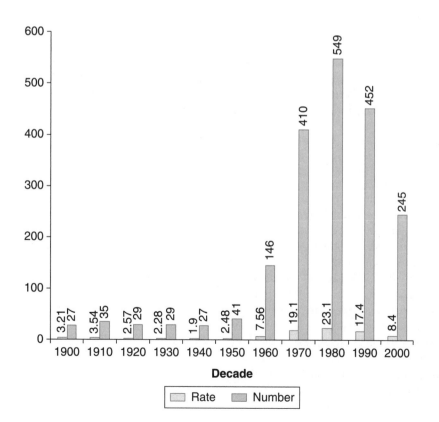

Figure 12.2

Number and Rate per Million Population of Known Serial Killers per Decade From 1900–1910 to 2000–2010

Source: Aamodt, 2013

types: visionary, mission-oriented, hedonistic, and power/control. These are not definitive categories that all serial killers can be neatly assigned to; many serial killers may evidence aspects of all types at various times.

- The **visionary serial killer** is typically out of touch with reality, may be psychotic, and feels impelled to commit murder by visions or "voices in my head." David Berkowitz ("The Son of Sam"), who shot mostly young lovers parked in their cars, was this type of killer. The sexual assault of victims is not usually a component of the visionary killer's pattern. The visionary killer is the stereotypical dysfunctional loner.

- The **mission-oriented serial killer** feels it is his mission in life to kill certain kinds of people, such as prostitutes. Unlike visionary killers, mission-oriented killers do not have visions or hear voices telling them to kill. They define their own "undesirables" and set out to eliminate as many as they can. The black Muslim group the Angels of Death, which operated during the 1970s in California, targeted "white devils" and may have killed more people than all other serial killers combined during that period. One estimate puts the total number of victims attributed to the group at 270 (Howard, 1979), although another source (Lubinskas, 2001) puts the "official" count at 71.

- The **hedonistic serial killer** is the majority of serial killers. He kills for thrills, engaging in perverted sexual activity. The hedonistic killer is such a self-centered psychopath that he considers someone's life less important than his sexual pleasure. Edmund Kemper is an example of this type. He had been diagnosed as psychotic as a teenager after killing both his grandparents, but he never claimed that "voices" made him kill.

- The **power/control serial killer** gains more satisfaction from exercising complete power over his victims rather than from "bloodlust," although sexual activity is almost always involved. Like the hedonistic killer, the power/control killer frequently suffers from some form of sexual inadequacy. Ted Bundy and Jeffrey Dahmer are examples of this type of killer. Both men would keep the bodies of their victims (women in Bundy's case, men in Dahmer's case) for some time after killing them, often washing and grooming them like dolls. Dahmer went several steps further and tried to create sex slave zombies of his victims by drilling holes in their heads and pouring acid into the holes. He also cannibalized several victims.

Theories of Serial Killing

Serial killing is not the result of any single "cause" but of several risk factors interacting in various ways, and becoming a serial killer is a long drawn-out process, not a discrete event. Any one factor or combination of factors can facilitate or expedite the onset of killing for some killers but have little or no effect on others. Keep in mind that when theorists attempt to explain something as bizarre as serial killing they are offering very broad and speculative generalities.

Elliott Leyton (1986) applied anomie theory to explain serial killing across the centuries, proposing that different social classes have dominated the ranks of serial killers at different periods because classes are differentially exposed to high aspirations and thus to crises to their social standing. During preindustrial times only the aristocracy could aspire to greater status, and thus only they would be susceptible to the strains of anomie. In the 19th century the middle class had opportunities to advance their social position, and serial killers were drawn from the ranks of those who failed. In the 20th century serial killers were drawn overwhelmingly from the ranks of ordinary working men as they aspired to the American Dream.

Significant changes in the prevalence of serial killers since the early 1960s point to some important social changes. The disinhibited counterculture that arose during the period had much to do with the increased prevalence because traditional values were questioned and rejected (Levin & Fox, 1985). Despite its rhetoric of flower power and peace, the counterculture was essentially about personal satisfaction ("Do your own thing") and not feeling bad about it ("Don't get hung up on guilt"). Following that period many more people crossed the line to engage in a variety of aberrant behaviors because of what has been called "society's recent war against guilt" (Levin & Fox, 1985, p. 72). The late 1960s also saw an explosion of pornography, some of which depicted scenes of bondage, torture, and violent rape, which may have fed and shaped the sexual fantasies of some people, a proportion of whom subsequently acted them out (Sears, 1991).

Whatever the social factors accounting for the increased prevalence of serial killing, only an infinitesimally small number of people experiencing them ever kill once, let alone become serial killers. Thus, the developmental histories of serial killers should be explored. Social control theory emphasizes the role of the family, and one factor linked to serial killers is an extreme level of maternal deprivation in childhood. The increasing breakdown of the family also provides serial killers with large numbers of rootless potential victims (Saffron, 1997). The neglect, abuse, and social isolation experienced by many serial killers in their early years leaves them angry and unable to relate to others in conventional ways, and eventually the resentment is detonated.

With sexuality being a central part of human life, extreme sexual dysfunction may result in deeply embedded feelings of worthlessness and powerlessness, the seeds of which may have already been implanted by childhood abuse and neglect. Kemper's fondness for sex with the dead was supposedly tied to concerns about his small penis. Serial killers may be trying to counteract feelings of inadequacy by controlling and destroying vulnerable others (i.e., women) whom they may see as the cause of their feelings. Many studies of serial murders reveal a pattern of long-standing preoccupation with fantasies devoted to sexualized violence and that children reared in abusive homes often retreat into a private fantasy world where they can escape their fears and exert control, thus gaining in their minds that which is unavailable in reality (Carlisle, 1993).

A theory popular among serial killer profilers is the so-called MacDonald triad, which consists of three childhood predictors—enuresis (frequent bedwetting past the age of 5), fire setting, and cruelty to animals. Some researchers see this triad as indicators of severe childhood abuse and dismiss it as an urban myth, but the triad is often seen in the childhood histories of serial killers, especially hedonistic killers (Levi-Minzi & Shields, 2007), as we will see when discussing the Green River Killer shortly.

The making of a serial killer is an extremely complicated process that may be very different for different killers. Stephen Giannangelo's (1996) diathesis-stress model attempts to integrate cultural, developmental, psychological, and biological concepts. The theory states that all serial killers have a congenital biological propensity (diathesis) to behave and think in ways that lead to serial killing if combined with environmental stressors such as abuse and neglect. This combination leads to self-esteem, self-control, and sexual dysfunction problems that feed back on one another and lead to maladaptive social skills, which move the person to retreat into his pornographic fantasy world. As he dwells longer and longer in this world, he enters a dissociative process in which he takes his fantasies to their moral limits. At this point the killer seeks out victims to act out his fantasies, but the actual kill never lives up to his expectations or to the thrill of the hunt, so the whole process is repeated and becomes obsessive-compulsive and ritualistic, much like drug addiction. Figure 12.3 illustrates this process.

Figure 12.3

Stephen Giannangelo's Diathesis-Stress Model of Serial Killing

Biological predisposition (low arousal levels, prefrontal cortex damage, etc.) ↕ Environmental trauma/stress (abuse, neglect) → Self-esteem and self-control problems ↕ Sexual dysfunction → Maladaptive coping skills ↕ Retreat into fantasy world → Dissociation → **First Kill**

THEORY IN ACTION: Gary Ridgway, America's Most Prolific Serial Killer

Photo 12.3

Gary Ridgway became known as the Green River Killer for his habit of depositing victims' bodies along this waterway. Serial killers frequently victimize marginalized groups, such as prostitutes. Some of his victims' bodies were discovered only years after their untimely deaths by searchers such as these, revisiting kill sites.

As noted in the text, one of the secrets of serial killers who remain at large for long periods of time (two or more decades) is the extraordinary ordinariness of their appearance and of the behavior they present to almost everyone except their victims. Gary Ridgway (the Green River Killer), the most prolific serial killer in U.S. history, unlike the typical violent street criminal, was married and had children, held respectable jobs, was a reliable employee, and was a fervent church member. In fact, he was something of a religious fanatic who constantly tried to convert others and was often seen to cry after sermons or Bible readings. Gary's son, Matthew, even remembers him as a typical "soccer dad," who was always there for him. Ridgway was also fascinated by police work and had unsuccessfully attempted to join the police.

Ridgway first spilled blood when he was only 16 years old, stabbing and severely wounding a 6-year-old boy in 1965 because "I always wanted to know what it was like to kill somebody." Although he was identified as the attacker, he was never prosecuted. His first known killing occurred in 1982 when the body of a 16-year-old girl was found in a field. His last known killing was in 1998. Ridgway had been a suspect in the so-called Green River murders almost from the start, but inconclusive physical evidence and the fact that he passed a polygraph test prevented his prosecution. Detectives secured a saliva sample from Ridgway in 1987, but DNA identification testing was underdeveloped at that time. Nothing came of it, and the investigatory task force slowly disbanded.

After the lead detective on the Green River Task Force, Dave Reichart, was elected sheriff of King County in 1997, he jump-started the case again. In 2001 DNA evidence secured in 1987 positively linked Ridgway to a number of the murders, and he was arrested in 2001, almost 20 years after his first known murder. He subsequently pled guilty in 2003 to 48 murders (mostly prostitutes) for which he received 48 life sentences. This is the largest count of verified murders of any known American serial killer, and detectives suspect that he may have been responsible for more than 70. In 2011 he was charged with a 49th murder, that of 20-year-old mother Becky Marrero in 1982, whose remains were found in Auburn, Washington.

Gary was born the middle of three sons into an intact family in Salt Lake City, Utah, in 1949, and raised in Seattle, Washington. There are a number of clues in his

THEORY IN ACTION (Continued)

early life that he might become violent, including enuresis and cruelty to animals. His mother would shame him for bedwetting and immediately wash him, paying special attention to his "naughty parts." He later told psychologists that he would fanaticize about having sex with his mother and then killing her. He was a very poor student and was found to have an IQ of only 82, although this did not stop him from amassing a credible work history as a spray painter. We might look to his mother's dominant role in the household combined with his father's meekness. One perhaps telling piece of information is that perhaps his father unwittingly introduced the idea of necrophilia to him. His father would tell stories of a coworker at the mortuary who engaged in necrophilia. These stories then may have become the subject of Ridgway's teenage sexual fantasies, and he frequently had sex with the dead bodies of his victims. His low IQ also illustrates the myth of all serial killers being evil geniuses and also shows that a low IQ is not necessarily a barrier to eluding the police for a very long time. The fact that he passed a polygraph in 1982 when he was initially suspected points to the low ANS arousal of the psychopath.

Ridgway falls into the hedonistic killer category because sex was his primary motive. Ridgway's three wives and several girlfriends report that he was sexually insatiable, and all his victims had been raped. But there was also a touch of the mission-oriented killer in him; as Ridgway said himself, "I picked prostitutes as my victims because I hate most prostitutes and I did not want to pay them for sex." This may have stemmed from his time in the Navy when he compulsively visited prostitutes and contracted gonorrhea, or perhaps it stemmed from the emotional conflict probably felt between his lust for prostitutes and his religious beliefs.

Discussion Questions

1. Ridgway had a childhood history of fire setting, cruelty to animals, and bedwetting. Look up these three factors as a unit and discuss how they may partially explain Ridgway's behavior.

2. How do you think that a poorly educated and low-IQ person such as Ridgway was able to evade being caught until 20 years after his first murder?

3. Why is sexual lust such a central part of most serial killing?

Sources: Blanco, n.d., Ridgway; Levi-Minzi & Shields, 2007; McGinnis, 2009.

Offender Profiling

Law enforcement agencies responded to the challenge presented by serial killers with the establishment of the FBI's Behavioral Science Unit (BSU) in the early 1970s. The BSU, now part of the National Center for the Analysis of Violent Crime (NCAVC), has developed methods of profiling serial killers and other violent offenders. Profiling is done by extensive interviewing and formal psychological testing of incarcerated killers in order to develop a typology (the classification of offenders into different types) based on personality and other offender characteristics (FBI, 2008). Law enforcement officials have always done some sort of rudimentary profiling based on their experiences regarding "what sort of person would have done this." Only recently has it been elevated to an art—it cannot as yet be considered a science because profiles do not always fit the persons eventually convicted of the crimes (Canter, 2004). Hazelwood and his FBI colleagues (1987) describe the qualities of successful profilers as "experienced in criminal investigation and research and possess[ing] common sense, intuition, and the ability to isolate their feelings about the crime, the criminal, and the victim. They have the ability to evaluate analytically the behavior exhibited in the crime and to think very much like the criminal responsible" (p. 148).

❖ Rape

Rape was called **forcible rape** until 2012 and defined as "the carnal knowledge of a female forcibly and against her will" (FBI, 2013). This definition included attempts to commit rape but excluded statutory rape (consensual sex with an underage female) and the rape of males. The new FBI (2013a) definition is "the penetration, no matter how slight, of the vagina or anus with any body part or object, or oral penetration by a sex organ of another person, without the consent of the victim." According to the 2013 UCR, there were 88,097 reported rapes in 2012, a rate of 52.9 per 100,000 females. By race, 65% of those arrested for rape were white, 32.5% black, and the remaining 2.5% were other races. Poor, young, unmarried, nonwhite females are disproportionately likely to be victimized, and poor, young, unmarried, nonwhite males are disproportionately likely to be perpetrators (Rand, 2009).

Some facts from 20 years of victimization surveys on rape include the following:

- About half of all rapes are committed by someone known to the victim.

- The offender was armed in about 20% of the cases. Stranger rapists were more likely to be armed (29%) than were rapists known to the victim.

- Among the victims who fought their attackers or yelled and screamed, more reported that it helped the situation rather than made it worse.

- Slightly more than half of the victims reported the assault to the police. Victims are more likely to report the incident if the perpetrator was armed or if they sustained physical injuries.

- As is the case with all other crimes, rape rates have fallen significantly over the last 35 years. (Walsh & Ellis, 2007)

Rape rates vary considerably from country to country; the *reported* rape rate in the United States is typically four times higher than that of Germany, 13 times higher than Britain's, and 20 times higher than Japan's (Schwartz, 1995). We emphasize *reported* because determining rape rates is extremely difficult, and comparing international rape rates is more difficult yet. Some countries include statutory rape in their rape reports (which would inflate the number of rapes in those countries relative to those in the United States), and others do not; some do not differentiate between rape and other sexual offenses (which would also inflate their rates). We also have to be sensitive to the degree of stigma attached to rape victims in different cultures. For instance, Egypt, a nation of about 54 million people, reported just three rapes to INTERPOL in 1991, while France, with approximately the same population, reported 4,582 (INTERPOL, 1992). Accusing someone of rape in some Islamic countries is not taken lightly. Proof requires the sworn eyewitness testimony of two males (or four women) of good Muslim character. As if the stigma of being raped that attaches to women in Islamic countries is not reason enough to forgo reporting the crime, if eyewitness testimony is not forthcoming the accuser may herself be punished with 100 lashes in some Islamic countries for making a "false accusation" (Walsh & Hemmens, 2011).

Theories of Rape

There are a variety of theories about the causes of rape with different assumptions. Feminist theories of rape assert that it is a learned behavior and is motivated by power rather than sexual desire, that all men are capable of it, and that it is a tactic potentially used by all men to control women (Brownmiller, 1975). Social learning theorists agree with some of these assumptions but view rapists as psychologically unhealthy males, not as "normal men." Therapists who work with rapists tend to agree that all men are *potential* rapists but assert that in most cases rape is sexually motivated and that violence (and other methods) is a tactic used to gain sexual compliance, not a goal (Mealey, 2003). Evolutionary psychologists also contend that rape is sexually motivated and that force is a tactic and not a goal. For them, rape is a maladaptive consequence of an adaptive male behavior; i.e., seeking multiple sexual partners (Thornhill & Palmer, 2000). Note that the adjectives *adaptive* and *maladaptive* are not moral statements; rather, they refer to biologists' assessment of how a behavior may have had reproductive benefits regardless of how repugnant the behavior may be.

Although attitudes about rape have changed dramatically since the 1980s (King & Roberts, 2011), a number of early surveys of high school and college students showed that a majority of males and a significant minority of females believe it is justifiable for a man to use some degree of force to obtain sex if the victim had somehow "led him on" (Herman, 1991). This seems to indicate that some people back then believed there could be an act labeled "justifiable rape" in the same sense that there is justifiable homicide. These surveys also indicate that many believe that rape victims are often at least partially responsible for their rape because of such factors as provocative dress and lifestyle (frequenting bars) and because of the belief that "nice girls don't get raped" (Bartol, 2002, p. 295). To put this in perspective, we would not get very far claiming we were justified in robbing a bank because the bank got us "all excited" by leading us to believe that it would give us a loan but later denied us the loan or that its location, gaudy advertising, and apparent lack of security meant that it was "asking to be robbed."

Most studies of rapists concentrate on the violent rapist, who is usually a stranger to his victim and who tends to have histories of other violent crimes (Mills, Anderson, & Kroner 2004; Freeman 2007). We know that among these subjects violence is an important component of the sexual excitement they obtain from their crimes, just as whips and other devices are important to masochists and sadists. This pattern of preferential violence is determined by comparing penile responses of convicted rapists with those of nonrapists when exposed to sexual stimuli with strong violence content. A device called a penile plethysmograph (PPG), which is like a blood pressure gauge that fits around the penis, is used to measures penile response by gauging the pressure of penile blood to ascertain how sexually excited subjects become when exposed to visual stimuli depicting sexual situations. Violent rapists become significantly more aroused than nonrapists or date rapists when exposed to images of sexual violence (Robertiello & Terry, 2007). For instance, if a rapist achieves a 30% erection when viewing nonviolent sex and an 80% erection when viewing violent sex, we can conclude that he is more interested in violent sex than consensual sex and is a dangerous individual (Walsh & Stohr, 2010). Table 12.1 provides some facts regarding a number of aspects relating to rape.

❖ Robbery

Robbery is "the taking or attempted taking of anything of value from the care, custody, or control of a person or persons by force or threat of force or violence and/or putting the victim in fear" (FBI, 2013a). In 2012, there were 354,520 reported robberies in the United States, a rate of 112.9 per 100,000, down almost 59% from the peak rate of 272.7 in 1991. Of those robbers arrested, 93% were male, 54.9% were black, 43.4% white, and the remaining 1.7% were other races. According to the FBI (2013a), in 2012, 632 robbery victims were murdered (557 males and 75 females) during the course of the robbery, and a total of $414 million was taken in robberies. Figure 12.4 shows the primary locations where reported robberies took place in 2012.

Table 12.1

Facts and Statistics About Rape

Rape Statistics	Percentage
Women who have experienced rape or attempted rape sometime in life	18
Men who have experienced rape or attempted rape sometime in life	3
Decline in rape rate since 1993	60
Rapes not reported to police or other authorities	60
Rapes where both victim and perpetrator were drinking	47
Percentage raped by friend or acquaintance	38
Percentage raped by an "intimate"	28
Percentage raped by a relative	7
Percentage raped by a stranger	26
Percentage of rapes occurring in perpetrator's home	31
Percentage of rapes occurring in victim's home	27
Percentage of rapes occurring in shared home of victim and perpetrator	10
Percentage at party	7
Percentage in vehicle	7
Percentage outdoors	4
Percentage in bar	2

Source: U.S. Bureau of Justice, 2013

Photo 12.4

Because robbery inherently involves force or the threat of force, being victimized in such a manner is a traumatic event.

The danger posed by resisting victims and the severe penalties attached to committing robbery make it a high-risk crime, which suggests that those who commit it may be among the most daring and dangerous of all criminals. Interviews of active street robbers (Wright & Decker, 1997) reveal them to be the least educated, most fearless, most impulsive, and most hedonistic of criminals. Obtaining legitimate work is simply not an option robbers entertain because work would seriously interfere with their "every night is Saturday night" lifestyles.

Jacobs and Wright (1999) focus on the motivating factors and decision-making processes of robbers and find that most robbers decide to commit their crimes impulsively with very little rational thought. The timing and motivation of street robbers are largely governed by their need for money, as the following statement from a robber in Jacobs and Wright (1999) explains:

> [The idea of committing a robbery] comes into your mind when your pockets are low; it speaks very loudly when you need things and you are not able to get what you need. It's things that you need, things that if you don't have the money, you have the artillery to go and get it. (p. 150)

The participation of robbers in street culture leads them to be blind to legitimate opportunities to the point where many seem to fatalistically believe that they have little choice but to rob. In other words, armed robbers appear to be so overwhelmed by their emotional, financial, and drug problems, and so into the "focal concerns" of their subcultures, that they perceive robbery as their only way to obtain money. Sometimes robberies are committed simply because the robber sees an opportunity he can't let pass:

> If I had $5,000, I wouldn't do [a robbery] like tomorrow. But if I got $5,000 today and I seen you walkin' down the street and you look like you got some money in your pocket, I'm gonna take a chance and see. It's just natural. . . . If you see an opportunity, you take that opportunity. It doesn't matter if I have $5,000 in my pocket. (Jacobs & Wright, 1999, p. 150)

There are a number of attractions to robbery in comparison with other crimes. Burglary takes time and requires the burglar to find buyers for stolen property, and burglars never know who or what they might run into inside a house. Drug selling means dealing with a lot of people, the risk of being robbed oneself, and most importantly, coping with the temptation of being one's own best customer. Robbery, on the other hand, allows the robber to pick the time, place, and victim at leisure and then complete the job in a matter of minutes or seconds. It is the perfect crime for those with a pressing and constant need for fast cash to feed a hedonistic lifestyle and who enjoy the adrenalin rush the crime affords them. Robbery, and flaunting the material trappings signaling its successful pursuit, is seen ultimately as a campaign for respect and status in the street culture in which most robbery specialists participate. As James Messerschmidt (1993) puts it,

> The robbery setting provides the ideal opportunity to construct an "essential" toughness and "maleness"; it provides a means with which to construct that certain type of masculinity—hardman. Within the social context that ghetto and barrio males find themselves, then, robbery is a rational practice for "doing gender" and for getting money. (p. 107)

Gender and Robbery

With the exception of rape, robbery is the most "male" of all crimes, but women constituted 11.2% of robbery arrestees in 2012 (FBI, 2013a). Most female robbers share the same street

Figure 12.4

Primary Locations of Robberies in 2012

Source: FBI, 2013a

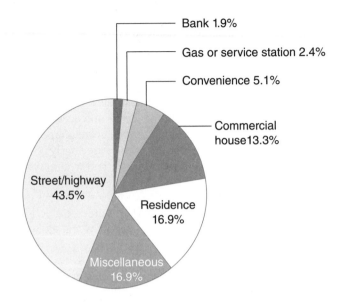

Bank 1.9%

Gas or service station 2.4%

Convenience 5.1%

Commercial house 13.3%

Street/highway 43.5%

Residence 16.9%

Miscellaneous 16.9%

culture with their male counterparts. A favorite ploy for female robbers is to appear sexually available (prostitution or otherwise) to a male victim and then, either alone or with the help of an accomplice, rob him. Female robbers will seldom rob males without an accomplice but practice their "art" mostly on other females. Much like their male counterparts, female robbers are totally educationally or motivationally unprepared for legitimate work and prefer their hedonistic "money for nothing" lifestyles (Miller, 1998).

Why are so few women involved in robbery compared with their involvement in other crimes of resource acquisition? The female percentage of arrests for larceny/theft in 2012, for instance, was 41.3%, or almost four times their proportion of arrests for robbery (FBI, 2013a). From an evolutionary perspective, Anne Campbell (1999) supports Messerschmidt's analysis explaining that while women need resources as much as men, the difference is that men seek status and dominance and the reputation as a "hardman" as well as the resources expropriated from their victims and that this "reflects a particularly masculine logic" (p. 210).

❖ Aggravated Assault

Aggravated assault is "an unlawful attack by one person upon another for the purpose of inflicting severe or aggravated bodily injury" (FBI, 2010). As opposed to simple assault, aggravated assault is one in which a weapon such as a knife or gun is used, although sometimes the use of hands and feet can result in a charge of aggravated assault. There were 760,739 aggravated assaults reported in 2012. This rate of 242.3 per 100,000 is a 45.2% drop from the all-time high of 441.8 in 1992. Blunt objects or "other dangerous weapons" were used in 32.6% of the cases, personal weapons such as hands and feet in 26.8%, firearms in 21.8%, and knives or other cutting instruments in 18.8%. About 40% of those arrested for aggravated assault were under the age of 25. Males made up 77.3%, and 62.8% were white, 34.2% were black, and 3% were other races.

Any case of aggravated assault can be viewed as a murder that never happened. Each incident of aggravated assault carries the potential threat of becoming a murder, because without the speedy access to modern medicine we enjoy today, many aggravated assaults would have turned into murders. A highly disproportionate number of aggravated assaults take place exactly where other kinds of crime take place—in socially disorganized neighborhoods—and much of them involve drug activity and disputes (Martínez, Rosenfeld, & Mares, 2008). Many other aggravated assaults are over trivial matters of "face saving" that occur when someone feels someone else has "dissed" him. As with homicides, a fair number of aggravated assaults are "victim precipitated," meaning the victim initiated the incident that resulted in his own victimization.

❖ Gun Violence

The horrendous events at Sandy Hook Elementary School in 2012 saw a resurgence of concern over gun use and control. In 2012, guns were used in 69.3% of murders, 41% of robberies, and 21.8% of aggravated assaults in the United States (FBI, 2013a). According to the United Nations Office on Drugs and Crime (UNODC; 2006), the United States has the highest gun ownership rate in the world at 88.8 per 100 people. This places the United States well out in front in gun ownership, with second-place country Yemen significantly behind at 54.8 per 100. However, and contrary to what a lot of people believe, the United States ranks 28th in its firearms murder rate. The highest rates of firearm murders are in Honduras, El Salvador, and Jamaica, countries that rank 88th, 92nd, and 74th, respectively, in gun ownership per 100 people. So, is the gun violence problem really a people violence problem? For instance, Switzerland is ranked number three in gun ownership, with 45.7 guns per 100 people, but had a homicide rate of 0.7 the same year. On the other hand, England and Wales had a homicide rate of 1.2 but were a joint 88th (with Honduras) in the world in gun ownership with 6.2 guns per 100 people. Of course, it is difficult (if not impossible) to make cause-effect statements on the basis of gross data such as these, but it does stop us from thinking that more guns automatically means more violence.

Barry and her colleagues' (2013) assessment of public opinion and gun policy noted that perpetrators of the Sandy Hook (December 2012; 26 victims), Aurora, Colorado (July 2012; 12 killed, 58 wounded), and Virginia Tech (April 2007; 32 killed, 17 wounded) mass shootings were apparently mentally ill. We can add to this list the Washington Navy Yard shooting in September 2013 that left 12 dead and 8 wounded. Barry and colleagues (2013) maintain that the real problem is the combination of mental illness and the availability of guns. They note that even 84% of members of the National Rifle Association support requiring universal background checks and the prohibition of gun ownership to convicted felons and the mentally ill. Figure 12.5 provides percentages of the

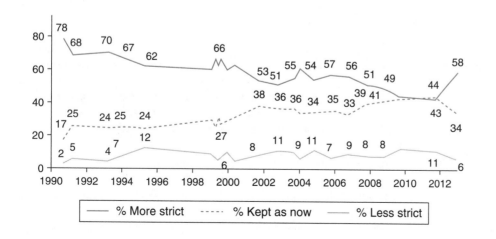

Figure 12.5

Gallup Poll of American Public Opinion Regarding Sale of Firearms

Source: Gallup, 2013

Photo 12.5

The combination of mental illness and the availability of guns has fueled recent mass shootings. James E. Holmes appeared in court nearly 6 months after a bloody rampage in a Colorado movie theater left 12 people dead, pleading not guilty by reason of insanity.

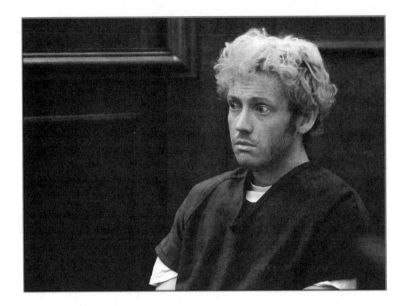

general public's belief that firearm laws should be stricter, stay the same, or be less strict. Public opinion always shifts in response to shocking events such as Sandy Hook. Note the rise in "more strict" responses following the spate of school shootings in the late 1990s, for instance.

This does not mean Americans favor a ban on gun ownership; they only favor more sensible laws. There are arguments such as those made by criminologist John Lott that the more guns there are in private hands the less crime there is. Lott (2010) provides statistical evidence that violent crime rates go down when states pass concealed-carry laws, and he also looks at the impact of different kinds of gun control laws on crime rates. Lott's work has garnered both praise from the pro-gun lobby and condemnation from those who call him a gun zealot, but we certainly cannot engage those interesting arguments here. Whatever your point of view on gun control, it is plain that guns are an integral part of American culture and are protected by the Second Amendment, so they won't be going away anytime soon. It would thus behoove us as a society to do everything possible to keep guns out of the hands of the mentally unstable and to do more for people who show violent tendencies because of mental issues.

❖ Theories of Violence

Let us be clear that peaceful cooperation defines our species more so than violent conflict. The great majority of humans are not attracted to violence, want to avoid it, and generally strongly condemn it, but that does not mean it is not a part of our evolutionary baggage. Most humans in modern Western societies probably go from cradle to grave without ever committing a serious act of violence (Collins, 2009), but we owe this state of affairs to the fact that we inhabit societies in which law enforcement and the judiciary are largely respected and trusted; violence emerges on a large scale when these things are absent.

Researchers in different disciplines ask different questions about violence, but they all add something of value to the overall picture. Sociologists might ask what it is about the social structure of a society or the norms of a subculture within it that leads to high rates of violence. Psychologists might ask what personality features, situations, or developmental experiences increase the risk of violence. Geneticists might inquire about the mix of genetic and environmental factors associated with violence in a particular population at a particular time. Neuroscientists will focus on questions about the brain structures and neurotransmitters associated with violence. Finally, evolutionary theorists will want to know why humans have a propensity for violence in the first place and what adaptive purposes did and does it serve.

According to Cao, Adams, and Jensen (1997), the subculture of violence thesis formulated by criminologists Wolfgang and Feracutti in 1967 "remains *the* definitive argument for society's role in creating violent criminal behavior" (p. 367, italics in original). A **subculture of violence** is one in which the norms, values, and attitudes of its members legitimize the use of violence to resolve conflicts. The thesis reminds us that violence is not evenly distributed among all groups and in all locations in society, and it is necessary to find out why it is more prevalent in some areas and among some groups than in others. Wolfgang and Feracutti (1967) reasoned that "by identifying the groups with the highest rates of homicide, we should find in the most intense degree a subculture of violence" (p. 153). They found such a culture in and based their theory on Philadelphia's black community in the mid-1950s, where the homicide rate for young black males was 27 times higher than that for young white males, and the black female rate was 23 times greater than that for white females.

Subcultural norms in such areas dictate that one is expected to settle matters "like a man" and to take care of his own beefs (don't involve the power structure). "Taking care of business" often involves violence in a subculture where it is not viewed as illicit. It is part of the street code that "emerges where the influence of the police ends and where personal responsibility for one's safety is felt to begin" (Anderson, 1999, p. 33). The successful application of aggression—as a manifestation of subcultural values *and* a disavowal of mainstream cultural values—is a source of pride (Anderson, 1999).

Subcultures of violence have always existed and have also been referred to as honor subcultures. **Honor subcultures** are defined as "communities in which young men are hypersensitive to insult, rushing to defend their reputation in dominance contests" (Mazur & Booth, 1998, p. 362). Cultural norms that allowed duels over trivial matters of "honor" were common among the most polished and cultivated "gentlemen" of Europe and the United States until about the middle of the 19th century. Such duels over matters of honor enhanced the duelists' reputations and provided them with public validation of their self-worth; i.e., they were "doing gender" (Baumeister, Smart, & Boden, 1996). Only with the establishment of modern law was dueling as a way to settle disputes brought into disrepute. Far from acting in pathological ways, males in our modern honor subcultures are acting in historically and evolutionarily normative ways. This does not make such behavior morally acceptable, but it makes it understandable.

When evolutionary biologists explore the behavioral repertoire of any species their first question is "What is the adaptive significance of this particular behavior?" With regard to violence, they want to know how violence was adaptive in evolutionary environments, what its function is, and what environmental circumstances are likely to evoke it. Evolutionary biologists assume that violence evolved to solve some set of adaptive problems; if it didn't solve some such problems it wouldn't be part of our behavioral repertoire. However, just because it is considered "natural" and just because evolutionary accounts show how it can be useful, it certainly does not mean it is good. There are many other natural things we would like to avoid, such as disease, death, and earthquakes.

But in what ways can violence be considered adaptive? Violence (at least credible threats of violence) is intimately related to reproductive success in almost all animal species through its role in attaining status and dominance and thus access to more resources and more females. Remember, this is what evolution by natural selection is all about. Reacting violently when some brute tries to steal your bananas, your cave, or your wife could be very useful in evolutionary environments when you just couldn't call 911 to have the police settle your problem. Having a reputation for violence would be even better because others would be aware of it and avoid your bananas, your cave, and your wife in the first place. In other words, in environments in which one is expected to take care of one's own beefs, violence or the threat of violence works to let any potential challenger know that it would be in his best interests to avoid you and your resources and look elsewhere. All this is why a "bad ass" reputation is so valued in honor subcultures, why those with such a reputation are always looking for opportunities to validate it, and why it is craved to such an extent that "many inner city young men . . . will risk their lives to attain it" (Anderson, 1994, p. 89).

Neuroscience and evolutionary research support the sociological research at different levels of analysis. Neuroscientists are interested in the effects on the brain of living in such cultures. As we saw in Chapter 10, the brain *physically* captures our experiences by molding and shaping neuronal circuitry in ways that make our behavior adaptive to the environments in which we find ourselves. The neurological literature is consistent with the evolutionary literature in suggesting that impulsiveness is the proximate behavioral expression of a brain wired by consistent exposure to violence (Niehoff, 2003). If our brains develop in violent environments, we expect hostility from others and behave accordingly. By doing so we invite the very hostility we are on guard against, thus confirming our belief that the world is a dangerous and hostile place and setting in motion a vicious circle of negative expectations and confirmations.

Neuroscience shares the sociological and evolutionary position that a major long-term factor in violence instigation is how much violence a person has been exposed to in the past. As Gaulin and Burney (2001) explain, when many acts of violence are observed, "there is a feedback effect; each violent act observed makes observers feel more at risk and therefore more likely to resort to preemptive violence themselves" (p. 83). Inner-city children witness a lot of violence. In one study in Chicago, 33% of school children had witnessed a homicide and 66% had witnessed a serious assault (Osofsky, 1995). Another study found that 32% of Washington, DC, and 51% of New Orleans children had been victims of violence, and 72% of Washington, DC, and 91% of New Orleans children had witnessed violence (Osofsky, 1995). Witnessing and experiencing so much violence cannot help but stamp on the brain circuitry of these children that the world is a dangerous place in which one must be prepared to protect one's interests with violence if necessary.

Violence and Inequality

It is frequently noted that impulsivity and discounting the future are maladaptive; that is, they are poor ways of adjusting to the conditions one finds oneself in. Wilson and Daly (1997) suggest, however, that discounting the future "may be a 'rational' response to information that indicates an uncertain or low probability of surviving to reap delayed benefits, for example, and 'reckless' risk taking can be optimal when the expected profits from safer courses of action are negligible" (p. 1271). In other words, when the young perceive little opportunity for legitimate success and when many people they know die at an early age, living for the present and engaging in risky violence to obtain resources makes excellent evolutionary sense. Wilson and Daly assert that natural selection has designed people to compete for the status and resources necessary for survival and reproductive success by whatever means are available to them in the cultural environments in which they live.

Wilson and Daly tested their assumption with homicide, income inequality, and life expectancy data from 77 neighborhoods in Chicago for the years 1988 through 1995. They hypothesized that neighborhoods with the lowest income levels and the shortest life expectancies (excluding homicides) would have the highest homicide rates. Life expectancy (effects of homicide mortality statistically removed) ranged from 54.3 years in the poorest neighborhood to 77.4 years in the wealthiest, and the attending homicide rates ranged from 1.3 per 100,000 in the wealthiest neighborhood to 156 in the poorest, a huge 120-fold difference. Wilson and Daly appeal to evolutionary logic to interpret these data, viewing it as reflecting escalations of risky competitive tactics that make sense from an evolutionary point of view given the conditions in which people in disadvantaged and disorganized neighborhoods live. As Bob Dylan sang, "When you ain't got nothin', you got nothin' to lose."

We remind you again not to confuse an *explanation* of the facts with a *moral evaluation* of them. Wilson and Daly are saying that natural selection has equipped us to respond to high levels of inequality and expectations of a short life by creating risky, high-stakes male-male competitions that all too frequently result in violence, including homicide. From a moral point of view, this is obviously something to be condemned, but to the extent that such contingent responses are the products of natural selection, they are not pathological from the point of view of evolutionary biology.

Summary

- Murder rates have been significantly higher in the past than they are today, primarily because of the lack of effective law enforcement and adequate medical attention. Homicide trends in the United States have fluctuated wildly over the years, and the United States is situated somewhere in the middle of nations in its homicide rate. In the United States, the typical perpetrator and victim of homicide is a young black male living in an urban center. Female/female homicide is very rare worldwide.

- Spree, mass, and serial murder have increased dramatically since the 1960s, especially serial murders. Serial murder is the murder of three or more victims over an extended period of time.

- The FBI addresses a number of myths prevalent in the media about serial killers; e.g., that they are limited to white males who are either insane or geniuses who travel the country looking for victims and really want to get caught. African Americans are overrepresented in the ranks of serial killers relative to their numbers in the population, and females are even more underrepresented than they are among other kinds of criminals. Asian Americans are underrepresented among serial killers.

- A popular typology of serial killers contains visionary, mission-oriented, hedonistic, and power/control types. Visionary killers are usually psychotic, and mission-oriented killers feel it is their duty to rid the world of people they consider undesirable. Hedonistic killers (the most common) kill for the pure joy of it, while power/control killers get more satisfaction from exerting complete control over their victims.

- There have been attempts to explain serial killing using traditional criminological theories. The diathesis-stress model integrates biological, psychological, and sociological variables and posits that serial killers have a biological disposition to kill that is exacerbated by severe environmental stress during childhood.

- Poor, young, unmarried, nonwhite females are disproportionately likely to be victimized by rape, and poor, young, unmarried, nonwhite males are disproportionately likely to be perpetrators. Feminist theories maintain that all men have a propensity to rape and that the act is about power, not sex. Social learning and feminist theory assert that rape is the result of male socialization, while evolutionary theorists maintain that it is a maladaptive consequence of male reproductive strategy.

- Robbery is a violent crime, and robbers tend to be the most impulsive, hedonistic, daring, and dangerous of all street criminals, as well as the least educated and conscientious. Robbery is also considered an excellent way to prove a certain kind of "manliness" in certain urban areas.

- Aggravated assault is the most frequently committed of the violent Part I crimes. Each such incident carries the threat of ending up as a criminal homicide, and but for speedy access to medical treatment, many of them would have done so.

■ Different disciplines study violence from different perspectives. The subculture of violence thesis is the most popular sociological theory for the influence of values and attitudes on violence. Evolutionary theories augment this model by showing why and how violence is part of the human behavioral repertoire, and neuroscience shows how constant exposure to violence is physically captured in the brain.

Exercises and Discussion Questions

1. Why is female/female homicide so rare, and why is it the case around the world?

2. Explain why homicide rates have dropped dramatically across the centuries.

3. What do you think of the idea that rape is only about violence and not sex?

4. Look up a famous female serial killer and discuss differences in motives and methods for committing her crimes compared to male serial killers.

5. Giannangelo's model of serial killers maintains that without a congenital disposition a person would not become a serial killer. What traits do you think would be "necessary" to become a serial killer when combined with environmental stressors?

Useful Websites

Bureau of Justice Statistics. www.bjs.gov.
Federal Bureau of Investigation. www.fbi.gov.
Rape, Abuse, and Incest National Network. www
.rainn.org.

Subculture of violence theory. www.criminology
.fsu.edu/crimtheory/wolfgang.htm.
Women Organized Against Rape. www.woar.org.

Chapter Terms

Aggravated assault

Aggravated or first-degree murder

Forcible rape

Hedonistic serial killer

Honor subcultures

Involuntary manslaughter

Mass murder

Mission-oriented serial killer

Murder

Negligent manslaughter

Power/control serial killer

Robbery

Second-degree murder

Serial murder

Spree murder

Subculture of violence

Violent crime

Visionary serial killer

Voluntary manslaughter

CHAPTER 13

Terrorism

On the morning of September 11, 2001, Americans woke to horrifying images seared into their memories forever. Nineteen Islamic terrorists led by Mohamed Atta, a shy 33-year-old son of a wealthy Egyptian lawyer, had hijacked four airliners and used them in coordinated attacks against symbols of America's financial and military might. At 8:45 a.m., American Airlines Flight 11 with 92 people on board crashed into the north tower of the World Trade Center. Eighteen minutes later, United Airlines Flight 175 with 64 people aboard smashed into the south tower. At 9:40, American Airlines Flight 77 carrying 64 people crashed into the Pentagon. Then at 10 a.m., United Airlines Flight 93 carrying 45 people crashed into a Pennsylvania field, having been prevented from accomplishing its mission (apparently to destroy the Capitol Building or the White House) by the courageous actions of its passengers. These actions cost the lives of close to three thousand people from 78 different countries, making it the deadliest terrorist attack in history anywhere. The financial cost of the attacks is estimated to be close to $285 billion. What were these people trying to accomplish by such a wanton act, and what drove them to sacrifice their own lives in the process?

On September 3, 2004, about 30 terrorists took over 1,000 adults and children hostage in Beslan, Russia. They held them huddled together in a gymnasium for at least two days in sweltering heat, telling them that they (the terrorists) had come to die in the name of Allah and that they were going to take the hostages with them. They did not feed or allow the children to use the bathrooms and shot and killed many of them trying to make their escapes. Some children died from dehydration or from unattended wounds, while others survived by drinking their own urine and eating flowers they had brought to school for their teachers. Ultimately, 340 hostages were killed and 700 others were wounded. Although much less costly in lives and property than the 9/11 attacks, the Beslan incident provides us with an even grimmer picture of the inhumane lengths to which terrorists will go to achieve their goals because they purposely targeted children.

LEARNING OBJECTIVES

- Understand what terrorism is and what its purposes are
- Know the distinction between terrorists and freedom fighters
- Understand the motives behind Islamic terrorist groups such as al-Qaeda and Hezbollah
- Know the extent of domestic terrorism in the United States
- Understand what factors are involved in people making the decision to join terrorist groups and commit brutal acts of terrorism
- Understand the link between terrorism and ordinary crime
- Understand the efforts and the difficulties involved in battling terrorism

❖ What Is Terrorism?

What kind of hatred, hostility, fanaticism, or cause could motivate individuals to board a plane or enter a school and look into the faces of innocent men, women, and children knowing that they were to be the instruments of their deaths? And in the case of the Beslan incident, mock and torture frightened little children? We may well ask with talk show host David Letterman, speaking to a shocked nation after 9/11, "If you live to be a thousand years old . . . will that [the 9/11 attacks] make any goddamn sense?" (Feeney, 2002, p. 191). These terrorist actions lead us to suppose that terrorists are subhuman creatures and that terrorism is something peculiar to the modern age. Although the average terrorist will never win any humanitarian awards, and terrorism is far more prevalent and deadly today than ever before, those suppositions are incorrect.

Terrorism has a long history; it is "as old as the human discovery that people can be influenced by intimidation" (Hacker, 1977, p. ix). The term *terrorism* itself is believed to have originated with the French Revolutionary Jacobins who instituted France's domestic Reign of Terror, killing over 400,000 people in the name of "liberty, fraternity, and equality" (Simonsen & Spindlove, 2004). The earliest known terrorist group was a Jewish nationalist/religious group called the Sicarii. They operated against occupying Roman forces around AD 70 using deadly savage methods against Romans and their Jewish collaborators (Veter & Perlstein, 1991). Another early group, the Ismailis, or Assassins, responding to what they considered religious oppression, carried out a reign of intimidation throughout the Islamic world from about the 11th to the mid-13th century (Wheeler, 1991).

The FBI defines **terrorism** as "the unlawful use of force or violence against persons or property to intimidate or coerce a government, the civilian population, or any segment thereof, in furtherance of political or social goals" (Smith, 1994, p. 8). Terrorism is a tactic used to influence the behavior of others through intimidation, although terrorists typically appeal to a higher moral "good," such as ethnic autonomy or some religious or political dogma to justify the killing of innocents. They strike at innocents because the essence of terrorism is public intimidation, and the randomness of terrorist action accomplishes this better than targeting specific individuals. Victims are incidental to the aims of terrorists, they are simply instruments in the objectives of publicizing the terrorists' cause, instilling in the general public a sense of personal vulnerability and provoking a government into unleashing repressive social control measures that may cost it public support (Simonsen & Spindlove, 2004).

Al-Qaeda's Osama bin Laden made it clear that the latter is one of the goals of his organization. He stated that in response to terrorist attacks the United States government will have to restrict many civil liberties its citizens enjoy. "Freedom and human rights in America are doomed," bin Laden said, adding that the United States will lead people of the Western world "into an unbearable hell and a choking life" (in Kurtz, 2002, p. 5). Russian president Vladimir Putin's decision to hand over sweeping new powers to the Kremlin in the wake of the Beslan attack is evidence that bin Laden may be right. Putin's decision was criticized by another former Russian president, Boris Yeltsin, as "the strangling of freedoms, the rollback of democratic rights—this can only mean that the terrorists have won" (in Walsh & Ellis, 2007, p. 345).

Thus, while terrorist violence is immoral, it is not "senseless" because it has an ultimate purpose, and terrorists justify evil means by the ends they seek. The terrorist attacks on trains in Madrid, Spain, on March 11, 2004 (exactly 911 days after the 9/11 attacks), which took the lives of at least 200 people, led to the fall of a conservative government that supported the U.S. action in Iraq and the election of a socialist government three days later. The new government immediately pulled Spanish troops out of Iraq, which was evidently the purpose of the bombings. Every time terrorists gain an objective they have sought, the rationality of terrorism is demonstrated along with its immorality.

❖ Is There a Difference Between Terrorists and Freedom Fighters?

Although many people accept the cliché that one person's terrorist is another's freedom fighter, this attitude has been called "sophomoric moral relativism" (Sederberg, 1989, p. 28). Of course, not everyone agrees that we can draw a sharp line between terrorists and freedom fighters, and the label one chooses to affix to a group has as much to do with one's politics as anything else. After all, Drummond (2002) points out that four individuals who engaged in or actively supported terrorism have actually been awarded Nobel Peace prizes (Sean McBride, Menachem Begin, Yasir Arafat, and Nelson Mandela).

All terrorists probably claim to be freedom fighters, or at least that their cause is righteous, but there are two important distinctions between terrorists and freedom fighters (or guerrillas) that do not imply their moral equivalence. First, freedom fighters are fighters in wars of national liberation against foreign occupiers or against oppressive domestic regimes they seek to overthrow. Terrorists are typically fighting to gain some sort of ethnic autonomy, right some perceived wrong, or rid the world of some perceived evil and rarely have illusions of overthrowing the government they are fighting against. While guerrillas may occasionally use terrorist tactics against noncombatants, widespread use of such tactics will deprive them of the popular support they need, and thus they tend to confine their activities to fighting enemy combatants (Garrison, 2004). Because of the political contexts in which they operate, guerrillas may have no choice other than armed insurgence to accomplish change because they are outside the system that oppresses them. Terrorists, on the other hand, often have access to the system but spurn the ballot box in favor of the bullet and bomb. Of course, not all claims of injustice can be righted at the polling stations, and thus the distinctions we have made here may be overdrawn to some extent. They are real enough, however, to conclude that the moral conflation of terrorist and freedom fighter is probably not warranted (Garrison, 2004).

❖ The Extent of Terrorism

Although terrorism has ancient roots, it is far more prevalent today. Of the 74 terrorist groups listed by the U.S. Department of State (USDS; 2004) in 2003, only three—the Irish Republican Army (IRA), Euskadi Ta Askatasuna (Basque Homeland and Freedom or ETA), and the Egyptian Muslim Brotherhood—operated before 1960. In order to be classified as a terrorist group by the USDS, the organization must be foreign, must engage or have the intent to engage in terrorist activity, and must threaten the security of the United States or its nationals (USDS, 2013). Of the 51 terrorist groups currently listed by the USDS, 39 are Islamic and the remaining 12 are either Marxist/Maoist (e.g., Peru's Shining Path) or criminal/nationalist groups such as the Real IRA or the Revolutionary Armed Forces of Colombia.

Terrorist groups and incidents rose dramatically after the 1960s, probably because the 1960s was the high point of conflict between the United States and Soviet Union, with each having their zones of influence and each supporting armed opposition to the other. The United States, for instance, supported the Taliban in Afghanistan both morally and financially when that organization was fighting the Soviet Union's occupation, and President Reagan even called them freedom fighters. This support has turned around to bite the United States, since we are now engaged in a bitter struggle against the Taliban.

Figure 13.1 provides data on the number of terrorist attacks and resulting fatalities worldwide in 2012 from the United State Department of State (2013). The total attacks in 2012 (6,771) were

Figure 13.1

Number of Deaths Due to Terrorism in 2012 and Tactics Used by Terrorist Groups in 2012

Source: U.S. Department of State, 2013

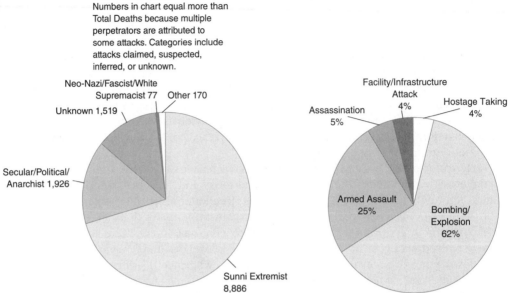

12,533 Total Deaths
Numbers in chart equal more than Total Deaths because multiple perpetrators are attributed to some attacks. Categories include attacks claimed, suspected, inferred, or unknown.

less than half the 2007 figure of 14,545, and fatalities were down 44.3%, from 22,508 to 12,533. These are tragic numbers, but to put them in perspective, these are worldwide figures, and as we have seen, there were 14,827 murders in the United States alone in 2012 (FBI, 2013a), more than twice the worldwide deaths attributed to terrorism.

Terrorism is also much easier to accomplish today than ever before. The Internet, e-mail, and cell phones give terrorists ready access to information and to each other, and economic globalization has led to open borders across which terrorists can easily flow (Jalata, 2011). Modern transportation systems allow terrorists to slip in and out of areas of operation with speed and efficiency, and the same systems provide terrorists with lots of victims by bringing large numbers of people together in places such as airports and railroad stations. Modern technology also makes the terrorist's life less complicated in that it provides easily concealed and relatively cheap weapons and explosives of great destructive power. The downing of Pan American Flight 103 over Lockerbie, Scotland, in 1988 that killed 281 people was accomplished with a small amount of Semtex explosive hidden in a cassette player. Even the enemy's technology can be turned against them. Before the advent of airplanes it would have taken a well-equipped army to topple structures like the World Trade Center; certainly 19 terrorists armed only with box cutters could not have accomplished it.

❖ Al-Qaeda

Very few Americans knew anything about al-Qaeda or Osama bin Laden prior to the 9/11 attacks orchestrated by that group; now the organization and the man are household names on par with *Nazi* and *Adolph Hitler* of earlier generations. **Al-Qaeda** is not a single terrorist group but rather the base (*al-Qaeda* means "the base") organization for a number of Sunni Muslim terrorist groups from around the world. Al-Qaeda also has cells operating in 100 countries around the world, including the United States (Berger & Hoffman, 2010).

Photo 13.1

Wreckage of Pan Am Flight 103 in Lockerbie, Scotland. With improved technology, terrorism has become easier to perpetrate than ever before—a small amount of Semtex explosive hidden in a cassette player downed this plane.

Al-Qaeda got its start under Osama bin Laden in the late 1980s and expanded dramatically in the 1990s. Bin Laden, who had fought the Russians during their invasion of Afghanistan throughout the 1980s, objected to the stationing of non-Muslim troops in Saudi Arabia, the country containing the two holiest sites in Islam—Mecca and Medina—after the first Gulf War in 1991. Because of his objections, bin Laden was exiled from Saudi Arabia and went to live in Sudan, an Islamic dictatorship. Bin Laden first built his worldwide terrorist network in Sudan, financing much of it through his vast personal fortune, as well as through the drug trade and criminal activities in a variety of countries (Simonsen & Spindlove, 2004).

After being ousted from Sudan, bin Laden and his henchmen moved to Afghanistan, where they found refuge and protection with the Taliban regime in power there, thanks to some extent to American support. Al-Qaeda set up terrorist training camps in Afghanistan from which terrorists were dispatched to wreak havoc around the world. Following the 9/11 attacks, President George W. Bush demanded the Taliban turn over bin Laden to U.S. authorities for trial. When the Taliban refused the demands, American and NATO forces (mostly British), aided by Afghan groups (mostly Shiite Muslims), drove the Taliban from power and scattered al-Qaeda. The group now seems to be operating primarily from Pakistan and Yemen (Berger & Hoffman, 2010). Bin Laden was and his organization still is virulently anti-West in general and anti-American in particular. In 1998, bin Laden issued a fatwa (an Islamic decree or command) and called for a jihad (holy war) in which he called on Muslims everywhere to kill Americans wherever they are found, whether military or civilian, man, woman, or child, and those who support America. However, on May 2, 2012, U.S. Navy SEALS found bin Laden hiding in "plain sight" in his luxury compound in the Pakistani city of Abbottabad and killed him, thus ending the biggest manhunt in human history. Osama's successor as leader of al-Qaeda is Ayman al-Zawahiri, bin Laden's former adviser and personal physician. Al-Zawahiri is the founder of the Egyptian Islamic Jihad, or Islamic Brotherhood, which opposes secular Egyptian government and seeks to overthrow it. Al-Zawahiri also "inherited" Osama bin Laden's

Photo 13.2

Ayman al-Zawahiri, successor to Osama Bin Laden as leader of al-Qaeda.

$25 million reward for his capture, becoming the current "world's most wanted man."

❖ Hezbollah

Hezbollah ("Party of God") is the best contemporary example of a state-sponsored terrorist organization. Directed and financed by Iran, Hezbollah is headquartered in Lebanon and has established cells in Europe, North and South America, and Africa (USSD, 2013). Hezbollah ultimately owes its existence to the religious split between Sunni Muslims, who believe in the legitimacy of the secular state, and Shi'ite Muslims, who do not. It was organized by the Shi'ite religious leader Ayatollah Khomeini to fight the secular rule of the Shah of Iran. It emerged on the international stage after the Israeli invasion of Lebanon in 1982, which drove the Palestine Liberation Organization (PLO) out of that country. Ironically, the PLO had been the chief opponent of the Lebanese Shi'ites prior to the invasion. Hezbollah fighters were sent to Lebanon by Khomeini, ostensibly to aid in the fight against Israel but with the long-range goal of establishing an Iranian-style Islamic regime in Lebanon. Hezbollah has claimed responsibility for a number of spectacular terrorist operations that helped hasten the withdrawal of American and Israeli forces from Lebanon (something no Arab army has ever accomplished). Among these actions were the bombing of the U.S. Marine barracks in 1983, killing 251 Americans and 56 French soldiers and marines, and the kidnapping and/or murder of several American and European citizens.

Hezbollah has a sense of engaging in a sacred mission that transcends the confines of Lebanon. Much as Christian crusaders several centuries before them saw the Muslim presence in the Holy Land as an affront to Christianity, the more radical among modern Shi'ites view the existence of a Jewish state in an area they also consider holy to be an affront to Islam (Kramer, 1990). They are fiercely anti-Israeli and anti-American, viewing the United States as the decadent, drug-infested, crime-ridden, sex-perverted "Great Satan" of the world. Oddly enough, the "A-team" of terrorist groups and its top contender (opinions vary as to whether al-Qaeda or Hezbollah is the A-team) are busy fighting and killing each other in Syria. Sunni al-Qaeda may be the most effective force fighting against Syrian president Assad's troops, and against Shi'ite Hezbollah, who are fighting to preserve Assad's rule (Wood, 2013). Al-Qaeda has committed many atrocities in this fight, including the slaughter of hundreds of Christians and the beheading of priests.

❖ Domestic Terrorism

The FBI divides terrorism into two broad categories—domestic and international. It defines domestic terrorism as "the unlawful use, or threatened use, of violence by a group or individual based and operating entirely within the United States (or its territories) without foreign direction committed against persons or property to intimidate or coerce a government, the civilian population, or any segment thereof, in furtherance of political or social objectives" (Watson, 2002). Groups such as al-Qaeda are known as transnational terrorists because they operate in and against many countries across the globe. Groups such as the IRA and ETA are domestic terrorists because they confine operations to domestic targets (the IRA in the United Kingdom and British bases overseas and ETA against Spanish interests). The United States also has its home-grown (domestic) terrorists.

Most terrorist activity takes place far away from the United States, but the bombings of the World Trade Center in 1993 and of the Oklahoma City Federal Building in April 1995 and the horrific events of 9/11 show that the United States is not immune from it. Although the World Trade Center attacks in 1993 and 2001 were the work of foreign Islamic terrorists, the Oklahoma City bombing that took 168 lives was carried out by "All-American" U.S. Army veteran Timothy McVeigh and his accomplices who belonged to a Michigan militia group called the Patriots (see Theory in Action box).

Perhaps the most disturbing trend in terrorism on the domestic front is "the increasing 'Americanization' of the leadership of al-Qaeda and aligned groups, and the larger number of Americans attaching themselves to these groups" (Berger & Hoffman, 2010, p. 14). Berger and Hoffman identify 63 American citizens or legal resident aliens who have been arrested and indicted, either in America or overseas, for Islamic terrorist acts from 2009 to September 2010. When Berger and Hoffman refer to the Americanization of al-Qaeda's leadership, they are referring to people like Anwar al-Awlaki, Adnan Shukrijumah, and Omar Hammmami.

The cleric al-Awlaki was raised in New Mexico and was an important operational organizer for al-Qaeda in Yemen until he was killed in 2011 by a U.S. drone attack in Lebanon. Shukrijumah, who grew up in New York and Florida, is al-Qaeda's director of external operations, and Hammmami, a convert from the Baptist faith from Alabama, was a key propagandist and military commander for al-Qaeda until killed by a rival faction of al-Qaeda called Al-Shabaab in Somalia in 2013. The three are the most notorious home-grown jihadists. Listed here is a sampling of conspiracies and attacks that took place from 2009 to 2013, for which American citizens or foreign nationals legally residing in the United States were responsible.

> *May 2009.* James Cromitie, David Williams, Onta Williams, and Laguerre Payen were arrested for plotting to blow up Jewish centers in the Bronx, New York, and to shoot down planes at an Air National Guard base. One was Afghan-born; the other three were African Americans converted to Islam in prison.

> *June 2009.* Abdulhakim Muhammed, a Muslim convert from Tennessee, killed one soldier and wounded another outside a military recruiting office in Little Rock, Arkansas.

Photo 13.3

Workers clearing rubble and searching for victims of the bombing of the Oklahoma City Federal Building.

September 2009. Afghan Najibullah Zazi was arrested after purchasing large quantities of chemicals used to make a bomb intended for detonation in the New York City subway.

September 2009. Jordanian Hosam Maher Husein Smadi was arrested in an attempt to plant a bomb in a Dallas skyscraper.

September 2009. Michael Finton, a prison convert to Islam, was arrested after attempting to detonate a car bomb outside the Federal Building in downtown Springfield, Illinois.

November 2009. U.S. Army major Nidal Malik Hasan opened fire on fellow soldiers in Fort Hood, Texas, killing 13 people and wounding 29 others.

December 2009. Nigerian Umar Farouk Abdulmutallab attempted to ignite an explosive device hidden in his underwear while aboard an airliner over Detroit.

May 2010. Faisal Shahzad, a Pakistani naturalized U.S. citizen, planted a car bomb in Times Square in New York. The bomb failed to detonate properly.

November 2010. Somali American Mohamed Osman Mohamud tried to detonate a van filled with dummy explosives supplied by the FBI in a sting operation.

July 2011. Army private Naser Jason Abdo, who grew up in Dallas, Texas, was arrested for plotting an attack on Fort Hood.

April 2013. Brothers Tamerlan and Dzhokhar Tsarnaev detonated bombs at the Boston Marathon, killing 3 and severely wounding more than 100.

Many of these attacks (and many more not mentioned here) were unsuccessful thanks to good undercover law enforcement, the amateurish efforts of poorly trained operatives whom their terrorist handlers considered expendable, or sheer good luck. The potential loss of life had some of these operations proved successful for the terrorists is staggering. As for the element of luck, we should remind ourselves that terrorists only have to get lucky once; their potential victims have to be lucky all the time.

❖ Other Domestic Groups

We should not equate terrorism only with Islamic groups. There are, and have been in the past, a number of other domestic groups with their own causes. Although many of these groups have been active for long periods and have perpetrated far more attacks within the United States than Islamic groups (Watson, 2002), they do not pose the same kinds of dire threat to the United States that groups like al-Qaeda do.

Ideological: Left Wing

According to the FBI (Watson, 2002), left-wing groups "generally profess a revolutionary socialist doctrine and view themselves as protectors of the people against the 'dehumanizing effects' of capitalism and imperialism. They aim to bring about change in the United States and believe this change can be realized through revolution rather than through the established political process." Leftist groups posed the most serious domestic terrorist threat to the United States from the 60s through the 1980s, but their fortunes changed as law enforcement dismantled the infrastructure of many of these groups, and the fall of communism in Eastern Europe left them without their ideological foundation and patronage.

Left-wing terrorism in the United States became most active during the turmoil of the 1960s. The most prominent group was the Weather Underground (WU). Solidly middle class, mostly white, and fiercely Marxist, the WU focused its attacks on symbols of "capitalist oppression" such as banks, corporate headquarters, and military facilities. It was thought to be defunct after the arrest of many of its leaders in the 1970s, but it renewed its robbery and bombing campaign in the 1980s (White, 1998). An even more radical group, The May 19 Communist Organization (M19CO), carried out bombing operations of U.S. military facilities and developed ties with foreign terrorist groups.

Another left-wing group was the Revolutionary Armed Task Force (RATF) forged from the alliance of the May 19th Coalition and the Black Liberation Army. Although this group earned its terrorist credentials by bombing a number of capitalist symbols, including the FBI's headquarters in New York, much of its activity seemed to be concentrated on conventional crimes such as robbery and drug trafficking. The RATF recruited from minority prisoners and parolees, especially those who saw themselves as victims of a capitalist and racist America (Albanese & Pursley, 1993). The activities of these left-wing groups began to wane in the 1980s, and according to most experts, their organizations are now defunct (Council on Foreign Relations, 2004). Groups like al-Qaeda attract the kinds of people formerly attracted to RATF.

Ideological: Right Wing

Most right-wing American groups espouse radical libertarian views ("get the government off my back") and tend to be anti-Semites and white supremacists. An example of a right-wing group is the Aryan Nations, founded in the mid-1970s and headquartered in Idaho until 2001. The group espouses white supremacy, anti-Semitism, tax resistance, and radical libertarianism. The group suffered a serious blow in 2000 when it lost a $6.3 million lawsuit, which cost them the real estate they owned in Idaho as well as automobiles and other property owned by the group (Law Enforcement Agency Resource Network, 2004).

The KKK is one of the oldest terrorist groups in the world, although today it is a generic name for a number of autonomous groups that range from those that never go beyond rhetoric and cross burning to those who actively practiced terrorism against black churches and Jewish synagogues (White, 1998). At its peak the KKK boasted a membership of 4 million, and some of its members engaged in murders, bombings, beatings, and cross burnings to intimidate blacks and white civil rights workers. The KKK shares with most other American right-wing extremist/terrorist organizations an extreme Christian fundamentalism, the advocacy of paramilitary survivalist training, and a conspiratorial view of politics. They refer to the United States government as ZOG (Zionist Occupational Government), which they say is run by Jews, liberals, and African Americans (Vetter & Perlstein, 1991). As was the case with the Aryan Nations, as a result of a lawsuit against the KKK in 2000 the organization had to "hand over all its assets and skulk off into virtual oblivion" (Walsh & Hemmens, 2011, p. 345).

The poison spread by such groups is apparently still influencing some to commit acts of violence, however. On March 8, 2011, Kevin Harpham, a former member of the white supremacist group the National Alliance, was arrested, convicted, and imprisoned for 32 years for leaving a bomb along a Martin Luther King Jr. Day parade route in Spokane, Washington. Luckily,

Photo 13.4

The burning cross of the KKK symbolizes the violent tactics used against African Americans and others.

the bomb was discovered and defused. The bomb was apparently quite sophisticated and could have killed and wounded many people (Machetta, 2011).

There are a number of groups in the United States that employ terrorist tactics that have no grand sociopolitical agenda but rather seek to resolve special issues. These groups include environmentalists seeking to protect the environment, animal rights groups seeking to protect animals, and antiabortion groups seeking to protect the rights of the unborn. The overwhelming majority of those who align themselves which such causes are nonviolent and seek their aims through political means. However, as with any group affiliated with almost any cause, there are extremists on the fringes that turn to violence to get their point across.

Leftist-oriented Animal Liberation Front (ALF) and the Earth Liberation Front (ELF) have emerged in the past several years as major domestic terror threats, with ELF being declared by the FBI as America's number one domestic terrorist group (Consumer Freedom, 2006), which seems like a gross exaggeration given the so-called "Americanization of al-Qaeda" noted earlier. This group has engaged in numerous acts of tree spiking, arson, sabotage of construction equipment, and other forms of vandalism that the Law Enforcement Agency Resource Network (2006) reports have caused more than $100,000 in damage (compare this to the financial cost of the 9/11 attacks put at close to $285 billion [Jalata, 2011]). According to the ELF website (Earth First, 2006), it sees itself as "working to speed up the collapse of industry, to scare the rich, and to undermine the foundations of the state."

ALF has close ties with ELF because of the closeness of their respective agendas. Like ELF, ALF subscribes to the principle of "leaderless resistance," organizing itself into small autonomous cells with no centralized chain of command. This minimizes the possibility of infiltration by law enforcement (Leader & Probst, 2006). According to James Jarboe (2002), the FBI estimated that ALF and ELF committed more than 600 criminal acts from 1996 to 2001. Despite the attention given to these two groups by the FBI, there have mercifully been no deaths attributed to the activities of ALF or ELF, although Leader and Probst (2006) see the groups as ready to turn to more violent tactics in the future.

THEORY IN ACTION: Timothy McVeigh and the Oklahoma Bombing

When we hear the word *terrorism*, the minds of most Americans quickly turn to Islamic terrorism. However, prior to the 9/11 attacks on the World Trade Center, the worst act of terrorism in American history was perpetuated by an "all-American" man named Timothy McVeigh, along with co-conspirator Terry Nichols. On April 19, 1995, McVeigh exploded a massive bomb that destroyed the Alfred P. Murrah Federal Building in Oklahoma City, killing 168 people and injuring 680 others. McVeigh was arrested just 90 minutes after the explosion by an Oklahoma state trooper, who stopped him for driving without a license plate and discovered McVeigh was carrying an unlawful weapon. Forensic evidence subsequently linked McVeigh and Nichols to the crime, and Nichols was arrested two weeks later.

What drove this young self-styled patriot to commit such an act? McVeigh was born the second of three children of William and Mildred McVeigh in Lockport, New York. His parents divorced when Timothy was 10, and he was raised by his father. He was apparently a target of school bullying, and although he grew up with the American flag flying in the front yard, he came to see the federal government as the ultimate bully. McVeigh was not abused, neglected, or deprived by his parents in any way, and he never showed any signs of trouble. He was always respectful and polite to others and even won a state Regents scholarship for exceptionally high scores on standardized tests. The only clues to his later actions were an obsession with guns, then with survivalist interests, and then association with extremist militia groups with profound distrust of the government. Much of his attraction to these antigovernment groups was his feeling of being discriminated against as a white male, seeing affirmative action and race norming of test scores as profoundly unfair.

After working a series of dead-end jobs, McVeigh joined the army, where his love of guns and explosives stood out. His army test scores showed exceptional intelligence, and he outshone his squad mates in everything and was quickly promoted to sergeant. Timothy was deployed to Iraq during the first Gulf War in 1991, and he was awarded the coveted Bronze Star and seven other medals. After a failed attempt to join Special Forces after his tour in Iraq, Timothy was let out of the army (and away from all his beloved guns) as it downsized.

The FBI believes McVeigh's violent antigovernment views evolved gradually after he left the army and became reacquainted with old army buddy Terry Nichols, who introduced him to radical right-wing militias. Two events that helped to shape McVeigh's radicalism were the 1992 shootout between federal agents and survivalist Randy Weaver in Idaho, killing Weaver's wife and son, and the attack on the Branch Davidian compound in Waco, Texas, in 1993 by federal agencies in which 80 followers of David Koresh died in a blazing inferno.

Timothy McVeigh was executed on June 10, 2001. He was reportedly calm as the hour of his death approached, maintaining an affable attitude and demeanor to the end but never really expressing remorse for the worst act of domestic terrorism in U.S. history.

Which, if any, theory of criminal behavior can explain Timothy McVeigh's horrible action in Oklahoma City? There is nothing in his background to suggest that he would ever do anything criminal. Indeed, he was a very respectful boy with high intellectual potential and a deep sense of social justice. It is this latter attribute that marks McVeigh as more similar to the typical terrorist than the typical criminal (see Laurence Miller's four cognitive stages involved in becoming a terrorist nearby). He saw racial preference programs and a number of other factors in terms of Miller's first two stages, the "It's not right" and the "It's not fair" stages. He then entered the "It's your

(Continued)

Photo 13.5

The Oklahoma City Bomber Timothy McVeigh was convicted of 11 federal offenses and sentenced to death. His execution took place on June 11, 2001.

fault" stage, in which the cause of injustice was identified as the federal government, and finally the "You are evil" stage in which the government is identified as the evil cause of his suffering, spurring him to strike back.

Discussion Questions

1. McVeigh saw himself as a patriot fighting against an increasingly intrusive federal government. Compose arguments supporting and denying his view.

2. Might differential association and social learning theories explain McVeigh's evolving radicalism?

3. Do you think McVeigh may have been a psychopath, given his love of war and guns and his lack of remorse?

Sources: Giordano, 2003; Linenthal, 2001; Wright, 2007

❖ Is There a Terrorist Personality?

Terrorists, like criminals in general, tend to be young unmarried males, although they *do not* fit the criminal profile in terms of being poorly educated relative to their peers or from single-parent families (LaFree & Ackerman, 2009). Despite self-selection for membership in terrorist groups, no study of terrorist psychology has ever produced a psychological profile, leading the majority of terrorist experts to suspect there is any such thing as a terrorist personality (Hudson, 1999). On the other hand, the absence of a uniform terrorist personality does not mean that certain traits are not disproportionately present among those who join terrorist groups. Some scholars view terrorists as people with marginal personalities drawn to terrorist groups because their deficiencies are both accepted and welcomed by the group (Johnson & Feldman, 1992). This may apply more to domestic terrorists such as Timothy McVeigh than to Islamic terrorists.

Johnson and Feldman (1992) view terrorist groups as made up of three types of people: the charismatic leader, the antisocial personality, and the follower. The charismatic leader is socially alienated, narcissistic, arrogant, and intelligent, with a deeply idealistic sense of right and wrong. The terrorist group provides a forum for his narcissistic rage and intellectual ramblings, and the subservience of group members feeds his egoism. Antisocial individuals have opportunities in terrorist groups to use force and violence to further their own personal goals, as well as the goals of the group. For the antisocial personality the group functions like an organized crime family, providing greater opportunity, action, and prestige than could be found outside the group (Perlman, 2002). The majority of terrorists, however, are simple followers who see the world purely in black ("them") and white ("us") and have deep needs for acceptance, which makes them susceptible to all sorts of religious, ideological, and political propaganda (Ardila, 2002).

Terrorist expert Bruce Hoffman views home-grown terrorists as disaffected self-radicalized individuals who actively seek contact with peers with similar views and who visit terrorist websites to make contact with radical groups. Yet aside from this there is little to set them apart from other Americans or immigrants to America. Hoffman (2010) described home-grown jihadists to the Committee on Homeland Security as a very mixed bunch, concluding that they are

good students and well-educated individuals and high school dropouts and jailbirds. Persons born in the U.S. or variously in Afghanistan, Egypt, Pakistan, and Somalia.

Teenage boys pumped up with testosterone and middle-aged divorcees. The only common denominator appears to be a newfound hatred for their native or adopted country, a degree of dangerous malleability, and a religious fervor justifying or legitimizing violence that impels these very impressionable and perhaps easily influenced individuals toward potentially lethal acts of violence. (pp. 38–39)

❖ Terrorism and Common Crime

Like any organization, terrorists must be financed. A certain amount of funding for terrorist groups comes from governments sympathetic to their cause or hostile to the governments against which the terrorists operate. The United States government has designated Cuba, Iran, Iraq (before the 2003 U.S.-led invasion), Libya, Sudan, Syria, and North Korea as terrorist-sponsoring nations, with Iran the most active (U.S. Department of State, 2004). Libya renounced terrorism in 2004, and it remains to be seen what we can say of Iraq in years to come. Some terrorist funding comes from private sympathizers, but most of it comes from common criminal activities like drug trafficking, extortion, and bank robbery. As William Reid (2002) sees it, terrorists cloak "themselves in a 'crusade' that is more accurately viewed as criminal behavior. Even groups that preach against capitalism spend much of their energy raising money and using money from capitalist endeavors" (p. 4). The IRA has raised vast sums by extorting "protection" money from the very people for whom they claim to be fighting. They have made so much money from this and other criminal activities that they have had to branch out into legitimate businesses and have launched money-laundering schemes (Dishman, 2001). Evidence suggests that many IRA groups now exist with the primary purpose of developing wealth for their members. However, some splinter groups such as the Real IRA (RIRA) and Continuity IRA (CIRA) continue to engage in bombing and assassinations as well as common crime. Dishman (2001) calls the IRA "a prime example of a *mutated* terrorist group who invested significant energies into committing profit-driven criminal acts" (p. 49, italics in original).

Many Islamic groups also obtain funding from nongovernmental organizations such as charity groups, from legitimate cover businesses, and from criminal activities, particularly drug trafficking (U.S. Department of State, 2013). Terrorist groups in South America such as the Marxist/Maoist Shining Path of Peru make enormous profits from drug trafficking, and European groups such as Germany's Red Army Faction and Italy's Red Brigades (both Marxist-oriented and now supposedly defunct) financed their activities through bank robberies and kidnapping. The widespread involvement of terrorist groups in such practices casts serious doubt on the ideological idealism they claim motivates their activities. The large amounts of money involved can corrupt the most dedicated ideologue in time, especially if fellow terrorists are lining their pockets. As Albanese and Pursley (1993) put it, "Gradually, the [criminal] activities become ends in themselves and terrorist groups begin to resemble ordinary criminal organizations hidden behind a thin political veneer" (p. 100). This is not true of groups motivated by Islamic fundamentalism, because many of the groups' members, especially its leaders, such as Osama bin Laden, often give up more than they gain in material terms.

❖ Theories of Terrorism

We have a tendency to think of terrorism as being caused by religious fanaticism and political radicalism. While terrorism is certainly fed by these things, they are not its causes—fanaticism and radicalism have to somehow turn ideology into action. There are as many causes of terrorism as there are terrorist groups because it cannot be understood without understanding the historical, social, political, and economic conditions behind the emergence of each group. Perhaps the one generality we can make is that all groups originate in response to some perceived injustice. Although certain kinds of people may be drawn to terrorism, terrorists are not a bunch of "sicko weirdos," running around the world killing for pleasure. If they were we would have defeated terrorism long ago. Most terrorist groups take pains not to recruit anyone showing signs of mental instability because such people are not trustworthy and would arouse the suspicion of their intended targets (Hudson, 1999).

Some terrorism theorists believe the bulk of terrorists are crusaders convinced of the moral rightness of their cause (White, 1998). If these theorists are right, we have to explain how "normal" people are persuaded to commit brutal acts against innocent people. When moral people are required to commit immoral acts there must be some sort of personal transformation that makes it possible. In other words, the willingness to perform terrorist acts may reflect a process of moral disengagement more than an indication of pathological and/ or criminal traits the individual brings to the terrorist group. If the essence of terrorism is "the complete transformation of sane human beings into brutal and indiscriminate killers" (Sprinzak, 1991, p. 58), terrorist acts may generate significant levels of guilt and doubt in the new recruit that must be resolved. Inconsistencies between attitudes and behavior (cognitive dissonance) are usually resolved by changing attitudes rather than behaviors. For the terrorist this typically means a deepening of the belief that the cause is just, the further dehumanizing of targets ("infidels," "capitalist pigs," and so on), viewing the slaughter of innocents as "collateral damage," and any of a number of other ways humans exorcize behavior-inhibiting guilt and doubt.

Laurence Miller (2011) presents four cognitive stages by which terrorist groups form and by which individuals evolve into people capable of slaughtering innocents. The first stage is the belief that some set of conditions in their lives is unpleasant and unacceptable, such as widespread poverty or rampant immorality. This is the "It's not right" stage. The second stage is "It's not fair," in which they perceive others as living a better life than the budding terrorists are living. Stage three is the "It's your fault" stage, in which the cause of injustice has been identified in other groups. The final stage is the "You are evil" stage, in which the group identified as the cause of the budding terrorists' suffering becomes dehumanized.

Differential association theory is relevant here. Many Islamic terrorists are recruited from religious schools known as **madrasas**. In these schools, all of Miller's four stages are present, and thus recruits are provided with an excess of definitions favorable to terrorism over definitions unfavorable to it. These schools teach secular subjects but focus mostly on religious texts and stress the immorality ("it's not right") and materialism ("it's not fair") of Western life and the need to convert all infidels to Islam (Armanios, 2003). The madrasas are appealing to poor Muslim families because they offer free education and free room and board. Many members of the Afghan Taliban (*Taliban* means "student") regime studied and trained in Pakistani madrasas stressing a strict form of Islam. Children are indoctrinated in these schools with anti-Israeli and anti-American propaganda from the earliest days of their lives (differential association's priority, duration, frequency, and intimacy). We might call socialization in the madrasas differential association and social learning theories on steroids, because the only definitions of reality students receive are that of the school, and they are amply rewarded (reinforced) for their acceptance and participation. Substitute radical right-wing politics in America for Islamic extremists and the various cultlike militias for the madrasas, and perhaps we might gain some understanding of Timothy McVeigh's actions.

The gruesome barbarity behind the Beslan school incident and the beheading deaths of Daniel Pearle in Pakistan in 2002, Nicholas Berg in Iraq in 2004, and Paul Johnson in Saudi

Arabia in 2004 (as well as other decapitation incidents before and after these), all videotaped and boastfully distributed, underline the psychopathic nature of much terrorist activity. There is certainly no glory in decapitating helpless individuals or terrorizing little children, and the individuals who actually ordered and carried out the acts were likely on the psychopathic fringes of the group. Musab al-Zarqawi certainly falls into that category. On September 20, 2004, al-Zarqawi's terrorist group released a grisly video in which al-Zarqawi is shown drawing a knife from his belt and cutting off the head of American hostage Eugene Armstrong. Such horrendous acts are designed to unnerve the enemy by essentially saying, "We are merciless and will stop at nothing." There is a degree of rationality underlying such evil if it accomplishes something terrorists want.

Suicide Bombers

A person nurtured on the hatred spouted in the madrasa is ideal material for recruitment as a martyr to the cause. Martyrdom brings with it the promise of immediate ascension into heaven, where he will find "rivers of milk and wine . . . lakes of honey, and the services of 72 virgins" (Hoffman, 2002, p. 305). The promise of a sexual paradise is powerful for young males in cultures that allow males to have multiple wives if they can afford them. This practice leaves other males, particularly the young, without access to women, a situation that must lead to great strains and frustrations. Young male suicide bombers take the Koran promise of sexual paradise seriously. They often take elaborate steps to protect their genitals from damage so they can enjoy the pleasures of paradise, and as one of them is supposed to have said, "Most boys can't stop thinking about the virgins" (Victoroff & Kruglanski, 2009, p. 127). However, it is not only religious fervor and sexual frustration that motivates suicide bombers. Many see themselves as altruists, saints, and heroes striving to achieve noble political goals on behalf of their people. They are also afforded tremendous status in their communities, and their families are often handsomely financially rewarded for their offsprings' sacrifice (Miller, 2011).

This supports rational choice theorists who say we should look at what terrorist groups have to offer if we want to understand why individuals join them. In addition to the rewards offered to Islamic terrorists just described, for terrorist "wannabes," "terrorism can provide a route for advancement, an opportunity for glamour and excitement, a chance of world renown, a way of demonstrating one's courage, and even a way of accumulating wealth" (Reich, 1990, p. 271). Terrorism is much like organized crime in that it provides illegitimate ways to get what most of us would like to have—fame and fortune, and in the case of Islamic suicide martyrs, an eternity of sexual bliss. Terrorists also have a bonus in that they, and their comrades and supporters, see themselves as romanticized warriors fighting for a just and noble cause, and in the case of religious terrorists, the favor of their God and the promise of a rewarding afterlife.

The need to belong appears to be particularly important for Islamic immigrants to Europe and the United States or to the offspring of these immigrants. Such people often feel alienated from the host country, which they may see as decadent and godless. They feel their differences in religion, language, dress, and culture very acutely, and their humiliation and alienation turns into hatred (LaFree & Ackerman, 2009). These are exactly the kinds of people that can be turned into terrorists by the rhetoric spouted by radical imams (preachers) in their mosques. This is aptly demonstrated by the recruitment of American-born sons (and sometimes daughters) of Islamic immigrants in certain mosques, as we have seen (Hoffman, 2010).

❖ Law Enforcement Response and Government Policy

There are any number of ways a democracy can respond to terrorism, ranging from making concessions to military intervention. Concessions are likely only when there is moral substance to the terrorist cause and when such concessions are reasonable. But the West cannot make any concessions to al-Qaeda and other such groups because they are not demanding any. What these groups say they want over and over is nothing less than the Islamification of the world, starting with the purification of existing Islamic regimes (as was done in Afghanistan by the Taliban) that do not match the terrorists' ideas of what an Islamic state should be.

Military intervention may be used when the terrorist threat is too big for civilian authorities to handle. But besides being distasteful to the democratic spirit, military intervention, even though successful in the short term, may be detrimental in the long term, as recent military interventions have aptly demonstrated. The Islamic terrorist threat comes from many nations fed by a constant stream of religious hatred poisoning the minds of young Muslim men. It is estimated that more than 50,000 terrorists were trained in Afghanistan who are now scattered around the globe, quietly integrated into local communities and awaiting their orders to strike (Simonsen & Spindlove, 2004). Former United States Defense secretary Donald Rumsfeld has expressed doubt the West can win the broader global fight against Islamic terrorism and wonders if the various groups "are turning out newly trained terrorists faster than the United States can capture or kill them" (R. Burns, 2004, p. 5). Clearly we cannot defeat the threat by military force alone.

International law has been applied against terrorists, sometimes successfully but often not. The principle of international law known as *aut dedire aut punire* (Latin for "either extradite or punish") obligates countries to either extradite terrorists to the country where their crimes were committed or to punish them themselves. Some countries neither extradite nor punish for one reason or another (they may support the terrorist's cause, or they may fear reprisals).

The United States has a clear-cut policy to combat terrorism (U.S. Department of State, 1995, p. iv):

1. Do not make deals with terrorists or submit to blackmail. We have found over the years that this policy works.

2. Treat terrorists as criminals and apply the rule of law.

3. Bring maximum pressure on states that sponsor and support terrorists by imposing economic, diplomatic, and political sanctions and urging other states to do likewise.

The Department of Homeland Security and the USA Patriot Act

Just 11 days after the 9/11 terrorist attacks, President George W. Bush appointed Pennsylvania governor Tom Ridge as the first director of the Department of Homeland Security, a new cabinet-level department. The office was mandated to oversee and coordinate multiple agencies under a comprehensive national strategy to safeguard the United States against future terrorist attacks. The department states its mission as follows: "Protecting the American people from terrorist threats is our founding principle and our highest priority." According to the department's website (2013), their counterterrorism responsibilities focus on three goals:

1. Prevent terrorist attacks

2. Prevent the unauthorized acquisition, importation, movement, or use of chemical, biological, radiological, and nuclear materials and capabilities within the United States

3. Reduce the vulnerability of critical infrastructure and key resources, essential leadership, and major events to terrorist attacks and other hazards

Put simply, the mission of the **Department of Homeland Security** is to detect, prevent, prepare for, and recover from terrorist attacks within the United States. Detection involves coordinated efforts on the part of federal, state, and local agencies to collect information in an attempt to identify terrorist activities within the United States. Prevention relates to the investigation of identified threats; the denial of entry of suspected terrorists, terrorist materials, and supplies into the United States; and the arrest, detention, and deportation of individuals suspected of membership in foreign terrorist groups. Preparedness refers to nationwide efforts to prepare for and lessen the impact of any terrorist attack. Recovery refers to efforts to quickly restore critical infrastructure facilities (distribution systems, utilities, telecommunications), the provision of adequate medical facilities, and the removal of hazardous materials in the event of a successful terrorist attack (White House, 2001).

Homeland security efforts were given "legal teeth" by the passage of the congressional **USA Patriot Act** on October 11, 2001. The Patriot Act is either loved as a powerful tool that will avert terrorist plots and put terrorists in jail, or it is feared as the beginning of the end of American civil liberties. The act grants federal agencies greater authority to track and intercept private communications, gives greater powers to the Treasury Department to combat corruption and prevent money laundering, and creates new crimes, penalties, and procedures for use against domestic and foreign terrorists (Doyle, 2002).

Many people feel that if the establishment of the Department of Homeland Security and the passage of the Patriot Act prevent another 9/11, it is all right with them. After all, if you are not engaged in terrorist activities, what have you to fear? While no one suggests law enforcement is interested in intercepting e-mail exchanges of cheesecake recipes or listening to your call home asking for money, the American Civil Liberties Union (ACLU) fears the inclusion of domestic terrorism in the Patriot Act's definition of terrorism has great potential for abuse. The ACLU claims the definition is broad enough to encompass the activities of several legitimate activist groups such as Greenpeace, Operation Rescue, and Environmental Liberation and that it could put participants in some protest activities at risk for the same enhanced criminal penalties and asset forfeitures applied to genuine terrorists (ACLU, 2002). In summary, the ACLU asserts that the Patriot Act increases the government's surveillance powers in four areas:

1. *Records searches*. It expands the government's ability to look at records on an individual's activity being held by third parties.

2. *Secret searches*. It expands the government's ability to search private property without notice to the owner.

3. *Intelligence searches*. It expands a narrow exception to the Fourth Amendment that had been created for the collection of foreign intelligence information.

4. *"Trap and trace" searches*. It expands another Fourth Amendment exception for spying that collects "addressing" information about the origin and destination of communications, as opposed to the content.

The mechanisms set up by the Department of Homeland Security can only work if the men and women on the front lines of security are constantly vigilant. Security was so tight in the first months after 9/11 that this period was probably the safest time to fly in the history of aviation. But the human tendency is to grow complacent after long periods in which nothing happens, and this is terrorism's great weapon. For instance, a U.S. government document published in 1999 predicted that al-Qaeda would retaliate "in a spectacular way" for the cruise missile attacks against their training facilities in 1998, ordered by President Clinton in retaliation for the 1998 attacks on U.S. embassies. This document stated that "suicide bomber(s) belonging to al-Qaeda's Martyrdom Battalion could crash an aircraft packed with high explosives (C-4 and semtex) into the Pentagon, the headquarters of the Central Intelligence Agency (CIA) or the White House" (Hudson, 1999, pp. 7–8). Al-Qaeda waited patiently for three years before doing almost exactly as predicted, and they did it with relative ease. Thus, all the intelligence in the world is of little use unless those in the day-to-day security trenches take it as seriously every day as they did immediately after September 11, 2001.

At the time of writing (November 2013), many Islamic states in Africa and the Middle East are in turmoil as regimes from Egypt to Yemen are being toppled or retoppled (in the case of Egypt) or are on the verge of toppling. If all this turmoil eventually results in real democracy in these states, it bodes well for the defeat of terrorism. On the other hand, we have seen previous promises of democracy in that region of the world that turned into Islamic dictatorships—"one man (no women allowed), one vote, one time." In power struggles such as these, the spoils usually go to the most organized, disciplined, and ruthless groups, adjectives that certainly define terrorist groups more accurately than democratic organizations. If Islamic extremists with their dreams of a universal caliphate (a global Islamic state) manage to gain power, there are only decades of more terrorism to look forward to.

Summary

- Terrorism is an ancient method of intimidating the public by the indiscriminate use of violence for social or political reasons. Terrorism increased rather dramatically from the 1960s to the mid-1980s, steadily dropped off in the 1990s, and has again increased in the 21st century.

- Terrorists are different from freedom fighters or guerrillas in that terrorists usually operate against democracies and freedom fighters against foreign colonialists or oppressive domestic regimes. Many terrorist groups tend to evolve into organized crime groups hidden behind an ideological veneer.

- Al-Qaeda is a "base" organization for a number of Islamic terrorist groups and is the group of most concern to Americans. Hezbollah, a radical pro-Iranian Islamic fundamentalist group, appears to be the most active and most deadly terrorist group presently operating not associated with al-Qaeda.

- Although American terrorists are decidedly amateur in comparison with their foreign counterparts, there are a fair number of terrorist groups operating in this country. The most disturbing trend is the Americanization of al-Qaeda, with a number of Islamic immigrants and Islamic converts taking up arms against the United States. Other domestic terrorist groups are divided into ideological (left- and right-wing) and special issue groups.

- There is no uniform terrorist personality, although there are certain traits found more frequently among terrorists than among the general population. The most common traits found are low self-esteem and a predilection for risk taking. Since most terrorists are not mentally ill, a process of moral disengagement is posited to explain their transition from sane human beings to killers.

- There are as many causes of terrorism as there are terrorist groups. Each group has its origins in some perceived injustice, but only a minuscule number of people react to such conditions by joining terrorist organizations.

■ Democracies have considerable difficulty responding to the terrorist threat because of legal restraints. The United States has a clear-cut policy of treating terrorists like common criminals and not making deals with them and imposing sanctions against nations that sponsor terrorism. The threat to democracies from terrorism is great, and the United States responded after 9/11 with the establishment of the Department of Homeland Security.

Exercises and Discussion Questions

1. Do you agree or disagree that there is a moral difference between terrorists and guerillas?

2. Discuss the ways in which terrorism is rational behavior.

3. Do you think extremist Muslims hate the United States because it has troops on soil they consider holy (Saudi Arabia)? If so, why don't we take the troops out of there? Or is it fear of losing Saudi oil that keeps them there?

4. Can you conceive of any circumstances under which you would commit the kinds of terrorist acts committed on 9/11 or the Beslan school, sacrificing your own life in the bargain?

5. Discuss why the Patriot Act does or does not make us safer from terrorist attacks. Are we giving up certain civil liberties for a measure of security?

6. Go to www.cfrterrorism.org and click on "groups." You will find a number of terrorist groups listed there with a variety of motives. Chose an Islamic and a Marxist group and write a short paper comparing and contrasting their motives and methods.

Useful Websites

Bureau of Justice Statistics. www.bjs.gov. Data on U.S.-based terrorism.

Council on Foreign Relations. www.cfr.org/issue/terrorism/ri135.

Intelligence Resource Program. www.fas.org/irp/threat/terror.htm.

U.S. Department of State. www.state.gov.

Chapter Terms

Al-Qaeda

Department of Homeland Security

Hezbollah

Madrasas

Terrorism

USA Patriot Act

CHAPTER 14
Property Crime

Jay Scott Ballinger was a property offender on a dark mission. He admitted in court to setting fire to anywhere from 30 to 50 churches in 11 states from 1994 to 1999. A volunteer firefighter was killed in one of the blazes, which also made Ballinger a murderer. Ballinger did not set these fires for profit or because he got some weird sexual kick from watching them burn; he did so on an anti-Christian mission. Ballinger, his girlfriend Angela Wood, and accomplice David Puckett traveled around the country seeking converts to satanism, and churches were the sanctuaries of the enemy. To finance their travels around the Midwest and South the trio would burglarize and shoplift, and Woods worked as a stripper.

It all came to an end when Ballinger was arrested after paramedics treating him for severe burns wondered why he waited two days to seek treatment (he had burns to 40% of his body and had to receive four skin grafts). A police officer who remembered Ballinger's name from a previous investigation questioned him and then summoned ATF (Alcohol, Tobacco, and Firearms) agents who found fire-setting paraphernalia and satanic literature at Ballinger's home. Among the writings agents found were 50 "contracts" signed by teenagers in their own blood pledging their souls to the devil and to do "all types of evil" for which they would be rewarded with wealth, power, and sex, the perennial male motivators. Ballinger, age 36 at the time of his arrest, was described as a misfit loner and high school dropout who was more comfortable with teens than people his own age. He was sentenced to 42 years in prison for his multistate arson spree. As the Ballinger case shows, crimes against property can sometimes morph into something much more deadly.

LEARNING OBJECTIVES

- Realize that although property crimes are les "sexy" than other types of crimes, they constitute the overwhelming majority of crimes committed in the United States
- Know the FBI definitions of each property crime discussed
- Understand the difference between simple burglary and home invasion and between simple motor vehicle theft and carjacking
- Know the difficulties involved in determining if a fire was intentionally started
- Be able to explain the differences between embezzlement, fraud, and forgery/counterfeiting

❖ What Is a Property Offense?

Although violent crime gets the lion's share of media and police attention, 88.1% (almost 9 out of 10) of the 10,189,905 offenses reported to the police in 2012 were property crimes (FBI, 2013a). Property crimes either involve the illegal acquisition of someone else's property (money or goods) or the malicious destruction of property (sometimes even including one's own if the intention is fraudulent). Just about everyone has been or will be victimized by a property offense at some time in life, but few of us will be victimized by a serious violent crime. It is also true that while the vast majority of us will never commit a violent crime, most of us have committed, or will commit, a property offense of some kind such as pilfering items from work or shoplifting. Thus the phrase "property crime" involves everything from teens vandalizing a mailbox to a sophisticated gang stealing property worth millions from museums and mansions. Figure 14.1 shows property crime trends in the United States over the past 5 years (FBI, 2013a). Property crime has dropped dramatically over that time (by over 1 million reported cases).

❖ Larceny-Theft

Larceny-theft is the most common property crime committed in the United States, accounting for 68.5% of all property offenses. **Larceny-theft** is defined as "the unlawful taking, leading, or riding away from the possession or constructive possession of another" (FBI, 2013a). The number of larceny-thefts reported in the United States in 2012 was an estimated 6,150,598, for a rate of 1,959 per 100,000 U.S. residents. The average loss due to larceny-theft was $987, for a total national loss of approximately $6 billion. Of those arrested for larceny-theft in 2012, 56.6% were males. Whites were 68.2 % of larceny-theft arrests, blacks 29%, and other races 2.1% (FBI, 2013a).

In early English common law, larceny only applied to persons who achieved possession of goods belonging to others by stealth or force; it did not cover persons who abused their victim's trust to steal from them. For instance, if farmer Jones gave farmer Smith a sheep to graze in his field, but Smith killed and ate the sheep, no larceny was committed because Jones voluntarily handed over the sheep to Smith. You can see the problems this would cause in today's society where every day numerous people hand over their money to bank tellers, their clothes to cleaners, and their vehicles and appliances to mechanics and repair persons. Lawmakers responded to this by enlarging the definition of larceny to include taking by fraud or false pretenses as well as by stealth and force. Taking by stealth has evolved into other crimes such as burglary, fraud, or embezzlement, and taking by force has evolved into the crime of robbery.

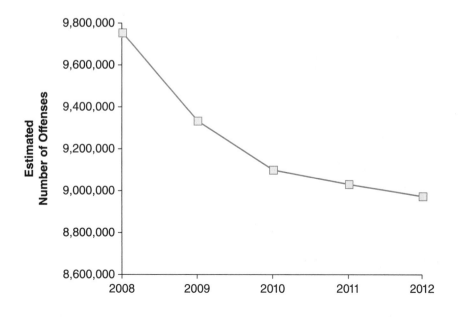

Figure 14.1

Five-Year Trend in U. S. Property Crime

Source: FBI, 2013a

Today larceny-theft covers most types of theft that do not include the use of threats or force. Larceny-theft includes grand theft (a felony) and petty theft (a misdemeanor), with the distinction depending on the value of the asset stolen. The cutoff value varies from state to state, but presently it is under $1,000 in every state. Whether a person is charged with grand or petty theft depends on the value of the item at the time it was stolen, not at the time it was purchased. A stolen computer worth $100 today is a petty theft no matter how much it cost initially, but a stolen guitar bought for $100 in 1955 that is now a classic valued at $10,000 is classified as a grand theft. Because the grand theft/petty theft distinction varies across states, the UCR considers both grand and petty theft as the same thing in its yearly larceny-theft tally. Figure 14.2 breaks down how most incidents of larceny-theft occurred in 2012 (FBI, 2013a).

Larceny-theft is subclassified into shoplifting, pocket picking, purse snatching, thefts from motor vehicles, theft of motor parts and accessories, theft of bicycles, and theft from buildings. Theft from motor vehicles is the most common type and includes thefts from just about any type of motorized vehicle, such as automobiles, trucks, buses, or motor homes. Purse snatching and pocket picking can easily be charged as robberies, however, because property is taken directly from the person.

Figure 14.2

Percentage Distribution of Larceny-Theft Offenses, 2012

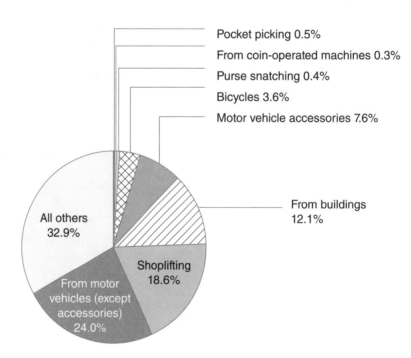

Pocket picking 0.5%

From coin-operated machines 0.3%

Purse snatching 0.4%

Bicycles 3.6%

Motor vehicle accessories 7.6%

From buildings 12.1%

All others 32.9%

From motor vehicles (except accessories) 24.0%

Shoplifting 18.6%

Shoplifting is theft of goods exposed for sale by a person other than an employee in a store and is the most studied subcategory of larceny-theft. According to the National Association of Shoplifting Prevention (2013), there are about 550,000 incidents of shoplifting every day in the United States. This results in more than $13 billion worth of goods stolen from retailers each year, which costs the average American family about $435 per year in increased prices imposed to cover the industry's losses. Shoplifting, in effect, is larceny committed against all of us.

About 8% of shoplifters say they engage in the practice as a primary source of income (Moore, 1984). These are the individuals with the greatest level of expertise who know how to minimize the risk of being caught, target the most expensive items, and steal almost exclusively for resale. Most shoplifters, however, are impulsive amateurs who shoplift relatively inexpensive items on the spur of the moment and for their own gratification (Lamontagne, Boyer, Hetu, & Lacerte-Lamontagne, 2000). One self-report study is consistent with rational choice theory in that shoplifters said they engaged in shoplifting simply because it is an easy, low-risk crime for which there are abundant opportunities (Tonglet, 2001). Some criminologists, especially cultural/anarchic criminologists, maintain that the reward received from crimes such as shoplifting often goes far beyond any material gain. They argue that a big part of the reward for engaging in crime comes from the sheer thrill of getting away with something in

the face of the possibility that one could get caught and point out that there is little economic gain from most shoplifting offenses. The "seduction" of crime, the conquering of fear, and the euphoric thrill of completion is the real payoff for many shoplifters (Young, 2003).

Repetitive impulsive stealing for the thrill of stealing and getting away with it is called kleptomania (Greek for "stealing madness"). This psychiatric label may be nothing more than an upscale "technique of neutralization" applied to affluent offenders to excuse their behavior and/or mitigate their punishment (Bartol, 2002). For instance, actress Winona Ryder was arrested in 2001 for shoplifting about $5,000 worth of goods from a Saks Fifth Avenue store in Beverly Hills (Mowbray, 2002). She could easily buy half the store without it having any major impact on her bank account, but she stole items she had little need for because of her "compulsion." Regardless of any skepticism one might have about the psychiatric label, there is a self-help organization similar to Alcoholics Anonymous (AA) called Cleptomaniacs and Shoplifters Anonymous (CASA) designed to treat what CASA prefers to call addictive-compulsive shoplifting (Shulman, 2003). A common theme for people who engage in "nonsensical shoplifting" is that they are often depressed and have other compulsive addictions (Lamontagne et al., 2000).

❖ Burglary

Burglary is "the unlawful entry of a structure to commit a felony or theft" (FBI, 2013a). This simple definition belies the hodgepodge of state laws that define burglary in a variety of ways. Burglary has always been considered a very serious offense under common law dating back many centuries because of the importance attached to the sanctity of the home as indicated by the ancient saying, "An Englishman's home is his castle." Residential burglary is one of the most traumatic crimes victims can experience, generating feelings of anger and fear and a profound sense of invasion of privacy and vulnerability in addition to financial loss. The original common law definition involved breaking and entering at nighttime with the intention of committing a felony whether or not a felony was committed. Burglary almost always involves theft, but burglary may be charged if no theft actually took place. The definition has evolved to include any unlawful entry (entry without right or permission), and thus a forceful entry ("breaking and entering") is no longer a necessary element of burglary. Of course, a forceful entry is obviously one method of unlawful entry. Entering through an unlocked door or open window still constitutes a burglary if the person has no legal right to be present in the structure.

Photo 14.2

Although this man entered through an unlocked window during the daytime, his crime is still classified as burglary.

Nor is nighttime entry any longer a necessary element. Nighttime entry was considered most seriously in early common law because it was assumed that home owners would be most likely to be at home during the night and thus at risk of violent confrontation with any intruders. This has also been recognized in modern statutes where nighttime burglaries (first-degree burglaries or aggravated burglaries) are punished more severely than daytime burglaries. Unlawful entries into motels, hotels, or vacation residences are considered residential burglaries committed against those who have temporarily rented or leased rooms in such places.

The number of burglaries reported to the police in 2013 was 2,103,787, for a rate of 723.5 per 100,000. Of these, 75.5% were residential with an average loss of $2,230, with the estimated loss for all burglaries at $4.7 billion. Of those arrested for burglary in 2013, 83.3% were male. Whites were 67.1%, blacks 30.8%, and the remaining 2.1% were of other races (FBI, 2013a).

As noted previously, burglary statutes are a hodgepodge of laws covering a variety of conduct. The unlawful entry element enables some states to define shoplifting as burglary if it can be shown that a suspect entered a store with the intention of stealing, thereby making the entry unlawful. Samaha (1993) lists a variety of offending scenarios for which offenders have been charged *and* convicted of burglary. These include shoplifting, pumping gas and leaving without paying, stealing a case of cigarettes from an open trunk, stealing popcorn from a sidewalk stand, and stealing a few coins from a pay telephone. None of these offenses included "breaking" and only the shoplifter "entered" a "structure" (unless a telephone booth is so defined). Regardless of state statutes, however, all these offenses must be reported to the FBI as a larceny-theft and not burglary. The absurdity of such broad definitions of burglary is that a 15-year-old girl who shoplifts a $1.50 lipstick and a 30-year-old man who enters an occupied residence at night and steals property worth thousands of dollars could both be charged with the same crime in some states, although they obviously would not receive the same penalty.

Home Invasion

Home invasion is a type of breaking and entering into a residential home in which the express purpose is to catch occupants at home so that criminals can rob, rape, or assault the occupants as well as steal their property. Being victimized by a home invasion is perhaps the most horrifying and potentially deadly experience a person can have. Home invasion is not a legally defined federal offense, but several states do have a separate statutory definition, such as the following from Connecticut:

> A person is guilty of home invasion when such person enters or remains unlawfully in a dwelling, while a person other than a participant in the crime is actually present in such dwelling, with intent to commit a crime therein, and, in the course of committing the offense: (1) Acting either alone or with one or more persons, such person or another participant in the crime commits or attempts to commit a felony against the person of another person other than a participant in the crime who is actually present in such dwelling.

The federal government and most other states do not have a separate statute for home invasion because although it is by definition a burglary, burglary is likely to be the least serious charge levied against anyone convicted of engaging in a home invasion. The most likely crimes to be charged in a home invasion are murder, rape, or aggravated assault in addition to burglary. Under the Connecticut statute, for instance, two parolees committed a home invasion in 2007 that resulted in three charges of murder (a mother and two daughters), the rape of a kidnapped person, aggravated assault (the husband and father), and arson. Both perpetrators were sentenced to death (Shahid, 2010).

Home invasion perpetrators typically work as teams of two or three so they can quickly overcome opposition and often pose as maintenance workers or deliverymen who simply ring the doorbell and force their way inside when someone answers. Home invasions provide criminals with more opportunities than burglarizing unoccupied homes.

They can more quickly access cash and other valuables, force occupants to open safes and reveal hidden values through torture or threats of torture, gain keys to family vehicles, and engage in sadistic assaults, rapes, or murders if such are their inclinations.

Figure 14.3 presents highlights from the closest thing we have to nationwide statistics on home invasions. Note that over the time period, about 28% of burglaries occurred while a household member was present (which was not necessarily the criminals' intention). Notice that actual violent victimization (15% simple assault and 3% rape) was not as common as we are often led to assume and that only 12% of the offenders were armed with a firearm (Catalano, 2010).

Burglars and Their Motives

The "typical" burglar is a young male firmly embedded in street culture. Burglars are perhaps a little less daring (intentional home invaders excepted) than robbers since there is less chance of victim contact, injury, and identification for burglary than for robbery, and the penalties and probability of arrest are lower (the national clearance rate for burglary in 2013 was 12.7 versus 28.1 for robbery [FBI, 2013a]). Yet burglars are the most likely of all criminals to be reconvicted (76%) within 2 years of being released from prison (Mawby, 2001). Almost all of the 105 active burglars interviewed by Wright and Decker (1994) admitted numerous other offenses they had

---

- An estimated 3.7 million burglaries occurred each year on average from 2003 to 2007.
- A household member was present in roughly 1 million burglaries and became victims of violent crimes in 266,560 burglaries.
- Simple assault (15%) was the most common form of violence when a resident was home and violence occurred. Robbery (7%) and rape (3%) were less likely to occur when a household member was present and violence occurred.
- Offenders were known to their victims in 65 % of violent burglaries; offenders were strangers in 28%.

- Overall, 61% of offenders were unarmed when violence occurred during a burglary while a resident was present. About 12% of all households violently burglarized while someone was home faced an offender armed with a firearm.
- Households residing in single-family units and higher-density structures of 10 or more units were least likely to be burglarized (8 per 1,000 households) while a household member was present.
- Serious injury accounted for 9% and minor injury accounted for 36% of injuries sustained by household members who were home and experienced violence during a completed burglary.

Figure 14.3

Highlights From Home Invasions Reported From 2003 to 2007

Source: Catalano, 2010

committed. They evidenced pride in their ability to exploit the range of criminal opportunities that came their way, but most considered burglary their preferred crime because it offers the greatest chance of success and reward with the least amount of risk.

Demographically, Wright and Decker's burglars come from poor, run-down, and socially disorganized neighborhoods rife with unemployment. They were poorly educated, unreliable, and resistant to taking orders, and most came from single-parent homes. Consistent with Walter Miller's focal concerns concept addressed in Chapter 4, there was a strong sense of toughness and masculine independence, fate ("I had little choice but to burgle"), excitement (sexual activity, drugs, alcohol), autonomy ("As a burglar I'm my own man"), and smartness (outwitting the law; getting something for nothing).

Wright and Decker (1994) state that burglars constantly need money quickly to finance their lifestyle, but many burglars also reported that they found the psychic rewards of committing burglaries a secondary benefit, describing the act as "an adventure," "a challenge," "fun," "exciting," and "thrilling," which once again points to the psychological payoff emphasized by cultural/anarchic criminologists for committing crimes (p. 58). Given the lack of legitimate skills and general untrustworthiness they see among burglars, Wright and Decker are dubious about the possibility of job creation programs changing burglars into law-abiding citizens because most burglars see burglary as being far more profitable than working. Rengert and Wasilchick (2000) also reject the notion that burglary is a default option of the jobless, claiming that many burglars give up jobs to concentrate on burglary: "Unemployment is not what caused crime. Crime caused the unemployment" (p. 47). Legitimate employment simply would not fit into these people's lives because for them party time is all the time. Almost all of the proceeds of Wright and Decker's burglars were spent on drugs, alcohol, and sex, and legitimate jobs provide neither adequate time nor money to engage in these pleasures to the extent desired.

Burglary and Gender

Although burglary is primarily a male crime, females commit it as well. In 2013, 16.7% of arrestees for burglary were females, which makes female arrests for burglary proportionately greater than for any other Part I index crime except larceny. Because females overwhelmingly commit burglaries in mixed-gender teams, it follows that they share most of the demographic characteristics of their male partners (Mullins & Wright, 2003). Mullins and Wright found that most of the women were initiated into burglary by their boyfriends and some were coerced ("If you love me, you'll do it") against their will. Unlike males, females prefer to work as part of a team and admit they lack the skills and knowledge to go solo.

Mullins and Wright also found that, in common with female robbers, female burglars capitalized on their sexuality to locate potential targets and gain access to homes they and their partners would burglarize later. Once inside a target's home they could assess potential valuables and entry points and perhaps even discover where their victim kept spare keys. They could also elicit other important information such as the target's schedule so that she and her partner could be sure to enter the house when the target is not at home. Female burglars were slightly more likely than their male counterparts to spend portions of their loot on necessities and clothing, but they too spend the greatest proportion on drugs.

Choosing Burglary Targets

Selecting a suitable home for burglary is an obvious concern for burglars. Working from a routine activities framework, Mawby (2001, p. 29) lists the four most important considerations in target selection as target exposure, guardianship, target attractiveness, and proximity.

- Target exposure refers to the visibility and accessibility of the home; i.e., isolation from other homes and easy access via side and back doors shielded by abundant trees and shrubs. Can the premises be seen by neighbors and passersby? Thus some homes are at a much greater risk for burglary than others simply because of location and the physical properties of the premises.

- Guardianship refers to how well the home is protected. Does the home show signs of occupancy such as cars in the driveway, lights on, or music playing? Is there a burglar alarm or dog present, mail in the mailbox, newspapers in the foyer, or a general silence about the place? Households in urban socially disorganized neighborhoods are not only vulnerable because they have numerous motivated offenders looking for opportunities to score but also because the neighborhood has low levels of collective efficacy (see Chapter 6).

- Target attractiveness refers to signs that there should be rich pickings in the house. Previous surveillance may have revealed high-priced cars in the driveway or delivery trucks delivering expensive items.

- Proximity refers to the distance between the target home and the burglar's home and/or to potential sources of loot disposal, such as pawnshops.

All these concerns are relative to the "professionalism" of the burglar. High-level burglars may travel miles to a particularly attractive target after very careful surveillance and planning, but the majority of burglars are low- to midlevel opportunists who engage only in minimal, even spur-of-the-moment planning. For these individuals the "planning" of a burglary is little more than opportunism. Proximity is important both because burglars are most familiar with their own areas and because many of them lack transportation. As one of Wright and Decker's (1994) subjects put it, "I ain't gonna go no further than 10 blocks; that's a ways to be carryin' stuff. . . . Since I'm on foot, I got to keep walkin' back and forth until I get it all" (p. 86). As is the case with murderers, robbers, and rapists, the great majority of low- and midlevel burglars prey on residents in the same neighborhoods in which they also reside. Target exposure and attractiveness is simply making the best of a bad deal for such burglars since the pickings are pretty slim in their neighborhoods.

Guardianship is the most important consideration for low- and midlevel burglars, with many choosing homes occupied by individuals known to them such as neighbors, acquaintances, and even friends (Mawby, 2001; Wright & Decker, 1994). Wright and Decker (1994) report the statement of one of their respondents: "I be knowin' what house I'm going to hit. It could be a friend of mine, I could be over at his house all last week, I know he got a new VCR, we be lookin' at movies. I know what time they work. I know where his wife at or he stay by himself" (p. 70). Typically the only planning such individuals do is to call and see if their intended victims are home. Some of those who victimize friends and acquaintances do report occasional pangs of guilt but justify their actions as the result of a desperate need to get money for another drug fix. Given their willingness to criminally exploit almost anyone, including so-called friends, we can easily see why Wright and Decker (1994) characterized their sample of burglars (who obviously lack the social emotions) as "self-centered individuals without notably strong bonds to other human beings; their allegiance seemed forever to be shifting to suit their own needs" (p. 72).

Disposing of the Loot

The most immediate pressure facing burglars after a successful burglary is to convert the stolen goods into cash. Burglars turn to a variety of sources to dispose of the loot, including the use of fences. A **fence** is a person who regularly buys stolen property and who often has a legitimate business to cover his activities. Only a minority of burglars (the high-level burglar) use a fence because fences prefer to deal only with people they trust. Fences are valued by burglars who use them because it is the fastest way of getting rid of "hot" property and they can be trusted to be discreet. Fencing is a UCR Part II crime that is formally known as receiving stolen property. Anyone knowingly buying or possessing stolen property can be charged with this crime.

Burglars without connections to a professional fence must turn to other outlets. One method is a pawnshop, but this is not a very popular outlet for most burglars because pawnbrokers must ask for identification, take pictures of people selling to them, and possess "hot sheets" of stolen goods. Some burglars who have developed a trusting relationship with certain pawnbrokers are able to sell "off camera," but because pawnbrokers always have the upper hand in negotiations and offer very little for the goods, only 13 of Wright and Decker's sample said that they regularly used them. A more popular outlet was the drug dealer because it can entail a strict "drugs-for-merchandise" deal without involving any middleman. Others regularly sold to relatives, friends, and acquaintances because few people can resist buying merchandise at below even "fire sale" prices. Because of the high value of the property they go after, high-level burglars would never use any of these alternatives to the professional fence.

THEORY IN ACTION: Colton Harris-Moore, the Barefoot Bandit

Colton Harris-Moore was born March 22, 1991, to an alcoholic mother and a drug-abusing father who was imprisoned when Colton was a toddler. He grew up in his mother's house in Camano Island, Washington, located in Puget Sound close to Seattle. His father tried to strangle him when he was 12 years old and then walked out on the family forever. Several neighbors reported his mother to child protective agencies for abuse and neglect during her frequent violent drinking bouts, but pro-

tective services did little to help him. His mother told probation authorities that "something was off" about him because of recurrent problems at school, and he was diagnosed with ADHD, depression, and intermittent explosive disorder (extreme anger, often to the point of uncontrollable rage disproportionate to the situation), although he has never been accused of a violent crime.

By the age of 7, Colton was already breaking into vacation homes to steal food, drink, and blankets and would then disappear into the woods for days to escape his abusive home life. He was first convicted of breaking and entering at 12 and walked away from a 3-year sentence in a halfway house in 2008, when he had just turned 17. He embarked on a crime spree across Washington, Idaho, South Dakota, Nebraska, Iowa, Illinois, and Canada, stealing everything from food and clothes to automobiles, speedboats, and even a light aircraft. He crashed the airplane in a field in Yakima, Washington, leaving behind his vomit. Evidently that did not deter him, because on July 4, 2010, he stole a Cessna from a Bloomington, Indiana, airport and flew to the Bahamas, crashing it once more into a field. He was caught by the Bahaman police and charged with illegal entry and illegally flying a plane, sentenced to 3 months in jail and assessed a $300 fine, and deported to the United States to face numerous charges.

Photo 14.3

The wanted poster of the "Barefoot Bandit." His face was also recognizable on social media where he became a minor celebrity for his crimes.

WANTED
BY THE FBI

INTERSTATE TRANSPORTATION OF A STOLEN AIRCRAFT

COLTON A. HARRIS-MOORE

Captured   Captured   Captured

Aliases: Colton A. Harris, Colton Harris, Colton Moore, Colton A. Moore, Colton Harris-Moore, Colton Koehler

DESCRIPTION

Date of Birth Used:	March 22, 1991	**Hair:**	Brown
Place of Birth:	Washington State	**Eyes:**	Green
Height:	6'5"	**Sex:**	Male
Weight:	205 pounds	**Race:**	White
NCIC:	W277849912	**Nationality:**	American
Occupation:	Unknown		
Scars and Marks:	Harris-Moore has a scar on his left arm from a knife wound.		
Remarks:	Harris-Moore may be in possession of stolen firearms.		

CAUTION

Colton A. Harris-Moore has been charged with interstate transportation of a stolen aircraft, and a federal warrant was issued for his arrest on December 11, 2009, in the United States District Court, Western District of Washington, Seattle, Washington. This stemmed from the theft of an airplane from Bonners Ferry, Idaho, on September 29, 2009. The plane crash-landed after running out of fuel 260 miles away near Snohomish, Washington.

Additionally, Harris-Moore is wanted locally for escaping from a Renton, Washington, group home in April of 2008. He had been ordered to stay there after pleading guilty to

Colton became known as the "Barefoot Bandit" because he allegedly committed some of his crimes barefooted. This baby-faced giant would occasionally leave footprints at the scene of his crimes, and on one occasion he actually drew a series of chalk footprints on the floor of a burgled store with the caption "See ya!" This is the sort of stuff that Facebook and YouTube are made for, and he garnered a fan page on Facebook with over 60,000 members. He has even had T-shirts and coffee mugs emblazoned with his likeness. There is also a film deal based on Colton's life in the works, and at least one book has been published about him (he cannot profit from either of these things since the law forbids criminals to profit from any type of merchandise capitalizing on their exploits). In 2011 he was sentenced in federal court to 6 years imprisonment and received 7 years from a Washington state court. During the latter sentencing, the judge described Colton's childhood as a "mind-numbing absence of hope."

Discussion Questions

1. Although born on an island where the median income is above the national average rather than in a poor disorganized neighborhood, Colton suffered deprivations and became criminal. However, he was never accused of committing a violent crime. Do you think the absence of violent role models in the community accounts for this?

2. Colton's ADHD, depression, and intermittent explosive disorder strongly predict violent crimes, but he was never accused of such crimes. What do you think was the protective factor against violence in Colton's life?

3. What is your opinion about social media making minor celebrities out of criminals?

Sources: Friel, 2012; Raftery, 2011

❖ Motor Vehicle Theft

Motor vehicle (MV) **theft** is simply "the theft or attempted theft of a motor vehicle"; i.e., any motorized land vehicles such as motorcycles, buses, automobiles, trucks, and snowmobiles, although the vast majority of thefts involve automobiles (FBI, 2013a). There were an estimated 721,053 MV thefts in 2013 for a rate of 229.7 per 100,000 population, down 42.8% from the 2003 estimate. The nationwide loss attributable to MV theft was approximately $4.3 billion. Of those arrested for MV theft, 80.1% were males. Whites were 66.1%, blacks 30.8%, and other races the remainder. Table 14.1 presents the top 10 most stolen vehicles in 2012 and the cities where they are most likely to be stolen. The older vehicles are stolen primarily for their parts.

The state of California accounted for eight of the top 10 auto theft hot spots, and the state of Washington the other two. The western region of the country saw an overall increase in MV theft of 10.65% year over year, while the Midwest, Northeast, and southern regions reported reductions of 3.1%, 7.9%, and 2.9%, respectively. California is a hotbed for auto theft because of its proximity to ports and to the Mexican border, which makes it relatively easier and quicker to get rid of stolen cars. The weather in California also keeps popular older models in good shape.

When juveniles commit MV thefts they usually do so strictly for fun (joyriding). Juveniles will spot a "cool" car with the keys in the ignition, steal it, drive it around until it runs out of gas, and then abandon it. Some of the more malicious joyriders will get an additional kick by smashing it up a little first (Rice & Smith, 2002). The high recovery rate of stolen vehicles (about 62%) indicates that most MV thefts are for expressive (to show off, to get some kicks) rather than instrumental reasons (financial gain) (Linden & Chaturvedi, 2005).

Table 14.1

The 10 Most Stolen Vehicles and 10 Cities With the Highest MV Theft Rates, 2012

1. 1994 Honda Accord	1. Modesto, California
2. 1998 Honda Civic	2. Fresno, California
3. 1997 Ford full-size pickup	3. Bakersfield, California
4. 1999 Chevy full-size pickup	4. Stockton–Lodi, California
5. 1991 Toyota Camry	5. Yakima, Washington
6. 2000 Dodge Caravan	6. San Francisco–Oakland–Hayward, California
7. 2004 Dodge full-size pickup	7. San Jose–Sunnyvale–Santa Clara, California
8. 1994 Acura Integra	8. Vallejo–Fairfield, California
9. 1997 Nissan Altima	9. Spokane–Spokane Valley, Washington
10. 1996 Nissan Maxima	10. Redding, California

Source: National Insurance Crime Bureau, 2013

Motor vehicles are also obviously stolen for profit. Most vehicles stolen for profit are taken to so-called chop shops where they are stripped of their parts and accessories. These items are easily sold to auto supply stores, repair shops, and individuals who get faster delivery at a cheaper price than they would from legitimate suppliers. Other stolen vehicles may be shipped abroad, where they are worth more than in the United States. Some professional auto thieves (called jockeys) even steal particularly high-value vehicles "to order" for specific customers.

The common theme that emerges from in-depth interviews of all types of criminals, including those who specialize in stealing automobiles, is the general disdain of legitimate employment and the unending pursuit of their self-indulging lifestyles (alcohol, drugs, sex, being a "sackhound" and one's "own man," and so on). Again, this is a "rational choice" but one that is severely bounded by offenders' knowledge, cognitive and emotional skills, and traits in the context of their developmental experiences in disorganized neighborhoods. The content of a series of interviews with car thieves on probation or parole by Copes (2003) is almost identical to our earlier discussion of robbers and burglars. Here is one example from Copes (2003) illustrating the kind of lifestyles to which the typical criminal is drawn:

> The life is mostly party. I don't think people understand that it's quite like that, but it is. In other words, you don't work. . . . When you get your money, you usually get it real fast and you have a lot of time to spend it. You can sleep all day if you want to and you can go out and get drunk, get high—you don't have to get up the next morning to go to work. (pp. 315–316)

Carjacking: MV Theft With an Attitude

The most serious form of MV theft is **carjacking** (the theft or attempted theft of a motor vehicle from its occupant by force or threat of force). Carjacking thus involves multiple crimes for which the offender may be charged, including robbery, assault, and MV theft. While auto theft is usually handled by local police departments, carjacking was made a federal crime in 1992 following the shooting death of a young Detroit woman who was forced off the road and had her car stolen.

Carjacking is now investigated by the FBI, but reliable statistics for this crime are not available since the FBI does not separate car theft and carjacking statistics, and the UCR's hierarchy rule means that the more serious crimes of robbery and/or aggravated assault will take recording precedence over the crime of auto theft.

Because cars have become increasingly difficult to steal by the "old-fashioned" method of breaking into and hotwiring them, carjacking has become significantly more common. The last government counting of carjacking cases listed an average of 34,000 incidents per

year from 1992 to 2002 (Klaus, 2004). Media accounts of carjacking have sparked many copycat offenders: "Hey, I can steal any vehicle I want without damaging it, I get the car keys, and I can rob the owner too; what a concept!" (McGoey, 2005, p. 1).

Victims report that 93% of carjackers were male, 3% involved a male/female team, and 3% were lone females. By race/ethnicity, 56% were African American, 21% white, and the remainder not identified by race. Approximately 32% of the victims of completed carjackings and 17% of attempted carjackings were injured. Two well-known victims of carjacking are singer-writer Marc Cohn and rapper Cam'ron, both of whom were shot and wounded in botched carjackings in 2005.

Interviews with active carjackers find they are more like street robbers in their demographics, motivations, and lifestyles than they are like professional car thieves. Much of it is motivated by the need to bankroll a hedonistic lifestyle and displays of status. Many times, carjacking is a spur-of-the-moment thing, as described by "Tall": "I was broke. I didn't have enough bus fare. I'm walking down the street, there's a guy sitting in his car. I go ask him for change. He was going for his pocket. I just grabbed him outta his car. Why just take his change when I can take his car and get a little bit more?" (Jacobs, Topoli, & Wright, 2003, p. 683). Carjacking may also be precipitated by the victim driving around "flossing"—that is, engaging in ostentatious displays of wealth and status that others see as an affront ("dissing") to neighborhood carjackers. One carjacker described his attitudes toward flossing as follows: "This motherfucker [was] . . . flossing . . . showboating and shit. He had all that shit in that motherfucking [car]. . . . He flossed his ass off. . . . So we was gonna get the motherfucker" (Jacobs et al., 2003, p. 681).

The sheer thrill, the rush, the dance with danger for its own sake is also a powerful motivator of carjacking: "It's a rush thing when you're pulling someone out of a car. . . . I mean, I feel good." Some carjackers also say they enjoy the opportunity to brutalize and humiliate their victims: "The way people look at you when they're scared and panicky and stuff . . . it is funny just to see them shaking an pissing all over theyself." "You get a kick out of seeing them screaming and hollering . . . especially when they all [acting as though they were] tough" (Jacobs et al., 2003, p. 683).

According to the U.S. Department of State (2002), carjacking is most likely to occur in the following places and situations:

- High-crime areas
- Less-traveled roads (rural areas)
- Intersections where you must stop
- Isolated areas in parking lots

- Residential driveways and gates
- Traffic jams or congested areas

And four of the most common methods of accomplishing carjacking are these:

The bump. The attacker bumps the victim's vehicle from behind. The victim gets out to assess the damage and exchange information. The victim's vehicle is taken.

The good Samaritan. The attacker(s) stage what appears to be an accident. They may simulate an injury. The victim stops to assist, and the vehicle is taken.

The ruse. The vehicle behind the victim flashes its lights or the driver waves to get the victim's attention. The attacker tries to indicate that there is a problem with the victim's car. The victim pulls over and the vehicle is taken.

The trap. Carjackers use surveillance to follow the victim home. When the victim pulls into his or her driveway waiting for the gate or garage door to open, the attacker pulls up behind and blocks the victim's car.

❖ Arson

Arson is "any willful or malicious burning or attempting to burn, with or without intent to defraud, a dwelling house, public building, motor vehicle or aircraft, personal property of another, etc." (FBI, 2013a). Arson was added to the UCR in 1979, and there is still a great deal of difficulty in gathering statistics from reporting agencies because of the problem of deciding whether a "suspicious" fire was arson. Only fires that have been determined by investigators to have been willfully and maliciously set are classified as arsons; fires labeled as suspicious or of unknown origin are excluded from the data presented here from the 2013 UCR.

- In 2012, 15,656 law enforcement agencies provided 1 to 12 months of arson data and reported 52,766 arsons.

- Nearly 47% of all arson offenses involved structures (e.g., residential, storage, public). Mobile property was involved in 23.1% of arsons, and other types of property (such as crops, timber, fences) accounted for 30.1% of reported arsons.

- The average dollar loss per arson was $12,796.

- Arsons of industrial/manufacturing structures resulted in the highest average dollar losses ($42,133).

- Nationwide, there were 18.7 arson offenses for every 100,000 inhabitants. Thirty-eight percent of all persons arrested for arson in 2013 were juveniles. Whites accounted for 73.6% of arson arrests and blacks for 23.6%. Males accounted for 81.8% of arson arrests.

Arson can have a variety of instrumental motivations such as financial gain, revenge, and intimidation or can be due to expressive motivations ("thrills"). For instance, an owner of a failing business may hire a professional arsonist (a torch) to burn down his or her place of business, a person may set fire to the property of another because of some perceived wrong suffered, or labor unionists may set fires in a labor dispute to intimidate management, as was the case with the massive Dupont Hotel fire in Puerto Rico in 1986 that led to the death of 97 people and injured 140 others.

Because juveniles who have reached the age of responsibility comprise only about 7% of the American population but are consistently arrested for over two-thirds of arson cases, expressive motivations are of great interest. Juvenile fire setting may be the result of curiosity and may never be repeated if the juvenile is caught and dealt with, but persistent fire setters are another matter. It is worth noting that fire setting is one of three childhood behaviors psychiatrists have long used to predict adult violence (Vaughn et al., 2010). This is the so-called MacDonald triad of fire setting, cruelty to animals, and enuresis discussed in Chapter 12 regarding serial killers.

A variety of studies have shown that compared with youths in general, persistent fire

Photo 14.6

One way police catch arsonists is to offer cash rewards for tips that will lead them to the perpetrator.

setters have higher levels of other antisocial behaviors such as hostility and impulsiveness and lower levels of sociability and assertiveness. They have also been shown to suffer more psychiatric symptoms and higher levels of depression and to come from families with low levels of affectionate expression and child monitoring (Brett, 2004; Hakkanen, Puolakka, & Santilla, 2004; Santtila, Hakkanen, Alison, & Whyte, 2003). The most ambitious of these studies comes from a nationally representative sample of over 43,000 U.S. residents 18 years of age and over (Vaughn et al., 2010). Vaughn and his colleagues found that the 407 respondents who admitted ever "setting fires on purpose to destroy someone else's property or just to see it burn" differed greatly from the rest of the sample on many variables. For instance, the odds of a fire setter forcing someone to have sex with him or her were over 18 times greater than the odds of a non–fire setter ever doing so, almost 13 times the odds of a non–fire setter for animal cruelty, and almost 20 times the odds of a non–fire setter ever committing a robbery.

❖ Crimes of Guile and Deceit: Embezzlement, Fraud, and Forgery/Counterfeiting

The property crimes we have discussed thus far are "physical" crimes committed largely by "street" people. The UCR lists three Part II property crimes—embezzlement, fraud, and forgery/counterfeiting—committed by a demographically broader range of people than we see committing such crimes as burglary and MV theft. Some criminologists consider these crimes committed by guile and deceit to be white-collar crimes. White-collar workers certainly commit these crimes, but blue- and pink-collar workers as well as the unemployed and welfare recipients commit them also. This is why most criminologists examine them as property crimes rather than white-collar crimes.

Embezzlement is the unlawful misappropriation or misapplication of money or property entrusted to the embezzler's care, custody, or control. Embezzlement is the rarest of property crimes, with only 7,912 cases reported in the UCR in 2013, down 32.7% from 2009. Males (51%) and females (49%) were almost equally likely to be arrested for embezzlement in 2013. Whites constituted 64.6% of arrests and blacks 33.2%.

Most embezzlers do what they do because they have some pressing financial problem or simply because they have access to money and the ability to hide any discrepancies for some time. After being exposed, many insist that they were only "borrowing the money" and that they fully intended to pay it back.

Banks have long been embezzlement targets, but the advent of computers has made the crime both easier to commit and more lucrative. In the first decade of the "computer revolution" in banking, arrests for embezzlement rose 56%, with the average loss to banks per computer embezzlement crime as high as $500,000, compared with the average loss per armed bank robbery of just over $3,000 (Rosoff, Pontell, & Tillman, 1998). A favorite method of stealing via the computer is known as the salami ("slicing off") technique whereby the embezzler will open up "phantom accounts" in his or her name and slice off a few cents from a large number of accounts whose owners are hardly likely to notice. This technique can garner the embezzler large sums of money over a period of time (Rosoff et al., 1998).

The most successful embezzler in U.S. history was Robert L. Vesco, who looted close to $250 million from a variety of mutual funds while he was head of a Swiss-based investment organization. When Vesco learned he was under investigation for criminal fraud in 1972, he fled to Costa Rica, avoiding extradition by "contributing" $300,000 to the Costa Rican president (Coleman, 1986). In 1982 Vesco settled down in Cuba where he set up a criminal empire, becoming a middleman and dealmaker to a variety of dictators and criminal elites in the Central American/Caribbean region. Justice prevailed in the end when the Cubans arrested him in 1995 on suspicion of being a foreign agent and sentenced him to 13 years in prison for "economic crimes against the state" (Associated Press, 1996). Vesco died in prison of lung cancer in 2007.

Fraud is theft by trick; i.e., obtaining the money or property of another through deceptive practices such as false advertising and impersonation. Confidence games and passing bad checks, except forgeries and counterfeiting, are included. The FBI (2013a) reported 117,706 arrests for fraud in 2013, of which 59.4% were males. Whites were 66.5%, blacks 31.6%, and the remainder Asian/Pacific Islander.

Obtaining resources by fraudulent means probably began when the first human being realized he or she could obtain them with less risk and effort by using brains rather than brawn. Examples of fraud include dishonest telemarketing, quack medical cures, phony faith healers, "cowboy" home repair companies, price gouging, and diploma mills promising "accredited" college degrees for a lot of money and little study. Your author was a victim of a minor mail fraud when, at the age of 16, he sent his $1 plus postage away to a con man who promised to teach him "how to kiss like a movie star." When the anxiously awaited envelope arrived, a piece of paper inside merely said, "Pucker up and suck."

Perhaps the most successful U.S. fraudster of the 20th century is penny stock king Robert E. Brennan. The penny stock business is a legitimate one but is almost designed for fraud. Penny stocks are shares/securities in small start-up companies in need of financing that are not listed on a recognized exchange and are sold "over the counter." Penny stock fraudsters such as Brennan purchase large blocks of virtually worthless stocks at as little as one-tenth of a cent per share and aggressively sell them at a higher price. When the stock reaches a predetermined price they dump their own shares (a practice known as "pump and dump"), leaving the hapless investors with worthless paper and the brokers with millions in ill-gotten gains. At his high point, Brennan had over 500,000 customers and a sales force of 1,200 brokers. The primary targets of Brennan's firm were the elderly, who were called by salespersons who were instructed to "never hang up until the customer buys or dies" (Griffin, 2002, p. 254). Brennan was eventually arrested and found guilty of securities fraud and ordered to pay $75 million to settle fraud claims. In 2001 Brennan was found guilty of money laundering and sentenced to prison; he was released in 2011. As of November 2013, Brennan was still fighting off lawsuits stemming from his trail of frauds (Diamond, 2013).

Forgery/counterfeiting is defined by the FBI (2013a) as "the altering, copying, or imitating of something, without authority or right, with the intent to deceive or defraud by passing the copy or thing altered or imitated as that which is original or genuine; or the selling, buying, or possession of an altered, copied, or imitated thing with the intent to deceive or defraud." In other words, it is the creation or alteration of documents to give them the appearance of legality and validity with the intention of gaining some fraudulent benefit from doing so. Strictly speaking, forgery is the "false writing" of a document, and uttering is the passing of that document to another with knowledge of its falsity with intent to defraud. One can thus commit a forgery without uttering (passing the document on) and can utter (passing a forged document on he or she did not forge) without committing a forgery.

Counterfeiting, the creation or altering of currency, is a special case of forgery. In most states forgery and counterfeiting are allied offenses, which is the reason they appear that way in the UCR. Would-be counterfeiters no longer need the engraver's fine craftsmanship to produce quality plates for professional counterfeiting. Printing currency with copiers available today has become an amateur's do-it-yourself enterprise (just feed in a $20 bill and press the button). Such bills are far more difficult to pass today due to new technology embedded in genuine currency and new detection technology in stores. There were 45,048 arrests for forgery/counterfeiting in 2012, of which 62.6% were males. By race, 65.6% were white and 32.7% black (FBI, 2013a).

The prince of all modern forgers is Frank Abagnale, whose first victim was his own father whom he conned out of $3,400. Abagnale netted millions of dollars in many audacious cons and scams, impersonating a security guard, airline pilot, physician, and lawyer, among many other disguises. He flew on over 250 flights to many countries during his stint as a pilot (never actually taking off or landing a plane) and survived for almost a year as the chief resident pediatrician in a Georgia hospital by passing on all complicated cases to interns. Abagnale was caught in France (he swindled the French too), served 6 months in jail, and was extradited to Sweden to face check forging charges there. When Frank heard that the next extradition request was from Italy (this guy really got around), he dropped objections to extradition to the United States and was duly sent home. Abagnale was sentenced to 12 years in a federal penitentiary but served only 5 years upon agreeing to use his expertise to help the FBI investigate similar forgery cases. Frank is now CEO of his own security consulting firm (Abagnale & Associates) used by many financial companies to protect themselves against forgery and counterfeiting (Abagnale & Redding, 2000).

Summary

- Property crimes constitute the vast majority of crimes committed in the United States. Larceny-theft is the most common of these crimes and is divided into misdemeanor and felony categories depending on the value of the stolen property. Shoplifting has received the most attention of all the subcategories of larceny-theft, largely because some people supposedly suffer from a psychiatric condition known as kleptomania.

- Burglary is a more serious property offense because it violates victims' homes and could lead to personal confrontation. Studies of burglars find them to be motivated by the need to get quick and easy cash to finance a hedonistic lifestyle. They are typically members of the lower class with the focal concerns of that class, such as seeking excitement and autonomy. Female burglars typically work as auxiliaries to male partners and they too spend much of their money on alcohol and drugs.

- Home invasion is the most horrifying form of burglary. About one-quarter of burglaries take place when household residents are present, and in about one-quarter of those cases the residents are violently victimized.

- Motor vehicle theft is a serious larceny often committed by joyriding juveniles, although many vehicles are stolen for profit. Carjacking is a relatively new method of stealing cars made "necessary" by the improvement of antitheft devices. There is a high degree of injury to the victim inherent in this crime, which is essentially a robbery.

- Arson is a particularly dangerous property crime because it can lead to deaths. Juveniles commit the majority of arsons, suggesting that it serves some expressive function for them. Compulsive fire setting signals some very serious underlying psychological problems.

- Crimes of guile and deceit included in the UCR property crime classification are embezzlement, fraud, and counterfeiting/forgery. There are only small gender differences in the commission of these crimes.

Exercises and Discussion Questions

1. Survey several friends or classmates and ask them if they have ever shoplifted and how they felt afterward. What were their motivations? Were some guilty, some proud about getting away with it? Did some get a thrill out of it?

2. According to the burglary researchers discussed in this chapter, would it be wise policy to implement job training and job creation programs for convicted burglars?

3. Go to www.sosfires.com and view the various youth fire-setting intervention programs listed there. Click on two or three of the research reports listed and report on what you have learned about juvenile fire setting and its treatment.

Useful Websites

FTCs identity theft site. www.ftc.gov/bcp/edu/microsites/idtheft.

InterFire. www.interfire.org.

Motor vehicle theft statistics. www.rmiia.org/auto/auto_theft/statistics.asp.

Property crime statistics. www.fbi.gov/about-us/cjis/ucr/crime-in-the-u.s/2010/crime-in-the-u.s.-2010/property-crime.

Property crime trends. www.cna.org/sites/default/files/research/Crime_Trends.pdf.

Chapter Terms

Arson	Embezzlement	Home invasion
Burglary	Fence	Larceny-theft
Carjacking	Forgery	Motor vehicle theft
Counterfeiting	Fraud	

CHAPTER 15

Public Order Crime

Joe Alladyce and Jared Livingston were both literally born drunk. Their mothers were heavy drinkers who continued to drink during their pregnancies, and if mothers drink, so do their fetuses. If the fetus survives this assault it is highly likely to be born with a condition called fetal alcohol syndrome (FAS), symptoms of which include neurological abnormalities, intellectual impairment, behavioral problems, and various bodily and facial imperfections. Joe and Jared were made wards of the court and sent to a special institution where staff did their best to educate and care for them. The boys formed a bond with each other and soothed each other's feelings of anger and depression. When they were both 17 they walked away from the home and made their way to the nearest town where they robbed a liquor store and went on a drinking binge. Walking down the street in a stupor, they came across Mr. and Mrs. Whelan and little 7-year-old Angela walking toward them. Angela made a remark about their behavior and appearance and started to giggle. Enraged, Jared smashed Angela over the head with the beer bottle he was carrying and Joe did the same thing to her father when he tackled Jared. Both boys mercilessly beat and kicked all three family members to death.

This tragic story illustrates the insidious nature of alcohol abuse. Joe and Jared didn't ask to be born with incurable disabilities, and according to many FAS experts could no more be held responsible for their actions than a blind person is for not recognizing faces. They have brains incapable of appreciating right from wrong and of linking cause and effect. Their mothers not only ruined their own lives but also the lives of their sons and the lives of surviving members of the Whelan family. There is a huge cost to society caused by what has been aptly named "the beast in the bottle" and by other substances that tear the rationality from our brains and replace it with all manner of monsters.

LEARNING OBJECTIVES

- Understand the concept of public order crime as different from other crime
- Be able to describe the link between alcohol abuse and criminal behavior in terms of alcohol's pharmacological properties and the context in which it is drunk
- Be able to describe the various general types of illicit substances
- Understand the link between drugs and violence according to Goldstein's model
- Be able to explain the harm reduction principle
- Know the issues related to legalizing prostitution

❖ What Are Public Order Crimes?

Public order crimes are a smorgasbord of offenses, some of which have been variously called vice offenses, consensual offenses, victimless crimes, or even nuisance offenses. Some public order crimes are considered very serious (the sale of drugs), and some are dismissed with a shrug of the shoulders or a look of disgust (drunken and disorderly behavior). Public order crimes are of the "moving target" type—legal in some places and at some times (prostitution in Nevada, drugs in Amsterdam, gambling in London) and illegal at other times and in other places. One school of thought maintains that allowing or ignoring public order offenses can only lead to more serious crimes because it signals that nobody cares for the community (Wilson & Kelling, 1982). This so-called broken-windows approach to crime control has had a major impact on policing and may be considered an approach akin to Sampson, Raudenbush, and Earls's (1997) collective efficacy concept discussed in Chapter 6.

All public order offenses cause some social harm, but whether or not the harm is great enough to warrant siphoning off criminal justice resources that could be applied to more serious crimes is a matter of debate. For instance, the debate about whether the use of mind-altering drugs should be legalized is not about the effects of these drugs—everyone realizes they are harmful—but rather about whether legalization or decriminalization would be less harmful to society overall than continuing the current "war on drugs."

The notion that public order offenses are "victimless" has been rejected by most criminologists today because there are always secondary victims (e.g., family members, friends) who may be profoundly harmed by the actions of the offender. The man who brings a sexually transmitted disease back to his wife after visiting a prostitute, the man who gambles away the family's money, and the woman who takes illicit drugs during her pregnancy are all causing great harm to many other people. The "victimless" act of drinking alcohol to excess by the mothers of Joe and Jared in this chapter's vignette started a horrible chain of events that took three lives and ruined many others. These two mothers caused more social, financial, and emotional harm than any two burglars or thieves probably ever did. Rather than victimless, most public order crimes are better conceived of as consensual *mala prohibita* acts that always have the potential for causing harm to others besides the person engaging in them.

❖ Alcohol and Crime

Humans have a love of ingesting substances that alter their moods. We swallow, sniff, inhale, and inject with a relish that suggests sobriety is a difficult state for us to tolerate. Alcohol has always been humans' favorite way of temporarily escaping reality. We drink this powerful drug to loosen our tongues, be sociable, liven up our parties, feel good, sedate ourselves, and anesthetize the pains of life. Benjamin Franklin once supposedly opined that "beer is proof positive that God loves us and wants us to be happy" (E. Burns, 2004, p. 2). Many centuries before, the ancient Sumerians and Egyptians were singing the praises of beer, wine, and the various spirits but also warning about the consequences of excessive use.

Of all the substances used to alter mood and consciousness, alcohol is the most directly linked to crime, especially violent crime (Martin, 2001). According to the U.K. Institute of Alcohol Studies (2013), in 2012, 47% of all violent incidents in England and Wales were committed by offenders under the influence of alcohol. An Australian study (Payne & Gaffney, 2012) reported that 33.3% of violent crimes were attributed to alcohol and only 12.4% to illicit drugs. It has been estimated that at least 84% of American prison inmates (National Center on Addiction and Substance Abuse, 2010) and 60% of British inmates (McMurren, 2003) are alcohol and/or drug addicted. The World Health Organization (2012) reported that alcohol deaths reached 2.5 million people worldwide in 2009, with only malnutrition and unsafe sex killing more.

Police officers spend more than half of their time on alcohol-related offenses, and it is estimated are that one-third of all arrests (excluding drunk driving) in the United States are for alcohol-related offenses (Mustaine & Tewksbury, 2004). About 75% of robberies and 80% of homicides involve a drunken offender and/or victim (Martin, 2001). The U.S. Department of Health and Human Services (2009) estimates the cost of alcohol abuse to society to be a staggering $185 billion.

Effects of Alcohol and Context on Behavior

The effects of alcohol (or any other drug) on behavior are a function of the interactions of the pharmacological properties of the substance, the individual's physiology and personality, and the social and cultural context in which the substance is ingested. Pharmacologically, alcohol is a depressant drug that inhibits the functioning of the higher brain centers. As more and more alcohol is drunk, behavior becomes less and less inhibited as the rational cortex surrenders its control of the drinker's demeanor to the more primitive limbic system (the "emotional" brain). What's going on in the drinker's brain to cause this? Although alcohol is a brain-numbing depressant, at low dosages it is actually a stimulant because it raises dopamine levels (Ruden, 1997). Alcohol also reduces inhibition by affecting a neurotransmitter called GABA, which is a major inhibitor of internal stimuli such as fear, anxiety, and stress (Buck & Finn, 2000). Additionally, alcohol decreases serotonin, reduces impulse control, and increases the likelihood of aggression (Walsh & Bolen, 2012). Alcohol's direct effects on the brain can thus help us to reinvent ourselves as "superior" beings: the fearful to become more courageous, the self-effacing to become more confident, and the timid to become more assertive.

As powerful a behavioral disinhibitor as alcohol is, it is not sufficient by itself to change anyone's behavior in the direction of serious law violations. Most people don't become violent or commit criminal offenses when drinking or even when they are "over the limit." Alcohol releases behaviors we normally keep under control but may be prone to exhibit when control is weakened. Hence, we may become silly, amorous, melancholic, maudlin, and even aggressive and violent when our underlying propensity to be these things is facilitated by alcohol and the social context in which it is drunk. In some social contexts drinking may lead to violence but not in others. Many violent incidents between strangers take place in or around drinking establishments in which both victims and perpetrators had been drinking (Richardson & Budd, 2003).

Groups of young men assembled in bars are recipes for trouble. Experimental research has shown that drinking increases fantasies of power and domination and that men who are the heaviest drinkers were the most likely to have them (Martin, 2001). With loosened inhibitions, such fantasies might lead to males flirting with the girlfriends of males from another group and then not backing off when challenged or interpreting some comment or gesture as threatening. If a male values his reputation as a macho tough guy, aggressive responses are more likely when his friends are present and he is looking to validate his reputation. There's an old saying among heavy drinkers: "It's not how many beers you drink, it's who you drink them with."

Cultural factors should also be considered when evaluating the alcohol/crime relationship. Two of the major cultural factors influencing the relationship between alcohol consumption and criminal behavior are "defining a drinking occasion as a 'time-out' period in which controls are loosened from usual behavior and a willingness to hold a person less responsible for their actions when drinking than when sober by attributing the blame to alcohol" (Martin, 2001, p. 146). If one's culture defines alcohol as a good-time elixir, the unfortunate (but often subjectively experienced as enjoyable) by-product of which is a loss of control over behavioral inhibitions, then one is granted cultural "permission" to do just that.

Binge Drinkers

The Substance Abuse and Mental Health Services Administration (SAMHSA; 2013) states that binge drinking is the most common pattern of alcohol abuse and defines it as drinking five or more drinks within 2 hours. This pattern of drinking brings a person's blood alcohol content (BAC) to 0.08 grams per deciliter of blood or above. **Binge drinkers** are typically college-age single young adults who drink solely to get drunk. SAMHSA's nationwide survey of 67,500 individuals found that 39.5% admitted binge drinking during the 30-day period prior to the survey. A study found that 40% of American college students reported at least one episode of binge drinking in the previous 2 weeks (Johnson, O'Malley, & Bachman, 2000), and a Russian nationwide study found that almost one-third of the men admitted binge drinking at least once a month (Pridemore, 2004). The cultures of both American college students and Russians in general have a high level of tolerance for heavy drinking. Richardson and Budd's (2003) British study found that 39% of binge drinkers admitted a criminal offense in the previous 12 months whereas 14% of other regular drinkers and 8% of occasional or nondrinkers did. The corresponding percentages for a violent crime were 17%, 4%, and 2%. A survey of 180,455 male and 3,664 female arrestees in major U.S. cities found that 47.9% of the males and 34.9% of the females reported engaging in binge drinking on at least one occasion in the 30 days preceding their arrest (Zhang, 2004).

But does heavy drinking plus social context *per se* cause increased antisocial behavior? It could well be that antisocial individuals are more prone to drink heavily and to be attracted to social contexts in which violence is most likely to occur. In this view, antisocial propensities are simply exacerbated under the influence of alcohol and social setting (Walsh & Bolen, 2012). Heavy alcohol intake certainly has a greater disinhibiting effect on behavior than heavy tea intake; so alcohol-induced disinhibition may be considered a cause of antisocial acts. Likewise, violence and other antisocial behaviors are assuredly more likely to occur in a biker bar than in a tearoom, and thus social context may be considered a cause as well. But a stricter standard of causation may want to consider that perhaps the substance and the setting are secondary in causal importance to the traits of individuals drinking the beverage of their choice in the settings of their choice.

Photo 15.1

Many alcohol researchers compare societies in which drinking alcohol is considered normal behavior from an early age with American society, in which youth alcohol drinking is illegal. In the United States, many teens drink anyway, and binge drinking rather than moderate use is a potential problem.

Drunk Driving

Traffic fatalities caused by drivers under the influence of alcohol (or some other drug) are another evil caused by the "beast in the bottle." In state statutes this crime is typically referred to as driving under the influence (DUI) or driving while intoxicated (DWI). According to the Insurance Information Institute (2009), 11,773 people died in alcohol-impaired crashes in 2008, down 9.7% from 13,041 in 2007. In 2008 there were 1,483,396 DUI arrests, 80.5% of whom were males and 84% white (FBI, 2009a).

Many people used to consider deaths due to drunk drivers as "accidents" rather than "crimes," and penalties were relatively light. Attitudes began to change with the founding of MADD (Mothers Against Drunk Driving) in 1980, an organization that has effectively lobbied for legislation nationwide to increase the legal drinking age and for stricter penalties for drunk drivers. MADD also lobbied to lower the blood alcohol count (BAC) level that defines intoxication from 0.10 to 0.08 grams per deciliter of blood. Every state in the union has now enacted these measures. As we see in Figure 15.1 from the National Highway Traffic Safety Commission (NHTSC; 2009), these combined measures reduced alcohol-related traffic fatalities by 57% from 1982 to 2008.

The 2009 NHTSC study of DUI offenders found that the average BAC at arrest was 0.24, or three times the legal limit, and that among drivers involved in fatal crashes, those who were above the legal limit were more than 4 times more likely to have a previous DUI than sober drivers. The average time for DUI offenders in jail was 11 months, and for offenders sent to prison it was 49 months (Maruschak, 1999). The significant drop in alcohol-related traffic fatalities following the lowered-tolerance, increased-penalties stance in criminal justice shows that general deterrence works but again, primarily only for those with a lot to lose.

Alcoholism: Type I and Type II

Alcoholism is a chronic disease condition marked by progressive incapacity to control alcohol consumption despite psychological, social, or physiological disruptions (Giancola, Josephs, Parrott, & Duke, 2010). It is a state of altered cellular physiology caused by chronic consumption of alcohol that manifests itself in physical disturbances (withdrawal symptoms) when alcohol use is suspended. While most alcoholics do not get into serious trouble with the law, numerous theorists have hypothesized that alcoholism and criminality are linked because they share a

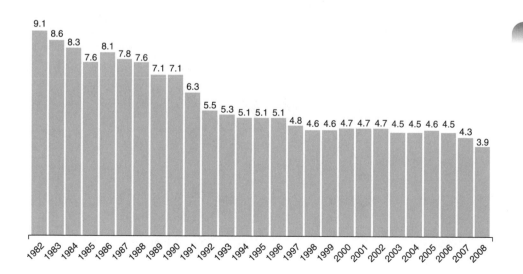

Figure 15.1

Alcohol-Related
Fatalities
per 100,000
Population,
1982–2008

Source: NHTSC, 2009

common cause and that it is probably dysregulation of the behavioral activating system (BAS—see Chapter 10) that leads to a "craving brain" (Gove & Wilmoth, 2003). Alcoholics have a saying that one drink is one too many and a hundred drinks are not enough. This seemingly contradictory statement tells us that a single drink activates the brain's pleasure centers and leads to such a craving for more that a hundred drinks will not satiate. Thus both alcoholics and serious criminals are "reward dominant" in their neurophysiology. Figure 15.2 shows the alcohol reward system. Alcohol stimulates the release of the "pleasure neurotransmitter" dopamine, which is made in the ventral tegmental area and then sent to the nucleus accumbens, the brain's major "pleasure center" (Oscar-Berman et al., 2009).

Although only about 14% of frequent alcohol users descend into the hell of addiction (Bierut et al., 2010), the abuse of alcohol by nonalcoholics constitutes the majority of criminal justice's problems because there are a lot more of them. This is because the acute effects of alcohol on violent behavior are much greater than the chronic effects; i.e., the immediate effects of impaired judgment experienced by anyone who drinks too much rather than the long-term effects on the physiology of alcoholics (Giancola et al., 2010). Nevertheless, it is a rare chronic offender who is not also a chronic abuser of alcohol and other kinds of mind-altering substances.

Estimates of the heritability of alcoholism range from 0.49 to 0.64 (Bevilacqua & Goldman, 2009). There are two types of alcoholics who can be likened to Moffitt's adolescent-limited and life course–persistent offenders discussed in Chapter 11: Type I and Type II. Crabbe (2002) describes the two types in this way: "**Type I alcoholism** is characterized by mild abuse, minimal criminality, and passive-dependent personality variables, whereas **Type II alcoholism** is characterized by early onset, violence, and criminality, and is largely limited to males" (p. 449). Type II alcoholics start drinking (and using other drugs) at a very early age and rapidly become addicted and have many character disorders and behavioral problems that *precede* their alcoholism. Type I alcoholics start drinking later in life than Type II's and progress to alcoholism slowly. Type I's typically have families and careers, and if they have character defects, these are induced by their alcohol problem and are not permanent (DuPont, 1997).

Heritability estimates for Type II alcoholism are about 0.90 and about 0.40 for Type I's (McGue, 1999), indicating that environmental factors are more important to understanding

Figure 15.2

The Alcohol Reward System and Other Areas Affected by Alcohol

Source: National Institute on Drug Abuse, 1996

ALCOHOL

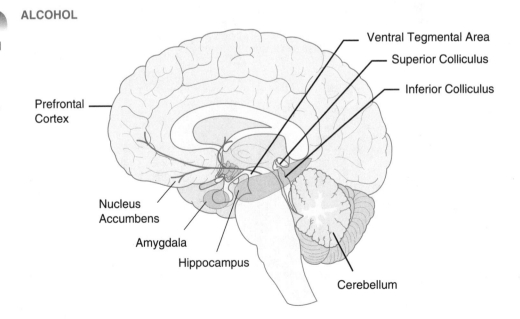

Type I alcoholism than Type II alcoholism (Crabbe, 2002). The genetic influence on alcoholism reflects genetic regulation of neurotransmitters such as GABA, dopamine, and serotonin (Buck & Finn, 2000) and/or regulation by enzymes such as the MAOA enzyme discussed in Chapter 10 (Demir et al., 2002).

THEORY IN ACTION: What "Happy Drunks" Cost Society: The Case of Henry Earl

We in the United States make celebrities out of some pretty weird folks doing some pretty bizarre things, but very little is more strange than the story of Henry Earl, the most famous drunk in the United States and perhaps in the world. Henry's claim to fame is his record for being the most arrested man in the United States. This man from Lexington, Kentucky, became famous in 2008 when it was revealed that Henry had been arrested for the 1,000th time. When the news was released it piqued the curiosity of the Facebook generation and TV clips of the story and mug shots were posted on YouTube. Henry now has his own fan club and webpage complete with RSS feed to current status, and people have been known to actually travel to Lexington from across the country to try to catch Henry during his few periods of freedom from lockup to buy him a drink.

Henry was born on October 24, 1949, in Lexington, Kentucky. His first recorded arrest was in 1970 for carrying a concealed weapon (CCW). The rest of that decade was relatively quiet by Henry's standard, being arrested "only" a total of 34 times. He may have been arrested elsewhere, but the only available source of his arrest record comes from the Lexington–Fayette County Jail website. This website, incidentally, has been shut down due to overuse by people (like this author) seeking updated information about Henry's arrests.

Despite alcohol's reputation as an instigator of violence, except for the 1970 CCW charge, Henry has never been arrested for anything other than drunk and disorderly or trespassing violations, and he typically leaves a bar when asked to without much fuss. Interviews with bartenders and tavern customers find that local college students take pleasure in feeding Henry's addiction by continually responding to his begging for drinks (apparently, he never begged for money) by allowing him to finish theirs in exchange for a "photo op" with the world's most famous drunk. By 2008, when the news of Henry's 1,000th arrest hit the airwaves, it was calculated that he

Photo 15.2

Mug shots from some of Henry Earl's numerous arrests.

had actually passed that milestone in 2002 and that by 2008, he had been arrested 1,333 times.

In 2009, Henry spent 5 months in an alcohol rehabilitation program by order of the court. This was the longest time Henry had gone without drinking since he was first introduced to the "beast in the bottle," but he was busted for public drunkenness before finishing the program. Henry was only a month away from completing the program and voiced his great disappointment at not being able to receive his certificate of completion. Henry's latest arrest at the time of writing was on October 4, 2013.

People like Henry are a tremendous burden on the taxpayer. According to Pierrette Shields (2012), a basic arrest for even a minor crime can cost $1,000, and an inmate who does not require mental or physical health medication and/or assistance costs the taxpayer $67 per day. Even if we stopped counting with Henry's 1,333rd

(Continued)

arrest in 2008, he has cost taxpayers $1,333,000 just in arrests. If each one of those arrests resulted in only a 10-day jail sentence, we reach a grand total of $13,330,000. This is a minimal estimate of the costs of just one man! Alcoholism is indeed expensive.

Discussion Questions

1. Given the huge financial burden posed by people such as Henry, is it wise to continually arrest him for nonviolent or public intoxication offenses? What might be a better alternative?

2. Based on what you know about Henry, would you classify him as a Type I or Type II alcoholic?

3. Why do you think people make celebrities out of people as dysfunctional and antisocial as Henry?

Sources: Monkey Gumbo, n.d.; Shields, 2012; Smoking Gun, 2008

❖ Illegal Drugs and Crime

Extent of the Illicit Drug Problem

Illicit drugs join with legal drug alcohol to become the diabolical duo of crime. Alcohol use is a legal and socially acceptable way of drugging oneself, but substances discussed in this section are not. This was not always the case, for many of these drugs have been legitimately used in religious rituals, for medical treatment, and for recreational use around the world and across the ages. Up until 1914, drugs now considered illicit were legally and widely used in the United States for medicinal purposes. Not fully aware of the dangers of addiction, many substances were openly advertised and sold as cures for all sorts of aliments and for refreshing "pick-me-ups." The most famous of these was Coca-Cola, which was made with the coca leaf (used to process cocaine) and kola nuts (hence the name) until 1903. Many patented medicines such as Cocaine Toothache Drops and Mother Barley's Quieting Syrup, used to "soothe" infants and young children, contained cocaine, morphine, or heroin.

Attitudes toward drug usage in America gradually began to changes as awareness of the addictive powers of many of these substances grew. As noted in Chapter 1, the **Harrison Narcotic Act** of 1914 was the benchmark for changing America's concept of drugs and their use. According to Richard Davenport-Hines (2002), "By the early 1920s, the conception of the addict changed from that of a middle-class victim accidentally addicted through medicinal use, to that of a criminal deviant using narcotics (or stimulants) for pleasure" (p. 14). The Harrison Act did initially reduce the number of addicts (estimated at around 200,000 in the early 1900s), but it also spawned criminal black market operations (as did the Volstead Act prohibiting the production and sale of alcohol in 1919) and ultimately many more addicts (Casey, 1978).

Figure 15.3 shows percentages of individuals participating in the 2013 National Household Survey on Drug Abuse (NHSDA) who admitted the use of any illicit drug during the month prior to being interviewed. As with delinquency and crime, drug use peaks in the 18-to-20 age category and then drops precipitously. The use of illicit drugs by most adolescents probably reflects experimentation (adolescent-limited use) while their continued use in adulthood (life course–persistent use) reflects a far more serious antisocial situation.

Drug Addiction

All addictive drugs mimic the actions of normal brain chemistry by inhibiting or slowing down the release of neurotransmitters, stimulating or speeding up their release, preventing their reuptake after they have stimulated neighboring neurons, or by breaking transmitters down more quickly. As we saw earlier (Figure 15.2), the brain contains evolved pleasure centers by which "Mother Nature" rewards us when we do things that lead to survival and reproductive success. That is, we are neurologically rewarded with a shot of dopamine to the nucleus accumbens when we eat, drink, have sex, reach safe havens, and enjoy the good company of others. Drugs produce more powerful, rapid, and predictable effects on our pleasure centers than are naturally obtained by the action of neurotransmitters in response to non–drug-induced pleasurable experiences. The euphoria obtained from unnatural pleasures hijacks the brain because they involve much greater dopamine signaling at the synapse, thus commandeering brain circuits that control responses to natural rewards. As Hyman (2007) explains, "Unlike natural rewards, addictive drugs always signal 'better than expected.' Neural circuits 'over-learn' on an excessive and grossly distorted dopamine signal" (p. 10).

People turn to illegal drugs for many of the same reasons they turn to alcohol—to be "with it," to be sociable, to conform, to induce pleasure, to escape stress, or to escape chronic boredom. Among those who experiment with drugs, some are genetically predisposed to develop addiction to their substance(s) of choice just as others are "sitting ducks" for alcoholism (Robinson & Berridge, 2003).

The Drug Enforcement Administration (DEA) defines **drug addiction** as "compulsive drug-seeking behavior where acquiring and using a drug becomes the most important activity in the user's life" and estimates that 5 million Americans suffer from drug addiction (2003, p. 13). Physical dependence on a drug refers to changes to the body that occur after repeated use of it and necessitate its continued administration to avoid withdrawal symptoms. **Physical dependence** is not synonymous with addiction as commonly thought, but **psychological dependence** (the deep craving for the drug and the feeling that one cannot function without it) is synonymous with addiction.

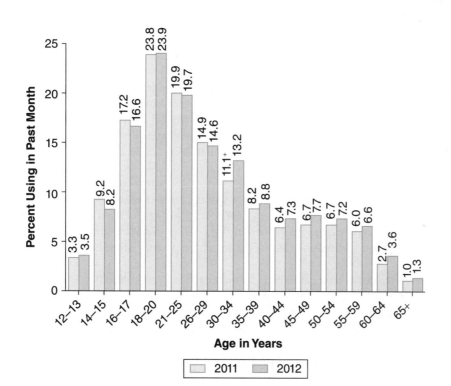

Figure 15.3

Illicit Drug Use in Past Month by Age, 2011–2012

Source: Substance Abuse and Mental Health Services Association, 2013

Regardless of the type of drug, addiction is not an invariable outcome of drug usage any more than alcoholism is an invariable outcome of drinking. The DEA (2003) estimates that about 55% of today's youth have used some form of illegal substance, but few descend into the hell of addiction (Kleber, 2003). Genetic differences are undoubtedly related to a person's chances of becoming addicted given identical levels of usage and an identical period of time using. The median heritability estimates for addiction to some of the drugs we discuss are provided here (Belivacqua & Goldman, 2009). Recall that heritability is the percentage of variance in a trait in a population that is attributable to genetics.

Hallucinogens: $h^2 = 0.39$

Cannabis: $h^2 = 0.42$

Opiates: $h^2 = 0.65$

Cocaine: $h^2 = 0.72$

Drug Classification

Drug classification schemes are determined by the purpose for which the classification is being made. We discuss the most popularly abused illegal drugs according to their pharmacological effects and their DEA schedule classification. This classification scheme divides chemical substances into five categories, or schedules. Schedule I substances are those that have high abuse liability and no medical use in the United States, such as heroin, peyote, and LSD. Schedule II substances have equally high (or higher) abuse liability but have some approved medical usage, such as opium or cocaine. Schedule III and IV substances have moderate to moderately high abuse liability and are legally available with prescription, and Schedule V substances can be purchased without prescription.

The Opiates

The opiates, or narcotics, are drugs that reduce the sense of pain, tension, and anxiety and produce a drowsy sense of euphoria. All drugs in this category have the potential for physical and psychological dependence, and all produce **tolerance** (the tendency to require larger and larger doses to produce the same effects after the body adjusts to lower dosages) and induce **withdrawal** symptoms (adverse physical reactions that occur when the body is deprived of the drug). Heroin is a Schedule I substance and is a derivative of morphine that wafts the individual into a euphoric state of sweet indifference, a state heroin users describe as the "floats." Intravenous injection of heroin ("mainlining") used to be the most popular method of administering the drug among hard-core addicts. This produces the famous "rush," a warm skin flush and orgasmic feeling, after which the user drifts off into a carefree world for anywhere up to 12 hours. Because of the increasing awareness of the dangers (e.g., AIDS, hepatitis) of sharing contaminated "works," many heroin addicts now snort or smoke heroin. It is possible to achieve about the same effect as mainlining using these methods because of the increased potency of the heroin available today (DEA, 2003).

The brain produces its own pain-killing substances called endorphins (for "endogenous morphinelike substances") that do for us naturally, if far less effectively, what heroin does artificially. The presence of these naturally occurring analgesics provides clues to the addictive process. Frequent use of heroin negatively affects the body's natural capacity to produce and release endorphins in response to the pains and stresses of life. If the brain has opiates running around from the outside, it is fooled into stopping the production of its own natural endorphins, and the addict may then be totally reliant on heroin to dull the pains of life (Alexander & Pratsinak, 2002).

The Stimulants

The stimulants have effects opposite to those of the narcotics. Cocaine is a Schedule II substance because it has legitimate medical uses as a local anesthetic. Cocaine works by blocking the reuptake of excitatory neurotransmitters at the synaptic terminals (see Figure 10.2), thus keeping the brain in an extended state of arousal. Cocaine is taken up by the brain quickly, producing the familiar euphoric rush, and when taken intravenously, the rush or "flash" takes only about 15 seconds.

Photo 15.3

This man is damaging his brain and all those who care about him.

Smokeable cocaine (crack) produces intense craving and may be the most addictive substance known. Crack is manufactured by combining cocaine, baking soda, and water, heating the mixture, which is then allowed to cool, and then breaking it into tiny pieces or "rocks." Crack produces the same high as powdered cocaine, if only for 5 to 10 minutes, but its relatively low price makes it attractive to those who formerly resisted the more expensive powder. Crack prices range from $5 to $25 for a rock compared with about $200 for a gram (about the amount of artificial sweetener contained in the typical Equal packet) of powdered cocaine.

Crack is a real shortcut to the nucleus accumbens, arriving there within seconds of being inhaled. Cocaine works by blocking the reuptake of dopamine into the sending synaptic knob, thus keeping the "joy juice" active in the synaptic gap for longer periods of time. Neurotransmitters not pumped back into the sending synaptic knob eventually are broken apart and cleared away by enzymes that balance their production and usage. Because cocaine blocks reuptake channels, enzymes eventually destroy so much dopamine trapped between the sending and receiving synaptic knobs that the brain's supply is depleted and the addict is unable to experience any kind of pleasure without cocaine (Walsh, Johnson, & Bolen, 2012).

Arrests for crack cocaine have dropped dramatically since 1990 (ADAM, 2013). This decrease may be due to a number of factors, such as severe penalties for sale and possession of crack and the danger from others trafficking in the market. It may also be that many individuals have decided not to try crack in the first place after seeing its consequences. Many inner-city youths have apparently determined that crack is not "cool" anymore, and this emerging norm has been attributed to the "younger brother syndrome." This syndrome essentially means that these youths have seen relatives and friends serving long prison sentences, killed or permanently disabled in drug deals gone wrong, or sick and dying because of their addiction (Witkin, 1998).

Methamphetamine is the strongest form of a class of stimulants called amphetamines, all of which accentuate and accelerate the visual, tactile, auditory, and olfactory impulses. The amphetamines are chemically similar to epinephrine (adrenaline), the hormone that provides the body with its "fight or flight" energy (Alexander & Pratsinak, 2002). They all act on the brain by stimulating the release of norepinepherine and dopamine and preventing their reuptake. While the stimulant effects of methamphetamine are slower in coming than are cocaine's, they last longer. Methamphetamine is the poor man's cocaine, enabling users to go on a "run" of several days at a cost of only a few hundred dollars compared with a few thousand for a cocaine run of similar duration. Chronic abuse of methamphetamine may produce schizophrenic-like effects (paranoia, auditory and visual hallucinations, picking at one's skin, and a preoccupation with one's inner thoughts) that can last for months or years after withdrawal from the drug (DEA, 2003).

Hallucinogens

Hallucinogens are mind-altering drugs such as lysergic acid diethylamide (LSD) and peyote and classified by the DEA as Schedule I. LSD is a clear, odorless, and tasteless liquid sold soaked in sugar cubes or on saturated blotting paper (microdots). LSD is produced from acid found on fungus that grows on grains such as rye called ergot. It is a drug primarily favored by inward-looking people who seek to increase awareness rather than to escape it. It causes hyperawareness and greatly enhances appreciation of stimuli in the user's perceptual field by disabling the brain's filtering system by inhibiting serotonin production, thus releasing the user's perceptual brakes (Alexander & Pratsinak, 2002). This flood of stimuli sometimes mimics psychotic-like behavior. LSD does not cause physical dependence, but psychological dependence may occur, and the drug rapidly produces tolerance.

Some classification systems include marijuana (Spanish for "Mary Jane") among the hallucinogens while others classify it separately under cannabis, which also includes hashish.

Marijuana is by far the most widely used illicit drug in the United States. Despite its classification as a Schedule I substance, it is only mildly hallucinogenic and moderately addictive and is available in some states for the treatment of glaucoma and for ameliorating the effects of chemotherapy. Today's marijuana is much stronger than that available in the days of the hippie pot smoker. Unlike alcohol, which is water soluble and quickly metabolized and excreted from the body, tetrahydrocannabinol, or THC (the active chemical in marijuana), is fat soluble, which means it penetrates the fatty areas of the body and may remain there for months or even years. There are many THC receptors in areas of the brain that influence pleasure but also in areas that influence concentration, memory, and coordination (National Institute on Drug Abuse, 2004). Marijuana users might want to consider that there are 421 chemicals in cannabis and about four times the carcinogenic tar in marijuana smoke than in tobacco smoke (Alexander & Pratsinak, 2002).

The Drugs/Violence Link

Illegal drugs are associated with violence in three ways: pharmacological, economic-compulsive, and systemic (Goldstein, 1985). **Systemic violence** is that associated with "doing business" (the growing, processing, transporting, and selling of drugs) in the criminal drug culture. There is so much systemic violence because the drug business is tremendously lucrative for those involved in it, and there is much competition for a slice of that business. The United Nations estimates the annual worth of the international illicit drug trade at $400 billion (Davenport-Hines, 2002).

As with any industry, the illicit drug industry consists of several levels of business between extracting the product from the ground and selling it to the eventual consumer. Cocaine and heroin both begin as natural products grown in fields, cocaine as the coca leaf and heroin as the poppy flower. According to the U.S. Department of State (2005), the number of acres used for coca cultivation in 2004 in South America was 60,787, down from 552,763 in 2001. This huge reduction was accomplished mainly by the aerial spraying of the coca crop with herbicides. On the down side, it was also reported that Afghanistan had 510,756 acres (798 square miles) devoted to cultivating poppies, up from a mere 4,164 acres under cultivation during the last full year (2001) of the Taliban regime.

After the crop has been picked, the raw material must be processed, packaged, and smuggled via various "pipelines" into the countries in which the customers for the product reside. Figure 15.4 show the trafficking routes for cocaine and heroin from points of origin to eventual destination. Once it is at its destination it is "cut" (mixed with various other substances) to increase its volume and then distributed it to street-level outlets for sale to drug users. Profit is

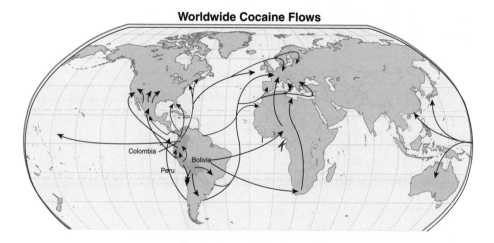

Worldwide Cocaine Flows

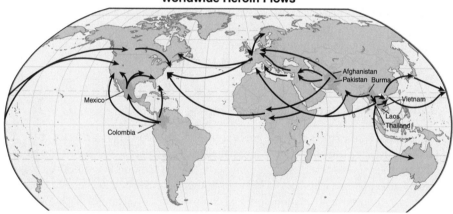

Worldwide Heroin Flows

Figure 15.4

Global Cocaine and Heroin Trafficking Routes: Countries of Origin and Major Countries of Destination

Source: National Drug Control Strategy, 2001

made along each step of the way. For instance, a kilogram (about 2.2 pounds) of heroin cost an average of $2,720 in Pakistan in 2002 but sold for an average of $129,380 on the streets in the United States, and a kilogram of coca base cost an average of $950 in Colombia in 1997 and sold for $25,000 in the United States (Davenport-Hines, 2002).

Systemic violence and other criminal activity begin with the bribery and corruption of law enforcement officials and political figures, or their intimidation and assassination, in the countries where raw materials are grown and through which the processed product is transported. On the streets of the United States, systemic violence is most closely linked with gang battles over control of drug market territory. Goldstein and his colleagues found that just over one-half of a sample of 414 murders committed in New York City in 1988 were drug related, with 90% of them involving cocaine. Figure 15.5 shows the flow of illegal drugs from the planting of the base crop to the sale of the finished product on the streets.

Economic-compulsive violence is that associated with efforts to obtain money to finance the high cost of illicit drugs. The drugs most associated with this type of activity are heroin and cocaine because they are most likely to lead to addiction among their users and the most expensive (Belivacqua & Goldman, 2009). Crimes committed to obtain drug money run the gamut from shoplifting, robbery, and prostitution to trafficking in the very substance the addict craves.

Figure 15.5

Illegal Drugs From Grower to Consumer

Grower →	Processor →	Transporter →	Wholesaler →	Retailer
Farmers plant and harvest poppy, coca, and marijuana crops	Use of chemicals such as motor oil, sulfuric acid, kerosene, and insecticides to refine product	Smugglers use planes, boats, trucks, and many other methods to get product to wholesaler	Organized criminal groups cut product and distribute it to dealers	Deals directly with consumer in crack houses or on street

A study of newly incarcerated drug users found that 72% claimed they committed their latest crime to obtain drug money (Lo & Stephens, 2002).

Pharmacological violence is that induced by the pharmacological properties of the drug itself. Violence induced by illicit drug use is rare compared with violence induced by alcohol, the legal drug. A criminal victimization survey found that less than 5% of victims of violent crimes perceived their assailants to be under the influence of illicit drugs versus 20% who perceived them to be under the influence of alcohol (Parker & Auerhahn, 1998).

What Causes Drug Abuse?

Sociological explanations of drug abuse mirror almost exactly their explanations for crime. Erich Goode (2005) illustrates the almost indistinguishable explanations offered for the causes of crime and drug abuse in his book *Drugs in American Society*. In anomie terms, drug abuse is a retreatist adaptation of those who have failed in both the legitimate and illegitimate worlds, and drug dealing is an innovative adaptation. In social control terms, drug abusers lack social bonds, in self-control terms drug abuse is the hedonistic search for immediate pleasures, and in social learning terms drug abuse reflects differential exposure to individuals and groups in which it is modeled and reinforced. Goode favors conflict theory most as an explanation. As the rich get richer and the poor poorer and economic opportunities are shrinking for the uneducated and unskilled, drug dealers have taken firm root among the increasingly demoralized, disorganized, and politically powerless "underclass." Goode (2005) notes that most members of this class do not succumb to addiction, but enough do "to make the lives of the majority unpredictable, insecure, and dangerous" (p. 77). He maintains that conflict theory applies "more or less exclusively to heavy, chronic, compulsive use of heroin or crack" (p. 74).

Although some people are genetically sitting ducks for addiction, addiction cannot occur without exposure to drugs, and exposure to drugs depends on time and culture. The counterculture of the 1960s and 1970s largely precipitated today's drug problem. Ask almost anyone who reached adulthood prior to that time, and they will probably tell you they were ignorant of the presence of illicit drugs in their environments, and perhaps most were not even aware of their existence at all. How different things are today. We saw that the DEA (2003) estimates that the majority of today's youth has used some form of illegal substance and that such experimenting serves as some kind of unofficial rite of passage. Certain drugs may even serve to define social groups (the feeling of "us-ness" or "we-ness"), as witnessed by the psychedelic movement of the '60s and '70s and today's rave/clubbing phenomenon defined primarily by MDMA, or what clubbers call "ecstasy." The sociable nature of ecstasy-centered raves is understandable when we note that taking MDMA causes the surge of serotonin (a natural antidepressant) and oxytocin (the "cuddle chemical"). Many friendship groups and sexual relationships are formed at raves. Moore and Miller (2008) share the response of one of their young research respondents describing his clubbing experience: "The music, dancing, the feeling/energy doing pills gives you; enjoying myself and seeing other people I know and care about enjoying themselves, sense of community and feeling special!" (p. 7).

It is easy for teens to appreciate the attraction of this drug at a time when they need a little confidence booster and are strongly susceptible to peer pressure. The downside, however, is not easily appreciated. As with all drugs that lead to "better than expected" overstimulation of brain areas, it will eventually lead to the downgrading of the systems involved (Walsh, Johnson, & Bolen, 2012). The long-term use of ecstasy can change a person's behavior from "ultrasocial" to "antisocial" (McGregor, Callaghan, & Hunt, 2008, p. 358), and studies have shown significantly decreased serotonin functioning in chronic MDMA users (e.g., Kish et al., 2010).

Does Drug Abuse Cause Crime?

Figure 15.6 shows the percentage of adult arrestees in five large American cities testing positive for illicit drugs from 2007 through 2012. With anywhere from 60% to 85% of arrestees testing positive for some illicit substance, clearly illicit drug abuse is strongly *associated* with criminal behavior. However, the question is "Is the association a *causal* one; that is, is illicit drug use a direct cause of criminal behavior?" There are three possible explanations for the connection between drugs and crime: (1) drug use causes high rates of offending, (2) high rates of offending cause drug use, and (3) there is no causal connection because certain individuals are predisposed to high levels of involvement in both drugs and crime.

A large body of research indicates that drug abuse does not appear to initiate a criminal career, although it does increase the extent and seriousness of one (Menard, Mihalic, & Huizinga, 2001; Quinn & Sneed, 2008). Drug abusers are not "innocents" driven into a criminal career by drugs, although this might occasionally be true. Rather, chronic drug abuse and criminality are part of a broader propensity of some individuals to engage in a variety of deviant and antisocial behaviors (Fishbein, 2003; McDermott et al., 2000). The reciprocal (feedback) nature of the drugs/

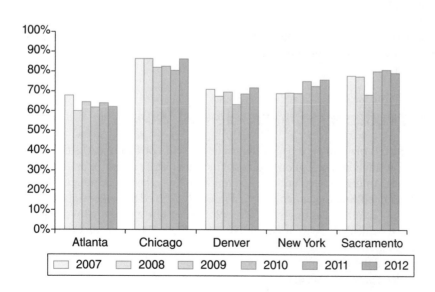

Figure 15.6

Adult Arrestees Testing Positive for Various Drugs, 2007–2012

Source: Office of Drug Control Policy, 2013

crime connection is explained by Menard et al. (2001) as follows: "Initiation of substance abuse is preceded by initiation of crime for most individuals (and therefore cannot be a cause of crime). At a later stage of involvement, however, serious illicit drug use appears to contribute to continuity in serious crime, and serious crime contributes to continuity in serious illicit drug use" (p. 295).

Drug Abuse and Harm Reduction

Clearly the use of illicit drugs is very harmful to individuals and their families and to society. What is even clearer, however, is that the "war on drugs," just like the war on alcohol during Prohibition, is the cause of more harm than it prevents. Most countries have abandoned their own war on drugs and reverted to harm reduction policies (i.e., policies aimed solely at minimizing harm). The United States is among only a handful of countries that reject harm reduction programs favored by agencies such as the World Health Organization (WHO) and the United Nations Children's Fund (UNICEF) (Wodak, 2007). Such programs involve syringe exchange programs, drug substitution programs (such as methadone for heroin), and most importantly, decriminalizing drug usage. Yes, such practices do upset many people's sense of morality, but it does seem to be a practical solution if our goal is to reduce the overall social harm of drugs in our society.

The International Harm Reduction Association (IHRA; 2012) defines **harm reduction** thusly:

> Harm reduction refers to policies, programmes and practices that aim to reduce the harms associated with the use of psychoactive drugs in people unable or unwilling to stop. The defining features are the focus on the prevention of harm, rather than on the prevention of drug use itself, and the focus on people who continue to use drugs.

The goal of the IHRA is not to reduce drug consumption, although it applauds efforts by others to do so, but rather to weigh the risks and harms caused by criminalizing drugs against the risks and harms associated with legalizing them. Like the WHO and UNICEF, the IHRA decries the presence of these dangerous substances in society but also that knows Pandora's box has been opened and there is no closing it. The object is to minimize the harm done by legalizing drugs so that criminal elements no longer control the market (as with alcohol after Prohibition was lifted). This has the added bonus of making substances cheaper and legally obtainable from licensed physicians, thus reducing addicts' need to engage in crime to feed their habits. How successful have harm reduction programs been in countries that have adopted the stance? According to drug expert Alex Wodak (2007), "No country which has started harm reduction programs has ever regretted that decision and then reversed their commitment" (p. 61).

❖ Prostitution and Commercialized Vice

No other crime has been subjected to shifts of attitudes and opinions across the centuries and cultures than prostitution. Throughout much of American history it was regarded as a "necessary evil." During the American Revolution "camp followers" who serviced the sexual needs of the troops were tolerated, and the term *hooker* is apparently derived from the women who serviced the Union troops commanded by General Joseph Hooker during the Civil War (Hagan, 2008). Prostitutes were particularly active in the old American West where women were rare. However, the scourge of venereal disease and the grip of Victorian morality marked a change in attitudes in the latter part of the 19th century, at which time many jurisdictions criminalized prostitution. In 1910 the federal government got into the act when Congress passed the White-Slave Traffic Act (the Mann Act) prohibiting prostitution and made it a felony to transport females across state lines for immoral purposes.

The FBI defines **prostitution** and commercialized vice in such a way as to cover people who sell their sexual services (prostitutes), those who recruit (procure) them, those who solicit clients (pander) for them, and those who house them. The common term for a procurer and panderer is a pimp, and a madam is the keeper of a

Photo 15.4

A female prostitute parleys with a prospective john.

bawdy house (a brothel). There were 56,575 arrests for prostitution and commercialized vice in 2012, down from 74,004 the previous year. This is obviously only the tiniest fraction of all such offenses that actually take place, and the approximately 31% decrease doubtless reflects police practices rather than an actual reduction of prostitution.

Exchanging sexual favors for some other valued resource is as old as the species, and prostitution has long been referred to as the world's oldest profession. It has not always had the same sordid reputation attached to it today, however. Many ancient societies employed prostitutes in temples of worship with whom worshipers "communed" and then deposited a sum of money into the temple coffers according to their estimation of the worth of the communion. In ancient Greece many women of high birth who had fallen on hard times became high-class courtesans called *hetaerae*, who supplied their wealthy clients with stimulating conversation and other cultured activities as well as sexual services. The lower classes had to content themselves with the brothel-based *pornae* or the prettier and more entertaining *auletrides* who would make house calls (Bullough & Bullough, 1994).

This ancient Greek hierarchy of sex workers (as most prostitutes like to be called) is mirrored in modern American society. The modern American hetaerae belong to the elite escort services and call houses and tend to be much better educated, more sophisticated, and better looking than other sex workers because they cater to a wealthy clientele who want to be made to feel special as well as sexually satisfied. These women (and sometimes men who cater to a gay clientele) can earn six-figure incomes annually and are able to sell their "date books" upon retiring for thousands of dollars (Kornblum & Julian, 1995, p. 109).

Brothel prostitutes are the modern auletrides. The only legal brothels in the United States are in certain counties of Nevada, but brothels—masquerading as massage parlors—probably exist in every town of significant size in the United States, although they are not as prominent a part of community life as they used to be. Brothel prostitutes must accept whatever client comes along but may make from $50 to $100 from each client. The streetwalker is the lowest member of the sex worker hierarchy. These prostitutes solicit customers on the streets and may charge only about $20 a trick (typically a quick act of oral sex).

Becoming a Prostitute

It has been estimated that prostitution is the primary source of income for over 1 million women in the United States, many of whom view sex work as the most financially lucrative option open to them (Bartol, 2002). Many brothel and streetwalker prostitutes typically progressed from casual promiscuity at an early age to reasoning that they could sell what they were giving away under the influence of peer pressure from more experienced girls and from pimps (Kornblum

& Julian, 1995). Pimps exploit the strong need for love and acceptance among vulnerable girls. They frequently take on the roles of father, protector, employer, lover, husband, and often drug supplier, thus making the girls totally dependent on them (Tutty & Nixon, 2003). The girls most vulnerable to pimps and other pressures to enter prostitution are those who have experienced high rates of physical, sexual, and emotional abuse at home and who are drug abusers (Bartol, 2002). Hwang and Bedford (2004), however, show that unlike many Western prostitutes, very few Taiwanese prostitutes cite their own economic motives for entering the profession. However, a certain number of the prostitutes in Taiwan are indentured to a brothel by their parents who were in desperate need of money. As is the case in the United States, many Taiwanese prostitutes ran away from home to escape abuse and were befriended by pimps who supplied them with drugs and a certain amount of affection.

Should Prostitution Be Legalized or Decriminalized?

Harm reduction principles also come into play with the issue of prostitution. What are the harms of prostitution, and are they sufficient to warrant state intervention? Most of the harms are obvious, ranging from the spread of sexually transmitted infections to concerns about the exploitation of women. The seamy world of prostitution is also closely related to the drug market and to other forms of serious criminality and to neighborhood blight. As discussed in Chapter 3, the worst exploitation is that of trafficking women and children from poor countries to work in the brothels of rich countries. Some of these women come with their eyes fully open, but most others are duped, coerced, or forced. Even so-called voluntary migrants are forced to sell themselves into prostitution by the poverty and lack of opportunities in their countries of origin (Raymond, 2003).

Prostitution is one of those things we can never really prevent, although the AIDS epidemic has greatly reduced it. One study found that about 40% of streetwalkers and 20% of call girls were HIV positive (Kornblum & Julian, 1995). If we can't stop it, should we legalize it and therefore make it safer? When the ancient Greek lawmaker Solon (638–559 BC) legalized and taxed prostitution he was widely praised: "Hail to you Solon! You bought public women [prostitutes] for the benefit of the city, for the benefit of the morality of a city that is full of vigorous young men who, in the absence of your wise institution, would give themselves over to the disturbing annoyance of better women" (Durant, 1939, p. 116). Taxes on prostitution enabled Athens to build the temple to Aphrodite (the goddess of love) and provided its "vigorous young men" safe outlets for their urges. To borrow a term from sociology, the citizens of Athens found prostitution to be *functional,* meaning it had a socially useful role to play. Such an attitude, however, ignores the important functional role of morality to society, and the issue of legalization becomes how much morality we are willing to sacrifice for the sake of expediency.

Legalizing prostitution means that it becomes a legitimate occupation and that the state can regulate it by licensing brothels and prostitutes, determining where they can be located and requiring regular health checkups. Holland is a country that has legalized prostitution. All parties—the prostitutes, pimps, procurers, and customers—are legally sanctioned as long as they remain in prescribed areas. The obnoxious downside of this is that about 70% of Dutch prostitutes are trafficked in from poorer countries because legalization has greatly expanded the demand for a variety of "exotic" foreign females (Raymond, 2003). Thus legalization has increased demand rather than decreased it.

Decriminalization simply means the removal of laws against prostitution without imposing regulatory controls on it. Decriminalization is the stance favored by the American Civil Liberties Union (ACLU) and prostitution rights groups. These groups oppose legalization since legalization requires regulation and further stigmatizes the "profession" (Weitzer, 1999). Police tolerance (and evidently the public's) of massage parlors in our cities constitutes de facto decriminalization in the United States. Decriminalization basically means business as usual for prostitutes and saves many millions of taxpayer dollars not expended arresting, prosecuting, and punishing women, most of whom are in the business because they perceive few alternatives or who may have been forced into it by pimps upon whom they rely for love, protection, and drugs (Tutty & Nixon, 2003).

The United Kingdom is an example of a country that has decriminalized prostitution. In the United Kingdom women are not penalized for selling sexual favors, but all third-party activities such as pimping, procuring, or in any way living off "immoral earnings" are criminalized. Whether prostitution is legalized or decriminalized, however, one inevitable upshot has always been an increase in demand as more men come to see it as no big deal ("it's legal, so it must be OK") or to engage in it because there is no longer risk of arrest. Sweden has decriminalized prostitution but also criminalizes purchasing prostitutes' services. If a prostitute and her john (customer) are caught engaging in sex, the man is arrested and the prostitute sent on her way. Since many customers are married or otherwise respectable members of society, an arrest experience has a very large deterrent effect. An American study of arrested johns found that only 18 out of 2,200 (0.8%) men arrested for soliciting were arrested again for soliciting over a 4-year period (Weitzer, 1999). This remarkably low recidivism rate is an example of specific deterrence working for those who were probably ordinary working men with families and therefore fearful of the stigma of arrest.

Summary

- Public order offenses are sometimes dismissed as minor nuisance offenses, but they can be quite serious. Criminologists now use the term *public order offenses* rather than *victimless crimes* with the realization that there are always secondary victims.
- Alcohol is humankind's favorite way of drugging itself and has always been associated with criminal and antisocial behavior. It reduces the inhibiting neurotransmitters and thus reduces impulse control. Contextual factors also play their part in producing the kinds of obnoxious behavior associated with drinking too much alcohol. So-called binge drinking is a major contextual problem.
- Driving under the influence is the most serious Part II offense because of its sometimes deadly consequences. More people are killed by drunken drivers in a typical year than are murdered by other means. Activism and legislation since the 1980s have succeeded in significantly reducing drunk driving.
- There are two types of alcoholism: Type I and Type II. Type I is associated with mild abuse, minimal violence, moderate heritability, and character disorders that result from alcoholism. Type II is characterized by early onset, violence, criminality, high

heritability, and character disorders that precede alcoholism. Type II alcoholics may have inherited disorders that drive both their alcoholism and criminality.
- Illicit drug use is also a major problem. Like delinquency, drug usage increases at puberty and drops off in early adulthood to almost zero by the age of 65. Drug addiction is fairly similar to alcoholism in terms of brain mechanisms. Drugs hijack the pleasure centers in the brain and make addicts crave drugs to gain any sort of pleasure at all. Most people who try drugs do not become addicted.
- Drugs are associated with violence in these ways: pharmacological, economic-compulsive, and systemic, with the latter having the strongest association. Systemic violence is part of "doing business" in the lucrative illicit drug business. The economic-compulsive link with violence is the result of addicts' efforts to gain money to purchase drugs, and the rarest link, pharmacological, is violence induced by ingested drugs.
- Most people arrested for a crime test positive for drugs, but this does not mean that drugs cause crime. Drug abuse is part of a broader propensity of some individuals to engage in all kinds of

antisocial behavior, and such behavior is usually initiated before drug abuse. Drug abuse does exacerbate criminal behavior, however.

■ Many countries have decided to cease their wars on drugs and adopt harm reduction principles.

■ Prostitution is as old as the species. While many individuals are coerced into prostitution, others become prostitutes because it is a lucrative business. There are many arguments for and against the legalization of prostitution.

Exercises and Discussion Questions

1. Discuss with classmates how each of you act—silly, aggressive, lusty, maudlin—when you have "gone over the limit" drinking alcohol. Why do you think the same substance "makes" different people react differently?

2. The traffic fatality rate attributable to drunk driving in 2008 was less than half what it was in 1982. Does this tell you anything about the deterrent effect of punishment in general or just about its effect on "ordinary folk"?

3. Get a discussion going among classmates who are not afraid to reveal that they have used some illicit drug other than marijuana and ask them how they felt under its influence and why they no longer (hopefully) use that drug.

4. Given what you know about the history of drug laws in the United States and the link between drug abuse and violence (and crime in general), would legalizing drugs be the lesser of two evils? Give reasons why or why not that include harm reduction principles.

5. Give reasons why we should or should not legalize or decriminalize prostitution using harm reduction principles.

Useful Websites

Crimes against public order and morality. www .drtomoconnor.com/3010/3010lect07.htm.

Maintaining public order. www.open.ac.uk/Arts/ history-from-police-archives/Met6Kt/PublicOrder/ poBiaPol.html.

Mothers Against Drunk Driving. http://www.madd.org.

Paraphilias. www.athealth.com/Consumer/disorders/ Paraphilias.html.

Prostitution Research and Education. www .prostitutionresearch.com.

Chapter Terms

Alcoholism

Binge drinkers

Drug addiction

Economic-compulsive violence

Harm reduction

Harrison Narcotic Act

Pharmacological violence

Physical dependence

Prostitution

Psychological dependence

Systemic violence

Tolerance

Type I alcoholism

Type II alcoholism

Withdrawal

CHAPTER 16

White-Collar Crime

On August 10, 1978, teenage sisters Judy and Lyn Ulrich and their cousin Donna were on a 20-mile journey to Goshen, Indiana, in their Ford Pinto when they were rear-ended by another car. As a result, gas spilled onto the highway and caught fire, and all three trapped girls died horrible fiery deaths. Pintos were fitted with gas tanks that easily ruptured and burst into flames in rear-end collisions of over 25 miles per hour. The problem could have been fixed at a cost of $11 per vehicle, but with 11 million Pintos and 1.5 million light trucks with the problem, Ford accountants calculated that it would cost $137 million to fix. It was calculated that not fixing it would result in 180 burn deaths, 180 serious burn injuries, and 2,100 burned vehicles, which they estimated would cost about $49.5 million dollars in lawsuits and other claims. Comparing those two figures, it was determined that in light of the $87.5 million it would save by not fixing the gas tank problem, to fix it would be unprofitable and irrational.

The consciences of Ford executives did not bother them because they openly used these figures to lobby against federal fuel leakage standards to show how unprofitable such standards would be! According to a Ford engineer, 95% of the 700 to 2,500 people who died in Pinto crashes would have survived if the problem had been fixed. If this is an accurate estimate of deaths caused by the defect, the executives who conspired to ignore it may be the worst multiple murderers in U.S. history. Yet no Ford executive was ever imprisoned, and many went on to bigger things. Lee Iacocca, whose personal maxim "safety doesn't sell" was still in evidence in 1986 when he opposed mandatory airbags for automobiles, went on to become president of Chrysler Corporation and to chair the committee for the centennial celebrations for the Statue of Liberty.

LEARNING OBJECTIVES

- Understand the concept of white-collar crime and the distinction between occupational and corporate white-collar crime
- Understand the basic causes of the S&L, Enron, and subprime scandals
- Know the concept of moral hazard and how it explains a lot of white-collar crime
- Be able to articulate some of the theoretical explanations of white-collar crime
- Understand the difficulties involved in investigating and prosecuting white-collar crime and the weapons law enforcement currently has to battle it
- Understand how the computer has made it easier for all of us to become victims

❖ The Concept of White-Collar Crime

What images pop into your head when you hear the word *crime*? Whatever images you conjured up, we wager one was not of a well-dressed, middle-aged person sitting in a leather recliner dictating a memo authorizing the marketing of defective automobiles or the dumping of toxic waste. We seldom think the chain of events set into motion by a business memo may do more harm than the activities of any "street punk." As sociologist Edward Ross (1907) pointed out over 100 years ago:

> The villain most in need of curbing is the respectable, exemplary, trusted personage who, strategically placed at the focus of a spider web of fiduciary relations, is able from his office chair to pick a thousand pockets, poison a thousand sick, pollute a thousand minds, or imperil a thousand lives. (p. 29)

Indeed, more money is stolen and more people die every year as the result of scams and willful corporate criminal activity than as the result of the activities of street criminals. Kappeler, Blumberg, and Potter (2000) estimate that crimes committed by corporations result in economic losses from 17 to 31 times greater than those resulting from street crimes. There is a huge grubby ring around the white collar that no amount of scrubbing will erase, and most criminologists agree that by virtually all criteria, our most serious crime problem is white-collar crime.

The term *white-collar crime* was coined in the 1930s by Edwin Sutherland (1940), who defined it as crime "committed by a person of respectability and high social status in the course of his occupation" (p. 9). In its Administration Improvement Act (AIA) of 1979, Congress defined **white-collar crime** as "an illegal act or series of illegal acts committed by non-physical means and by concealment or guile, to obtain money or property, or to obtain business or personal advantage" (Weisburd, Wheeler, Waring, & Bode, 1991, p. 6). This definition focuses on characteristics of the offense as opposed to Sutherland's focus on the offender as a high-status person, because most white-collar crime is not committed by "high-status persons." The AIA definition, however, fails to differentiate between persons who commit crimes for personal gain and those who do so primarily on behalf of an employer. Our analysis of white-collar crime differentiates between individuals who steal, defraud, and cheat both in and out of an occupational context and those who commit the variety of offenses attributed to business corporations. We follow Rosoff, Pontel, and Tillman (1998) in using the term *occupational crime* for the former and *corporate crime* for the latter.

❖ Occupational Crime

Occupational crime is committed by working-class to upper-middle-class individuals in the course of their employment. It includes crimes committed by businesses against individuals, such as stores knowingly selling faulty goods, lawyers overbilling clients, and physicians persuading patients to have unneeded medical procedures, and crimes committed by individuals against businesses. Such crimes might range from the draining of company funds by sophisticated computer techniques to stealing pens and paper clips or vandalizing company property by scrambling computer data or scratching graffiti on newly painted walls. Although such activities may seem relatively mundane to most of us, according to the business insurance industry, employee activities such as theft, fraud, and vandalism cost American businesses an estimated $660 billion in 2003 (Parekh, 2004), or $840 billion in 2014 dollars. Just as we all pay for street crime through taxes that support the criminal justice system, we all pay for employee crime because companies merely pass on their losses to customers. Employee crime may also lead to businesses going bankrupt and employees losing their jobs.

Professional occupational crimes are committed by professionals such as physicians and lawyers in the course of their practices. Medical fraud is perhaps the most costly of all occupational crimes. In many respects, Medicare and Medicaid programs are welfare programs for physicians; fraud within these programs is estimated to cost from $50 to $80 billion per year (FBI, 2009b). The American system of fee-for-service medicine covered by private insurance companies is almost an open invitation for fraud. Wong (2012) writes, "The U.S. spends more than twice as much per person on health care as all other industrialized countries despite being the only developed country that doesn't provide basic health insurance for all its citizens." For instance, despite having lower life expectancy than such countries as Canada, France, and the United Kingdom, the cost of American surgical procures may be two or three times higher than in those countries, and the prices of drugs are three or four times higher (Brill, 2013). Medical fraud resulting from unnecessary and overpriced medical tests and treatments, administrative fees, and other medical fraud was estimated at $750 billion in 2009 (Wong, 2012).

Crimes committed by health care doctors (physicians, dentists, chiropractors, psychologists, and so on) include practices such as filing insurance claims for tests or procedures not performed, performing unnecessary operations, steering patients to laboratories or pharmacies in which the doctor has financial stakes, and referrals to other doctors in return for kickbacks. An estimated 16,000 American patients die annually from unnecessary operations (Friedrichs, 2010), although, of course, the physicians may have genuinely believed them to be necessary in many cases. Anyone who has seen charges of $8 an aspirin, $500 for a nursing bra, or $200 for a pair of crutches on their hospital bill knows how hospitals rip patients off.

Most lawyers also work on a fee-for-service basis, thus generating the same temptations to increase their incomes by fraudulent means. Frauds perpetrated by lawyers can include embezzlement of clients' funds, bribery of witnesses and judges, persuading clients to pursue fraudulent or frivolous lawsuits, billing clients for hours not worked, filing unnecessary motions, and complicating a simple legal matter to keep clients on the hook—"I will defend you all the way to your last dollar." Many crimes by lawyers are committed via the power of attorney granted to them by clients, which gives attorneys access to all sorts of client information and opportunities to steal from them.

I would be remiss if I did not also discuss academic occupational crime, because professors commit it too. Professors are sometimes the recipients of multimillion-dollar grants from government agencies and private companies to perform research. This creates opportunities to steal and the temptation to fudge data to provide results the funding agency is looking for. A professor at Tufts University was even convicted of murdering a prostitute he paid for with grant funds (Friedrichs, 2010), and *Breaking Bad*'s Walter White had a real-life counterpart in Dr. John Buettner-Janusch, an anthropologist who was convicted of using university labs to manufacture illegal drugs (Carpenter, 1989). It seems that every occupational category generates a considerable number of criminals, and the higher the prestige of the occupation the more their criminal activities costs the general public.

Causes of Occupational White-Collar Crime: Are They Different?

According to Hirschi and Gottfredson (1987), while anyone can commit a common street crime, occupational crime differs only in that it is committed by people in a position to do so. Medicaid fraud can typically only be committed by health care providers and bank embezzlement by bank employees in positions of trust. The motives of occupational criminals are the same as those of street criminals: to obtain benefits quickly with minimal effort, and the age, sex, and race profiles of occupational criminals are not that much different from those of street criminals. Hirschi and Gottfredson (1987) concluded that "when opportunity is taken into account, demographic differences in [occupational] white collar crime are the same as demographic differences in ordinary crime" (p. 967). Walters and Geyer (2004) examined this assertion using indicators of criminal thinking patterns and attitudes. They found that white-collar criminals with prior arrests for non-white-collar crimes were not significantly different from street criminals in their demographics, lifestyle, and criminal thinking patterns but were significantly different from white-collar criminals with no history of arrest for non-white-collar crimes.

❖ Corporate Crime

In *The Wealth of Nations*, economist and founder of modern capitalism Adam Smith (1776/1953) wrote, "Seldom do members of a profession meet . . . that is does not end up in some conspiracy against the public or some contrivance to raise prices" (p. 137). Smith was referring to what we call corporate crime today. **Corporate crime** is criminal activity on *behalf* of a business organization committed during the course of fulfilling the legitimate role of the corporation. During much of American history, the primary legal stance relating to the activities of business was laissez-faire (leave it alone to do as it will). American courts traditionally adopted the view that government should not interfere with business, so for a very long period in our history, victims of defective and dangerous products could not sue corporations for damages because the guiding principle was *caveat emptor* (let the buyer beware). Unhealthy and dangerous working conditions in mines, mills, and factories were excused under the freedom of contract clause of the Constitution (Walsh & Hemmens, 2008).

Corporate crime is everywhere, but just as there are neighborhoods where street crime is rampant, there are corporations where corporate crime is rampant. One of the first systematic examinations of corporate recidivism found that 98% of the nation's 70 largest corporations were recidivists with an average of 14 regulatory or criminal decisions against them (Sutherland, 1956). A study of 477 major U.S. corporations found that 60% of them were known to have violated the law and that 13% of violator companies accounted for 52% of all violations, with an average of 23.5 violations per company (Clinard & Yeager, 1980). And a study of brokerage firms found that many of the biggest names in the business, such as Prudential, Paine Webber, and Merrill Lynch, have had an average of two or more serious violations *per year* since 1981 (Wells, 1995). "Three-strikes-and-you're-out" laws evidently do not apply in the world of pinstriped suits. We could go on for another few hundred pages documenting specific instances of corporate crime but will concentrate on the three most costly in American history: the S&L, Enron, and subprime mortgage scandals.

The S&L Scandal: The Best Way to Rob a Bank Is to Own One

Although the political and legal climate in the 20th century changed considerably from the previous century, the public continued to be victimized by corporate criminals. For instance, the savings and loan (S&L) scandal of the 1980s amounted to one of the most costly crime sprees in American history and cost the U.S. taxpayer $150 billion in bailouts, with a total cost of $473 billion after factoring in what the Federal Deposit Insurance Corporation (FDIC) covered in bank deposits (the FDIC covered up to $100,000 in personal accounts at the time) (Wallison, 2009). This staggering amount is many times greater than losses from all the "regular" bank robberies in American history put together (Schmalleger, 2004). Government bailouts of these financial institutions dropped the country into recession and portended the much deeper recession of 2007.

How did it happen? The hyperinflation of the 1970s left S&Ls holding low-interest mortgages, and many began to fail. The S&L industry was deregulated in 1980 under the assumption that the free market cures all economic problems. Deregulation allowed for massive embezzlement of funds by S&L owners and executives, thus making these crimes hybrids of occupational and corporate crime in that they constituted crime *by* the corporation *against* the corporation (but ultimately against the taxpayers of the United States). Most of the looting took the form of extravagant salaries, bonuses, and perquisites that executives awarded themselves as their banks sank ever further into debt. Other methods involved selling land back and forth ("land flipping") within a few days until its paper value far exceeded its real value and then finding "sucker" institutions to buy it at the inflated price and loans made back and forth between employees of different banks with the knowledge that the loans would never be called in. A variety of scams with their own playful names such as "cash for trash," "kissing the paper," "daisy chains," and "dead cows for dead horses" convey the contempt these upper-middle-class executives had for their victims and the gamelike way in which they viewed their activities (Calavita & Pontell, 1994).

Of the 1,098 defendants charged in S&L cases, only 451 were sentenced to prison, with the majority (79%) sentenced to less than 5 years, and the average sentence was 3.4 years (Calavita, Pontell, & Tillman, 1999). The most notorious figure in the scandal was Charles Keating, the CEO of Lincoln Savings of Irvine, California, who in 1993 received 5 years for fraud, racketeering, and conspiracy. Keating's attempts to avoid criminal investigation of his operation led to a political scandal known as the Keating Five. Keating made substantial political "contributions" to five influential U.S. senators totaling $1.3 million. These senators were subsequently accused of improperly intervening in the investigation of Keating's bank by the Federal Home Bank Loan Board, which backed off taking action against Lincoln (Binstein & Bowden, 1993). Three senators—Alan Cranston (D-Calif.), Don Riegle (D-Mich.), and Dennis DeConcini (D-Ariz.)—were "reprimanded" and as a result had their political careers cut short. The other two senators—John Glenn (D-Ohio) and John McCain (R-Ariz.)—were cleared.

The close relationship between business and politicians for purposes of lining each other's pockets is commonly referred to as **crony capitalism** and sometimes as state-corporate crime. Shover and Cullen (2008) define state-corporate crime as occurring when "state agencies are willfully or negligently lax in oversight [and can] also take the form of complicity in crime committed by profit-seeking organizations" (p. 161). Political interference with investigations of corporate wrongdoing was also central to the subprime mortgage scandal that led to the 2007 recession.

The Enron Scandal: Crooks Cooking Books

The first major scandal of the 21st century was Enron, which has been called "one of the most intricate pieces of financial chicanery in history," that for its stockholders and employees was "the financial disaster of a lifetime, a harrowing, nerve-racking disaster from which they may never recover" (English, 2004, p. 1). The Enron scandal (and other similar scandals in the first two years of the 21st century) did tremendous damage to the economy and "created a crisis of investor confidence the likes of which hasn't been seen since the Great Depression" (Gutman, 2002, p. 1).

Enron was a $100 billion corporate empire with over 200,000 employees in 40 countries that controlled about one-quarter of all trading in natural gas and electricity in the United States (Fox, 2003). The company poured millions of dollars into political campaigns and lobbyists arguing for further deregulation of the energy markets. The Enron hierarchy expected never-ending innovation and growth from its executives to feed this monster enterprise. In response, executives created imaginary markets, "paper partnerships," and phantom growth that enabled them to report profits that didn't exist and hide debts that did. Executives were accomplished at cooking the financial books in many ingenious ways, which kept Enron's stock price rising and thus their

Photo 16.1

Former Enron CEO Jeff Skilling (*left*) leaves the federal courthouse with his attorney Daniel Petrocelli (*right*) after being sentenced to 292 months in federal prison.

own compensation. Because much of the compensation received by Enron executives was stock based, they had major incentives to make the company look as good as possible to investors by reporting higher profits than the company actually earned to the Security and Exchange Commission (SEC). Inflated reports of company profits sent the company's stock higher, and thus with it the bonuses of its executives.

The SEC is a government regulatory agency that has power to regulate activities related to the stock exchange and securities markets. That is, it can investigate, charge, and penalize illegal activities via fines and injunctions, but it cannot impose criminal sanctions. If an SEC investigation uncovers criminally fraudulent behavior, it turns the case over to law enforcement agencies, typically the FBI.

The victimization of Enron's employees lies largely in the fact that they were all strongly encouraged to plow their retirement accounts into Enron stock, which Enron bureaucrats had convinced them would continue to rise. The tragedy is that from its high of $90 in 2000, it plummeted to a piddling 36 cents, which is "junk bond" status (Fox, 2003, p. 2). This plunge effectively wiped out the retirement savings of thousands of Enron employees and cost outside investors millions of dollars. With the benefit of insider knowledge, however, top executives cashed in their stock before the implosion and "walked off with small fortunes" (McLean & Elkind, 2003, p. 409). Criminal profiles of the two Enron top executives are presented in Table 16.1.

The Subprime Mortgage Scandal: The Road to Hell Is Paved With Good Intentions

Although the S&L and Enron scandals badly hurt the economy, the subprime mortgage meltdown of 2007 pushed the American economy and economies around the world into the worst recession since the Great Depression. Subprime loans extend credit to people who would not otherwise have access to it. This was a well-meaning attempt to spread the American Dream around, but it ultimately led to millions of foreclosures as economic reality set in. Because of government bailouts of financial institutions and banks considered "too big to fail," the national

Table 16.1

Ten Infamous White-Collar Criminals and Their Crimes

Name and Job Title	Crime, Sentence, and Year Sentenced	Synopsis of Offenses
Ivan Boesky Stock trader and CEO of Beverly Hills Hotel Corp.	Insider trading; 3.5 years prison, $100 million fine; 1986	Boesky was convicted of engaging a large number of insider trades. Insider trading is buying or selling by corporate insiders based on information originating within the company. Insider trading is harmful to the economy and unfair to investors who do not have access to information that is lucrative to those who do.
Michael Milken Wall Street financier	Securities fraud; 10 years, later reduced to 2, $600 million fine; 1989	Milken has been described as the epitome of Wall Street greed and nicknamed the "Junk Bond King." Boesky implicated Milken in several illegal transactions, such as stock manipulation, securities fraud, and insider trading, in a plea bargain deal. Some have placed a great deal of blame on Milken for the S&L fiasco.
Sholam Weiss Businesman	Racketeering, wire fraud, and money laundering (78 counts); 845 years; 2000	Weiss basically looted the National Heritage Life Insurance Company of $450 million, which led to the largest insurance failure in history at the time. After Weiss was convicted, he fled the country but was eventually extradited from Austria. His 845-year sentence in the longest in U.S. history.
Herman Beebe Banker, Mafia associate	Bank fraud; 1 year prison, 5 years probation; 1985	Beebe is considered the godfather of the corrupt Texas S&Ls. He began his career in the insurance business and eventually moved to banking. Beebe eventually directly or indirectly controlled 55 banks and 29 S&Ls in eight states.
Bernard Ebbers WorldCom CEO	Fraud, false financial reporting; 25 years; 2005	Bernard Ebbers was the cofounder of long-distance telecommunications company WorldCom. WorldCom misstated its true earning to the tune of $11 billion, which subsequently led to investors losing $100 billion.
Andrew Fastow Enron's chief financial officer (CFO)	Fraud, money laundering, and conspiracy; 6 years, $23.8 million fine; 2006	As CFO of Enron, Fastow was able to set up a web of companies to just do business with Enron and in which the company could hide its massive losses from the SEC. This enabled Enron's balance sheets to appear debt free to auditors while, in fact, it owed more than $30 billion.
Dennis Kozlowski CEO of Tyco International	Thirty-eight counts of fraud; 8 to 25 years; 2005	Kozlowski was found guilty of 38 felony counts of fraud and stock manipulation that enabled him to pocket $170 million from the company and $430 million through tainted sales of stock. Tyco paid $30 million in stockholder money for Kozlowski's lavish New York apartment. He was released in January of 2014 after serving 9 years.
John and Timothy Rigas, CEO and CFO of Adelphia Communications	Bank, wire, and securities fraud; John 15 years, Timothy, 20 years; 2005	John Rigas (father of Timothy) was the primary founder of Adelphia Communications Corporation, one of the largest cable TV companies in the United States. The Rigases had conspired to hide $2.3 billion in Adelphia debt, had stolen $100 million of Adelphia funds, and lied about the company's financial condition. They used Adelphia funds to cover personal investment losses and purchase luxuries.
Jeffrey Skilling CEO of Enron	Fraud and insider trading; 24 years, $45 million fine; 2006	Skilling was indicted on 35 counts of fraud, insider trading, conspiracy, and making false statements. Based on insider information about the pending bankruptcy of Enron, he sold $60 million in Enron shares while their value was still high. Skilling had his sentence reduced to 14 years in 2013 on condition that he release $40 million to his victims.
Lawrence Duran Owner of American Therapeutic Corp.	Medicaid and various other health care frauds; 50 years, $87.5 million restitution; 2011	American Therapeutic Corporation (ATC) owners and operators submitted $205 million in fraudulent claims to Medicare. They paid kickbacks to other facilities to provide bogus mentally ill "patients" for unneeded therapeutic programs. Over 20 other ATC franchise owners were indicted and charged, with at least one other owner receiving serious prison time.

debt rose from 66% of gross domestic product (GDP; GDP is the value of all goods and services produced within a country in a specific time period) to well over 100% of GDP, millions saw their bank accounts and retirement funds seriously depleted, and 5.4 million Americans lost their jobs (*The Economist*, 2013).

The subprime scandal occurred in a political climate that almost guaranteed it would occur. Housing and Urban Development (HUD) policies designed to make home buying "more affordable" led to millions of people taking on mortgages they could not afford, and many bought houses they subsequently lost or were saddled with homes worth much less than what they paid for them (Leonnig, 2008). In 1995, President Clinton loosened housing loan rules by rewriting and vigorously enforcing a 1977 act called the Community Reinvestment Act (CRA), which put pressure on banks to lend to low-income borrowers ("No credit? No job? No problem!"). According to the *New York Times*'s Steven Holmes (1999), "Fannie Mae, the nation's biggest underwriter of home mortgages, has been under increasing pressure from the Clinton administration to expand mortgage loans among low and moderate income people and felt pressure from stock holders to maintain its phenomenal growth in profits."

Unlike other white-collar scandals, this one became ideological. That is, who or what is ultimately to blame for the mess is contested by conservatives, who blame government policies, and liberals, who blame Wall Street. For instance, Thomas DiLorenzo (2012) writes that the scandal was "the direct result of thirty years of government policy that has forced banks to make bad loans to un-creditworthy borrowers" (p. 1). The liberal view blames the entire thing on the "exhaustion of American capitalism rather than being the result of specific policy failures" (Pally, 2010, p. 33).

Because the issue is politicized, it is wise to go to someone both highly respected in the economic world and who does not have a dog in the fight. Such a person is Oonagh McDonald (2012), whose thoroughly researched and heavily documented book *Fannie Mae and Freddie Mac: Turning the American Dream Into a Nightmare* has become the bible for those seeking to understand the largest white-collar crime (or rather series of crimes) in history. McDonald is a former Labour member of the British Parliament and is its spokeswoman on financial matters. Her analysis in a nutshell is as follows:

> Clinton set the wheels in motion; Bush did little to stop the juggernaut of "affordable" or "subprime lending," which rolled on without any obstacles in its way. But when house prices began to fall and interest rates began to rise, almost half of all outstanding mortgages were revealed as subprime. When it all went wrong, politicians both in the US and elsewhere sought to deflect attention from their own actions by the ever-popular sport of attacking and blaming the banks. Of course, many of the banks played their part as well, but the prime responsibility is a political one of seeking to increase home ownership at any price. (2012, pp. 328–329)

Government's role in the scandal is not disputed because government-sponsored enterprises (GSEs) such as Fannie Mae and Freddie Mac largely control the American mortgage market, and the Clinton administration did set the ball rolling by practically mandating the distortion of normal lending procedures. However, as McDonald asserts, there is enough blame to go around.

To grasp the essence of the scandal it is important to understand what economists call moral hazard. **Moral hazard** is the tendency to take unwarranted risks when costs are not borne by the party taking the risk. Mark Zandi (2008) considers moral hazard to be at the root of the mortgage scandal, writing, "The risks inherent in mortgage lending became so widely dispersed that no one was forced to worry about the quality of any single loan. As shaky mortgages were combined, diluting any problems into a larger pool, the incentive for responsibility was undermined" (p. 3).

This is privatizing the profit and socializing the risk, since it is the taxpayer who bears the burden. Likewise, Arnold and Stevens (2011) see mixing economic interventions with social agenda as the quintessential moral hazard.

The relationship of moral hazard to mortgage lending is this: When someone gets a mortgage, the bank granting the mortgage typically sells it to a GSE because banks cannot tie up their funds for 15 to 30 years. GSEs obtain funds to buy trillions of dollars worth of mortgages by selling government bonds to investors, who obtain a much lower interest rate than the mortgage rate the homeowner has to pay. The difference between what the GSEs pay in interest to their investors and what homeowners pay on their mortgage amounts to profits of billions of dollars a year (Eggert, 2009). A high proportion of these "toxic" mortgages were then bundled and sold as lots by GSEs to private financial organizations around the world. Many of these organizations went bankrupt with the meltdown, throwing the economies of their parent countries into a wild tailspin that is yet to stop.

Just as political scandals dotted the S&L landscape, so they did in the subprime meltdown. Ike Brannon (2013) characterizes Fannie and Freddie as exemplifying the worst horrors on crony capitalism, writing that "for years these fiefdoms were run as little more than piggy banks for connected politicians." According to a *U.S. News and World Report* story (Barone, 2008), the Bush administration called for tighter regulation of GSEs no fewer than 17 times, but the House never passed a bill in response. Barney Frank (D-Mass.), who was then the ranking member of the House Financial Services Committee, did his best to prevent any tightening of mortgage lending standards, stating, "I want to roll the dice a little bit more in this situation towards subsidized housing." Frank had been in a sexual relationship with a high-ranking Fannie Mae executive, Herb Moses (Frank had recommended him for the job). Even though his association with Moses was over in 1998, Frank continued to block efforts to make Fannie Mae more transparent in its accounting practices up to 2007 (Barone, 2008).

But Mr. Frank's is not the only instance of crony capitalism involved. According to an Office of Federal Housing Enterprise Oversight (OFHEO; 2006) report, senior executives of Fannie Mae interfered with all attempts to reign in their activities or to examine its accounting practices by lobbying congressional support to thwart such attempts. According to the Federal Elections Commission, Fannie Mae "contributed" millions of dollars for such support. The top recipients were Barack Obama, Christopher Dodd, John Kerry, and Hillary Clinton (Hancock, 2012). This political interference is similar to that of the Keating Five in the S&L scandal, but similar congressional action has not been taken against those complicit in attempts to impede regulatory efforts to reign in the GSEs.

Recall that the Enron scandal was the use of false and illegal accounting to inflate reported earnings. The Enron scandal piqued the interest of SEC investigators because Freddie Mac (which had already been successfully investigated for accounting fraud) and Enron shared the same accounting firm. This sparked SEC and OFHEO investigations of Fannie Mae, which eventually uncovered widespread accounting fraud that enabled executives to garner big—really big—bonuses. For instance, Fannie's CEO, Franklin Raines, who took "early retirement" in 2004, made over $91 million from 1999 to 2004, $52.6 million of which was made in bonuses based on fraudulently reported profits (Gordon, 2008). Raines eventually had to pay back $24.7 million to settle a lawsuit (the OFHEO asked for $100 million), although most of this was paid by Fannie Mae insurance, not by Raines personally. Raines made his bogus bonuses the same way Enron executives and other corporate crooks highlighted in Table 16.1 did, but neither he nor any other GSE executive has been criminally investigated. Apparently, there are people too big to jail, as well as financial institutions too big to fail.

Everyone involved in real estate benefited from the careless lending standards of the 1990s through 2007, from GSE executives and their outsized salaries and bonuses down to the real estate agents on the front lines. Banks were willing to make loans to people they knew could not honor them as long as they could unload their mortgages onto GSEs. GSEs accepted them, both because they were mandated to and because they could bundle and sell them to Wall Street speculators and their equivalent around the world. Real estate brokers and agents were happy as long as the commissions kept coming from listing and selling overpriced houses. The people who suffered and are still suffering are the taxpayers in every country hit by the scandal, particularly those subprime loans were supposed to help. A statement by British novelist and philosopher C. S. Lewis (1970) seems appropriate here: "Of all tyrannies, a tyranny exercised for the good of its victims may be the most oppressive" (p. 292).

Theories on the Causes of Corporate Crime

A number of theorists have tried to explain white-collar crime using their favored theory. Theories emphasizing things such as low IQ or low self-control cannot be applied to people who have spent many years of disciplined effort to achieve their positions. Anomie/strain theorists have gotten into the act by stressing that all companies and their executives are exposed to the capitalist ethos and the strain of seeking their elevated versions of the American Dream. For strain theorists, corporate criminals are "high-class innovators." But strain can only be invoked as a *motive* for corporate crime, not for the *choice* to engage in it. So what differentiates "innovators" from the other modes of adaptation available in the corporate world?

Differential association/social learning theorists highlight the fact that newcomers entering corporate environments are socialized into the prevailing way of doing things. If the newcomer does not fit in and conform to the company ways, he or she is not likely to remain employed there. This process can produce a sort of moral apathy in executives striving to do their jobs in their own and their company's best interests. If each small bending of the rules that brings profit to the company brings the rule bender appreciation and bonuses, the individual's behavior will be almost imperceptibly molded in the direction of ever-greater wrongdoing. If he or she is rewarded through the usual stock-based nature of the executive compensation there is further incentive to engage in illegal behavior. Although stock-based compensation is designed to increase executives' focus on stockholders' profits, as we have seen, it is a situation ripe for insider trading, falsifying accounts, fraudulent trading, and an emphasis on short-term earnings rather than the long-term success of the corporation (Thornburn, 2004).

Conflict theorists have no trouble explaining white-collar crimes invoking their version of the Golden Rule ("those with the gold make the rules"). The people who define the seriousness of criminal acts are the same people who own or have large interests in many of the institutions and corporations that commit the acts in question. The same people may also play an "active part in crafting the laws and regulatory standards that circumscribe their conduct" (Shover & Hochstetler, 2000, p. 264). Such people are thus hardly likely to want to define shady corporate acts as criminal.

Shover, Hochstetler, and Alalehto's (2013) integrated rational choice model is perhaps the best and most comprehensive of all attempts to explain white-collar crime. They view white-collar crime as a function of three factors working together at the aggregate, organizational, and personal levels. At the aggregate level, they posit that the lack of credible oversight by regulatory agencies is behind most large-scale corporate scandals, as was made abundantly clear in our discussions of the S&L, Enron, and subprime scandals. At the organizational level, they see a crime-facilitating corporate culture focused on profit maximization and stock-based compensation for executives. At the individual level, they see such traits as aggressiveness, thrill seeking, and a sense of entitlement. This model is presented in Figure 16.1.

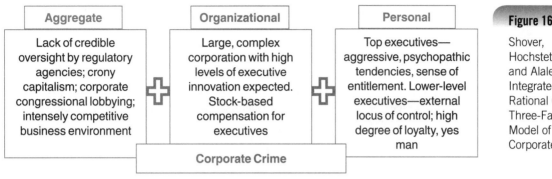

Aggregate		Organizational		Personal
Lack of credible oversight by regulatory agencies; crony capitalism; corporate congressional lobbying; intensely competitive business environment	✚	Large, complex corporation with high levels of executive innovation expected. Stock-based compensation for executives	✚	Top executives—aggressive, psychopathic tendencies, sense of entitlement. Lower-level executives—external locus of control; high degree of loyalty, yes man

Corporate Crime

Figure 16.1

Shover, Hochstetler, and Alalehto's Integrated Rational Choice Three-Factor Model of Corporate Crime

We have seen that rational choice theorists share the classical assumption that human behavior can be understood in terms of striving to maximize pleasure and minimize pain and thus have no difficulty appreciating why individuals engage in corporate crime. Opportunities abound in corporate America to gain wealth beyond what individuals could earn legitimately. The weakness of formal and informal controls over business activities, the extreme difficulties involved in investigating and prosecuting white-collar crimes, and the relatively lenient penalties formerly imposed on white-collar criminals make corporate crime a rational and an immoral choice.

Greek philosopher Plato's allegory of the ring of Gyges is useful in helping us understand the rational choice position on white-collar crime. Gyges was a young shepherd in the service of the king of Lydia. The gist of the story is that Gyges came upon a gold ring in a cave that allowed him to become invisible whenever he turned it on his finger. When he realized the possibilities this opened for him, he went to the court, seduced the queen, murdered the king, and took over the kingdom. Plato's story makes the point that with the gift of invisibility no one could resist all temptation to act unjustly in the name of self-interest:

> No man can be imagined to be of such an iron nature that he would stand fast in justice. No man would keep his hands off what is not his own when he could safely take what he liked out of the market, or go into houses and lie with anyone at his pleasure, to kill or release from prison whom he would, and in all respects be like a God among men. (Plato, 1960, p. 44)

White-collar crime is often invisible, with lax regulatory oversight and corporate culture functioning as a kind of ring of Gyges. As such, we have a corporate version of Quetelet's judgment that "society prepares the crime and the guilty is only the instrument by which it is accomplished" (in Vold & Bernard, 1986, p. 132). We have also seen that different people respond in different ways to similar situations, and thus criminologists studying white-collar crime have been "bringing the offender back in" (Benson, 2013, p. 324).

In terms of white-collar offenders' characteristics, it appears that people who choose business careers tend to have lower ethical and moral standards than people who choose other legitimate careers. A number of studies have concluded that business students are, on average, less ethical than students in other majors—even law! (Tang, Chen, & Sutarso, 2008).

Other studies have focused on the traits of locus of control, moral reasoning, and Machiavellianism. People with an internal locus of control believe they can influence life outcomes and are relatively resistant to coercion from others. People with an external locus feel that circumstances have more influence over situations than they themselves do. Those who engage in corporate crime tend to have an external locus of control, and whistle-blowers tend to have an internal locus of control (Trevino & Youngblood, 1990). Furthermore, people with an internal locus of control operate at higher stages of moral development and tend to behave according to their own beliefs about right and wrong. People at lower stages of moral development tend to emphasize conformity to group norms (external locus of control) (Weber, 1990).

Machiavellianism is the manipulation of others by any means necessary for personal gain. People high on this trait are shallow individuals who exploit superiors and equals by deceit and ingratiation and subordinates by bullying, classical tactics of psychopaths. Simon (2002) describes those who make it to the top of bureaucratic organizations: such an individual "exudes charisma via a superficial sense of warmth and charm," and he or she exhibits "free floating hostility, competitiveness, a high need for socially approved success, unbridled ambition, aggressiveness [and] impatience" (p. 277). Simon's description sounds very much like that of a psychopath and reminds us of Gordon Gekko in the 1987 movie *Wall Street* and its 2010 sequel.

It is not too far-fetched to characterize many top corporate figures as possible psychopaths. Frank Perri (2011) tells us that "Dr. Hare [the psychologist who developed the psychopathic checklist discussed in Chapter 9] once indicated that if he was not studying psychopaths in prison, he would be studying them at the Stock Exchange" (p. 226).

Indeed, in one study 203 corporate professionals participating in management development programs were assessed using Hare's Psychopathy Checklist–Revised (PCL–R) in conjunction with copious other data supplied by their parent companies (Babiak, Neumann, & Hare, 2010). It was found that 3% of participants had PCL–R scores at or above the 30 cut-point used for defining psychopathy, compared to 0.2% of individuals in a large community sample, and 5.9% had scores indicative of "potential" or "possible" psychopathy compared to 1.2% in the community sample.

Law Enforcement's Response to Corporate Crime

The invisibility of white-collar crime is a huge obstacle to law enforcement. With street crimes there is a body in the street, a house burgled, a dazed mugging victim, or a car stolen. These easily defined discrete events quickly come to the attention of the police. With many white-collar crimes, victims often do not even know they have been victimized, and the sequence of events is often quite the opposite: "White-collar crime investigators start with a suspected con artist, and their question is, What did he or she do, and can we prove it?" (Calavita et al., 1999, p. 7). White-collar criminals leave behind no bloody fingerprints or DNA evidence, and what evidence there is often requires thousands of hours and millions of dollars to unravel and may well have influential politicians behind the scenes working to destroy, hide, or discredit whatever evidence does exist.

As we saw in Chapter 2, white-collar crimes are investigated by various white-collar crime units of the FBI and reported in the *Financial Crimes Report to the Public*. Other tallies of corporate wrongdoings are collected and distributed each year by state and federal regulatory agencies such as the FTD (Federal Trade Commission) and the SEC (Securities and Exchange Commission). However, these agencies do not come under the jurisdiction of the Justice Department and thus lack the law enforcement powers of the FBI's Financial Crimes Section. Further complicating things, these agencies cite organizations rather than individuals for wrongdoings, and any one citation may include multiple crimes committed by multiple individuals.

Corporate wrongdoing is thus monitored and responded to by a variety of criminal, administrative, and regulatory bodies. However, very few corporate crooks in the past received truly meaningful sanctions. Their power to avoid such sanctions may be gauged by the 1990 U.S. Justice Department's withdrawal of its support for proposed tougher sentences for corporate offenders in response to heavy lobbying of powerful politicians (crony capitalism again) by many prominent industries, the very targets of the proposal (Hagan, 1994). It is doubtful that street criminals would get very far lobbying against proposals for stricter penalties for them.

The cascade of corporate scandals and failures in the first decade of the 21st century finally awakened American law enforcement to the realities of the harm done by elite criminals. As a result of congressional hearings and public outcry, Congress passed the **Sarbanes-Oxley Act** (SOA) of 2002. The SOA increased penalties for corporate criminals, increased the budgets of agencies charged with investigating corporate crime, and made prosecution easier. Because of the SOA, Burr (2004) contends that "prosecutors are driven to go after corporate fraud with an almost evangelical zeal" (p. 10). Perhaps the days of leniency for white-collar criminals are over, as may be seen by the sentences imposed on major corporate crooks reported in Table 16.1.

An important part of the SOA is the White-Collar Crimes Penalty Enhancement Act. This act creates new offenses with significantly enhanced penalties. It also relaxes some procedural evidentiary requirements for prosecutors who formerly had to prove "willfulness" in white-collar cases (i.e., prove beyond a reasonable doubt that the defendant took some action knowing that it violated a specific law). Prosecutors now have only to show that defendants did what they did, period, which has always been the standard in other criminal cases ("ignorance of the law is no excuse"). Relaxed standards for proving obstruction of justice (and penalties of up to 20 years if convicted of it) are also included. There are also significant protections for whistle-blowers, making it a crime punishable by up to 10 years in prison for retaliating against them. These protections and relaxed evidentiary standards make it easier for guiltless employees to reveal what they know to investigators.

According to Lowell and Arnold (2003), "Congress clearly intended to send a message to the law enforcement community to be tougher on violators of business law and regulations. Further, Congress's message will echo to prosecutors and sentencing judges who will avail themselves of the new SOA maximums or use previously available means to enhance maximum penalties" (p. 228). SEC investigators and prosecutors are clearly taking advantage of the tools provided by the SOA.

THEORY IN ACTION: Ponzi Schemes From Charles Ponzi to Bernie Madoff

Many people looking for higher interest rates on their money than paid by banks search out investment opportunities. The risks of losing money are greater than if the money were tucked away in the bank, but so are the rewards. A Ponzi scheme is one such investment opportunity, but unbeknownst to its investors, it is fraudulent. In a Ponzi operation, initial investors are actually paid handsome interest or returns on their money, which encourages further investment and also encourages others to join. Such schemes can continue to operate as long as there is a continual stream of investments, but when demands for payments exceed funds coming in from new investors the scheme collapses. Ponzi schemes are thus an example of robbing Peter to pay Paul. Anytime the buzzwords "high-yield investment program" or "offshore investment" are seen you should be aware that you are probably being invited to participate in some sort of Ponzi scheme.

The man who gave his name to the Ponzi scheme was Italian-born (1882) Charles Ponzi, who arrived in New York in 1903 "with $2.50 in cash and $1 million in hopes." Ponzi moved to Montreal in 1907, took a job in a bank, and subsequently fled to Mexico with a chunk of its money. He returned to the United States in 1911 and set up his Ponzi scheme in Boston, telling people he could double their investment in 90 days. Many early investors got what was promised, and by 1920 Ponzi had millions from investors who mortgaged their homes and invested their life savings to join his scheme.

Suspicions were soon aroused when a *Boston Post* article claimed Ponzi's scheme was mathematically impossible and that rather than being $7 million in the black, he was $2 million in the red. The *Post* also later reported on Ponzi's theft from the Montreal bank, leading to Ponzi being arrested, charged with fraud, and sentenced to 5 years. His investors lost about $20 million ($226,656,898 in 2013 money). After his release from prison, Ponzi tried his hand at various other investment frauds and was again imprisoned. He died penniless in Brazil in 1949.

(Continued)

THEORY IN ACTION (Continued)

Photo 16.2

Mug shots of Charles Ponzi (*right*), the namesake of the Ponzi Scheme, and Bernard Madoff (*left*), the most infamous recent perpetrator of such a scheme.

Bernard "Bernie" Madoff is an American fraudster born in 1938 who out-Ponzied Ponzi. Madoff founded his company as a penny stock trading company in 1960 and claims that it was legitimate until 1990, although investigators believe that it hadn't been strictly legal since the early 1980s. Madoff's company was a major player on Wall Street, and he was on the board of governors of the regulatory body that was supposed to oversee securities dealers like himself. Even more indicative of the way Bernie had everyone fooled about his trustworthiness, Nasdaq (a stock market exchange like Dow Jones) made him its chairman and the SEC appointed him to security industry panels. Madoff made contributions to political candidates of close to $250,000 since the 1990s, and when he sensed trouble on the horizon, began "donating" $25,000 per year from 2005 to 2008 to the Democratic Senatorial Campaign Committee. He was also a "dear friend" of SEC chairperson Mary Schapiro. In the world of white-collar crime it is wise to curry favor among the powerful.

After years of investment returns in the range of 12% to 15%, the returns began to tumble because of the housing meltdown. Madoff was suddenly confronted with $7 billion in redemptions, which eventually led to the uncovering of his Ponzi scheme. In 2008, Madoff's sons reported to the FBI Bernie's confession to them that most of his business amounted to a massive Ponzi scheme, and Bernie was arrested the next day. In 2009, Madoff pled guilty to 11 counts of fraud, money laundering, false statements, and perjury. His indictment claimed that for a period of at least 20 years Madoff had defrauded his clients out of $65 billion. Madoff was sentenced to 150 years in federal prison and had most of his assets seized.

How do we explain these crimes? Do we really need fancy explanations? After all, think of Gyges and his ring and the slim chances of being caught weighed against the truly huge gains that white-collar crimes have to offer. How many of us placed in a position of trust and tempted by the ultralavish lifestyles led by most white-collar criminals and the low probability of being caught would, as Plato asked, "be of such an iron nature that he would stand fast in justice"? Ponzi seemed to have set out as a crook, but Madoff seemed to have started out honest. Madoff slowly, and perhaps imperceptibly, became seduced by the many opportunities to become wealthy beyond imagination (he now earns $40 a month doing menial labor in prison). On the other hand, his fellow inmates portray him as a prison celebrity who is past apologizing. One fellow prisoner claims that Madoff is contemptuous of his victims, stating, "Fuck my victims, I carried them for 20 years and now I'm doing 150."

Discussion Questions

1. Discuss honestly with your classmates if you would "stand fast in justice" if you had a ring such as the one Gyges found.

2. Do you think the provisions of the Sarbanes-Oxley Act are sufficiently punitive to deter white-collar crimes such as those Ponzi and Madoff committed?

3. Given the traits of psychopaths discussed in Chapter 9, and given the way influential people seemed to have trusted Madoff, do you think we could classify him as a psychopath? What else might lead you to that conclusion?

Sources: Arvedlund, 2009; Dunn, 2004; Oppenheimer, 2009; Zuckoff, 2005

❖ Cybercrime: Oh, What a Tangled World Wide Web We Weave!

Cybercrime is the use of computer technology to criminally victimize unwary individuals or groups. Any invention that *can* be used by criminals to exploit others or to further their criminal enterprises has been, but few of these inventions have been as useful as the computer. Now even the weak and timid who would never dream of using a gun to rob or otherwise victimize someone can steal, assault, and harass in the comfort of his or her home with little or no risk involved. Everyone who enters cyberspace, uses a credit card, and/or has a social security number—which means just about everybody—is a potential victim of cybercrime. We have seen that conventional criminals such as robbers and burglars typically operate in their own or nearby neighborhoods, but the global reach of the Internet now allows someone in Birmingham, England, to victimize someone in Birmingham, Alabama, or vice versa, without leaving home. The number of offenses it is possible to classify under cybercrime is a legion, ranging from terrorism (the targeting of a country's computer-run infrastructures such as air traffic control and power grid systems) to simple e-mail harassment. As computer technology gets more sophisticated, more possibilities open up for cybercrooks to ply their nefarious trades.

The Silk Road: Amazon.com for Crooks, Creeps, and Crackheads

The Silk Road is the name given to ancient trading routes between China and Europe that greatly benefitted both East and West by providing each with access to products and ideas indigenous to the other. The modern Silk Road was a website were people anywhere in the world could access all sorts of illegal goods and services, such as drugs, child pornography, unlicensed weapons, forged passports and other official documents, counterfeit cash, and even genuine hit men. This emporium of vice displayed bricks of cocaine and counterfeit passports on its website as attractively as Amazon displays its products.

The Silk Road site was buried in what is called the "deep web" or the "dark web," accessible only by downloading a router called TOR ("the onion router"). TOR directs Internet traffic through more than four thousand relays manned by volunteers to conceal a user's location, thus supposedly assuring anonymity (Grossman & Newton-Small, 2013). Goods and services available on websites such as Silk Road are paid for with an online currency called bitcoin. Bitcoin is peer-to-peer virtual money that has no physical reality but is a trusted currency that fuels the deep web with about 55,000 transactions every day (Grossman & Newton-Small, 2013).

The Silk Road website was started in 2011 by Eagle Scout, physics graduate, and radical libertarian ("Get the government off my back!") Ross Ulbricht, aka "Dread Pirate Roberts." Ulbricht was arrested and the site shut down by the FBI in October 2013. According to information in Ulbricht's federal indictment, during its 2 ½ years of operation it provided almost a million customers with $1.2 billion worth of contraband. Ulbricht's indictment charges him with conspiracy to traffic narcotics, money laundering, computer hacking, and attempted murder. The FBI also seized $28.5 million in bitcoin from him (Thompson & Wynters, 2013). The FBI's investigation swept up dealers and buyers in the United States, United Kingdom, Australia, and Sweden who had used Silk Road. Online buying and selling on Silk Road apparently turned out not to be so anonymous after all.

A second federal indictment charges Ulbricht with hiring a hit man to eliminate a former employee who apparently stole bitcoins and got arrested. Ulbricht wanted him dead because he was afraid he would squeal about Ulbricht's operation. The FBI computer crime squad had already been able to trace the origins of the Silk Road website, and the "hit man" hired was actually an undercover FBI agent. Ulbricht agreed to pay $80,000 for the hit, depositing half before the job and half after the undercover officer e-mailed him several pictures of the staged killing (Hume, 2013).

The Silk Road website had its deep-web competitors in sites such as Sheep Marketplace and Black Market Reloaded; both dealt in child pornography, drugs, fraudulent documents, and guns. However, both have shut down, claiming they could not handle the increase in users after Silk Road shut down, could no longer guarantee their customers' anonymity, and were fearful of apprehension. However, on November 5, 2013, Silk Road 2.0 came online offering a "new and improved" version of Ulbricht's website administered by someone also using the moniker Dread Pirate Roberts. By the following day it already had close to 500 drug listings, ranging from marijuana to ecstasy to cocaine (Greenberg, 2013). The website boasts that it is now more secure than the old version and that "you can't keep a good idea down."

Denial of Service Attacks: Virtual Kidnapping and Extortion

Denial of service (DoS) attacks occur when criminals "kidnap" a business website or threaten to kidnap it so that business cannot be conducted. DoS attacks are accomplished by overloading the computational resources of the victim's system by flooding it with millions of bogus messages and useless data. Sometimes an attack is simply malicious mischief carried out by computer-savvy disgruntled employees, customers, or just someone who has a bone to pick with the services the company provides. Other times DoS attacks are committed by criminals who demand ransom. Online gambling sites are prime targets for cyberextortionists because a "kidnapped" website cannot accept bets, and its owners stand to lose millions. Paying the ransom is cheaper than losing business, especially if the threat comes during peak operation times. Millions of dollars have been paid to cyberextortionists with only a miniscule few ever reported to the police (Kshetri, 2006). Not that the police could do much anyway, as many of these attacks originate overseas.

Who Are the Hackers?

A **hacker** may be simply defined as someone who illicitly accesses someone else's computer system. Hackers may be seen as the upscale version of Albert Cohen's lower-class delinquents we met in Chapter 4 who engaged in malicious, destructive, and nonutilitarian vandalism "just for the heck of it." We do not include in this categorization people who hack into computers for instrumental or political reasons, such as professional criminals or cyberterrorists.

Some hackers are purely interested in the intellectual challenge of breaking into difficult systems and do so without damaging them, while others (sometimes known as cyberpunks or virtual vandals) break into systems and implant viruses to destroy data. Most, however, appear to be intellectual thrill seekers who enjoy the challenge of doing something illegal and getting away with it (Voiskounsky & Smyslova, 2003). There is something of a counterculture among these people analogous to graffiti artists and gang members. They take on cybernames such as Nightcrawler and Kompking and romanticize and tell stories about their accomplishments, as well as the accomplishments of "legendary" hackers. Gaining the respect of fellow hackers serves as a source of psychological reinforcement for them in ways similar to ordinary street delinquents (Kshetri, 2006). Hackers tend to be young white males, loners, "nerdy," high-IQ, and idealistic but also unpopular with others, prone to lying and cheating, and perhaps prone to drug and/or alcohol abuse (Voiskounsky & Smyslova, 2003).

Photo 16.3

FBI cyber agents work to combat cyberhackers and pirates.

Software Piracy

Software piracy is illegally copying and distributing software for free or for sale. The Business Software Alliance (BSA) has estimated the worldwide cost of software piracy in 2004 at $31 billion. Although the United States has the lowest piracy rate (ratio of legitimate to pirate market) in the world, it leads the world in losses to piracy—about $7 billion annually (BSA, 2005). In the United States, the illegal market is 21% of the total market, whereas in countries such as China, Vietnam, and Russia the illegal market is around 90% of the total. The BSA estimates that worldwide for every $2 worth of software purchased, $1 worth was illegally obtained.

Software piracy is a crime, but few people see it as such unless multiple copies are made and sold for profit. Many view making copies for friends the same way they view loaning books to them—"I bought it; shouldn't I be able to give it to whomever I please?" Having purchased something legally, they see no reason why the law should mandate they only be allowed rights to it. A large survey of university employees found that this was indeed the attitude of many. Forty-four percent of the respondents said they had obtained unauthorized copies of software, and 31% said they had made such copies (Seale, Polakowski, & Schneider, 1998).

Summary

- White-collar crime is the costliest and most deadly form of crime and divided into occupational and corporate crime. Occupational crime is committed against an employer or the general public in the course of an individual's employment.

- Except for those requiring high-status occupations for their crimes, most white-collar criminals are not all that different from street criminals and occupy a middle position between street criminals and "respectable" people in terms of criminal convictions.

- Corporate crime is criminal activity on behalf of an organization. Corporate crimes involve multiple individuals both as perpetrators and victims and include the loss of billions of dollars and, in some cases, hundreds of lives.

- Corporate crime is explained by a variety of factors, including the juxtaposition of lucrative opportunities and lenient penalties. Personal characteristics associated with corporate criminality include an external locus of control, a low level of cognitive moral development, and a high level of Machiavellianism.
- Corporate wrongdoing is typically investigated and punished by administrative agencies and has typically been treated leniently. New weapons in the fight against white-collar crime, such as the Sarbanes-Oxley Act, have resulted in meaningful penalties imposed on individual executives of corporations involved in corporate crime.
- Cybercrime is a form of victimization for which anyone who enters cyberspace is at risk. Criminals use the Internet for all sorts of illegal things, such as "deep web" sites that offer a multitude of illegal goods and services "anonymously." Hackers also worm their way into the websites of others to steal, destroy, or even kidnap data and hold it for ransom.

Exercises and Discussion Questions

1. Do you think there is really any moral difference between setting off a bomb outside a building for some political reason knowing that a certain number of people would be killed and marketing 11 million defective automobiles knowing that a certain proportion of them will explode into flames when rear-ended and burn the occupants alive?

2. Do you think white-collar crime (occupational and corporate) can be explained by the same principles as street crime? Read one or two of the relevant cited articles for guidance.

3. Do you think a single-payer medical system like those in place in all other Western societies would solve the health care fraud problem and make health care more affordable and accessible?

4. Is corporate crime worse, not as bad, or the same as street crime in your view?

5. Many major corporate scandals are made possible by crony capitalism. How should we as a society react to corporate and political collusion?

6. Would limiting campaign contributions to politicians effectively put an end to crony capitalism in your opinion?

Useful Websites

FBI: White-Collar Crime. www.fbi.gov/whitecollarcrime.htm.

Institute for Intergovernmental Research. www.iir.com/WhatWeDo/Information_Sharing/NW3C.

National Check Fraud Center. www.ckfraud.org/whitecollar.html.

National White Collar Crime Center. www.nw3c.org.

Chapter Terms

Corporate crime

Crony capitalism

Cybercrime

Hacker

Moral hazard

Occupational crime

Sarbanes-Oxley Act (SOA)

Software piracy

White-collar crime

CHAPTER 17

Organized Crime

Mobster turned snitch Henry Hill was born to working-class parents in Brooklyn, New York, in 1943. He grew up fascinated by the world of gangsters and always wanted to become one. Henry got his break at the age of 14 when he began working for the Lucchese crime family as a bagman. Hill slowly moved up the family ladder but could not become a "made man" because he was not Italian. His first arrest was at age 16, but Henry's finest hour was when he put together a small team in 1967 to steal $420,000 (close to $3 billion in 2013 dollars) from the Air France cargo terminal at JFK airport.

At this time Hill was making anywhere from $15,000 to $40,000 a week but managed to blow it in short order on dope, fast women, and slow horses. After a drug-related arrest in 1980, the FBI played Hill a wiretap in which gang members were recorded planning to kill him because he was a "junkie," and they were afraid he would rat on them for their involvement in yet another JFK heist. As a consequence, Henry agreed to testify against his old associates, eventually leading to 50 mob convictions. In exchange for his cooperation, Hill and his family were placed in the Witness Protection Program (WPP). Due to numerous arrests, he was expelled from the WPP in the 1990s and embarked on a legitimate career as a chef and restaurateur. Despite having a contract on his head, Hill was never "whacked." He died peacefully in his bed in Los Angeles in 2012.

Henry Hill's story, told in the movie GoodFellas, graphically illustrates the allure of a life of crime. The allure of being one's own man, the admiration and respect shown to a Mafia associate by fellow gangsters and assorted wannabes, and the promise of wealth well beyond that of what he referred to as the "average schmuck" all led Henry to choose a life he freely and gladly embraced. His story also shows how difficult it is for someone seduced by such a life to go straight. His frequent arrests while in the WPP and his subsequent expulsion from it while he had a price on his head speaks volumes about the mind-set of career criminals. Keep this in mind as you read this chapter and wonder why people would get involved in such a perilous life as an organized crime member.

LEARNING OBJECTIVES

- Be able to differentiate organized crime from other types of criminal groups
- Understand the role of corruption in the origin, perpetuation, and growth of organized crime
- Know the history of organized crime in the United States
- Be able to identify and expound on Russian, Japanese, African American, and Latino organized crime groups
- Recognize the roles various criminological theories play in trying to understand organized crime
- Identify methods of law enforcement to battle organized crime

❖ What Is Organized Crime?

Organized crime has probably existed in one form or another since our ancestors lived in caves, but criminologists have a difficult time defining it. For instance, which criminal groups can be characterized as *organized*, just how organized is organized crime, and how does organized crime differ (if it does) from corporate crime? Some argue that "any distinction between organized and white-collar crime may be artificial inasmuch as both involve the important elements of organization and the use of corruption and/or violence to maintain immunity" (Albanese, 2000, p. 412). Corporate crime is indeed "organized crime" in some senses; by definition corporations are organized, and when their members commit illegal acts they are engaging in crime. But corporate criminals don't fit whistle-blowers with concrete footwear or bomb their competitors out of business. The major difference between corporate and organized crime is that corporate criminals are created from the opportunities available to them in companies organized around doing legitimate business. Organized crime members, on the other hand, must be accomplished criminals before they enter such groups, which are organized around creating criminal opportunities. Thus, the former make a crime out of business and the latter make a business out of crime.

Some definitions of organized crime are so broad as to encompass almost any kind of planned crime committed by more than one individual, while others are so narrow they miss key characteristics that should be included. An excellent definition based on a fairly wide consensus of organized crime scholars is that **organized crime** is "a continuing criminal enterprise that works rationally to profit from illicit activities that are often in great public demand. Its continuing existence is maintained through the use of force, threats, and/or corruption of public officials" (Albanese & Pursley, 1993, p. 58). This section expands on this definition, drawing from findings of the President's Commission on Organized Crime (PCOC; 1986) and concentrating on **La Cosa Nostra** (literally, "our thing"), also commonly referred to as the Mafia. It should not be inferred from this that La Cosa Nostra (LCN) and organized crime are synonymous. There are many other organized crime groups in the United States and around the world.

Structure

The first characteristic that differentiates organized crime groups from other criminal groups such as street gangs is its formal structure. According to the PCOC, LCN groups are structured in a hierarchy reflecting levels of power and specialization. There are alleged to be 24 LCN families with a national ruling body known as the **Commission**, established by Salvatore "Lucky" Luciano in 1931 (PCOC, 1986). The Commission is a kind of "board of directors" and consists of the bosses of the five New York families and four bosses from other important families located in other cities. The Commission arbitrates disputes among the various families, facilitates joint ventures, approves of new members, authorizes the executions of errant members, and acts as a go-between for American and Sicilian factions of LCN (Lyman & Potter, 2004). Members know and respect the hierarchy of authority in their organization just as corporate executives know and respect ordered ranks of authority in their corporations. Although there are occasional family squabbles and coups that remove individuals from the hierarchy, the structure remains intact. The formal structure of an LCN family is diagrammed in Figure 17.1.

At the top of the family structure is the boss (the *don* or *capo*), whose rule within is absolute, although he may be overruled by the Commission. Beneath the boss are a counselor (*consigliere*) or advisor and an underboss (*sotto capo*). The counselor is usually an old family member, often a lawyer, who is wise in the ways of crime, and the underboss is a sort of vice president being groomed for succession to the top position. Beneath the underboss are the

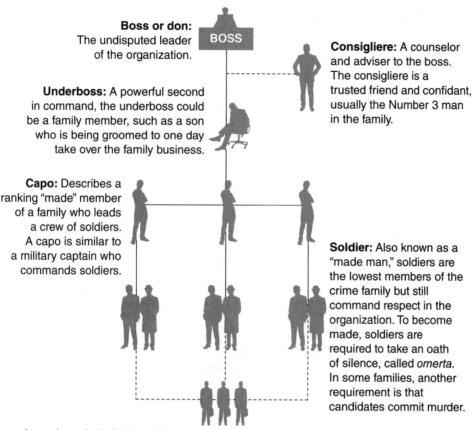

Boss or don: The undisputed leader of the organization.

BOSS

Consigliere: A counselor and adviser to the boss. The consigliere is a trusted friend and confidant, usually the Number 3 man in the family.

Underboss: A powerful second in command, the underboss could be a family member, such as a son who is being groomed to one day take over the family business.

Capo: Describes a ranking "made" member of a family who leads a crew of soldiers. A capo is similar to a military captain who commands soldiers.

Soldier: Also known as a "made man," soldiers are the lowest members of the crime family but still command respect in the organization. To become made, soldiers are required to take an oath of silence, called *omerta.* In some families, another requirement is that candidates commit murder.

Associate: An individual who is part of a crew but has not been "made" and commits crimes under the protection/direction of made members and remits a share of his illegal proceeds to his direct made superior.

Figure 17.1

Mafia Family Organization Flow Chart

Source: FBI, 2001

lieutenants (*caporegimas*) who supervise the day-to-day operation of the family and enjoy considerable power. Below the lieutenants are the soldiers (*soldati*), known as *made men, wiseguys,* or *button men.* Although soldiers are the lowest-ranking members of the family, they may each run their own crew of nonmember associates.

LCN members are not employees of the family in the sense that they earn a regular income from the organization. Membership in the family entitles members to run their own rackets using the family's connections and status. A percentage of a soldier's earnings is paid to his lieutenant, who also has his own enterprises on which he pays a percentage to the underboss, and so on up the line.

This is known as the **corporate model** because of its similarity to corporate structure; i.e., a formal hierarchy in which the day-to-day activities of the organization are planned and coordinated at the top and carried out by subordinates. Although it is the model favored by the PCOC, some criminologists favor the **feudal model**. The feudal system was a social system in medieval Europe in which the king granted land to his nobles. In return, the nobles swore oaths of loyalty to the king and promised to support him in his wars. The nobles also granted land to lesser nobles, who swore allegiance to the lord and promised to support him in war when he had to support the king. Then came the villeins, freemen who received land for working on the lord's manor and who could employ serfs, the lowest members of the feudal system.

This feudal model of the LCN views it as a loose collection of criminal groups held together by kinship and patronage. The Commission may be seen as the king and his ministers who rarely if ever interfered with their nobles; the individual family bosses may be seen as the lords, the lieutenants as the lesser nobility, the made men as the villeins, and the associates as the serfs. The oaths of loyalty, the autonomous operations of each family, the semiautonomous operations of the soldiers and lieutenants, and the provision of status and protection from the family in exchange for a cut of their earnings provides evidence that LCN bosses are more like feudal lords than corporate CEOs.

Continuity

Organized crime is like a mature corporation (or a feudal system for that matter) in that it continues to operate beyond the lifetime of its individual members. It does not disintegrate when key leaders are arrested, die, or otherwise absent. The criminal group takes on a life of its own, and members subordinate their personal interests to those of the family. This makes organized crime quite different from gangs that spring up and die with their leaders.

Membership

LCN is not an equal-opportunity employer; it is restricted to males of Italian descent of proven criminal expertise. Prospective members must be sponsored by made men (established members of the family), who are responsible for the behavior of those they sponsor during their probationary period. Applicants are screened carefully for their criminal activity and loyalty before being allowed to apply, and only the most promising applicants are accepted. A lifetime commitment to the family is required from the newcomer, and in return he receives a guaranteed lucrative criminal career as part of an organization of great prestige and respect in the underworld. A promising criminal (such as Henry Hill) not of Italian descent, but who has qualities useful to the organization, may become an associate member. The FBI estimates that for every formal member of LCN there are 10 associates (PCOC, 1986).

Criminality

Like any other kind of business, organized crime seeks to make a profit. Most of organized crime's income is derived from supplying the public with goods and services not available in the legitimate market, such as drugs, gambling, and prostitution. Much of organized crime's income is funneled into legitimate businesses after its "dirty" (illicit) money is "laundered." Thus, although organized crime is roughly structured similarly to legal business enterprises and is energized by the profit motive, it differs from them in the illicit nature of its product and its reason for being.

❖ Political Corruption and Organized Crime

Organized crime would have a very difficult time surviving were it not for the corruption of powerful individuals not directly associated with it. Corruption (dishonest and unethical conduct by people in power) is a continuum ranging from the beat cop accepting a small bribe to "look the other way" to corruption at the highest levels of government. The Center for the Study of Democracy

(CSD; 2010) observes that "in its most advanced form, organised crime is so thoroughly integrated into the economic, political, and social institutions of legitimate society that it may no longer be recognizable as a criminal enterprise" (p. 40). The CSD (2010) provides the example of former Italian prime minister Giulio Andretti's protection of Italian Mafia figures in exchange for the Mafia's electoral support, and Adelstein (2010) notes that the Japanese *yakuza* have funded and supported Japan's Liberal Democratic Party since its founding in 1955.

There is thus no doubt that a high level of business and political corruption walk hand in hand with organized crime. Dutch criminologist Jan Van Dijk (2008) carried out a book-length research project on this issue using data from 163 nations around the world. He examined the rule of law (the extent to which a country has an independent judiciary and the general population's respect for the law), the World Bank's corruption index (surveys of the perceived level of corruption in a country), wealth (gross domestic product), and the extent of organized crime. The results are summarized in Figure 17.2.

Interpreting the model, we see that (1) the lower the rule of law in a country the higher the level of organized crime. (2) The greater the organized crime the greater the level of corruption. (3) The greater the corruption the lower the wealth. (4) The greater the rule of law the greater the wealth. (5) The greater the wealth the greater the level of organized crime. The direction of the arrows is arbitrary in a causal sense; for instance, does greater organized crime cause greater corruption, or is it the other way around? It could be either in different countries, but these things really have a reciprocal relationship with one another; that is, each has a causal feedback impact on the other.

The United States was seen as "medium" on the composite organized crime index with a score of 36.4 out of a possible 100, with 100 representing the country with the highest level of organized crime (Haiti). The country with the lowest score was Finland (10.4). The United States was ranked first in wealth and 17th in the world on the rule of law (Iceland was first; the Democratic Republic of Congo was last). A later publication by Transparency International (2013), a global coalition against corruption, ranked the United States 19th (a score of 73 out of 100) in low levels of corruption, with New Zealand and Demark tied for first (least corrupt; score of 91) and Somalia last (the most corrupt; score of 8). The United States is ranked very favorably with regard to low levels of organized crime and corruption and high levels of the rule of law. Only the countries of Western Europe and Australasia seem to do better.

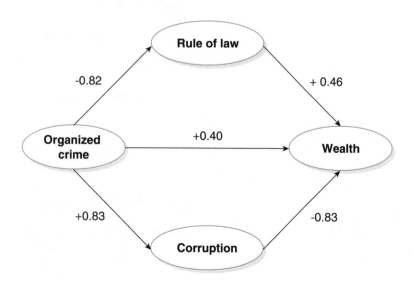

Figure 17.2

Statistical Model of the Relationship Among Prevalence of Organized Crime, Corruption, the Rule of Law, and Country Wealth

Source: Van Dijk, 2008

❖ A Brief History of Organized Crime in the United States

According to Mafia historian Nick Tosches (1992), "The first that America heard of what it would later call the Mafia was in newspaper accounts of certain events in New Orleans" (p. 35). He recounts that the 1869 articles state that a certain district of the city "had become infested by 'well-known and notorious Sicilian murderers, counterfeiters and burglars, who, in the last month, have formed a sort of general co-partnership or stock company for the plunder and disturbance of the city'" (p. 35). Accounts such as this have led to the widespread view that organized crime is an alien conspiracy of Italian origin. However, organized crime groups existed long before there was any major Italian presence in the United States, and most organized crime scholars believe the phenomenon is a "normal" product of the competitive and freewheeling nature of societies such as ours. The two major candidates for the origin of organized crime as we have defined it are the Society of Saint Tammany, founded in 1786, and Prohibition in 1920.

The **Tammany Society** began as a fraternal and patriotic society but soon evolved into a corrupt political machine. Tammany, which became synonymous with the Democratic Party in New York City, ran the city well into the 20th century from the "Hall" (Tammany Hall). Tammany Hall, pictured nearby, was featured in the movie *Gangs of New York*. Tammany political bosses made use of street gangs to threaten and intimidate political rivals. Prominent among these gangs were the vicious Whyos and Five Points gangs. In order for a new member to be accepted by the Whyos, which at its peak had over 500 members, he had to have killed at least once. The Whyos plied their trade among New York's citizenry by passing out price lists on the streets for the services they provided (ranging from $2 for punching to $100 for murder) as casually as pizza vendors (Browning & Gerassi, 1980). The Five Points gang was a confederation of neighborhood gangs and was said to have over 1,500 members at one time. Among the future luminaries of organized crime associated with the Whyos were Al Capone and Lucky Luciano (Abadinsky, 2003).

Photo 17.1

Tammany Hall, pictured here, housed the Tammany Society, a corrupt political machine that "ran" New York City and originated many of the characteristics of organized crime.

Organized crime existed on its earnings from gambling, prostitution, protection, extortion, and labor racketeering during the early part of the 20th century. During this period, members of these criminal organizations were often employed by politicians, who used them as errand boys and enforcers, a relationship that was to reverse itself after 1920. In 1920, the United States Congress handed every petty gang in America an initiation to unlimited expansion and wealth with the ratification of the Eighteenth Amendment (the Volstead Act, or **Prohibition**), which prohibited the sale, manufacture, or importation of intoxicating liquors within the United States. Prohibition ushered in a vicious 10-year period of crime, violence, and political corruption as gangsters fought over the right to provide the drinking public with illicit alcohol.

Photo 17.2

Notorious Prohibition-era gangster Al Capone.

Johnny Torrio, a product of New York's Five Points gang, became the leading figure in Chicago's gangland. A master strategist, he realized that violence was counterproductive and was able to broker a truce among warring factions and organize them into a sort of loose confederation. The confederation ended when members of a rival Irish gang critically wounded Torrio. After recovering from his wound, Torrio returned to New York in 1924, leaving his protégé, Al "Scarface" Capone, in charge of the Chicago operation.

The Capone era provided America with its stereotypical image of organized gangsters. Capone was a ruthless criminal and a flamboyant man whose generosity endeared him to many members of the media and to many of Chicago's poor people for whom he provided soup kitchens and shelter. Only 25 years of age when he succeeded Torrio, he soon established a criminal empire that at the height of Prohibition consisted of over 700 gunmen (Abadinsky, 2003). The wealth Capone accumulated from his bootlegging and prostitution enterprises got him into the *Guinness Book of Records* as having the highest gross income ($105 million, or $1,409,329,310 in 2013 dollars) of any private citizen in America in 1927. But all good things come to an end. The Depression cut into Capone's income, and the Supreme Court ruled that unlawful income, as well as lawful income, was subject to taxation. It was this law that spelled his doom. He was sentenced to 11 years in prison for tax evasion in 1931. So, this murderer, pimp, robber, extortionist, and thief was brought down by a relatively petty white-collar crime.

With the repeal of the Eighteenth Amendment in 1933, organized crime entered a new and quieter phase, but the modern face of LCN was already beginning to take form in New York. There were two main factions in Italian organized crime in New York at this time, one headed by Giuseppe Masseria and the other by Salvatore Maranzano, who were struggling for supremacy. This struggle, known as the Castellammarese War, ended with the deaths of both leaders in 1931. The Castellammarese War saw the end of the reigns of the old Sicilian "mustache petes" and the emergence of an Americanized LCN (Lyman & Potter, 2004). Lucky Luciano, Bugsy Siegel, and Meyer Lansky were all instrumental in this process. The Americanization of LCN saw the emergence of the five New York families active today. It also saw Lucky Luciano become the major figure in LCN, enabling him to set up the organization's national commission and to claim the title of founding father of Italian American organized crime (Lupsha, 1987).

❖ Affirming the Existence of Organized Crime

Law enforcement interest in organized crime activities waned considerably after WWII, and many officials refused to acknowledge its existence. Three events—the Kefauver Committee, the Apalachin "summit," and the McClellen Commission—affirmed the reality of its existence, however. The (Senator Estes) Kefauver Committee formed in 1950 to investigate organized crime's involvement in interstate commerce. The committee hearings called in to testify such important organized crime figures as Meyer Lansky, Frank Castello, and Bugsy Siegel, exposing them to the public for the first time.

The Apalachin meeting, held in Apalachin, New York, in 1957, provided further evidence for the existence of a national and coordinated crime syndicate, once again riveting national attention on it. Major LCN figures met on this occasion supposedly to confirm Vito Genovese as the *capo di tutti capi* ("boss of bosses") and to discuss other LCN matters. The police (who stumbled on the meeting purely by accident) raided the meeting and arrested 63 people, including the bosses and underbosses of New York's LCN families. All arrestees refused to answer questions about the purpose of the meeting and were indicted for obstruction of justice. No convictions came out of these indictments, but it destroyed LCN's hope that it could stay out of the public spotlight. According to the PCOC (1986) it finally confirmed the existence of organized crime, and law enforcement began to focus more seriously on combating it.

The (Senator John L.) McClellan Commission formed in 1956 to look into financial irregularities in the Teamsters Union, but the star witness was a made man in the Genovese family named Joe Valachi. While in prison on drug charges, another made man accused Valachi of being an informer, which meant to Valachi that he was marked for death. Rather than face this prospect, he decided to testify as to what he knew about the Mafia in front of the McClellan Commission. Valachi revealed much about the operation of the Mafia, including the fact that members of Italian organized crime no longer used that name, if they ever did. According to Valachi, the organization called itself *Cosa Nostra*, a term unfamiliar to law enforcement officials up to then. Senator Robert Kennedy called Valachi's testimony the "biggest intelligence breakthrough yet in combating organized crime" (in Wilson, 1984, p. 566).

LCN is still very much a major crime threat, although it is not as powerful as it once was. The government prosecuted hundreds of organized crime figures in the so-called Commission trials (a reference to the LCN Commission) of the 1980s. The leaders of 16 of the 24 LCN families were indicted with the leaders of the Genovese, Lucchesi, and Columbo families and sentenced to 100 years imprisonment each. The leader of the Gambino family, Paul Castellano, avoided prosecution by getting himself murdered. Castellano's successor (and the man who ordered his murder), John Gotti, was sentenced to life in prison in 1992 after being convicted of 13 federal charges (he died of cancer in prison in 2002). Known as "the Teflon Don" because of his ability to avoid prosecution and/or conviction, Gotti was betrayed by his former underboss, Salvatore "The Bull" Gravano, who testified against him in exchange for a lenient 5-year sentence (he openly admitted to killing 19 people "give or take a few"). John Gotti Jr. took control of the Gambino family after his father's imprisonment but was himself imprisoned for racketeering in 1999. He was further indicted in 2004 for ordering a hit on Curtis Sliwa, talk show host and founder of the citizen anticrime volunteer patrols, the Guardian Angels (McShane, 2004). Hope that LCN was on its deathbed faded after the terrorist attacks of 9/11. Before 9/11, the FBI's two areas of focus were counterespionage and organized crime, but 9/11 moved the focus onto counterterrorism. This gave the mob a new lease on life. Crime family bosses learned from the flamboyance of bosses like John Gotti that the spotlight is not a good place to occupy and reverted to maintaining low profiles. In January of 2011, the public became aware that LCN is still with us as the FBI swept up over 120 LCN mobsters on a variety of charges (Raab, 2011). This has again weakened LCN, but we have learned that it is almost impossible to kill it. Even if we could kill it, there are plenty of other crime groups ready, willing, and able to take its place.

❖ Other Organized Crime Groups

The Russian "Mafiya"

The Russian "Mafiya" is a catch-all phrase for a group of organized gangs that many experts consider to be the most serious organized crime threat in the world today (Rush & Scarpitti, 2001). There has been an explosion of crime in Russia since the breakup of the Soviet Union, but even in the old Soviet Union there had been significant organized crime activity as the "shadow economy" exploited the shortage of all kinds of consumer goods created by the socialist centrally planned economy. The crime, bribery, and political and police corruption in modern Russia make the Prohibition period in America look positively benign. As James Finckenauer (2004) put it, "Organized crime has been able to penetrate Russian businesses and state enterprises to a degree inconceivable in most other countries" (p. 62).

Russian organized crime (ROC) has existed since at least the 17th century and became firmly entrenched in Russian society in the 1920s. The major group in ROC is known as the *vory v zakone* (thieves-in-law), which began as a large group of political prisoners following the Communist Revolution in 1917. The Soviet prison system used this group to maintain order over the general prison population in exchange for many favors. These "elite" prisoners developed their own structural hierarchy and strict code of conduct or "laws" (hence *thieves-in-law*). One of their strictest rules was that there was to be absolutely no cooperation with legitimate authority for any reason.

Because of the ethnic diversity of ROC, it is loosely organized and may be undergoing the weeding-out and consolidation phases the LCN underwent in the 1930s. ROC is the biggest factor threatening Russia's democratization, economic development, and security. It threatens democratization because if a democratic government cannot control it, an authoritarian one will. It threatens the economy because foreign companies are reluctant to make the much-needed investments in an economy rife with the murder and extortion of business leaders. It threatens public security because many police officers and KGB personnel have left public service for the more lucrative opportunities available with organized crime (Carter, 1994).

Russian organized crime metastasized to the United States with the influx of Russian immigrants in the 1970s and 1980s who brought with them a cultural heritage. One aspect of that heritage similar to that of the earlier Sicilian/Italian immigrants is a deep distrust of government. This distrust allows criminal elements among the new arrivals to criminally exploit their fellow immigrants with relative impunity. Another piece of cultural baggage born from the communist heritage is a disdain for the work ethic. Both the distrust of the authorities and the alleged attitude toward legitimate work provide fertile ground for the growth of criminal activity (Rosner, 1995).

Unlike the largely uneducated Mafioso driven out of Italy by Mussolini in the 1920s, many of Russian émigré criminals are highly educated. Some, driven out by economic hardship, even held professional positions in Russia (Rush & Scarpitti, 2001). This level of intelligence and expertise should make them more of a threat than the unsophisticated peasant class that made up most of the early Sicilian/Italian mobsters. ROC groups are difficult to infiltrate because they do not organize along the hierarchical structure of LCN groups but rather "form their networks based on the skills needed for particular crimes" (Finklea, 2010, p. 17). Nevertheless, Rush and Scarpitti (2001) write that "it has been speculated by intelligence agencies such as the IRS, FBI, and CIA that because of their higher level of criminal sophistication Russian organized crime groups will present a greater overall threat to American society than the traditional Italian-American crime families ever have" (p. 538). According to Finklea (2010), these speculations rang true because the FBI now considers ROC to be the top organized crime threat in the United States.

The Japanese Yakuza

Japanese organized crime (JOC) groups are probably the oldest and largest in the world, with total membership larger than LCN and estimated at 90,000 (Lyman & Potter, 2004). The official Japanese term for organized criminals is *Boryokudan* (violent ones), but they are more commonly referred to as *yakuza* (useless person). As with the Sicilian Mafia, the yakuza has its roots in rural lawlessness and is likewise clouded in a dubious and romanticized history (Hill, 2003). The group is commonly believed to have evolved from *ronin*, or masterless samurai warriors, who contracted their services out for assassinations and other illegal purposes. Like the Sicilian Mafia, they also protected the peasants from other marauding bandits as a sort of vigilante–law enforcement group. The defeat of Japan in WWII and the ensuing chaos provided the catalyst for the growth of JOC. This period saw many gang wars erupt over control of lucrative illicit markets. As in the United States, these gang wars led to the elimination of some gangs and to the consolidation and strengthening of others. The Kobe-based *Yamaguchi-gumi* (*gumi* means *group*), with an estimated membership of over 10,000, is the largest of these groups (Iwai, 1986).

THEORY IN ACTION: James "Whitey" Bulger and the Winter Hill Gang

James "Whitey" Bulger was born in 1929, the first of three sons born to Johnny and Jane Bulger. After Johnny lost an arm in an industrial accident, the family was reduced to poverty and forced to move into a public housing project in Boston. Both of Jimmy's younger brothers did well in school, with William eventually becoming president of the Massachusetts Senate and Johnny becoming a court clerk magistrate. But for Whitey things were different; he hated school and was expelled for punching a teacher in the face when he was 14. As an adult,

Photo 17.3

Whitey Bulger's mug shot taken after his 16 years on the run came to an end.

Bulger stood 5'8" tall and weighed in at 155 pounds, but despite his size he was a fearsome fighter and one of the most feared men in Boston.

Whitey's extensive criminal career commenced with his first arrest for stealing when he was 14 years old. As a juvenile, he was arrested for larceny, forgery, assault and battery, and armed robbery, garnering him 5 years in a juvenile reformatory. He joined the Air Force upon his release, spending a good portion of his time in military jail for assault and going AWOL before being discharged in 1952.

After returning to Boston, Whitey resumed his life as a criminal, committing a string of bank robberies in states ranging from Rhode Island to Indiana. He was sentenced to 25 years in federal prison in June of 1956 but was released after serving only 9 years. Bulger soon resumed his life of crime upon returning to Boston, becoming an enforcer for a notorious Irish gang called the Winter Hill Gang headed by Donald Killeen. After Killeen was gunned down in 1972, Bulger rapidly rose through the ranks of the gang and became quickly known as a shrewd, ruthless, and cunning mobster who sanctioned and/or committed numerous killings (19 in all). He rapidly became a major figure in the organized crime world of Boston in the late 1970s after assuming gang leadership. He controlled a large portion of Boston's drug, bookmaking, and loan sharking operations.

While engaged in all this criminal activity, and unbeknownst to associates, Bulger was an FBI informant from 1975 through 1990. He became an informant because he wanted to bring down Boston's Italian American Patriarca crime family in order to build up his own crime

THEORY IN ACTION (Continued)

network. He was able to do this by taking advantage of his relationship with the FBI, his brother William's position in the Massachusetts State Senate, and his friendships in the city and state police forces forged in childhood. As a result of his value to the FBI and his other connections, the behavior of Bulger's crime network was largely ignored by law enforcement.

When the news media exposed Whitey's connections to powerful political and law enforcement people, as well as criminal actions on the part of law enforcement people tied to him, his world began to unravel. In December of 1994, when Whitey was 65 years old, he was tipped off by his former FBI handler that he was about to be indicted under the RICO act. Upon hearing this, Bulger fled Boston and went into hiding for 16 years, landing on the FBI's Ten Most Wanted list for 12 of those years. The $2 million reward for his capture was second only to Osama bin Laden's $25 million.

After traveling the world under assumed names with his longtime girlfriend Catherine Greig, at the age of 81 Whitey was finally arrested in Santa Monica, California, and extradited to Massachusetts. FBI agents found more than $800,000 in cash, fake IDs, and 30 guns in Bulger's apartment. After a 3-month trial, on August 12, 2013, Whitey was convicted of 11 counts of murder and 31 counts of various other crimes. Calling Whitey a "little sociopath" who "committed one heinous crime after another," the prosecutor urged the judge to sentence him to life in prison. He was sentenced to two consecutive life sentences plus 5 years. He may also be facing two additional murder charges in Florida and Oklahoma.

James "Whitey" Bulger exemplifies many of the points made in this chapter. He was an intelligent individual, but how far would he have gotten in the underworld without his political and law enforcement connections? Although his family was dirt poor, Whitey was not "forced" into crime; both of his brothers had successful and legitimate careers. Bulger was seduced by the "every night is party night" life of the criminal. The money, respect, reputation, and independence such a life offers trumped the dangers inherent in such a lifestyle. His fearlessness, callousness, and ruthlessness marks him as a psychopath, the personality type most likely to succeed in organized crime—after all, Whitey was the ripe old age of 81 when he was finally arrested.

Discussion Questions

1. Look up articles on Whitey's brother, William Bulger, and see if you can recognize any similarities in personality in the two brothers.

2. Whitey and his two brothers all took different paths in life; make a case using labeling theory on why Whitey took the criminal route.

3. To what extent do you think Whitey's criminal activities were made possible by political and law enforcement corruption?

Sources: Cullen & Murphy, 2013; Lehr & O'Neill, 2001

Members of JOC groups are recruited heavily from the two outcast groups in Japanese society—the *burakumin* (outcasts because their ancestors worked at trades that dealt with dead flesh, such as butchery, tanning, and grave digging, which was seen as unclean in the Buddhist religious tradition) and Japanese-born Koreans. Once admitted, a member must pledge absolute loyalty to his superiors and, like his LCN counterpart, must generate his own income and contribute part of it to the *ikka* (the family).

JOC enjoys a unique position in Japanese society. Despite their lowly beginning as burakumin, the yakuza have been able to acquire a level of legitimacy not afforded to LCN or ROC. Their historical connection with the samurai; their espousal of traditional norms of duty, loyalty, and manliness; their support for nationalistic programs; and their "law enforcement" functions (as in Mafia neighborhoods in America, yakuza neighborhoods are safe from common criminals) endow them with a certain level of respect and admiration among the Japanese. In fact, when a major earthquake hit Kobe in 1995, the Yamaguchi-gumi's relief efforts exceeded those of the Japanese government (Abadinsky, 2003). Similarly, in the aftermath of the 2011 tsunami and earthquake, JOC groups were the first workers on the scene, aiding in rescue and recovery and donating $500,000 worth of food and supplies (Fisher, 2012).

Indicative of their status in Japanese society, the yakuza are not shadowy underworld figures. Their gang affiliations are proudly displayed on insignia worn on their clothes and on their offices and buildings, and they publish their own newsletter. The headquarters of one crime group, complete with the gang emblem hanging proudly outside, is only three doors away from the local police station (Johnson, 1990). With their openness, extensively tattooed bodies, gang colors, and service-for-hire tradition, the yakuza seem more like outlaw motorcycle gangs than La Cosa Nostra.

The police have tended to tolerate yakuza activity in certain areas as long as it involves only the provision of certain illicit goods and services demanded by the public, but they have cracked down hard when firearms and drugs are trafficked or when innocent civilians are harmed. With the introduction of the Boryokudan Countermeasures Law of 1992, however, the relationship between the police and the yakuza has become more antagonistic, and there have been many police crackdowns (Hill, 2003).

Outlaw Motorcycle Gangs

There are some 900 motorcycle gangs in the United States, with the "big four"—the Hells Angels, Outlaws, Bandidos, and Pagans—having evolved into a serious organized crime problem (Quinn, 2001). Outlaw motorcycle gangs (OMGs) are of American heritage, but they have been copied around the world. The California-based Hells Angels is the largest of these gangs, with an estimated membership in the United States of 1,000 (Lyman & Potter, 2004).

The organizational structure of OMGs typically consists of a president, vice president, secretary-treasurer, sergeant at arms, road captain, and enforcer. Each chapter or club belongs to a regional entity and to a national organization headed by a mother club, which is usually the founder club. As with LCN "wannabes," prospective OMG members must be sponsored by an active club member and be willing to demonstrate their worth by committing a serious criminal act in front of "made" members, which enables the club to weed out the weak as well as possible police infiltrators.

Photo 17.4

Hells Angels ride together displaying their club colors and patches. Bikers in outlaw motorcycle gangs like this one aim to project the impression of toughness and boldness.

Women can join the gangs, but their status is little more than sexual playthings. Wives or steady girlfriends of gang members are referred to as old ladies and are the exclusive "property" of their men, wearing denim jackets with that designation embroidered on them. Other women associates are referred to as mammas or sheep and are the sexual property of any gang member desiring to use them or to prostitute them to nonmembers (Abadinsky, 2003).

Bikers revel in and flaunt their antisocial attitudes, wearing patches on their club colors such as FTW ("fuck the world"), 666 (the sign of Satan), and 1%, which owes its origin to a statement that outlaw bikers were only 1% of motorcyclists (Abadinsky, 2003). Bikers are also intensely concerned with maintaining a personal aura of boldness, strength, and toughness and have a deep fascination with power. Borrowing from Merton's anomie theory, James Quinn (2001) views bikers' social adaptations as "extremes of retreatism, rebellion, and innovation in combinations that vary across groups, regions, and time periods" (p. 382). Certainly all OMGs are involved in many crimes. The manufacturing and distribution of drugs is their main source of income, with extortion, contract murder, gunrunning, prostitution, pornography, and massage parlors being other sources (Lyman & Potter, 2004). The Hells Angels and the Outlaws, often in bitter conflict with each other, are known to have ties to LCN and to have performed contract killings for it. An Alcohol, Tobacco, and Firearms (ATF) agent stated that the big four OMGs are "priority ATF targets" and are "the largest—and best armed—criminal organizations in the country" (in Quinn, 2001, p. 381).

African American Organized Crime

Powerful black organized crime groups have existed in the United States since at least the 1920s, meeting the illicit needs for drugs, alcohol, gambling, and prostitution in black communities (Schatzberg & Kelly, 1996). African American organized crime began with the policy syndicates in Harlem in the 1920s, but they were often either muscled out of business or functioned as local franchise operators for white gangsters (Schatzberg & Kelly, 1996). The Vietnam War enabled African American organized crime to gain its independence from white organized crime by establishing its own connections with Asian drug dealers. The Vietnam War was to African American organized crime what Prohibition was to white organized crime, giving birth to such gangs as the Crips and Bloods and to the kind of inter- and intragang warfare that characterized Prohibition-era white gangs (Adamson, 2000).

The Gangster Disciples, formed in Chicago in 1969 by the merger of two former rival gangs—the Disciples and the Supreme Gangsters—became an organization that comes closest to matching LCN in scope and sophistication. Membership in the Gangster Disciples has been estimated to be from 6,000 to 50,000 in 35 states (Abadinsky, 2003). The group is a formal, hierarchical, and authoritarian organization and has alliances with other black groups such as the Crips (Knox & Fuller, 1995). Despite this level of organization, Adamson (2000) disputes their status as a "black mafia" because they lack sophistication, stating that "at best, they are a proto-mafia" (p. 289). Yet it is precisely the lack of sophistication that makes such groups more violent and dangerous than traditional organized crime groups (Cureton, 2009).

Although the strong ethnic sense of belonging that helped to cement LCN groups together does not exist among African American groups, just because they do not fit the Mafia prototype does not mean they cannot be organized. Ianni (1998) claims that "instead of family or kinship . . . the blacks may be able to use black militancy as their organizing principle" (p. 125). Many blacks are recruited into crime networks from youth gangs and prison groups. Experiences within these groups lay down a foundation for disrespect of the law and a sense of belongingness and "specialness," which organized crime groups depend on to maintain discipline and loyalty.

Latino Groups

After the 1959 revolution that saw Fidel Castro assume power in Cuba, many Cubans fled their homeland, some of them taking to crime. The so-called Marielitos originated with the Mariel Harbor boatlift from Cuba in 1980 in which Castro rid himself of about 125,000 Cuban dissidents by shipping them to Florida. Among these refugees were a number of common criminals (estimates range from 2,500 to 8,750). The Marielitos teamed up with other Cuban criminal elements as enforcers and executioners but soon branched off on their own. Today they are said to exist in a number of states and are active primarily in drug trafficking (Lyman & Potter, 2004).

The Marielitos have connections with the South American drug trafficking groups. Organized crime thrives where political corruption comes easy, and it comes very easy in Mexico. There are a large number of drug cartels operating in Mexico and sending their wares to the United States. The cartels make full use of the United States' inability to control illegal immigration because they can use any number of Mexicans desperate to get into the United States as mules. These cartels are known to have hundreds of politicians and law enforcement officials on their payroll and may have been instrumental in getting the Mexican government to print their Migrant Guide, instructing their nationals on how to avoid detection when trying to enter the United States illegally (Walsh, 2005). Howard Abadinsky (2003) quotes the director of the DEA with regard to the danger of Mexican organized crime to the United States:

> Organized crime figures in Mexico have at their disposal an army of personnel, an arsenal of weapons and the finest technology money can buy. They run transportation and financial empires and an insight in how they conduct their day-to-day business leads . . . to the conclusion that the United States is facing a threat of unprecedented proportions and gravity. (p. 186)

❖ Theories of Organized Crime

Criminologists ask the same questions about organized crime that they do about white-collar crime: What causes it? Are these causes unique to it? Are the external social and economic causes of it more important than individual-level causes? Some argue that we create our own organized crime problem by creating laws that prevent members of the public from acquiring goods and services (e.g., alcohol, drugs, gambling, prostitution) they desire and demand (Lyman & Potter, 2004). When such demands are not met legally there are always those willing to supply them illegally. And, as already noted, on a macro-scale widespread corruption in the political, legal, and business realms provides fertile territory for organized crime to flourish.

To say that organized crime exists because of huge economic incentives to supply people with goods and services legally denied them is only part of the causal equation. It looks at the social sources of the criminal opportunities made available but not why those who take advantage of them do so. Early theories of organized crime relied on the anomie/strain tradition to explain it, describing the gangster as "a man with a gun, acquiring by personal merit what was denied him by complex orderings of stratified society" and viewing each successive wave of immigrants as ascending a "queer ladder of social mobility" in American society (Bell, 1962, p. 128).

According to this **ethnic succession theory**, upon arrival in the United States each ethnic group was faced with prejudicial and discriminatory attitudes that denied them legitimate means to success. The Irish, Jews, and Italians were each prominent in organized crime before they became assimilated into American culture and gained access to legitimate means of social mobility. More recently, African Americans, Russians, and Asians have been prominent in organized crime and, according to this view, may have to climb their own "queer ladder" until they gain full acceptance in American society.

The memoirs of a number of LCN figures, however, do not support the notion that they turned to crime because they were denied legitimate opportunities. Many of them had received good educations, came from involved and intact families, and had many opportunities to enter legitimate careers (Firestone, 1997). Rather, these men saw organized crime as a more lucrative and desirable career than any legitimate alternative. Michael Franzese, a former caporegima of the Columbo family, for instance, gave up his premed studies to join the mob because the mob was a quicker and easier way to monetary success. Similarly, Bill Bonanno, former consigliere of the Bonanno family, had a boarding school education and studied agricultural engineering at university (Firestone, 1997). However, these memoirs were mostly written by high-ranking figures born into the mob, so the lack of legitimate opportunities remains a possible factor explaining the participation of the more numerous mob associates.

It is difficult to claim that anyone in the United States today is literally denied opportunities to succeed in the legitimate world, although opportunities are certainly more available to some than to others. The idea of opportunity denial implies that those allegedly denied them would have gladly taken advantage of them if they existed and would have spurned crime. In this view, a criminal career is simply the default option undertaken by the downtrodden, with the unspoken corollary being that no one would actively seek criminal opportunities if legitimate options were available. But organized crime, like white-collar crime, affords those who commit it huge rewards for relatively little risk. Given this, we might well ask with social control theorists why most of us don't seek out these criminal opportunities rather than why some of us do.

Part of the answer to this question is that just as we all don't have equal access to lucrative legitimate opportunities, as Cloward and Ohlin (1960) stress in their opportunity structure theory discussed in Chapter 6, access to lucrative illegitimate opportunities is not equally available to everyone that might desire them. If you wanted to become part of an organized crime group, how would you go about it? As most of us know, networking, or establishing interconnecting lines of communication among friends and acquaintances "in the know," is very useful when seeking legitimate employment opportunities. Similarly, you would have to have access to someone who is "connected" to become involved in organized crime.

Differential association theory may provide an explanation. We know that criminal acts arise from the interaction of environmental instigation and individual risk factors. The environmental risk factors are particularly powerful in some neighborhoods, and therefore the threshold for engaging individual risk factors is lowered for those living in them. If you grew up in subcultural enclaves where organized crime was established and flourishing, you would stand a good chance of at least having a shot at joining the mob if you were so inclined. Almost all mob members lived in neighborhoods where they were constantly surrounded by criminals and criminal values. They grew up hero-worshiping the neighborhood made men, emulating their dress and mannerisms, and dreaming of becoming one of them. It was the mobster who had the beautiful women, the sleek cars, the fancy clothes, and the respect, not the legitimate "working stiff" (Firestone, 1997). Such neighborhoods proved to be fertile ground for the constant cultivation of new batches of criminals because they provided their young inhabitants with exposure to an excess of definitions favorable to law violation.

Because membership in some gangs is so valued that there is always a surplus of contenders for mob positions living in these neighborhoods, aspiring hoods have to prove they have the "right stuff." If they can make the grade, the joy and enthusiasm with which they describe their acceptance makes nonsense of the idea that gangsters are poor deprived individuals making the best of a bad deal. A newly initiated member of the Bonanno family makes plain how much he valued his new status: "Getting made is the greatest thing that could ever happen to me. . . . I've been looking forward to this day ever since I was a kid." And a made man in the Columbo family gushes: "Since I got made I got a million fuckin' worshipers hanging around" (Abadinsky, 2003, pp. 23–24).

Men with attitudes such as these could be described as narcissistic, a trait said to be very prevalent among organized gangsters (Hill, 2003). It would not be too much of a stretch to posit that many men attracted to the outlaw lifestyle are predatory psychopaths or sociopaths. For instance, Al Capone could smash a suspected "rat's" head in with a baseball bat as casually as patting him on the back, and Sammy Gravano explained that after killing he "felt good. Like high. Like powerful, maybe even superhuman." Then there's caporegime Joe Armore's statement to Gambino family capo Paul Castellano: "But you know, Paul, I think some guys just take so much pleasure from breaking heads that they'd almost rather not get paid" (Abadinsky, 2003, p. 41).

Not only made men find the life of organized crime appealing. The biography of Henry Hill featured in this chapter's vignette illustrates how young men admire and seek to emulate the men with "juice" in their neighborhoods: "I used to watch them from my window and I dreamed of being like them. At the age of twelve my ambition was to be a gangster. To be a wiseguy. To me being a wiseguy was better than being President of the United States" (in Pileggi, 1985, p. 13). As with common inner-city street robbers, the attitude toward legitimate employment and those who pursued it was the polar opposite. Citing Henry Hill, Pileggi (1985) writes, "Anyone who stood waiting his turn on the American pay line was beneath contempt. . . . To wiseguys, 'working guys' were already dead" (p. 37).

Yet most young men in neighborhoods infested with organized crime saw the same things and did not become criminals, nor are there any outcast groups analogous to the burakumin in the United States. Although there are criminogenic neighborhoods that produce proportionately more criminals than other neighborhoods, there is no reason to assume that the rank-and-file gangster is any different in background and personal characteristics than the ordinary unaffiliated street criminal or the street criminal affiliated with ad hoc criminal gangs. The leadership of organized crime groups may be intelligent and shrewd men who hatch complicated criminal plots, but their subordinates engage in mundane crimes like burglary and robbery to support themselves and their masters. Their strong desire to belong and to gain instant respect by displays of "manliness" and aggression, their fatalism, their sensation seeking, their lack of empathy, and their involvement in many high-risk/low-profit crimes mark them as very ordinary street criminals.

❖ Law Enforcement's Response to Organized Crime

Joe Valachi's testimony before the McClelland Committee, along with a number of other events, led to the passage of federal legislation that has enabled law enforcement to launch massive attacks on organized crime. Among the most important new tools forged for law enforcement are the Organized Crime Control Act (OCCA) and the Bank Secrecy Act (BSA), both passed in 1970. Included in the provisions of OCCA are witness immunity from prosecution, the witness protection program, and the **Racketeer Influenced and Corrupt Organizations** (RICO) **statutes**.

The witness immunity provision allows federal prosecutors to grant lower-level members of organized crime groups immunity from prosecution for their own crimes in exchange for testimony incriminating higher-level members. Witnesses who do not want to testify or be granted immunity are immunized anyway and then forced to testify under pain of contempt of court charges, which could result in indefinite imprisonment. If witnesses are still reluctant to testify despite the grant of immunity because they realize that doing so places their lives in jeopardy, they may join the **Witness Protection Program**. The program, administered by the U.S. Marshals Service, provides for around-the-clock protection while witnesses are awaiting court appearances. After testifying, witnesses in the program are provided with new identification documents, employment, housing, and other assistance until they become reestablished. Jay Albanese (2000) reports that there are about 12,400 persons (witnesses or informants and their families) in the Witness Protection Program at an annual cost of $25 million.

An interesting sideline underscoring the difficulties in rehabilitating confirmed criminals is that despite being given a new start in life, 21% of criminals entering the Witness Protection Program are arrested under their new identities within 2 years of entry (Albanese & Pursley, 1993). Because criminals (such as Henry Hill) in the Witness Protection Program were used to relatively high incomes made in a life filled with excitement and personal power and independence, many find it very difficult to adjust to a mundane job with minimal financial rewards. For instance, Sammy Gravano, former Gambino family underboss, placed in the program after testifying against his boss John Gotti, was arrested in 2000 and sentenced to 19 years in prison for masterminding a drug ring in Arizona (Abadinsky, 2003). Arrested program members become exposed and thus place themselves and their families at risk for murder by cohorts of those they had betrayed. Peter Gotti, brother of John Gotti, was convicted in December 2004 in a plot to kill Gravano, which was only thwarted by Gravano's arrest (Neumeister, 2004). According to Abadinsky (2003), about 30 people who left the program have been murdered, while none who have remained in it and complied with its rules have.

The RICO statutes address ordinary crimes such as murder, robbery, extortion, fraud, and kidnapping, but they differ from traditional statutes relevant to these same crimes in that they specifically target the continuing racketeering activities of organized criminals. RICO statutes provide for more severe penalties for the same crimes that fall under traditional criminal statutes and also provide for the seizure of property and assets obtained from or involved in illegal activities. RICO even provides for the seizure of the assets of a legitimate business if the business was used for money laundering.

The primary function of the BSA (supplemented by the Money-Laundering Control Act of 1986) is the prevention and detection of money laundering. Money laundering—making illegitimate money appear legitimate—is a vital component of organized crime's ability to carry on its activities. The vast amount of illicit money that flows through the hands of organized crime must be "laundered" into legitimate money so that income taxes can be paid on it (the lesson of Al Capone's conviction for income tax evasion was not lost on organized crime) and it can be openly used. Under this act, banks must file a report if funds over $10,000 in cash are either deposited or withdrawn, and a report must be filed with the U.S. Customs Service if more than $10,000 in cash enters or leaves the United States.

Summary

- Organized crime (OC) is defined by its formal structure, continuity, and restricted membership. La Cosa Nostra (LCN) is a confederation of families, the leaders of which are of Italian heritage, that restricts membership to ethnic Italians.

- American OC grew out of the corrupt political machine and its supporting street gangs known as Tammany Hall and received its biggest boost from Prohibition. Many of the gangsters who rose to national prominence during this period got their start in the variety of gangs that supported Tammany Hall.

- The repeal of Prohibition ushered in a quiet period in OC's history, particularly after the founding of

- the Commission by Lucky Luciano as a judicial body to settle interfamily disputes without resorting to war.

- The Russian Mafiya is considered to be the biggest OC threat in the world today. The widespread chaos and corruption following the breakup of the Soviet Union allowed Russian OC to come out of the closet and proliferate. The special danger of Russian OC is that many of its members are highly intelligent and educated men who held professional jobs in the old Soviet Union.

- The Japanese yakuza is the oldest OC group in the world. Having evolved from masterless samurai warriors, it received a major boost by the chaos in Japan after its defeat in WWII. The yakuza has many characteristics in common with LCN, but it operates openly and proudly, even publishing its own newsletter.

■ Other OC groups such as outlaw motorcycle gangs and African American and Asian gangs point to the widespread existence of organized crime.

■ Theories of organized crime tend to be in the anomie/strain tradition whereby gangsters are presumed to be mainly from disadvantaged groups climbing the "queer (illegitimate) path to success."

■ Law enforcement in the United States has used a variety of ways to combat organized crime, the most useful being the various RICO statutes such as the Witness Protection Program.

Exercises and Discussion Questions

1. Looking back at all the theories presented in this book, make a case for one of them as the best at explaining organized crime.

2. What do you think the relationship (if any) is between the general level of morality in society and the prevalence (that is, the increase or decrease in the number of individuals involved in it) of organized crime?

3. Some observers believe law enforcement's response to organized crime in America (e.g., the RICO statutes) goes too far and threatens everyone's civil liberties. Do you agree?

4. Gang Land News provides information of many famous wiseguys. Go to www.ganglandnews.com and write a report on one of them to share with classmates.

Useful Websites

Criminal Justice Resources: Organized Crime. http://staff.lib.msu.edu/harris23/crimjust/orgcrime.htm.
FBI: Organized Crime. www.fbi.gov/hq/cid/orgcrime/ocshome.htm.

RICO Act. http://www.ricoact.com.
United Nations Office on Drugs and Crime: Organized Crime. www.unodc.org/unodc/en/organized-crime/index.html.

Chapter Terms

Commission

Corporate model

Ethnic succession theory

Feudal model

La Cosa Nostra

Organized crime

Prohibition

RICO (Racketeer Influenced and Corrupt Organizations) statutes

Tammany Society

Witness Protection Program

Glossary

Actus reus: Literally *guilty act*, it refers to the principle that a person must commit some forbidden act or neglect some mandatory act before he or she can be subjected to criminal sanctions.

Adaptive behavior: Any behavior that contributes directly or indirectly to an individual's survival and reproductive success.

Adolescent-limited (AL) offenders: The vast majority of youth who offend during adolescence and desist.

Age-crime curve: The statistical count of the number of known crimes committed in a population over a given period mapped according to age.

Age-graded theory: Theory stressing the power of informal social controls to explain onset, continuance, and desisting from crime. Emphasizes the concepts of social capital, turning points in life, and human agency.

Aggravated assault: An unlawful attack by one person upon another for the purpose of inflicting severe or aggravated bodily injury.

Aggravated or first-degree murder: The most serious kind of murder that requires the act be committed with malice and aforethought, deliberation, and premeditation.

Agreeableness: The tendency to be friendly, considerate, courteous, helpful, and cooperative with others.

Alcoholism: A chronic disease condition marked by a progressive incapacity to control alcohol consumption despite psychological, social, or physiological disruptions.

Alienation: A condition that describes the estrangement or distancing of individuals from something, such as another person or from society in general.

Allele: An alternate form of the same gene; i.e., a "blue" allele versus a "brown" allele of the gene coding for eye color.

Al-Qaeda: Not a single terrorist group but rather the base (*al-Qaeda* means "the base") organization for a number of Sunni Muslim terrorist groups from around the world.

Altruism: The action component of empathy; i.e. an *active* concern for the well-being of others.

Anelpis: A term meaning "without hope" applied by cultural criminologists to describe the lowest segment of society ruled primarily by their emotions and marked by cynicism and nihilism, no realistic expectations, no hope, and no fear of authority.

Anomie: A term meaning "lacking in rules" or "normlessness" used by Durkheim to describe a condition of normative deregulation in society.

Antisocial personality disorder: A psychiatric label described as "a pervasive pattern of disregard for, and violation of, the rights of others that begins in childhood or early adolescence and continues into adulthood."

Arraignment: A court proceeding in which the defendant answers to the charges against him or her by pleading guilty, not guilty, or no contest (nolo contendere).

Arrest: The act of being legally detained to answer criminal charges on the basis of an arrest warrant or a law enforcement officer's probable cause to believe the person arrested has committed a felony crime.

Arson: Any willful or malicious burning or attempting to burn, with or without intent to defraud, a dwelling house, public building, motor vehicle or aircraft, or personal property of another.

Atavism: Cesare Lombroso's term for his "born criminals," meaning evolutionary "throwbacks" to an earlier life form.

Attachment: One of the elements of the social bonds in social control theory; the emotional component of conformity referring to one's attachment to others and to social institutions.

Attention deficit with hyperactivity disorder (ADHD): A chronic neurological condition manifested as constant restlessness, impulsiveness, difficulty with peers, disruptive behavior, short attention span, academic underachievement, risk-taking behavior, and extreme boredom.

Autonomic nervous system: Part of the peripheral nervous system that carries out the basic housekeeping functions of the body by funneling messages from the environment to the various internal organs; the physiological basis of the conscience.

Background of crime: Everything that person is (age, race, gender, impulsive, drug abuser) or has experienced (abuse, poverty, broken home, drugs) that may have led him or her to commit a crime.

Behavior genetics: A branch of genetics that studies the relative contributions of heredity and environment to behavioral and personality characteristics.

Behavioral activating system: A reward system associated chemically with the neurotransmitter dopamine and anatomically with pleasure areas in the limbic system.

Behavioral inhibition system: Inhibits or modulates behavior and associated with serotonin.

Belief: Refers to the acceptance of the social norms regulating conduct.

Binge drinkers: People who frequently consume anywhere from 5 to 10 drinks in a few hours' time (go on a binge).

Bourgeoisie: In Marxism, the owners of the means of production.

Burglary: The unlawful entry of a structure to commit a felony or theft.

Carjacking: The theft or attempted theft of a motor vehicle from its occupant by force or threat of force.

Cartographic criminologists: Criminologists who employ maps and other geographic information in their research to study where and when crime is most prevalent.

Causation: A legal principle stating that there must be an established proximate causal link between the criminal act and the harm suffered.

Cheats: Individuals in a population of cooperators who gain resources from others by signaling their cooperation and then defaulting.

Chicago Area Project: A project designed by Clifford Shaw to "treat" communities from which most delinquents came.

Choice structuring: A concept in rational choice theory referring to how people decide to offend and defined as "the constellation of opportunities, costs, and benefits attaching to particular kinds of crime."

Class struggle: Marxist concept stating that all history is the history of class struggles.

Classical school: The classical school of criminology was a nonempirical mode of inquiry similar to the philosophy practiced by the classical Greek philosophers.

Classical conditioning: A mostly passive visceral form of learning depending on ANS arousal that forms an association between two paired stimuli.

Cleared offense: A crime is cleared by the arrest of a suspect or by exceptional means (cases in which a suspect has been identified but he or she is not immediately available for arrest).

Cognitive dissonance: A form of psychological discomfort resulting from a contradiction between a person's attitudes and his or her behavior.

Collective efficacy: The shared power of a group of connected and engaged individuals to influence an outcome the collective deems desirable.

Commission: A national ruling body of La Cosa Nostra consisting of the bosses of the five New York families and four bosses from other important families.

Commitment: One of the four social bonds in social bonding theory; the rational component of conformity referring to a lifestyle in which one has invested considerable time and energy in the pursuit of a lawful career.

CompStat: A police management and accountability process that has been implemented across the nation.

Concurrence: The legal principle stating that the act (*actus reus*) and the mental state (*mens rea*) concur in the sense that the criminal intention actuates the criminal act.

Conduct disorder: The persistent display of serious antisocial actions that are extreme given the child's developmental level and have a significant impact on the rights of others.

Conformity: The most common of Merton's modes of adaptation; i.e., the acceptance of cultural goals and the legitimate means of obtaining them.

Conscience: A complex mix of emotional and cognitive mechanisms acquired by internalizing the moral rules of one's social group in the ongoing socialization process.

Conscientiousness: A personality trait composed of several secondary traits, such as well organized, disciplined, scrupulous, responsible, and reliable at one pole and disorganized, careless, unreliable, irresponsible, and unscrupulous at the other.

Consensus or **functionalist perspective:** A view of society as a system of mutually sustaining parts and characterized by broad normative consensus.

Constrained vision: One of the two so-called ideological visions of the world. The constrained vision views human activities as constrained by an innate human nature that is self-centered and largely unalterable.

Contrast effect: The effect of punishment on future behavior depends on how much the punishment and the usual life experience of the person being punished differ or contrast.

Corporate crime: Criminal activity on behalf of a business organization.

Corporate model: A model that sees La Cosa Nostra as similar to corporate structure; i.e., a formal hierarchy in which the day-to-day activities of the organization are planned and coordinated at the top and carried out by subordinates.

Corpus delicti: Refers to the five elements of criminal liability that must be proven beyond a reasonable doubt in order to convict a person of a crime.

Counterfeiting: The creation or altering of currency.

Crime: An intentional act in violation of the criminal law committed without defense or excuse and penalized by the state.

Crime mapping: The use of modern technology such as Geographic Information Systems (GIS) by police departments to "map" and analyze patterns of crime.

Crime rate: The rate of a given crime is the actual number of reported crimes standardized by some unit of the population.

Criminality: A continuously distributed trait composed of a combination of other continuously distributed traits that signals the willingness to use force, fraud, or guile to deprive others of their lives, limbs, or property for personal gain.

Criminaloid: One of Lombroso's criminal types. They had none of the physical peculiarities of the born or insane criminal and were considered less dangerous.

Criminology: An interdisciplinary science that gathers and analyzes data on crime and criminal behavior.

Critical criminology: An umbrella term for a variety of theories united only by the assumption that conflict and power relations between various classes of people best characterize the nature of society.

Crony capitalism: The close relationship between business and politicians for purposes of lining each other's pockets.

Cultural criminology: A theory sometimes called anarchic criminology that is opposed to the state. It champions the role of emotions in instigating crime (the thrill and rush) rather than rationality.

Cybercrime: A wide variety of crimes committed with computer technology.

Dark figure of crime: The dark (or hidden) figure of crime refers to all of the crimes committed that never come to official attention.

Decommodification: The process of freeing social relationships from economic considerations.

Defensible space: A model for residential environments that inhibit crime by creating the physical expression of a social fabric that defends itself.

Definitions: Term used by Edwin Sutherland to refer to the meanings our experiences have for us and our attitudes, values, and habitual ways of viewing the world.

Delinquency: A legal term that distinguishes between youthful (juvenile) offenders and adult offenders. Acts forbidden by law are called delinquent acts when committed by juveniles.

Department of Homeland Security: Organization whose mission is to detect, prevent, prepare for, and recover from terrorist attacks within the United States.

Determinism: The position that events have causes that precede them.

Deterrence: The prevention of criminal acts by the use or threat of punishment; deterrence may be either specific or general.

Developmental theories: Emphasize that individuals develop along different pathways, and as they do, factors that were previously meaningful to them (e.g., acceptance by antisocial peers) no longer are, and factors that previously meant little to them (marriage and a career) become meaningful.

Differential association theory: Criminological theory devised by Edwin Sutherland asserting that criminal behavior is learned through association with others who communicate their values and attitudes.

Differential reinforcement: The balance of anticipated or actual rewards and punishments that follow or are consequences of behavior.

Discrimination: A term applied to stimuli that provide clues signaling whether a particular behavior is likely to be followed by reward or punishment.

Domestic violence: Any abusive act (physical, sexual, or psychological) that occurs within the family setting. Intimate-partner violence is the most common form.

Drug addiction: Compulsive drug-seeking behavior where acquiring and using a drug becomes the most important activity in the user's life.

Ecological fallacy: The process of making inferences about individuals and groups on the basis of information derived from a larger population of which they are a part.

Economic-compulsive violence: Violence associated with efforts to obtain money to finance the cost of illicit drugs.

Economic marginalization hypothesis: Argues that much of female crime is related to economic need.

Emancipation hypothesis: Rita Simon's view that increased participation in the workforce affords women greater opportunities to commit job-related crime without undergoing "masculinization."

Embezzlement: The misappropriation or misapplication of money or property entrusted to the embezzler's care, custody, or control.

Emotions: Subjective feelings of varying strength prompted by nervous system arousal in response to some perceived event. Emotions are divided into primary and secondary emotions.

Empathy: The emotional and cognitive ability to understand the feelings and distress of others as if they were one's own—to be able to "walk in another's shoes."

Enlightenment: A major intellectual shift in the way people viewed the world and their place in it, questioning traditional religious and political values and substituting humanism, rationalism, and naturalism for supernaturalism.

Ethnic succession theory: Theory about the causes of organized crime positing that upon arrival in the United States each ethnic group was faced with prejudicial and discriminatory attitudes that denied it legitimate means to success in America.

Evolutionary psychology: A way of thinking about human behavior using a Darwinian evolutionary theoretical framework.

Fence: A person who regularly buys stolen property for resale and who often has a legitimate business to cover his activities.

Fetal alcohol syndrome (FAS): A chronic condition affecting the brain resulting from an individual's prenatal alcohol exposure.

Financial Crimes Report: The FBI's annual tally of financial ("white-collar") crimes in the United States.

Flight/fight system: An autonomic nervous system mechanism that mobilizes the body for action in response to threats by pumping out epinephrine.

Flynn effect: The upward creep in average IQ scores taking place across the last three or four generations in all countries examined.

Focal concerns: Miller's description of the value system and lifestyle of the lowest classes; they are trouble, toughness, excitement, smartness, fate, and autonomy.

Forcible rape: The carnal knowledge of a female forcibly and against her will.

Forgery: The creation or alteration of documents to give them the appearance of legality and validity with the intention of gaining some fraudulent benefit from doing so.

Foreground of crime: The immediate situation and the thought processes of the individual criminal at the time of committing the crime.

Fraud: Obtaining the money or property of another through deceptive practices such as false advertising, impersonation, and other misrepresentations.

Free will: That which enables human beings to purposely and deliberately choose to follow a calculated course of action.

Feudal model: Sees La Cosa Nostra as similar to the old European feudal system based on patronage, oaths of loyalty, and semiautonomy.

Gender ratio problem: An issue in feminist criminology asking why always and everywhere females commit far less crime than males.

Gene/environment correlation: The notion that genotypes and the environments they find themselves in are related because parents provide children with both.

Gene/environment interaction: The interaction of a genotype with its environment: people are differentially sensitive to identical environmental influences because of their genes and will thus respond in different ways to them.

General deterrence: The assumed preventive effect of the threat of punishment on the general population; i.e., *potential* offenders.

General strain theory: Agnew's extension of anomie theory into the realm of social psychology stressing multiple sources of strain and how people cope with it.

Generalizability problem: An issue in feminist criminology asking if traditional theories based on male offender samples apply to women offenders.

Genes: Strands of DNA that code for the amino acid sequences of proteins.

Genetic polymorphisms: Variations in the same gene allele (alternate form of a gene) such as SNPs and VNTRs.

Genotype: A person's genetic makeup.

Grand jury: An investigatory jury composed of seven to 23 citizens before which the prosecutor presents evidence that sufficient grounds exist to try the suspect for a crime. If the prosecutor is successful, he or she obtains an indictment from the grand jury listing the charges a person is accused of.

Hacker: A person who illicitly accesses someone else's computer system.

Harm: The legal principle stating that a crime must have a negative impact on either the victim or the general values of the community to be a crime.

Harm reduction: Refers to policies, programs, and practices that aim to reduce the harms associated with the use of psychoactive drugs in people unable or unwilling to stop.

Harrison Narcotic Act: A 1914 congressional act that criminalized the sale and use of narcotics.

Hedonism: A doctrine assuming that the achievement of pleasure or happiness is the main goal of life.

Hedonistic calculus: Combining hedonism and rationality to logically weigh the anticipated benefits of a given course of action against its possible costs.

Hedonistic serial killer: A killer that kills for the pure thrill and joy of it.

Hegemonic masculinity: Concept in structured action theory positing the cultural ideal of masculinity men are expected to live up to; i.e., "work in the paid-labor market, the subordination of women, heterosexism, and the driven uncontrollable sexuality of men."

Heritability: A concept defined by a number ranging from 0 to 1 indicating the extent to which variance in a phenotypic trait in a population is due to genetic factors.

Hezbollah ("Party of God"): The best contemporary example of a state-sponsored terrorist organization. Directed and financed by Iran, Hezbollah is headquartered in Lebanon and has established cells in Europe, North and South America, and Africa.

Hierarchy rule: A rule requiring the police to report only the most serious offense committed in a multiple-offense single incident to the FBI and to ignore the others.

Home invasion: A type of breaking and entering into a residential home in which the express purpose is to catch occupants at home so that criminals can rob, rape, or assault the occupants as well as steal their property.

Honor subcultures: Communities in which young men are hypersensitive to insult, rushing to defend their reputation in dominance contests.

Human agency: A concept that maintains humans have the capacity to make choices and the responsibility to make moral ones regardless of the internal or external constraints on one's ability to do so.

Human ecology: Describes the interrelations of human beings and the environments in which they live and views the city as a kind of superorganism with areas differentially adaptive for different ethnic groups.

Human trafficking: The recruitment, transportation, transfer, harboring, or receipt of persons by means of threat or use of force or other forms of coercion, of abduction, of fraud, of deception, of the abuse of power or of a position of vulnerability, or of the giving or receiving of payments or benefits to achieve the consent of a person having control over another person for the purpose of exploitation.

Hypotheses: Statements about relationships between and among factors we expect to find based on the logic of our theories.

Identity theft: The use of someone else's personal information without their permission to perform an illegal act.

Ideology: A way of looking at the world, a general emotional picture of "how things should be" that forms, shapes, and colors our concepts of the phenomena we study.

Impulsiveness: A personality trait reflecting people's varying tendencies to act on matters without giving much thought to the possible consequences (not looking before one leaps).

Insane criminal: One of Lombroso's criminal types. Insane criminals bore some stigmata but were not born criminals. Among their ranks were alcoholics, kleptomaniacs, nymphomaniacs, and child molesters.

Institutional anomie theory: Messner and Rosenfeld's extension of anomie theory avering that high crime rates are intrinsic to the structural and cultural arrangements of American society.

Integrated cognitive antisocial potential (ICAP) theory: Theory based on the notion that people have varying levels of antisocial propensity due to a variety of environmental and biological factors.

Intellectual imbalance: A significant difference between a person's verbal and performance IQ scores.

Intelligence: The aggregate or global capacity of the individual to act purposefully, think rationally, and deal effectively with his or her environment.

Involuntary manslaughter: A criminal homicide where an unintentional killing results from a reckless act.

Involvement: A direct consequence of commitment; part of an overall conventional pattern of existence.

Italian school of criminology: Positivist school of criminology associated with Cesare Lombroso, Raffael Garofalo, and Enrico Ferri.

La Cosa Nostra (literally, "our thing"): An organized crime group of Italian/Sicilian origins; also commonly referred to as the Mafia.

Larceny-theft: The unlawful taking, leading, or riding away from the possession or constructive possession of another.

Latent trait: An assumed "master trait" such as self-control said to influence behavioral choices across time and situations.

Left realists: Group of Marxist criminologists who want to work within the system to make things better for the working classes.

Level of analysis: That segment of the phenomenon of interest that is measured and analyzed; e.g., individuals, families, neighborhoods, states.

Life course–persistent (LCP) offenders: Individuals who begin offending prior to puberty and continue well into adulthood and who are saddled with neuropsychological and temperamental deficits manifested in low IQ, hyperactivity, inattentiveness, negatively emotionality, and low impulse control.

Lifestyle theory: A theory stressing that crime is not just a behavior but a general pattern of life.

***Lumpenproletariat*:** The lowest ("criminal class") class in Marxist theory.

Madrasas: Islamic religious schools that stress the immorality and materialism of Western life and the need to convert all infidels to Islam.

***Mala in se*:** Universally condemned crimes that are "inherently bad."

***Mala probibita*:** Crimes that are "bad" simply because they are prohibited.

Masculinization hypothesis: Freda Adler's idea that as females increasingly adopt male roles they will increasingly masculinize their attitudes and behavior and become as crime-prone as men.

Mass murder: The killing of several people at one location within minutes or hours.

Mating effort: The proportion of total reproductive effort allotted to acquiring sexual partners; traits facilitating mating effort are associated with antisocial behavior.

Maturity gap: In Moffitt's theory, the gap between the average age of puberty and the acquisition of socially responsible adult roles.

Mechanical solidarity: A form of social solidarity existing in small, isolated, prestate societies in which individuals sharing common experiences and circumstances share common values and develop strong emotional ties to the collectivity.

Mens rea: "Guilty mind." Criminal liability does not attach based on actions alone; there must also be criminal intent.

Middle-class measuring rods: According to Cohen, because low-class youths cannot measure up to middle-class standards they experience status frustration, and this frustration spawns an oppositional culture.

Minority power groups: Groups whose interests are sufficiently on the margins of mainstream society so that just about all their activities are criminalized.

Mission-oriented serial killer: A killer that feels it to be a mission in life to kill certain kinds of people.

Modes of adaptation: Robert Merton's concept of how people adapt to the alleged disjunction between cultural goals and structural barriers to the means of obtaining them. These modes are conformity, ritualism, retreatism, innovation, and rebellion.

Moffitt's dual-pathway developmental theory: Theory based on the notion of two main pathways to offending: One pathway is followed by individuals with neurological and temperamental difficulties exacerbated by inept parenting, the other by "normal" individuals temporarily derailed during adolescence.

Moral hazard: The tendency to take unwarranted risks when costs are not borne by the party taking the risk.

Motor vehicle theft: The theft or attempted theft of a motor vehicle.

Murder: The willful (nonnegligent) killing of one human being by another.

National Crime Victimization Survey (NCVS): A biannual survey of a large number of people and households requesting information on crimes committed against individuals and households (whether reported to the police of not) and circumstances of the offense (time and place it occurred, perpetrator's use of a weapon, any injuries incurred, and financial loss).

National Incident-Based Reporting System (NIBRS): A comprehensive crime statistic collection system currently a component of the UCR program and eventually expected to replace it entirely.

Negative emotionality: A personality trait that refers to the tendency to experience many situations as aversive and to react to them with irritation and anger more readily than with positive affective states.

Negligent manslaughter: An unintentional homicide charged when a death or deaths arise from some negligent act that carries a substantial risk of death to others.

Neurons: Brain cells consisting of the cell body, an axon, and a number of dendrites.

Neurotransmitters: Brain chemicals that carry messages from neuron to neuron across the synaptic gap.

Nonshared environment: That part of the environment referring to the unique experiences that make children from the same family different.

Occupational crime: Crime committed by individuals in the course of their employment.

Operant psychology: A perspective on learning asserting that behavior is governed and shaped by its consequences (reward or punishment).

Opportunity: In self-control theory, opportunity is a situation that presents itself to those with low self-control by which they can immediately satisfy their needs with minimal effort.

Opportunity structure theory: An extension of anomie theory claiming that lower-class youth join gangs as a path to monetary success.

Organic solidarity: A form of social solidarity characteristic of modern societies in which there is a high degree of occupational specialization and weak normative consensus.

Organized crime: A continuing criminal enterprise that works rationally to profit from illicit activities often in great public demand. Its continuing existence is maintained through the use of force, threats, and/or corruption of public officials.

Parenting effort: The proportion of total reproductive effort invested in rearing offspring; traits facilitating parenting effort are associated with prosocial behavior.

Part I offenses (or index crimes): The four violent (homicide, assault, forcible rape, and robbery) and four property offenses (larceny/theft, burglary, motor vehicle theft, and arson) reported in the Uniform Crime Reports.

Part II offenses: The less serious offenses reported in the Uniform Crime Reports and recorded based on arrests made rather than cases reported to the police.

Patriarchy: Any social system that is male dominated at all levels from the family to the highest reaches of government and supported by the belief of male superiority.

Peacemaking criminology: Theory based on the postmodernist tradition that rejects the notion that the scientific view is better than any other view and believes that any method of understanding can be objective.

Perceptual deterrence theory: A theory of deterrence that refers to offenders' perception of the likelihood of arrest and how severe they believe the punishment will be for a crime if caught.

Personality: The relatively enduring, distinctive, integrated, and functional set of psychological characteristics that results from people's temperaments interacting with their cultural and developmental experiences.

Pharmacological violence: Violence induced by the pharmacological properties of a drug.

Phenotype: The observable and measurable behavioral and personality characteristics of any living thing as a result of genes interacting with the environment.

Physical dependence: The state in which a person is physically dependant on a drug because of changes to the body that have occurred after repeated use of it and necessitates its continued administration to avoid withdrawal symptoms.

Policy: A course of action designed to solve some problem and selected by appropriate authorities from among alternative courses of action.

Positivism: An extension of the scientific method—from which more *positive* knowledge can be obtained—to social life.

Power/control serial killer: A killer that gains most satisfaction from exercising complete power over his victims.

Power-control theory: A feminist theory that views gender differences in criminal and delinquent behavior to be a function of power differentials in the family.

Prefrontal cortex: Occupies about one-third of the front part of the brain's cerebrum. It has many connections with other brain structures and plays the major integrative and supervisory roles in the brain.

Primary deviance: In labeling theory, the initial nonconforming act that comes to the attention of the authorities resulting in the application of a criminal label.

Primitive rebellion hypothesis: Marxist idea that crime is simply the product of people rebelling against unjust and alienating social conditions.

Principle of utility: Posits that human action should be judged moral or immoral by its effect on the happiness of the community and that the proper function of the legislature is to promulgate laws aimed at maximizing the pleasure and minimizing the pain of the largest number in society—"the greatest good for the greatest number."

Prohibition: Common term for the Volstead Act that prohibited the sale, manufacture, or importation of intoxicating liquors within the United States.

Proletariat: The working class in Marxist theory.

Prostitution: The provision of sexual services in exchange for money or other tangible reward as the primary source of income.

Psychological dependence: The deep craving for a drug and the feeling that one cannot function without it; psychological dependence is synonymous with addiction.

Psychopathy: A syndrome characterized by the inability to tie the social emotions with cognition. Psychopaths come from all social classes and may or may not be criminals.

Psychopathy Checklist–Revised: The major "pencil and paper" instrument used worldwide to assess psychopathy.

Punishment: A process intended to lead to the weakening or eliminating of the behavior preceding it.

Rape trauma syndrome: A syndrome sometimes suffered by rape victims similar to post-traumatic stress syndrome (reexperiencing the event via "flashbacks," avoiding anything associated with the event, and a general numbness of affect).

Rational: Rational behavior is consistent with logic; a logical "fit" between the goals people strive for and means they use to achieve them.

Rational choice theory: A neoclassical theory asserting that offenders are free actors responsible for their own actions. Rational choice theorists view criminal acts as specific examples of the general principle that all human behavior reflects the rational pursuit of benefits and advantages. People are conscious social actors free to choose crime, and they will do so if they perceive that its utility exceeds the pains they might conceivably expect if discovered.

Recidivism: Refers to "falling back" into criminal behavior after having being punished.

Reinforcement: A process that leads to the repetition and strengthening of behavior.

Restorative justice: A system of mediation and conflict resolution oriented toward justice by repairing the harm caused by the crime using a face-to-face confrontation between victim and perpetrator.

Reticular activating system: A small bundle of cells at the top of the spinal cord that filter all incoming stimuli from all human senses and determine which of those stimuli are important to pay immediate attention to.

Reward dominance theory: A neurological theory based on the proposition that behavior is regulated by two opposing mechanisms, the behavioral activating system (BAS) and the behavioral inhibition system (BIS).

RICO statutes: Statutes that specifically target the continuing racketeering activities of organized criminals and provide for more severe penalties for the same crimes that fall under traditional criminal statutes and for the seizure of property and assets obtained from or involved in illegal activities.

Risk factor: Something in individuals' personal characteristics or their environment that increases the probability of offending.

Robbery: The taking or attempted taking of anything of value from the care, custody, or control of a person or persons by force or threat of force or violence and/or putting the victim in fear.

Routine activities theory: A neoclassical theory pointing to the routine activities in that society or neighborhood that invite or prevent crime. Routine activities are defined as "recurrent and prevalent activities which provide for basic population and individual needs." Crime is the result of motivated offenders meeting suitable targets that lack capable guardians.

Routine activities/lifestyle theory: A victimization theory that states there are certain lifestyles (routine activities) that disproportionately expose some people to high risk for victimization.

Sarbanes-Oxley Act (SOA): An act passed in 2002 in response to numerous corporate scandals. Provisions include increased funding for the Security Exchange Commission, penalty enhancement for white-collar crimes, and the relaxing of some legal impediments to gaining convictions.

Secondary deviance: Deviance that results from society's reaction to offenders' primary deviance.

Second-degree murder: The intentional killing of another human being without premeditation and deliberation.

Self-control: The extent to which people are vulnerable to the temptations of the moment.

Self-control theory: Theory developed by Gottfredson and Hirschi that maintains all crime is attributable to an individual's lack of self-control.

Self-report surveys: The collecting of data by criminologists themselves asking people to disclose their delinquent and criminal involvement on anonymous questionnaires.

Sensation seeking: The active desire for novel, varied, and extreme sensations and experiences often to the point of taking physical and social risks to obtain them.

Serial murder: The killing of three or more victims over an extended period of time.

Shared environment: The environment experienced by children reared in the same family (parental SES, religion, values and attitudes, parenting style, family size, intactness of home, and neighborhood) assumed to make them similar.

Short-run hedonism: The seeking of immediate gratification of desires without regard for any long-term consequences.

Social bond theory: A theory focusing on a person's bonds to others. The four elements of the social bond are attachment, commitment, involvement, and belief. The absence of these bonds in criminals does not cause crime; it permits it.

Social capital: The store of positive relationships in social networks built on norms of reciprocity and trust developed over time upon which the individual can draw for support.

Social control: Mechanisms designed to minimize nonconformity and deviance.

Social defense: A theory of punishment asserting that its purpose is not to deter or to rehabilitate but to defend society against criminals.

Social disorganization: The central concept of the Chicago school of social ecology. It refers to the breakdown or serious dilution of the power of informal community rules to regulate conduct in poor neighborhoods.

Social ecology: Term used by the Chicago school to describe the interrelations of human beings and the communities in which they live.

Social learning theory: A theory designed to explain how people learn criminal behavior using the psychological principles of operant conditioning.

Social push hypothesis: The idea that if an individual lacks environmental risk factors that predispose toward antisocial behavior yet still engages in antisocial behavior, the causes of this behavior are more likely to be biological than social.

Social sentiments: Willem Bonger's proposition that individuals vary in their risk for crime because they vary in the innate social sentiments of altruism and egoism.

Social structure: How society is organized by social institutions—the family and educational, religious, economic, and political institutions—and stratified on the basis of various roles and statuses.

Sociopaths: All sociopaths are criminals by definition. They development of sociopathy is not as closely tied to genetics as it is in psychopaths but is developed primarily through inadequate socialization and hostile childhood experiences.

Software piracy: Illegally copying and distributing computer software.

Specific deterrence: The effect of punishment on the future behavior of the person who experiences the punishment.

Spree murder: The killing of several people at different locations over several days.

Status frustration: A form of frustration experiences by lower-class youth who desire approval and status but who cannot meet middle-class criteria and thus seek status via alternate means.

Staying-alive hypothesis: Campbell's thesis that staying alive is more crucial to a mother's reproductive success than to a father's and that greater fear in females is a result.

Strain theory: The inability to attain resources legitimately generates unhappiness (strain) and sometimes leads to efforts to obtain them illegitimately.

Structured action theory: A feminist theory formulated by James Messerschmidt that focuses on how individuals "do gender."

Subculture of violence: A part of a larger culture in which the norms, attitudes, and values of its people legitimizes the use of violence.

Super traits theory: A developmental theory asserting that five life domains interact over the life course once individuals are set on a particular developmental trajectory by their degree of low self-control and irritability.

Symbolic interactionism: A perspective in sociology that focuses on how people interpret and define their social reality and the meanings they attach to it in the process of interacting with one another via language (symbols).

Systemic violence: Violence associated with aggressive patterns of interaction within the system of drug distribution and use.

Tammany Society: A corrupt political machine that ran New York into the early 20th century associated with the Democratic Party and with organized crime.

Techniques of neutralization: Techniques by which offenders justify their behavior as "acceptable" on a number of grounds.

Temperament: An individual characteristic identifiable as early as infancy that constitutes a habitual mode of emotionally responding to stimuli.

Terrorism: The FBI defines terrorism as "the unlawful use of force or violence against persons or property to intimidate or coerce a government, the civilian population, or any segment thereof, in furtherance of political or social goals."

Theory: A set of logically interconnected propositions explaining how phenomena are related and from which a number of hypotheses can be derived and tested.

Thinking errors: Criminals' typical patterns of faulty thoughts and beliefs.

Tolerance: The tendency to require larger and larger doses of a drug to produce the same effects after the body adjusts to lower dosages.

Transition zone: An area or neighborhood in the process of being "invaded" by members of "alien" racial or ethnic groups bringing with them values and practices that conflict with those established by the "natural" inhabitants of the area.

Turning points: Transition events in life (getting married, finding a job, moving to a new neighborhood) that may change a person's life trajectory in prosocial directions.

Type I alcoholism: A form of alcoholism characterized by mild abuse, minimal criminality, and a passive-dependent personality.

Type II alcoholism: A form of alcoholism characterized by early onset, violence, and criminality and largely limited to males.

Unconstrained vision: One of the two so-called ideological visions of the world. The unconstrained vision denies an innate human nature, viewing it as formed anew in each culture.

Uniform Crime Reports (UCR): Annual report compiled by the Federal Bureau of Investigation (FBI) containing crimes known to the nation's police and sheriff departments, the number of arrests made by these agencies, and other crime-related information.

USA Patriot Act: Grants federal agencies greater authority to track and intercept private communications, grants greater powers to the Treasury Department to combat corruption and prevent money laundering, and creates new crimes, penalties, and procedures for use against domestic and foreign terrorists.

Victim precipitation theory: A theory in victimology that examines how violent victimization may have been precipitated by the victim by he or she acting in certain provocative ways.

Victimology: A subfield of criminology that specializes in studying the victims of crime.

Violent crime: The use of force exercised without excuse or justification to achieve a goal at the expense of a victim.

Visionary serial killer: A killer that feels impelled to commit murder by visions or "voices in my head."

Voluntary manslaughter: The intentional killing of another human being without malice and aforethought, often in response to the mistaken belief that self-defense required the use of deadly force or to adequate provocation while in the heat of passion.

Wertrationalitat: One of Max Weber's forms of rationality. It is rationality related to a value such as honor and duty to some revered entity rather than a self-serving rationality.

White-collar crime: An illegal act or series of illegal acts committed by nonphysical means and by concealment or guile to obtain money or property or to obtain a business or personal advantage.

Withdrawal: A process involving a number of adverse physical reactions that occur when the body of a drug abuser is deprived of his or her drugs.

Witness Protection Program: Program administered by the U.S. Marshals Service that provides witnesses awaiting court appearances with around-the-clock protection and new identification documents, employment, housing, and other assistance after testifying.

Zweckrationalitat: One of Max Weber's forms of rationality. It is an instrumental self-serving means-ends rationality that Weber assumed to be innate in everyone.

References

Aamodt, M. (2013). *Serial killer IQ*. Radford University Serial Killer Information Center. http://maamodt.asp.radford.edu/Serial%20Killer%20Information%20Center/Serial%20Killer%20IQ.htm.

Abadinsky, H. (2003). *Organized crime* (7th ed.). Belmont, CA: Wadsworth.

Abagnale, F., & Redding, S. (2000). *Catch me if you can: The amazing true story of the youngest and most daring con man in the history of fun and profit!* New York: Broadway Books.

ADAM. (2013). *2012 annual report*. www.whitehouse.gov/sites/default/files/ondcp/policy-and-research/adam_ii_2012_annual_rpt_final_final.pdf

Adams, J. (1971). *In defense of the Constitution of the United States* (Vol. 1). New York: De Capo Press. (Original work published 1778)

Adamson, C. (2000). Defensive localism in black and white: A comparative history of European-American and African-American youth gangs. *Ethnic and Racial Studies, 23,* 272–298.

Adelstein, J. (2010). The last yakuza. *World Policy Journal, 27,* 63–71.

Adler, F. (1975). *Sisters in crime: The rise of the new female criminal.* New York: McGraw-Hill.

Adler, F., Mueller, G., & Laufer, W. (2001). *Criminology and the criminal justice system.* Boston: McGraw-Hill.

Agnew, R. (1994). The techniques of neutralization and violence. *Criminology, 32,* 555–580.

Agnew, R. (1997). Stability and change in crime over the life-course: A strain theory explanation. In T. Thornberry (Ed.), *Developmental theories of crime and delinquency* (pp. 101–132). New Brunswick, NJ: Transaction.

Agnew, R. (2002). Foundation for a general strain theory of crime. In S. Cote (Ed.), *Criminological theories: Bridging the past to the future* (pp. 113–124). Thousand Oaks, CA: Sage.

Agnew, R. (2005). *Why do criminals offend? A general theory of crime and delinquency.* Los Angeles: Roxbury.

Agnew, R., Brezina, T., Wright, J., & Cullen F. (2002). Strain, personality traits, and delinquency: Extending general strain theory. *Criminology, 40,* 43–72.

Akers, R. (1994). *Criminological theories: Introduction and evaluation.* Los Angeles: Roxbury.

Akers, R. (1997). *Criminological theories: Introduction, evaluation, and application.* Los Angeles: Roxbury.

Akers, R. (1998). *Social learning and social structure: A general theory of crime and deviance.* Boston: Northeastern University Press.

Akers, R. (1999). Social learning and social structure: Reply to Sampson, Morash, and Krohn. *Theoretical Criminology, 3,* 477–493.

Akers, R. (2002). A social learning theory of crime. In S. Cote (Ed.), *Criminological theories: Bridging the past to the future* (pp. 135–143). Thousand Oaks, CA: Sage.

Akers, R. (2009). *Social learning and social structure: A general theory of crime and deviance.* New Brunswick, NJ: Transaction.

Albanese, J. (2000). The causes of organized crime. *Journal of Contemporary Criminal Justice, 16,* 409–432.

Albanese, J., & Pursley, R. (1993). *Crime in America: Some existing and emerging issues.* Englewood Cliffs, NJ: Regents/Prentice Hall.

Alexander, R. (2013). Sweden's rape rate under the spotlight. *BBC News Magazine,* September 14.

Alexander, R., & Pratsinak, G. (2002). *Arresting addictions: Drug education and relapse.* Lanham, MD: American Correctional Association.

Alzheimer's Disease Education and Referral Center. (2011). *Alzheimer's disease: Unraveling the mystery.* www.nia.nih.gov/alzheimers/publication/alzheimers-disease-unraveling-mystery.

Amateau, S., & McCarthy, M. (2004). Induction of PGE2 by estradiol mediates: Developmental masculinization of sex behavior. *Nature Neuroscience, 7,* 643–650.

American Civil Liberties Union. (2002). *How the USA Patriot Act redefines "domestic terrorism."* www.aclu.org/NationalSecurity.cfm?ID=11437&c=111.

American Psychiatric Association. (1994). *Diagnostic and statistical manual of mental disorders* (4th ed.). Washington, DC: American Psychiatric Association.

Amir, M. (1971). *Patterns of forcible rape.* Chicago: University of Chicago Press.

Anderson, E. (1994). The code of the streets. *The Atlantic Monthly, 5,* 81–94.

Anderson, E. (1999). *Code of the street: Decency, violence, and the moral life of the inner city.* New York: W. W. Norton.

Andrews, D., & Bonta, J. (1998). *The psychology of criminal conduct.* Cincinnati, OH: Anderson.

Ardila, R. (2002). The psychology of the terrorist: Behavioral perspectives. In C. Stout (Ed.), *The psychology of terrorism* (Vol. I, pp. 9–15). Westport, CT: Praeger.

Armanios, F. (2003). *Islamic religious schools, madrasas: Background. Report for Congress.* Congressional Research Service, Report # RS21654. The Library of Congress.

Arnold, T., & Stevens, J. (2011). Mixed agendas and government regulation of business: Can we clean up the mess? *University of Richmond Law Review, 45,* 1059–1089.

Arvedlund, E. (2009). *Too good to be true: The rise and fall of Bernie Madoff.* London: Penguin.

Associated Press. (1996, August 27). U.S. fugitive convicted in Cuba. *Idaho Statesman*, p. 6a.

Babiak, P., Neumann, C., & Hare, R. (2010). Corporate psychopathy: Talking the walk. *Behavioral Sciences and the Law, 28*, 174–193.

Badcock, C. (2000). *Evolutionary psychology: A critical introduction*. Cambridge, England: Polity Press.

Baines, H. (1996). *The Nigerian scam masters: An expose of a modern international gang*. Hauppauge, NY: Nova Science.

Baker, L., Bezdjian, S., & Raine, A. (2006). Behavior genetics: The science of antisocial behavior. *Law and Contemporary Problems, 69*, 7–46.

Barak, G. (1998). *Integrating criminologies*. Boston: Allyn & Bacon.

Barash, D., & Lipton, J. (2001). Making sense of sex. In D. Barash (Ed.), *Understanding violence* (pp. 20–30). Boston: Allyn & Bacon.

Barber, N. (2004). Single parenthood as a predictor of cross-national variation in violent crime. *Cross Cultural Research, 38*, 343–358.

Barkow, J. (Ed.). (2006). *Missing the revolution: Darwinism for social scientists*. Oxford: Oxford University Press.

Barnett, R., Zimmer, L., & McCormack, J. (1989). P>V sign and personality profiles. *Journal of Correctional and Social Psychiatry, 35*, 18–20.

Barnum, A., & Gregory, T. (2009, November 12). Jeanine Nicarico murder: Tears of joy as Brian Dugan gets death penalty. *Chicago Tribune*.

Barone, M. (2008, October 6). Democrats were wrong on Fannie Mae and Freddie Mac. *US News and World Report*. www.usnews.com/opinion/blogs/barone/2008/10/06/democrats-were-wrong-on-fannie-mae-and-freddie-mac_print.html.

Barry, C., McGinty, E., Vernick, J., & Webster, D. (2013). After Newton—Public policy on gun policy and mental illness. *The New England Journal of Medicine*. doi:10.1056/NEJMp1300512

Bartol, C. (2002). Criminal behavior: A psychosocial approach (6th ed.). Englewood Cliffs, NJ: Prentice Hall.

Bartol, C., & Bartol, A. (1989). *Juvenile delinquency: A systems approach*. Englewood Cliffs, NJ: Prentice Hall.

Bartollas, C. (2005). *Juvenile delinquency* (7th ed.). Boston: Allyn & Bacon.

Baumeister, R., Smart, L., & Boden, J. (1996). Relation of threatened egoism to violence and aggression: The dark side of self-esteem. *Psychological Review, 103*, 5–33.

Baumer, E., & Wolff, K. (2012). Evaluating contemporary crime drop(s) in America, New York City, and many other places. *Justice Quarterly*. doi:1080/07418825.2012

BBC News. (1999). Jimmy Boyle's life less ordinary. http://news.bbc.co.uk/2/hi/special_report/1999/08/99/edinburgh_festival_99/431661.st.

Beaver, K. (2009). Molecular genetics and crime. In A. Walsh & K. Beaver, *Biosocial criminology: New directions in theory and research* (pp. 50–72). New York: Routledge.

Beaver, K., Wright, J., & DeLisi, M. (2008). Delinquent peer group formation: Evidence of a gene x environment correlation. *Journal of Genetic Psychology, 169*, 227–244.

Beaver, K., Wright, J., & Walsh, A. (2008). A gene-based evolutionary explanation for the association between criminal involvement and number of sex partners. *Biodemography and Social Biology, 54*, 47–55.

Beccaria, C. (1963). *On crimes and punishment* (H. Paulucci, Trans.). Indianapolis, IN: Bobbs-Merrill. (Original work published 1764)

Bell, D. (1962). *The end of ideology*. New York: Collier Books.

Bellinger, D. (2008). Neurological and behavioral consequences of childhood lead exposure. *PLoS Medicine, 5*, 690–692.

Bennett, S., Farrington, D., & Huesmann, L. (2005). Explaining gender differences in crime and violence: The importance of social cognitive skills. *Aggression and Violent Behavior, 10*, 263–288.

Benson, M. (2010). *Killer twins*. New York: Pinnacle Books.

Benson, M. (2013). Editor's introduction—White-collar crime: Bringing the offender back in. *Journal of Contemporary Criminal Justice, 29*, 324–330.

Bentham, J. (1948). *A fragment on government and an introduction to the principles of morals and legislation* (W. Harrison, Ed.). Oxford: Basil Blackwell. (Original work published 1789)

Berger, P., & Hoffman, B. (2010). *Assessing the terrorist threat: Report to the Bipartisan Policy Center's National Security Preparedness Center*. www.bipartisanpolicy.org/ library/ report/assessing-terrorist-threat.

Berk, R., Li, A., & Hickman, L. (2005). Statistical difficulties in determining the role of race in capital cases: A re-analysis of the data from the state of Maryland. *Journal of Quantitative Criminology, 21*, 365–390.

Bernard, T., Snipes, J., & Gerould, A. (2010). *Vold's theoretical criminology*. New York: Oxford University Press.

Bevilacqua, L., & Goldman, D. (2009). Genes and addictions. *Clinical and Pharmacological Therapy, 85*, 359–361.

Bierut, L., Agrawal, A., Bucholz, K., Doheny, K., Laurie, C., Pugh, E., et al. (2010). A genome-wide association study of alcohol dependence. *Proceedings of the National Academy of Sciences, 107*, 5082–5087.

Bing, L. (1991). *Do or die*. New York: HarperCollins.

Binstein, M., & Bowden, C. (1993). *Trust me: Charles Keating and the missing billions*. New York: Random House.

Birkenhead, T, & Moller, A. (1992, July). Faithless females seek better genes. *New Scientist*, 34–38.

Blair, R. (2008). The amygdala and ventromedial prefrontal cortex: Functional contributions and dysfunctions in psychopathy. *Philosophical Transactions of the Royal Society: Biological Sciences, 363*, 2557–2565.

Blanco, J. (n.d.). *Gary Leon Ridgway*. Murderpedia. www.murderpedia .org/male.R/r/ridgway-gary.htm

Blanco, J. (n.d.). *Robert Bruce Spahalski*. Murderpedia. www .murderpedia. org/male.S/s/spahalski-robert.htm.

Blanco, J. (n.d.). *Lionel Tate*. Murderpedia. www.murderpedia.org/ male.T/t/tate-lionel.htm.

Blonigen, D. (2010). Explaining the relationship between age and crime: Contributions from the developmental literature on personality. *Clinical Psychology Review, 30*, 89–100.

Bobb, A., Castellanos, F., Addington, A. & Rapoport, J. (2005). Molecular genetic studies of ADHD: 1991 to 2004. *American Journal of Medical Genetics—Neuropsychiatric Genetics, 132*, 109–125.

Bohm, R. (2001). *A primer on crime and delinquency* (2nd ed.). Belmont, CA: Wadsworth.

Bonger, W. (1969). *Criminality and economic conditions*. Bloomington: Indiana University Press.

Bostaph, L. (2004). *Race and repeat victimization: Does the repetitive nature of police motor vehicle stops impact racially biased policing?* Unpublished doctoral dissertation, University of Cincinnati.

Brannigan, A. (1997, October). Self-control, social control and evolutionary psychology: Towards an integrated perspective on crime. *Canadian Journal of Criminology*, 403–431.

Brannon, I. (2013). Fannie Mae and Freddie Mac exemplify the horrors of crony capitalism. *Forbes Magazine.* www.forbes.com/sites/realspin/2013/11/22/fannie-mae-and-freddie-mac-exemplify-the-horrors-of-crony-capitalism.

Brebner, J. (2003). Gender and emotions. *Personality and Individual Differences, 34,* 387–394.

Brennan, P., Grekin, E., & Sarnoff, M. (1999). Maternal smoking during pregnancy and adult male criminal outcomes. *Archives of General Psychiatry, 56,* 215–219.

Brennan, P., Raine, A., Schulsinger, F., Kirkegaard-Sorenen, L., Knop, J., Hutchings, B., et al. (1997). Psychophysiological protective factors for male subjects at high risk for criminal behavior. *American Journal of Psychiatry, 154,* 853–855.

Brett, A. (2004). "Kindling theory" in arson: How dangerous are firesetters? *Australian and New Zealand Journal of Psychiatry, 38,* 419–425.

Brill, S. (2013, March). Bitter pill: How outrageous pricing and egregious profits are destroying our health care. *Time, 181,* 16–55.

British Foreign Office. (2013). *Information pack for British prisoners in Saudi Arabia.* www.gov.uk/government/.../saudi-arabia-prisoner-pack.

Broidy, L., & Agnew, R. (1997). Gender and crime: A general strain theory perspective. *Journal of Research in Crime and Delinquency, 34,* 275–306.

Browning, F., & Gerassi, J. (1980). *The American way of crime.* New York: G. P. Putnam.

Brownmiller, S. (1975). *Against our will: Men, women, and rape.* New York: Simon & Schuster.

Buck, K., & Finn, D. (2000). Genetic factors in addiction: QTL mapping and candidate gene studies implicate GABAergic genes in alcohol and barbiturate withdrawal in mice. *Addiction, 96,* 139–149.

Bullough, B., & Bullough, V. (1994). Prostitution. In V. Bullough & B. Bullough (Eds.), *Human sexuality: An encyclopedia* (pp. 494–499). New York: Garland Press.

Burgess, R., & Akers, R. (1966). A differential association-reinforcement theory of criminal behavior. *Social Problems, 14,* 128–147.

Burns, E. (2004). *The spirits of America: A social history of alcohol.* Philadelphia: Temple University Press.

Burns, R. (2004, June 6). Rumsfeld fearful of losing broader battle against extremists. *Idaho Statesman,* p. 5a.

Burr, M. (2004, December). SEC gains power, prestige in post Enron era. *Corporate Legal Times,* pp. 10–13.

Bushway, S., & Reuter, P. (2008). Economists' contribution to the study of crime and the criminal justice system. *Crime and Justice, 37,* 389–451.

Business Software Alliance. (2005). *2005 piracy study.* www.bsa.org/globalstudy.

Buss, D. (2005). *The murderer next door: Why the mind is designed to kill.* New York: Penguin.

Button, T., Corley, R., Rhee, S., Hewitt, J., Young, S., & Stallings, M. (2007). Delinquent peer affiliation and conduct problems: A twin study. *Journal of Abnormal Psychology, 116,* 554–564.

Buzawa, E., & Buzawa, C. (2003). *Domestic violence: The criminal justice response* (3rd ed.). Thousand Oaks, CA: Sage.

Calavita, K., & Pontell, H. (1994). "Head I win, tails you lose": Deregulation, crime, and crisis in the savings and loan industry. In D. Curran & C. Renzetti (Eds.), *Contemporary societies: Problems and prospects* (pp. 460–480). Upper Saddle River, NJ: Prentice Hall.

Calavita, K., Pontell, H., & Tillman, R. (1999). *Big money game: Fraud and politics in the savings and loan crisis.* Berkeley: University of California Press.

Campbell, A. (1999). Staying alive: Evolution, culture, and women's intrasexual aggression. *Behavioral and Brian Sciences, 22,* 203–214.

Campbell, A. (2006). Feminism and evolutionary psychology. In J. Barkow (Ed.), *Missing the revolution: Darwinism for social scientists* (pp. 63–99). Oxford: Oxford University Press.

Campbell, A. (2008). Attachment, aggression and affiliation: The role of oxytocin in female social behavior. *Biological Psychology, 77,* 1–10.

Campbell, A. (2009). Gender and crime: An evolutionary perspective. In A. Walsh & K. Beaver (Eds.), *Criminology and biology: New directions in theory and research* (pp. 117–136). New York: Routledge.

Canter, D. (2004). Offender profiling and investigative psychology. *Journal of Investigative Psychology and Offender Profiling, 1,* 1–15.

Cao, L. (2000). Is American society more anomic? A test of Merton's theory with cross-national data. *International Journal of Comparative and Applied Criminal Justice, 28,* 15–32.

Cao, L. (2004). *Major criminological theories: Concepts and measurement.* Belmont, CA: Wadsworth.

Cao, L., Adams, A., & Jensen, V. (1997). A test of the black subculture of violence thesis: A research note. *Criminology, 35,* 367–369.

Carey, G. (2003). *Human genetics for the social sciences.* Thousand Oaks, CA: Sage.

Carlisle, A. L. (1993). The divided self: Toward an understanding of the dark side of the serial killer. *American Journal of Criminal Justice,* 17:23–26.

Carpenter, T. (1989). *Missing beauty.* New York: Zebra Books.

Carter, D. (1994). International organized crime: Emerging trends in entrepreneurial crime. *Journal of Contemporary Criminal Justice, 10,* 239–266.

Cartwright, J. (2000). *Evolution and human behavior.* Cambridge, MA: MIT Press.

Casey, E. (1978). *History of drug use and drug users in the United States.* Schaffer Library of Drug Policy. www.druglibrary.org/schaffer/History/CASEY1.htm.

Caspi, A. (2000). The child is the father of the man: Personality continuities from childhood to adulthood. *Journal of Personality and Social Psychology, 78,* 158–172.

Caspi, A., McClay, J., Moffitt, T., Mill, J., Martin, J., Craig, I., et al. (2002). Evidence that the cycle of violence in maltreated children depends on genotype. *Science, 297,* 851–854.

Caspi, A., & Moffitt, T. (1995). The continuity of maladaptive behavior: From description to understanding in the study of antisocial behavior. In D. Cicchetti & D. Cohen (Eds.), *Manual of developmental psychology* (pp. 472–511). New York: Wiley.

Caspi, A., Moffitt, T., Silva, P., Stouthamer-Loeber, M., Krueger, R., & Schmutte, P. (1994). Are some people crime-prone?

Replications of the personality-crime relationship across countries, genders, races, and methods. *Criminology, 32,* 163–194.

Casswell, S., Pledger, M., & Hooper, R. (2003). Socioeconomic status and drinking patterns in young adults. *Addiction, 98,* 601–610.

Catalano, S. (2006). *Criminal victimization, 2005.* Washington, DC: Bureau of Justice Statistics.

Catalano, S. (2007). *Intimate partner violence in the United States.* Washington, DC: Bureau of Justice Statistics.

Catalano, S. (2010). *Victimization during household burglary.* Washington, DC: Bureau of Justice Statistics.

Catalano, S. (2012). *Intimate partner violence, 1993–2010.* Washington, DC: Bureau of Justice Statistics.

Cauffman, E., Steinberg, L., & Piquero, A. (2005). Psychological, neuropsychological and physiological correlated of serious antisocial behavior in adolescence: The role of self-control. *Criminology, 43,* 133–175.

Cecil K., Brubaker, C., Adler, C., Dietrich, K., Altaye, M., Egelhoff, J., et al. (2008). Decreased brain volume in adults with childhood lead exposure. *PLoS Medicine, 5,* 742–750.

Center for the Study of Democracy. (2010). *Examining the links between organized crime and corruption.* Sofia, Bulgaria: CSD.

Cernkovich, S., Giordano, P., & Rudolph, J. (2000). Race, crime, and the American dream. *Journal of Research in Crime and Delinquency, 37,* 131–170.

Chambliss, W. (1976). *Criminal law in action.* Santa Barbara, CA: Hamilton.

Chamorro-Premuzic, T., & Furnham, A. (2005). Intellectual competence. *The Psychologist, 18,* 352–354.

Champion, D. (2005). *Probation, parole, and community corrections* (5th ed.). Upper Saddle River, NJ: Prentice Hall.

Chapple, C., & Johnson, K. (2007). Gender differences in impulsivity. *Youth Violence and Juvenile Justice, 5,* 221–234.

Chesney-Lind, M. (1995). Girls, delinquency and juvenile justice: Toward a feminist theory of young women's crime. In B. Price & N. Sokoloff (Eds.), *The criminal justice system and women: Offenders, victims, and workers* (pp. 71–88). New York: McGraw-Hill.

Clarke, R., & Cornish, D. (2001). Rational choice. In R. Paternoster & R. Bachman (Eds.), *Explaining criminals and crime: Essays in contemporary criminological theory* (pp. 23–42). Los Angeles, Roxbury.

Cleveland, H., Wiebe, R., & Rowe, D. (2005). Sources of exposure to smoking and drinking friends among adolescents. *Journal of Genetic Psychology, 166,* 153–169.

Cleveland, H., Wiebe, R., van den Oord, E., & Rowe, D. (2000). Behavior problems among children from different family structures: The influence of genetic self-selection. *Child Development, 71,* 733–751.

Clinard, M., & Yeager, P. (1980). *Corporate crime.* New York: Free Press.

Cloward, R., & Ohlin, L. (1960). *Delinquency and opportunity.* New York: Free Press.

Coates, R. (1990). Victim-offender reconciliation programs in North America. In B. Galaway & J. Hudson (Eds.), *Criminal justice, restitution, and reconciliation* (pp. 245–265). Monsey, NY: Criminal Justice Press.

Cohen, A. (1955). *Delinquent boys.* New York: Free Press.

Cohen, L., & Felson, M. (1979). Social change and crime rate trends: A routine activities approach. *American Sociological Review, 44,* 588–608.

Coleman, J. (1986). *The criminal elite: The sociology of white collar crime.* New York: St. Martin's Press.

Collins, R. (2004). Onset and desistence in criminal careers: Neurobiology and the age-crime relationship. *Journal of Offender Rehabilitation, 39,* 1–19.

Collins, R. (2009). The micro-sociology of violence. *British Journal of Sociology, 60,* 566–576.

Connell, R., & Messerschmidt, J. (2005). Hegemonic masculinity: Rethinking the concept. *Gender and Society, 19,* 829–859.

Consumer Freedom. (2006). *America's number one terrorists.* http://consumerfreedom.com.

Coolidge, F., Thede, L., & Young, S. (2000). Heritability and the comorbidity of attention deficit hyperactivity disorder with behavioral disorders and executive function deficits: A preliminary investigation. *Developmental Neuropsychology, 17,* 273–287.

Cooper, J., Walsh, A., & Ellis, L. (2010). Is criminology ripe for a paradigm shift? Evidence from a survey of American criminologists. *Journal of Criminal Justice Education, 2,* 332–347.

Copes, H. (2003). Streetlife and the rewards of auto theft. *Deviant Behavior, 24,* 309–332.

Cornish, D., & Clarke, R. (1987). Understanding crime displacement: An application of rational choice theory. *Criminology, 25,* 933-947.

Council on Foreign Relations. (2004). *American militant extremists.* http://cfrterrorism.org/groups/American_print.html.

Covell, C., & Scalora, M. (2002). Empathetic deficits in sexual offenders: An integration of affective, social, and cognitive constructs. *Aggression and Violent Behavior, 37,* 251–270.

Crabbe, J. (2002). Genetic contributions to addiction. *Annual Review of Psychology, 53,* 435–462.

Crockett, M., Clark, L., Lieberman, M., Tabinia, G., & Robbins, T. (2010). Impulsive choice and altruistic punishment are correlated and increase in tandem with serotonin depletion. *Emotion, 10,* 855–862.

Crowell, S., Beauchaine, T., Gatzke-Kopp, L., Sylvers, P., Mead, H., & Chipman-Chacon, J. (2006). Autonomic correlates of attention-deficit/hyperactivity disorder and oppositional defiant disorder in preschool children. *Journal of Abnormal Psychology, 115,* 174–178.

Cullen, F. (2005). Challenging individualistic theories of crime. In S. Guarino-Ghezzi & J. Trevino (Eds.), *Understanding crime: A multidisciplinary approach* (pp. 55–60). Cincinnati, OH: Anderson.

Cullen, F., & Agnew, R. (2006). *Criminological theory: Past to present.* Los Angeles: Roxbury.

Cullen, K., & Murphy, S. (2013). *Whitey Bulger: America's most wanted gangster and the manhunt that brought him to justice.* New York: W. W. Norton.

Cureton, S. (2009). Something wicked this way comes: A historical account of black gangsterism offers wisdom and warning for African American leadership. *Journal of Black Studies, 40,* 347–361.

Curran, D., & Renzetti, C. (2001). *Theories of crime.* Boston: Allyn & Bacon.

Currie, E. (1989). Confronting crime: Looking toward the twenty-first century. *Justice Quarterly, 6,* 5–25.

Daigle, L., Fisher, B. & Cullen, F. (2008). The violent and sexual victimization of college women: Is repeat victimization a problem? *Journal of Interpersonal Violence, 23,* 1296–1313.

D'Alessio, S., & Stolzenberg, L. (2003). Race and the probability of arrest. *Social Forces, 81,* 1381–1397.

Daly, K., & Chesney-Lind, M. (2002). Feminism and criminology. In S. Cote (Ed.), *Criminological theories: Bridging the past to the future* (pp. 267–284). Thousand Oaks, CA: Sage.

Daly, M. (1996). Evolutionary adaptationism: Another biological approach to criminal and antisocial behavior. In G. Bock & J. Goode (Eds.), *Genetics of criminal and antisocial behaviour* (pp. 183–195). Chichester, England: Wiley.

Daly, M., & Wilson, M. (1996). Violence against stepchildren. *Current Directions in Psychological Science, 5,* 77–81.

Daly, M., & Wilson, M. (2000). Risk-taking, intersexual competition, and homicide. *Nebraska Symposium on Motivation, 47,* 1–36.

Davenport-Hines, R. (2002). *The pursuit of oblivion: A global history of narcotics.* New York: W. W. Norton.

David-Ferdon, C., & Hertz, M. F. (2009). *Electronic media and youth violence: A CDC issue brief for researchers.* Atlanta, GA: Centers for Disease Control.

Davidson, J. (2010). New slavery, old binaries: Human trafficking and the borders of "freedom." *Global Networks, 10,* 244–261.

Day, J., & Carelli, R. (2007). The nucleus accumbens and Pavlovian reward learning. *The Neuroscientist, 13,* 148–159.

Death Penalty Information Center. (2011). Deterrence: States without the death penalty have had consistently lower murder rates. www.deathpenaltyinfo.org/deterrence-states-without-death-penalty-have-had-consistently-lower-murder-rates.

De Haan, W., & Vos, J. (2003). A crying shame: The over-rationalized conception of man in the rational choice perspective. *Theoretical Criminology, 7,* 29–54.

DeLisi, M. (2009). Psychopathy is the unified theory of crime. *Youth Violence and Juvenile Justice, 7,* 257–273.

DeLisi, M., Beaver, K., Vaughn, M., & Wright, J. (2009). All in the family: Gene x environment interaction between DRD2 and criminal father is associated with five antisocial phenotypes. *Criminal Justice and Behavior, 36,* 1187–1197.

DeLisi, M., & Conis, P. (2012). *Violent offenders: Theory, research, policy, and practice.* Burlington, MA: Jones & Bartlett.

Demir, B., Ucar, G., Ulug, B., Ulosoy, S., Sevinc, I., & Batur, S. (2002). Platelet monoamine oxidase activity in alcoholism subtypes: Relationship to personality traits and executive functions. *Alcohol and Alcoholism, 37,* 597–602.

Department of Homeland Security. (2013). *Prevent terrorism and enhance security.* www.dhs.gov/prevent-terrorism-and-enhance-security.

Depue, R., & Collins, P. (1999). Neurobiology of the structure of personality: Dopamine, facilitation of incentive motivation, and extraversion. *Behavioral and Brain Sciences, 22,* 491–569.

DeVoe, J., Bauer, L., & Hill, M. (2012). *Student victimization in U.S. schools.* Washington, DC: U.S. Department of Education.

de Waal, F. (2008). Putting the altruism back into altruism: The evolution of empathy. *Annual Review of Psychology, 59,* 279–300.

Diamond, M. (2013, November 7). Ex-penny stock pitchman working at club he once owned. *Asbury Park Press.*

Dickens, W., & Flynn, J. (2001). Heritability estimates versus large environmental effects: The IQ paradox resolved. *Psychological Review, 108,* 346–349.

Dieter, R. (2009). *Smart on crime: Reconsidering the death penalty in a time of economic crisis.* Washington, DC: Death Penalty Information Center.

DiLorenzo, T. (2012). *The government-created subprime mortgage meltdown.* www.lewrockwell.com/dilorenzo/dilorenzo125.html.

Dinkes, R., Kemp, J., Baum, K., & Snyder, T. (2010). *Indicators of school crime and safety, 2009.* Washington, DC: Bureau of Justice Statistics.

Dishman, C. (2001). Terrorism, crime, and transformation. *Studies in Conflict & Terrorism, 24,* 43–58.

District of Columbia. (2014). *DC police crime mapping.* http://crimemap.dc.gov.

Doerner, W., & Lab, S. (2002). *Victimology* (3rd ed.). Cincinnati, OH: Anderson.

Doyle, C. (2002). The USA Patriot Act: A sketch. Washington, DC: Congressional Research Service, Library of Congress.

Drapkin, I. (1989). *Crime and punishment in the ancient world.* Lexington, MA: Lexington Books.

Drug Enforcement Administration. (2003). *Drugs of abuse.* Arlington, VA: U.S. Department of Justice.

Drummond, J. (2002). From the northwest imperative to global jihad: Social psychological aspects of the construction of the enemy, political violence, and terror. In E. Stout (Ed.), *The psychology of terrorism* (Vol. 1, pp. 49–95). Westport, CT: Praeger.

Dugdale, R. (1895). *"The Jukes": A study in crime, pauperism, disease, and heredity.* New York: Putnam. (Original work published 1877)

Dunn, D. (2004). *Ponzi: The incredible true story of the king of financial cons.* New York: Broadway.

Dunworth, T. (2001). Criminal justice and the IT revolution. *Criminal Justice, 3,* 371–426.

DuPont, R. (1997). *The selfish brain: Learning from addiction.* Washington, DC: American Psychiatric Press.

Durant, W. (1939). *The life of Greece.* New York: Simon & Schuster.

Durkheim, E. (1951). *The division of labor in society.* Glencoe, IL: Free Press.

Durkheim, É. (1982). *Rules of sociological method.* New York: Free Press.

Durrant, W., & Durrant, A. (1968). *The lessons of history.* New York: Simon & Schuster.

Durston, S. (2003). A review of the biological bases of ADHD: What have we learned from imaging studies? *Mental Retardation and Developmental Disabilities, 9,* 184–195.

Earth First. (2006). *Communique from the Earth Liberation Front.* www.iiipublishing.com/elf.htm.

The Economist. (2013, November 29). America's economic difficulties are mostly political, p. 11.

Eggert, K. (2009). The great collapse: How securitization caused the subprime meltdown. *Connecticut Law Review, 41,* 1257–1312.

Eisener, M. (2001). Modernization, self-control, and lethal violence: The long-term dynamics of European homicide rates in theoretical perspective. *British Journal of Criminology, 41,* 618–638.

Elliot, D., Huizinga, D., & Menard, S. (1989). *Multiple problem youth: Delinquency, substance abuse, and mental health problems.* New York: Springer-Verlag.

Ellis, L. (2003). Genes, criminality, and the evolutionary neuroandrogenic theory. In A. Walsh & L. Ellis (Eds.), *Biosocial criminology: Challenging environmentalism's supremacy* (pp. 12–34). Hauppauge, NY: Nova Science.

Ellis, L., Hartley, R., & Walsh, A. (2010). *Research methods in criminal justice and criminology*. Lanham, MD: Rowman & Littlefield.

Ellis, L., & Hoffman, H. (1990). Views of contemporary criminologists on causes and theories of crime. In L. Ellis & H. Hoffman (Eds.), *Crime in biological, social, and moral contexts* (pp. 50–58). New York: Praeger.

Ellis, L., & Walsh, A. (2000). *Criminology: A global perspective*. Boston: Allyn & Bacon.

Ellis, L., & Walsh, A. (2003). Crime, delinquency and intelligence: A review of the worldwide literature. In H. Nyborg (Ed.), *The scientific study of general intelligence: A tribute to Arthur Jensen* (pp. 343–365). Amsterdam: Pergamon.

Ember, M., & Ember, C. (1998, October). Facts of violence. *Anthropology Newsletter*, 14–15.

English, S. (2004). Enron legal bills will cost $780m. *Business Telegraph*. www.telegraph.co.uk/money.jhtml?xml=/money/2004/1.

Eppig, C., Fincher, C., & Thornhill, R. (2010). Parasite prevalence and the worldwide distribution of cognitive ability. *Proceedings of the Royal Society: Biological Science*. doi:10.1098/rspb.2010.0973

Eppig, C., Fincher, C., & Thornhill, R. (2011). Parasite prevalence and the distribution of intelligence among the states of the USA. *Intelligence, 29,* 155–160.

Farrell, G. (2010). Situational crime prevention and its discontents: Rational choice and harm reduction versus "cultural criminology." *Social Policy and Administration, 44,* 40–66.

Farrell, G., Phillips, C., & Pease, K. (1995). Like taking candy from a baby: Why does repeat victimization occur? *British Journal of Criminology, 35,* 384–399.

Farrington, D. (1982). Longitudinal analyses of criminal violence. In M. Wolfgang & N. Weiner (Eds.), *Criminal violence*. Beverly Hills, CA: Sage.

Farrington, D. (2003). Developmental and life-course criminology: Key theoretical and empirical issues—The 2002 Sutherland Award address. *Criminology, 41,* 221–255.

Fast Track Project. (2005). *Fast track project overview*. www.fasttrackproject.org/fasttrackoverview.htm.

Federal Bureau of Investigation. (2001). *Mafia family chart*. www.fbi.gov/news/stories/2011/january/mafia_012011/image/mafia-family-tree/view.

Federal Bureau of Investigation. (2005). *Uniform Crime Reports Handbook*. Washington, DC: U.S. Government Printing Office.

Federal Bureau of Investigation. (2008). *Serial murder-multidisciplinary perspectives for investigators*. www.fbi.gov/publications/serial_murder.htm.

Federal Bureau of Investigation. (2009a). *Crime in the United States: 2008*. Washington DC: U.S. Government Printing Office.

Federal Bureau of Investigation. (2009b). *Financial crimes report to the public, fiscal year 2008*. Washington, DC: Government Printing Office.

Federal Bureau of Investigation. (2010). *Crime in the United States: 2009: Uniform Crime Reports*. Washington DC: U.S. Government Printing Office.

Federal Bureau of Investigation. (2012). *Financial Crimes Report, 2010–2011*. www.fbi.gov/stats-services/publications/financial-crimes-report-2012.

Federal Bureau of Investigation. (2013a). *Crime in the United States: 2012*. Washington DC: U.S. Government Printing Office.

Federal Bureau of Investigation. (2013b). *Today's FBI: Facts and figures: 2013–2014*. Washington, DC: U.S. Department of Justice.

Federal Trade Commission. (2010). *Consumer sentinel network data book*. Washington, DC: Federal Trade Commission.

Feeney, D. (2002). Enhancement in Islamic fundamentalism. In C. Stout (Ed.), *The psychology of terrorism* (Vol. III, pp. 192–209). Westport, CT: Praeger.

Felson, M. (1998). *Crime and everyday life* (2nd ed.). Thousand Oaks, CA: Pine Forge Press.

Ferguson, C. (2010). Genetic contributions to antisocial personality and behavior: A meta-analytic review from an evolutionary perspective. *Journal of Social Psychology, 150,* 160–180.

Fergusson, D., Swain-Campbell, N., & Horwood, J. (2004). How does childhood economic disadvantage lead to crime? *Journal of Child Psychology and Psychiatry, 45,* 956–966.

Ferrell, J. (2004). Boredom, crime and criminology. *Theoretical Criminology, 8,* 287–302.

Ferri, E. (1917). *Criminal sociology*. Boston: Little, Brown. (Original work published 1897)

Finckenauer, J. (2004, July/August). The Russian "mafia." *Society*, 61–64.

Finkelhor, D. (1984). *Child sexual abuse: New theory and research*. New York: Free Press.

Finklea, K. (2010). *Organized crime in the United States: Trends and issues for congress*. Washington, DC: Congressional Research Service.

Firestone, T. (1997). Mafia memoirs: What they tell us about organized crime. In P. Ryan & G. Rush (Eds.), *Understanding organized crime in global perspective* (pp. 71–86). Thousand Oaks, CA: Sage.

Fishbein, D. (1992). The psychobiology of female aggression. *Criminal Justice and Behavior, 19,* 99–126.

Fishbein, D. (2001). *Biobehavioral perspectives in criminology*. Belmont, CA: Wadsworth.

Fishbein, D. (2003). Neuropsychological and emotional regulatory processes in antisocial behavior. In A. Walsh & L. Ellis (Eds.), *Biosocial criminology: Challenging environmentalism's supremacy* (pp. 185–208). Hauppauge, NY: Nova Science.

Fisher, B., Cullen, F., & Turner, M. (2001). *The sexual victimization of college women*. Washington DC: National Institute of Justice.

Fisher, E. (2012). From outcasts to overlords: The legitimacy of the yakuza in Japan. *The Undergraduate Journal of Social Studies, 3,* 1–12.

Flynn, J. (2007). *What is intelligence? Beyond the Flynn effect*. Cambridge, England: Cambridge University Press.

Fox, J., & Levin, J. (2001). *The will to kill: Making sense of senseless murder*. Boston: Allyn & Bacon.

Fox, L. (2003). *Enron: The rise and fall*. Hoboken, NJ: John Wiley.

Franklin, T., Gau, J., & Pratt, T. (2010). *Key ideas in criminology and criminal justice*. Thousand Oaks, CA: Sage.

Fredrickson, B. (2003). The value of positive emotions. *American Scientist, 91,* 330–335.

Freeman, N. (2007). Predictors of rearrest for rapists and child molesters on probation. *Criminal Justice and Behavior, 34,* 752–758.

Freud, S. (1976). The ego and the id (J. Strachey, Ed. and Trans.). *The complete psychological works of Sigmund Freud* (Vol. 19). New York: Norton. (Original work published 1923)

Friedman, L. (2005). *A history of American law*. New York: Simon & Schuster.

Friedrichs, D. (2010). *Trusted criminals* (4th ed.). Belmont, CA: Wadsworth.

Friel, B. (2012). *The barefoot bandit: The true tale of Colton Harris-Moore, new American outlaw*. New York: Hyperion.

Gallup. (2013). *Americans' reaction to Obama gun proposals is positive*. www.gallup.com/poll/1645/guns.aspx.

Gao, Y., Raine, A., Venerables, P., Dawson, M., & Mednick, S. (2010). Association of poor childhood fear conditioning and adult crime. *American Journal of Psychiatry, 167,* 56–60.

Garofalo, R. (1968). *Criminology*. Montclair: NJ: Patterson Smith. (Original work published 1885)

Garrison, A. (2004). Defining terrorism: Philosophy of the bomb, propaganda by deed and change through fear and violence. *Criminal Justice Studies, 17,* 259–279.

Gatzke-Kopp, L., Raine, A., Loeber, R., Stouthamer-Loeber, M., Steinhauer, S. (2002). Serious delinquent behavior, sensation seeking, and electrodermal arousal. *Journal of Abnormal Child Psychology, 30,* 477–486.

Gaulin, S., & McBurney, D. (2001). *Psychology: An evolutionary approach*. Upper Saddle River, NJ: Prentice Hall.

Geary, D. (2000). Evolution and proximate expression of human paternal investment. *Psychological Bulletin, 126,* 55–77.

Giancola, P., Josephs, R., Parrott, D., & Duke, A. (2010). Alcohol myopia revisited: Clarifying aggression and other acts of disinhibition through a distorted lens. *Perspectives on Psychological Science, 5,* 265–278.

Giannangelo, S. (1996). *The psychopathology of serial murder: A theory of violence*. Westport, CT: Praeger.

Gibson, M. (2002). *Born to crime: Cesare Lombroso and the origins of biological criminology*. Westport, CT: Praeger.

Gilsinian, J. (1990). *Criminology and public policy: An introduction*. Englewood Cliffs, NJ: Prentice Hall.

Giordano, G. (2003). *The Oklahoma City bombing*. New York: Rosen.

Given, J. (1977). *Society and homicide in thirteenth-century England*. Stanford, CA: Stanford University Press.

Gluckman, P., & Hanson, M. (2006). Changing times: The evolution of puberty. *Molecular and Cellular Endocrinology, 255,* 26–31.

Glueck, S. (1956). Theory and fact in criminology: A criticism of differential association theory. *British Journal of Criminology, 7,* 92–109.

Glueck, S., & Glueck, E. (1934). *Five hundred delinquent women*. New York: Knopf.

Glueck, S., & Glueck, E. (1950). *Unraveling juvenile delinquency*. New York: Commonwealth Fund.

Goddard, H. (1931). *The Kallikak family: A study in the heredity of feeble-mindedness*. New York: Macmillan. (Original work published 1912)

Goldberg, E. (2001). *The executive brain: Frontal lobes and the civilized mind*. New York: Oxford University Press.

Goldstein, P. (1985). The drugs/violence nexus: A tripartite conceptual framework. *Journal of Drug Issues, 15,* 493–506.

Goldstein, P., Browstein, H., Ryan, P., & Belluci, P. (1989, Winter). Crack and homicide in New York City 1988: A conceptually based event analysis. *Contemporary Drug Problems,* 651–687.

Goode, E. (2005). *Drugs in American Society* (6th ed.). Boston: McGraw Hill.

Goodlett, C., Horn, K., & Zhou, F. (2005). Alcohol teratogenesis: Mechanisms of damage and strategies for intervention. *Developmental Biology and Medicine, 230,* 394–406.

Gordon, N. (2008, April 18). Franklin Raines to pay $24.7 million to settle Fannie Mae lawsuit. *Seattle Times*. http://seattletimes.com/html/businesstechnology/2004358433_webraines18.html.

Gottfredson, L. (2011). Intelligence and social inequality: Why the biological link? In T. Chamorro-Premuzic, S. von Stum, & A. Furnham (Eds.), *The Wiley-Blackwell handbook of individual differences* (pp. 538–575). Hoboken, NJ: Wiley-Blackwell.

Gottfredson, M. (2006). The empirical status of control theory in criminology. In F. Cullen, J. Wright, & K. Blevins (Eds.), *Taking stock: The status of criminological theory* (pp. 77–100). New Brunswick, NJ: Transaction.

Gottfredson, M., & Hirschi, T. (1990). *A general theory of crime*. Stanford, CA: Stanford University Press.

Gottfredson, M., & Hirschi, T. (1997). National crime control policies. In M. Fisch (Ed.), *Criminology 97/98* (pp. 27–33). Guilford, CT: Dushkin.

Gove, W., & Wilmoth, C. (2003). The neurophysiology of motivation and habitual criminal behavior. In A. Walsh & L. Ellis (Eds.), *Biosocial criminology: Challenging environmentalism's supremacy* (pp. 227–245). Hauppauge, NY: Nova Science.

Graham-Kevan, N., & Archer, J. (2009). Control tactics and partner violence in heterosexual relationships. *Evolution and Human Behavior, 30,* 445–452

Grana, S. (2002). *Women and (in) justice: The criminal and civil effects of the common law on women's lives*. Boston: Allyn & Bacon.

Grasmick, H., Tittle, C., Bursik, R., & Arneklev, B. (1993). Testing the core empirical implication of Gottfredson and Hirschi's general theory of crime. *Journal of Research in Crime and Delinquency, 30,* 5–29.

Greenberg, A. (2013). "Silk Road 2.0" launches, promising a resurrected black market for the dark web. *Forbes Magazine*. www.forbes.com/sites/andygreenberg/2013/11/06/silk-road-2-0-launches-promising-a-resurrected-black-market-for-the-dark-web.

Greenberg, D. (1981). *Crime and capitalism: Readings in Marxist criminology*. Palo Alto, CA: Mayfield.

Griffin, S. (2002). Actors or activities? On the social construction of "white-collar crime" in the United States. *Crime, Law, and Social Change, 37,* 245–276.

Grossman, L., & Newton-Small, J. (2013). The deep web. *Time, 182,* pp. 26–33.

Gudjonsson, G., Sigurddsson, J., Young, S., Newton, A., & Peersen, M. (2009). Attention deficit hyperactivity disorder (ADHD). How do ADHD symptoms relate to personality among prisoners? *Personality and Individual Differences, 47,* 64–68.

Guo, G., Tong, Y., & Cai, T. (2008). Gene by social context interactions for number of sexual partners among white male youths: Genetics-informed sociology. *American Journal of Sociology, 114,* S36–66.

Gutman, H. (2002). Dishonesty, greed, and hypocrisy in corporate America. *Statesman* (Kalkota, India). www.commondreams .org/cgi-bin/print.cgi?file=/views.

Hacker, F. (1977). *Crusaders, criminals, crazies: Terror and terrorism in our time.* New York: Norton.

Hacking, I. (2006). Genetics, biosocial groups & the future of identity. *Daedalus, 135,* 81–95.

Hagan, F. (1994). *Introduction to criminology.* Chicago: Nelson-Hall.

Hagan, F. (2008). *Introduction to Criminology* (6th ed.) Thousand Oaks, CA: Sage.

Hagan, J. (1985). *Modern criminology: Crime, criminal behavior and its control.* New York: McGraw-Hill.

Hagan, J. (1989). *Structural criminology.* New Brunswick, NJ: Rutgers University Press.

Haidt, J. (2001). The emotional dog and its rational tail: A social intuitionist approach to moral judgment. *Psychological Review, 108,* 814–834.

Hakkanen, H., Puolakka, P., & Santilla, P. (2004). Crime scene actions and offender characteristics in arsons. *Legal and Criminological Psychology, 9,* 197–214.

Hall, S. (2000). Paths to anelpis: Dimorphic violence and the pseudo-pacification process. *Paralax, 6,* 36–53.

Hall, S., & Winlow, S. (2004). Barbarians at the gate: Crime and violence in the breakdown of the pseudo-pacification process. In J. Ferrell, K. Hayward, W. Morrison, & M. Presdee (Eds.), *Cultural criminology unleashed* (pp 275–286). London: Glass House Press.

Hampton, R., Oliver, W., & Magarian, L. (2003). Domestic violence in the African American community. *Violence Against Women, 9,* 533–557.

Hancock, T. (2012). *Housing bubble, financial crisis: What happened, who is responsible?* http://tjhancock.wordpress.com/housing-bubble-financial-crisis-detailed-comprehensive-assessment.

Hare, R. (1993). *Without conscience: The disturbing world of the psychopaths among us.* New York: Pocket Books.

Hare, R. (1996). Psychopathy: A clinical construct whose time has come. *Criminal Justice and Behavior, 23,* 25–54.

Hargrove, T. (2010). Unsolved murder rate increasing. *Scripps Howard News Service.* www.newsnet5.com/dpp/news/crime/unsolved-murder-rate-increasing#ixzz2Vjwsqtps.

Harrell, E. (2011). *Workplace violence, 1993–2009.* Washington, DC: Bureau of Justice.

Harrendorf, S., Heiskanen, M., & Malby, S. (2010). *International statistics on crime and justice.* Helsinki, Finland: European Institute for Crime Prevention and Control.

Harris, A., Thomas, S., Fisher, G., & Hirsch, D. (2002). Murder and medicine: The lethality of criminal assault 1960–1999. *Homicide Studies, 6,* 128–166.

Harris, G., Skilling, T., & Rice, M. (2001). The construct of psychopathy. In M. Tonry (Ed.), *Crime and justice: A review of research* (pp. 197–264). Chicago: University of Chicago Press.

Harris, J. (1998). *The nurture assumption: Why children turn out the way they do.* New York: Free Press.

Harris, K. (1991). Moving into the new millennium: Toward a feminist view of justice. In H. Pepinsky & R. Quinney (Eds.),

Criminology as peacemaking (pp. 83–97). Bloomington: Indiana University Press.

Hawley, A. (1944). Ecology and human ecology. *Social Forces, 22,* 398–405.

Hawthorne, N. (2003). *The scarlet letter.* New York: Barnes & Noble Classics. (Originally published 1850)

Hayward, K. (2007). Situational crime prevention and its discontents: Rational choice theory versus the "culture of now." *Social Policy and Administration, 41,* 332–350.

Hayward, K. (2012). Response to Farrell. *Social Policy and Administration, 46,* 21–34.

Hayward, K., & Young, J. (2004). Cultural criminology: Some notes on the script. *Theoretical Criminology, 8,* 259–273.

Hazelwood, R., Ressler, R., Depue, K., & Douglas, J. (1987). Criminal personality profiling: An overview. In R. Hazelwood & A. Burgess (Eds.), *Practical aspects of rape Investigation: A multidisciplinary approach* (pp. 137–149). New York: Elsevier.

Henry, B., Caspi, A., Moffitt, T., & Silva, P. (1996). Temperament and familial predictors of violent and non-violent criminal convictions: From age 3 to age 8. *Developmental Psychology, 32,* 614–623.

Herman, J. (1991). Sex offenders: A feminist perspective. In W. Marshall, D. Laws, & H. Barbaree (Eds.), *Handbook of sexual assault: Issues, theories, and treatment of the offender* (pp. 177–193). New York: Plenum.

Hermans, E., Putman, P., & van Honk, J. (2006). Testosterone reduces empathetic mimicking in healthy young women. *Psychoneuroendocrinology, 31,* 859–866.

Herrnstein, R., & Murray, C. (1994). *The bell curve: Intelligence and class structure in American society.* New York: Free Press.

Hickey, E. (2006). *Serial murderers and their victims* (4th ed.). Belmont, CA: Wadsworth.

Hill, P. (2003). *The Japanese mafia: Yakuza, law, and the state.* Oxford, England: Oxford University Press.

Hill, R., & Robertson, R. (2003). What sort of future for critical criminology? *Crime, Law, & Social Change, 39,* 91–115.

Hindelang, M., Hirschi, T., & Weis, J. (1981). *Measuring delinquency.* Beverly Hills, CA: Sage.

Hirschi, T. (1969). *The causes of delinquency.* Berkeley: University of California Press.

Hirschi, T. (2004). Self-control and crime. In R. Baumeister & K. Vohs (Eds.), *Handbook of self-regulation research, theory, and applications* (pp. 537–552). New York: Guilford.

Hirschi, T., & Gottfredson, M. (1983). Age and the explanation of crime. *American Journal of Sociology, 89,* 552–584.

Hirschi, T., & Gottfredson, M. (1987). Causes of white-collar crime. *Criminology, 25,* 949–974.

Hirschi, T., & Hindelang, M. (1977). Intelligence and delinquency: A revisionist review. *American Sociology Review, 42,* 571–587.

Hoffman, B. (2010, Fall). The evolving nature of terrorism. *The Social Contract,* 33–40.

Hoffman, C. (2002). Rethinking terrorism and counterterrorism since 9/11. *Studies in Conflict & Terrorism, 25,* 303–316.

Holmes, R., & DeBurger, J. (1998). Profiles in terror: The serial murderer. In R. Holmes & A. Holmes (Eds.), *Contemporary perspectives on serial murder* (pp. 1–16). Thousand Oaks, CA: Sage.

Holmes, S. (1999, September 30). Fannie Mae eases credit to aid mortgage lending. *New York Times.* www.nytimes

.com/1999/09/30/business/fannie-mae-eases-credit-to-aid-mortgage-lending.html.

Hopcroft, R. (2009). Gender inequality in interaction: An evolutionary account. *Social Forces, 87,* 1845–1872.

Howard, C. (1979). *Zebra: The true account of the 179 days of terror in San Francisco.* New York: Richard Marek.

Huber, J. (2008). Reproductive biology, technology, and gender inequality: An autobiographical essay. *Annual Review of Sociology, 34,* 1–13.

Hudson, R. (1999). *The sociology and psychology of terrorism: Who becomes a terrorist and why?* Washington, DC: Library of Congress, Federal Research Division.

Hughes, V. (2010). Head case. *Nature, 464,* 140–142.

Huizink, A., & Mulder, E. (2006). Maternal smoking, drinking or cannabis use during pregnancy and neurobehavioral and cognitive functioning in human offspring. *Neuroscience and Biobehavioral Reviews, 30,* 24–41.

Hume, T. (2013). How the FBI caught Ross Ulbricht, alleged creator of criminal marketplace Silk Road. *CNN News.* www.cnn.com/2013/10/04/world/americas/silk-road-ross-ulbricht.

Hunnicutt, G., & Broidy, L. (2004). Liberation and economic marginalization: A reformulation and test of (formerly?) competing models. *Journal of Research in Crime and Delinquency, 41,* 130–155.

Hurd, M. (2003). *The psychology of junior sniper Lee Malvo.* www.capmag.com.

Hwang, S., & Bedford, O. (2004). Juveniles' motivations for remaining in prostitution. *Psychology of Women Quarterly, 28,* 136–146.

Hyman, S. (2007). The neurobiology of addiction: Implications for voluntary control of behavior. *American Journal of Bioethics, 7,* 8–11.

Ianni, F. (1998). New mafia: Black, Hispanic, and Italian styles. *Society, 35,* 116–129.

Incident-Based Reporting Resource Center. (2013). *Background and status of incident-based reporting and NIBRS.* www.jrsa.org/ibrrc/background-status/top_25.shtml.

Institute of Alcohol Studies. (2013). *UK alcohol-related crimes statistics.* www.ias.org.uk/Alcohol-knowledge-centre/Crime-and-social-impacts/Factsheets/UK-alcohol-related-crime-statistics.aspx.

Insurance Information Institute. (2009). *Teen drivers.* www.iii.org/media/hot-topics/insurance/teendrivers.

International Harm Reduction Association. (2012). *What is harm reduction?* www.ihra.net/files/2010/08/10/Briefing_What_is_HR_English.pdf.

INTERPOL. (1992). *International crime statistics.* Lyons, France.

Irwin, K., & Chesney-Lind, M. (2008). Girls' violence: Beyond dangerous masculinity. *Sociology Compass, 2/3,* 837–855.

Iwai, H. (1986). Organized crime in Japan. In R. Kelly (Ed.), *Organized crime: A global perspective* (pp. 208–233). Totowa, NJ: Rowman & Littlefield.

Jacobs, B., Topalli, V., & Wright, R. (2003). Carjacking, streetlife and offender motivation. *British Journal of Criminology, 43,* 673–688.

Jacobs, B., & Wright, R. (1999). Stick-up, street culture, and offender motivation. *Criminology, 37,* 149–173.

Jafee, S., Moffitt, T., Caspi, A., & Taylor, A. (2003). Life with (or without) father: The benefits of living with two biological parents depend on the father's antisocial behavior. *Child Development, 74,* 109–126.

Jalata, A. (2011). Terrorism from above and below in the age of globalization. *Sociology Mind, 1,* 1–15.

Jarboe, J. (2002). *The threat of domestic terrorism. Testimony of Congressional Committee on Forests and Forest Health.* www.fbi.gov/congress/congress02/jarboe021202.htm.

Johnson, E. (1990). Yakuza (criminal gangs) in Japan: Characteristics and management in prison. *Journal of Contemporary Criminal Justice, 6,* 113–126.

Johnson, L., O'Malley, P., & Bachman, J. (2000). *Monitoring the future National Survey Results on drug use, 1975–1999.* Bethesda, MD: National Institute of Drug Abuse.

Johnson, P., & Feldman, T. (1992). Personality types and terrorism: Self-psychology perspectives. *Forensic Reports, 5,* 293–303.

Jones, M. (2009). The Pinocchio effect: On making Italians (1860–1920). *Journal of the Association for the Study of Modern Italy, 14,* 359–361.

Kanazawa, S. (2003). A general evolutionary psychological theory of criminality and related male-typical behavior. In A. Walsh & L. Ellis (Eds.), *Biosocial criminology: Challenging environmentalism's supremacy* (pp. 37–60). Hauppauge, NY: Nova Science.

Kappeler, V., Blumberg, M., & Potter, G. (2000). *The mythology of crime and criminal justice* (3rd ed.). Prospect Heights, IL: Waveland.

Karmen, A. (2005). *Crime victims: An introduction to victimology* (5th ed.). Belmont, CA: Wadsworth.

Katz, J. (1988). *Seductions of crime: Moral and sensual attractions in doing evil.* New York: Basic Books.

Keel, T., Jarvis, J., & Muirhead, Y. (2009). An exploratory analysis of factors affecting homicide investigations. *Homicide Studies, 13,* 50–68.

Keeney, B., & Heide, K. (1995). Serial murder: A more accurate and inclusive definition. *International Journal of Offender Therapy and Comparative Criminology, 39,* 299–306.

Kendler, K., Jacobson, K., Gardner, C., Gillespie, N., Aggen, S., & Prescott, C. (2007). Creating a social world: A developmental twin study of peer group deviance. *Archives of General Psychiatry, 64,* 958–965.

Kesteren, J. van, Mayhew, P., & Nieuwbeerta, P. (2000). *Criminal victimization in seventeen industrialised countries: Key findings from the 2000 international crime victims survey.* The Hague, Netherlands: Ministry of Justice.

Kim, J., Fendrich, M., & Wislar, J. (2000). The validity of juvenile arrestees' drug use reporting: A gender comparison. *Journal of Research in Crime and Delinquency, 37,* 429–432.

Kim-Cohen, J., Caspi, A., Taylor, A., Williams, B., Newcombe, R., Craig, I., et al. (2006). MAOA, maltreatment, and gene-environment interaction predicting children's mental health: New evidence and a meta-analysis. *Molecular Psychiatry, 11,* 903–913.

Kimura, D. (1992). Sex differences in the brain. *Scientific American, 267,* 119–125.

King, L., & Roberts, J. (2011). Traditional gender role and rape myth acceptance: From the countryside to the big city. *Women & Criminal Justice, 21,* 1–20.

Kirchgassner, G. (2011). Econometric estimates of deterrence of the death penalty: Facts or ideology? *Kyklos, 64,* 448–478.

Kirman, A., Livet, P., & Teschl, M. (2010). Rationality and emotions. *Philosophical Transactions of the Royal Society B: Biological Sciences, 365*(1538), 215–219.

Kish, S., Lerch, J., Furukawa, Y., Tong, J., McCluskey, T., Wilkins, D., et al. (2010). Decreased cerebral cortical serotonin transporter binding in ecstasy users: A positron emission tomography/DASB and structural brain imaging study. *Brain, 133,* 779–797.

Klaus, P. (2004). *Carjacking, 1993–2002.* Washington, DC: Bureau of Justice Statistics Crime Data Briefs. U.S. Department of Justice.

Kleber, H. (2003). Pharmacological treatments for heroin and cocaine dependence. *American Journal on Addictions, 12,* S5–S18.

Knox, G., & Fuller, L. (1995). The gangster disciples: A gang profile. *Journal of Gang Research, 3,* 58–76.

Kochanska, G., & Aksan, N. (2004). Conscience in childhood: Past, present, and future. *Merrill-Palmer Quarterly, 50,* 299–310.

Koller, K., Brown, T., Spurfeon, A., & Levy, L. (2004). Recent developments in low-level lead exposure and intellectual impairment in children. *Environmental Health Perspectives, 112,* 987–994.

Kornblum, W., & Julian, J. (1995). *Social problems* (8th ed.). Englewood Cliffs, NJ: Prentice Hall.

Kornhauser, R. (1978). *Social sources of delinquency: An appraisal of analytical methods.* Chicago: University of Chicago Press.

Kramer, M. (1990). The moral logic of Hizballah. In W. Reich (Ed.), *Origins of terrorism: Psychologies, ideologies, theologies, states of mind* (pp. 131–157). New York: Cambridge University Press.

Krueisi, M., Leonard, H., Swedo, S., Nadi, S., Hamburger, S., Lui, J., et al. (1994). Endogenous opioids, childhood psychopathology, and Quay's interpretation of Jeffrey Gray. In D. Routh (Ed.), *Disruptive behavior disorders in childhood* (pp. 207–219). New York: Plenum.

Kruk, E. (2012). Arguments for an equal parental responsibility presumption in contested child custody. *American Journal of Family Therapy, 40,* 33–55.

Kshetri, N. (2006, January/February). The simple economics of cybercrimes. *IEEE Security & Privacy,* 33–39.

Kumar, M., & Chandrasekar, C. (2011). CIS technologies in crime analysis and crime mapping. *International Journal of Soft Computing and Engineering, 1,* 2231–2307.

Kurtz, H. (2002, February 2–3). America is "doomed" Bin Laden says on tape. *International Herald Tribune,* p. 5.

Lacourse, E., Nagin, D., Vitaro, F., Côté, S., Arseneault, L., Tremblay, R. E. (2006). Prediction of early-onset deviant peer group affiliation: A 12-year longitudinal study. *Archives of General Psychiatry, 63,* 562–568.

LaFree, G., & Ackerman, G. (2009). The empirical study of terrorism: Social and legal research. *Annual Review of Law and Social Science, 5,* 347–374.

LaFree, G., Drass, K., & O'Day, P. (1992). Race and crime in postwar America: Determinants of African-American and white rates. *Criminology, 30,* 157–185.

Lamontagne, Y., Boyer, R., Hetu, C., & Lacerte-Lamontagne, C. (2000). Anxiety, significant losses, depression, and irrational beliefs in first-offense shoplifters. *Canadian Journal of Psychiatry, 45,* 63–66.

Lanier, M., & Henry, S. (1998). *Essential criminology.* Boulder, CO: Westview.

Lanier, M., & Henry, S. (2010). *Essential criminology* (3rd ed.). Boulder, CO: Westview.

Laub, J., & Sampson, R. (2003). *Shared beginnings, divergent lives: Delinquent boys at age 70.* Cambridge, MA: Harvard University Press.

Law Enforcement Agency Resource Network. (2004). *Aryan Nations/Church of Jesus Christ Christian.* www.adl.org/learn/ext_us/Aryan_Nations.asp?xpicked=3&.

Leader, S., & Probst, P. (2006). *The Earth Liberation Front and environmental terrorism.* http://www1.umn.edu/des/earthliberationfront3pub.htm.

Lehr, D., & O'Neill, G. (2001). *Black mass: The true story of an unholy alliance between the FBI and the Irish mob.* New York: HarperCollins.

Lemert, E. (1974). Beyond Mead: The societal reaction to deviance. *Social Problems, 21,* 457–468.

Leonard, E. (1995). Theoretical criminology and gender. In B. Price & N. Sokoloff (Eds.), *The criminal justice system and women: Offenders, victims, and workers* (pp. 54–70.) New York: McGraw-Hill.

Leonnig, C. (2008, June 10). How HUD mortgage policy fed the crisis. *Washington Post.*

Lepowsky, M. (1994). Women, men, and aggression in egalitarian societies. *Sex Roles, 30,* 199–211.

Lester, D. (2010). Suicide in mass murderers and serial killers. *Suicidology, 1,* 19–27.

Levi-Minzi, M., & Shields, M. (2007). Serial sexual murderers and prostitutes as their victims: Difficulty profiling perpetrators and victim vulnerability as illustrated by the Green River case. *Brief Treatment and Crisis Intervention, 7,* 77–89.

Levin, J., & Fox, J. (1985). *Mass murder: America's growing menace.* New York: Plenum.

Levin, Y., & Lindesmith, A. (1971). English ecology and criminology of the past century. In H. Voss & D. Petersen (Eds.), *Ecology, crime, and delinquency* (pp. 47–76). New York: Appleton-Century-Crofts.

Levy, F., Hay, D., McStephen, M., Wood, C., & Waldman, I. (1997). Attention-deficit hyperactivity disorder: A category or a continuum? Genetic analysis of a large-scale twin study. *Journal of the American Academy of Child and Adolescent Psychiatry, 36,* 737–744.

Levy, S., & Stone, B. (2005). Grand theft identity. *Newsweek.* http://msnbc.com/id/835i692/site/newsweek/print/1/displaymode/1098.

Lewis, C. S. (1970). *God in the dock: Essays on theology and ethics* (W. Hooper, Ed.). London: Eerdmans.

Leyton, E. (1986). *Hunting humans: Inside the minds of mass murderers.* New York: Pocket Books.

Lilly, J., Cullen, F., & Ball, R. (2007). *Criminological theory: Context and consequences* (3rd ed.). Thousand Oaks, CA: Sage.

Lilly, J., Cullen, F., & Ball, R. (2011). *Criminological theory: Context and consequences* (5th ed.). Thousand Oaks, CA: Sage.

Linden, R., & Chaturvedi, R. (2005). The need for comprehensive crime prevention planning: The case of motor vehicle theft. *Canadian Journal of Criminology and Criminal Justice, 47,* 251–270.

Linenthal, E. (2001). *The unfinished bombing: Oklahoma City in American memory.* New York: Oxford University Press.

Lo, C., & Stephens, R. (2002). The role of drugs in crime: Insights from a group of incoming prisoners. *Substance Use and Misuse, 37,* 121–131.

Loeber, R., Kalb, L., & Huizinga, D. (2001). Juvenile delinquency and serious injury victimization. *Juvenile Justice Bulletin.* Washington, DC: U.S. Department of Justice.

Lombroso, C. (1876). *Criminal man*. Milan: Hoepli.

Lombroso, C. (1968). *Crime: Its causes and remedies* (H. Horton, Trans.). Montclaire, NJ: Patterson Smith. (Originally published 1911)

Lombroso-Ferrero, G. (1972). *Criminal man according to the classification of Cesare Lombroso*. Montclaire, NJ: Patterson Smith. (Originally published 1911)

Lott, J. (2010). *More guns, less crime: Understanding crime and gun control laws*. Chicago: University of Chicago Press.

Lowell, A., & Arnold, K. (2003). Corporate crime after 2000: A new law enforcement challenge or déjà vu? *American Criminal Law Review, 40,* 219–240.

Lubinskas, J. (2001). *Remembering the zebra killings*. www.gnosticliberationfront.com/remembering_the_zebra_killings.htm.

Lupsha, P. (1987). La Cosa Nostra in drug trafficking. In T. Bynum (Ed.), *Organized crime in America: Concepts and controversies* (pp.31–41). Monsey, NY: Willow Tree Press.

Lykken, D. (1995). *The antisocial personalities*. Hillsdale, NJ: Lawrence Erlbaum.

Lyman, M., & Potter, G. (2004). *Organized crime* (3rd ed.). Upper Saddle River, NJ: Prentice Hall.

Lynam, D. (1996). Early identification of chronic offenders: Who is the fledgling psychopath? *Psychological Bulletin, 120,* 209–234.

Lynam, D., Moffitt, T., & Stouthamer-Loeber, M. (1993). Explaining the relation between IQ and delinquency: Class, race, test motivation, school failure, or self control? *Journal of Abnormal Psychology, 102,* 187–196.

Lynn, R. (2009). What has caused the Flynn effect? Secular increases in the development quotients of infants. *Intelligence, 37,* 16–24.

Lytton, H., & Romney, D. (1991). Parents' differential socialization of boys and girls: A meta-analysis. *Psychological Bulletin, 109,* 267–296.

MacDonald, K., & MacDonald, T. (2010). The peptide that binds: A systematic review of oxytocin and its prosocial effects in humans. *Harvard Review of Psychiatry, 18,* 1–21.

Machetta, J. (2011). *Washington bomb suspect linked to Kirksville white supremacist*. www.missourinet.com/.../washington-bomb-suspect-linked-to-kirksville-white-*supremacist-website*.

Macmillan, R. (2001). Violence and the life course: The consequences of victimization for personal and social development. *Annual Review of Sociology, 27,* 1–22.

Mallon, R. (2007). A field guide to social construction. *Philosophy Compass, 2,* 93–108.

Mann, C. (1990). Black female homicides in the United States. *Journal of Interpersonal Violence, 5,* 176–201.

Martin, S. (2001). The links between alcohol, crime and the criminal justice system: Explanations, evidence and interventions. *American Journal on Addictions, 10,* 136–158.

Martínez, R. Jr., Rosenfeld, R., & Mares, D. (2008). Social disorganization, drug market activity, and neighborhood violent crime. *Urban Affairs Review, 43,* 846–874.

Maruschak, L. (1999). *DWI offenders under correctional supervision*. Washington, DC: Bureau of Justice Statistics.

Marx, K., & Engels, F. (1948). *The communist manifesto*. New York: International.

Marx, K., & Engels, F. (1965). *The German ideology*. London: Lawrence and Wishart.

Massey, D. (2002). A brief history of human society: The origin and role of emotion in social life. *American Sociological Review, 67,* 1–29.

Matarazzo, J. (1976). *Weschler's measurement and appraisal of adult intelligence*. Baltimore: Williams & Wilkins.

Mauer, M. (2005). *Comparative international rates of incarceration: An examination of causes and trends*. Washington, DC: The Sentencing Project.

Maughan, B. (2005). Developmental trajectory modeling: A view from developmental psychopathology. *Annals of the American Academy of Political and Social Science, 602,* 118–130.

Mawby, R. (2001). *Burglary*. Cullompton, Devon, England: Willan.

May, P., & Gossage, P. (2008). *Estimating the prevalence of fetal alcohol syndrome: A summary*. Washington, DC: National Institute of Alcohol Abuse and Alcoholism. National Institute of Health. http://pubs.niaaa.nih.gov/publications/arh25–3/159–167.hm.

Maynard, R., & Garry, E. (1997). *Adolescent motherhood: Implications for the juvenile justice system*. OJJDP Fact Sheet #50. Washington, DC: U.S. Department of Justice.

Mazur, A., & Booth, A. (1998). Testosterone and dominance in men. *Behavioral and Brain Sciences, 21,* 353–397.

McCollister, K., French, M., & Fang, H. (2010). The cost of crime to society: New crime-specific estimates for policy and program evaluation. *Drug and Alcohol Dependence, 108,* 98–109.

McCrae, R., Costa, P., Ostendorf, F., Angleitner, A., Hrebickova, M., Avia, M., et al. (2000). Nature over nurture: Temperament, personality, and life span development. *Journal of Personality and Social Psychology, 78,* 173–186.

McDermott, P., Alterman, A., Cacciola, J., Rutherford,M., Newman, P., & Mulholland, E. (2000). Generality of Psychopathy Checklist—Revised factors over prisoners and substance-dependent patients. *Journal of Consulting and Clinical Psychology, 68* 181–186.

McDonald, O. (2012). *Fannie Mae and Freddie Mac: Turning the American dream into a nightmare*. New York: Bloomsbury Academic.

McGinnis, K. (2009). The Buller-McGinnis model of serial homicidal behavior: An integrated approach. *Journal of Criminology and Criminal Justice Research*. www.scientificjournals.org/journals2009/articles/1441.pdf?pagewanted=all.

McGoey, C. (2005). *Carjacking facts: Robbery prevention advice*. www.crimedoctor.com.carjacking.htm.

McGregor, I., Callaghan, P., & Hunt, G. (2008). From ultrasocial to antisocial: A role for oxytocin in the acute reinforcing effects and long-term adverse consequences of drug use? *British Journal of Pharmacology, 154,* 358–368.

McGue, M. (1999). The behavioral genetics of alcoholism. *Current Directions in Psychological Science, 8,* 109–115.

McGue, M., Bacon, S., & Lykken, D. T. (1993). Personality stability and change in early adulthood: A behavioral genetic analysis. *Developmental Psychology, 29,* 96–109.

McLean, B., & Elkind, P. (2003). *The smartest guys in the room: The amazing rise and scandalous fall of Enron*. New York: Portfolio.

McMurren, M. (2003). Alcohol and crime. *Criminal Behaviour and Mental Health, 13,* 1–4.

McShane, L. (2004, October 24). Mob midlife crisis: "Junior" Gotti turns 40. *Idaho Statesman*, p. 8.

Meadows, R., & Kuehnel, J. (2005). *Evil minds: Understanding and responding to violent predators*. Upper Saddle River, NJ: Prentice Hall.

Mealey, L. (1995). The sociobiology of sociopathy: An integrated evolutionary model. *Behavioral and Brain Sciences, 18,* 523–541.

Mealey, L. (2003). Combating rape: Views of an evolutionary psychologist. In R. Bloom & N. Dess (Eds.), *Evolutionary psychology and violence* (pp. 83–113). Westport, CT: Praeger.

Mears, D., Ploeger, M., & Warr, M. (1998). Explaining the gender gap in delinquency: Peer influence and moral evaluations of behavior. *Journal of Research in Crime and Delinquency, 35,* 251–266.

Menard, S, (2002, February). Short- and long-term consequences of adolescent victimization. *Youth Violence Research Bulletin.* Washington, DC: U.S. Department of Justice.

Menard, S., Mihalic, S., & Huizinga, D. (2001). Drugs and crime revisited. *Justice Quarterly, 18,* 269–299.

Merton, R. (1938). Social structure and anomie. *American Sociological Review, 3,* 672–682.

Messner, S., & Rosenfeld, R. (2001). *Crime and the American dream* (3rd ed.). Belmont, CA: Wadsworth.

Miller, J. (1998). Up it up: Gender and the accomplishment of street robbery. *Criminology, 36,* 37–65.

Miller, J., & Lynam, D. (2001). Structural models of personality and their relation to antisocial behavior: A meta-analytic review. *Criminology, 39,* 765–798.

Miller, L. (1987). Neuropsychology of the aggressive psychopath: An integrative review. *Aggressive Behavior, 13,* 119–140.

Miller, L. (2011). The terrorist mind: A psychological and political analysis. In A. Walsh & C. Hemmens (Eds.), *Introduction to criminology: A text/reader* (2nd ed., pp. 423–432). Thousand Oaks, CA: Sage.

Miller, W. (1958). Lower-class culture as a generating milieu of gang delinquency. *Journal of Social Issues, 14,* 5-19.

Mills, J., Anderson, D., & Kroner, D. (2004). The antisocial attitudes of sex offenders. *Criminal Behavior and Mental Health, 14,* 134–145.

Messerschmidt, J. (2002). On gang girls, gender and a structured action theory. *Theoretical Criminology, 6,* 461–475.

Moehringer, J. R. (2012). *Sutton.* New York: Hyperion Books.

Moffitt, T. (1993). Adolescent-limited and life-course-persistent antisocial behavior: A developmental taxonomy. *Psychological Review, 100,* 674–701.

Moffitt, T., Caspi, A., Rutter, M., & Silva, P. (2001). *Sex differences in antisocial behaviour: Conduct disorder, delinquency and violence in the Dunedin longitudinal study.* Cambridge, England: Cambridge University Press.

Moffit, T., & the E-Risk Study Team. (2002). Teen-aged mothers in contemporary Britain. *Journal of Child Psychology and Psychiatry, 43,* 1–16.

Moffitt, T., & Walsh, A. (2003). The adolescence-limited/Life course–persistent theory and antisocial behavior: What have we learned? In A. Walsh & L. Ellis (Eds.), *Biosocial criminology: Challenging environmentalism's supremacy* (pp. 125–144). Hauppauge, NY: Nova Science.

Monkey Gumbo. (n.d.). *What's up with Henry Earl?* www.monkeygumbo.com/wee/news/henryearl.

Moore, J., & Hagedorn, J. (2001). Female gangs: Focus on research. *OJJDP Juvenile Justice Bulletin.* Washington, DC: U.S. Department of Justice.

Moore, K., & Miller, S. (2008). Living the high life: The role of drug taking in young people's lives. In H. Wilson (Ed.), *Drugs, society, and behavior* (pp. 5–8). Dubuque, IA: McGraw-Hill.

Moore, R. (1984). Shoplifting in middle-America: Patterns and motivational correlates. *International Journal of Offender Therapy and Comparative Criminology, 23,* 29–40.

Morley, K., & Hall, W. (2003). Is there a genetic susceptibility to engage in criminal acts? *Trends and Issues in Crime and Criminal Justice, 263,* 1–10. Canberra: Australian Institute of Criminology.

Mowbray, J. (2002). *Justice interrupted.* www.nationalreview.com.

Mullins, C., & Wright, R. (2003). Gender, social networks, and residential burglary. *Criminology, 41,* 813–839.

Muñoz, L., & Anastassiou-Hadjicharalambous, X. (2011). Disinhibited behaviors in young children: Relations with impulsivity and autonomic psychophysiology. *Biological Psychology, 86,* 349–359.

Mustaine, E., & Tewksbury, R. (2004). Alcohol and violence. In S. Holmes & R. Holmes (Eds.), *Violence: A contemporary reader* (pp. 9–25). Upper Saddle River, NJ: Prentice Hall.

Nagin, D., & Land, K. (1993). Age, criminal careers, and population heterogeneity: Specification and estimation of a nonparametric, mixed poisson model. *Criminology, 31,* 327–362.

Nagin, D., & Pepper, J. (Eds.). (2012). *Deterrence and the death penalty.* Washington, DC: Committee on Law and Justice: National Academies Press.

National Association of Crime Victim Compensation Board. (2005). *FY 2004 compensation to victims continues to increase.* www.nacvcb.org.

National Association of Shoplifting Prevention. (2013). *The shoplifting problem in the nation.* www.shopliftingprevention.org/TheIssue.htm.

National Center for Policy Analysis. (1998). *Falsified crime data.* www.ncpa.org/pi/crime/aug98a.html.

National Center for Victims of Crime. (2010). *Child sexual abuse statistics.* www.victimsofcrime.org/media/reporting-on-child-sexual-abuse/child-sexual-abuse-statistics.

National Center for Victims of Violence. (2012). *Workplace violence.* www.victimsofcrime.org/library/crime-information-and-statistics/workplace-violence.

National Center on Addiction and Substance Abuse. (2010). *Behind bars II: Substance abuse and America's prison population.* www.casacolumbia.org/articlefiles/575-report2010behindbars2.pdf.

National Coalition Against Domestic Violence. (2009). *Domestic violence facts.* www.ncadv.org/files/DomesticViolenceFactSheet%28National%29.pdf.

National Drug Control Strategy. (2001). *2000 annual report.* Washington, DC: U.S. Government Printing Office.

National Highway Traffic Safety Commission. (2009). *Traffic safety facts.* Washington, DC: U.S. Department of Transportation.

National Institute on Drug Abuse. (1996). *The brain's drug reward system (NIDA Notes 11).* Washington, DC: Department of Health and Human Services.

National Institute on Drug Abuse. (2004). *Resource guide.* www.aamc.org/research/adhocgp/pdfs/nida.pdf.

National Insurance Crime Bureau. (2013). *2012 hot wheels.* www.nicb.org/newsroom/ news-releases/hot-wheels-2012.

National Youth Gang Center. (2012). *National Youth Gang Survey Analysis.* www.nationalgangcenter.gov/Survey-Analysis/Demographics#anchorregm.

Nedelec, J., & Beaver, K. (2012). The association between sexual behavior and antisocial behavior: Insights from an evolutionary informed analysis. *Journal of Contemporary Criminal Justice, 28,* 329–345.

Neisser, U., Boodoo, G., Bouchard, T., Boykin, A., Brody, N., Ceci, S., et al. (1995). *Intelligence: Knowns and unknowns: Report of a task force established by the Board of Scientific Affairs of the American Psychological Association.* Washington, DC: American Psychological Association.

Nettler, G. (1978). *Explaining crime.* New York: McGraw-Hill.

Nettler, G. (1984). *Explaining crime* (3rd ed.). New York: McGraw-Hill.

Neumeister, L. (2004). Gotti brother convicted in plot to kill Mafia turncoat. *San Diego Union-Tribune.* www.signonsandiego.com/news/nation/20041222-1310.petergotti.html.

Newman, O. (1972). *Defensible space.* New York: Macmillan.

Newton, M. (2000). *The encyclopedia of serial killers.* New York: Checkmark.

Niehoff, D. (2003). A vicious circle: The neurobiological foundations of violent behavior. *Modern Psychoanalysis, 28,* 235–245.

Nisbett, R., Aronson, J., Blair, C., Dickens, W., Flynn, J., Halpern, D, et al. (2012). Intelligence: New findings and theoretical developments. *American Psychologist, 67,* 130–159.

O'Brien, R. (2001). Crime facts: Victim and offender data. In J. Sheley (Ed.), *Criminology: A contemporary handbook* (pp. 59–83). Belmont, CA: Wadsworth.

Office of Drug Control Policy. (2013). *ADAM II 2012 annual report.* Washington, DC: U.S. Government printing Office.

Office of Federal Housing Enterprise Oversight. (2006). *Report of the special examination of Fannie Mae.* www.fhfa.gov/webfiles/747/fnmspecialexam.pdf.

Office of the Surgeon General. (2001). *Youth violence: A report of the surgeon general.* Washington, DC: U.S. Department of Health and Human Services.

Olds, D., Hill, P., Mihalic, S., & O'Brien, R. (1998). *Blueprints for violence prevention, book seven: Prenatal and infancy home visitation by nurses.* Boulder, CO: Center for the Study and Prevention of Violence.

Olson, S., & Dzur, A. 2004. Revisiting informal justice: Restorative justice and democratic professionalism. *Law and Society Review, 38,* 139–176.

O'Manique, J. (2003). *The origins of justice: The evolution of morality, human rights, and law.* Philadelphia: University of Philadelphia Press.

Oppenheimer, J. (2009). *Madoff with the money.* Hoboken, NJ: John Wiley.

Oscar-Berman, M., Valmas, M., Sawyer, K., Kirkley, S., Gansler, D., Merritt, D., et al. (2009). Frontal brain dysfunction in alcoholism with and without antisocial personality disorder. *Neuropsychiatric Disease and Treatment, 5,* 309–326.

Osgood, D., & Chambers, J. (2003, May). Community correlates of rural youth violence. *Juvenile Justice Bulletin.* Washington, DC: U.S. Department of Justice.

Osofsky, J. (1995). The effects of exposure to violence on young children. *American Psychologist, 50,* 782–788.

Palermo, G. (1997). The berserk syndrome: A review of mass murder. *Aggression and Violent Behavior, 2,* 1–8.

Pally, T. (2010). America's exhausted paradigm: Macroeconomic causes of the financial crisis and great recession. *New School Economic Review, 4,* 15–43.

Parekh, R. (2004). Fraud by employees on the rise, survey finds. *Business Insurance, 38,* 4–6.

Parker, N., & Auerhahn, K. (1998). Alcohol, drugs, and violence. *Annual Review of Sociology, 24,* 291–311.

Passas, N. (1995). Continuities in the anomie tradition. In F. Adler & W. Laufer (Eds.), *The legacy of anomie theory* (pp. 91–112). New Brunswick, NJ: Transaction.

Paternoster, R. (2010). How much do we really know about criminal deterrence? *Journal of Criminal Law and Criminology, 100,* 765–823.

Paternoster, R., & Iovanni, L. (1989). The labeling perspective and delinquency: An elaboration of the theory and an assessment of the evidence. *Justice Quarterly, 6,* 359–394.

Patrick, C. (2006). Back to the future: Cleckley as a guide to the next generation of psychopathy research. In C. Patrick (Ed.), *Handbook of psychopathy* (pp. 605–617). New York: Guilford Press.

Paus, T. (2010). Population neuroscience: Why and how. *Human Brain Mapping, 31,* 891–903.

Payne, J., & Gaffney, A. (2012). *How much crime is drug or alcohol related?* www.aic.gov.au/publications/current%20series/tandi/421–440/tandi439.html.

Perlman, D. (2002). Intersubjective dimensions of terrorism and its transcendence. In C. Stout (Ed.), *The psychology of terrorism* (Vol. III, pp. 57–81). Westport, CT: Praeger.

Perri, F. (2011). White collar criminals: The "kinder, gentler" offender? *Journal of Investigative Psychology and Offender Profiling, 8,* 217–241.

Perry, B., & Pollard, R. (1998). Homeostasis, stress, trauma, and adaptation: A neurodevelopmental view of childhood trauma. *Child and Adolescent Psychiatric Clinics of America, 7,* 33–51.

Pessoa, L. (2008). On the relationship between emotion and cognition. *Nature/Neuroscience, 9,* 148–158.

Petrosino, A., Turpin-Petrosino, C., & Guckenburg, S. (2010). Formal system processing of juveniles: Effects on delinquency. *Campbell Systematic Reviews, 1,* 1–88.

Pileggi, N. (1985). *Wiseguy: Life in a mafia family.* New York: Simon & Schuster.

Pinel, J. (2000). *Biopsychology* (4th ed.). Boston: Allyn & Bacon.

Pitchford, I. (2001). The origins of violence: Is psychopathy an adaptation? *Human Nature Review, 1,* 28–38.

Plato. (1960). *The republic and other works.* Garden City, NY: Doubleday.

Pollock, J. (1999). *Criminal women.* Cincinnati, OH: Anderson.

Pope, C., & Snyder, H. (2003). Race as a factor in juvenile arrests. *Juvenile Justice Bulletin.* Washington, DC: Office of Juvenile Justice and Delinquency Prevention.

Posthumus, J., Böcker, K., Raaijmakers, M., Van Engeland, H., & Matthys, W. (2009). Heart rate and skin conductance in four-year-old children with aggressive behavior. *Biological Psychology, 82,* 164–168.

President's Commission on Organized Crime. (1986). *The impact: Organized crime today.* Washington, DC: U.S. Government Printing Office.

Pridemore, W. (2004). Weekend effects on binge drinking and homicide: The social connection between alcohol and violence in Russia. *Addiction, 99,* 1034–1041.

Quartz, S., & Sejnowski, T. (1997). The neural basis of cognitive development: A constructivist manifesto. *Behavioral and Brain Sciences, 20,* 537–596.

Quinn, J. (2001). Angels, bandidos, outlaws, and pagans: The evolution of organized crime among the big four 1% motorcycle clubs. *Deviant Behavior, 22,* 379–399.

Quinn, J., & Sneed, Z. (2008). Drugs and crime: An empirically based interdisciplinary model. *Journal of Teaching in the Addictions, 70,* 16–28.

Quinney, R. (1974). *Critique of the legal order: Crime control in capitalist society.* Boston: Little, Brown.

Quinsey, V. (2002). Evolutionary theory and criminal behavior. *Legal and Criminological Psychology, 7,* 1–14.

Raab, S. (2011, January 22). Omerta may be dead; the Mafia isn't. *New York Times.*

Radelet, M., & Lacock, T. (2009). Do executions lower homicide rates? The views of leading criminologists. *Journal of Criminal Law and Criminology, 99,* 489–508.

Radzinowicz, L., & King, J. (1979). *The growth of crime: The international experience.* Middlesex, England: Penguin Books.

Raftery, I. (2011). "Barefoot Bandit" gets prison for stealing from neighbors. *New York Times.* www.nytimes.com/2011/12/17/us/colton-harris-moore-the-barefoot-bandit-is-sentenced-for-stealing-from-neighbors.html.

Raine, A. (1997). Antisocial behavior and psychophysiology: A biosocial perspective and a prefrontal dysfunction hypothesis. In D. Stoff, J. Breiling, & J. Maser (Eds.), *Handbook of antisocial behavior* (pp. 289–304). New York: John Wiley.

Raine, A., Meloy, J., Bihrle, S., Stoddard, J., LaCasse, L., & Buchsbaum, M. (1998). Reduced prefrontal and increased subcortical brain functioning assessed using positron emission tomography in predatory and affective murderers. *Behavioral Sciences and the Law, 16,* 319–332.

Rand, M. (2009). *Criminal victimization, 2008.* Washington, DC: Bureau of Justice Statistics.

Raymond, J. (2003). Ten reasons for not legalizing prostitution and a legal response to the demand for prostitution. *Journal of Trauma Practice, 2,* 315–332. http://www.prostitutionresearch.com/laws/000022.html.

Raz, A. (2004, August). Brain imaging data of ADHD. *Neuropsychiatry,* 46–50.

Reckdenwald, A., & Parker, K. (2008). The influence of gender inequality and marginalization on types of female offending. *Homicide Studies, 12,* 208–226.

Reich, W. (1990). Understanding terrorist behavior: The limits and opportunities of psychological inquiry. In W. Reich (Ed.), *Origins of terrorism: Psychologies, ideologies, theologies, states of mind* (pp. 261–279). New York: Cambridge University Press.

Reid, J., & Sullivan, C. (2009). A model of vulnerability for adult sexual victimization: The impact of attachment, child maltreatment, and scarred sexuality. *Violence and Victims, 24,* 485–501.

Reid, W. (2002). Controlling political terrorism: Practicality, not psychology. In C. Stout (Ed.), *The psychology of terrorism: Public understanding* (pp. 1–8). Westport, CT: Praeger.

Rengert, G., & Wasilchick, J. (2001). *Suburban burglary: A tale of two suburbs.* Springfield, IL: Charles C Thomas.

Rennie, Y. (1978). *The search for criminal man.* Lexington, MA: Lexington Books.

Rennison, C. (2003). *Intimate partner violence, 1993–2003.* Washington, DC: Bureau of Justice Statistics Report. U.S. Department of Justice.

Restak, R. (2001). *The secret life of the brain.* New York: Dana Press and Joseph Henry Press.

Restivo, E., & Lanier, M. (2013). Measuring the contextual effects of mitigating factors of labeling theory. *Justice Quarterly.* doi:10.1080/07418825.2012.756115

Rhee, S., & Waldman, I. (2002). Genetic and environmental influences on antisocial behavior: A meta-analysis of twin and adoption studies. *Psychological Bulletin, 128,* 490–529.

Rice, K., & Smith, W. (2002). Socioecological models of automotive theft: Integrating routine activities and social disorganization approaches. *Journal of Research in Crime and Delinquency, 39,* 304–336.

Richardson, A., & Budd, T. (2003). Young adults, crime and disorder. *Criminal Behaviour and Mental Health, 13,* 5–17.

Roach, J., & Pease, K. (2013). *Evolution and crime.* New York: Routledge.

Robertiello, G., & Terry, K. (2007). Can we profile sex offenders? A review of sex offender typologies. *Aggression and Violent Behavior, 12,* 508–518.

Robinson, M. (2004). *Why crime? An integrated systems theory of antisocial behavior.* Upper Saddle River, NJ: Prentice Hall.

Robinson, M. (2009). No longer taboo: Crime prevention implications of biosocial criminology. In A. Walsh & K. Beaver (Eds.), *Biosocial criminology: New directions in theory and research* (pp. 243–263). New York: Routledge.

Robinson, T., & Berridge, K. (2003). Addiction. *Annual Review of Psychology, 54,* 25–53.

Rodkin, P., Farmer, T., Pearl, R., & Van Acker, R. (2000). Heterogeneity of popular boys: Antisocial and prosocial configurations. *Developmental Psychology, 36,* 14–24.

Romano, S., Levi-Minzi, M., Rugala, E., & Van Hasselt, V. (2011). Workplace violence and prevention: Readiness and response. *FBI Law Enforcement Bulletin.* www.fbi.gov/stats-services/publications/law-enforcement-bulletin/january2011/workplace_violence_prevention.

Rosenbaum, D., Lurigio, A., & Davis, R. (1998). *The prevention of crime: Social and situational strategies.* Belmont, CA: West/Wadsworth.

Rösler, M., Retz, W., Retz, P., Hengesch, G., Scneider, M., & Supprian, T. (2004). Prevalence of attention deficit-hyperactivity disorder and comorbid disorders in young male prison inmates. *European Archives of Psychiatry Clinical Neuroscience, 254,* 365–371.

Rosner, L. (1995). Organized crime IV: The Russian connection. *Contemporary Criminal Justice, 11,* vi–viii.

Rosoff, S., Pontell, H., & Tillman, R. (1998). *Profit without honor: White-collar crime and the looting of America.* Upper Saddle River, NJ: Prentice Hall.

Ross, E. (1907). *Sin and society: An analysis of latter-day iniquity.* New York: Houghton, Mifflin.

Rothbart, M. (2012). Advances in temperament: History, concepts and measures. In M. Zentner & L. Shiner (Eds.), *Handbook of temperament* (pp. 3–20). New York: Guilford.

Rowe, D. (1996). An adaptive strategy theory of crime and delinquency. In J. Hawkins (Ed.), *Delinquency and crime: Current theories* (pp. 268–314). Cambridge, England: Cambridge University Press.

Rowe, D. (2002). *Biology and crime.* Los Angeles: Roxbury.

Ruden, R. (1997). *The craving brain: The biobalance approach to controlling addictions.* New York: HarperCollins.

Rush, R., & Scarpitti, F. (2001). Russian organized crime: The continuation of an American tradition. *Deviant Behavior, 22,* 517–540.

Saffron, I. (1997, February 2). Chance leads to capture in serial killer-cannibal case. *Idaho Statesman,* p. 19a.

Samaha, J. (1993). *Criminal law* (5th ed.). Minneapolis/St. Paul: West.

Sampson, R. (2000). Whither the sociological study of crime. *Annual Review of Sociology, 26,* 711–714.

Sampson, R. (2004). Neighborhood and community: Collective efficacy and community safety. *New Economy, 11,* 106–113.

Sampson, R., & Laub, J. (1999). Crime and deviance over the life-course: The salience of adult social bonds. In F. Scarpitti & A. Nielsen (Eds.), *Crime and criminals: Contemporary and classical readings in criminology* (pp. 238–246). Los Angeles: Roxbury.

Sampson, R., & Laub, J. (2005). A life-course view of the development of crime. *Annals of the American Academy of Political and Social Sciences, 602,* 12–45.

Sampson, R., Raudenbush, S., & Earls, F. (1997). Neighborhoods and crime: A multilevel study of collective efficacy. *Science, 277,* 918–924.

Sanders, W. (1994). *Gangbangs and drivebys: Grounded culture and juvenile gang violence.* New York: Aldine De Gruyter.

Sanchez-Jankowski, M. (2003). Gangs and social change. *Theoretical Criminology, 7,* 191–216.

Sanjiv, K., & Thaden, E. (2004, January). Examining brain connectivity in ADHD. *Psychiatric Times,* 40–41.

Santtila, P., Hakkanen, H., Alison, L., & Whyte, C. (2003). Juvenile firesetters: Crime scene actions and offender characteristics. *Legal and Criminological Psychology, 8,* 1–20.

Sawhill, I., & Morton, J. (2007). *Economic mobility: Is the American dream alive and well?* Washington, DC: The Economic Mobility Project/Pew Charity Trusts.

Scarpa, A., & Raine, A. (2003). The psychophysiology of antisocial behavior: Interactions with environmental experiences. In A. Walsh & L. Ellis (Eds.), *Biosocial criminology: Challenging environmentalism's supremacy* (pp. 209–226). Hauppauge, NY: Nova Science.

Schaffer, J., & Ruback, B. (2002). *Violent victimization as a risk factor for violent offending among juveniles.* Washington, DC: Juvenile Justice Bulletin. U.S. Department of Justice.

Schatzberg, R., & Kelly, R. (1996). *African American organized crime: A social history.* New York: Garland.

Schilling, C., Walsh, A., & Yun, I. (2011). ADHD and criminality: A primer on the genetic, neurobiological, evolutionary, and treatment literature for criminologists. *Journal of Criminal Justice, 39,* 3–11.

Schmalleger, F. (2004). *Criminology today* (3rd ed.). Upper Saddle River, NJ: Prentice Hall.

Schwartz, B. (1995). Characteristics and typologies of sex offenders. In B. Schwartz & H. Cellini (Eds.), *The sex offender: Corrections, treatment, and legal practice* . Kingston, NJ: Civic Research Institute.

Scott, A. (2012). Holding out for a hero: Patty Hearst and American culture in the seventies. *Reviews in American History, 40,* 139–144.

Seale, D., Polakowski, M., & Schneider S. (1998). It's not really theft! Personal and workplace ethics that enable software piracy. *Behavior and Information Technology, 17,* 27–40.

Sears, D. (1991). *To kill again: The motivation and development of serial murder.* Wilmington, DE: Scholarly Resources.

Sederberg, P. (1989). *Terrorist myths: Illusions, rhetoric, and reality.* Englewood Cliffs, NJ: Prentice Hall.

Segrave, K. (1992). *Women serial and mass murderer: A worldwide reference, 1580 through 1990.* Jefferson, NC: McFarland.

Seligman, D. (1992). *A question of intelligence: The IQ debate in America.* New York: BirchLane.

Shahid, A. (2010). Steven Hayes sentenced to death in Connecticut home invasion of mom, daughters, of Dr. Petit. *NYDailyNews.com.* www.nydailynews.com/news/national/steven-hayes-sentenced-death-connecticut-home-invasion-murders-mom-daughters-dr-petit-article-1.470958.

Sharp, B. (2006). *Changing criminal thinking: A treatment program.* Alexandria, VA: American Correctional Association.

Shaw, C., & McKay, H. (1972). *Juvenile delinquency and urban areas* (rev. ed.). Chicago: University of Chicago Press.

Shea, C. (2009, January 9). The nature-nurture debate, redux: Genetic research finally makes its way into the thinking of sociologists. *Chronicle of Higher Education: Chronicle Review,* p. B6. http://chronicle.com/free/v55/i18/18b00601.htm.

Shelden, R., Tracy, S., & Brown, W. (2001). *Youth gangs in American society* (2nd ed.). Belmont, CA: Wadsworth.

Shepherd, J. (2005). Deterrence versus brutalization: Capital punishment's differing impacts among states. *Michigan Law Review, 104,* 203–256.

Sherman, L., Gottfredson, D., McKenzie, D., Eck, J., Reuter, P., & Bushway, S. (1997). *Preventing crime: What works, what doesn't, what's promising.* Washington, DC: U.S. Department of Justice.

Shields, P. (2012). *Repeat, low-level offenders costly for Boulder County Jail.* www.timescall.com/ci_20399008.

Shore, R. (1997). *Rethinking the brain: New insights into early development.* New York: Families and Work Institute.

Shover, N., & Cullen, F. (2008). Studying and teaching white-collar crime: Populist and patrician perspectives. *Journal of Criminal Justice Education, 19,* 155–174.

Shover, N., & Hochstetler, A. (2000). Crimes of privilege. In J. Shelly (Ed.), *Criminology: A contemporary handbook* (pp. 287–319). Belmont, CA: Wadsworth.

Shover, N., Hochstetler, A., & Alalehto, T. (2013). Choosing white-collar crime. In F. Cullen & P. Wilcox (Eds.) *The Oxford handbook of criminological theory* (pp. 475–493). Oxford, England: Oxford University Press.

Shulman, T. (2003). *Some facts about shoplifters.* http://shopliftersanonymous.com.

Siegel, L. (1986). *Criminology.* Belmont, CA: Wadsworth.

Siegel, L. (1992). *Criminology* (4th ed.). St. Paul, MN: West.

Silfver, M., & Klaus, H. (2007). Empathy, guilt, and gender: A comparison of two measures of guilt. *Scandinavian Journal of Psychology, 48,* 239–246.

Simon, D. (2002). *Elite deviance* (7th ed.). Boston: Allyn & Bacon.

Simon, R. (1975). *Women and crime.* Lexington, MA: Lexington Books.

Simonsen, C., & Spindlove, J. (2004). *Terrorism today: The past, the players, the future.* Upper Saddle River, NJ: Prentice Hall.

Smith, A. (1953). *The wealth of nations.* Cambridge, MA: Harvard University Press. (Originally published 1776)

Smith, B. (1994). *Terrorism in America: Pipe bombs and pipe dreams.* Albany: State University of New York Press.

Smith, E., & Farole, D. (2009). *Profile of intimate partner violence cases in large urban counties.* Washington, DC: Bureau of Justice Statistics, Report # NCJ 228193.

Smith, H. (2011). Sex trafficking: Trends, challenges, and the limitations of international law. *Human Rights Review, 12,* 271–286.

Smith, H., & Bohm, R. (2008). Beyond anomie: Alienation and crime. *Critical Criminology: An International Journal, 16,* 1–15.

Smith, H., Pettigrew, T., Pippin, G., & Bialosiewitz, S. (2012). Relative deprivation: A theoretical and meta-analytical review. *Personality and Social Psychology Review, 16,* 203–232.

Smith, R. (1984). Grendon, the Barlinnie Special Unit, and the Wormwood Scrubs Annexe: Experiments in penology. *British Medical Journal, 288,* 472–476.

Smoking Gun. (2008). *Henry Earl: Setting the record straight.* www.thesmokinggun.com/documents/crime/henry-earl-setting-record-straight.

Snell, T. (2011). *Capital punishment, 2010: Statistical tables.* Washington, DC: Bureau of Justice Statistics.

Sowell, T. (1987). *A conflict of visions: Ideological origins of political struggles.* New York: William Morrow.

Spear, L. (2000). Neurobehavioral changes in adolescence. *Current Directions in Psychological Science, 9,* 111–114.

Spergel, I. (1995). *The youth gang problem: A community approach.* New York: Oxford University Press.

Sprinzak, E. (1991). The process of delegitimization: Towards a linkage theory of political terrorism. In C. McCauley (Ed.), *Terrorism research and public policy* (pp. 50–68). London: Frank Cass.

Steffensmeier, D., & Haynie, D. (2000). Gender, structural disadvantage, and urban crime: Do macrosocial variables also explain female offending rates? *Criminology, 38,* 403–438.

Steffensmeier, D., Zhong, H., Ackerman, J., Schwartz, J., & Agha, S. (2006). Gender gap trends for violent crimes, 1980 to 2003: A UCR-NCVS comparison. *Feminist Criminology, 1,* 72–98.

Stiles, B., Liu, X., & Kaplan, H. (2000). Relative deprivation and deviant adaptations: The mediating effects of negative self-feelings. *Journal of Research in Crime and Delinquency, 37,* 64–90.

Stiles, F. (2007). *Evil brothers: A true crime story.* Parker, CO: Outskirts Press.

Stohr, M., & Walsh, A. (2012). *Corrections: The essentials.* Thousand Oaks, CA: Sage.

Substance Abuse and Mental Health Services Administration. (2013). *Results from the 2012 National Survey on Drug Use and Health.* http://www.samhsa.gov/data/NSDUH/2012SummNatFindDetTables/NationalFindings/NSDUHresults2012.pdf.

Sutherland, E. (1939). *Principles of criminology.* Philadelphia: J. B. Lippincott.

Sutherland, E. (1940). White collar criminality. *American Sociological Review, 5,* 1–20.

Sutherland, E. (1956). *The Sutherland papers* (A. Cohen, A. Lindesmith, & K. Schuessler, Eds.). Bloomington: Indiana University Press.

Sutherland, E., & Cressey, D. (1974). *Criminology* (9th ed.). Philadelphia: J. B. Lippincott.

Sutton, W., & Linn, E. (1976). *Where the money was: Memoirs of a bank robber.* New York: Viking.

Suwa, G., Asfaw, B., Kono, R., Kubo, D., Lovejoy, C., & White, T. (2009). The Ardipithecus ramidus skull and its implications for hominid origins. *Science, 326,* 68e1–68e8.

Sykes, G., & Matza, D. (2002). Techniques of neutralization: A theory of delinquency. In S. Cote (Ed.), *Criminological theories: Bridging the past to the future* (pp. 144–150). Thousand Oaks, CA: Sage.

Syngelaki, E., Fairchild, G., Moore, S., Savage, J., & van Goozen, S. (2012). Fearlessness in juvenile offenders is associated with offending rate. *Developmental Science.* doi:10.1111/j.1467-7687.2012.01191.x

Talbot, T., Gilligan, L., Carter, M., & Matson, S. (2002). *An overview of sex offender management.* Washington, DC: Center for Sex Offender Management.

Tang, T., Chen, Y., & Sutarso, T. (2008). Bad apples in bad (business) barrels: The love of money, Machiavellianism, risk tolerance, and unethical behavior. *Management Decision, 46,* 243–263.

Tannenbaum, F. (1938). *Crime and community.* New York: Columbia University Press.

Tanner, M. (2012). *The American welfare state. How we spend nearly $1 trillion a year fighting poverty—and fail.* Policy Analysis No. 694. Washington, DC: Cato Institute.

Tappan, P. (1947). Who is the criminal? *American Sociological Review, 12,* 96–112.

Taylor, I. (1999). Crime and social criticism. *Social Justice, 26,* 150–168.

Taylor, S. (2006). Tend and befriend: Biobehavioral bases of affiliation under stress. *Current Directions in Psychological Science, 15,* 273–277.

Thompson, C., & Wynters, J. (2013). Clearing the haze. *Medicus, 53,* 22–25.

Thornberry, T., Huizinga, D., & Loeber, R. (2004). The causes and correlates studies: Findings and policy implication. *Juvenile Justice, 9,* 3–19.

Thornburn, K. (2004). Corporate governance and financial distress. In H. Sjogren & G. Skogh (Eds.), *New perspectives on economic crime* (pp. 76–94). Cheltenham, England: Edward Elgar.

Thornhill, R., & Palmer, C. (2000). *A natural history of rape: Biological bases of sexual coercion.* Cambridge, MA: MIT press.

Tibbetts, S. (2003). Selfishness, social control, and emotions: An integrated perspective on criminality. In A. Walsh & L. Ellis (Eds.), *Biosocial criminology: Challenging environmentalism's supremacy* (pp. 83–101). Hauppauge, NY: Nova Science.

Tibbetts, S., & Hemmens, C. (2010). *Theoretical criminology.* Thousand Oaks, CA: Sage.

Tittle, C. (1983). Social class and criminal behavior: A critique of the theoretical foundation. *Social Forces, 62,* 334–358.

Tittle, C. (2000). Theoretical developments in criminology. *National Institute of Justice 2000, Vol.1. The nature of crime: Continuity and change.* Washington, DC: National Institute of Justice.

Tolan, P., Gorman-Smith, D., & Henry, D. (2006). Family violence. *Annual Review of Psychology, 57,* 557–583.

Tonglet, M. (2001). Consumer misbehavior: An exploratory study of shoplifting. *Journal of Consumer Behaviour, 1,* 336–354.

Topalli, V. (2005). When being good is bad: An expansion of neutralization theory. *Criminology, 43,* 797–835.

Tosches, N. (1992). *Dino: Living high in the dirty business of dreams.* New York: Dell.

Transparency International. (2013). *Corruption perception index, 2012.* www.transparency.org.surveys.indicescpi.2013.

Tremblay, R. (2008). Understanding development and prevention of physical aggression: Towards experimental epigenetic studies. *Philosophical Transactions of the Royal Society: B Biological Sciences, 363,* 2613–2622.

Trevino, L., & Youngblood, S. (1990). Bad apples in bad barrels: A causal analysis of ethical decision-making behavior. *Journal of Applied Psychology, 78,* 378–385.

Truman, J., Langton, L., & Planty, M. (2013). *Criminal victimization, 2012*. Washington, DC: Bureau of Justice Statistics.

Tseloni, A., & Pease, K. (2003). Repeat personal victimization. *British Journal of Criminology, 43,* 196–212.

Turner, H., Finkelhor, D., & Ormrod, R. (2006). The effects of lifetime victimization on the mental health of children and adolescents. *Social Science and Medicine, 62,* 13–27.

Tutty, L., & Nixon, K. (2003). Selling sex? It's really like selling your soul: Vulnerability to and the experience of exploitation through child prostitution. In K. Gorkoff & J. Runner (Eds.), *Being heard: The experience of young women in prostitution* (pp. 29–45). Black Point, Nova Scotia: Fernwood.

Udry, J. R. (2003). *The National Longitudinal Study of Adolescent Health (Add Health)*. Chapel Hill: Carolina Population Center, University of North Carolina.

Umbreit, M. S., Coates, R. B., & Kalanj, B. (1994). *Victim meets offender: The impact of restorative justice and mediation* (pp. 53–64). Monsey, NY: Criminal Justice Press.

United Nations. (2004). *Convention against transnational organized crime and the protocols thereto*. New York: United Nations.

United Nations Office on Drugs and Crime. (2012). *UNODC homicide statistics*. www.unodc.org/unodc/en/data-and-analysis/homicide.html.

Unnever, J., Cullen, F., & Pratt, T. (2003). Parental management, ADHD, and delinquent involvement: Reassessing Gottfredson and Hirschi's general theory. *Justice Quarterly, 20,* 471–500.

U.S. Bureau of Justice Statistics. (1998). *What is the sequence of events in the criminal justice system?* www.bjs.gov/content/justsys.cfm.

U.S. Bureau of Justice Statistics. (2007). *Recidivism*. www.bjs.gov/index.cfm?ty=tp&tid=17.

U.S. Bureau of Justice Statistics. (2010). *Homicide trends in the U.S.* http://dailykenn.com/522.pdf.

U.S. Bureau of Justice Statistics. (2013). *Rape statistics*. www.statisticbrain.com/rape-statistics.

U.S. Census Bureau. (2012). *Homicide victims by race and sex: 1980–2008*. www.census.gov/compendia/statab/2012/tables/12s0313.pdf.

U.S. Department of Health and Human Services. (2009). *National household survey on drug abuse*. Washington, DC: U.S. Department of Health and Human Services.

U.S. Department of Justice. (2004). *Nineteen individuals indicted in Internet "carding" conspiracy*. www.cybercrime.gov/montovaniIndict.html.

U.S. Department of State. (1995). *Patterns of global terrorism: 1994*. Washington, DC.

U.S. Department of State. (2002). *Carjacking—Don't become a victim*. www.state.gov/m/ds/rls/rpt/19782.htm.

U.S. Department of State. (2004). *Patterns of global terrorism: 2003*. Washington, DC.

U.S. Department of State. (2005). *International Narcotics Control Strategy Report*. Washington, DC: United States Department of State.

U.S. Department of State. (2012). *Trafficking in persons report*. www.state.gov/j/tip/rls/tiprpt/2012.

U.S. Department of State. (2013). *Country reports on global terrorism*. www.state.gov/j/ct/rls/crt/2012.

U.S. Immigration and Customs Enforcement. (2013). *Human trafficking*. www.ice.gov/human-trafficking.

van Berlo W., & Ensink, B. (2000). Problems with sexuality after sexual assault. *Annual Review of Sex Research, 11,* 235–257.

van den Haag, E. (2003). Justice, deterrence and the death penalty. In J. Aker, R. Bohm & C. Lanier (Eds.), *America's experiment with capital punishment* (pp. 233–249). Durham, NC: Carolina Academic Press.

Van Dijk, J. (2008). *The world of crime*. Thousand Oaks, CA: Sage.

Van Honk, J., Harmon-Jones, E., Morgan, B., & Schutter, D. (2010). Socially explosive minds: The triple imbalance hypothesis of reactive aggression. *Journal of Personality, 78,* 67–94.

Vaughn, M., Fu, Q., DeLisi, M., Wright, J., Beaver, K., Perron, B., et al. (2010). Prevalence and correlates of fire-setting in the United States: Results from the National Epidemiological Survey on Alcohol and Related Conditions. *Comprehensive Psychiatry, 51,* 217–223.

Vetter, H., & Perlstein, G. (1991). *Perspectives on terrorism*. Pacific Grove, CA: Brooks/Cole.

Victoroff, J., & Kruglanski, A. (2009). *Psychology of terrorism: Classic and contemporary insights*. New York: Psychology Press.

Vila, B. (1994). A general paradigm for understanding criminal behavior: Extending evolutionary ecological theory. *Criminology, 32,* 311–358.

Vila, B. (1997). Human nature and crime control: Improving the feasibility of nurturant strategies. *Politics and the Life Sciences, 16,* 3–21.

Voiskounsky, A., & Smyslova, O. (2003). Flow-based model of computer hackers' motivation. *CyberPsychology & Behavior, 6,* 171–180.

Vold, G., & Bernard, T. (1986). *Theoretical criminology*. New York: Oxford University Press.

Vold, G., Bernard, T., & Snipes, J. (1998). *Theoretical criminology* (4th ed.). New York: Oxford University Press.

von Hentig, H. (1941). Remarks on the interaction of perpetrator and victim. *Journal of Criminal Law, Criminology, and Police Science, 31,* 303–309.

Wakschlag, L., Pickett, K., Cook, E., Benowitz, N., & Leventhal, B. (2002). Maternal smoking during pregnancy and severe antisocial behavior in offspring: A review. *American Journal of Public Health, 92,* 966–974.

Wallace, W. (1990). Rationality, human nature, and society in Weber's theory. *Theory and Society, 19,* 199–223.

Wallison, P. (2009, February). The true origins of this financial crisis. *The American Spectator*.

Walmsley, R. (2012). *World prison population list*. www.idcr.org.uk/wp-content/uploads/2010/09/WPPL-9-22.pdf.

Walsh, A. (2000). Evolutionary psychology and the origins of justice. *Justice Quarterly, 17,* 841–864.

Walsh, A. (2002). *Biosocial criminology: Introduction and integration*. Cincinnati, OH: Anderson.

Walsh, A. (2003). Intelligence and antisocial behavior. In A. Walsh & L. Ellis (Eds.), *Biosocial criminology: Challenging environmentalism's supremacy* (pp. 105–124). Hauppauge, NY: Nova Science.

Walsh, A. (2006). Evolutionary psychology and criminal behavior. In J. Barkow (Ed.), *Missing the revolution: Darwinism for social scientists* (pp. 225–268). Oxford, England: Oxford University Press.

Walsh, A. (2009). *Biology and criminology: The biosocial synthesis*. New York: Routledge.

Walsh, A. (2011a). *Feminist criminology through a biosocial lens.* Durham, NC: Carolina Academic Press.

Walsh, A. (2011b). *Social class and crime: A biosocial approach.* New York: Routledge.

Walsh, A. (2014). *Criminological theory: Assessing philosophical assumptions.* Waltham, MA: Anderson/Elsevier.

Walsh, A., & Bolen, J. (2012). *The neurobiology of criminal behavior: Gene-brain culture co-evolution.* Farnham, England: Ashgate.

Walsh, A., & Ellis, L. (2004). Ideology: Criminology's Achilles' heel? *Quarterly Journal of Ideology, 27,* 1–25.

Walsh, A., & Ellis, L. (2007). *Criminology: An interdisciplinary approach.* Thousand Oaks, CA: Sage.

Walsh, A., & Hemmens, C. (2000). *From law to order: The theory and practice of law and justice.* Lanham, MD. American Correctional Association.

Walsh, A., & Hemmens, C. (2008). *Law, justice, and society: A socio-legal introduction.* New York: Oxford University Press.

Walsh, A., & Hemmens, C. (2011). *Law, justice, and society: A sociolegal introduction* (2nd ed.). New York: Oxford University Press.

Walsh, A., Johnson, H., & Bolen, J. (2012). Drugs, crime, and the epigenetics of hedonic allostasis. *Journal of Contemporary Criminal Justice, 28,* 314–328.

Walsh, A., & Stohr, M. (2010). *Correctional assessment, casework, and counseling* (5th ed.). Alexandria, VA: American Correctional Association.

Walsh, A., & Wu, H-H. (2008). Differentiating antisocial personality disorder, psychopathy, and sociopathy: Evolutionary, genetic, neurological, and sociological considerations. *Criminal Justice Studies, 21,* 135–152.

Walsh, A., & Yun, I. (2011). Developmental neurobiology from embryonic neuron migration to adolescent synaptic pruning: Relevance for antisocial behavior. In M. DeLisi and K. Beaver (Eds.), *Criminological theory: A life-course approach* (pp. 69–84). Boston: Jones & Bartlett.

Walters, G. (1990). *The criminal lifestyle.* Newbury Park, CA: Sage.

Walters, G., & Geyer, M. (2004). Criminal thinking and identity in male white-collar offenders. *Criminal Justice and Behavior, 31,* 263–281.

Walters, G., & White, T. (1989). The thinking criminal: A cognitive model of lifestyle criminality. *Criminal Justice Research Bulletin.* Sam Houston State University.

Ward, D., & Tittle, C. (1994). IQ and delinquency: A test of two competing explanations. *Journal of Quantitative Criminology, 10,* 189–212.

Warr, M. (2002). *Companions in crime: The social aspects of criminal conduct.* New York: Cambridge University Press.

Watson, D. (2002, February 6). *Testimony before the Senate Select Committee on Intelligence.* Washington, DC.

Weber, J. (1990). Managers' moral reasoning: Assessing their responses to three moral dilemmas. *Human Relations, 43,* 687–702.

Weber, M. (1978). *Economy and society: An outline of interpretative sociology* (Vol. 2, G. Roth & C. Wittich, Eds.). Berkeley: University of California Press.

Webster, C., MacDonald, R., & Simpson, M. (2006). Predicting criminality? Risk factors, neighborhood influence and desistance. *Youth Justice, 6,* 7–22.

Webster, D. (1990). Nobody's Patsy: Versions of Patty Hearst. *Critical Quarterly, 32,* 3–21.

Wechsler, D. (1958). *The measurement and appraisal of adult intelligence.* Baltimore: Williams and Wilkin.

Weisburd, D., Wheeler, S., Waring, E., & Bode, N. (1991). *Crimes of the middle classes: White-collar offenders in the federal courts.* New Haven, CT: Yale University Press.

Weitzer, R. (1999). Prostitution control in America. *Crime, Law, and Social Change, 32,* 83–102.

Wells, R. (1995, June 16). Study finds fines don't deter Wall St. cheating. *Idaho Statesman,* pp. 1e–2e.

Wheeler, E. (1991). Terrorism and military theory: An historical perspective. In C. McCauley (Ed.), *Terrorism research and public policy* (pp. 6–33). London: Frank Cass.

White, A. (2004). *Substance use and the adolescent brain: An overview with the focus on alcohol.* Chapel Hill, NC: Duke University Medical Center.

White, J. (1998). *Terrorism: An introduction* (2nd ed.). Belmont, CA: West/Wadsworth.

White House. (2001). *The Office of Homeland Security.* www.white house.gov/news/release/2001/10/print.

Widom, C., & Brzustowicz, L. (2006). MAOA and the "cycle of violence": Childhood abuse and neglect: MAOA genotype and the risk for violent and antisocial behavior. *Biological Psychiatry, 60,* 684–689.

Wiebe, R. (2004). Psychopathy and sexual coercion: A Darwinian analysis. *Counseling and Clinical Psychology Journal, 1,* 23–41.

Wiebe, R. (2011). The nature and utility of low self-control. In K. Beaver & A. Walsh (Eds.), *The Ashgate research companion to biosocial theories of crime* (pp. 369–395). Farnham, England: Ashgate.

Wiebe, R. (2012). Integrating criminology through adaptive strategy and life history theory. *Journal of Contemporary Criminal Justice, 28,* 346–365.

Wikstrom, P., & Loeber, R. (2000). Do disadvantaged neighborhoods cause well-adjusted children to become adolescent delinquents? A study of male juvenile serious offending, individual risk and protective factors and neighborhood context. *Criminology, 38,* 1109–1142.

Willoughby, M. (2003). Developmental course of ADHD symptomology during the transition from childhood to adolescence: A review with recommendations. *Journal of Child Psychology and Psychiatry, 43,* 609–621.

Wilson, C. (1984). *A criminal history of mankind.* London: Panther Books.

Wilson, H., & Hoge, R. (2013). The effect of youth diversion programs on recidivism: A meta-analytic review. *Criminal Justice and Behavior, 40,* 497–518.

Wilson, J. Q. (1976). *Thinking about crime.* New York: Basic Books.

Wilson, J. Q. (1987). *The truly disadvantaged.* Chicago: University of Chicago Press.

Wilson, J. Q., & Herrnstein, R. (1985). *Crime and human nature.* New York: Simon & Schuster.

Wilson, J. Q., & Kelling, G. L. (1982, March). Broken windows: The police and neighborhood safety. *The Atlantic Monthly,* pp. 29–38.

Wilson, M., & Daly, M. (1997). Life expectancy, economic inequality, homicide and reproductive timing in Chicago neighborhoods. *British Medical Journal, 314,* 1271–1274.

Witkin, G. (1998, May 25). The crime bust. *U.S. News and World Report.*

Wodak, A. (2007). Ethics and drug policy. *Psychiatry, 6,* 59–62.

Wolfgang, M., & Ferracutti, F. (1967). *The subculture of violence: Towards an integrated theory in criminology.* London: Tavistock.

Wong, J. (2012, September 6). *US health care system "wasted" $750 billion in 2009.* ABC News Medical Unit.

Wood, J. (2013). *Hezbollah rolls the dice in Syria.* http://america.aljazeera.com/articles/2013/9/10/hezbollah-rolls-thediceinsyria.html.

Wood, P., Gove, W., Wilson, J., & Cochran, J. (1997). Nonsocial reinforcement and habitual criminal conduct: An extension of learning theory. *Criminology, 35,* 335–366.

Wood, S., & Wood, E. (1997). *The world of psychology.* Boston: Allyn & Bacon.

Woodhouse, B. (2010). *Hidden in plain sight: The tragedy of children's rights from Ben Franklin to Lionel Tate.* Princeton, NJ: Princeton University Press.

World Health Organization. (2012). *Alcohol fact sheet.* www.who.int/mediacentre/factsheets/fs349.

Wright, J. (2009). Inconvenient truths: Science, race and crime. In A. Walsh & K. Beaver (Eds.), *Biosocial criminology: New directions in theory and research* (pp. 137–153). New York: Routledge.

Wright, J. (2011). Prenatal insults and the development of persistent criminal behavior. In M. DeLisi & K. Beaver (Eds.), *Criminological theory: A life-course approach* (pp. 51–67). Boston: Jones & Bartlett.

Wright, J., & Beaver, K. (2012). The behavioral genetics of predatory criminal behavior. In M. DeLisi & P. Conis (Eds.), *Violent offenders: Theory, research, policy, and practice* (pp. 109–123). Burlington, MA: Jones & Bartlett.

Wright, J., Beaver, K., Delisi, M., & Vaughn, M. (2008). Evidence of negligible parenting influence on self-control, delinquent peers, and delinquency in a sample of twins. *Justice Quarterly, 25,* 544–569.

Wright, J., & Cullen, F. (2012). The future of biosocial criminology: Beyond scholars' professional ideology. *Journal of Contemporary Criminal Justice, 28,* 237–253.

Wright, R., & Decker, S. (1994). *Burglars on the job: Streetlife and residential break-ins.* Boston: Northeastern University Press.

Wright, R., & Decker, S. (1997). *Armed robbers in action.* Boston: Northeastern University Press.

Wright, S. (2007). *Patriots, politics, and the Oklahoma City bombing.* Cambridge, England: Cambridge University Press.

Young, J. (2003). Merton with energy, Katz with structure: The sociology of vindictiveness and the criminology of transgression. *Theoretical Criminology, 7,* 389–414.

Zandi, M. (2008). *Financial shock: A 360 degree look at the subprime mortgage implosion, and how to avoid the next financial crisis.* New York: Financial Times Press.

Zechel, J., Gamboa, J., Peterson, A., Puchowicz, M., Selman, W., & Lust, D. (2005). Neuronal migration is transiently delayed by prenatal exposure to intermittent hypoxia. *Birth Defects Research, 74,* 287–299.

Zhang, Z. (2004). *Drug and alcohol use and related matters among arrestees, 2003.* Washington, DC: National Institute of Justice.

Zimring, F. (2013). What New York City teaches about police and prisons. *ACJS Today, 38,* 12–13.

Zuckerman, M. (1990). The psychophysiology of sensation-seeking. *Journal of Personality, 58,* 314–345.

Zuckoff, M. (2005). *Ponzi's scheme: The true story of a financial legend.* New York: Random House.

Photo Credits

Chapter 1 opening photo: STRDEL/Stringer/AFP/Getty Images
Photo 1.1: Doug Menuez/Photodisc/Thinkstock
Photo 1.2: Stockbyte/Thinkstock
Photo 1.3: Public domain
Photo 1.4: Ablestock.com/Thinkstock
Photo 1.5: ©Allan Grant/Time & Life Pictures/Getty Images
Chapter 2 opening photo: ©iStockphoto.com/Chris Schmidt
Photo 2.1: Brunswyk
Photo 2.2: ©iStockphoto.com/JackF
Photo 2.3: Stockbyte/Thinkstock
Photo 2.4: ©iStockphoto.com/JackF
Chapter 3 opening photo: ©iStockphoto.com/stray_cat
Photo 3.1: ©iStockphoto.com/MachineHeadz
Photo 3.2: Photodisc/Thinkstock
Photo 3.3: ©iStockphoto.com/monkeybusinessimages
Photo 3.4: ©iStockphoto.com/Wavebreak
Chapter 4 opening photo: Stockbyte/Thinkstock
Photo 4.1: Public domain
Photo 4.2: Henry William Pickersgill
Photo 4.3: *The Works of Jeremy Bentham,* vol. 4, 172–173
Photo 4.4: Robert Ashby Collection
Photo 4.5: Public domain
Chapter 5 opening photo: ©AP Photo
Photo 5.1: ©iStockphoto.com/coloroftime/
Photo 5.2: ©iStockphoto.com/EdStock
Photo 5.3: AP Photo
Photo 5.4: John Foxx/Stockbyte/Thinkstock; and Jupiterimages/Stockbyte/Thinkstock
Chapter 6 opening photo: ©Susan Ragan/AP Photo
Photo 6.1: Cecil Greek
Photo 6.2: ©iStockphoto.com/Yuri
Photo 6.3: *Toledo Blade*

Photo 6.4: ©Daniel Lainé/CORBIS
Chapter 7 opening photo: ©Daniel Lainé/CORBIS
Photo 7.1: ©Daniel Lainé/CORBIS
Photo 7.2: ©iStockphoto.com/dolgachov
Photo 7.3: Comstock Images/Stockbyte/Thinkstock
Photo 7.4: Marsha Halper/Pool Miami Herald/AP Photo
Chapter 8 opening photo: Photos.com/Thinkstock
Photo 8.1: Cecil Greek
Photo 8.2: ©iStockphoto.com/ozgurdonmaz
Photo 8.3: ©AP Photo
Chapter 9 opening photo: Creatas/Thinkstock
Photo 9.1: An image from Henry H. Goddard's *The Kallikak Family,* 1912.
Photo 9.2: Ferdinand Schmutzer
Photo 9.3: Karl Weatherly/Photodisc/Thinkstock
Photo 9.4: ©Bettmann/CORBIS
Chapter 10 opening photo: Stockbyte/Thinkstock
Photo 10.1: ©JASON REED/Reuters/Corbis
Photo 10.2: AP Photo/M. Spencer Green
Photo 10.3: Illinois Department of Corrections
Photo 10.4: Jack Hollingsworth/Digital Vision/Thinkstock
Chapter 11 opening photo: ©iStockphoto.com/rez-art
Photo 11.1: ©iStockphoto.com/Shane Hansen
Photo 11.2: Cecil Greek
Photo 11.3: Comstock Images/Stockbyte/Thinkstock; and Jupiterimages/liquidlibrary/Thinkstock
Photo 11.4: Ulf Andersen/Hulton Archive/Getty Images
Chapter 12 opening photo: ©David Goldman/AP Photo
Photo 12.1: ©iStockphoto.com/piranka

Photo 12.2: Jacksonville Police Department; Florida Department of Corrections; and Los Angeles Police Department
Photo 12.3: King County Sheriff's Office
Photo 12.4: ©iStockphoto.com/4X6
Photo 12.5: RJ Sangosti/AP Photo
Chapter 13 opening photo: ©iStockphoto.com/danhowl
Photo 13.1: FBI
Photo 13.2: FBI
Photo 13.3: Federal Emergency Management Agency
Photo 13.4: National Photo Company, Library of Congress
Photo 13.5: Justice Department
Chapter 14 opening photo: Jupiterimages/Photos.com/Thinkstock
Photo 14.1: ©iStockphoto.com/AmmentorpDK
Photo 14.2: ©iStockphoto.com/IS_ImageSource
Photo 14.3: FBI
Photo 14.4: ©iStockphoto.com/cookelma
Photo 14.5: Creative Commons
Photo 14.6: ©iStockphoto.com/Michael Krinke
Chapter 15 opening photo: ©iStockphoto.com/EduardSV
Photo 15.1: ©ThinkStock/Sean Murphy
Photo 15.2: Public Domain
Photo 15.3: Thinkstock
Photo 15.4: ©iStockphoto.com/microgen
Chapter 16 opening photo: ©Bettmann/CORBIS
Photo 16.1: ©David J. Phillip/AP Photo
Photo 16.2: U.S. Department of Justice
Photo 16.3: FBI
Chapter 17 opening photo: AP Photo
Photo 17.1: Public Domain
Photo 17.2: Public Domain
Photo 17.3: U.S. Marshals Service/U.S. Department of Justice
Photo 17.4: Lee Brimelow

Index

NOTE: Page numbers referring to boxes, figures, photos, and tables are followed by (box), (fig.), (photo), and (table).

About the Author

Anthony Walsh received his PhD from Bowling Green State University, Ohio. He is currently a professor at Boise State University in Idaho, where he teaches criminology, statistics, law, and correctional casework and counseling. He has field experience in both law enforcement and corrections and is the author or co-author of 34 books and approximately 150 other publications. He also has a drop-dead gorgeous wife whom he has loved with all his being for 27 years.

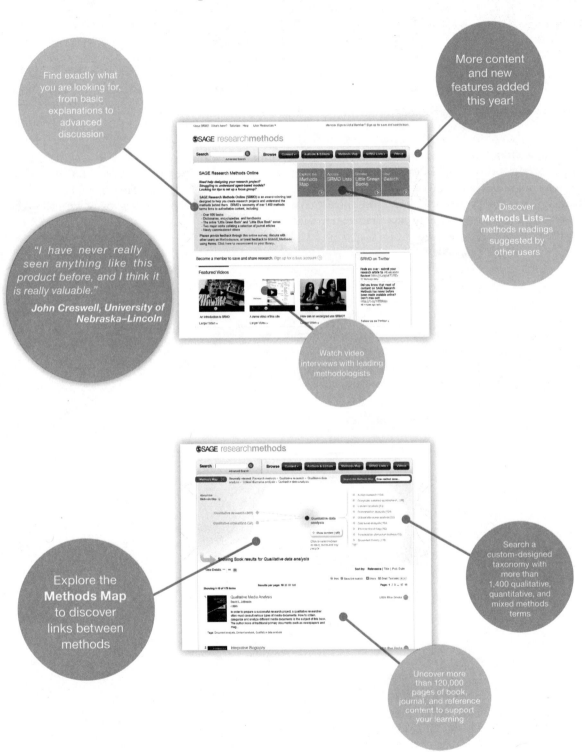

SAGE researchmethods

The essential online tool for researchers from the world's leading methods publisher

Find exactly what you are looking for, from basic explanations to advanced discussion

More content and new features added this year!

"I have never really seen anything like this product before, and I think it is really valuable."

John Creswell, University of Nebraska–Lincoln

Discover **Methods Lists**— methods readings suggested by other users

Watch video interviews with leading methodologists

Explore the **Methods Map** to discover links between methods

Search a custom-designed taxonomy with more than 1,400 qualitative, quantitative, and mixed methods terms

Uncover more than 120,000 pages of book, journal, and reference content to support your learning

Find out more at
www.sageresearchmethods.com